# QA
# **Compact**

## SECOND EDITION

### LYNN QUITMAN TROYKA

### DOUGLAS HESSE

**Prentice Hall**

Upper Saddle River   London   Singapore
Toronto   Tokyo   Sydney   Hong Kong   Mexico City

VP/Publisher: Joe Opiela
Editor in Chief: Craig Campanella
Executive Editor: Kevin Molloy
Project Manager, Editorial: Jessica A. Kupetz
Editorial Assistant: Gina Aloe
VP/Director of Marketing: Tim Stookesbury
Executive Marketing Manager:
    Megan Galvin-Fak
Senior Marketing Manager: Susan E. Stoudt
Marketing Assistant: Jessica Nelson
Assistant Managing Editor: Melissa Feimer
Text Permissions Specialist: Jane Scelta
Development Editor in Chief: Mary Ellen Curley
Development Editor: Paul Sarkis
Permissions Assistant: Peggy Davis
Senior Operations Specialist: Sherry Lewis
Manager, Image Rights and Permissions:
    Zina Arabia

Manager, Visual Research: Beth Brenzel
Manager, Cover Visual Research and
    Permissions: Karen Sanatar
Image Permissions Coordinator:
    Ang'John Ferreri
Image Researcher: Beth Brenzel
Senior Art Director: Nancy Wells
Art Director: Anne Nieglos
AV Project Manager: Mirella Signoretto
Interior and Cover Designer: Anne DeMarinis
Cover Art: "Mulberry Tree" 1889 by Vincent Van
    Gogh © The Gallery Collection/Corbis
Full-Service Project Management: Karen Berry,
    Laserwords Maine
Copyeditor: Tally Morgan
Composition: Laserwords Maine
Printer/Binder: Courier Companies
Cover Printer: Lehigh Phoenix

This book was set in 10/12 Adobe Garamond.

Credits and acknowledgements borrowed from other sources and reproduced, with permission, in this book appear on page 515.

**Library of Congress Cataloging-in-Publication Data**

Troyka, Lynn Quitman
    Quick access compact / Lynn Quitman Troyka, Douglas Hesse. — 2nd ed.
        p. cm.
    Includes index.
    ISBN 0-205-68734-2
1.  English language—Rhetoric—Handbooks, manuals, etc.   2. English language—Grammar—
Handbooks, manuals, etc.   3. Report writing—Handbooks, manuals, etc.   I. Hesse, Douglas
Dean.   II. Title.
    PE1408.T6955 2009
    808'.042—dc22
                                                                        2009000984

10   9   8   7   6   5   4   3   2   1

**Prentice Hall**
is an imprint of

PEARSON

www.pearsonhighered.com

Student ISBN-13:
978-0-205-68734-3
Student ISBN-10:
0-205-68734-2
Exam ISBN-13:
978-0-205-69968-1
Exam ISBN-10:
0-205-69968-5

# Why Do You Need This New Edition?

The second edition of *QA Compact* has been revised to provide more useful instruction and examples for writing students and instructors. Some of the helpful features that you'll find only in this new edition are:

**1** **The most up-to-date coverage of documentation styles**: the second edition features the most current standards for MLA and APA documentation, which you'll need in first-year composition as well as in many courses in your field of study.

**2** New and revised **Quick Reference boxes** highlight the most important must-have concepts for easy use. These are key to finding the information you need in the handbook.

**3** New Chapters 2 and 7, **"Essential Processes for Academic Writing"** and **"Strategies for Writing Typical Kinds of College Papers,"** give not only general writing advice but also specific strategies for producing the most common types of academic writing in first-year composition and other courses. This makes the second edition a great resource

for any class, not just first-year composition.

**4** A new **Chapter 8, "Style and Tone in Writing,"** illustrates the importance of *how* you say something in addition to *what* you say.

**5** New Chapters 39 and 40, **"Business and Professional Writing"** and **"Writing for the Public,"** are great resources for writing outside of your classroom when you are creating **resumés, cover letters,** and **personal Web sites**.

**6** The book's **exercises**, which are popular as assignments for many instructors, have been thoroughly revised.

**7** **Coverage and support for writing with new media,** including making oral presentations and using multimedia, document and visual design, and using audio and video.

# CONTENTS

To David, the love of my life

LYNN QUITMAN TROYKA

To my Illinois State
English 101 students

DOUG HESSE

■ ■ ■ ■ ■

# Personal Message to Students

## FROM LYNN TROYKA AND DOUG HESSE

As writers, many of you have much in common with both of us. Sure, we've been at it longer, so we've had more practice, and most rules have become cemented in our heads. However, we share with you a common goal: to put ideas into words worthy of someone else's reading time.

We also share the constant desire to become better writers. Given our extensive teaching experience, this probably sounds odd. However, writing is a lifelong enterprise. Just as we did, you'll write not only in composition classes, but also in other courses throughout college. Writing will likely be an important part of your career, of your role as a public citizen, and even of your personal life. It has certainly been central to ours. Whenever we get stuck in an unfamiliar writing situation or while learning new writing technology, we rummage through strategies we've developed over time. We talk to friends and colleagues, in person, by phone, and by e-mail, and they consult us, too.

We offer this book to you, then, as our partners in the process of writing. We hope that its pages help you give voice to your thoughts—now and years from now. We trust you'll find our advice useful in the wide range of writing situations you're bound to encounter in college and in life. You're always welcome to write us at troykalq@nyc.rr.com or dhesse@du.edu to share your reactions to this book and your experiences as writers. We promise to answer.

Each of us would like to end this message with a personal story.

*From Doug:* I first glimpsed the power of writing in high school, when I wrote sappy—but apparently successful—love poems. Still, when I went to college, I was surprised to discover all I didn't know about writing. Fortunately, I had good teachers and developed lots of patience. I needed it. I continue to learn from my colleagues, my students, and my coauthor, Lynn.

*From Lynn:* When I was an undergraduate, handbooks for writers weren't common. Questions about writing nagged at me. One day, browsing in the library, I found an incorrectly shelved, dust-covered book whose title included the words *handbook* and *writing.* I read it hungrily and kept checking it out from the library. Back then, I could never have imagined that someday I might write such a book myself. Now that we've completed the second edition of *QA Compact,* I'm amazed that I ever had the nerve to begin. This proves to me—and I hope to you—that anyone can write. Students don't always believe that. I hope you will.

With cordial regards,

*Lynn Quitman Troyka*                    *Doug Hesse*

# How to Use QA Compact

*QA Compact* is designed to help you find what you need to become a better writer. You will find many features intended to highlight key concepts and develop your skills. We are confident that you will find *QA Compact* to be a useful tool throughout college and beyond.

The following list of *QA Compact* tools will help you find the information you need quickly and easily.

- **The brief Table of Contents** on the inside front cover lists all parts and chapters in the book. Locate the general topic you need to reference and then turn to the chapter as needed.

- **A detailed Table of Contents** starts on page v. Use this version of the Table of Contents if you are looking for a more specific topic than those that are referenced on the inside front cover.

- **A list of supplementary material available with this book**, including information about the book's Web site, can be found in the Preface.

- **Quick Reference** boxes throughout give easy access to some of the most common and important issues that will come up as you write.

- An easy-to-reference and comprehensive subject **Index** can be found in the back of the book.

- **A list of Response Symbols** and **Proofreading Marks** is provided on the inside back cover. Consult this list if your instructor uses revision and proofreading symbols when commenting on your writing.

The sample page to the right illustrates how to navigate the content of the book from page to page.

Indicates the last section on the current page.

Chapter and section

Page number

# 44j  What is pronoun case?

Indicates new section of a chapter.

**Case** applies in different ways to pronouns and to nouns. For pronouns, case refers to three pronoun forms: **subjective** (pronoun SUBJECTS), **objective** (pronoun OBJECTS), and **possessive** (pronouns that are possessive). For nouns, case refers to only one noun form: possessive. (For using apostrophes in the possessive case, see Chapter 60.)

Words printed in bold or in small capital letters are discussed elsewhere in the book.

---

### Quick Reference 44.2                                 ■ ■ ■ ■ ■

#### Choosing between *that* and *which*

In informal writing, you can use either *that* or *which* in a restrictive clause (a clause that is essential to the sentence's meaning), as long as you do so consistently in each piece of writing. However, in academic writing, your instructor and peers usually expect you to use *that*.

> The zoos **that most children like** display newborn and baby animals. [The point of this sentence is to identify the kind of zoos that children like. Therefore, the clause *that most children like* is essential to the meaning of the sentence; if you remove it, the meaning changes substantially.]

Use *which* in a **nonrestrictive clause** (a clause that isn't essential to the sentence's meaning).

> Zoos, **which most children like**, attract more visitors if they display newborn and baby animals. [This sentence concerns what attracts more visitors to zoos. The clause *which most children like* is not essential to the meaning of the sentence; if you remove it, the meaning of the sentence doesn't change substantially.]

Quick Reference boxes highlight key information.

---

**❗ Alert:** The expression *he or she* operates as a single unit and therefore calls for a singular antecedent. Generally, however, try to avoid this awkward expression by switching to plural forms. ●

Alerts call attention to important rules and best practices.

**ESOL Tip:** The word *to* has several functions, each of which is discussed in Chapter 46. As part of the INFINITIVE *to eat*, the word *to* modifies (limits) the PRONOUN *nothing*. ●

ESOL icons call out information of particular use for multilingual students.

xv

■ ■ ■ ■ ■

# PREFACE

## For the Instructor

**Prentice Hall Resources for Writing.** This series is a specially designed set of supplements for the instructor that support timely classroom and composition topics. These supplements are available upon adoption of *QA Compact,* Second Edition.

* *Teaching Writing Across the Curriculum* by Art Young is written for college teachers in all disciplines and provides useful advice on teaching writing across the curriculum.

* *Teaching Civic Literacy* by Cheryl Duffy offers advice on how to integrate civic literacy into the composition classroom.

* *Teaching Visual Rhetoric* by Susan Loudermilk provides an illustrated look at visual rhetoric and offers guidance on how to incorporate this topic into the classroom.

* *Teaching Writing for ESL Students* by Ruth Spack addresses various strategies that can be employed to teach writing to nonnative speakers.

## For the Instructor and Student

**MyCompLab.** The new MyCompLab uniquely integrates proven resources and new assessment tools with a student's own writing. This seamless and flexible application, built for writers by writers, will help instructors and students accomplish everyday composition tasks more easily and effectively.

**Prentice Hall WAC Resources.** A compilation of resources designed to facilitate teaching and learning, Writing Across the Curriculum (WAC) includes *Papers Across the Curriculum* (a series of sample student papers edited by Judith Ferster) and *A Prentice Hall Pocket Reader: Writing Across the Curriculum* (by Stephen Brown, University of Nevada Las Vegas). If you would like to put additional emphasis on WAC in your composition course(s), please contact your Pearson sales representative for more information.

**Dictionary, Thesaurus, Writer's Guides, Workbooks, and Pocket Readers.** The following resources can be packaged with *QA Compact,* Second Edition. These valuable student resources provide additional depth on specialized topics that may only be touched upon in the text, and allow you to customize the handbook to your specific needs. Contact your local Pearson representative for additional information.

- *The New American Webster Handy College Dictionary*
- *The New American Roget's College Thesaurus*
- *A Writer's Guide to Research and Documentation*
- *A Writer's Guide to Oral Presentations and Writing in the Disciplines*
- *A Writer's Guide to Document and Web Design*
- *A Writer's Guide to Writing About Literature*
- *The Prentice Hall Grammar Workbook*
- *The Prentice Hall ESL Workbook*
- *Applying English to Your Career (Workbook)*
- *A Prentice Hall Pocket Reader: Argument*
- *A Prentice Hall Pocket Reader: Literature*
- *A Prentice Hall Pocket Reader: Patterns*
- *A Prentice Hall Pocket Reader: Themes*
- *A Prentice Hall Pocket Reader: Purposes*
- *A Prentice Hall Pocket Reader: Writing Across the Curriculum*
- *Papers Across the Curriculum*

# ABOUT THE AUTHORS

**Lynn Quitman Troyka,** Adjunct Professor in the Graduate Program in Language and Literature at the City College (CCNY) of the City University of New York (CUNY), has also taught at Queensborough Community College. Former editor of the *Journal of Basic Writing,* she has had her writing and research published in major journals and various scholarly collections. She also conducts workshops in the teaching of writing. Dr. Troyka is co-author of the *Simon & Schuster Handbook for Writers,* Ninth Edition, Pearson Prentice Hall; *Quick Access Reference for Writers,* Sixth Edition, Pearson Prentice Hall; the Canadian editions of her *Simon & Schuster Handbook for Writers* and *Quick Access Reference for Writers; Structured Reading,* Seventh Edition, Prentice Hall; and *Steps in Composition,* Eighth Edition, Prentice Hall.

Dr. Troyka is a past chair of the Conference on College Composition and Communication (CCCC); the Two-Year College Association (TYCA) of the National Council of Teachers (NCTE); the College Section of NCTE; and the Writing Division of the Modern Language Association (MLA). She received the 2001 CCCC Exemplar Award, the highest CCCC award for scholarship, teaching, and service; the Rhetorician of the Year Award; and the TYCA Pickett Award for Service.

"This information," says Dr. Troyka, "tells what I've done, not who I am. I am a teacher. Teaching is my life's work, and I love it."

**Doug Hesse,** Professor of English and Director of Writing at the University of Denver, previously held several positions at Illinois State University, including Director of the Honors and Writing Programs, and Director of the Center for the Advancement of Teaching. Dr. Hesse earned his PhD from the University of Iowa. He has also taught at the University of Findlay, Miami University (as Wiepking Distinguished Visiting Professor), and Michigan Tech.

Dr. Hesse is a past chair of the Conference on College Composition and Communication (CCCC), the nation's largest professional association of college writing instructors. A past president, as well, of the Council of Writing Program Administrators (WPA), Dr. Hesse edited that organization's journal, *Writing Program Administration.* He has been a member of the executive committee of the National Council of Teachers of English (NCTE) and chaired the Modern Language Association (MLA) Division on Teaching as a Profession.

He is the author of over fifty articles and book chapters, in such journals as *College Composition and Communication, College English, JAC, Rhetoric Review,* and the *Journal of Teaching Writing* and in such books as *Essays on the Essay; Writing Theory and Critical Theory; The Writing Program Administrator's Sourcebook; Literary Nonfiction; The Private, the Public, and the Published;* and *Passions, Pedagogies, and 21st Century Technologies.* He is also coauthor with Lynn Quitman Troyka of the *Simon & Schuster Handbook for Writers,* Ninth Edition, Pearson Prentice Hall, and *Quick Access Reference for Writers,* Sixth Edition, Pearson Prentice Hall. He has consulted at over forty colleges and universities.

The writing program he directs at the University of Denver is only one of twenty-five internationally to receive the CCCC Certificate of Excellence. "Of all these accomplishments," says Dr. Hesse, "the one that matters most to me was being named Distinguished Humanities Teacher. That one came from my students and suggests that, in however small a way, I've mattered in their education and lives."

# 1 ■ ■ ■ ■

# Understanding College and Other Writing Situations

## 1a   What is a writing situation?

Think of the following situations: writing a text message to a friend; a research paper for a history class; a job application letter; a Web site for a museum. These situations result in texts widely different in length, format, content, organization, style, and so on. A **writing situation** is the combination of several elements: your topic, your purpose, your audience, your role as a writer, and your context and special requirements.

You'll often be assigned a **topic,** the subject you need to write about and, perhaps, the sources (7b) that you'll need to use. Topics can be very general ("Write about poverty") or very specific ("Analyze the factors that led to James Ferguson's poverty"); you'll be more successful if you narrow broad topics (2b.3).

It may surprise you to learn that you can take on different **roles** (personalities or identities) for different writing situations. The **context** of your purpose and audience can affect the writing situation. Context refers to the circumstances in which your readers will encounter your writing. **Special requirements** are practical matters such as how much time you're given to complete the assignment and the required length of your writing.

Understanding a writing situation guides your writing process and shapes your final draft. A writing process that might be effective in one situation might not be appropriate for another, and the final drafts would have different characteristics. For example, writing a history paper in the short, informal style of a text message definitely won't impress a professor. Similarly, texting your friends in long paragraphs will make them impatient (and perhaps wonder who's using your cell phone).

Your writing situation also helps determine the tone of your writing. Tone refers to the attitude conveyed in writing, mostly by the writer's word choice. A tone can be formal, informal, laid back, pompous, sarcastic, concerned, judgmental, sympathetic, and so on. The tone you use greatly affects your readers' sense of the ROLE* you've chosen.

---

*Terms in SMALL CAPITAL LETTERS have been defined elsewhere in this text. To find a definition, look up the term in the index and turn to the page number in **bold type.**

# 1b  What does "purpose" mean for writing?

A writer's purpose motivates what and how he or she writes. Quick Reference 1.1 lists four major purposes for writing.

## ■ What is expressive writing?

**Expressive writing** is writing to express your personal thoughts, feelings, and opinions. Some expressive writing is for the writer's eyes only, such as that in diaries, personal journals, or exploratory drafts. Other people, however, express themselves in e-mails to friends and colleagues or in blogs for all the world to see. A crucial reason for much of this kind of writing is simply for people to make connections with others. Social networking sites like Facebook, for example, do impart information and, occasionally, try to persuade others; however, their main purpose is to establish and deepen human contact. This purpose, which is as old as personal letter writing, has been invigorated by digital communication.

---

### Quick Reference 1.1                        ■ ■ ■ ■ ■

#### Purposes for writing

- To express yourself or build connections with others
- To inform a reader
- To persuade a reader
- To create a literary work

In this handbook, we concentrate on two major purposes for most forms of college writing: to **inform** and to **persuade.** The two remaining purposes listed above are important for contributing to human thought and culture, but they relate less to what most college writing involves.

---

Finally, some expressive writing for public audiences falls into the category of literary writing. The excerpt here comes from a memoir intended for public reading.

> For much of her life my mother longed, passionately longed, for a decent house. One with a yard that did not have to be cleared with an ax. One with a roof that kept out the rain. One with a floor that you could not fall through. She longed for a beautiful house of wood or stone. Or of red brick, like the houses her many sisters and their husbands had. When I was thirteen she found such a house. Green-shuttered, white-walled. Breezy. With a lawn and a hedge and giant pecan trees. A porch swing. There her gardens flourished in spite of the shade, as did her youngest daughter, for whom she sacrificed her

life doing hard labor in someone else's house, in order to afford peace and prettiness for her child, to whose grateful embrace she returned each night.

—Alice Walker, "My Mother's Blue Bowl"

## ■ What is informative writing?

Informative writing seeks to give information to readers and usually to explain it. Another name for this type of writing is expository writing because it expounds on—sets forth in detail—observations, ideas, facts, scientific data, and statistics. You can find informative writing in textbooks, encyclopedias, technical and business reports, manuals, nonfiction books, newspapers, and many magazines.

The essential goal of informative writing is to educate your readers about something. Like all good educators, therefore, you want to present your information clearly, accurately, completely, and fairly. Quick Reference 1.2 gives you a checklist to assess your informative writing.

---

**Quick Reference 1.2**  ■ ■ ■ ■ ■

### Informative writing

- Is its information clear?
- Does it present facts, ideas, and observations that can be verified?
- Does its information seem complete and accurate?
- Is the writer's TONE reasonable and free of distortions? (8d)

---

## ■ What is persuasive writing?

**Persuasive writing,** also called *argumentative* writing, seeks to persuade readers to support a particular opinion. When you write to persuade, you deal with debatable topics—those that people can consider from more than one point of view. Your goal is to change your readers' minds—or at least to bring your readers' opinions closer to your point of view. To succeed, you want to evoke a reaction in your audience so that they think beyond their present position (for example, reasoning why free speech needs to be preserved) or take action (for example, register to vote). Examples of persuasive writing include newspaper editorials, letters to the editor, opinion essays in magazines, reviews, sermons, advertising, fund-raising letters, books that argue a point of view, business proposals, and so on.

In general terms, persuasive writing means you need to move beyond merely stating your opinion. You need to give the basis for that opinion. You support your opinion by using specific, illustrative details to back up your **generalizations,** which are usually very broad statements.

Quick Reference 1.3 gives you a checklist to assess your persuasive writing.

---

### Quick Reference 1.3    ■ ■ ■ ■ ■

#### Persuasive writing

- Does it present a point of view about which opinions vary?
- Does it support its point of view with specifics?
- Does it provide sound reasoning and logic?
- Are the parts of its argument clear?
- Does it intend to evoke a reaction from the reader?

---

**EXERCISE 1-1**    For each paragraph, decide if the dominant purpose is informative, persuasive, or expressive. Then, use the information in section 1b to explain your answers.

A.    Trees are living archives, carrying within their structure a record not only of their age but also of precipitation and temperature for each year in which a ring was formed. The record might also include the marks of forest fires, early frosts and, incorporated into the wood itself, chemical elements the tree removed from its environment. Thus, if we only knew how to unlock its secrets, a tree could tell us a great deal about what was happening in its neighborhood from the time of its beginning. Trees can tell us what was happening before written records became available. They also have a great deal to tell us about our future. The records of past climate that they contain can help us to understand the natural forces that produce our weather, and this, in turn, can help us plan.

—James S. Trefil, "Concentric Clues
from Growth Rings Unlock the Past"

B.    Actual physical location threatens to evaporate everywhere we look. Information, we are everywhere taught, has annihilated distances. Surgeons can cut you open from a thousand miles away. Facsimile Las Vegas casinos deliver Rome and New York on the same daily walk. You don't have to go to the office to go to the office. You can shop in your kitchen and go to school in your living room. And, sadly enough, when you actually do go out shopping, one mall seems much like another. For what actually matters, physicality doesn't matter anymore. Even with money; now, we are told, information about money is more important than the actual green.

—Richard Lanham, *The Economics of Attention*

C.    Although Littleman, my eleven-year-old poodle, has never been separated from his thirteen-year-old mother, Simone, they are remarkably different. Simone weighs in at about five kilograms with very delicate, sophisticated features and coarse, curly hair. Slightly shorter, Littleman tops the scale at no more than three kilograms and is quite handsome with his teddy-bear features and soft wavy hair. Simone was the first dog in the family and is a pedigreed poodle. In many ways she is the picture of a thoroughbred, with her snobby attitude and nonchalant manners. On the other hand,

Littleman came into the family a year later with four other puppies of pure breeding, but they were never registered. Unlike his mother, Littleman is very friendly, almost to the point of being pesty at times.

—Linda Neal, student

# 1c What does "audience" mean for writing?

Your **audience** consists of everyone who will read your writing, but it especially refers to readers to whom you're most directly aiming your words. Thinking about audience means figuring out how to reach your audience in various kinds of situations. Effective writers know they need to adjust their writing for different tasks and audiences.

After college, your audiences are likely to be readers of your business, professional, and public writing (Chapters 39–40). In college, you'll surely address a mix of audience types that expect to read ACADEMIC WRITING. Here's a list of categories of those audiences, each of which is detailed in the section listed in parentheses.

- General educated audiences
- Specialist audiences
- Your instructor (who represents your general or specialized readers)
- Your peers (classmates, co-workers, friends, or others like yourself) (6a)

The more specifics you understand about each of your audiences, the better your chances of communicating with them successfully.

**ESOL Tips:** (1) If you do not share a cultural background with your readers, it may be difficult for you to estimate how much your readers know about your topic. Discussing your topic with friends or classmates might help you decide what background information you need to include in your paper.

(2) As someone from a non-US culture, you might be surprised—even offended—by the directness with which people speak and write in the United States. If so, we hope you'll read our open letter to multilingual students about honoring their cultures on page 484. ●

## ◼ What is a general educated audience?

A **general educated audience** is composed of experienced readers who regularly read newspapers, magazines, and books, not only because they have to but because they want to. These readers typically have a general knowledge of many subjects and are likely to understand something about your topic. If your writing contains too many technical details or unusual references, your writing may confuse and alienate these readers. Consequently, for general educated readers you need to avoid using specialized terms without plainly defining them, or referring to uncommon information without explaining it.

General educated readers usually approach a piece of writing expecting to become interested in it, to learn about a new topic, to add to their store of knowledge about a subject, or to see a subject from a perspective other than their own. As a writer, work to fulfill those expectations. While some readers aren't particularly knowledgeable or open to new ideas, your goal in most writing that's not intended for specialized audiences needs to be targeting a general audience, as defined above.

## ■ What is a specialist audience?

A **specialist audience** is composed of readers who have a thorough knowledge of specific subjects or who are particularly committed to certain interests or viewpoints. Many people are experts in their occupational fields, and some become experts in areas that simply interest them, such as astronomy or raising orchids. People from a particular group background (for example, Democrats, Republicans, Catholics, or military veterans) are knowledgeable in those areas.

Specialist readers may also share certain assumptions and beliefs. Additionally, whenever you introduce a concept that might be new to a specialist audience, explain the concept thoroughly rather than assuming the audience will understand it right away.

## ■ What is my instructor's role as audience?

As your audience, your instructor functions in three ways. First, your instructor assumes the role of your target audience by reading and responding to your writing as though he or she is one of your intended general or specific readers. Second, your instructor acts as a coach who is dedicated to helping improve your writing. Third, your instructor evaluates your final drafts.

Although instructors know that few students are experienced writers or experts on the subjects they write about, they expect your writing to reflect your having taken the time to learn something worthwhile about a topic and then to write about it clearly. They can recognize a minimal effort almost immediately.

Don't assume that your instructor can mentally fill in what you leave out of your writing. Instructors—indeed, all readers—can't be mind readers, and they expect students' writing to fully explore their chosen topic.

## 1d   What resources can help me with writing?

Computers are important tools for creating documents, finding resources, managing work, and communicating with others. Almost all writing projects, whether in college or beyond, require them. Although some instructors make allowances for students with no access to a computer, they clearly prefer word-processed final drafts.

In addition to helping you produce and revise writing, computers can help you find SOURCES. Nearly all library catalogs and databases are now searchable electronically, both from within the library and remotely through the Internet. Catalogs and databases are large collections of references that experts have gathered and organized. Some of those references exist only in print, but increasingly, they're also available online.

A **dictionary** is indispensable. Most college bookstores offer a variety of hardback "college dictionaries." Before buying one, browse through a few definitions, check the format and accessories (information in the front and back), and choose the book you like best. Keeping a lightweight paperback abridged dictionary in your book bag can be very handy for checking unknown words on the spot. Also, many dictionaries and other reference books can be downloaded onto a **personal digital assistant (PDA)** for even greater portability.

Another valuable resource for writers is a **thesaurus,** which is a collection of *synonyms.* The alphabetically arranged ones are the easiest to use. Be sure you check for this feature since some thesauruses are not organized alphabetically. *Roget's 21st Century Thesaurus* is an excellent volume arranged alphabetically.

**College libraries**, sometimes called *learning resource centers*, are essential for writers. Libraries are fully stocked with all manner of reference books, circulating books, resources for online access, and more. Some resources are available online, in "full text versions," through the library's Web site. It's helpful to know what resources are available at your library so that you can dive right in when you need to get information.

# 2

■ ■ ■ ■

# Essential Processes for Academic Writing

## 2a　What processes do academic writers use?

Many people think that professional writers can sit down at their computers, think of ideas, and magically produce a finished draft, word by perfect word. Experienced writers know better. They know that writing is a process, a series of activities that starts the moment they begin thinking about a subject and ends with proofreading the final draft. Experienced writers also know that good writing is rewriting, again and yet again. Their drafts are filled with additions, deletions, rewordings, and rearrangements.

> ~~Chapter One discusses what writing is. This chapter explains~~
>
> ~~how writing happens.~~ Many people think that professional writers
>
> can sit down at their computers, think of ideas, and ^magically^ produce a
>
> finished draft, word by perfect word. Experienced writers know
>
> better. They know that writing is a process. ~~The writing process is~~
>
> a series of activities that starts the moment ^they begin^ thinking about a subject
>
> ~~begins~~ and ends with the ^proofreading^ final draft. Experienced writers also know
>
> that good writing is rewriting, again and yet again. *Their drafts*
>
> *are filled with additions, deletions, rewordings, and rearrangements.*

**Draft and revision of Lynn Troyka's first paragraph in Chapter 2**

For example, see above how Lynn revised the paragraph you just read. She didn't make all the changes at the same time, even though it looks that way on the example. She went through the paragraph four times before she was satisfied with it. Notice that she deleted two sentences, combined two sentences, added a sentence at the end, and changed wording throughout.

Writing is an ongoing process of considering alternatives and making choices. Knowing and practicing a few general processes will help you with almost every writing situation in college and beyond.

In this chapter, we discuss each part of the writing process separately. In real life, the steps overlap. They loop back and forth, which is why writing is called a recursive process. Quick Reference 2.1 lists the steps.

## Quick Reference 2.1    ■ ■ ■ ■ ■

### Steps in the writing process

- **Planning** means discovering and compiling ideas for your writing.
- **Shaping** means organizing your material.
- **Drafting** means writing your material into sentences and paragraphs.
- **Revising** means evaluating your draft and then rewriting it by adding, deleting, rewording, and rearranging.
- **Editing** means checking for correct grammar, spelling, punctuation, and mechanics.
- **Proofreading** means reading your final copy to eliminate typing or handwriting errors.

Do you like, as we do, to visualize a process? If so, see the drawing on page 10. The arrows show movement. You might move back before going ahead (perhaps as you revise, you realize you need to plan some more); or you might skip a step and come back to it later (perhaps in the middle of revising, you jump into editing for a few minutes because a punctuation or grammar rule affects how you express your point), and so on.

As you work with the writing process, allow yourself to move freely through each step to see what's involved. Notice what works best for you. As you develop a sense of your preferred writing methods, adapt the process to fit each writing situation. No single way exists for applying the writing process.

Our personal advice from one writer to another is this: Most writers struggle some of the time with ideas that are difficult to express, sentences that won't take shape, and words that aren't precise. Be patient with yourself. Don't get discouraged. The more you write, the easier it will become—though writing never happens magically.

## 2b  How do I begin a college writing project?

Begin every writing assignment by carefully analyzing the writing situation you're given. Some assignments are very specific, and students need to do precisely what's asked, taking care not to wander off the topic. More often, however, writing-class assignments aren't specific. Often, you'll be expected to select your own topic or even your own purpose and audience.

### ■ Selecting your own topic or purpose

If you have to choose a topic, don't rush. Take time to think through your ideas. Avoid getting so deeply committed to one topic that you cannot change to a more suitable topic in the time allotted.

Not all topics are suitable for ACADEMIC WRITING. Your topic needs to have ideas and issues meaty enough to demonstrate your thinking and writing abilities. Think through potential topics by breaking each one down into its logical subsections. Then, make sure you can supply sufficiently specific details to back up each general statement. Conversely, make sure you aren't bogged down with so many details you can't figure out what GENERALIZATIONS they support.

Work toward balance by finding a middle ground. Beware of topics so broad that they lead to well-meaning but vague generalizations (for example, "Education is necessary for success"). Also, beware of topics so narrow that they lead nowhere after a few sentences (for example, "Jessica Max attends Tower College").

Most instructors put each assignment in writing, in a handout, on a Web site, or perhaps on the board. But some instructors give assignments orally during class, expecting you to write them down. Try to record every word. Don't hesitate to ask questions if you don't catch all the words or if something isn't

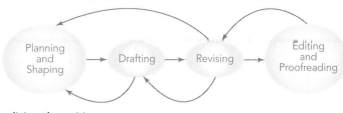

**Visualizing the writing process**

clear—and be sure to write down the answers because they often tend to slip from memory. Listen, too, to questions other students ask.

In the rest of this chapter, we present the writing processes of two college students, Sara Cardini and Alex Garcia, as they plan and shape their material. You'll see Cardini's essay evolving through three separate, complete drafts. Later, in Chapter 5, you'll see how Garcia's essay developed. To start, here are the written assignments each student received.

---

**Sara Cardini received this assignment:**

Addressing an educated audience, write an essay of 900 to 1,300 words discussing something you learned outside of a classroom. Your writing purpose can be informative or persuasive. Expect to write three drafts. (1) Your first draft, typed double-spaced, is due two classes from today. (2) Your clean second draft, typed double-spaced, without notes or comments, is due two classes later. Clip to it your first draft showing all notes you made to yourself or from comments your peer-response group made; you can handwrite notes and comments. I'll read your second draft as an "essay in progress" and will make comments to help you toward a third (and final) draft. (3) The third draft, typed double-spaced, is due one week after I return your second draft with my comments.

**Alex Garcia was given this assignment:**

Write an essay of 1,000 to 1,500 words that argues for a particular action on an issue that interests you. Your final draft is due in two weeks.

---

Cardini's first step was to analyze her writing situation. She looked at the very general topic—explain to an educated audience something you learned outside of a classroom—and she saw that she needed to narrow it considerably. She tentatively decided her purpose would be informative, though she thought she might have to switch to a persuasive purpose as she went along. She knew that she would share her first draft with her peer-response group to help her toward her second draft. She also understood that her instructor would be her final audience. She was aware of the requirements for time and length.

Garcia also read his assignment and analyzed his writing situation. Because the topic was very broad, he knew he would have to spend a good deal of time deciding what he wanted to write about. On the other hand, he understood that his assigned purpose was persuasive. The audience was not specified; he knew that his instructor would be the main audience, but he also decided to write in a way that would address a broader public audience. He kept in mind the requirements for time and length.

## ■ Broadening a narrow topic

You know a topic is too narrow when you realize there's little to say after a few sentences. When faced with a too-narrow topic, think about underlying concepts. For example, suppose you want to write about Oprah Winfrey. If you chose "Oprah Winfrey's television show debuted in 1986," you'd be working with a single fact rather than a topic. To expand beyond such a narrow thought, you could think about the general area that your fact fits into—say, the impact of television shows on American culture. Although that is too broad to be a useful topic, you're headed in the right direction. Next, you might think of a topic that relates to Oprah's influence, such as "What impact has Oprah Winfrey's television show had on American culture since she began broadcasting in 1986?" Depending on your WRITING SITUATION (1a), you might need to narrow your idea further by focusing on Oprah's impact in a single area, such as how her book club influenced publishing and reading habits, how her guests and topics brought certain issues to national visibility, or how the style of her show affected other talk shows.

## ■ Narrowing a broad topic

Narrowing a broad topic calls for you to break the topic down into subtopics. Most broad subjects can be broken down in hundreds of ways, but you need not think of all of them. Settle on a topic that interests you, one narrowed enough—but not too much—from a broad topic. Here are two examples.

| | |
|---|---|
| SUBJECT | *music* |
| WRITING SITUATION | freshman composition class |
| | informative purpose |
| | instructor as audience |
| | 500 words; one week |
| POSSIBLE TOPICS | "How music affects moods" |
| | "The main characteristics of country music" |
| | "The types of songs in Disney animations" |

|                   |                                                        |
|-------------------|--------------------------------------------------------|
| SUBJECT           | *cities*                                               |
| WRITING SITUATION | sociology course                                       |
|                   | persuasive purpose                                     |
|                   | peers and then instructor as audience                  |
|                   | 950 to 1,000 words; ten days                           |
| POSSIBLE TOPICS   | "The importance of public transportation"              |
|                   | "Discomforts of city living"                           |
|                   | "How open spaces enhance the quality of city life"     |

Sara Cardini knew that her very general assigned topic—"Explain to an educated audience something you learned outside of a classroom"—was too broad. To narrow it, she used the following structured techniques for discovering and compiling ideas: browsing her journal, FREEWRITING, and MAPPING. They helped her decide that she wanted to discuss how she learned about a culture other than her own. In the end, she chose "Japanese videos" and, even more specifically, a kind of Japanese animation called "anime" (commonly pronounced AN-a-may).

Alex Garcia also needed to narrow his topic to suit a 1,000- to 1,500-word essay. To explore several possible topics, he used BRAINSTORMING. Once he had chosen a topic (whether buying organic food was worthwhile), he used the "journalist's questions" to compile more ideas and then a subject tree (2e) to check whether he was ready to begin drafting.

## 2c How can I come up with ideas and information?

If you've ever felt you'll never think of anything to write about, don't despair. Instead, use structured techniques, sometimes called *prewriting strategies* or *invention techniques,* for discovering and compiling ideas. Professional writers use them to uncover hidden resources in their minds. For a list of the techniques, see Quick Reference 2.2.

⬣ **ESOL Tip:** The structured techniques discussed here aim to let your ideas flow out of you without your judging them right away. If it's difficult for you to implement these techniques using English, consider doing several in your primary language. Then, choose one that seems to have potential for your writing and do it over again in English. ●

### ▨ Using an idea log or journal

As you develop the habits of mind and behavior of a writer, your ease with writing will grow. One such habit is keeping an idea log. Professional writers are always on the lookout for ideas to write about and details to develop their

> **Quick Reference 2.2**    ■ ■ ■ ■ ■
>
> ### Ways to discover and compile ideas for writing
>
> - Keep an idea log and a journal.
> - Freewrite.
> - Brainstorm.
> - Ask the "journalist's questions."
> - Map.
> - Talk it over.
> - Read, browse, or search.
> - Incubate.

ideas. They listen, watch, talk with people, and generally keep an open mind. Because they know that good ideas can evaporate as quickly as they spring to mind, they're always ready to jot down their thoughts and observations. Some carry a pocket-size notepad, while others use a personal digital assistant (PDA) or a laptop. If you use an idea log throughout your college years, you'll see your powers of observation increase dramatically.

Additionally, many professional writers keep a daily writing **journal.** Doing this will allow you to have a conversation in writing with yourself. Your audience is you, so the content and tone can be as personal and informal as you wish. Even fifteen minutes a day can be enough.

Unlike a diary, a journal isn't a record of what you do each day. A journal is for your thoughts from your reading, your observations, even your dreams. You can respond to quotations, react to movies or plays, or reflect on your opinions, beliefs, and tastes. Keeping a journal can help you in three ways. First, writing every day gives you the habit of productivity; the more you write and the more you feel words pouring out of you onto paper, the more easily you'll write in all situations. Second, a journal instills the practice of close observation and discovery, two habits of mind that good writers cultivate. Third, a journal is an excellent source of ideas for assignments.

### ■ Freewriting

**Freewriting** is writing nonstop. You write down whatever comes into your mind without stopping to wonder whether the ideas are good or the spelling is correct. When you freewrite, don't do anything to interrupt the flow. Don't censor any thoughts or flashes of insight. Don't go back and review. Don't delete.

Freewriting helps get you used to the "feel" of your fingers rapidly hitting computer keys or your pen moving across paper. Freewriting works best if you set a goal—perhaps writing for fifteen minutes or filling one or two pages. Keep going until you reach that goal, even if you have to write one word repeatedly until a new word comes to mind. Some days when you read over your freewriting, it might seem mindless, but other days your interesting ideas may startle you.

In **focused freewriting,** you write from a specific starting point—a sentence from your general freewriting, an idea, a quotation, or anything else you choose. Except for this initial focal point, focused freewriting is the same as regular freewriting. Write until you meet your time or page limit, and don't censor yourself. If you go off the topic, that's fine: See where your thoughts take you. Just keep moving forward.

Like a journal, freewriting is a good source of ideas and details.

### ■ Brainstorming

**Brainstorming** means listing everything you can think of about a topic. Let your mind roam freely, generating quantities of ideas. Write words, phrases, or sentence fragments—whatever comes to you. If you run out of ideas, ask yourself exploratory questions, such as *What is it? What is it the same as? How is it different? Why or how does it happen? How is it done? What causes it or results from it? What does it look, smell, sound, feel, or taste like? Who benefits from it? Who loses?*

After you've compiled a list, go to step two: Look for patterns, ways to group the ideas into categories. You'll probably find several categories. Set aside any items that don't fit into a group. If a category interests you but has only a few items, brainstorm that category alone.

You can brainstorm in one concentrated session or over several days, depending on how much time you have for an assignment. Brainstorming with other writers can be especially fruitful: One person's ideas bounce off the next person's, and collectively more ideas come to mind. Chapter 6 explains strategies for working with others.

Brainstorming was a technique Alex Garcia used to find his topic about the benefits of organic foods. Brainstorming helped him think through several topics and generate some ideas about the one that most appealed to him.

### ■ The "journalist's questions"

When journalists report a story, they gather and write about information by asking who did what, when it happened, where it happened, and why and how it happened. The same questions come in handy for writers exploring a topic. The **journalist's questions** are *Who? What? When? Where? Why?* and *How?*

Alex Garcia used the journalist's questions to expand his thinking on the value of eating organic foods. His answers, listed below, showed him that he had enough material for a good essay.

| | |
|---|---|
| **WHO?** | **Who** benefits from buying or selling organic food? |
| **WHAT?** | **What** kinds of organic foods are available? |
| **WHEN?** | **When** did the practice of growing organic foods begin? |
| **WHERE?** | **Where** can I find evidence if organic foods are healthier? |
| **WHY?** | **Why** do some people doubt the value of organic foods? |
| **HOW?** | **How** exactly should someone evaluate the evidence? |

## ■ Mapping

**Mapping,** also called *clustering,* is a visual form of brainstorming. Some writers find that they begin to think more creatively if they can actually see ways that their ideas connect. Other writers use mapping to help them check the logical relationships between ideas.

To map, write your topic in the middle of a sheet of paper and draw a circle around it. Now, moving out from the center, use lines and circles to show ideas that are subtopics of the topic in the center circle. Continue to subdivide and add details. At any time, you can move to a blank space on your map and start a new subtopic. Try to keep going without censoring yourself.

Sara Cardini used mapping to prompt herself to discover ideas about Japanese animation. When she finished, she was satisfied that she'd have enough to say in her essay.

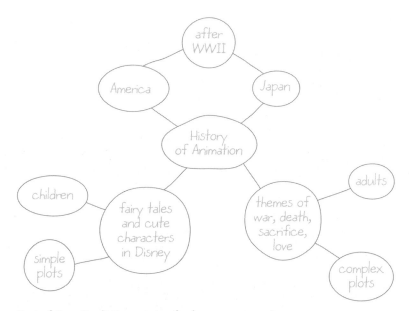

**Part of Sara Cardini's mapping for her essay on anime**

### ■ Reading and browsing

Reading newspapers, magazines, and books can provide a constant source of ideas. While it might sound old-fashioned, academic writers do this all the time. Spending time in the PERIODICALS or new books section of a library or browsing a good bookstore can alert you to fresh topics.

Of course, **Internet searches** also help you find topics and locate specific information. Chapter 33 provides extensive guidelines for searching the WORLD WIDE WEB. Briefly, however, access the Yahoo! directory at http://dir.yahoo.com or the Google directory at http://www.google.com/dirhp. You'll see a screen that lists broad subject areas.

On the Google directory, click on the broad subject "Society" to see a number of slightly more specific topics, including one on "Relationships." Note that each of them would be much too broad to write about. However, if you keep clicking on topic headings, you'll move to more and more specific subjects. Browsing through the layers of topics can help you think of several ideas for your writing. If you know a general topic area, you can type it in the search window of the program and then click on more specific subcategories.

**Screen shot of Google directory**

**EXERCISE 2-1**  Explore some of the following topics by typing them into the search window of a search engine. Be ready to explain the sequence of topics you discover.

1. global warming
2. sustainability
3. weightlifting
4. world music
5. disability

## ■ Incubation

**Incubation** refers to giving your ideas time to grow and develop. This technique works especially well when you need to step back and evaluate what you've discovered and compiled for your writing. For example, you might not see how your material can be pulled together at first, but if you let it incubate, you might discover connections you didn't see originally. Conversely, if some parts of your essay seem too thin in content, incubation gives you distance from your material so that you can decide what works.

## 2d  What is a thesis statement?

A **thesis statement** is the central message of an essay. The thesis statement presents the TOPIC of your essay, your particular focus on that topic, and your PURPOSE for writing about that topic. As a writer, you want to write a thesis statement with great care so that it prepares your readers for what follows. Quick Reference 2.3 lists the basic requirements for a thesis statement.

| Quick Reference 2.3                    ■ ■ ■ ■ ■ |
|---|
| **Basic requirements for a thesis statement** |
| • It states the essay's subject—the topic that you discuss. |
| • It conveys the essay's purpose—either informative or persuasive. |
| • It indicates your focus—the assertion that presents your point of view. |
| • It uses specific language, not vague words. |
| • It may briefly state the major subdivisions of the essay's topic. |

Some instructors add to these basic requirements for a thesis statement. You might, for example, be asked to put your thesis statement at the end of your introductory paragraph. Some instructors require that the thesis statement be contained in one sentence; other instructors permit two sentences if the topic is complex. All requirements, basic and additional, are designed to help you develop a thesis statement that will guide the writing of your essay and help you communicate clearly with your reader. By the way, never confuse the role of a thesis statement with the role of an essay's title.

Most writers find that their thesis statement changes somewhat with each successive draft of an essay, so you shouldn't feel locked into your first thesis draft. Still, when you revise its language, be sure to stick to the essential idea you want to communicate. A thesis statement is a guide; it helps you stay on the topic and develop your ideas. To start, make an **assertion**—a sentence stating your topic and the point you want to make about it. This assertion focuses your thinking as you develop a preliminary thesis statement. Next, move toward a final thesis statement that most accurately reflects the content of your essay.

### THESIS STATEMENTS FOR INFORMATIVE ESSAYS

For essays with an informative purpose, here are more examples of thesis statements for 900- to 1,300-word essays. The NO versions are assertions or preliminary thesis statements. The YES versions are good because they fulfill the requirements in Quick Reference 2.3.

> **TOPIC**    *Reality television*
>
> **NO**    There are many kinds of reality television shows.
>
> **YES**    A common feature of reality television shows is a villain, a contestant that viewers love to hate.
>
> **TOPIC**    *Women artists*
>
> **NO**    Paintings by women are getting more attention.
>
> **YES**    During the past ten years, the works of the artists Mary Cassatt and Rosa Bonheur have finally gained widespread critical acclaim.

## 2e    How do I plan and organize my ideas?

After you've generated ideas and information, you need to decide the best way to organize it. A plan helps you start drafting. Like a story, an essay needs a beginning, a middle, and an end: a shape. The essay's introduction sets the stage; the essay's body paragraphs provide the substance of your message in a sequence that makes sense; the concluding paragraph ends the essay logically. Each paragraph's length in an informative essay needs to be in proportion to its function. Introductory and concluding paragraphs are usually shorter than body paragraphs. Body paragraphs need to be approximately equal to each other in length. If one body paragraph becomes overly long in relation to the others, consider breaking it into two paragraphs. The major elements in an informative essay are listed in Quick Reference 2.4.

Shaping an essay takes place on two levels. One is grouping individual ideas or pieces of information into paragraphs. The other is arranging those paragraphs into the best possible order and relationship to each other.

### Quick Reference 2.4

■ ■ ■ ■ ■

#### Elements in an informative essay

1. **Introductory paragraph:** Leads into the topic of the essay and tries to capture the reader's interest (see 3c).

2. **Thesis statement:** States the central message of the writing. The thesis statement usually appears at the end of the introductory paragraph (2d).

3. **Background information:** Provides a context for understanding the points that a writer wants to make. You can integrate background information into the introductory paragraph. More complex information may require a separate paragraph of information (as in the second paragraph in Sara Cardini's essay, in section 2l).

4. **Points of discussion:** Supports the essay's thesis statement. They're the essential content of the body paragraphs in an essay (3d). Each point of discussion consists of a general statement backed up by specific details.

5. **Concluding paragraph:** Ends the essay smoothly, flowing logically from the rest of the essay (3k).

To group your information, look for topics that are related to each other and, within them, search for layers of generality. Which ideas or information can fit under which topics?

A **subject tree** shows you visually whether you have sufficient content, at varying levels of generality or specificity, to start a first draft of your writing. A subject tree also visually demonstrates whether you have a good balance

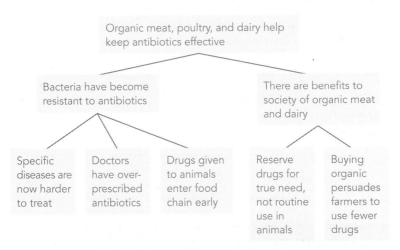

**Alex Garcia's subject tree for the fifth paragraph in his essay**

of general ideas and specific details. If what you have are mostly general ideas—or, the other way around, mostly specific details—go back to techniques for discovering and compiling ideas (2c) so that you can come up with the sorts of materials that are missing. Alex Garcia created a subject tree, shown on page 19, using software tools to help him shape the fifth paragraph in his essay (5j).

Once you've sorted your ideas and information into groups organized by generalizations, you're ready to shape your work at another level. You need to figure out the best order for the sections and paragraphs that you've planned. Of course, like all elements of the writing process, organizing is recursive. Although an initial plan might change considerably as you revise your work, a plan is still helpful for writing your first draft.

# 2f   What is outlining?

An **outline** lays out the relationships among ideas in a piece of writing. Outlines can lead writers to see how well their writing is organized. Many instructors require outlines either before or with an essay.

An outline can be *informal* or *formal.* Try outlining at various steps of the WRITING PROCESS: before drafting, to arrange ideas; while you draft, to keep track of your material; while you revise, to check the logical flow of thought or to reveal what information is missing, repeated, or off the topic; or in whatever other ways you find helpful.

## INFORMAL OUTLINES

An **informal outline** is a working plan that lays out the major points of an essay. Because it's informal, it doesn't need to use the numbering and lettering conventions of a formal outline. Complete sentences aren't required; words and phrases are acceptable. Sara Cardini used an informal outline for planning her essay. Here is part of an informal outline for the third paragraph of her essay.

### Sara Cardini's Informal Outline

*Thesis statement:* Anime has traditions and features that distinguish it from American cartoons and make it sophisticated enough to appeal to adults.

> qualities of anime
>> quick movements
>> jazz and rock music
>> large eyes for characters
>> complicated drawings
>> *Samurai X* as an example

## FORMAL OUTLINES

A traditional **formal outline** follows long-established conventions for using numbers and letters to show relationships among ideas. MLA STYLE (see Chapter 35) doesn't officially endorse using an outline or, indeed, any one outline style. However, many instructors do assign outlines, and they prefer the traditional format shown here. Some instructors prefer a less traditional format for a formal outline, one which includes the content of the introductory and the concluding paragraphs. Either of these styles of formal outline—the traditional or the less traditional—can be a sentence outline, composed entirely of complete sentences, or a topic outline, composed only of words and phrases. So that you can compare the two styles of outlines, both examples below outline the third paragraph of Sara Cardini's essay on Japanese anime. Never mix the two styles in one outline.

Writers who use formal outlines say that a sentence outline brings them closer to drafting than a topic outline does. This makes sense because topic outlines contain less information. But you have to find out which type works better for you.

### Topic Outline

*Thesis statement:* Anime has traditions and features that distinguish it from American cartoons and make it sophisticated enough to appeal to adults.

  I.  Anime qualities

      A.  Quick images

      B.  Jazz and rock soundtracks

      C.  Character eyes and features

      D.  Colorful, complicated art

          1.  *Samurai X* as example

          2.  *Samurai X* about nineteenth-century warrior

          3.  *Samurai X* art like old Japanese prints

### Sentence Outline

*Thesis statement:* Anime has traditions and features that distinguish it from American cartoons and make it sophisticated enough to appeal to adults.

  I.  Complex plots are but one of the distinctive features of anime.

      A.  Anime images move quickly, with a style often more frantic than in American cartoons.

      B.  Their soundtracks frequently use jazz and rock music rather than symphonic music.

C. Most striking are the large eyes and sharp features of the characters.

D. The drawing is more colorful, more complicated, and often more abstract than that in most American cartoons.

1. A TV series called *Samurai X* is one of the most popular anime series with both American and Japanese audiences.

2. *Samurai X* is set in the nineteenth century and tells the story of one warrior's life.

3. *Samurai X* art is drawn beautifully to look both like older Japanese art prints and like more contemporary movies such as *Crouching Tiger, Hidden Dragon.*

# 2g What can help me write a first draft?

**Drafting** means you get ideas onto paper or into the computer, in sentences and paragraphs. In everyday conversation, people use the word *writing* to talk about drafting, but writing is too broad a term here. The word *drafting* more accurately describes what you do when you write your first attempt—your first *draft*—to generate words.

A **first draft** is the initial version of a piece of writing. Before you begin a first draft, seek out places and times of the day that encourage you to write. You might write best in a quiet corner of the library, or at 4:30 a.m. at the kitchen table before anyone else is awake, or outside alone with nature, or with a steady flow of people walking by. Most experienced writers find they concentrate best when they're alone and won't be interrupted. But individuals differ, and you may prefer background noise—a crowded cafeteria, with the low hum of conversation at the next table or in the next room, for example.

Finally, resist delaying tactics. While you certainly need a computer or a pad of paper and a pencil, you don't need fifteen perfectly sharpened pencils neatly lined up on your desk.

Quick Reference 2.5 offers suggestions for ways to move from planning and shaping into drafting. Experiment to see what works best for you. And be ready to adjust what works according to each WRITING SITUATION.

Now, dive in. Using the planning and shaping you've done as a basis, start writing. The direction of drafting is forward: Keep pressing ahead. If you wonder about the spelling of a word or a point of grammar, don't stop. Use a symbol or other signal to alert you to revisit the question later. Use whatever you like: boldface, underlining, a question mark before and after, an asterisk, or all capital letters. If the exact word you want escapes you while you're drafting, substitute an easy synonym and mark it to go back to later. If you question your sentence style or the order in which you present supporting details, boldface or underline the passage or insert a symbol or the word *Style?* or *Order?* nearby so

**Quick Reference 2.5**                    ■ ■ ■ ■ ■

### Ways to start drafting

- **Write a discovery draft.** Put aside all your notes from planning and shaping, and write a discovery draft. This means using FOCUSED FREEWRITING to get ideas on paper or onto your computer screen so that you can make connections that spring to mind as you write. Your discovery draft can serve as a first draft or as one more part of your notes when you write a more structured first draft.

- **Work from your notes.** Sort your notes from planning and shaping into groups of subtopics. When you start writing, you can systematically concentrate on each subtopic without having to search repeatedly through your pile of notes. Arrange the subtopics in what seems to be a sensible sequence, knowing you can always go back later and resequence the subtopics. Now, write a first draft by working through your notes on each subtopic. Draft either the entire essay or chunks of a few paragraphs at one time.

- **Use a combination of approaches.** When you know the shape of your material, write according to that structure. When you feel "stuck" and don't know what to say next, switch to writing as you would for a discovery draft.

that you can return to it later. If you begin to run out of ideas, reread what you have written—not to start revising prematurely, but only to propel yourself to keep moving ahead with your first draft. Once you finish your draft, search for marks that you've used to alert yourself to reconsider something. If it's a word, you can use the "Edit > Find" function on your word processing program toolbar.

A first draft is a preliminary or *rough draft.* Its purpose is to get your ideas onto disk or into computer memory or on paper. Never are first drafts meant to be perfect.

## 2h   How can I overcome writer's block?

If you're afraid or otherwise feel unable to start writing, perhaps you're being stopped by **writer's block.** You want to get started but somehow can't. Often, writer's block occurs because the writer harbors a fear of being wrong. To overcome that fear, or any other cause of your block, first admit it to yourself. Face it honestly so that you can understand whatever is holding you back. Writer's block can strike professional as well as student writers, and a variety of techniques to overcome it have become popular.

Quick Reference 2.6 lists reliable strategies writers have developed to overcome writer's block. If you feel blocked, experiment to discover which works best for you. Also, add your own ideas about how to get started. As you use the list

### Quick Reference 2.6

■ ■ ■ ■ ■

## Ways to overcome writer's block

- **Avoid staring at a blank page.** Relax and move your hand across the keyboard or page. Write words, scribble, or draw while you think about your topic. The physical act of getting anything on paper can stir up ideas and lead you to begin drafting.

- **Visualize yourself writing.** Many professional writers say that they write more easily if they first picture themselves doing it. Before getting out of bed in the morning or while waiting for a bus or walking to classes, mentally construct a visual image of yourself in the place where you usually write, with the materials you need, busy at work.

- **Picture an image or a scene, or imagine a sound that relates to your topic.** Start writing by describing what you see or hear.

- **Write about your topic in a letter or e-mail to a friend.** This technique helps you relax and makes drafting nothing more than a chat on paper with someone you feel comfortable with.

- **Write a draft to a different audience.** If it feels intimidating writing for your instructor, imagine you're writing for a roommate or parent or someone much younger.

- **Try writing your material as if you were someone else.** When they take on a role, many writers feel less inhibited about writing. Pretend you're an expert, for example, and imagine that everyone wants to know what you think.

- **Start by writing the middle of your essay.** Skip the introduction and begin with a body paragraph, and write from the center of your essay out, instead of from beginning to end.

- **Use** FREEWRITING or FOCUSED FREEWRITING.

- **Change your method of writing.** If you usually use a computer, try writing by hand. When you write by hand, switch between pencil and pen or ink colors and treat yourself to good-quality paper so that you can enjoy the pleasure of writing on smooth, strong paper. Often that pleasure propels you to keep going.

- **Switch temporarily to writing about a topic that you care about passionately.** Write freely about that topic. Once writing starts to pour out of you, you can often use the momentum to switch back to the topic of your assignment.

in Quick Reference 2.6, suspend judgment of your writing. Let things flow. Don't find fault with what you're typing or writing. Your goal is to get yourself under way. You can evaluate and improve your writing when you're revising it. According to research, premature revision stops many writers cold—and leads to writer's block. Your reward for waiting to revise until after you finish your first draft is the comfort of having a springboard for the revision work in front of you.

# **2i** How do I revise?

**Revising** is rewriting. To revise, you evaluate, change, and reevaluate your draft to figure out ways to improve it. To do this, you need to read your writing honestly, without losing confidence or becoming defensive. As you work, look at whatever you change and evaluate the revision first on its own and then in the context of the surrounding material. Continue until you're satisfied that your essay is the best you can make it, in light of your specific WRITING SITUATION.

Whenever possible within your time frame, distance yourself from each draft. The best way is to leave a chunk of time between finishing a first draft and starting to revise. Doing so helps you develop an objective sense of your work.

Also, as you're revising, don't start EDITING too soon. Editing comes after revising. Research shows that premature editing distracts writers from dealing with the larger issues that revision involves. Your goal during revision is to improve your draft at three levels: content, organization, and ideas.

To revise successfully, you need to understand that writing is revising. You can engage in the activities of revision, listed in Quick Reference 2.7, by hand or on the computer, which allows you to make both large and small changes easily.

## ■ The role of a thesis statement in revision

The THESIS STATEMENT of your essay has great organizing power because it controls and limits what your essay can cover. Therefore, as you revise, keep checking the accuracy of your thesis statement. Use the thesis statement's controlling power to bring it and your essay into line with each other. Adjust your thesis if necessary, for example, if revisions have resulted in more interesting or effective ideas—or have even changed your position. When your essay is finished, the thesis statement and what you say in your essay need to match. If they don't, you need to revise either the thesis statement or the essay—or sometimes both.

Every writer's experience with revising a thesis statement varies from essay to essay. Sara Cardini, the student you met earlier in this chapter as she did her planning and shaping, wrote several versions of her thesis statement for her drafts. You can read Cardini's three complete drafts, along with comments, at the end of this chapter.

---

### Quick Reference 2.7    ■ ■ ■ ■ ■

#### Major activities during revision

- **Add:** Insert needed words, sentences, paragraphs, or ideas. If your additions require new content, return to the structured techniques shown in section 2b.
- **Cut:** Get rid of whatever goes off the topic or repeats what has already been said.
- **Replace:** As needed, substitute new words, sentences, and paragraphs for what you have cut.
- **Move:** Change the sequence of paragraphs if the material isn't presented in logical order. Move sentences within paragraphs or to other paragraphs when your PARAGRAPH ARRANGEMENT does not allow the material to flow.

---

### ■ The role of a title in revision

Your **title** can also show you what needs revising because it clarifies the overall point of the essay. An effective title sets you on your course and tells your readers what to expect. Some writers like to begin their first drafts with a title at the top of the page to focus their thinking. Then, as they revise drafts, they revise the title. If, however, no title springs to mind, don't be concerned. Often, a good title doesn't surface until after drafting, revising, and even editing. Whatever you do, never tack on a title as an afterthought right before handing in your essay. A suitable title is essential for readers to think about as they begin focusing on your essay.

Titles can be direct or indirect. A **direct title** tells exactly what the essay will be about—for example, "The Characteristics of Japanese Animation." A direct title contains key words under which the essay could be cataloged in a library or an online database. A direct title shouldn't be too broad.

An **indirect title** only hints at the essay's topic. It tries to catch the reader's interest by presenting a puzzle that can be solved by reading the essay. When writing an indirect title, you don't want to be overly obscure or too cute.

🔴 **Alert:** When you write the title at the top of the page or on a title page, never enclose it in quotation marks or underline it. Let your title stand on its own, without decoration. Where you place it will depend on which DOCUMENTATION STYLE you're using. ●

Whether direct or indirect, your essay title stands on its own. Never does the first sentence of an essay refer to the essay's title. For example, Cardini's essay, titled "The Appeal of Japanese Animation for Adults," would suffer a major blow if the first sentence were "It certainly does have appeals" or "I am the proof." Rather, the first sentence starts the flow of the essay's content.

## ■ The role of unity and coherence

Chapter 3 shows you many techniques for achieving unity and coherence in an essay, but here we need to preview those concepts because they're central concerns as you revise.

An essay has **unity** when all of its parts relate to the THESIS STATEMENT and to one another. Does each paragraph—especially each body paragraph—contain examples, reasons, facts, and details that relate directly to your thesis and contribute to your writing situation? As you revise, do you notice that anything in the essay is off the topic? An essay achieves **coherence** through closely built relationships among ideas and details that are built on word choice, use of TRANSITIONAL EXPRESSIONS, clear use of PRONOUNS, and effective PARALLELISM.

## ■ Using a revision checklist

A revision checklist can focus your attention as you evaluate and revise your writing. Use such a checklist, either one provided by your instructor or one that you compile on your own, based on Quick Reference 2.8.

---

### Quick Reference 2.8   ■ ■ ■ ■ ■

#### Revision

Your goal is to answer *yes* to each question on the following list. If you answer *no,* you need to revise your writing accordingly. The section numbers in parentheses tell you where to look in this handbook for help.

1. Is your essay topic suitable and sufficiently narrow?
2. Does your thesis statement communicate your topic, focus, and purpose? (2d, Quick Reference 2.3)
3. Does your essay show that you are aware of your audience? (1c)
4. Have you checked for places where your reader would be confused or need more information?
5. Have you checked for places where a skeptical reader would object to your argument or not be convinced?
6. Is your essay arranged effectively?
7. Have you checked for material that strays off the topic?
8. Does your introduction prepare your reader for the rest of the essay? (3c)
9. Do your body paragraphs express main ideas in topic sentences as needed? (3e) Are your main ideas clearly related to your thesis statement? (2d)
10. Do you provide specific, concrete support for each main idea? (3f)
11. Do you use transitions and other techniques to connect ideas within and between paragraphs? (3j)
12. Does your conclusion give your essay a sense of completion?

## 2j    How do I edit?

Editing means checking the sentence-level wording and the technical correctness of your writing. You carefully examine your writing for correct grammar, spelling, punctuation, capitalization, and use of numbers, italics, and abbreviations. You see if you can improve the style of your sentences. Some people use the terms *editing* and *revising* interchangeably, but these terms refer to very different steps in the writing process. Revising refers to making changes that affect the content, meaning, and organization of a paper. In contrast, editing involves fine-tuning the surface features of your writing.

Editing is crucial. No matter how much attention you've paid to planning, shaping, drafting, and revising, you need to edit carefully. Slapdash editing distracts and annoys your reader; lowers that reader's opinion of you and what you say in your essay; and, in a college assignment, usually earns a lower grade.

Our best advice to you about editing is this: Don't rush. Editing takes time. Resist any impulse to hurry. Be systematic and patient. Checking grammar and punctuation takes your full concentration, along with time to look up and apply the rules in this handbook.

Word-processing programs include editing tools such as a spell-checker, style-checker, thesaurus, and readability analyzer. However, each of these tools has shortcomings serious enough to create new errors. Yet, if you use the tools intelligently, with their shortcomings in mind, they can be useful.

Whenever possible, edit on a paper copy of your writing. It's much easier to spot editing errors on a printed page than on a computer screen. Double-space your paper before printing it for revising or editing. The extra space gives you room to write your changes clearly so that you can read them easily later. After you finish editing, you can transfer your corrections to the computer. If you must edit on-screen, highlight every two or three sentences and read each slowly. By working in small segments, you reduce the tendency to read too quickly and miss errors.

Using an editing checklist—either one provided by your instructor or one based on Quick Reference 2.9 that you tailor to your particular needs—can help you find errors by moving through editing systematically.

## 2k    How do I proofread?

To **proofread,** check your final draft for accuracy and neatness before handing it in. In contrast to editing, which is a check for technical correctness, proofreading is a check for typographical accuracy. This is your last chance to catch typing (or handwriting) errors and to make sure that you hand in a clean transcription of your final draft. You don't want all your hard efforts drafting, revising, and editing to be undercut by not taking this final step.

## Quick Reference 2.9

### Editing

Your goal is to answer *yes* to each question below. If you answer *no,* you need to edit. The numbers in parentheses tell you which chapters in this handbook to go to for more information.

1. Are your sentences concise? (Chapter 11)
2. Are your sentences interesting? Do you use parallelism, variety, and emphasis correctly and to increase the impact of your writing? (Chapters 9–10)
3. Have you used exact words? (Chapter 12)
4. Is your usage correct and your language appropriate? (Chapter 13)
5. Have you avoided sexist or stereotypical language? (Chapter 12)
6. Is your grammar correct? (Chapters 14–22)
7. Is your spelling correct? (Chapter 31)
8. Have you used commas correctly? (Chapter 24)
9. Have you used all other punctuation correctly? (Chapters 23 and 25–29)
10. Have you used capital letters, italics, abbreviations, and numbers correctly? (Chapter 30)
11. Have you used the appropriate citation and documentation formats? (Chapters 35–36)

When proofreading, read your work carefully line by line, looking for typing errors such as "form" vs. "from," letters or words accidentally omitted, words typed twice in a row, wrong indents to start each paragraph, and similar typos or slips. Then, print out a complete fresh copy. Reprinting just one page is often difficult because of reflowing text. Never expect your instructor to make allowances for handwritten corrections.

Some techniques for proofreading include: (1) using a ruler under each line as you read it to prevent yourself from looking beyond that line; (2) reading backwards, sentence by sentence, to prevent yourself from being distracted by the content of the paper; and (3) proofreading your final draft aloud, to yourself or to a friend, so that you can hear errors that have slipped past your eyes. As with revising and editing, whenever possible, print and proofread a double-spaced paper copy of your writing. Again, it's much easier to spot errors on a printed page than onscreen. If you must proofread onscreen, highlight every two or three sentences and read each slowly. Enlarging the type onscreen is another useful trick to help you focus word by word.

## 2l    A student essay in three drafts

The following sections observe Sara Cardini, a student, planning to write on the topic of Japanese animation. Elsewhere in this chapter, you'll find her writing assignment (2b), how she used an entry in her journal, mapped her ideas, wrote her thesis statement (2d), and outlined (2f).

### ◼ The first draft of a student essay

Here's Cardini's first draft showing her own notes to herself about revisions to make in the second draft. The notes resulted from comments from other students in her peer-response group (6c) and from her personal rereading of her draft.

Sara Cardini

Mr. Bantham

English 101    *[I know. It's not specific enough]*

10 April 2009

Japanese Videos    *[Oops. The opening sentence shouldn't continue the title]*

There certainly are many reasons to like it. Like most

people, I watched cartoons as a child, consuming daily doses

*[Remember to italicize titles in final draft]* of Hey, Arnold and Doug and watching The Lion King over

and over again. Then, I discovered Sailor Moon and an entirely

different approach to animation. Sailor Moon is just one

of hundreds of animated television series to come from the

*[I'd better show pronunciation]* creative minds of Japan. These series and thousands of

films are called anime. Because much anime is created for

adults, I have continued to watch it as I have gotten older.

→

**Sara Cardini's first draft, with notes**

*in my interest*

I am not alone. In recent years, (anime rocks) Still, people  *Tone*
                                                              *appropriate?*

who are unfamiliar with anime may wonder why adults

would waste their time watching cartoons. (Some careful

analysis makes the answer clear.) Anime is a sophisticated

Japanese cartoon style.   *Need to add thesis concept that*
                          *anime differs from American cartoons.*

Someone watching (animes) for the first time notices several

*Check*
*plural*  distinctive qualities: ~~The most obvious difference between~~

Japanese and American cartoons is, of course, the language.

Most anime will let you choose between a dubbed version

(with actors speaking English) and a subtitled version (in

*I think*  which the English is written at the bottom of the screen). True
*I'm*
*going*   ~~anime fans will never want to the dubbed version. As a result,~~
*off*
*track*
*here.*    American viewers are barraged with Japanese voices that seem
*Are*
*these*    to use a high-pitched, very fast speaking style. Of course, the
*points*
*important*
*to my*     film depicts Japanese houses, trees, rooms, and such in a way
*comparison?*
           ~~that shows the contrasts between their country and ours.~~  *Keep*
                                                                         *verb*
           Anime images move quickly, with a style often more frantic *tenses*
                                                                        *consistent.*
           than in American cartoons. Their soundtracks frequently (used)

                          *symphonic*
*Too*      jazz and rock rather than ~~traditional~~ music. People in anime are
*itsy*
*bitsy.*   very stylized, not realistic. The drawing is colorful. It is more
*Make*
*into*      complicated. It is often more abstract than most American
*one*
*sentence*                                                            →

**Sara Cardini's first draft, with notes, continued**

cartoons. ~~E.G.~~ *For example,* ⟨take⟩ a TV series called <u>Samurai X</u> the most

popular anime cartoons with both American and Japanese

audiences. <u>Samurai X</u> is set in the nineteenth century and

*"take" isn't the right verb—fix*

tells the story of one warrior's life. It is drawn beautifully in

*wordy* → a way that looks both like older Japanese art prints and like

more contemporary movies such as <u>Crouching Tiger, Hidden</u>

<u>Dragon.</u>

*Bet this is a fragment. Check Chapter 19.*

~~While~~ *Whereas* Americans considered animation entertainment

for children. The Japanese viewed it as ~~entertaining primarily~~ *mainly*

for adults. Since the beginning of print, cartooning in Japan

has been aimed at adults, so anime was a natural step. It's *in this tradition*

interesting how graphic novels were important in Japan long

before they were here, but lately you see more and more

graphic novels. In America, aside from editorial cartoons

and newspaper funny pages, comics were ⟨aimed⟩ primarily

*adolescent males*

at ~~boys~~. American animation in the 1940s and 1950s was

*Used same word twice. Get out my thesaurus.*

different. Think of Walt Disney. Japanese cartoons were

developed for both kids and old people, male and female

audiences. In Japan, animated cartoons take on adult subjects

often absent from American cartoons. ← *Examples needed*

*There must be a better word*

The ⟨special⟩ style of anime comes largely from the films

→

**Sara Cardini's first draft, with notes, continued**

being produced for [narrow] audiences. The animators were *Right word?*

creating works only for a Japanese market, at least until

quite recently. Therefore, they did not take into account the

traditions of other cultures. Indeed, US animation was

produced for an international audience, which called for

recognizable themes that came out of familiar European

traditions. For ~~rookie~~ *uninitiated* viewers then, anime provides a crash

course in ~~a~~ *an Eastern* culture quite different from their own. Nearly

all serious anime fans own guides that explain such things *Add more detail here*

as Japanese social hierarchies. For instance, several anime

feature a *hagoromo* or feathered cloak worn by a mythological

figure known as the tennyo. Knowing that this figure has a

*symbolic* certain meaning for a Japanese viewer and is not just a

random decoration or character adds to the depth of a scene

in which it appears. Decoding some of these cultural

references is undoubtedly some of the fun and challenge for

the true *otakon*, or anime fan.

Japanese television has many daily animated series

that vary in terms of sophistication and audience. Some of

these have extremtly ~~complicated~~ *complex* scripts, while others are

bad by nearly any standard. Several of these television series

→

**Sara Cardini's first draft, with notes, continued**

*Add examples*

now appear in the United States. A wide range of anime

feature films is readily available on DVD, and many have

even found their way into American theaters. For instance,

Akira is a film about life thirty years after a nuclear war.

Probably the most famous theatrical anime in the United    *Better look at this sentence again!*

States is Spirited Away. Directed by Hayao Miyasaki, in

which a young girl, Chihiro, is able to free her parents from

*probably*

a spell after many magical adventures. The movie will become

a ~~probably~~ classic. Anime appears in all kinds of types and

genres, from childish works like Pokémon to dark science

fiction like Ghost in the Shell.    *I think I should move this up as the topic sentence for this paragraph.*

*Best word?*    One reason grown-ups enjoy anime is because they

missed a form they loved as children. Anime gives them    *of design, creativity, sophistication and content*

*Verb tense ok?*    animated art but adds an adult level. While there have

been a few American cartoons aimed at adults (The Simpsons,

South Park), the animation is less detailed and the tone is

usually satiric. There is no such barrier in anime.

By studying anime, I also learned more about Japan.

I met people who took Japanese language classes and had

traveled to cities such as Tokyo and Osaka. I found out about

Japanese popular culture and how much fashion, music, etc.,

→

**Sara Cardini's first draft, with notes, continued**

the Japanese borrow from Americans and how much we

borrow from them. I discovered that while the Japanese are

very different in some traditions, they are very much like us

in terms of their love of movies, TV, and music. For the first

time, I became very interested in how people in another

*Does this para relate directly to my thesis?*

country live. Now I am considering traveling to Japan

As Americans come to embrace anime, the form may

*watered down*

change. Some fans fear that the art of anime will be ~~wasted~~
$\wedge$

in the bid for popularity and profits. Others celebrate the

combination of styles as some American animators borrow

from the Japanese. In this essay I have explained Japanese

rmimation.

*I shouldn't declare what I have done. My ending needs work.*

**Sara Cardini's first draft, with notes, continued**

## ■ The second draft of a student essay

For her second draft, Cardini revised by working systematically through the notes she had written on the draft. The notes came from her own thinking as well as from the comments of the peer-response group with which she had shared her paper.

From the assignment (2b), Cardini knew that her instructor would consider this second draft an "essay in progress." Her instructor's responses would help her write a final draft. She expected two types of comments: questions to help her clarify and expand on some of her ideas, and references to some of this handbook's section codes (designated by number-letter combinations) to point out errors. Here is her second draft.

Sara Cardini

Mr. Bantham

English 101

14 April 2005

*[Think about the title as you clarify the overall point of your essay.]*

Japanese Anime

*[What might be an attention-catching opening line?]*

Like most people, I watched cartoons as a child, consuming daily doses of *Hey, Arnold* and *Doug* and watching *The Lion King* over and over again. *[When?]* Then, I discovered *Sailor Moon* and an entirely different approach to animation. *Sailor Moon* is just one of hundreds of animated television series to come from the creative minds of Japan. These series and *[What personal background do you have in this area?]* thousands of films are called anime (commonly pronounced AN-ah-may). Because much anime is created for adults, I have continued to watch it as I have gotten older. I am not alone in my interest. In recent years, anime has become hugely popular in the United States. Still, people who are *[If this sentence is necessary, why put it in parentheses?]* unfamiliar with anime may wonder why adults waste their time watching cartoons. (Some careful analysis makes the answer clear.) The purpose of this paper is to

*[For comma use, see 24c]*

→

**Sara Cardini's second draft, with her instructor's responses**

*Indicate the purpose of your paper without announcing it.*

explain Japanese anime and how it differs from the style of American cartoons.

*Should this para come after the background information?*

*Think about a stronger link between paragraphs*

Someone watching anime for the first time notices several distinctive qualities. Anime images move quickly, with a style often more frantic than in American cartoons. Their soundtracks frequently use jazz and rock rather

*Interesting, but I'd like to know more detail*

than symphonic music. People in anime are very stylized, not realistic. The drawing is more colorful, more complicated, and often more abstract than in most American cartoons. For example, a TV series called *Samurai X* is one of the most popular anime cartoons with both American and Japanese audiences. *Samurai X* is set in the nineteenth century and

*Since this para gives background information, does it belong here?*

tells the story of one warrior's life.

*Why is it popular?*

Whereas Americans considered animation entertainment for children, the Japanese viewed it as mainly for adults. Since the beginning of print, cartooning in Japan has targeted adults,

*This para needs a stronger topic sentence.*

so anime was a natural step in this tradition. It's interesting how graphic novels were important in Japan long before they

*Off topic?*

were here, but lately you see more and more graphic novels.

→

**Sara Cardini's second draft, with her instructor's responses, continued**

In the United States, aside from editorial cartoons and newspaper funny pages, comics were aimed primarily at adolescent males. American animation in the 1940s and 1950s was different. Think of Walt Disney. Japanese cartoons were developed for both kids and old people, male and female audiences. In Japan, animated cartoons take on adult subjects often absent from American cartoons. These subjects include war, death, sacrifice, love, Japan's historical past and future, and even occasionally sex and violence.

The unique style of anime comes largely from the films being produced for narrow audiences. The animators were creating works only for a Japanese market, at least until quite recently. Therefore, it did not take into account the traditions of other cultures. Indeed, American animation was produced for an international audience, which called for recognizable themes that came out of familiar European traditions. For uninitiated viewers, then, anime provides a crash course in an Eastern culture quite different from their own. Nearly all serious anime fans own guides that explain such

*[Handwritten instructor's notes:]*
- A little more guidance, please.
- From what?
- Off topic?
- A link to the next para would be welcome here.
- Right word? [pointing to "narrow"]
- What does it refer to? See 16p
- Right word? [pointing to "Indeed,"]

→

**Sara Cardini's second draft, with her instructor's responses, continued**

things as Japanese social hierarchies, clothing, dining habits,

traditions, rituals, and mythology. For instance, several anime See next page.

feature a *hagoromo*, or feathered cloak, worn by a mythological

figure known as the *tennyo*. Knowing that this figure has a

symbolic meaning for a Japanese viewer and is not just a

random decoration or character adds to the depth of a scene

in which it appears. Decoding some of these cultural references

*Excellent point!*

is undoubetedly some of the fun and challenge for the true

*otakon*, or anime fan.

Anime appears in all kinds of types and genres, from

*Do you really mean childish?*

childish works like *Pokémon* to dark science fiction like *Ghost

In the Shell*. Japanese television has many daily animated series

that vary in terms of sophistication and audience. Some of

*Meaning what?*

these have extremely complex scripts, while others are bad

by nearly any standard. Several of these television series

now appear in the United States, with some of the best known

including *Inuyasha* and *Evangelion*. A wide range of anime

feature films are readily available on DVD, and many have

even found their way into American theaters.

→

**Sara Cardini's second draft, with her instructor's responses, continued**

*See previous page.*

(For instance,) *Akira* is a film about life thirty years after a nuclear war. Probably the most famous theatrical anime video in the United States is *Spirited Away*, directed by Hayao Miyasaki, in which a young girl, Chihiro, is able to free her parents from a spell after many magical adventures. The movie will probably become a classic.

*More detail would make this vivid.*

One reason American adults enjoy anime is because they miss a form they loved as children. Anime gives them animated art but adds an adult level of design, creativity, sophistication, and content. While there have been a few American cartoons aimed at adults (*The Simpsons, South Park*). the animation is less detailed and the tone is usually satiric. There are no such barriers in anime.

*Interesting concluding thoughts*

As Americans come to embrace anime, the form may change. Some fans fear that the art of anime will be watered down in the bid for popularity and profits. Others celebrate the combination of styles as some American animators borrow from the Japanese. In this essay I have proved that anime deserves our attention.

*Bringing in your voice again makes for an effective ending.*

*But avoid making an absolute claim like this.*

**Sara Cardini's second draft, with her instructor's responses, continued**

## ■ A student's final draft

For her final draft, Cardini worked systematically through her second draft with an eye on her instructor's responses. Also, she revised in places where her instructor hadn't commented. As another check, Cardini referred to the revision checklist (Quick Reference 2.8).

Next, to edit her final draft, Cardini looked up the handbook codes (number-letter combinations) her instructor wrote on her second draft. She also consulted the editing checklist (Quick Reference 2.9). Then, before she started to proofread, she took a break from writing so she could refresh her ability to see typing errors. Distance from her work, she knew, would also help her see it more objectively.

Cardini's final draft appears on the following pages with notes in the margins to point out elements that help the essay succeed. These notes are for you only; don't write any notes on your final drafts.

**Sara Cardini's final draft**

Places name
and page
number at
top right

Sara Cardini

Mr. Bantham

English 101

13 April 2008

Includes name,
course information,
and date; double-
spaced and flush left

Centers title

The Appeal of Japanese Animation for Adults

Includes
attention-
getting
first line

I confess that I am an animation addict. Like most people,
I watched cartoons as a child, consuming daily doses of *Hey,
Arnold* and *Doug* and watching *The Lion King* over and over
again. Then in junior high, just about the time I was getting
tired of cartoons, I discovered *Sailor Moon* and an entirely
different approach to animation. *Sailor Moon* is just one of
hundreds of animated television series to come from the
creative minds of Japan. These series and thousands of films
are called *anime* (commonly pronounced AN-ah-may). Because
much anime is created for adults, I have continued to watch

Provides her
credentials on
this topic

it as I have gotten older. In fact, my interest has grown so
strong that I have studied Japanese, have attended anime
conferences, and am now studying filmmaking. I am not alone
in my interest. In recent years, anime has become hugely

Introduces
a question

popular in the United States. Still, people who are unfamiliar
with anime may wonder why adults would waste their time
watching cartoons. Some careful analysis makes the answer

Offers a
thesis

clear. Anime has traditions and features that distinguish it
from American cartoons and make it sophisticated enough to
appeal to adults.

continued >>

(Proportions shown in this paper are adjusted to fit space limitations of this book. Follow
actual dimensions given in this book and your instructor's directions.)

Cardini 2

Animation developed differently in Japan and America after World War II. Whereas Americans considered animation entertainment for children, the Japanese viewed it as mainly for adults. Since the beginning of print, cartooning in Japan has targeted adults, so anime was a natural step in this tradition. In America, aside from editorial cartoons and newspaper funny pages, comics were aimed primarily at adolescent males. Therefore, American animation in the 1940s and 1950s was different from the type developed in Japan. The early work of Walt Disney, for example, came from fairy tales, or it featured cute animal characters. In Japan, animated cartoons take on adult subjects often absent from American cartoons. These subjects include war, death, sacrifice, love, Japan's historical past and future, and even occasionally sex and violence. The plot lines are often extremely complex. Stories that would be kept simple in a Disney film to avoid viewer confusion have no such restrictions in Japan.

Complex plots are but one of the distinctive features of anime. Anime images move quickly, with a style often more frantic than in American cartoons. Their soundtracks frequently use jazz and rock rather than symphonic music. However, perhaps most striking are the large eyes and sharp features of the characters. People in anime are very stylized, not realistic. The drawing is more colorful, more complicated, and often more abstract than most American cartoons. For example, a TV series called *Samurai X* is one of the most popular anime cartoons with both American and Japanese audiences. *Samurai X* is set in the nineteenth century and tells the story of one warrior's life. It is drawn beautifully in a way

**Provides background on topic**

**Uses comparison and contrast to develop paragraph**

**Uses specific details to explain anime**

**Provides a concrete example**

continued >>

Cardini 3

that looks both like older Japanese art prints and like more contemporary movies such as *Crouching Tiger, Hidden Dragon.*

**Uses cause and effect to explain differences**

The unique style of anime comes largely from the films being produced for specific audiences. The animators were creating works only for a Japanese market, at least until quite recently. Therefore, they did not take into account the traditions of other cultures. In contrast, American animation was produced for an international audience, which called for recognizable themes that came out of familiar European traditions. For uninitiated viewers, then, anime provides a crash course in an Eastern culture quite different from their own. Nearly all serious anime fans own guides that explain such things as Japanese social hierarchies, clothing, dining habits, traditions, rituals, and mythology. To cite one small

**Cites a very specific example**

example, several anime feature a *hagoromo,* or feathered cloak, worn by a mythological figure known as the *tennyo.* Knowing that this figure has a symbolic meaning for a Japanese viewer and is not just a random decoration or character adds to the depth of a scene in which it appears. Decoding some of these cultural references is undoubtedly some of the fun and challenge for the true *otakon,* or anime fan.

**Uses classification to explain types**

Anime appears in all kinds of types and genres, from children's works like *Pokémon* to dark science fiction like *Ghost in the Shell.* Japanese television has many daily animated series that vary in terms of sophistication and audience. Some of these have extremely complex scripts, while others are painfully simplistic. Several of these television series now appear in America, with some of the best known

continued >>

Cardini 4

including *Inuyasha* and *Evangelion*. A wide range of anime feature films are readily available on DVD in America, and many have even found their way into theaters. For example, *Akira* is a film about life thirty years after a nuclear war. A misfit boy, Tetsuo, accidentally discovers the government experiments that led to that war and then learns that scientists are starting similar experiments once again. Probably the most famous theatrical anime films in the United States are *Howl's Moving Castle* and *Spirited Away*. In the last one, directed by Hayao Miyasaki, a young girl, Chihiro, is able to free her parents from a spell after many magical adventures. The movie will probably become a classic.

One reason American adults enjoy anime is because they miss a form they loved as children. Anime gives them animated art but adds an adult level of design, creativity, sophistication, and content. While there have been a few American cartoons aimed at adults (*The Simpsons, South Park*), the animation is not very detailed and the tone is usually satiric. There are no such barriers in anime.

As Americans come to embrace anime, the form may change. Some fans fear that the art of anime will be watered down in the bid for popularity and profits. Others celebrate the combination of styles as some American animators borrow from the Japanese. As an animation addict, I welcome more American animation for adults. Still, I would be disappointed if the distinctive qualities of anime disappeared. I fervently hope the Japanese animators will maintain their exotic creativity.

*Provides specific titles as examples*

*Focuses at length on one prominent example*

*States a reason in the topic sentence*

*Contrasts American cartoons with anime*

*Speculates about the future in concluding strategy*

*Uses final comment to return to her opening idea*

# 3

■ ■ ■ ■

# Writing Paragraphs, Shaping Essays

## 3a How do I shape essays?

A good essay has an effective beginning, middle, and end. The key word is *effective.* Beginnings interest your reader and create expectations for the rest of the essay, usually through a THESIS STATEMENT, your main point. Middles explain or provide arguments for the thesis, usually through a series of statements and supporting details or evidence. Writers organize their main ideas to build a logical and engaging sequence. What separates most good writing from bad is the writer's ability to move back and forth between main ideas and specific details. Endings provide closure. They make readers feel that the writing achieved its purpose and that the writer had a skilled sense of his or her audience to the very end. One key to shaping essays is understanding how paragraphs work.

## 3b How do paragraphs work?

A **paragraph** is a group of sentences that work together to develop a unit of thought. Paragraphing permits writers to divide material into manageable parts. When a group of paragraphs works together in logical sequence, the result is a complete essay or other whole piece of writing.

To signal the start of a new paragraph, indent the first line about one-half inch. Skip no extra lines between paragraphs. Business writing (Chapter 39) is an exception: It calls for BLOCK STYLE for paragraphs, which means you do not indent the first line but rather leave a double space between paragraphs.

## 3c How can I write effective introductory paragraphs?

An **introductory paragraph** leads the reader to sense what's ahead. It sets the stage. It also, if possible, attempts to arouse a reader's interest in the topic.

A THESIS STATEMENT can be an important component in an introduction. Many instructors require students to place the thesis statement at the end of the opening paragraph. Doing so disciplines students to state early the central point of the essay. If an introduction points in one direction, and the rest of the essay goes off in another, the essay isn't communicating a clear message. Professional writers don't necessarily include a thesis statement in their introductory paragraphs. Most have the skill to maintain a line of thought without overtly stating a main idea. Introductory paragraphs, as well as concluding paragraphs (3k), are often shorter than body paragraphs (3d).

Be careful not to tack on a sloppy introduction at the last minute. The introductory paragraph plays too important a role to be tossed off with merely a few shallow lines. That doesn't mean you have to write an introduction first; you might put down ideas and a thesis to start, then return during the revision process to write an effective, polished introduction. For a list of specific strategies to use and pitfalls to avoid for introductory paragraphs, see Quick Reference 3.1.

---

### Quick Reference 3.1

#### Introductory paragraphs

**STRATEGIES TO USE**

- Providing relevant background information
- Relating briefly an interesting story or anecdote
- Giving one or more pertinent—perhaps surprising—statistics
- Asking one or more provocative questions
- Using an appropriate quotation
- Defining a KEY TERM
- Presenting one or more brief examples (3i)
- Drawing an ANALOGY (3i)

**STRATEGIES TO AVOID**

- Don't write statements about your purpose, such as "I am going to discuss the causes of falling oil prices."
- Don't apologize, as in "I am not sure this is right, but this is my opinion."
- Don't use overworked expressions, such as "Haste makes waste, as I recently discovered" or "Love is grand" or "According to Webster's dictionary."

---

Always integrate an introductory device into the paragraph so that it leads smoothly into the thesis statement. Some examples follow. In this chapter, each example paragraph has a number to its left for your easy reference. Here's an introductory paragraph that uses two brief examples to lead into the thesis statement at the end of the paragraph.

1   On seeing another child fall and hurt himself, Hope, just nine months old, stared, tears welling up in her eyes, and crawled to her mother to be comforted—as though she had been hurt, not her friend. When 15-month-old Michael saw his friend Paul crying, Michael fetched his own teddy bear and offered it to Paul; when that didn't stop Paul's tears, Michael brought Paul's security blanket from another room. Such small acts of sympathy and caring, observed in scientific studies, are leading researchers to trace the roots of empathy—the ability to share another's emotions—to infancy, contradicting a long-standing assumption that infants and toddlers were incapable of these feelings.

—Daniel Goleman, "Researchers Trace Empathy's Roots to Infancy"

In paragraph 2, the opening quotation sets up a dramatic contrast with the thesis statement.

2   "Alone one is never lonely," says May Sarton in her essay "The Rewards of Living a Solitary Life." Most people, however, don't share Sarton's opinion: They're terrified of living alone. They're used to living with others—children with parents, roommates with roommates, friends with friends, spouses with spouses. When the statistics catch up with them, therefore, they're rarely prepared. Chances are high that most adult men and women will need to know how to live alone, briefly or longer, at some time in their lives.

—Tara Foster, student

**EXERCISE 3-1**    Write an introduction for each of the three essays informally outlined below. Then, for more practice, write one alternative introduction for each. If you have a peer-response group, share the various written introductions and decide which are most effective. For help, see section 3c.

1. Play at school
   *Thesis statement:* School recesses today differ tremendously from recess a generation ago.
   Body paragraph 1: types of recess activities thirty years ago
   Body paragraph 2: types of games now, including ultimate frisbee
   Body paragraph 3: other activities, including climbing walls and free running

2. Cell phones
   *Thesis statement:* Cell phones have changed how some people behave in public.
   Body paragraph 1: driving
   Body paragraph 2: restaurants
   Body paragraph 3: movies and concerts
   Body paragraph 4: sidewalks, parks, and other casual spaces

3. Identity theft
   *Thesis statement:* Taking some simple precautions can reduce the danger of identity theft.
   Body paragraph 1: discarding junk mail
   Body paragraph 2: watching store purchases
   Body paragraph 3: Internet security

# 3d What are body paragraphs?

In most academic writing, each **body paragraph,** the several paragraphs between an introductory paragraph (3c) and a concluding paragraph (3k), consists of a main idea and support for that idea. To be effective, a body paragraph needs three characteristics: development (3f), unity (3g), and coherence (3g). Quick Reference 3.2 gives an overview of all three characteristics.

---

**Quick Reference 3.2** ■ ■ ■ ■ ■

### Characteristics of effective body paragraphs

- **Development:** Have you included detailed and sufficient support for the main idea of the paragraph? (3f)
- **Unity:** Have you made a clear connection between the main idea of the paragraph and the sentences that support, develop, or illustrate the main idea? (3g)
- **Coherence:** Have you progressed from one sentence to the next in the paragraph smoothly and logically? (3g)

---

Paragraph 3 is an example of an effective body paragraph.

> **3** The Miss Plastic Surgery contest, trumpeted by Chinese promoters as "the world's first pageant for artificial beauties," shows the power of cosmetic surgery in a country that has swung from one extreme to another when it comes to the feminine ideal. In the 10th century, Emperor Li Yu ordered his consort to bind her feet; women practiced the painful ritual for more than 900 years in the belief that small feet were more alluring. In contrast, at the height of the Cultural Revolution in the 1960s and 1970s, Maoist officials condemned any form of personal grooming or beautification as "unrevolutionary" and regularly beat women for owning hairbrushes, wearing blush, or painting their nails.
>
> —Abigail Haworth, "Nothing About These Women Is Real"

Paragraph 3 has UNITY (3g) in that the main idea—the feminine ideal in China has swung from one extreme to another—stated in the TOPIC SENTENCE (3e) is supported by detailed examples. It has COHERENCE (3g) in that the content of every sentence ties into the content of the other sentences. Also, the paragraph *coheres*—sticks together—because of the use of transitional phrases

("In the 10th century" and "In contrast," for example). It has PARAGRAPH DE-VELOPMENT (3f) in that the details provide support for the main idea.

## 3e    What are topic sentences?

A **topic sentence** contains the main idea of a paragraph and controls its content. Often, the topic sentence comes at the beginning of a paragraph, though not always. Professional essay writers, because they have the skill to carry the reader along without explicit signposts, sometimes decide not to use topic sentences. However, instructors often require students to use topic sentences. As apprentice writers, students might have more difficulty writing unified paragraphs.

### TOPIC SENTENCE STARTING A PARAGRAPH

In ACADEMIC WRITING, most paragraphs begin with a topic sentence so that readers know immediately what to expect. Paragraph 4 is an example.

**4**    Music patronage was at a turning point when Mozart went to Vienna in the last part of the eighteenth century. Many patrons of music continued to be wealthy aristocrats. Haydn's entire career was funded by a rich prince. Mozart's father and, for a time, Mozart himself were in the employ of another prince. But when Mozart went to Vienna in 1781, he contrived to make a living from a variety of sources. In addition to performances at aristocratic houses and commissions for particular works, Mozart gave piano and composition lessons, put on operas, and gave many public concerts of his own music.

—Jeremy Yudkin, "Composers and Patrons in the Classic Era"

### TOPIC SENTENCE ENDING A PARAGRAPH

Some paragraphs give supporting details first and wait to state the topic sentence at the paragraph's end. This approach is particularly effective for building suspense or for creating a bit of drama. Paragraph 5 is an example.

**5**    Once the Romans had left, the political situation in Britain deteriorated rapidly. Softened by their dependence on the Roman legions, the Romanized Britons were ill equipped to defend themselves from renewed attacks by the Picts in the north. Then, even as the Britons were trying to cope with their fiercer northern neighbors, a much more calamitous series of events took place: waves of Germanic-speaking people from the Continent began to invade the island. The "English" were coming to England.

—C. M. Millward, "The Arrival of the English"

### TOPIC SENTENCE IMPLIED, NOT STATED

Some paragraphs are a unified whole even without a single sentence that readers can point to as the topic sentence. Yet, most readers can catch the main idea anyway. Paragraph 6 is an example. What do you think might be a straightforward topic sentence for it?

6  It is easy to identify with the quest for a secret document, somewhat harder to do so with a heroine whose goal is identifying and understanding the element radium, which is why in dramatic biography writers and directors end up reverting to fiction. To be effective, the dramatic elements must, and finally will, take precedence over any "real" biographical facts. We viewers do not care—if we wanted to know about the element radium, we would read a book on the element radium. When we go to the movies to see *The Story of Marie Curie* we want to find out how her little dog Skipper died.

—David Mamet, *Three Uses of the Knife:*
*On the Nature and Purpose of Drama*

**EXERCISE 3-2**   Working individually or with a group, identify the topic sentences in the following paragraphs. If the topic sentence is implied, write the point the paragraph conveys. For help, consult section 3e.

A.  A good college program should stress the development of high-level reading, writing, and mathematical skills and should provide you with a broad historical, social, and cultural perspective, no matter what subject you choose as your major. The program should teach you not only the most current knowledge in your field but also—just as important—prepare you to keep learning throughout your life. After all, you'll probably change jobs, and possibly even careers, at least six times, and you'll have other responsibilities, too—perhaps as a spouse and as a parent and certainly as a member of a community whose bounds extend beyond the workplace.

—Frank T. Rhodes, "Let the Student Decide"

B.  The once majestic oak tree crashes to the ground amid the destructive flames, as its panic-stricken inhabitants attempt to flee the fiery tomb. Undergrowth that formerly flourished smolders in ashes. A family of deer darts furiously from one wall of flame to the other, without an emergency exit. On the outskirts of the inferno, firefighters try desperately to stop the destruction. Somewhere at the source of this chaos lies a former campsite containing the cause of this destruction—an untended campfire. This scene is one of many that illustrate how human apathy and carelessness destroy nature.

—Anne Bryson, student

C.  Rudeness isn't a distinctive quality of our own time. People today would be shocked by how rudely our ancestors behaved. In the colonial period, a French traveler marveled that "Virginians don't use napkins, but they wear silk cravats, and instead of carrying white handkerchiefs, they blow their noses either with their fingers or with a silk handkerchief that also serves as a cravat, a napkin, and so on." In the 19th century, up to about the 1830s, even very distinguished people routinely put their knives in their mouths. And when people went to the theater, they would not just applaud politely—they would chant, jeer, and shout. So, the notion that there's been a downhill slide in manners ever since time began is just not so.

—"Horizons," *U.S. News & World Report*

# 3f How can I develop my body paragraphs?

You develop a **body paragraph** by supplying detailed support for the main idea of the paragraph communicated by your TOPIC SENTENCE (3e), whether stated or implied. **Paragraph development** is not merely a repetition, using other words, of the main idea. When this happens, you're merely going around in circles. We've deliberately manipulated paragraph 3 above to create paragraph 10. It is an example of a poorly developed paragraph. It goes nowhere; rather, it restates one idea three times in different words.

**NO**

**10**

The Miss Plastic Surgery contest, trumpeted by Chinese promoters as "the world's first pageant for artificial beauties," shows the power of cosmetic surgery in a country that has swung from one extreme to another when it comes to the feminine ideal. In past decades, China did not promote personal grooming. Beautification is a recent development.

To check whether you are providing sufficient detail in a body paragraph, use the RENNS Test. Each letter in the made-up word *RENNS* cues you to remember a different kind of supporting detail at your disposal, as listed in Quick Reference 3.3.

---

### Quick Reference 3.3

#### The RENNS test: Checking for supporting details

**R = Reasons** provide support.

Jules Verne, a nineteenth-century writer of science fiction, amazes readers today **because he imagined inventions impossible to develop until recent years.**

**E = Examples** provide support.

**For example,** he predicted submarines and moon rockets.

**N = Names** provide support.

He forecast that the moon rockets would take off from an area in the **state of Florida.**

**N = Numbers** provide support.

Specifically, he declared as the point of departure **27 degrees North Latitude and 5 degrees West Longitude.**

**S = Senses**—sight, sound, smell, taste, touch—provide support.

Today, space vehicles are **heard blasting off** from Cape Kennedy, only eighty miles from the site Verne chose.

Use the RENNS Test to check the quality of your paragraph development. Of course, not every paragraph needs all five kinds of RENNS details, nor do the supporting details need to occur in the order of the letters in *RENNS*. Paragraph 11 contains three of the five types of RENNS details. Identify the topic sentence and as many RENNS as you can before reading the analysis that follows the paragraph.

**11** U.S. shores are also being inundated by waves of plastic debris. On the sands of the Texas Gulf Coast one day last September, volunteers collected 307 tons of litter, two-thirds of which was plastic, including 31,733 bags, 30,295 bottles, and 15,631 six-pack yokes. Plastic trash is being found far out to sea. On a four-day trip from Maryland to Florida that ranged 100 miles offshore, John Hardy, an Oregon State University marine biologist, spotted "Styrofoam and other plastic on the surface, most of the whole cruise."

—"The Dirty Seas," *Time*

In paragraph 11, the first sentence serves as the topic sentence. Supporting details for that main idea include examples, names, and numbers. The writer provides examples of the kinds of litter found washed up on the beach and floating offshore. The writer names many specific things: Texas Gulf Coast, September, bags, bottles, six-pack yokes, Maryland, Florida, John Hardy, Oregon State University, marine biologist, and Styrofoam. And the writer uses specific numbers to describe the volume of litter collected (307 tons), to give counts of specific items (such as 31,733 bags), and to tell how far from shore (100 miles) the litter had traveled.

**EXERCISE 3-3**    Working individually or with a peer-response group, look again at the paragraphs in Exercise 3-2. Identify the RENNS in each paragraph. For help, consult 3f.

## **3g**  How can I create unity and coherence in paragraphs?

A paragraph has **unity** when the connection between the main idea and its supporting sentences is clear. A paragraph has **coherence** when its sentences relate to each other not only in content but also in choice of words and grammatical structures. Unity emphasizes meaning; coherence emphasizes structure.

Unity is ruined when any sentence in a paragraph "goes off the topic," which means its content doesn't relate to the main idea or to the other sentences in the paragraph.

In a coherent paragraph, the sentences follow naturally from one to the next. Techniques for achieving coherence are listed in Quick Reference 3.4; refer to the sections shown in parentheses for complete explanations.

### Quick Reference 3.4 ■ ■ ■ ■ ■

#### Techniques for achieving coherence

- Using appropriate transitional expressions
- Using pronouns when possible
- Using deliberate repetition of a key word
- Using parallel structures
- Using coherence techniques to create connections among paragraphs

### ■ Using transitional expressions for coherence

**Transitional expressions** are words and phrases that signal connections among ideas. **Transitions** are bridges that lead your reader along your line of thought. They offer cues about what follows. Commonly used transitional expressions are listed in Quick Reference 3.5.

**!** **Alert:** In ACADEMIC WRITING, set off a transitional expression with a comma, unless the expression is one short word (24c and 24g). ●

### Quick Reference 3.5 ■ ■ ■ ■ ■

#### Transitional expressions and the relationships they signal

| | |
|---|---|
| ADDITION | also, in addition, too, moreover, and, besides, furthermore, equally important, then, finally |
| EXAMPLE | for example, for instance, thus, as an illustration, namely, specifically |
| CONTRAST | but, yet, however, nevertheless, nonetheless, conversely, in contrast, still, at the same time, on the one hand, on the other hand |
| COMPARISON | similarly, likewise, in the same way |
| CONCESSION | of course, to be sure, certainly, granted |
| RESULT | therefore, thus, as a result, so, accordingly, consequently |
| SUMMARY | hence, in short, in brief, in summary, in conclusion, finally |
| TIME | first, second, third, next, then, finally, afterward, before, soon, later, meanwhile, subsequently, immediately, eventually, currently |
| PLACE | in the front, in the foreground, in the back, in the background, at the side, adjacent, nearby, in the distance, here, there |

The three brief examples below demonstrate how to use transitional expressions for each context.

### COHERENCE BY ADDITION

Woodpeckers use their beaks to find food and to chisel out nests. *In addition,* they claim their territory and signal their desire to mate by using their beaks to drum on trees.

### COHERENCE BY CONTRAST

Most birds communicate by singing. Woodpeckers, *however,* communicate by the duration and rhythm of the drumming of their beaks.

### COHERENCE BY RESULT

The woodpecker's strong beak enables it to communicate by drumming on dry branches and tree trunks. *As a result,* woodpeckers can communicate across greater distances than songbirds can.

Paragraph 12 demonstrates how transitional expressions (shown in **bold**) enhance a paragraph's COHERENCE. The TOPIC SENTENCE is the final sentence.

**12**  Before the days of television, people were entertained by exciting radio shows such as *Superman, Batman,* and "War of the Worlds." **Of course,** the listener was required to pay careful attention to the story if all details were to be comprehended. **Better yet,** while listening to the stories, listeners would form their own images of the actions taking place. When the broadcaster would give brief descriptions of the Martian space ships invading earth, **for example,** every member of the audience would imagine a different space ship. **In contrast,** television's version of "War of the Worlds" will not stir the imagination at all, for everyone can clearly see the actions taking place. All viewers see the same space ship with the same features. Each aspect is clearly defined, and **therefore,** no one will imagine anything different from what is seen. **Thus,** television can't be considered an effective tool for stimulating the imagination.

—Tom Paradis, "A Child's Other World"

## ■ Using pronouns for coherence

**Pronouns**—words that refer to nouns or other pronouns—allow readers to follow your train of thought from one sentence to the next without boring repetition. Without pronouns, you would have to repeat nouns over and over. For example, this sentence uses no pronouns and therefore has needless repetition: *The woodpecker scratched the woodpecker's head with the woodpecker's foot.* In contrast, with pronouns the sentence can be *The woodpecker scratched **its** head with **its** foot.* Paragraph 13 illustrates how pronouns (shown in **bold**) contribute to COHERENCE.

**13** After Gary Hanson, now 56, got laid off from **his** corporate position in 2003, **he, his** wife, Susan, and **his** son, John, now 54 and 27, respectively, wanted to do a spot of cleaning. Though **they** are hard at work, **they** are not scrubbing floors or washing windows. **They** are running **their** very own housecleaning franchise, *The Maids Home Services,* which **they** opened in February.

—Sara Wilson, "Clean House: Getting Laid Off
from His Corporate Job Gave This Franchisee a Fresh Start"

### ■ Using deliberate repetition for coherence

A key word or phrase is central to the main idea of the paragraph. **Repetition** of key words or phrases is a useful way to achieve COHERENCE in a paragraph. The word or phrase usually appears first in the paragraph's TOPIC SENTENCE (3e) and then again throughout the paragraph. The idea of repetition is to keep a concept in front of the reader. Use this technique sparingly to avoid being monotonous. Paragraph 14 contains repeated words and phrases (shown in **bold**) closely tied to the concept of anthropology that make the paragraph more coherent.

**14** **Anthropology,** broadly defined, is the study of **humanity,** from its evolutionary origins millions of years ago to its present great numbers and worldwide diversity. Many other disciplines, of course, share with **anthropology** a focus on one aspect or another of **humanity. Like** sociology, economics, political science, psychology, and other behavioral and social sciences, **anthropology** is concerned with the way people organize their lives and relate to one another in interacting, interconnected groups—societies—that share basic beliefs and practices. **Like** economists, **anthropologists are interested in** society's material foundations—in how people produce and distribute food and other valued goods. **Like** sociologists, **anthropologists are interested in** the way people structure their relations in society—in families, at work, in institutions. **Like** political scientists, **anthropologists are interested in** power and authority: who has them and how they are allocated. And, **like** psychologists, **anthropologists are interested in** individual development and the interaction between society and individual people.

—Nancy Bonvillain, "The Study of Humanity"

### ■ Using parallel structures for coherence

**Parallel structures** are created when grammatically equivalent forms are used in series, usually of three or more items, but sometimes only two (see PARALLELISM, Chapter 10). Using parallel structures helps to give a paragraph coherence. The repeated parallel structures reinforce connections among ideas, and they add both tempo and sound to the sentence. Look back to paragraph 14 and the succession of sentences that begin with the word *like.*

In paragraph 15, the authors use several parallel structures (shown in **bold**): a parallel series of words (*the sacred, the secular, the scientific*); parallel phrases (*sometimes smiled at, sometimes frowned upon*); and six parallel clauses (the first being *banish danger with a gesture*).

> Superstitions are **sometimes smiled at** and **sometimes frowned upon** as observances characteristic of **the old-fashioned, the unenlightened,** children, peasants, servants, immigrants, foreigners, or backwoods people. Nevertheless, they give all of us ways of moving back and forth among the different worlds in which we live—**the sacred, the secular,** and **the scientific.** They allow us to keep a private world also, where, smiling a little, we can **banish danger with a gesture** and **summon luck with a rhyme, make the sun shine in spite of storm clouds, force the stranger to do our bidding, keep an enemy at bay,** and **straighten the paths of those we love.**

**15**

> —Margaret Mead and Rhoda Metraux, "New Superstitions for Old"

### ■ Creating coherence among paragraphs

The same techniques for achieving COHERENCE in a paragraph apply to showing connections among paragraphs in a piece of writing. All four techniques help: transitional expressions, pronouns, deliberate repetition, and parallel structures.

Example 16 shows two short paragraphs and the start of a third. The writer achieves coherence among the paragraphs by repeating the key word *gratitude* and the related words *grateful, thankful,* and *thank* and by using them as a transition into the next paragraph. The writer also uses PARALLELISM within the paragraphs in this example.

> To me, gratitude and inner peace go hand in hand. The more genuinely grateful I feel for the gift of my life, the more peaceful I feel. Gratitude, then, is worthy of a little practice.
>
> If you're anything like me, you probably have many people to be thankful for: friends, family members, people from your past, teachers, gurus, people from work, someone who gave you a break, as well as countless others. You may want to thank a higher power for the gift of life itself, or for the beauty of nature.
>
> As you think of people to be grateful for, remember that it can be anyone—someone who held a door open for you, or a physician who saved your life. . . .

**16**

**EXERCISE 3-4**   Working individually or with a peer-response group, locate the coherence techniques in each paragraph. Look for transitional expressions, pronouns, deliberate repetition, and parallel structures. For help, consult 3g.

A.   Kathy sat with her legs dangling over the edge of the side of the hood. The band of her earphones held back strands of straight copper hair that had come loose from two thick braids that hung down her back. She swayed with the music that only she could hear. Her shoulders raised, making circles in the warm air. Her arms reached out to her side; her open hands

**17**

reached for the air; her closed hands brought the air back to her. Her arms reached over her head; her opened hands reached for a cloud; her closed hands brought the cloud back to her. Her head moved from side to side; her eyes opened and closed to the tempo of the tunes. Kathy was motion.

—Claire Burke, student

B.   Newton's law may have wider application than just the physical world. In the social world, racism, once set into motion, will remain in motion unless acted upon by an outside force. The collective "we" must be the outside force. We must fight racism through education. We must make sure every school has the resources to do its job. We must present to our children a culturally diverse curriculum that reflects our pluralistic society. This can help students understand that prejudice is learned through contact with prejudiced people, rather than with the people toward whom the prejudice is directed.

—Randolph H. Manning, "Fighting Racism with Inclusion"

C.   The snow geese are first, rising off the ponds to breakfast in the sorghum fields up the river. Twenty thousand of them, perhaps more, great white birds with black wing tips rising out of the darkness into the rosy reflected light of dawn. They make a sweeping turn, a cloud of wings rising above the cottonwoods. But cloud is the wrong word. They don't form a disorderly blackbird rabble but a kaleidoscope of goose formations, always shifting, but always orderly. The light catches them—white against the tan velvet of the hills. Then they're overhead, line after line, layer above layer of formations, and the sky is filled with the clamor of an infinity of geese.

—Tony Hillerman, *Hillerman Country*

**EXERCISE 3-5**   Working individually or with a peer-response group, use RENNS (3f) and techniques for achieving coherence (3g) to develop three of the following topic sentences into paragraphs. When finished, list the RENNS and the coherence techniques you used in each paragraph.

1. Video games reflect current concerns in our culture.

2. The content of trash in the United States says a great deal about US culture.

3. Reality shows on television tend to have several common elements.

4. In many respects, our culture is very wasteful.

5. College students face several true challenges.

# 3h   How can I arrange a paragraph?

During DRAFTING, you concentrate on getting ideas onto the page or screen. Later, during REVISION, you can experiment to see how your sentences might be arranged for greatest impact. You may find sometimes that only one possible arrangement can work. For example, if you're explaining how to bake a cake, you want to give the directions in a particular order. At other times, you may find that more than one arrangement is possible. For example, if you're writing about solving a problem and therefore using the problem-to-solution arrangement, you might also use the technique of ordering from least to most important—or its reverse. Quick Reference 3.6 lists the most common ways to arrange a paragraph.

---

### Quick Reference 3.6                              ■ ■ ■ ■ ■

#### Ways to arrange sentences in a paragraph

- By time
- By location
- From general to specific
- From specific to general
- From least to most important
- From most to least important
- From problem to solution

---

## 3i   How can rhetorical patterns help me write paragraphs?

**Rhetorical patterns** (sometimes called *rhetorical strategies*) are techniques for presenting ideas clearly and effectively in academic and other situations. You choose a specific rhetorical strategy according to what you want to accomplish.

Often, your TOPIC SENTENCE will steer you toward a particular pattern. For example, if a topic sentence is "Grilling a great hot dog is easy," the implied pattern—or rhetorical strategy—is to explain the process of how to grill a hot dog. Or if a topic sentence is "To see many different styles of architecture in one US city, visit Chicago," the implied pattern—or rhetorical strategy—is to give examples.

Sometimes, you need to use a combination of rhetorical strategies. For example, in a paragraph on types of color blindness, you might use a combination of definition and classification. A paragraph explaining why one brand of house paint is superior to another might call for comparison and contrast combined with description—and, perhaps, also definition and examples.

### NARRATIVE

**Narrative** writing tells a story. A *narration* relates what is happening or what has happened. Paragraph 20 is an example.

**20**   Gordon Parks speculates that he might have spent his life as a waiter on the North Coast Limited train if he hadn't strolled into one particular movie house during a stopover in Chicago. It was shortly before World War II began, and on the screen was a hair-raising newsreel of Japanese planes attacking a gunboat. When it was over the camera operator came out on stage and the audience cheered. From that moment on Parks was determined to become a photographer. During his next stopover, in Seattle, he went into a pawnshop and purchased his first camera for $7.50. With that small sum, Parks later proclaimed, "I had bought what was to become my weapon against poverty and racism." Eleven years later, he became the first black photographer at *Life* magazine.

—Susan Howard, "Depth of Field"

## DESCRIPTION

Writing a **description** is a rhetorical strategy that appeals to a reader's senses—sight, sound, smell, taste, and touch. *Descriptive writing* paints a picture in words. Paragraph 21 is an example.

**21** Walking to the ranch house from the shed, we saw the Northern Lights. They looked like talcum powder fallen from a woman's face. Rouge and blue eye shadow streaked the spires of a white light which exploded, then pulsated, shaking the colors down—like lives—until they faded from sight.

—Gretel Ehrlich, "Other Lives"

## PROCESS

Writing about a **process** reports a sequence of actions or pattern by which something is done or made. A process usually proceeds chronologically—first do this, then do that. A process's complexity dictates the level of detail in the writing. For example, paragraph 22 provides an overview of a complicated process. Paragraph 23, on the other hand, gives explicit step-by-step directions.

**22** Making chocolate isn't as simple as grinding a bag of beans. The machinery in a chocolate factory towers over you, rumbling and whirring. A huge cleaner first blows the beans away from their accompanying debris—sticks and stones, coins and even bullets can fall among cocoa beans being bagged. Then they go into another machine for roasting. Next comes separation in a winnower, shells sliding out one side, beans falling from the other. Grinding follows, resulting in chocolate liquor. Fermentation, roasting, and "conching" all influence the flavor of chocolate. Chocolate is "conched"—rolled over and over against itself like pebbles in the sea—in enormous circular machines named conches for the shells they once resembled. Climbing a flight of steps to peer into this huge, slow-moving glacier, I was expecting something like molten mud but found myself forced to conclude it resembled nothing so much as chocolate.

—Ruth Mehrtens Galvin, "Sybaritic to Some, Sinful to Others"

**23** Traditionally, oil was extracted by pressing the olives between granite millstones. Many nonindustrial mills now use a modern continuous-cycle system. The olives are conveyed up a belt, washed, and cut into pulp. The resulting paste is kneaded and centrifugally "decanted" to separate it into solids, water, and oil.

—Lori de Mori, "Making Olive Oil"

## EXAMPLES

A paragraph developed by **examples** presents particular instances of a larger category. For instance, examples of the category "endangered animals" could include the black rhinoceros, South China tiger, Bulmer's fruit bat, and silvery gibbon. Paragraph 24 is an example of this strategy. On the other hand, sometimes one **extended example,** often called an *illustration,* is useful. Paragraph 25 is an example of this technique.

24     It's hard for us to imagine what it must have been like to live in a culture before the advent of printed books or before you could carry around a ballpoint pen and paper to jot notes. "In a world of few books, and those mostly in communal libraries, one's education had to be remembered, for one could never depend on having continuing access to specific material," writes Mary Carruthers, author of *The Book of Memory,* a study of the role of memory techniques in medieval culture. "Ancient and medieval people reserved their awe for memory. Their greatest geniuses they describe as people of superior memories." Thirteenth-century theologian Thomas Aquinas, for example, was celebrated for composing his *Summa Theologica* entirely in his head and dictating it from memory with no more than a few notes. Roman philosopher Seneca the Elder could repeat 2,000 names in the order they'd been given to him. Another Roman named Simplicius could recite Virgil by heart—backward. A strong memory was seen as the greatest of virtues since it represented the internalization of a universe of external knowledge. Indeed, a common theme in the lives of the saints was that they had extraordinary memories.

—Joshua Foer, "Remember This"

25     He was one of the greatest scientists the world has ever known, yet if I had to convey the essence of Albert Einstein in a single word, I would choose *simplicity.* Perhaps an anecdote will help. Once, caught in a downpour, he took off his hat and held it under his coat. Asked why, he explained, with admirable logic, that the rain would damage the hat, but his hair would be none the worse for its wetting. This knack of going instinctively to the heart of the matter was the secret of his major scientific discoveries—this and his extraordinary feeling for beauty.

—Banesh Hoffman, "My Friend, Albert Einstein"

## DEFINITION

When you define something, you give its meaning. **Definition** is often used together with other rhetorical strategies. If, for example, you were explaining how to organize a seashell collection, you'd probably want to define the two main types of shells: bivalve and univalve. You can also develop an entire paragraph by using definition, called an **extended definition.** An extended definition discusses the meaning of a word or concept in more detail than a dictionary definition. If the topic is very abstract, the writer tries to put the definition in concrete terms. Sometimes a definition tells what something is not, as well as what it is, as in paragraph 26.

**26**    Chemistry is that branch of science that has the task of investigating the materials out of which the universe is made. It is not concerned with the forms into which they may be fashioned. Such objects as chairs, tables, vases, bottles, or wires are of no significance in chemistry; but such substances as glass, wool, iron, sulfur, and clay, as the materials out of which they are made, are what it studies. Chemistry is concerned not only with the composition of such substances, but also with their inner structure.

—John Arrend Timm, *General Chemistry*

### ANALYSIS

**Analysis,** sometimes called *division,* divides things up into their parts. It usually starts, often in its topic sentence, by identifying one subject and continues by explaining the subject's distinct parts, as in paragraph 27.

**27**    Jazz is by its very nature inexact, and thus difficult to define with much precision: humble in its roots, yet an avenue to wealth and fame for its stars; improvised anew with each performance, but following a handful of tried-and-true formulas; done by everybody but mastered by an elite few; made by African Americans, but made the definition of its age by white bands—and predominantly white audiences. Jazz is primarily an instrumental idiom, but nearly all jazz is based on songs with words, and there are great jazz singers. "If you have to ask what jazz is," said Louis Armstrong, "you'll never know."

—D. Kern Holoman, "Jazz"

### CLASSIFICATION

**Classification** groups items according to an underlying, shared characteristic. Paragraph 28 groups—classifies—interior violations of building-safety codes.

**28**    A public health student, Marian Glaser, did a detailed analysis of 180 cases of building code violation. Each case represented a single building, almost all of which were multiple-unit dwellings. In these 180 buildings, there were an incredible total of 1,244 different recorded violations—about seven per building. What did the violations consist of? First of all, over one-third of the violations were exterior defects: broken doors and stairways, holes in the walls, sagging roofs, broken chimneys, damaged porches, and so on. Another one-third were interior violations that could scarcely be attributed to the most ingeniously destructive rural southern migrant in America. There were, for example, a total of 160 instances of defective wiring or other electrical hazards, a very common cause of the excessive number of fires and needless tragic deaths in the slums. There were 125 instances of inadequate, defective, or inoperable plumbing or heating. There were 34 instances of serious infestation by rats and roaches.

—William Ryan, "Blaming the Victim"

## COMPARISON AND CONTRAST

A paragraph developed by *comparison* deals with similarities; a paragraph developed by *contrast* deals with differences. **Comparison and contrast** writing is usually organized one of two ways: You can use *point-by-point organization,* which moves back and forth between the items being compared; or you can use *block organization,* which discusses one item completely before discussing the other.

Paragraph 29 is structured point by point, going back and forth between the two children (whose names are in **boldface**) being compared.

29 My husband and I constantly marvel at the fact that our two sons, born of the same parents and only two years apart in age, are such completely different human beings. The most obvious differences became apparent at their births. Our firstborn, **Mark,** was big and bold—his intense, already wise eyes, broad shoulders, huge and heavy hands, and powerful, chunky legs gave us the impression he could have walked out of the delivery room on his own. Our second son, **Wayne,** was delightfully different. Rather than having the football physique that **Mark** was born with, **Wayne** came into the world with a long, slim, wiry body more suited to running, jumping, and contorting. **Wayne's** eyes, rather than being intense like **Mark's,** were impish and innocent. When **Mark** was delivered, he cried only momentarily, and then seemed to settle into a state of intense concentration, as if trying to absorb everything he could about the strange, new environment he found himself in. Conversely, **Wayne** screamed from the moment he first appeared. There was nothing helpless or pathetic about his cry either—he was darn angry!

—Rosanne Labonte, student

Paragraph 30 uses the block pattern for comparison and contrast. The writer first discusses games and then business (each key word is in **boldface**).

30 Games are of limited duration, take place on or in fixed and finite sites, and are governed by openly promulgated rules that are enforced on the spot by neutral professionals. Moreover, they're performed by relatively evenly matched teams that are counseled and led through every move by seasoned hands. Scores are kept, and at the end of the game, a winner is declared. **Business** is usually a little different. In fact, if there is anyone out there who can say that the business is of limited duration, takes place on a fixed site, is governed by openly promulgated rules that are enforced on the spot by neutral professionals, competes only on relatively even terms, and performs in a way that can be measured in runs or points, then that person is either extraordinarily lucky or seriously deluded.

—Warren Bennis, "Time to Hang Up the Old Sports Clichés"

## ANALOGY

An **analogy** is an extended comparison between objects or ideas from different classes —things not normally associated. Analogy is particularly effective in explaining unfamiliar or abstract concepts because a comparison can be drawn between what is familiar and what is not. An analogy often begins with a simile or metaphor (12c), as in paragraph 31.

**31**  Casual dress, like casual speech, tends to be loose, relaxed, and colorful. It often contains what might be called "slang words": blue jeans, sneakers, baseball caps, aprons, flowered cotton housedresses, and the like. These garments could not be worn on a formal occasion without causing disapproval, but in ordinary circumstances, they pass without remark. "Vulgar words" in dress, on the other hand, give emphasis and get immediate attention in almost any circumstances, just as they do in speech. Only the skillful can employ them without some loss of face, and even then, they must be used in the right way. A torn, unbuttoned shirt or wildly uncombed hair can signify strong emotions: passion, grief, rage, despair. They're most effective if people already think of you as being neatly dressed, just as the curses of well-spoken persons count for more than those of the customarily foul-mouthed do.

—Alison Lurie, *The Language of Clothes*

## CAUSE-AND-EFFECT ANALYSIS

**Cause-and-effect analysis** examines outcomes and the reasons for those outcomes. Causes lead to an event or an effect, and effects result from causes. (For a discussion of correct logic for assessing CAUSE AND EFFECT, see 4h.) Paragraph 32 discusses how science (the cause) becomes indispensable (the effect) to creating tasty foods.

**32**  Once upon a time, flavor research was a matter of asking housewives to munch a few potato chips in the hopes that the company had stumbled on the perfect formula for reconstituting potatoes. But as the science became more sophisticated, and market pressures demanded more novelty and authenticity, flavor scientists had to create new varieties like "Mesquite BBQ" chips to sit alongside regular barbecue flavor. To fill that hungry maw, Dewis and his colleagues work to analyze hundreds of thousands of substances and develop compounds that will please the buying public in four ways—through smell, taste, sensation and emotion. To do so flavor scientists are homing in on molecules, receptors, brain structures and genetic code that will enable them to create flavors tailored to consumers' palates, health condition, demographics, even genotype. The industry doesn't just talk about things tasting good anymore. Now it's about providing an exceptional "flavor experience."

—Tamara Holt, "The Science of Yummy"

**EXERCISE 3-6** Working individually or with a peer-response group, decide what rhetorical strategies are used in each of paragraphs 33–37. Choose from any one or a combination of narrative, description, process, example, definition, analysis, classification, comparison and contrast, analogy, and cause and effect. For help, consult 3i.

A.    Another way to think about metamessages is that they frame a conversation, much as a picture frame provides a context for the images in the picture. Metamessages let you know how to interpret what someone is say-
**33**  ing by identifying the activity that is going on. Is this an argument or a chat? Is it helping, advising, or scolding? At the same time, they let you know what position the speaker is assuming in the activity, and what position you are being assigned.

—Deborah Tannen, *You Just Don't Understand*

B.    I retain only one confused impression from my earliest years: it's all red, and black, and warm. Our apartment was red: the upholstery was of red moquette, the Renaissance dining-room was red, the figured silk hangings over the stained-glass doors were red, and the velvet curtains in Papa's
**34**  study were red too. The furniture in this awful sanctum was made of black pear wood; I used to creep into the kneehole under the desk and envelop myself in its dusty glooms; it was dark and warm, and the red of the carpet rejoiced my eyes. That is how I seem to have passed the early days of infancy. Safely ensconced, I watched, I touched, I took stock of the world.

—Simone de Beauvoir, *Memoirs of a Dutiful Daughter*

C.    In the case of wool, very hot water can actually cause some structural changes within the fiber, but the resulting shrinkage is minor. The fundamental cause of shrinkage in wool is felting, in which the fibers scrunch together
**35**  in a tighter bunch, and the yarn, fabric, and garment follow suit. Wool fibers are curly and rough-surfaced, and when squished together under the lubricating influence of water, the fibers wind around each other, like two springs interlocking. Because of their rough surfaces, they stick together and can't be pulled apart.

—James Gorman, "Gadgets"

D.    After our lunch, we drove to the Liverpool public library, where I was scheduled to read. By then, we were forty-five minutes late, and on arrival we saw five middle-aged white women heading away toward an old car across the street. When they recognized me, the women came over and apologized: They were really sorry, they said, but they had to leave or
**36**  they'd get in trouble on the job. I looked at them. Every one of them was wearing an inexpensive, faded housedress and, over that, a cheap and shapeless cardigan sweater. I felt honored by their open-mindedness in having wanted to come and listen to my poetry. I thought and I said that it was I who should apologize: I was late. It was I who felt, moreover, unprepared: What in my work, to date, deserves the open-minded attention

of blue-collar white women terrified by the prospect of overstaying a union-guaranteed hour for lunch?

—June Jordan, "Waiting for a Taxi"

E.    Lacking access to a year-round supermarket, the many species—from ants to wolves—that in the course of evolution have learned the advantages of hoarding must devote a lot of energy and ingenuity to protecting their stashes from marauders. Creatures like beavers and honeybees, for example, hoard food to get them through cold winters. Others, like desert rodents that face
**37**    food scarcities throughout the year, must take advantage of the short-lived harvests that follow occasional rains. For animals like burying beetles that dine on mice hundreds of times their size, a habit of biting off more than they can chew at the moment forces them to store their leftovers. Still others, like the male MacGregor's bowerbird, stockpile goodies during mating season so they can concentrate on wooing females and defending their arena d'amour.

—Jane Brody, "A Hoarder's Life: Filling the Cache—and Finding It"

## 3j    What is a transitional paragraph?

**Transitional paragraphs** form a bridge between one long discussion on a single topic that requires a number of paragraphs and another discussion, usually lengthy, of another topic. Paragraph 38 is an example of a transitional paragraph that allows the writer to move from a long discussion of the extent and sources of anger in our society to a long discussion of possible remedies.

So is there any hope for you and your anger? Is there any reason to believe
**38**    that you will be able to survive the afternoon commute without screaming or tailgating or displaying choice fingers?

—Andrew Santella, "All the Rage"

## 3k    What are effective concluding paragraphs?

A **concluding paragraph** ends the discussion smoothly by following logically from the essay's introductory paragraph (3c) and the essay's body paragraphs (3d). Always integrate a concluding device into the final paragraph so that the discussion does not end abruptly. A conclusion that is hurriedly tacked on is a missed opportunity to provide a sense of completion and a finishing touch that adds to the whole essay. Quick Reference 3.7 lists strategies for concluding your essay as well as strategies to avoid.

The same writers who wait to write their introductory paragraph until they've drafted their body paragraphs often also wait to write their concluding paragraph until they've drafted their introduction. They do this to coordinate the beginning and end so that they can make sure they don't repeat the same strategy in both places.

## Quick Reference 3.7

■ ■ ■ ■ ■

### Strategies for concluding paragraphs

**STRATEGIES TO TRY**

- A strategy adapted from those used for introductory paragraphs (3c)—but be careful to choose a different strategy for your introduction and conclusion
- Relating a brief concluding interesting story or anecdote
- Giving one or more pertinent—perhaps surprising—concluding statistics
- Asking one or more provocative questions for further thought
- Using an appropriate quotation to sum up the THESIS STATEMENT
- Redefining a key term for emphasis
- An ANALOGY that summarizes the thesis statement
- A SUMMARY of the main points, but only if the piece of writing is longer than three to four pages
- A statement that urges awareness by the readers
- A statement that looks ahead to the future
- A call to readers

**STRATEGIES TO AVOID**

- Introducing new ideas or facts that belong in the body of the essay
- Rewording your introduction
- Announcing what you've discussed, as in "In this paper, I have explained why oil prices have dropped."
- Making absolute claims, as in "I have proved that oil prices don't always affect gasoline prices."
- Apologizing, as in "Even though I'm not an expert, I feel my position is correct."

Paragraph 39 is a concluding paragraph that summarizes the main points of the essay.

**39** Now the equivalent to molecule fingerprints, DNA profiles have indeed proven to be valuable investigative tools. As the FBI Laboratory continues to develop innovative technologies and share its expertise with criminal justice professionals worldwide, it takes great strides in bringing offenders to swift and sure justice, while clearing innocent individuals and protecting crime victims.

—"DNA Profiling Advancement: The Use of DNA Profiles in Solving Crimes," *The FBI Law Enforcement Bulletin*

# 4 ▪ ▪ ▪ ▪

# Thinking Critically About Ideas and Images

## 4a What is critical thinking?

Thinking isn't something you choose to do, any more than a fish chooses to live in water. To be human is to think. But while thinking may come naturally, being deliberate about how you think doesn't.

**Critical thinking** means taking control of your conscious thought processes. If you don't, you risk being controlled by the ideas of others. The essence of critical thinking is thinking beyond the obvious—beyond the flash of images on a television screen, the alluring promises of glossy advertisements, the evasive statements by some people in the news, the half-truths of propaganda. Thinking critically means identifying the weaknessess—and the strengths—of an idea, a text, an image, or a presentation. It means analyzing the quality of evidence and how writers or speakers make their cases. It means interpreting, considering implications, imagining alternatives, connecting information and ideas in one situation to information and ideas in another.

The word *critical* here has a neutral meaning. It doesn't mean taking a negative view or finding fault, as when someone criticizes another person for doing something incorrectly. Rather, the term means examining ideas thoroughly and deeply.

## 4b What are the elements of critical thinking?

Quick Reference 4.1 describes the general steps of critical thinking, steps that are just as fluid as those in the WRITING PROCESS. Expect sometimes to combine steps, reverse their order, and return to parts of the process you thought you had completed.

## 4c How do I read to comprehend?

When you read to comprehend, you try to understand the basic, literal meaning of a text. Your goal is to discover the main ideas, the supporting details, or, in a work of fiction, the central details of plot and character.

### Quick Reference 4.1                                    ■ ■ ■ ■ ■

#### Steps in the critical thinking process

1. **Comprehend** or **summarize.** Understand the **literal** meaning: the "plain" meaning on the surface of the material. Be able to extract and re-state its main message or central point or to accurately and objectively describe an image, event, or situation. Add nothing. Read "on the lines."

2. **Analyze.** Examine the material by breaking it into its component parts. Ask about the nature or meaning of each part and how it contributes to the overall meaning or effect.

3. **Infer.** Read "between the lines" to see what's not stated but implied.

4. **Synthesize.** Connect what you've summarized, analyzed, and inferred with your prior knowledge or experiences, with other ideas or perspectives, or with other readings, texts, or situations.

5. **Evaluate.** Read "beyond the lines." Judge the quality of the material or form your own informed opinion about it. Answer such questions as "Is it reasonable? Fair? Accurate? Convincing? Ethical? Useful? Comprehensive? Important?"

#### ■ Reading closely and actively

Reading is an active process—a dynamic, meaning-making interaction between the page and your brain. The secret to **reading closely and actively** is to annotate as you read. Annotating means writing notes to yourself in a book or article's margins and using asterisks and other codes to alert you to special material.

**Close reading** means annotating for content. You might, for example, number and briefly list the steps in a process or summarize major points in the margin. When you review, your marginal notes help you glance over the material and quickly recall what it's about.

**Active reading** means annotating to make connections between the material and your own knowledge or experiences. This is your chance to converse on paper with the writer. Consider yourself a partner in the making of meaning, a full participant in the exchange of ideas that characterizes a college education. Active reading is a key to ANALYSIS (section 4d), INFERENCE (4e), SYNTHESIS (4f), and EVALUATION (4g).

#### ■ Reading systematically

To **read systematically** is to use a structured plan: **Preview, Read,** and **Review.**

1. **Preview:** Before you begin reading, start making predictions. When your mind is reading actively, it is guessing what's coming next, either confirming or revising its prediction, and moving on to new predictions.

- To preview a book, first look at the table of contents. What topics are included? What seems to be the main emphasis? Which sections will be most important? If there's an Introduction or preface, skim it.

- To preview a particular reading (for example, a chapter or an article), read all the headings, large and small. Note the **boldfaced** words (in darker print), and all visuals and their captions, including photographs, drawings, figures, tables, and boxes.

- Check for introductory notes about the author and head notes, which often precede individual works in collections of essays or short stories. Read pivotal paragraphs, such as the opening and (unless you're reading for suspense) closing.

- Jot a few questions that you expect—or hope—the reading will answer.

2. **Read:** Read the material closely and actively. Identify the main points and start thinking about how the writer supports them.

3. **Review:** Go back to questions you jotted during previewing. Did the reading answer them? (If not, either your predictions could have been wrong, or you didn't read carefully; reread to determine which.) Also, look

---

### Quick Reference 4.2                                  ■ ■ ■ ■ ■

#### Ways to help your reading comprehension

- **Make associations.** Link new material to what you already know, especially when you're reading about an unfamiliar subject. You may even find it helpful to read an encyclopedia article or an easier book or article on the subject first in order to build your knowledge base.

- **Simplify tough sentences.** If the author's writing style is complex, "unpack" the sentences: Break them into smaller units or reword them in a simpler style.

- **Make it easy for you to focus.** If your mind wanders, do whatever it takes to concentrate. Arrange for silence or music, for being alone or in the library with others who are studying. Try to read at your best time of day.

- **Allot the time you need.** To comprehend new material, you must allow sufficient time to read, reflect, reread, and study. Discipline yourself to balance classes, working, socializing, and family activities. Alas, reading for comprehension takes time.

- **Master the vocabulary.** If you don't understand key terms in your reading, you can't fully understand the concepts. As you encounter new words, try to figure out their meanings from context clues. Also, many textbooks list key terms and their definitions (called a *glossary*) at the end of each chapter or of the book. Of course, nothing replaces having a good dictionary at hand.

at the annotations you made through close and active reading. What do
these add up to? Where are places you need to go back? Keep in mind
that collaborative learning can reinforce what you learn from reading. Ask
a friend or classmate to discuss the material with you and quiz you.

# 4d   How do I analyze a reading?

To analyze something is to break it into parts, just as a chemist does, for example, in order to figure out the compounds in a particular mixture. However, it's
easier to define analysis than to understand and apply it to reading. The key is
knowing what parts to examine and how.

---

### Quick Reference 4.3   ■ ■ ■ ■ ■

#### Elements of analysis

1. Separate facts from opinions.
2. Identify the evidence.
3. Identify cause and effect.
4. Describe the tone.

---

## ■ Separating facts from opinions

A helpful step in analyzing a reading is to distinguish **fact** from **opinion.** *Facts*
are statements that can be verified. *Opinions* are statements of personal beliefs.
While facts can be verified by observation, research, or experimentation, opinions are open to debate. Problems arise when a writer blurs the distinction between fact and opinion. Critical readers will know the difference.

For example, here are two statements, one a fact, the other an opinion.

1. Women can never make good mathematicians.

2. Although fear of math isn't purely a female phenomenon, girls tend to
   drop out of math classes sooner than boys, and some adult women have
   an aversion to math and math-related activity that is akin to anxiety.

Reading inferentially, you can see that statement 1 is clearly an opinion. Is it
worthy of consideration? Perhaps it could be open to debate, but the word
*never* implies that the writer is unwilling to allow for even one exception. Conversely, statement 2 at least seems to be factual, though research would be necessary to confirm or deny the position.

You may find it practical to label key sentences "facts" or "opinions" as
part of your analysis. You could put an "F" or "O" in the margin next to those

sentences. Or, you could include a brief note to yourself explaining why certain sentences are opinions.

**EXERCISE 4-1**    Working individually or with a collaborative group, decide which of the statements below are facts and which are opinions. When the author and source are provided, explain how that information influenced your judgment. For help, consult 4c and 4d.

1.  The life of people on earth is better now than it has ever been—certainly much better than it was 500 years ago.
    > —Peggy Noonan, "Why Are We So Unhappy When We Have It So Good?"

2.  The fast food industry pays the minimum wage to a higher proportion of its workers than any other American industry.
    > —Eric Schlosser, *Fast Food Nation*

3.  Grief, when it comes, is nothing we expect it to be.
    > —Joan Didion, *The Year of Living Dangerously*

4.  A mind is a terrible thing to waste.
    > —United Negro College Fund

5.  History is the branch of knowledge that deals systematically with the past.
    > —*Webster's New World College Dictionary*, Fourth Edition

## ■ Identifying the evidence

For any opinions or claims, you next need to identify and analyze the evidence that the writer provides. **Evidence** consists of facts, examples, the results of formal studies, and the opinions of experts. Quick Reference 4.4 provides a checklist for evaluating sources.

### EVALUATING EVIDENCE

You can evaluate evidence by asking the following questions to guide your judgment.

- **Is the evidence sufficient?** To be sufficient, evidence can't be skimpy. As a rule, the more evidence, the better. Readers have more confidence in the results of a survey that draws on a hundred respondents rather than on ten. As a writer, you may convince your reader that violence is a serious problem in high schools on the basis of only two examples, but you'll be more convincing with additional examples.

- **Is the evidence representative?** Evidence is representative if it is typical. As a reader, assess the objectivity and fairness of evidence. Don't trust a claim or conclusion about a group based on only a few members rather than on a truly typical sample.

- **Is the evidence relevant?** Relevant evidence is directly related to the conclusion you're drawing. Determining relevance often demands subtle thinking.

## Quick Reference 4.4

■ ■ ■ ■ ■

### Evaluating sources

- **Is the source authoritative?** Did an expert or a person you can expect to write credibly on the subject write it? If it's a memoir or eyewitness account, does it have the kind of detail and perspective that makes the writer credible?

- **Is the source published in a reliable place?** Does the material appear in a reputable publication—a book published by an established publisher, a respected journal or magazine—or on a reliable Internet site?

- **Is the source well known?** Is the source cited elsewhere as you read about the subject? (If so, the authority of the source is probably widely accepted.)

- **Is the tone balanced?** Is the language relatively objective (and therefore more likely to be reliable), or is it slanted (probably not reliable)?

- **Is the source current?** Is the material up-to-date and therefore more likely to be reliable, or has later authoritative and reliable research made it outdated? ("Old" isn't necessarily unreliable. In many fields, classic works of research remain authoritative for decades or even centuries.)

- **Are its findings valid (if a primary source)?** Did the experiment, survey, interview, or study seem to be conducted rigorously? Are the conclusions justified by the data?

- **Is it accurate and complete (if a secondary source)?** Does it accurately summarize and interpret the primary resource? Does it leave out anything important?

---

- **Is the evidence accurate?** Accurate evidence is correct and complete. To be accurate, evidence must come from a reliable source. Equally important, evidence must be presented honestly, not misrepresented or distorted.

- **Is the evidence qualified?** Reasonable evidence doesn't make extreme claims. Claims that use words such as *all, always, never,* and *certainly* are disqualified if even one exception is found. Conclusions are more sensible and believable when qualified with words such as *some, many, may, possibly, often,* and *usually.*

## ■ Identifying cause and effect

**Cause and effect** describes the relationship between one event (cause) and another event that happens as a result (effect). The relationship also works in reverse: One event (effect) results from another event (cause). Whether you begin with a cause or with an effect, you're using the same basic pattern.

Cause A → produces → effect B

You may seek to understand the effects of a known cause:

More studying → produces → ?

Or you may seek to determine the cause or causes of a known effect:

? → produces → recurrent headaches

When you're analyzing a reading, look for any claims of cause and effect. (Of course, not all readings will have them.) For any that you find, think carefully through the relationship between cause A and effect B. Just because A happened before B or because A and B are associated with each other doesn't mean A caused B. Consult the guidelines in Quick Reference 4.5.

---

### Quick Reference 4.5    ■ ■ ■ ■ ■

#### Assessing cause and effect

- **Is there a clear relationship between events?** Related causes and effects happen in sequence: A cause occurs before an effect. First the wind blows, then a door slams, then a pane of glass in the door breaks. But CHRONOLOGICAL ORDER merely implies a cause-and-effect relationship. Perhaps someone slammed the door shut. Perhaps someone threw a baseball through the glass pane. A cause-and-effect relationship must be linked by more than chronological sequence. The fact that B happens after A doesn't prove that A causes B.

- **Is there a pattern of repetition?** Scientific proof depends on a pattern of repetition. To establish that A causes B, every time A is present, B must occur. Or, put another way, B never occurs unless A is present.

- **Are there multiple causes and/or effects?** Avoid oversimplification. The basic pattern of cause and effect—single cause, single effect (A causes B)—rarely represents the full picture. Multiple causes and/or effects are more typical of real life. Similarly, one cause can produce multiple effects.

---

### ■ Describing the tone

**Tone** refers to the attitude conveyed in writing, mostly by the writer's word choice. A tone can be formal, informal, laid back, pompous, sarcastic, concerned, judgmental, sympathetic, and so on. We discuss tone at greater length in section 8d.

For now, however, as a critical reader, be suspicious of a highly emotional tone in writing. If you find it, chances are the writer is trying to manipulate the audience. As a writer, if you find your tone growing emotional, step back and rethink the situation. No matter what point you want to make, your chance of communicating successfully to an audience depends on your using a moderate, reasonable tone. For instance, the exaggerations below in the NO example (*robbing treasures, politicians are murderers*) might hint at the truth of a few cases, but they're too extreme to be taken seriously. The language of the YES version is far more likely to deliver its intended message.

**NO**   Urban renewal must be stopped. Urban redevelopment is ruining this country, and money-hungry capitalists are robbing treasures from law-abiding citizens. Corrupt politicians are murderers, caring nothing about people being thrown out of their homes into the streets.

**YES**   Urban renewal is revitalizing our cities, but it has caused some serious problems. While investors are trying to replace slums with decent housing, they must also remember that they're displacing people who don't want to leave their familiar neighborhoods. Surely, a cooperative effort between government and the private sector can lead to creative solutions.

## 4e   How do I draw inferences?

When you read for **inferences,** you're reading to understand what's suggested or implied but not explicitly stated. Drawing inferences takes practice. Quick Reference 4.6 lists questions to help you read "between the lines." A discussion of each point follows the box.

---

### Quick Reference 4.6   ▪ ▪ ▪ ▪ ▪

#### Drawing inferences during reading

- What is the point, even if the writer doesn't state it outright?
- How might the writer's position influence his or her perspective?
- Can I detect BIAS in the material?
- What are the implications of the reading?

---

### ▪ The writer's position

As a reader, when you can "consider the source"—that is, find out exactly who made a statement—you can open up new perspectives. For example, you would probably read an essay for or against capital punishment differently if you knew the writer was an inmate on death row rather than a noninmate who wished to express an opinion.

Although considering the source can help you draw inferences, take care that you don't fall prey to ARGUMENT TO THE PERSON (4i). Just because someone you don't respect voices an opinion doesn't mean that the position is necessarily wrong.

### ■ Bias

For inferential reading, you want to detect **bias**, also known as **prejudice**. When writing is distorted by hatred or distrust of individuals, groups of people, or ideas, you as a critical reader want to suspect the accuracy and fairness of the material. Bias can be worded in positive language, but critical readers aren't deceived by such tactics. Similarly, writers can merely imply their bias rather than state it outright.

### ■ What are implications of the reading?

An **implication** takes the form, "If this is true (or if this happens), then that might also be true (or that might be the consequence)." One way to consider implications, especially for readings that contain a proposal, is to ask, "Who might benefit from an action, and who might lose?" For example, consider the following short argument.

> Because parking downtown is so limited, we should require anyone putting up a new building to construct a parking lot or contribute to parking garages.

It doesn't take much to infer who might benefit: people driving downtown who are looking for places to park. With a little more thought, you can see how store owners could benefit if shoppers have an easier time finding parking. Who might lose? Well, having to provide parking will add to building costs, and these may be passed to customers. More room for parking means less room for building, so the downtown could sprawl into neighborhoods. More parking can encourage more driving, which contributes to congestion and pollution.

## 4f   How do I synthesize?

To **synthesize** is to put things together. When analysis and inference generate specific ideas, try to put them together with things you know from your experience or previous learning or from other readings. For example, suppose you read an opinion that reminds you of a similar opinion by an expert you respect. Making that connection is an act of critical thinking. It takes you beyond the reading itself. Or suppose that someone provides evidence for a claim, but that some further reading shows you that their facts are incomplete or even inaccurate. This synthesis allows you to read the first source more critically.

Synthesis also happens between a reading and your own experience. Take the following example.

> Probably no time in life is as liberating or stimulating as the college
> years. Freed from the drudgery of a career and the obligations of family

life, college students have the luxury to explore new ideas and pursue new paths of knowledge. College is a joyful time of endless possibility.

If you're a single parent taking classes at night or someone who is working a couple of jobs and worrying about paying back loans, your perspective probably differs from the author's. Synthesizing the reading and your experience would result in a critical evaluation.

# 4g    How do I evaluate?

When you read to evaluate, you're judging the writer's work. **Evaluative reading** comes after you've summarized, analyzed, and synthesized the material (see Quick Reference 4.1). Reading "between the lines" is usually concerned with recognizing tone, detecting prejudice, differentiating fact from opinion, and determining the writer's position. Reading to evaluate "beyond the lines" requires an overall assessment of the soundness of the writer's reasoning, evidence, or observations, and the fairness and perceptiveness the writer shows, from accuracy of word choice and tone to the writer's respect for the reader.

# 4h    How do I assess reasoning processes critically?

To think, read, and write critically, you need to distinguish *sound reasoning* from *faulty reasoning*. **Induction** and **deduction** are two basic reasoning processes, natural thought patterns people use every day to help them think through ideas and make decisions.

## ■ Inductive reasoning

Inductive reasoning moves from particular facts or instances to general principles. Suppose you go to the Registry of Motor Vehicles to renew your driver's license and have to stand in line for two hours. A few months later you return to get new license plates, and once again you have to stand in line for two hours. You mention your annoyance to a couple of friends who say they had exactly the same experience. You conclude that the registry is inefficient and indifferent to the needs of its patrons. You've arrived at this conclusion by means of induction. Quick Reference 4.7 shows the features of inductive reasoning.

## ■ Deductive reasoning

**Deductive reasoning** is the process of reasoning from general claims to a specific conclusion. Suppose you know that students who don't study for Professor Sanchez's history tests tend to do poorly. If your friend tells you that she

**Quick Reference 4.7** ▪ ▪ ▪ ▪ ▪

### Inductive reasoning

- **Inductive reasoning moves from the specific to the general.** It begins with specific evidence—facts, observations, or experiences—and moves to a general conclusion.

- **Inductive conclusions are considered reliable or unreliable, not true or false.** Because inductive thinking is based on a sampling of facts, an inductive conclusion indicates probability—the degree to which the conclusion is likely to be true—not certainty.

- **An inductive conclusion is held to be reliable or unreliable in relation to the quantity and quality of the evidence** (4g) on which it's based.

- **Induction leads to new "truths."** It can support statements about the unknown based on what's known.

didn't study, you can make a reasonable conclusion about her grade. Your reasoning might go something like this:

| | |
|---|---|
| **PREMISE 1** | Students who don't study do poorly on Professor Sanchez's exams. |
| **PREMISE 2** | My friend didn't study. |
| **CONCLUSION** | Therefore, my friend probably did poorly on the exam. |

Deductive arguments have three parts: two **premises** and a conclusion. This three-part structure is known as a **syllogism.** The first and second premises of a deductive argument may be statements of fact or assumptions. They lead to a conclusion, which is the point at which you want to think as precisely as possible because you're into the realm of *validity.*

Whether or not an argument is **valid** has to do with its form or structure. Here, the word *valid* isn't the general term people use in conversation to mean "acceptable" or "well grounded." In the context of reading and writing logical arguments, the word *valid* has a very specific meaning. A deductive argument is *valid* when the conclusion logically follows from the premises; a deductive argument is *invalid* when the conclusion doesn't logically follow from the premises. For example:

**VALID DEDUCTIVE ARGUMENT**

| | |
|---|---|
| **PREMISE 1** | When it snows, the streets get wet. [fact] |
| **PREMISE 2** | It is snowing. [fact] |
| **CONCLUSION** | Therefore, the streets are getting wet. |

INVALID DEDUCTIVE ARGUMENT

**PREMISE 1**   When it snows, the streets get wet. [fact]

**PREMISE 2**   The streets are getting wet. [fact]

**CONCLUSION**   Therefore, it is snowing.

Here's the problem with the invalid deductive argument: It has acceptable premises because they are facts. However, the argument's conclusion is wrong because it ignores other reasons why the streets might be wet. For example, the street could be wet from rain, from street-cleaning trucks that spray water, or from people washing their cars. Therefore, because the conclusion doesn't follow logically from the premises, the argument is invalid.

Another problem in a deductive argument can occur when the premises are implied but not stated—called **unstated assumptions.** An argument can be logically valid even though it is based on wrong assumptions. To show that such an argument is invalid, you need to attack the assumptions, not the conclusion, as wrong. Whenever there's an unstated assumption, you need to state it outright and then check that it's true. Quick Reference 4.8 summarizes deductive reasoning.

---

### Quick Reference 4.8    ■ ■ ■ ■ ■

#### Deductive reasoning

- **Deductive reasoning moves from the general to the specific.** The three-part structure that makes up a deductive argument, or SYLLOGISM, includes two premises and a conclusion drawn from them.

- **A deductive argument is valid if the conclusion logically follows from the premises.**

- **A deductive conclusion may be judged true or false.** If both premises are true, the conclusion is true. If the argument contains an assumption, the writer must prove the truth of the assumption to establish the truth of the argument.

- **Deductive reasoning applies what the writer already knows.** Though it doesn't yield new information, it builds stronger arguments than inductive reasoning because it offers the certainty that A conclusion is either true or false.

---

# **4i**  How can I recognize and avoid logical fallacies?

**Logical fallacies** are flaws in reasoning that lead to illogical statements. Though logical fallacies tend to occur when ideas are argued, they can be found in all types of writing. Interestingly, most logical fallacies masquerade as reasonable statements, but in fact, they're attempts to manipulate readers by appealing to their emotions instead of their intellects, their hearts rather than their heads. The name for each logical fallacy indicates the way that thinking has gone wrong.

## HASTY GENERALIZATION

A **hasty generalization** draws conclusions from inadequate evidence. Suppose someone says, "My hometown is the best place in the state to live," and gives only two examples to support the opinion. That's not enough. And others might not feel the same way, perhaps for many reasons. Therefore, the person who makes such a statement is indulging in a hasty generalization.

**Stereotyping,** sexism, and agism are other kinds of hasty generalization.

## FALSE ANALOGY

A **false analogy** draws a comparison in which the differences outweigh the similarities or the similarities are irrelevant. For example, "Old Joe Smith would never make a good president because an old dog can't learn new tricks" is a false analogy. Joe Smith isn't a dog. Also, learning the role of a president bears no comparison to a dog's learning tricks. Homespun analogies like this appear to have an air of wisdom about them, but they tend to fall apart when examined closely.

## BEGGING THE QUESTION

**Begging the question,** also called *circular reasoning,* tries to offer proof by simply using another version of the argument itself. For example, the statement "Wrestling is a dangerous sport because it is unsafe" begs the question. Because *unsafe* is a synonym for *dangerous,* the statement goes around in a circle, getting nowhere. Here's another example of circular reasoning but with a different twist: "Wrestling is a dangerous sport because wrestlers get injured." Here, the support given in the second part of the statement, "wrestlers get injured," is the argument made in the first part of the statement. Obviously, wrestling can be safe when undertaken with proper training and practice.

## IRRELEVANT ARGUMENT

An **irrelevant argument** reaches a conclusion that doesn't follow from the premises. Irrelevant argument is also called *non sequitur* (Latin for "it does not follow"). An argument is irrelevant when a conclusion doesn't follow from the premises. Here's an example: "Jane Jones is a forceful speaker, so she'll make a good mayor." You'd be on target if you asked "What does speaking ability have to do with being a good mayor?"

## FALSE CAUSE

A **false cause** assumes that because two events are related in time, the first caused the second. False cause is also known as *post hoc, ergo propter hoc* (Latin for "after this, therefore because of this"). For example, if someone claims that a new weather satellite launched last week has caused the rain that's been falling ever since, that person is connecting two events that, while related in time, have no causal relationship to each other. The launching didn't cause the rain.

## SELF-CONTRADICTION

**Self-contradiction** uses two premises that can't both be true at the same time. Here's an example: "Only when nuclear weapons have finally destroyed us will we be convinced of the need to control them." This is self-contradictory because no one would be around to be convinced if everyone has been destroyed.

## RED HERRING

A **red herring,** also called *ignoring the question,* tries to distract attention from one issue by introducing a second that's unrelated to the first. Here's an example: "Why worry about pandas becoming extinct when we haven't solved the plight of the homeless?" You'd be on target if you asked, "What do homeless people have to do with pandas?" If the argument were to focus on proposing that the money spent to prevent the extinction of pandas should go instead to the homeless, the argument would be logical; however, the original statement is a fallacy. By using an irrelevant issue, a person hopes to distract the audience, just as putting a herring in the path of a bloodhound would distract it from the scent it's been following.

## ARGUMENT TO THE PERSON

An **argument to the person** means attacking the person making the argument rather than the argument itself. It's also known as the *ad hominem* (Latin for "to the man") attack. When someone criticizes a person's appearance, habits, or character instead of the merits of that person's argument, the attack is a fallacy. Here's an example: "We'd take her position on child abuse seriously if she were not so nasty to her husband." You'd be on target if you were to ask, "What does nastiness to an adult, though not at all nice, have to do with child abuse?"

## GUILT BY ASSOCIATION

**Guilt by association** means that a person's arguments, ideas, or opinions lack merit because of that person's activities, interests, or companions. Here's an example: "Jack belongs to the International Hill Climbers Association, which declared bankruptcy last month. This makes him unfit to be mayor of our city." The fact that Jack is a member of a group that declared bankruptcy has nothing to do with Jack's ability to be mayor.

## JUMPING ON THE BANDWAGON

**Jumping on the bandwagon** means something is right or permissible because "everyone does it." It's also called *ad populum* (Latin for "to the people"). This fallacy operates in a statement such as "How could snowboarding be dangerous if thousands of people have done it?" Following the crowd in this example doesn't work because research shows that many people who snowboard eventually suffer serious knee injuries.

## FALSE OR IRRELEVANT AUTHORITY

Using **false** or **irrelevant authority** means citing the opinion of someone who has no expertise in the subject at hand. This fallacy attempts to transfer prestige from one area to another. Many advertisements containing celebrity endorsements rely on this tactic—a famous athlete praising a brand of energy drink or a popular movie star lauding a wireless phone service provider.

## CARD-STACKING

**Card-stacking,** also known as *special pleading,* ignores evidence on the other side of a question. From all available facts, people choose only those facts that show the best (or worst) possible case. Many television commercials use this strategy. For example, after three slim, happy consumers praise a diet plan, the announcer adds—in a very low and speedy voice—that results vary. Indeed, even that statement is vague and uninformative.

## THE EITHER-OR FALLACY

The **either-or fallacy,** also called *false dilemma,* offers only two alternatives when more exist. Such fallacies tend to touch on emotional issues, so many people accept them until they analyze the statement. Here's an example: "Either go to college or forget about getting a job." This rigid, two-sided statement ignores the truth that many jobs don't require a college education.

## TAKING SOMETHING OUT OF CONTEXT

**Taking something out of context** deliberately distorts an idea or a fact by removing it from its previously surrounding material. For example, suppose that a newspaper movie critic writes, "The plot was predictable and boring, but the music was sparkling." The next day, an advertisement for the movie claims "critics call it 'sparkling.'" Clearly, the ad has taken the critic's words out of context (only the music was called "sparkling"), and it thereby distorts the original meaning.

## APPEAL TO IGNORANCE

**Appeal to ignorance** tries to make an incorrect argument based on something never having been shown to be false—or, the reverse, never having been shown to be true. Here's an example: "Because it hasn't been proven that eating food X doesn't cause cancer, we can assume that it does." The statement is a fallacy because the absence of opposing evidence proves nothing. Such appeals can be very persuasive because they prey on people's superstitions or lack of knowledge. Often, they're stated in the fuzzy language of DOUBLE NEGATIVES.

## AMBIGUITY AND EQUIVOCATION

**Ambiguity** and **equivocation** are statements open to more than one inter-pretation, thus concealing the truth. Here's an example: Suppose a person is asked, "Is she doing a good job?" and the person answers, "She's performing as expected." The answer is a fallacy because it's open to positive or negative interpretation.

# 4j How can I view images critically?

Our digital age surrounds us with images in publications, on computers, on tel-evision, on cell phones. These images shape attitudes and beliefs, often in sub-tle ways. As a result—and as we suggested in the beginning of this chapter—you need to use critical thinking to analyze images as well as words. Doing so height-ens your sensitivity to how others use images and equips you to use them ef-fectively yourself.

You can view images critically in the same way that you can read texts critically by using summary, analysis, synthesis, and evaluation (Quick Refer-ence 4.1) and by using literal, analytic inferential, and evaluative reading (see section 4c).

Many texts—from Web pages to advertisements, posters, brochures, and so on—are multimodal in that they combine words and images. Critically an-alyzing multimodal texts means considering the images and the words separately, and then analyzing how the two elements combine to create a single effect.

*Document design* is the name given to the overall arrangement of words and visuals in a text. Chapter 41 explains several principles of document design.

Occasionally, you might be tempted to add images to your writing be-cause you want to add visual interest. That is a laudable goal, as long as the images support or enhance the message your writing is trying to deliver. How-ever, be wary of throwing in one or more images merely for the sake of includ-ing an image. Your readers will rightly assume your images are communicating a message related to the text, and if none emerges, your entire document loses credibility.

# 5 ▪ ▪ ▪ ▪

# Writing Arguments

## 5a  What is a written argument?

When you write an **argument,** you attempt to convince a reader to agree with you on a topic open to debate. You support your position, proposal, or interpretation with EVIDENCE, reasons, and examples. Some people use the terms *argumentative writing* and *persuasive writing* interchangeably. When people distinguish between them, *persuasive writing* is the broader term. It includes advertisements, letters to editors, and emotional speeches, as well as the kind of formal written arguments expected in college courses and other formal situations.

A written argument consists of two main elements: the **claim** states the issue and then takes a position on a debatable topic (the position can be written as a THESIS STATEMENT); facts and logical reasoning provide **support** for the claim (the support needs to be in the form of evidence, reasons, and examples).

For academic writing, as well as business and public writing, arguments are ways of demonstrating CRITICAL THINKING, calmly and respectfully. On difficult issues, your goal is to persuade an audience to consider your ideas with an open mind, which means that your audience's viewpoints and values need to influence your decisions about content, organization, and style. The passion that underlies a writer's position comes not from angry words but from the force of a balanced, well-developed, clearly written presentation.

In this chapter, you'll learn how to develop an effective claim, or thesis, how to generate support, and how to organize your argument using two strategies: the classical pattern and the Rogerian pattern. In addition, you'll find information about how to analyze and refute opposing arguments.

## 5b  How do I choose a topic for an argument?

When you choose a topic for written argument, be sure that it's open to debate. Don't confuse matters of information (facts) with matters of debate. An essay becomes an argument when it makes a claim—that is, *takes a position*—about a debatable topic. An effective way to develop a position is to ask two (or more) opposing questions about a topic.

> **FACT**  Students at Calhoon College must study a foreign language.

| DEBATABLE | Should Calhoon College require students to study a foreign language? |
|---|---|
| **ONE SIDE** | Calhoon College should not require students to study a foreign language. |
| **OTHER SIDE** | Calhoon College should require students to study a foreign language. |

Though you need to select one side of a debatable question to defend in your essay, always keep the other side (or sides) in mind. Devoting some space to state and counter opposing viewpoints shows readers that you're well informed and fair-minded. If you neglect to mention opposing views, your readers could justifiably assume you're not well informed, fair-minded, or disciplined as a thinker.

Instructors sometimes assign students a topic and even the position to take. In such cases, you need to fulfill the assignment skillfully even if you disagree with the point of view. Indeed, experienced debate teams practice arguing all sides of an issue.

If you choose your own topic and position, select one that has sufficient substance for college writing. Readers expect you to take an intelligent, defensible position and to support it reasonably and convincingly. For example, "We should prot of censorship in public libraries" is worthy of a college-level essay; "People should wear yellow baseball caps" is not.

## 5c  How do I develop a claim and a thesis statement for my argument?

A CLAIM is a statement that expresses a point of view on a debatable topic. It can be supported by evidence, reasons, and examples (including facts, statistics, names, experiences, and expert testimony). The exact wording of the claim rarely finds its way into the essay, but the claim serves as a focus for your thinking. Later, it serves as the basis for developing your THESIS STATEMENT.

| TOPIC | Wild animals as domestic pets |
|---|---|
| **CLAIM** | People should not be allowed to own wild animals. |
| **CLAIM** | People should be allowed to own wild animals. |

Alex Garcia, the student who wrote the argument essay that appears in section 5j, chose his own topic for a written argument in a first-year college writing class. Alex was a biology major who was fascinated about genetic engineering, especially of food. While exploring this topic, he became interested in the broader issue of organic food and whether it was really better. As a consumer himself, he had a direct stake in this matter. When he began reading articles he found through library research, he thought they would all come out clearly in favor of organic foods. When he found that not all of them did, he knew that the controversy would make a good topic for his argument. Here's how Alex progressed from topic to claim to thesis statement.

| | |
|---|---|
| **TOPIC** | Whether organic foods are better than regular ones |
| **MY POSITION** | I think people should buy organic foods when they can. |
| **THESIS STATEMENT (FIRST DRAFT)** | It is good for people to buy organic foods. [This is a preliminary thesis statement. It clearly states the writer's position, but the word *good* is vague.] |
| **THESIS STATEMENT (SECOND DRAFT)** | In order to achieve health benefits and to improve the quality of the environment, organic foods should be purchased by consumers. [This revised thesis statement is better because it states not only the writer's claim but also a reason for the claim. However, it suffers from a lack of conciseness and from the unnecessary passive construction "should be purchased."] |
| **THESIS STATEMENT (FINAL DRAFT)** | Research shows that the health and environmental benefits of organic foods outweigh their extra costs. [This final version works well because it states the writer's claim clearly and concisely, with all verbs in the active voice. The writer now has a thesis statement suitable for the time and length given in his assignment. Also, it meets the requirements for a thesis statement given in Quick Reference 2.3.] |

**EXERCISE 5-1** Working individually or with a peer-response group, develop a claim and a thesis statement for each of the topics listed at the end of the exercise. You may choose any defensible position. For help, consult sections 5a through 5c.

EXAMPLE **TOPIC:** Book censorship in high school

**CLAIM:** Books should not be censored in high school.

**THESIS STATEMENT:** When books are taken off high school library shelves or are dropped from high school curricula because they are considered inappropriate to read, students are denied an open exchange of ideas.

1. Commercials for weight loss pills on television
2. Taxing new cars according to their mileage
3. Athletes' use of steroids and performance drugs
4. Requiring students to undertake volunteer or community service

## 5d What is the structure of a classical argument?

No single method is best for organizing all arguments, but a frequently used structure is the **classical argument.** The ancient Greeks and Romans developed this six-part structure, which is described in Quick Reference 5.1.

---

### Quick Reference 5.1 ■ ■ ■ ■ ■

#### The structure of a classical argument

1. **Introductory paragraph:** Sets the stage for the position argued in the essay. It gains the reader's interest and respect (3c).

2. **Thesis statement:** States the topic and position you want to argue (2d).

3. **Background information:** Gives readers the basic information they need for understanding your thesis and its support. As appropriate, you might include definitions of key terms, historical or social context, prior scholarship, and other related material. You can include this as part of your introductory paragraph, or it can appear in its own paragraph placed immediately after the introduction.

4. **Evidence and reasons:** Supports the position you're arguing on the topic. This is the core of the essay. Each reason or piece of evidence usually consists of a general statement backed up with specific details, including examples and other RENNS (that is, reasons, examples, names, numbers, and senses). (See section 3f.) Evidence needs to meet the standards for critical thinking (Chapter 4). Depending on the length of the essay, you might devote one or two paragraphs to each reason or type of evidence.

5. **Response to opposing position:** Sometimes referred to as the *rebuttal* or *refutation.* This material mentions and defends against an opposite point of view. Often this refutation, which can be lengthy or brief according to the overall length of the essay, appears in its own paragraph or paragraphs, usually immediately before the concluding paragraph or immediately following the introductory paragraph, as a bridge to the rest of the essay.

6. **Concluding paragraph:** Ends the essay logically and gracefully— never abruptly. It often summarizes the argument, elaborates its significance, or calls readers to action (3k).

# 5e    What types of appeals can provide support?

An effective argument relies on three types of **persuasive appeals:** logical appeals, emotional appeals, and ethical appeals. The ancient Greeks called these appeals *logos, pathos,* and *ethos.* Quick Reference 5.2 summarizes how to use the appeals.

---

**Quick Reference 5.2**                                     ■ ■ ■ ■ ■

### Guidelines for persuasive appeals

- **Be logical:** Use sound reasoning (*logos*).
- **Enlist the emotions of the reader:** Appeal to the values and beliefs of the reader by arousing the reader's "better self" (*pathos*).
- **Establish credibility:** Show that you as the writer can be relied on as a knowledgeable person with good sense (*ethos*).

---

The **logical appeal** (*logos*) is the most widely used and intellectually solid and sound appeal in arguments. Sound reasoning involves using effective evidence and reasons. When the student writer Alex Garcia argues that certain foods carry health risks, he cites research that points to specific diseases (5j). Logical writers analyze CAUSE AND EFFECT correctly. Also, they use appropriate patterns of INDUCTIVE REASONING and DEDUCTIVE REASONING, and they distinguish clearly between fact and opinion. Finally, sound reasoning means avoiding LOGICAL FALLACIES. One strategy for generating logical appeals is the **Toulmin model,** developed by the philosopher Stephen Toulmin, discussed in 5f.

When you use **emotional appeals** (*pathos*), you try to persuade your readers by appealing to their hearts more than their minds. Such appeals are generally more effective when you combine them with logical appeals.

Emotional appeals can use descriptive language and concrete details or examples to create a mental picture for readers, which is an approach that leads them to feel or understand the importance of your claim. You want, however, to avoid manipulating your readers with biased, SLANTED LANGUAGE. Readers see through such tactics and resent them.

When you use **ethical appeals,** or *ethos,* you establish your personal credibility with your audience. Audiences don't trust a writer who states opinions as fact, distorts evidence, or makes claims that can't be supported. They do trust a writer who comes across as honest, knowledgeable, and fair. Ethical appeals can't take the place of logical appeals, but the two work well together. One effective way to make an ethical appeal is to draw on your personal experience. Another way to make an ethical appeal is to consider a variety of perspectives, reasonably and fairly addressing opposing viewpoints (Quick Reference 5.1). Using reliable SOURCES and a reasonable TONE all communicate that you're being fair-minded.

# 5f What is the Toulmin model for argument?

One powerful method for generating logical appeals and for analyzing the arguments of others is the Toulmin model. The Toulmin model defines three essential elements in an effective argument: the claim, the support, and the warrants. They describe concepts that you've encountered before (as Quick Reference 5.3 explains). For example, identifying the **warrants** (assumptions that are often unstated) is a good critical thinking strategy.

---

### Quick Reference 5.3                    ■ ■ ■ ■ ■

### The Toulmin model for argument

- **Claim:** A variation of a thesis statement. If needed, the claim is qualified or limited.

- **Support:** REASONS and EVIDENCE, moving from broad reasons to specific data and details, support the claim.

- **Warrants:** The writer's underlying assumptions, which are often implied rather than stated. Warrants may also need support (also called *backing*).

---

The concept of *warrant* is similar to the concept of *inferences,* a key component of critical thinking (4a). Inferences are not stated outright but are implied "between the lines" of the writing. Similarly, warrants are unspoken underlying assumptions in an argument.

The concepts in the Toulmin model can help you write arguments with a critical eye. They can be quite useful on their own as well as applied to the CLASSICAL ARGUMENT structure (Quick Reference 5.1). As you read and revise your own arguments, identify the claim, support, and warrants. If you don't have a clear claim or support, you'll probably have to assume that your argument is weak. Furthermore, make sure that all of your warrants will be convincing to readers. If they aren't, you need to provide backing, or reasons why the warrants are reasonable. For example, consider the following argument: "People should not receive a driver's license until the age of 25 because the accident rate for younger drivers is much higher than for older ones." One of the warrants here is that reducing the number of accidents should have highest priority. Obviously, many 18-to-24-year-old readers will not find that warrant convincing.

**EXERCISE 5-2** Individually or with a peer-response group, discuss these simple arguments. Identify the claim, support, and warrants for each.

EXAMPLE    The college should establish an honor code. Last semester more than fifty students were caught cheating on exams.

CLAIM: The college should establish an honor code.

SUPPORT: Last semester, more than fifty students were caught cheating on exams.

**WARRANTS:**

A. Enough students cheat on exams that the college should address the problem.

B. Cheating should be prevented.

C. Students would not have cheated if there had been an honor code.

1. The college should raise student tuition and fees. The football stadium is in such poor repair that the coach is having trouble recruiting players.

2. Vote against raising our taxes. In the past two years, we have already had a 2 percent tax increase.

3. The college should require all students to own laptop computers. Most students will have to use computers in their jobs after graduation.

# 5g  What part does audience play in my argument?

The PURPOSE of written argument is to convince your AUDIENCE either to agree with you or to be open to your position. In writing an argument, you want to consider what your readers already know or believe about your topic. Will the audience be hostile or open-minded to your position? Will it resist or adopt your point of view? What values, viewpoints, and assumptions will your audience hold?

Unfortunately, some members of some audiences can be persuaded by purely sensational or one-sided claims. Witness the effects on some readers of highly charged advertising or of narrowly one-sided ultraconservative or ultraliberal claims. However, such arguments rarely change the minds of people who don't already agree with them. Critical thinking quickly reveals the weaknesses of such arguments, including a frequent use of LOGICAL FALLACIES (4i). That's why academic audiences expect a higher standard and value, above all, logical appeals and appropriate, adequate support.

**Rogerian argument** seeks common ground between points of view. The Rogerian approach is based on the principles of communication developed by the psychologist Carl Rogers. According to Rogers, communication is eased when people find common ground in their points of view. Quick Reference 5.4 explains the structure of a Rogerian argument, which can be an effective alternative to CLASSICAL ARGUMENT structure.

As you write a Rogerian argument, remember that your audience wants to see how effectively you've reasoned and presented your position. This stance approaches that of a formal oral debate in which all sides are explored with similar intellectual rigor.

| Quick Reference 5.4 | ■ ■ ■ ■ ■ |
|---|---|

### The structure of a Rogerian argument

1. **Introduction:** Sets the stage for the position that is argued in the essay. It gains the reader's interest and respect (3c).

2. **Thesis statement:** States the topic and position you want to argue (5b and 5c).

3. **Common ground:** Explains the issue, acknowledging that your readers probably don't agree with you. Speculates about and respectfully gives attention to the points of agreement you and your readers might share, especially concerning underlying problems or issues. For example, people on both sides of the gun control issue can share the desire for fewer violent crimes with guns. You might even acknowledge situations in which your reader's position may be desirable. This may take one paragraph or several, depending on the complexity of the issue.

4. **Discussion of your position:** Gives evidence and reasons for your stand on the topic, as in classical argument (see Quick Reference 5.1).

5. **Concluding paragraph:** Summarizes why your position is preferable to your opponent's (3k). You might, for example, explain why a particular situation makes your position desirable.

# 5h  What is a reasonable tone in an argument?

A reasonable TONE tells your audience that you're being fair-minded. When you anticipate opposing positions and refute them with balanced language and emphasis, you demonstrate that you respect the other side. No matter how strongly you disagree with opposing arguments, never insult the other side.

**EXERCISE 5-3**    Here is the text of a notorious e-mail fraud that has been sent to many people. Hundreds of variations of this e-mail exist, but usually the writer claims to have a large amount of money that he or she wants to transfer to an American bank. The writer wants the recipient's help in making the transfer. This is a complete lie. The writer has no money and is trying to trick people into revealing their bank account numbers to steal their money.

Either alone or in a small group, examine the ways this writer tries to establish emotional and ethical appeals. *Note:* We've reproduced the e-mail with the often incorrect original wording, grammar, and punctuation.

Good day,

It is my humble pleasure to write this letter irrespective of the fact that you do not know me. However, I came to know of you in my private search for a reliable and trustworthy person that can handle a confidential transaction of this nature in respect of this, I got your contact through an uprooted search on the internet. Though I know that a transaction of this magnitude will make any one apprehensive and worried, but I am assuring you that all will be well at the end of the day.

I am Ruth Malcasa, daughter of late Mr. James Malcasa of Somalia, who was killed by the rebel forces on the 24th of December, 2007 in my country Somalia. When he was still alive, he deposited one trunk box containing the sum of USD$10 million dollars in cash (Ten Million dollars). with a private security and safe deposit company here in Lagos Nigeria. This money was made from the sell of Gold and Diamond by my mother and she has already decided to use this money for future investment of the family.

My father instructed me that in the case of his death, that I should look for a trusted foreigner who can assist me to move out this money from Nigeria immediately for investment. Based on this, I solicit for your assistance to transfer this fund into your Account, but I will demand for the following requirement: (1) Could you provide for me a safe Bank Account where this fund will be transferred to in your country after retrieving the box containing the money from the custody of the security company. (2) Could you be able to introduce me to a profitable business venture that would not require much technical expertise in your country where part of this fund will be invested?

I am a Christian and I want you to handle this transaction based on the trust I have established on you. For your assistance in this transaction, I have decided to compensate you with 10 percent of the total amount at the end of this business. The security of this business is very important to me and as such, I would like you to keep this business very confidential. I shall expect an early response from you. Thank you and God bless. Yours sincerely, Ruth Malcasa.

## 5i    How do I handle opposing arguments?

Dealing with opposing positions is crucial to writing an effective argument. If you don't acknowledge arguments that your opponents might raise and explain why they are faulty or inferior, you create doubts that you have thoroughly explored the issue. You risk seeming narrow-minded.

If your research doesn't generate opposing arguments, you need to develop them yourself. Imagine that you're debating someone who disagrees with you; what positions would that person take and why?

Once you have generated opposing arguments, you need to refute them, which means you want to show why they're weak or undesirable. Imagine that you're writing about national security and individual rights. You believe that the government shouldn't be allowed to monitor a private citizen's e-mail without a court order, and you have developed a number of reasons for your position. To strengthen your paper, you also generate some opposing arguments, including "People will be safer from terrorism if police can monitor e-mail," "Only people who have something to hide have anything to fear," and "It is unpatriotic to oppose the government's plans." How might you refute these or other opposing claims? Following are some suggestions.

- **Examine the evidence for each opposing argument** (4d–4h). Look especially for missing or contradictory facts. In the given example, you might question the evidence that people would be safer from terrorism if police could monitor e-mail.

- **Use the Toulmin model to analyze the opposing argument** (5f). What are the claims, support, and warrants? Often, it's possible to show that the warrants are questionable or weak. For example, a warrant in the counterarguments above is that the promise of increased safety is worth the price of privacy or individual rights. You might show why this warrant is undesirable.

- **Demonstrate that an opposing argument depends on emotion rather than reasoning.** The assertion that it's unpatriotic to oppose the government is primarily an emotional one.

- **Redefine key terms.** The term *patriotism* can be defined in various ways. You might point out, for example, that at the time of the American Revolution, "patriots" were the people who were opposing the British government then in power.

- **Explain the negative consequences of the opposing position.** Imagine that the opposing position actually won out, and explain how the results would be damaging. For example, if everyone knew that government officials might monitor their computer use, consider how this might affect free speech.

- **Concede an opposing point, but explain that doing so doesn't destroy your own argument.** For example, you might decide to concede that governmental monitoring of e-mails could reduce terrorism. However, you might argue that the increase in safety is not worth the threat to privacy and personal freedom.

- **Explain that the costs of the other position are not worth the benefits.**

**EXERCISE 5-4**  Individually or with a peer-response group, practice developing objections to specific arguments and responses to those objections. To do this, choose a debatable topic and brainstorm a list of points on that topic, some on one side of the topic, some on another. Following are some arguments to get you started. If you're part of a group, work together to assign the different positions for each topic to different sets of students. Then, conduct a brief debate on which side has more merit, with each side taking turns. At the end, your group can vote for the side that is more convincing.

1. It should be legal/illegal to ride motorcycles without a helmet.

2. Political candidates should/should not use negative advertising.

3. Students should/should not be required to take certain courses in order to graduate.

## **5j**   How did one student draft and revise his argument essay?

In his first draft, Alex Garcia focused on how organic farming would benefit the environment, and he found lots of studies of how traditional farming practices affect water and soil quality. However, he realized that this argument alone might seem remote to many readers, so he explored how agricultural chemicals affect consumers. Extensive research resulted in a second draft that included not only immediate concerns for individuals but also society at large. While doing that research, he was surprised to encounter evidence that organic foods weren't necessarily more nutritious. Initially, Alex wanted just to ignore it, but then he decided his paper would be stronger if he included and dealt with this opposing viewpoint in his third draft. That draft also was where he developed his introductory paragraph, which until this point he had just sketched generally. Throughout the process, he found the need to check facts and sources in library databases. Before completing the paper, he looked carefully at his use of *pathos* and *ethos* and consulted the revision checklist (see Quick Reference 2.8). Finally, he referred to the special checklist for revising written arguments in Quick Reference 5.5.

---

### Quick Reference 5.5                                       ■ ■ ■ ■ ■

**Revising written arguments**

- Is the thesis statement about a debatable topic? (5b and 5c)
- Do the reasons or evidence support the thesis statement? Are the generalizations supported by specific details? (5c)
- Does the argument deal with reader needs and concerns? (5g)
- Does the argument appeal chiefly to reason? Is it supported by an ethical appeal? If it uses an emotional appeal, is the appeal restrained? (5e)
- Is the tone reasonable? (5h)
- Is the opposing position started and refuted? (5i)

---

**EXERCISE 5-5**   Working individually or with a peer-response group, choose a topic from this list. Then, plan an essay that argues a debatable position on the topic. Apply all the principles you've learned in this chapter.

1. Animal experimentation
2. Genetically engineered food
3. Cloning of human beings
4. Taxpayer support for public colleges
5. Home schooling

Alex Garcia

WRIT 1122

Professor Brosnahan

4 May 2008

Why Organic Foods are Worth the Extra Money

A small decision confronts me every time I walk into the grocery store. I see a display of enticing apples for around $1.79 per pound. Next to them is a similar display of the same kind of apples, perhaps just a little smaller and just a little less perfect. These sell for $2.29 per pound. The difference between the two is the tiny sticker that reads "organic." Are those apples worth the extra money, especially when my budget is tight and the other ones appear just fine? Millions of shoppers face this same decision whenever they decide whether to buy organic food, and the right answer seems complicated, especially when the US Department of Agriculture "makes no claims that organically produced food is safer or more nutritious than conventionally produced food" (National). However, current research shows that the health and environmental benefits of organic foods outweigh their extra costs.

Organic foods are produced without using most chemical pesticides, without artificial fertilizers, without genetic engineering, and without radiation (National). In the case of organic meat, poultry, eggs, and dairy products, the animals are raised without antibiotics or growth hormones. As a result, people sometimes use the term "natural" instead of organic, but "natural" is less precise. Before 2002, people could never be quite sure what they were getting when they bought supposedly organic food, unless they bought it directly from a

continued >>

farmer they knew personally. In 2002, the US Department of
Agriculture established standards that food must meet in order
to be labeled and sold as organic.

According to environmental scientist Craig Minowa,
organic foods tend to cost about 15 percent more than
nonorganic, mainly because they are currently more difficult to
mass-produce (Minowa). Farmers who apply pesticides often
get larger crops from the same amount of land because there is
less insect damage. Artificial fertilizers tend to increase the
yield, size, and uniformity of fruits and vegetables, and
herbicides kill weeds that compete with desirable crops for
sun, nutrients, and moisture. Animals who routinely receive
antibiotics and growth hormones tend to grow more quickly
and produce more milk and eggs. In contrast, organic farmers
have lower yields and, therefore, higher costs. These get
passed along as higher prices to consumers.

Still, the extra cost is certainly worthwhile in terms of
health benefits. Numerous studies have shown the dangers
of pesticides for humans. An extensive review of research by
the Ontario College of Family Physicians concludes that
"Exposure to all the commonly used pesticides . . . has shown
positive associations with adverse health effects" (Sanborn
173). The risks include cancer, psychiatric effects, difficulties
becoming pregnant, miscarriages, and dermatitis. Carefully
washing fruits and vegetables can remove some of these
dangerous chemicals, but according to the prestigious
journal *Nature*, even this does not remove all of them (Giles
797). Certainly, if there's a way to prevent these poisons
entering our bodies, we should take advantage of it. The few
cents saved on cheaper food can quickly disappear in doctor's

continued >>

Garcia 3

bills needed to treat conditions caused or worsened by chemicals.

Organic meat, poultry, and dairy products can address another health concern: the diminishing effectiveness of antibiotics. In the past decades, many kinds of bacteria have become resistant to drugs, making it extremely difficult to treat some kinds of tuberculosis, pneumonia, staphylococcus infections, and less serious diseases (Dangerous 1). True, this has happened mainly because doctors overly prescribed antibiotics to patients who expect a pill for every illness. However, routinely giving antibiotics to all cows and chickens means that these drugs enter our food chain early, giving bacteria lots of chances to develop resistance. A person who switches to organic meats won't suddenly experience better results from antibiotics; the benefit is a more gradual one for society as a whole. However, if we want to be able to fight infections with effective drugs, we need to reserve antibiotics for true cases of need and discourage their routine use in animals raised for food. Buying organic is a way to persuade more farmers to adopt this practice.

Another benefit of organic foods is also a societal one: Organic farming is better for the environment. In his review of several studies, Colin Macilwain concluded that organic farms nurture larger numbers and more diverse kinds of plants and animals than regular farms (797). Organic farms also don't release pesticides and herbicides that can harm wildlife and run into our water supply, with implications for people's health, too. Macilwain notes that those farms also can generate less carbon dioxide, which will help with global warming; also, many scientists believe that organic farming is more

continued >>

sustainable because it results in better soil quality (798). Once again, these benefits are not ones that you will personally experience right away. However, a better natural environment means a better quality of living for everyone and for future generations.

Some critics point out that organic products aren't more nutritious than regular ones. Physician Sanjay Gupta, for example, finds the medical evidence for nutritional advantages is "thin" (60). The *Tufts University Health and Nutrition Letter* also reports that the research on nutritional benefits is mixed, with one important study showing "no overall differences" ("Is Organic" 8). Nutritional value, which includes qualities such as vitamins and other beneficial substances, is a different measure than food safety. At this point, it seems that nutrition alone is not a sufficient reason to buy organic foods. Perhaps future research will prove otherwise; a 2007 study, for example, showed that organically raised tomatoes have higher levels of flavonoids, nutrients that appear to have many health benefits (Mitchell). In the meantime, however, environmental quality and, most importantly, avoiding chemicals remain convincing reasons to purchase organic food, even if the same cannot yet be claimed for nutrition.

Despite the considerable benefits for purchasing organic products, there remains each consumer's decision in the grocery store. Are the more expensive apples ultimately worth their extra cost to me? It's true that there are no easily measurable one-to-one benefits, no way to ensure that spending fifty cents more on this produce will directly improve my quality of life by fifty cents. However, countless

continued >>

Garcia 5

people are rightly concerned these days about our personal
health and the health of the world in which we live, and I
am one of them. It's nearly impossible to put a value on a
sustainable, diverse natural environment and having the
physical health to enjoy it. The long-term benefits of buying
organic, for anyone who can reasonably afford to, far
outweigh the short-term savings in the checkout line.

Garcia 6

### Works Cited

"Dangerous Bacterial Infections Are on the Rise." *Consumer
Reports on Health* 19 (Nov. 2007): 1-4. Print.

Giles, Jim. "Is Organic Food Better for Us?" *Nature* 428.6985 (22
Apr. 2004): 796-97. Print.

"Is Organic Food Really More Nutritious?" *Tufts University
Health and Nutrition Letter* 25 (Sep. 2007): 8. Web. 25 Apr.
2008.

Gupta, Sanjay, and Shahreen Abedin. "Rethinking Organics."
*Time* (20 Aug. 2007): 60. Print.

Macilwain, Colin. "Is Organic Farming Better for the
Environment?" *Nature* 428.6985 (22 Apr. 2004): 797-98. Print.

Minowa, Craig. Interview by Louise Druce. "FYI on Organics:
Organic Q & A." Organic Consumers Assn. 29 June 2004.
Web.

Mitchell, Alyson E., Yun-Jeong Hong, Eunmi Koh, Diane M.
Barrett, D. E. Bryant, R. Ford Denison, and Stephen Kaffka.
"Ten-Year Comparison of the Influence of Organic and

continued >>

Garcia 7

Conventional Crop Management Practices on the Content of Flavonoids in Tomatoes." *Journal of Agricultural Food Chemistry* 55.15 (2007): 6154-59. Web. 30 Apr. 2008.

National Organic Program. "Organic Food Labels and Standards: The Facts." *Agricultural Marketing Service:* US Department of Agriculture. Jan. 2007. Web. 26 Apr 2008.

Sanborn, Margaret, Donald Cole, Kathleen Kerr, Cathy Vakil, Luz Helena Sanin, Kate Bassil. *Pesticides Literature Review: Systematic Review of Pesticide Human Health Effects.* Toronto: Ontario College of Family Physicians, 2004. Web. 28 Apr. 2008.

# 6

# Writing with Others

## 6a   What is writing with others?

Although it may often seem like a lonely act, a surprising amount of writing depends on two or more people working together. Anytime you ask someone else to read your draft and give you feedback for revision, you're working with others. The other person could be a friend, a classmate, a coworker, a writing tutor (in a campus writing center), or an instructor—after all, your instructor's comments on a draft are designed to guide your revision.

Collaborative writing assignments are increasingly popular in college courses across the curriculum, especially in business, the sciences, and the social sciences. Even if they aren't required to write full papers, small groups are commonly asked to brainstorm a topic together before individual writing tasks, to discuss various sides of a debatable topic, or to share reactions to an essay or piece of literature the class reads, and so on.

Writing collaboratively enhances confidence when writers support one another. Experience in collaborative writing has benefits beyond your college years because working well with others is a skill that employers value.

**Alert:** Some instructors and students use the terms *peer-response group* and *collaborative writing* to mean the same thing. In this handbook, we assign the terms to two different situations. We use *collaborative writing* (6b) for students writing an essay, a research paper, or a report together in a group. We use *peer-response group* (6c) for students getting together in small groups to help one another write and revise. ●

## 6b How can I collaborate with other writers?

Three qualities are essential to collaborative writing. The first is careful planning. Your group needs to decide when and how it will meet (in person, in a telephone call, in an online discussion); what steps it will follow and what the due dates will be; what software you'll use; and who will be responsible for what. Everyone in the group needs to commit to the plan, making changes only after deliberation by everyone.

The second essential quality is a fair division of labor. During early planning meetings, the group should figure out the tasks involved in the project and estimate how much time and effort each will take. (You can rebalance things during later meetings, if necessary.)

The third essential element of collaborative projects is clear communication. Open and honest communication is vital, and people need to put aside their own egos to build a productive and trusting atmosphere. Keep notes for every meeting so that the group has a clear record of what was decided; one way to do this is to have someone send an e-mail summarizing each meeting.

**EXERCISE 6-1**   Working in a small group, plan how your group would proceed on one or more of the following collaborative projects, satisfying each of the three essential criteria for group work. (*Note:* You don't actually have to complete the project; the purpose of this exercise is to develop your planning skills.)

- A report for a public audience in which you evaluate new car models.
- A research project in which you analyze the political views of students on your campus.
- A persuasive paper in which you argue whether the United States should pass laws to make it harder for American companies to move jobs to other countries.

Be prepared to explain your planning to your instructor or to class members in a way that shows your group has been thoughtful and thorough.

## 6c How can I give useful feedback to others?

There are two main ways to give feedback to other writers. One is in a small group, usually three to five people, who together discuss each group member's draft out loud. Another way is to work in pairs, providing oral or, more often, written comments for each other.

### ■ Working in peer-response groups

In some writing classes, instructors divide students into PEER-RESPONSE GROUPS. A peer is an "equal": another writer like you. Participating in a peer-response group makes you part of a respected tradition of colleagues helping colleagues. Professional writers often seek comments from other writers to improve their rough drafts. As a member of a peer-response group, you're not expected to be a writing expert. Rather, you're expected to offer responses as a practiced reader and as a fellow student writer who understands what writers go through.

Peer-response groups are set up in different ways. One arrangement calls for students to pass around and read one another's drafts silently, writing down reactions or questions in the margins or on a response form created by the instructor. In another arrangement, students read their drafts aloud, and then each peer responds either orally or in writing on a response form. Yet another arrangement asks for focused responses to only one or two features of each draft (perhaps each member's thesis statement, or topic sentences and supporting details, or use of transitional words, for example).

Whatever the arrangement of your group, you want to be clear about exactly what you are expected to do, both as a peer-responder and as a writer. If your instructor gives you guidelines for working in a group, follow them carefully. If you've never before participated in a peer-response group, or in the particular kind of group that your instructor forms, consult the guidelines in Quick Reference 6.1; watch what experienced peers do; and ask your instructor questions (your interest shows a positive, cooperative attitude). Otherwise, just dive in knowing that you'll learn as you go.

### ■ Giving peer response as an individual

Often an instructor will have two people exchange drafts and provide responses and suggestions to each other. All of the general guidelines for peer response in groups apply to situations when you're the only person giving feedback, especially being helpful, specific, and polite.

**Quick Reference 6.1**    ■ ■ ■ ■ ■

### Guidelines for participating in peer-response groups

One major principle needs to guide your participation in a peer-response group: Always take an upbeat, constructive attitude, whether you're responding to someone else's writing or receiving responses from others.

- Think of yourself as a coach, not a judge.

- Consider all writing by your peers as "works in progress."

- After hearing or reading a peer's writing, briefly summarize it to check that you and your peer are clear about what the peer said or meant to say.

- Start with what you think is well done. No one likes to hear only negative comments.

- Be honest in your suggestions for improvement.

- Base your responses on an understanding of the writing process, and remember that you're reading drafts, not finished products. All writing can be revised.

- Give concrete and specific responses. General comments such as "This is good" or "This is weak" don't offer much help. Describe specifically what is good or weak.

- Follow your instructor's system for putting your comments in writing so that your fellow writer can recall what you said. If one member of your group is supposed to take notes, speak clearly so that the person's notes can be accurate. If you're the note taker, be accurate and ask the speaker to repeat what he or she said if the comment went by too quickly.

As with peer response, your instructor may have you use a response form or follow a set of questions. Here are some other questions you might find useful:

- What part of the paper was most interesting or effective?

- If you had to remove one paragraph, which would you sacrifice and why?

- If you had to rearrange two parts of the paper, which would you change and why?

- What is one additional fact, argument, or piece of information that might improve the paper?

Another good strategy is for the writer to generate a couple of questions that he or she would particularly like the reviewer to answer. Avoid questions that require only a *yes* or *no* response. For example:

**NOT EFFECTIVE**    Is paragraph two on page three effective?

**EFFECTIVE**    How can I improve paragraph two on page three?

| **NOT EFFECTIVE** | Do you like my tone in the paper? |
| **EFFECTIVE** | How would you describe my tone in this paper? |

## 6d　How can I benefit from others' help?

Turning to the sometimes sticky issue of how to accept criticism of your writing, we offer you two pieces of personal advice from our own experience.

First, keep in mind that most students don't like to criticize their peers. They worry about being impolite or inaccurate, or losing someone's friendship. Try, therefore, to cultivate an attitude that encourages your peers to respond as freely and as helpfully as possible. It's particularly important to show that you can listen without getting angry or feeling intruded on.

Second, realize that most people tend to be at least a little defensive about even the best-intentioned and most tactful criticism. Of course, if a comment is purposely mean or sarcastic, you and all the others in your peer-response group have every right to say so, and to not tolerate such comments.

⊕ **ESOL Tip:** Students from cultures other than those in the United States or Canada might feel uncomfortable in the role of critic or questioner of other people's writing. Please know, however, that peer-response groups are fairly common in schools and at jobs because people usually think that "two heads are better than one." Sharing and questioning others' ideas—as well as how they are expressed in writing—is an honorable tradition in the United States and Canada. Peer-response groups help writers politely but firmly explore concepts and language, so please feel free to participate fully. In fact, some instructors grade you on your open participation in such activities. ●

# 7

# Strategies for Writing Typical Kinds of College Papers

## 7a What are typical kinds of papers I'll write in college?

Arguments and research papers are two of the most common types of college writing. In a written argument you try to persuade readers to take an action, adopt a position, or see a viewpoint as legitimate even if they ultimately disagree with it. Research papers (sometimes called term papers or seminar papers) involve gathering information from several sources, which you then summarize, analyze, and synthesize. Because arguments are such a vital part of college writing, we devote all of Chapter 5 to them. In addition, since there are many elements in writing a research paper, we devote Chapters 32–34 to this kind of writing.

College students face many types of writing, and expecting one set of guidelines to be perfect for every single variety would be unrealistic. Analyzing the WRITING SITUATION (Chapter 1) and understanding the WRITING PROCESS (Chapter 2) are important and useful for all writing.

Consider the following writing assignments you might get in college:

- A lengthy library research paper
- A summary of a reading
- A report on a laboratory experiment
- A proposal
- A personal essay
- An essay exam
- A critical response to a reading

These types of writing obviously differ in terms of length, PURPOSE, CONTEXT, and SPECIAL CONSIDERATIONS. But notice how each type also uses different SOURCES (readings vs. experiences vs. observations, for example), how the writer's ROLE changes (for example, from an impartial observer who keeps in the background to a center of attention whose experience and personality are foregrounded), and how format and style can vary. Knowing a few strategies will help you with different kinds of writing.

## 7b   What sources will I use in college writing?

A source is any form of information that provides ideas, examples, information, or evidence. Commonly, people think of readings (books, articles, Web sites, and so on) when they think of sources, and clearly readings are crucial.

There are other kinds of sources, too. Your own memories and experiences are a source, even though you may not think of them that way. Some academic situations allow or even require personal experiences, while others would definitely exclude them.

Another kind of source is direct observation. For example, you might be asked to attend a lecture and summarize what the speaker had to say or, additionally, to write a reaction to it. You might be asked to gather instances of a particular social or cultural phenomenon and, using analysis, inference, or synthesis, explore the meaning of that phenomenon.

An additional kind of source is statistical or quantitative information, which comes to us in the form of numbers ("217 people liked mushroom pizza"), as percentages ("14 percent liked mushroom pizza"), or other data. Of course, you might find this information in a published written source. Alternatively, you may be collecting the data yourself.

Finally, we note that many assignments mix sources. You might be asked to asked to relate one of your experiences to a reading in which someone else reports their own. You might do a study that combines direct observations with a survey.

**EXERCISE 7-1**   Working alone or in a group, discuss the kinds of sources you might use in each of the following writing questions.

1. Scholar Kyung Kim offers three suggestions for improving American high schools. Would her suggestions have worked at the high school you attended?

2. Are most students at your college liberal or conservative? What about students around the country?

3. What qualities generally seem true of romantic comedy movies that have been released in the past year?

## 7c   How can I write about experiences?

Some writing assignments may ask you to write about your memories or experiences. Generally, such writings will involve effectively telling a story, often accompanied by some reflection on or analysis of that story.

### ■ Memoirs and personal essays

In *memoirs,* writers tell what they remember about something that happened to them. While memoirs, like autobiographies, can cover most of a person's life, they often focus on smaller slices, such as a particular incident or a related set of incidents.

Personal essays are closely related to memoirs (in fact, your instructor may use the terms interchangeably). Once again, you'll want to tell about an experience. Personal essays tend to contain more reflection and to make their points more explicitly. They answer the question "What does this experience mean?" or "How does my experience illustrate a particular idea?"

### Important Elements of Memoirs and Personal Essays

- A well-told story. Your readers will want to know what happened. They will also want to know enough background information and context so they can fully understand and appreciate what happened and why it made an impression.

- Lively details. Help your readers see and hear, perhaps even smell, taste, and feel what you were experiencing. Recreate the place and time, the people who were involved. Give readers reason to like (or dislike, as the case may be) the places or people involved by the way you characterize them.

- Reflective or analytic paragraphs or passages. In addition to telling readers what happened, also tell them what you were thinking during the experience (take us inside your head at the time) or what you make of it now, looking backward.

- An effective use of STYLE and TONE (Chapter 8).

### ■ Literacy narratives

A literacy narrative is a specific kind of memoir in which you tell the story of how you developed as a reader and writer. Generally, these stories stretch from your earliest memories to the present day, and we find that students are often surprised at the memories they dig up while writing. First year writing instructors sometimes assign literacy narratives, as do some education or social sciences instructors.

### Important Elements of Literacy Narratives

- The elements important to memoirs and personal essays also matter for literacy narratives: a good story, lively details, and reflection.

- Examples of your previous reading, writing, or other language experiences. This may take the form of book titles, papers you remember writing, specific people important in your development as a reader and writer, scenes from school or home, and so on.

## 7d   How can I write about observations?

Writing about observations means writing about things you directly and intentionally see or experience. *Intentionally* is the important word. Sometimes you write about things that you just happened to notice or experience. However, in academic writing situations, observations are almost always purposeful and deliberate. You observe as a writer with a specific goal.

### ■ Reports of observations

Sometimes your assignment is to report about an event. You're asked to attend a presentation or lecture and summarize the talk. You go to a concert, play, or sporting event with the goal of explaining what happened. In these writing situations, your purpose is to inform, and your role is to be an objective reporter, much like a journalist. Other times you may be asked to describe a scene (a landscape, theatre set, classroom), a person, a process, an object (a sculpture, building, machine), or an image.

#### Important Elements of a Report

- A clear description of what you observed, which is complete and appropriately detailed—but not excessively detailed.
- Objectivity.
- The proper format that your instructor requires.

### ■ Reviews or evaluations

A *review* is a report plus an evaluation: a "reasoned judgment" of whether something is good or bad, fair or unfair, true or false, effective or useless. You're familiar with movie, music, and product reviews, which are designed to help you decide whether to invest your time, attention, or money. Reviews in academic situations show how thoughtfully you can evaluate a presentation, performance, product, event, art work, or some other object.

#### Important Elements of Reviews

- Your review needs to contain both a summary or description and one or more evaluations of the source's quality or significance. Your thesis needs to take the form of an evaluation.
- You need to provide reasons for your evaluation, and you need to provide evidence for those reasons.
- Be sure to answer any specific questions your instructor asks and to follow any special considerations of the assignment.

### ■ Interpretations

An interpretation makes an argument about what something means or why it's significant. You might be familiar with interpretations from studying fiction or poetry, and we will talk more about that kind of writing in section 7f and in Chapter 37. However, interpretation is hardly restricted to readings.

#### Important Elements of an Interpretation

- A clear explanation of the event, phenomenon, or object that you're interpreting.

- Statements about what the subject of your interpretation means or why it's significant.

- Convincing support, including reasoning, to show why your interpretive statements are convincing.

## ■ Case studies

Some **case studies** are careful descriptions and interpretations of individuals, usually focusing on some set of features in relation to a specific situation or issue. The word *case* might suggest a hospital case to be solved, and indeed medical journals publish these kinds of cases; however, *case* also has a more neutral sense of an "instance," and people in case studies usually don't have anything wrong with them, physically or otherwise.

Case studies are important in psychology, social work, education, medicine, and similar fields in which it's useful to form a comprehensive portrait of people in order to understand them and, in some cases, to help them. In some fields, such as education, people do case studies in order to understand or test theories and practices.

Case studies can also lead to theories or other kinds of research. People about whom you write case studies are called **subjects.** A kind of writing related to a case study is a **profile,** in which you create a portrait in words of a person.

### Important Elements of Case Studies of Individuals

- A combination of observation, interview, and discussion of any artifacts you might have from your subject (writings, test results, creative works, and so on).

- A focus on particular traits important to the purpose of the study.

- A combination of report and interpretation or analysis.

- Depending on the type of case study and its purpose, it may include recommendations for a course of action, a discussion of implications, or a commentary on a theory.

## ■ Ethnographies

The term *case studies* also refers to a kind of research about a particular group of people or situation (consider studies of online video game players, of college basketball players and their study habits, of a store's marketing strategy, of homeless life in Seattle, and so forth). They are closely related to **ethnographies,** in that both generally are comprehensive studies of people interacting in a particular situation. Situational case studies and ethnographies commonly occur in courses in business, education, or the social sciences, with anthropology and sociology being prime examples of disciplines that use these studies.

### Important Elements of Situational Case Studies or Ethnographies

- Thick description. The anthropologist Clifford Geertz coined the term *thick description* to explain the kinds of details needed in ethnographies. Pay attention to everything, from the setting, to observed interactions, to what people say.

- Interpretation. The purpose of an ethnography is to offer an explanation of what the situation means in context.

## 7e    How can I write about quantitative data or information?

Quantitative information or data comes in the form of numbers. Of course, such information can be an important source of detail and evidence in almost any kind of writing. However, some writings especially require writers to translate numbers into words and to explain what they mean.

### ■ Reports of data

Reporting data is parallel to summarizing. You need to present information clearly and objectively, translating numbers into words. The challenge with these types of assignments is that the numbers seem to "speak for themselves." In other words, if you have a table of information it might seem pointless to write about it. A table is an efficient way to present information, and converting absolutely everything into words would be a waste of time; as a result, reports usually combine words and numbers.

### Important Elements of Reporting Data

- Clear and accurate translations of numbers into language.
- Judicious selection and summary of data to report.
- Objective reporting, unless your task is to go a step further to analyze or interpret.

### ■ Analyses of data

Most papers that emphasize quantitative information go beyond reporting and into analysis or synthesis: drawing conclusions about what the information means or connecting it to other pieces of information or ideas. When you analyze data, you interpret it, going beyond translating numbers into language.

### Important Elements of Analyses

- A clear report of the data.
- Statements that make interpretations, inferences, or evaluations of the data.
- Reasoning and support that convince readers that your statements are justified.

## ■ Lab reports and empirical studies

A **lab report** is a specific and formal way of presenting and discussing the results of experiments or laboratory measurements, in fields such as chemistry, biology, physics, engineering, and other sciences. Lab experiments are one kind of **empirical research,** a name that generally refers to attempts to measure something (from physical substances to behaviors) in order to prove or disprove a theory or hypothesis. Disciplines other than the sciences use experiments, too; among them are psychology and other social sciences, some areas of education (for example, "Does this teaching strategy work better than that teaching strategy?"), economics, and so on. However, those disciplines also use sources like surveys or very specific observations to collect data. Both lab reports and other kinds of empirical research studies tend to have the same standard elements.

### Important Sections of Lab Reports and Similar Empirical Studies

- **Introduction.** State your purpose, present background materials (for example, a review of previous studies), and your hypothesis.
- **Methods and materials.** Describe the equipment and procedures.
- **Results.** Accurately and objectively provide information that you acquired through your study.
- **Discussion.** Interpret and evaluate your results, including whether they supported your hypothesis and why or why not.
- **Conclusion.** Discuss the implications of your work, along with any limitations. Suggest further studies.

Take care to keep clear distinctions among each of these sections. Lab reports and empirical studies frequently include two other parts. One is an ABSTRACT, a short overview of the entire report, which appears directly after your title. The other is a list of REFERENCES, which is crucial if you discuss other published research.

## **7f** How can I write about readings?

Nearly all types of writing about observations have counterparts in writing about reading. You may be asked to write summaries, critical responses, analyses or interpretations, and syntheses.

## ■ Summaries

To *summarize* is to extract the main messages or central points of a reading and restate them in a much briefer fashion. A summary doesn't include supporting evidence or details. It's the gist, the hub, the seed of what the author is saying. Also, it isn't your personal reaction to what the author says. How you summarize depends on your situation and assignment. For example, you can summarize an entire 500-page book in a single sentence, in a single page, or in five or six pages. Most of the time when you get an assignment to write a summary, your instructor will tell you how long it needs to be; if he or she doesn't, it's reasonable for you to ask.

### Important Elements of Summaries

- Inclusion of only the source's main ideas.

- Proportional summary of the source. This means that longer and more important aspects of the original need to get more space and attention in your summary.

- Use of your own words. If there are particular key terms or phrases, include them in quotation marks, but otherwise put everything into your own words.

- Accurate DOCUMENTATION of the original source.

## ■ Critical responses

A **critical response** essay has two missions: to provide a SUMMARY of a source's main idea and to respond to that idea.

A well-written critical response accomplishes these two missions with style and grace. That is, it doesn't say, "My summary is . . ." or "Now, here's what I think. . . ." Instead, you want the two missions to blend together as seamlessly as possible. A critical response essay may be short or somewhat long, depending on whether you're asked to respond to a single passage or to an entire work.

### Important Elements of Critical Responses

- A clear and concise representation of the source.

- Statements of agreement, disagreement, or qualified agreement (you accept some points but not others), accompanied by reasons and evidence for your statements.

## ■ Interpretations and analyses

Interpretations and analyses resemble critical response in that both make claims about a reading. Critical responses ask whether a source is "good," but interpretations and analyses ask what a source "means." You might be most familiar with this kind of writing from previous English or literature courses in which a teacher asked you to interpret a poem, play, or story.

## ■ Syntheses

To *synthesize* is to weave together material from several sources. Unsynthesized ideas and information are like separate spools of thread, neatly lined up, possibly coordinated but not integrated. Synthesized ideas and information are threads woven into a tapestry. By synthesizing, you show evidence of your ability to bring ideas together. Synthesis goes beyond summary and comes after it in the critical thinking process (section 4b).

One common synthesizing task is to connect two or more readings or source materials into a single piece of writing. You complete this synthesis after you have summarized, analyzed, and evaluated each of the source materials. Another common type of synthesis is to connect material to what you already know, creating a new final product that is your own.

### SYNTHESIZING MULTIPLE SOURCES

Your goal in synthesizing multiple sources is to join two or more texts together into a single writing. The resulting text needs to be more than just a succession of summaries. That is, avoid merely listing who said what about a topic. Such a list isn't a synthesis. It does not create new connections among ideas.

#### Advice on Process

- Make comparisons with—or contrasts between—concepts, ideas, and information. Do the sources generally agree or generally disagree? What are the bases of their agreement or disagreement? Are there subtle differences or shades of meaning or emphasis?

- Create definitions that combine and extend definitions you encounter in the separate sources.

- Use examples or descriptions from one source to illustrate ideas in another.

- Use processes described in one source to explain those in others.

- In revising, ask, "Have I truly synthesized the sources, or have I just written about one and then the other?"

### SYNTHESIZING WITH ONE SOURCE

If you're working with only one source, you need to make connections between the source and your prior knowledge, whether from experience, films or television, classes or conversations, or previous readings. Don't be afraid to synthesize. We're always surprised when we find that some students assume that what they think has no value. Nothing could be further from the truth.

#### Advice on Process

- Use your powers of play. Mentally toss ideas around, even if you make connections that seem outrageous. Try opposites (for example, read about athletes and think about the most nonathletic person you know). Try turning an idea upside down (for example, if you have read about the value of being a good sport, list the benefits of being a bad sport).

- Use the technique of clustering to lay out visually the relationships among elements in your source and other ideas that come to mind.

- Discuss the source with another person. Summarize its content and elicit the other person's opinion or ideas. Deliberately debate that opinion or challenge those ideas.

- Write your personal response to the material. Explain whether you agree or disagree and also the reasons why you respond as you do.

## ■ Essays that apply theories or concepts (essays of application)

Essays that apply theories or concepts (or **essays of application**) take general information from one source (usually a reading but perhaps from a lecture) and apply it to another, usually for the purpose of interpretation or evaluation.

Assignments like these require a form of synthesis, in that they combine two or more sources into a single piece of writing. However, the sources have characteristics that distinguish essays of application from other syntheses, which is why we explain them separately. One source explains a theory, concept, or definition; even if it's based on details from formal research or study, its purpose is to offer a generalization about something. The other source is more specific, consisting of stories, experiences, scenarios, observations, quantitative data, or reports of events, with little or no analysis or interpretation.

Instructors sometimes assign essays of application to test how well you grasp concepts; being able to apply an idea to a new situation demonstrates your deeper understanding of it. They may also assign such essays to help you analyze or interpret a situation or body of information in ways you might not have considered.

### Important Elements of Essays of Application

- A clear and accurate summary of the theory or concept you're applying.

## ■ Annotated bibliographies

An annotated bibliography is a list of sources that includes, for each one, publishing information, a brief summary, and usually your commentary on the content. Such commentary often addresses how a particular source relates to the other sources in the bibliography (32j).

## ■ Essay exams

"Essay exam" is a broadly-used term for questions that require you to answer in sentences, usually in a timed situation. Prepare for essay exams by rereading your class material and by actually doing some writing. Making up a few possible questions is an excellent way of studying, and having yourself answer those practice questions under pressure is good preparation for the real thing.

When you receive an essay question, resist the urge to dive right in to writing. Use a margin or scratch paper to jot an informal outline or series of points you want to make. Especially take care to understand the question and respond directly to it. For example, if the question asks you to RESPOND, ANALYZE, SYNTHESIZE, or APPLY, you don't just want to SUMMARIZE. While an essay exam may, rarely, simply invite you to dump information, most of the time it will ask you to perform a very specific task. After you've drafted your answer, save some time to proofread. It's easy to introduce errors when you're writing under pressure.

# Style and Tone in Writing

## 8a  What do style and tone in writing involve?

**Style** and tone both refer to *how* you say something, in contrast with *what* you're saying. The sentence structures you shape, from the simple to more complex, contribute to the style of your writing. The words you choose for your sentences create the tone in your sentences. They work in concert.

## 8b  How do style and tone operate in writing?

Style and tone operate together through a combination of the varying levels of formality and personality that you employ. The level of **formality** in writing can be roughly divided into three categories. Formal writing belongs in the structures and language of ceremonies, contracts, policies, or some literary writing. **Informal writing** is casual, colloquial, and sometimes playful, usually found in e-mails, text messages on cell phones, Facebook postings, and certain BLOGS. Semiformal writing, which sits between these poles, is the style and tone found in academic writing, as well as in much business and public writing. For an audience expecting such communication, its style is clear and efficient, and its tone is reasonable and evenhanded.

The level of **personality** refers to how much the writer reveals about him- or herself with patterns of sentence structure and choice of words. An intimate style and tone, which treats the reader as a close friend, includes specific personal experiences and opinions. A familiar or polite style and tone includes some experiences or personal thoughts, but only of a kind you might share in a professional relationship with an instructor, supervisor, or colleague. An impersonal style reveals nothing about the writer, so that the content is all that the reader is aware of.

| | |
|---|---|
| **INTIMATE** | When our eighth grade teacher assigned Huckleberry Finn by Mark Twain, I got cranky and angry after the first chapter. Why did he lay something so hard on us? I couldn't catch the story or figure out what the dialect was saying. |
| **FAMILIAR/ POLITE** | The next day in class, I was greatly relieved to discover that most other students had run into the same problems as I had reading Huckleberry Finn by Mark Twain. |
| **IMPERSONAL** | Our teacher explicated the story line and clarified how to decode the dialect, which enabled the class to appreciate the narrative and its underlying message. |

## 8c   How do I write with style?

A well-respected style manual states,

> Style, with a capital S, achieves what a rule book never can: it lights the page, draws in readers, earns their delight, makes them gasp or weep, and sometimes captures a place in memory.

> —*The New York Times Manual of Style and Usage*

Writing with style comes more naturally with lots of practice. It rarely shows up on most first drafts. The pleasure of creating a graceful, engaging style in your writing results from experimenting with different structures. And every so often, writers surprise themselves with sentences and passages of enormous power and impact that emerge almost unbidden on the page. Those are magical moments. To write with style, refer to Quick Reference 8.1; as you do, add your own personal hints so that you can make the material your own.

---

### Quick Reference 8.1                    ■ ■ ■ ■ ■

#### How to create good writing style

- Try out different sentence types to maintain readers' interest (see 9a, 9n, 9r).
- Use sentence coordination and subordination to vary the pace (see 9d–9m).
- Vary sentence length to keep your readers' attention (see 9c).
- Experiment with diction or word choice (see 12d, 12e)

continued >>

---

**Quick Reference 8.1**        (continued)        ■ ■ ■ ■ ■

- Use figurative language (see 12c)
- Employ the gracefulness of parallelism in sentences and larger sections for the pleasure of your readers (see Chapter 10).
- Be consistent in your level of formality and personality (see 8b)

---

# 8d  How do I write with appropriate tone?

Tone in writing involves choosing the right words to deliver your meaning. Tone operates like tone of voice, except that you can't rely on facial expressions and voice intonations to communicate your written message. The language you choose in your writing creates the tone you relay to your readers.

Your choice of words determines the degree to which your readers notice the language itself along with the content that the language is conveying. Well written figurative language (see 12c) can create pleasant surprises for readers. However, if you draw too much attention to your language without communicating a clear message, your writing suffers. Conversely, if you use only simple, one syllable words that create a dull drone, your writing suffers.

Your word choice can result in a wide range of possible tones, some desirable and some not. We list several in Quick Reference 8.2.

---

**Quick Reference 8.2**        ■ ■ ■ ■ ■

## Some examples of desirable and undesirable tone

| | |
|---|---|
| SERIOUS | The advent of space travel supported the predictions of science fiction, especially that of Jules Verne, who wrote in the nineteenth century. |
| LIGHT OR BREEZY | What a trip to flip through Verne's *From the Earth to the Moon* and find space ships taking off from Tampa, Florida, only 130 miles from today's Cape Canaveral. |
| SARCASTIC | Some poor slobs probably think Verne is worth worshiping like a god. |
| MEAN | Verne also made some dumb forecasts. |
| CONDESCENDING | Although most people struggle to read Jules Verne's sometimes complex books, those who succeed can consider themselves at least reasonably competent readers. |
| WHINING | Why should Jules Verne be the third most translated writer in the world? He's no big deal. If I put my mind to it, I could write as well as he did. |

Achieving the tone you want in each piece of your writing calls for experimenting with different words with similar meanings. If you consult a thesaurus (which can be a very productive activity), be sure to check the definition of any synonym that's new to you.

As with style in writing, appropriate tone results from your private trials, rejections, and explorations. Good tone rarely shows up on most first drafts. Quick Reference 8.3 offers you some suggestions for achieving an appropriate tone in your writing. Add your own advice to the list to personalize it.

---

### Quick Reference 8.3                    ■ ■ ■ ■ ■

#### How to use appropriate tone in writing

- Reserve a highly informal tone for conversational writing.
- Use a semiformal level of formality in your academic writing and when you write for supervisors, professionals, and other people you know only from a distance.
- Avoid an overly formal, ceremonious tone.
- Choose a tone that suits your topic and your readers.
- Whatever tone you choose, be consistent in each piece of your writing.

---

**EXERCISE 8-1**    Revise each of the sentences to create a very different tone. The sentences in Quick Reference 8.2 provide some examples. For a further challenge, see how many different tones you can create.

1. Many Americans spend much of their leisure time watching professional sports.

2. If you want to waste your money buying organic foods, who am I to stop you?

3. When considering the purchase of clothing in order to possess a serviceable wardrobe, it is imperative to select items in which the color combinations are harmonious and pleasing.

# 9

# Sentence Variety and Style

## 9a How do sentences affect style?

Sentences affect style through their length (9c), structures like COORDINATION and SUBORDINATION (9f and 9j), and types. The main sentence types in English are SIMPLE, COMPOUND, COMPLEX, and COMPOUND-COMPLEX (14o). When any one type dominates a piece of writing, it affects the style, especially if the sentences are also generally the same length.

A flurry of short, simple sentences creates a blunt, direct style. Such a style often gains in clarity but loses in interest. A series of long complex or compound-complex sentences creates a lofty, sometimes even stuffy, style. It may achieve sophistication but sacrifice clarity.

## 9b What are variety and emphasis in writing?

When you write sentences of different lengths and types within a piece of writing, you create **sentence variety.** Working in concert with sentence variety, **emphasis** allows you to add weight to ideas of special importance.

Using techniques of variety and emphasis adds style and clarity to your writing. When readers see variety in your writing, they see you as versatile and in control of language. Usually, the best time to apply the principles of variety and emphasis is while you are REVISING.

## 9c How do different sentence lengths create variety and emphasis?

To emphasize one idea among many others, you can express it in a sentence noticeably different in length from the sentences surrounding it. In the following example, a four-word sentence between two longer sentences carries the key message of the passage (**boldface** added).

> Today is one of those excellent January partly cloudies in which light chooses an unexpected landscape to trick out in gilt, and then shadow sweeps it away. **You know you're alive.** You take huge steps, trying to feel the planet's roundness arc between your feet.

> —Annie Dillard, *Pilgrim at Tinker Creek*

Sometimes a string of short sentences creates impact and emphasis. Yet, at other times, a string of short sentences can be dull to read. Similarly, a string of COMPOUND SENTENCES can be monotonous to read and may fail to communicate relationships among ideas.

**EXERCISE 9-1**   The following paragraph is dull because it has only short sentences. Combine some of the sentences to make a paragraph that has a variety of sentence lengths.

> There is a problem. It is widely known as sick-building syndrome. It comes from indoor air pollution. It causes office workers to suffer. They have trouble breathing. They have painful rashes. Their heads ache. Their eyes burn.

## 9d   What are coordination and subordination?

Two important sentence structuring methods are COORDINATION and SUBORDINATION, which reflect relationships between ideas that you seek to express. Coordination shows the equality of ideas, while subordination shows one idea is more important than others. Using these structures effectively creates variety and emphasis. We explain each of them in sections 9e and 9i, below, but an example will help you see the basic principle:

| | |
|---|---|
| **TWO SENTENCES** | The sky turned dark gray. The wind died down. |
| **USING COORDINATION** | The sky turned dark gray, **and** the wind died down. |
| **USING SUBORDINATION 1** | **As** the sky turned dark gray, the wind died down. [Here, the wind is the focus.] |
| **USING SUBORDINATION 2** | **As** the wind died down, the sky turned dark gray. [Here, the sky is the focus.] |

## 9e   What is coordination of sentences?

**Coordination** of sentences is a grammatical strategy to communicate that the ideas in two or more INDEPENDENT CLAUSES are equivalent or balanced. Coordination can produce harmony by bringing related elements together. Whenever you use the technique of coordination of sentences, make sure that it works well with the meaning you want to communicate.

The sky turned **brighter, and** people emerged happily from buildings.

The sky turned **brighter;** people emerged happily from buildings.

## 9f   What is the structure of a coordinate sentence?

A **coordinate sentence,** also known as a *compound sentence* (14o), consists of two or more INDEPENDENT CLAUSES joined either by a semicolon or by a comma working in concert with a COORDINATING CONJUNCTION (*and, but, for, or, nor, yet, so*).

## 9g   What meaning does each coordinating conjunction convey?

Each COORDINATING CONJUNCTION has its own meaning. When you choose one, be sure that its meaning accurately expresses the relationship between the equivalent ideas that you want to convey.

- **and** means addition
- **but** and **yet** mean contrast
- **for** means reason or choice
- **or** means choice
- **nor** means negative choice
- **so** means result or effect

 Alert:  Always use a comma before a coordinating conjunction that joins two INDEPENDENT CLAUSES (24b). ●

## 9h   How can I use coordination effectively?

COORDINATION is effective when each INDEPENDENT CLAUSE is related or equivalent. If they aren't, the result looks like a coordinated sentence, but the ideas are unrelated.

> **NO**  Computers came into common use in the 1970s, and they sometimes make costly errors. [The statement in each independent clause is true, but the ideas are not related or equivalent.]

> **YES**  Computers came into common use in the 1970s, and now they are indispensable business tools.

Coordination is also most effective when it's not overused. Simply stringing sentences together with COORDINATING CONJUNCTIONS makes relationships among ideas unclear—and the resulting sentence lacks style.

# 9i   What is subordination in sentences?

**Subordination** is a grammatical strategy to communicate that one idea in a sentence is more important than another idea in the same sentence. To use subordination, you place the more important idea in an INDEPENDENT CLAUSE and the less important—the subordinate—idea in a DEPENDENT CLAUSE. The information you choose to subordinate depends on the meaning you want to deliver.

> INDEPENDENT CLAUSE                              DEPENDENT
> Two cowboys fought a dangerous Colorado snowstorm **while they**

> CLAUSE                          DEPENDENT CLAUSE
> **were looking for cattle. When they came to a canyon,**

> INDEPENDENT CLAUSE
> they saw outlines of buildings through the blizzard.

To illustrate the difference in writing style when you use subordination, here's a passage with the same message as the example above, but without subordination.

> Two cowboys fought a dangerous Colorado snowstorm. They were looking for cattle. They came to a canyon. They saw outlines of buildings through the blizzard.

# 9j   What is the structure of a subordinate sentence?

A subordinate sentence starts the DEPENDENT CLAUSE with either a SUBORDINATING CONJUNCTION or a RELATIVE PRONOUN.

> **If** they are very lucky, the passengers may glimpse dolphins breaking water playfully near the ship.
>
> —Elizabeth Gray, student

> Pandas are solitary animals, **which** means they are difficult to protect from extinction.
>
> —Jose Santos, student

For patterns of subordination with dependent clauses, see Quick Reference 9.1. Dependent clauses are of two types: ADVERB CLAUSES and ADJECTIVE CLAUSES. An adverb clause starts with a subordinating conjunction. An adjective clause starts with a relative pronoun.

## Quick Reference 9.1

### Subordination

**SENTENCES WITH ADVERB CLAUSES**

- **Adverb clause,** independent clause.

    **After the sky grew dark,** the wind died suddenly.

- Independent clause, **adverb clause.**

    Birds stopped singing, **as they do during an eclipse.**

- Independent clause **adverb clause.**

    The stores closed **before the storm began.**

**SENTENCES WITH ADJECTIVE CLAUSES**

- Independent clause **restrictive (essential)\* adjective clause.**

    Weather forecasts warned of a storm **that might bring a thirty-inch snowfall.**

- Independent clause, **nonrestrictive (nonessential)\* adjective clause.**

    Spring is the season for tornadoes, **which may have wind speeds over 220 miles an hour.**

- Beginning of independent clause **restrictive (essential)\* adjective clause** end of independent clause.

    Anyone **who lives through a tornado** remembers its power.

- Beginning of independent clause, **nonrestrictive (nonessential)\* adjective clause,** end of independent clause.

    The sky, **which had been clear,** turned greenish black.

\*For an explanation of RESTRICTIVE and NONRESTRICTIVE ELEMENTS, see section 24f.

## 9k  What meaning does each subordinating conjunction convey?

Each SUBORDINATING CONJUNCTION has its own meaning. When you choose one, be sure that its meaning accurately expresses the relationship between the ideas that you want to convey. Quick Reference 9.2 lists subordinating conjunctions according to their different meanings.

## 9l  How can I use subordination effectively?

To be effective, a SUBORDINATING CONJUNCTION must communicate a sensible relationship between the INDEPENDENT CLAUSE and the DEPENDENT CLAUSE. See Quick Reference 9.2 for a list of subordinating conjunctions and their different meanings.

**NO** **Because** Beethoven was deaf when he wrote them, his final symphonies were masterpieces. [*Because* is illogical here; it says the masterpieces resulted from the deafness.]

**YES** **Although** Beethoven was deaf when he wrote them, his final symphonies were masterpieces. [*Although* is logical here; it says Beethoven wrote masterpieces in spite of his being deaf.]

---

### Quick Reference 9.2  ■ ■ ■ ■ ■

#### Subordinating conjunctions and their meanings

**TIME**
*after, before, once, since, until, when, whenever, while*

> **After** you have handed in your report, you cannot revise it.

**REASON OR CAUSE**
*as, because, since*

> **Because** you have handed in your report, you cannot revise it.

**PURPOSE OR RESULT**
*in order that, so that, that*

> I want to read your report **so that** I can evaluate it.

**CONDITION**
*even if, if, provided that, unless*

> **Unless** you have handed in your report, you can revise it.

**CONTRAST**
*although, even though, though, whereas, while*

> **Although** you have handed in your report, you can ask to revise it.

**CHOICE**
*than, whether*

> You took more time to revise **than** I did before the lab report deadline.

**PLACE OR LOCATION**
*where, wherever*

> **Wherever** you say, I'll come to hand in my report.

---

Subordination is also most effective when you avoid overusing it and crowding too many ideas together in one sentence. This causes readers to lose track of the message. Whenever you write a sentence with two or more dependent clauses, check that your message is clear. If it isn't, you've probably overused subordination.

**NO**   A new technique for eye surgery, **which is supposed to correct nearsightedness, which previously could be corrected only by glasses,** has been developed, **although many eye doctors do not approve of the new technique because it can create unstable vision, which includes intense glare from headlights on cars and many other light sources.** [The base sentence *A new technique for eye surgery has been developed* is crowded with five dependent clauses attached to it.]

**YES**   A new technique for eye surgery, **which is supposed to correct nearsightedness,** has been developed. Previously, only glasses could correct nearsightedness. Many doctors do not approve of the new technique **because it can create unstable vision.** The problems include intense glare from car headlights and many other sources of light. [In this revision, one long sentence has been broken into four sentences, which makes the material easier to read and the relationships among ideas clearer. Two dependent clauses remain, which balance well with the other sentence constructions. Some words have been moved to new positions.]

🌐 **ESOL Tip:** If your instructor, manager, or peer reviewers advise that your sentences are too long and complex, limit the number of words in each sentence. Many ESOL instructors recommend that you revise any sentence that contains more than three independent and dependent clauses in any combination. ●

**EXERCISE 9-2**   Working individually or with a group, correct illogical or excessive subordination in this paragraph. As you revise according to the message you want to deliver, use some dependent clauses as well as some short sentences. (Also, if you wish, apply the principles of coordination discussed in sections 9d through 9h.) For help, consult 9j.

Although many people in the United States consider the hot dog an American invention, it actually originated in Germany in 1852 when butchers in Frankfurt, Germany, stuffed meat into a long casing, which, in honor of the town, they called a "frankfurter." Because one butcher noticed that the frankfurter resembled the shape of his dog, a dachshund, he decided to name the meat roll a "dachshund sausage," a name which caught on in Germany. When Germans brought dachshund sausages to the United States, peddlers sold them on the streets, although the dachshund sausages were so hot that people often burned their fingers because they had trouble holding the meat. When one clever peddler put the sausage in a bun, a *New York Times* cartoonist decided to draw a picture of hot dachshund sausages in buns, although he called them "hot dogs" because he didn't know how to spell *dachshund*.

## 9m How can I effectively use coordination and subordination together?

Your writing style improves when you use a logical and pleasing variety of SENTENCE TYPES, utilizing COORDINATION and SUBORDINATION to improve the flow of ideas. Here's a paragraph that demonstrates a good balance in the use of coordination and subordination.

> When I was growing up, I lived on a farm just across the field from my grandmother. My parents were busy trying to raise six children and to establish their struggling dairy farm. It was nice to have Grandma so close. While my parents were providing the necessities of life, my patient grandmother gave her time to her shy, young granddaughter. I always enjoyed going with Grandma and collecting the eggs that her chickens had just laid. Usually, she knew which chickens would peck, and she was careful to let me gather the eggs from the less hostile ones.
>
> —Patricia Mapes, student

When you use both coordination and subordination, never use both a COORDINATE CONJUNCTION and a SUBORDINATE CONJUNCTION to express one relationship in one sentence.

**NO**   **Although** the story was well written, **but** it was too illogical.
[The subordinating conjunction *although* expresses the contrast, so also using *but* is incorrect.]

**YES**   **Although** the story was well written, it was too illogical.

**YES**   The story was well written, **but** it was too illogical.

## 9n How do occasional questions, commands, or exclamations create variety and emphasis?

The majority of sentences in English are DECLARATIVE—they tell something by making a statement. Declarative sentences offer an almost infinite variety of structures and patterns. For variety and emphasis, you might want to use three alternative types of sentences occasionally.

A sentence that asks a question is called INTERROGATIVE. Occasional questions, placed appropriately, tend to involve readers. A sentence that issues a mild or strong command is called IMPERATIVE. Occasional mild commands, appropriately used, gently urge a reader to think along with you. A sentence that makes an exclamation is called EXCLAMATORY. An occasional exclamatory sentence, appropriate to the context, can enliven writing, but you should use this sentence type only rarely in ACADEMIC WRITING.

## 9o   What are cumulative and periodic sentences?

The **cumulative sentence** is the most common sentence structure in English. Its name reflects the way information accumulates in the sentence until it reaches a period. Its structure starts with a SUBJECT and VERB and continues with modifiers. Another term for a cumulative sentence is *loose sentence* because it lacks a tightly planned structure.

For greater impact, you might occasionally use a **periodic sentence,** also called a *climactic sentence,* which reserves the main idea for the end of the sentence. This structure tends to draw in the reader as it moves toward the period. If overused, however, periodic sentences lose their punch.

| | |
|---|---|
| **CUMULATIVE** | A car hit a shoulder and turned over at midnight last night on the road from Las Vegas to Death Valley Junction. |
| **PERIODIC** | At midnight last night, on the road from Las Vegas to Death Valley Junction, a car hit a shoulder and turned over. |

—Joan Didion, "On Morality"

## 9p   How can modifiers create variety and emphasis?

MODIFIERS can expand sentences to add richness to your writing and create a pleasing mixture of variety and emphasis. Your choice of where to place modifiers to expand your sentences depends on the focus you want each sentence to communicate, either on its own or in concert with its surrounding sentences. Be careful where you place modifiers because you don't want to introduce the error known as a MISPLACED MODIFIER.

| | |
|---|---|
| **BASIC SENTENCE** | The river rose. |
| **ADJECTIVE** | The **swollen** river rose. |
| **ADVERB** | The river rose **dangerously.** |
| **PREPOSITIONAL PHRASE** | The river rose **above its banks.** |
| **PARTICIPIAL PHRASE** | **Swelled by melting snow,** the river rose. |
| **ABSOLUTE PHRASE** | **Uprooted trees swirling away in the current,** the river rose. |
| **ADVERB CLAUSE** | **Because the snows had been heavy that winter,** the river rose. |
| **ADJECTIVE CLAUSE** | The river, **which runs through vital farmland,** rose. |

● **EXERCISE 9-3** Working individually or with a group, expand each sen-
● tence by adding each kind of modifier illustrated in section 9p.

1. We bought a house.
2. The roof leaked.
3. I remodeled the kitchen.
4. Neighbors brought food.
5. Everyone enjoyed the barbeque.

# **9q** How does repetition affect style?

You can repeat one or more words that express a main idea when your message
is suitable. This technique creates a rhythm that focuses attention on the main
idea. Here's an example that uses deliberate repetition along with a variety of
sentence lengths to deliver its meaning.

> Coal is **black** and it warms your house and cooks your food. The night is
> **black,** which has a moon, and a million stars, and is beautiful. Sleep is **black,**
> which gives you rest, so you wake up feeling **good.** I am **black.** I feel very
> **good** this evening.
>
> —Langston Hughes, "That Word *Black*"

# **9r** How else can I create variety and emphasis?

## CHANGING WORD ORDER

**Standard word order** in English places the SUBJECT before the VERB.

> The **mayor** *walked* into the room. [*Mayor,* the subject, comes before
> the verb *walked.*]

Any variation from standard word order creates emphasis. For example,
**inverted word order** places the verb before the subject.

> Into the room *walked* the **mayor.** [*Mayor,* the subject, comes after the
> verb *walked.*]

## CHANGING A SENTENCE'S SUBJECT

The subject of a sentence establishes the focus for that sentence. To create the
emphasis you want, you can vary each sentence's subject. All of the sample sentences below express the same information, but the focus changes in each according to the subject (and its corresponding verb).

> **Our study** *showed* that 25 percent of college students' time is spent eat-
> ing or sleeping. [Focus is on the study.]

**College students** *eat or sleep* 25 percent of the time, according to our study. [Focus is on the students.]

**Eating or sleeping** *occupies* 25 percent of college students' time, according to our study. [Focus is on eating and sleeping.]

**Twenty-five percent of college students' time** *is spent* eating or sleeping, according to our study. [Focus is on the percentage of time.]

# 10

# Parallelism

## 10a  What is parallelism?

When you write words, PHRASES, or CLAUSES within a sentence to match
in their grammatical forms, the result is **parallelism.** Parallelism serves to
emphasize information or ideas in writing. The technique relates to the concept of parallel lines in geometry, lines that run alongside each other and
never meet.

> The deer often come to eat their grain, the wolves to destroy their
> sheep, the bears to kill their hogs, and the foxes to catch their poultry.
> [The message of the multiple, accumulating assaults is echoed by the
> parallel structures.]
> > —J. Hector St. Jean de Crèvecoeur, *Letters from an American Farmer*

Many writers attend to parallelism when they are REVISING. If you think
while you're DRAFTING that your parallelism is faulty or that you can enhance
your writing style by using parallelism, underline or highlight the material
and keep moving forward. When you revise, you can return to the places
you've marked.

A **balanced sentence** is a type of parallelism in which contrasting content is delivered. The two parallel structures are usually, but not always,
INDEPENDENT CLAUSES. A balanced sentence uses COORDINATION. The two coordinate structures are characterized by opposites in meaning, sometimes with
one structure cast in the negative.

> By night, the litter and desperation disappeared as the city's glittering lights
> came on; by day, the filth and despair reappeared as the sun rose.
> > —Jennifer Kirk, student

**❶ Alert:**  Authorities differ about using a comma, a semicolon, or nothing
between the parts of a short balanced sentence. In ACADEMIC WRITING, to avoid
appearing to make the error of a COMMA SPLICE, use a semicolon (or revise in
some other way), as in the following sentence.

> Mosquitoes don't bite; they stab. ●

## 10b How do words, phrases, and clauses work in parallel form?

When you put words, PHRASES, and CLAUSES into parallel form, you enhance your writing style with balance and grace.

**PARALLEL WORDS**  Recommended exercise includes running, swimming, and cycling.

**PARALLEL PHRASES**  Exercise helps people maintain healthy bodies and handle mental pressures.

**PARALLEL CLAUSES**  Many people exercise because they want to look healthy, because they need to increase stamina, and because they hope to live longer.

## 10c How does parallelism deliver impact?

Parallel structures serve to emphasize the meaning that sentences deliver. Deliberate, rhythmic repetition of parallel forms creates an effect of balance, reinforcing the impact of a message.

> Go back to Mississippi, go back to Alabama, go back to South Carolina, go back to Georgia, go back to Louisiana, go back to the slums and ghettos of our northern cities, knowing that somehow this situation can and will be changed.
>
> —Martin Luther King Jr., "I Have a Dream"

If King had not used PARALLELISM, his message would have made less of an impact on his listeners. His structures reinforce the power of his message. A sentence without parallelism could have carried his message, but with far less effect: *Return to your homes in Mississippi, Alabama, South Carolina, Georgia, Louisiana, or the northern cities, and know that the situation will be changed.*

## 10d How can I avoid faulty parallelism?

**Faulty parallelism** usually results when you join nonmatching grammatical forms.

### PARALLELISM WITH COORDINATING CONJUNCTIONS

The coordinating conjunctions are *and, but, for, or, nor, yet,* and *so.* To avoid faulty parallelism, write the words that accompany coordinating conjunctions in matching grammatical forms.

|     |                                         |
| --- | --------------------------------------- |
| **NO**  | Love *and* **being married** go together. |
| **YES** | Love *and* **marriage** go together. |
| **YES** | **Being in love** *and* **being married** go together. |

## PARALLELISM WITH CORRELATIVE CONJUNCTIONS

Correlative conjunctions are paired words such as *not only . . . but (also), either . . . or,* and *both . . . and.* To avoid faulty parallelism, write the words joined by correlative conjunctions in matching grammatical forms.

| | |
| --- | --- |
| **NO** | Differing expectations for marriage *not only* **can lead to disappointment** *but also* **makes the couple angry.** |
| **YES** | Differing expectations for marriage *not only* **can lead to disappointment** *but also* **can make the couple angry.** |

## PARALLELISM WITH *THAN* AND *AS*

To avoid faulty parallelism when you use *than* and *as* for comparisons, write the elements of comparison in matching grammatical forms.

| | |
| --- | --- |
| **NO** | **Having a solid marriage** can be more satisfying *than* **the acquisition of wealth.** |
| **YES** | **Having a solid marriage** can be more satisfying *than* **acquiring wealth.** |
| **YES** | **A solid marriage** can be more satisfying *than* **wealth.** |

## PARALLELISM WITH FUNCTION WORDS

**Function words** include ARTICLES (*the, a, an*); the *to* of the INFINITIVE (*to* love); PREPOSITIONS (for example, *of, in, about*); and sometimes RELATIVE PRONOUNS. When you write a series of parallel structures, be consistent in the second and successive structures about either repeating or omitting a function word. Generally, repeat function words only if you think that the repetition clarifies your meaning or highlights the parallelism that you intend.

| | |
| --- | --- |
| **NO** | **To assign** unanswered letters their proper weight, **free** us from the expectations of others, **to give** us back to ourselves—here lies the great, the singular power of self-respect. |
| **YES** | **To assign** unanswered letters their proper weight, **to free** us from the expectations of others, **to give** us back to ourselves—here lies the great, the singular power of self-respect. |

—Joan Didion, "On Self-Respect"

**EXERCISE 10-1**    Revise these sentences by putting appropriate information in parallel structures. For help, consult sections 10a through 10d.

1. According to the psychologist Harry Levinson, the five main types of bad
   boss are the workaholic, the kind of person you would describe as bullying, a person who communicates badly, the jellyfish type, and someone
   who insists on perfection.

2. As a way of getting ahead, to keep their self-respect, and for survival purposes, wise employees handle problem bosses with a variety of strategies.

3. To cope with a bad-tempered employer, workers can both stand up for
   themselves and reasoning with a bullying boss.

4. Often, bad bosses communicate poorly or fail to calculate the impact
   of their personality on others; being a careful listener and sensitivity to
   others' responses are qualities that good bosses possess.

5. Employees who take the trouble to understand what makes their bosses tick,
   engage in some self-analysis, and staying flexible are better prepared to cope
   with a difficult job environment than suffering in silence like some employees.

# 10e   How does parallelism work in outlines and lists?

All items in formal OUTLINES and lists must be parallel in grammar and structure. (For more about outline format and outline development, see section 2f.)

**OUTLINES**

> **NO**    Reducing Traffic Fatalities
>
> I. Stricter laws
>     A. Top speed should be 55 mph on highways.
>     B. Higher fines
>     C. Requiring jail sentences for repeat offenders
> II. The use of safety devices should be mandated by law.
>
> **YES**    Reducing Traffic Fatalities
>
> I. Passing stricter speed laws
>     A. Making 55 mph the top speed on highways
>     B. Raising fines for speeding
>     C. Requiring jail sentences for repeat offenders
> II. Mandating by law the use of safety devices

**LISTS**

> **NO**    Workaholics share these characteristics:
>     1. They are intense and driven.
>     2. Strong self-doubters
>     3. Labor is preferred to leisure by workaholics.

**YES** Workaholics share these characteristics:
1. They are intense and driven.
2. They have strong self-doubts.
3. They prefer labor to leisure.

# 11

# Conciseness

## 11a What is conciseness?

**Conciseness** requires you to craft sentences that are direct and to the point. Its opposite, **wordiness,** means you are filling sentences with empty words and phrases that increase the word count but contribute nothing to meaning. Wordy writing is padded with deadwood, forcing readers to clear away the branches and overgrowth—an annoying waste of time that implies the writer isn't skilled. Usually, the best time to work on making your writing more concise is while you're REVISING.

**WORDY**  As a matter of fact, the television station which is situated in the local area wins a great many awards in the final analysis because of its type of coverage of all kinds of controversial issues.

**CONCISE** The local television station wins many awards for its coverage of controversial issues.

## 11b What common expressions are not concise?

Many common expressions we use in informal speech are not concise. Quick Reference 11.1 lists some and shows you how to eliminate them.

### Cutting unnecessary words and phrases

| Empty Word or Phrase | Wordy Example Revised |
| --- | --- |
| as a matter of fact | Many marriages, ~~as a matter of fact,~~ end in divorce. |
| at the present time | The revised proposal for outdoor lighting angers many villagers *now* ~~at the present time.~~ |
| because of the fact that, in light of the fact that, due to the fact that | Because ~~of the fact that~~ the museum has a special exhibit, it stays open late. |
| by means of | We traveled by ~~means of a~~ car. |
| factor | The project's final cost was ~~the~~ essential ~~factor~~ to consider. |
| for the purpose of | Work crews arrived ~~for the purpose of~~ *to* fixing the potholes. |
| have a tendency to | The team ~~has a tendency~~ *tends* to lose home games. |
| in a very real sense | ~~In a very real sense,~~ *A*ll firefighters are heroes. |
| in the case of | ~~In the case of~~ *T*he election~~, it~~ will be close. |
| in the event that | ~~In the event that~~ *If* you're late, I will buy our tickets. |
| in the final analysis | ~~In the final analysis,~~ *N*o two eyewitnesses agreed on what they saw. |
| in the process of | We are ~~in the process of~~ reviewing the proposal. |
| it seems that | ~~It seems that~~ *T*he union went on strike over health benefits. |
| manner | The child spoke *reluctantly.* ~~in a reluctant manner.~~ |
| nature | The movie review was ~~of a~~ sarcastic ~~nature~~. |
| that exists | The crime rate ~~that exists~~ is unacceptable. |
| the point I am trying to make | ~~The point I am trying to make is~~ *T*elevision reporters invade our privacy. |
| type of, kind of | Gordon took a relaxing ~~type of~~ vacation. |
| What I mean to say is | ~~What I mean to say is~~ I love you. |

**EXERCISE 11-1**   Revise these sentences in two steps. First, underline all words that interfere with conciseness. Second, revise each sentence to make it more concise. (You'll need to drop words and replace or rearrange others.)

EXAMPLE   It seems that most North Americans think of motor scooters as vehicles that exist only in European countries.

1. It seems that most North Americans think of motor scooters as <u>vehicles that exist</u> only in European countries.

2. Most North Americans think of motor scooters as only European vehicles.

1. As a matter of fact, in the popular imagination, motor scooters are the very essence of European style.

2. Today, over one million scooters are purchased by people in Europe each year, compared with a number that amounts to only 70,000 buyers in the United States.

3. In fact, Europeans have long used fuel-efficient, clean-running scooters for the purpose of getting around in a manner that is relatively easy in congested cities.

4. The use of these brightly colored, maneuverable scooters allows city dwellers to zip through traffic jams and thereby to save time and to save gas.

5. However, sales of scooters, it might interest you to know, are in the process of increasing in North America.

## 11c What sentence structures usually work against conciseness?

Two sentence structures, although appropriate in some contexts, often work against CONCISENESS because they can lead to WORDINESS: writing EXPLETIVE constructions and writing in the PASSIVE VOICE.

### AVOIDING EXPLETIVE CONSTRUCTIONS

An expletive construction starts with *it* or *there* followed by a form of the VERB *be.* When you cut the expletive construction and revise, the sentence becomes more direct.

~~It is necessary for~~ students ^S^ to ^must^ fill in both questionnaires.

~~There are~~ ^E.^ eight instructors ~~who~~ teach in the Computer Science Department.

### AVOIDING THE PASSIVE VOICE

In general, the passive voice is less concise—as well as less lively—than the ACTIVE VOICE. In the active voice, the subject of a sentence does the action named by the verb. In the passive voice, the subject of a sentence receives the action named by the verb. Unless your meaning justifies using the passive voice, choose the active voice. (For more information, see sections 15n through 15p.)

**PASSIVE**   Volunteer work was done by students for credit in sociology. [The passive phrase *was done by students* is unnecessary for the intended meaning. *Students*, not *volunteer work*, are doing the action and should get the action of the verb.]

**ACTIVE**   **The students did** volunteer work for credit in sociology.

**ACTIVE**   **Volunteer work earned** students credit in sociology. [Since the verb has changed to *earned*, *volunteer work* performs the action of the verb.]

# 11d   How else can I revise for conciseness?

Four other techniques can help you achieve CONCISENESS: eliminating unplanned repetition; combining sentences; shortening CLAUSES; and shortening PHRASES and cutting words. These techniques involve matters of judgment.

## ■ Eliminating unplanned repetition

Unplanned repetition lacks conciseness because it delivers the same message more than once, usually in slightly different words. Unplanned repetition, or redundancy, implies that the writer lacks focus and judgment. The opposite—planned repetition—reflects both focus and judgment, as it creates a powerful rhythmic effect (see section 10c). As you revise, check that every word is necessary for delivering your message.

**NO**   Bringing **the project** to **final completion** three weeks early, the supervisor of **the project** earned our **respectful regard.** [*Completion* implies *bringing to final; project* is used twice in one sentence; and *regard* implies *respect.*]

**YES**   Completing the project three weeks early, the supervisor earned our respect. [Eighteen words reduced to eleven by cutting all redundancies.]

## ■ Combining sentences

Look at sets of sentences in your writing to see if you can fit information contained in one sentence into another sentence. (For more about combining sentences, see Chapter 9, particularly sections 9c, 9e, 9h, and 9m.)

|                       |                                                                                                                                                                                 |
| --------------------- | ------------------------------------------------------------------------------------------------------------------------------------------------------------------------------- |
| **TWO SENTENCES**     | The *Titanic* hit an iceberg and sank. Seventy-three years later, a team of French and American scientists located the ship's resting site.                                      |
| **SENTENCES COMBINED** | Seventy-three years after the *Titanic* hit an iceberg and sank, a team of French and American scientists located the ship's resting site.                                      |

### ■ Shortening clauses

Look at clauses in your writing to see if you can more concisely convey the same information. For example, sometimes you can cut a RELATIVE PRONOUN and its verb.

|             |                                                                       |
| ----------- | --------------------------------------------------------------------- |
| **WORDY**   | The *Titanic,* **which was** a huge ocean liner, sank in 1912.         |
| **CONCISE** | The Titanic, a huge ocean liner, sank in 1912.                         |

Sometimes you can reduce a clause to a word.

|             |                                                                                                  |
| ----------- | ------------------------------------------------------------------------------------------------ |
| **WORDY**   | The scientists held a memorial service for the passengers and crew **who had drowned.**           |
| **CONCISE** | The scientists held a memorial service for the **drowned** passengers and crew.                   |

### ■ Shortening phrases and cutting words

Sometimes you can reduce a phrase or redundant word pair to a single word. Redundant word pairs and phrases include *each and every, one and only, forever and ever, final and conclusive, perfectly clear, few* (or *many*) *in number, consensus of opinion,* and *reason . . . is because.*

|         |                                                                             |
| ------- | --------------------------------------------------------------------------- |
| **NO**  | The **consensus of opinion** was that the movie was disappointing.           |
| **YES** | The **consensus** was that the movie was disappointing.                      |
| **YES** | **Everyone agreed** that the movie was disappointing.                        |

## 11e   How do verbs affect conciseness?

ACTION VERBS are strong verbs. *Be* and *have* are weak verbs that often lead to wordy sentences. When you revise weak verbs to strong ones, you can both increase the impact of your writing and reduce the number of words in your sentences. Strong verbs come into play when you revise your writing to reduce PHRASES and to change NOUNS to verbs.

| WEAK VERB | The plan before the city council **has to do with** tax rebates. |
|---|---|
| STRONG VERB | The plan before the city council **proposes** tax rebates. |

## REPLACING A PHRASE WITH A VERB

Phrases such as *be aware of, be capable of, be supportive of* can often be replaced with one-word verbs.

I **envy** [not *am envious of*] your mathematical ability.

I **appreciate** [not *am appreciative of*] your modesty.

Your skill **illustrates** [not *is illustrative of*] how hard you studied.

## REVISING NOUNS INTO VERBS

Many nouns are derived from verbs. Such nouns usually end with *-ance, -ment,* and *-tion* (*tolerance, enforcement, narration*). When you turn such wordy nouns back into verbs, your writing is more concise.

| NO | The **accumulation of** paper lasted thirty years. |
|---|---|
| YES | The paper **accumulated** for thirty years. |

**12**

# The Impact of Words

## 12a What is American English?

Evolving over centuries into a rich language, **American English** is the variation of English spoken in the United States. It demonstrates that many cultures have created the US "melting pot" society. Food names are good examples: Africans brought the words *okra, gumbo,* and *goober* (peanut); Spanish and Latin American peoples contributed *tortilla, taco, burrito,* and *enchilada;* Greek speakers gave us *pita,* Cantonese speakers *chow,* Japanese speakers *sushi,* and so on.

## 12b What is edited American English?

**Edited American English,** also known as STANDARD ENGLISH, reflects the standards of the written language expected of a textbook. With edited American English, you can achieve the medium or semiformal language level required in ACADEMIC WRITING.

Edited American English isn't a special or fancy dialect for elite groups. Rather, it's a form of the language used by educated people to standardize communication in the larger world. Edited American English conforms to widely established rules of grammar, sentence structure, punctuation, and spelling—as covered in this handbook.

**Nonstandard English** is legitimately spoken by some groups in our society. With its own grammar and usage customs, it communicates clearly to other speakers of nonstandard English. Speakers of nonstandard English often benefit when they can switch, as an academic, business, or public WRITING SITUATION requires, to a more formal level of language.

It's true that advertising language and some trendy writings intended for mass audiences frequently ignore the conventions of edited American English. However, such departures from edited American English are not appropriate in academic writing.

## 12c What is figurative language?

**Figurative language** uses words for more than their literal meanings. Such words aren't merely decorative or pretentious (12g). Figurative language greatly enhances meaning. It makes comparisons and connections that draw on one idea or image to explain another. Quick Reference 12.1 explains the different types of figurative language and describes one type you should avoid, the **mixed metaphor.**

---

### Quick Reference 12.1　　　　■ ■ ■ ■ ■

### Types of figurative language

- **Analogy:** Comparing similar traits shared by dissimilar things or ideas. Its length can vary from one sentence (which often takes the form of a simile or metaphor) to a paragraph.

  A **cheetah sprinting across the dry plains** after its prey, the **base runner dashed** for home plate, cleats kicking up dust.

- **Irony:** Using words to suggest the opposite of their usual sense.

  Told that a minor repair on her home would cost $2,000 and take two weeks, she said, **"Oh, how nice!"**

continued >>

---

**Quick Reference 12.1** (continued) ▪ ▪ ▪ ▪ ▪

- **Metaphor:** Comparing otherwise dissimilar things. A metaphor doesn't use the word *like* or *as* to make a comparison. (See below about not using mixed metaphors.)

  > Rush-hour **traffic** in the city **bled out through major arteries** to the suburbs.

- **Personification:** Assigning a human trait to something not human.

  > The **book begged** to be read.

- **Overstatement** (also called *hyperbole*): Exaggerating deliberately for emphasis.

  > If this paper is late, the professor will **kill** me.

- **Simile:** Comparing dissimilar things. A simile uses the word *like* or *as*.

  > Langston Hughes observes that a deferred **dream dries up "like a raisin in the sun."**

- **Understatement:** Emphasizing by using deliberate restraint.

  > It feels **warm** when the temperature reaches **105 degrees.**

- **Mixed metaphor:** Combining two or more inconsistent images in one sentence or expression. Never use a mixed metaphor.

  **NO**  The violence of the hurricane reminded me of a train ride. [A train ride is not violent, stormy, or destructive.]

  **YES**  **The violence of the hurricane reminded me of a train's crashing into a huge tractor trailer.**

---

# 12d  How can using exact diction enhance my writing?

**Diction,** the term for choice of words, affects the clarity and impact of any writing you do. Your best chance of delivering your intended message to your readers is to choose words that fit exactly with each piece of writing. To choose words correctly—that is, to have good diction—you need to understand the concepts of *denotation* and *connotation* in words.

## ■ What is denotation in words?

The **denotation** of a word is its exact, literal meaning. It's the meaning you find when you look up the word in a dictionary. A dictionary is your ultimate authority for a word's denotation.

🌐 **ESOL Tip:** *The Oxford Dictionary of American English* (Cambridge: Oxford UP, 2005) is particularly useful for students who speak English as a second (or third) language. ●

### ■ What is connotation in words?

**Connotation** refers to ideas implied by a word. Connotations are never completely fixed, for they can vary in differing contexts. Connotations involve associations and emotional overtones that go beyond a word's definition. For example, *home* usually evokes more emotion than its denotation "a dwelling place" or its synonym *house*. *Home* carries the connotation, for some, of the pleasures of warmth, security, and love of family. For others, however, *home* may carry unpleasant connotations, such as abusive experiences or the impersonal atmosphere of an institution to house the elderly.

#### USING A THESAURUS

Sometimes a good college dictionary explains the small differences among synonyms, but a thesaurus is devoted entirely to providing synonyms for words. In distinguishing among **synonyms**—the other words close in meaning to a word—a thesaurus demonstrates connotation in operation. As you use a thesaurus, remain very alert to the subtle shades of meaning that create distinctions among words.

**❶ Alert:** Most word-processing programs include a thesaurus. But be cautious in using it. Unless you know the exact meaning of an offered synonym, as well as its part of speech, you may choose a wrong word or introduce a grammatical error into your writing. For example, one word-processing program's thesaurus offers these synonyms for *deep* in the sense of "low (down, inside)": *low, below, beneath*, and *subterranean*. None of these words could replace *deep* in a sentence such as *The crater is too deep* [not *too low, too below, too beneath*, or *too subterranean*] *to be filled with sand or rocks.* ●

**EXERCISE 12-1**    Look at each list of words and divide the words among three headings: "Positive" (good connotations); "Negative" (bad connotations); and "Neutral" (no connotations). If you think that a word belongs under more than one heading, you can assign it more than once, but be ready to explain your thinking. For help, consult a good dictionary and 12d.

EXAMPLE    grand, big, bulky, significant, oversized
   *Positive:* grand, significant; *Negative:* bulky, oversized; *Neutral:* big

1. harmony, sound, racket, shriek, melody, music, noise, pitch, voice

2. talkative, articulate, chattering, eloquent, vocal, verbose, gossipy, fluent, gabby

3. decorative, beautiful, modern, ornate, overelaborate, dazzling, flashy, elegant, sparkling

4. long, lingering, enduring, continued, drawn-out, stretched, never-ending, unbreakable, incessant

5. calculating, shrewd, crafty, ingenious, keen, sensible, sly, smooth, underhanded

## 12e   How can using specific words enhance my writing?

**Specific words** identify individual items in a group (*Ford, Honda*). **General words** relate to an overall group (*car*). **Concrete words** identify what can be perceived by the senses, by being seen, heard, tasted, felt, smelled (*padded black leather dashboard*), and convey specific images and details. **Abstract words** denote qualities (*kind*), concepts (*speed*), relationships (*friends*), acts (*cooking*), conditions (*bad weather*), and ideas (*transportation*) and are more general.

Usually, specific and concrete words bring life to general and abstract words. Therefore, whenever you use general and abstract words, try to supply enough specific, concrete details and examples to illustrate them.

| | |
|---|---|
| **GENERAL** | His car gets good gas mileage. |
| **SPECIFIC** | His Miser gets about 35 mpg on the highway and 30 mpg in the city. |

What separates most good writing from bad is the writer's ability to move back and forth between the general and abstract and the specific and concrete. Consider these sentences that effectively use a combination of general and specific words to compare cars:

GENERAL   CONCRETE   |   SPECIFIC ———————   ABSTRACT
My car, a midnight-black Corvette LS1 convertible, has a powerful

┌— SPECIFIC —┐   GENERAL   SPECIFIC   GENERAL
5.7-liter V8 engine with ride controls, the Tour for regular driving and

SPECIFIC   ┌— CONCRETE —┐   GENERAL
the Sport for a close-to-the-road feel. In contrast, Harvey's automobile,

CONCRETE   ┌———— SPECIFIC ————┐   ABSTRACT
a bright red Dodge Viper SRT-10 convertible, has a mighty

┌———————— SPECIFIC ————————┐
8.3-liter V10 engine with 6-speed manual transmission.

**EXERCISE 12-2**   Revise this paragraph by providing specific and concrete words and phrases to explain and enliven the ideas presented here in general and abstract language. You may revise the sentences to accommodate your changes in language. For help, consult 12e.

I hope to get a job as an administrative assistant in the company. At the interview, the person who would be my supervisor was pleasant. We seemed to get along well. The other assistants in the division appeared to be nice. My college courses clearly have prepared me for the position. I think the job would teach me a great deal more. The salary is a bit less than I had hoped for, but the Human Resources representative promised me raises at regular intervals if my work is good. Also, my trip to work would not take too much time for me. If my interviewer calls to offer me the job, I will accept it.

## 12f   What is gender-neutral language?

**Gender-neutral language,** also referred to as *gender-free* or *nonsexist language,* relies on terms that don't communicate whether the person is male or female (for example, in replacing *policeman* with *police officer* or *doctors' wives* with *doctors' spouses*).

**Sexist language** assigns roles or characteristics to people based on their sex and gender. Most people recognize that sexist language discriminates against both men and women. For example, it inaccurately assumes that every nurse and homemaker is female (and therefore referred to as "she"), and that every physician and stockbroker is male (and therefore referred to as "he"). One common instance of sexist language occurs when the pronoun *he* is used to refer to someone whose sex is unknown or irrelevant. Although tradition holds that *he* is correct in such situations, most people believe that using masculine pronouns to represent all humans excludes women and thereby distorts reality.

Nearly all businesses and professional organizations require gender-neutral language in written communications. Their policies exist not only for reasons of accuracy and fairness but also for sound business practice, as they want to be inclusive of potential clients and customers.

Gender-neutral language rejects demeaning STEREOTYPES or outdated assumptions, such as "women are bad drivers" and "men can't cook." In your writing, never describe women's looks, clothes, or age unless you do the same for men or doing so is important to the context. Never use a title for one spouse and the first name for the other spouse: *Phil Miller* (not *Mr. Miller*) and *his wife, Jeannette,* travel on separate planes; or *Jeannette and Phil Miller* live in Idaho. Quick Reference 12.2 gives you guidelines for using gender-neutral language.

### Quick Reference 12.2   ▪ ▪ ▪ ▪ ▪

#### How to avoid sexist language

- Avoid using only the masculine pronoun to refer to males and females together. The *he or she* and *his or hers* constructions act as singular PRONOUNS, and they therefore call for singular VERBS. Try to avoid using *he or she* constructions, especially more than once in a sentence or in consecutive sentences. A better solution is revising to the plural. You can also revise to omit the gender-specific pronoun.

continued >>

## Quick Reference 12.2 (continued) ■ ■ ■ ■ ■

**NO** A **doctor** has little time to read outside **his** specialty.

**YES** A **doctor** has little time to read outside **his or her** specialty.

**NO** A successful **stockbroker** knows **he** has to work long hours.

**YES** Successful **stockbrokers** know **they** have to work long hours.

- Avoid using *man* when referring to both men and women.

**NO** **Man** is a social animal.

**YES** **People** are social animals.

**NO** The history of **mankind** is predominately violent.

**YES** **Human** history is predominately violent.

- Avoid stereotyping jobs and roles by gender when referring to both men and women.

| NO | YES |
| --- | --- |
| chairman | chair, chairperson |
| policeman | police officer |
| businessman | businessperson, business executive |
| statesman | statesperson, diplomat |
| teacher . . . she | teachers . . . they |
| principal . . . he | principals . . . they |

- Avoid expressions that seem to exclude one sex.

| NO | YES |
| --- | --- |
| the common man | the average person |
| man-sized sandwich | huge sandwich |
| old wives' tale | superstition |

- Avoid using demeaning and patronizing labels.

| NO | YES |
| --- | --- |
| male nurse | nurse |
| gal Friday | assistant |
| coed | student |
| My girl can help. | My secretary can help. (*Or, better still:* Ida Morea can help.) |

🔵 **Alert:** Increasingly, you see "they" or "their" used as a singular pronoun, as in "If someone puts in the effort, they should be rewarded." The English language continually changes, and perhaps in a few years this growing usage will become perfectly acceptable because it fills a need: English lacks a gender-neutral singular pronoun. Today, however, it is still nonstandard in almost all academic and professional settings. ●

## **12g** What other types of language do I want to avoid?

Language that distorts or tries to manipulate a reader needs to be avoided in ACADEMIC WRITING. These and other types of language to avoid in an academic LEVEL OF FORMALITY are listed, with examples, in Quick Reference 12.3.

---

### Quick Reference 12.3 ■ ■ ■ ■ ■

#### Language to avoid in academic writing

- Never use **slanted language,** also called *loaded language;* readers feel manipulated by the overly emotional TONE and DICTION.

  **NO**   Our senator is a deceitful, crooked thug.

  **YES**   Our senator lies to the public and demands bribes.

- Never use **pretentious language;** readers realize you're showing off.

  **NO**   As I alighted from my vehicle, my clothing became besmirched with filth.

  **YES**   My coat got muddy as I got out of my car.

- Never use **sarcastic language;** readers realize you're being nasty.

  **NO**   He was a regular Albert Einstein with my questions. [This is sarcastic if you mean the opposite.]

  **YES**   He had trouble understanding my questions.

- Never use **colloquial language;** readers sense you're being overly casual and conversational.

  **NO**   Christina tanked chemistry.

  **YES**   Christina failed chemistry.

- Never use **euphemisms,** also called *doublespeak;* readers realize you're hiding the truth (more in 12j).

  **NO**   Our company will **downsize** to meet efficiency standards.

  **YES**   Our company has to cut jobs to maintain our profits.

---

## 12h  What are clichés?

A **cliché** is a worn-out expression that has lost its capacity to communicate effectively because of overuse. Many clichés are SIMILES or METAPHORS, once clever but now flat. For example, these are clichés: *dead as a doornail, gentle as a lamb,* and *straight as an arrow.*

If you've heard certain expressions repeatedly, so has your reader. Instead of a cliché, use descriptive language that isn't worn out. If you can't think of a way to rephrase a cliché, drop the words entirely.

## 12i  When is jargon unnecessary?

**Jargon** is the specialized vocabulary of a particular group. Jargon uses words that people outside that group might not understand. Specialized language exists in every field: professions, academic disciplines, business, various industries, government departments, hobbies, and so on.

Reserve jargon for a specialist AUDIENCE. As you write, keep your audience in mind as you decide whether a word is jargon in the context of your material. When you must use jargon for a nonspecialist audience, be sure to explain any special meanings.

## 12j  What are euphemisms?

**Euphemisms** attempt to avoid the harsh reality of truth by using more pleasant, "tactful" words. Good manners dictate that euphemisms sometimes be used in social situations: For example, in US culture, *passed away* is, in some situations, thought to be gentler than *died.* Such uses of euphemisms are acceptable.

In other situations, however, euphemisms drain meaning from truthful writing. Unnecessary euphemisms might describe socially unacceptable behavior (for example, *Johnny has a wonderfully vivid imagination* instead of *Johnny lies*). They also might try to hide unpleasant facts (for example, *She is between assignments* instead of *She's lost her job*). Avoid unnecessary euphemisms.

## 12k  What is bureaucratic language?

**Bureaucratic language** uses words that are stuffy and overblown. Bureaucratic language (or *bureaucratese,* a word created to describe this style) is marked by unnecessary complexity. This kind of language can take on a formality that complicates the message and makes readers feel left out.

**NO**  In reference to situations delineated above, corporate associates shall determine the existence of extraneous circumstances sufficient to preclude substantive action by management. In the event the evaluation of said circumstances results in an affirmative finding, the associate is directed to enact the policy mandated in section 4.b.7 of the procedures manual, unless said implementation would enact legal pursuits or other actions injurious to the company.

—from a corporate human resources manual

We would like to give a YES alternative for this example but regret that we can't understand enough of it to do so. If you, gentle reader, can, please contact us at dhesse@du.edu or troykalq@nyc.rr.com.

**13**

# Usage Glossary

A usage glossary presents the customary manner of using particular words and phrases. "Customary manner," however, is not as firm in practice as the term implies. Usage standards change. If you think a word's usage might differ from what you read here, consult a dictionary published more recently than the current edition of this handbook.

The meaning of *informal* or *colloquial* in the definition of a word or phrase is that it's found in everyday or conversational speech, but it needs to be avoided in ACADEMIC WRITING. Another term, *nonstandard,* indicates that the word or phrase, although widely understood in speech and dialect writing, isn't suitable in standard spoken or written English.

**a, an**  Use *a* before words that begin with a consonant (*a dog, a grade, a hole*) or a consonant sound (*a one-day sale, a European*). Use *an* before words or acronyms that begin with a vowel sound or a silent *h* (*an owl; an hour; an MRI,* because the *M* is sounded "em"). American English uses *a,* not *an,* before words starting with a pronounced *h: a* (not *an*) *historical event.*

**accept, except** The verb *accept* means "agree to; receive." As a preposition, *except* means "leaving out." As a verb, *except* means "exclude; leave out."

The workers wanted to **accept** [verb] management's offer **except** [preposition] for one detail: They wanted the limit on overtime **excepted** [verb] from the contract.

**advice, advise** *Advice,* a noun, means "recommendation." *Advise,* a verb, means "recommend; give advice."

I **advise** [verb] you to follow your car mechanic's **advice** [noun].

**affect, effect** As a verb, *affect* means "cause a change in; influence." (*Affect* is a noun in psychology.) As a noun, *effect* means "result or conclusion"; as a verb, *effect* means "bring about."

Loud music **affects** people's hearing for life, so some bands have **effected** changes to lower the volume. Many fans, however, don't care about the harmful **effects** of high decibel levels.

**aggravate, irritate** *Aggravate* is used colloquially to mean "irritate." In academic writing, use *aggravate* only to mean "intensify; make worse." Use *irritate* to mean "annoy; make impatient."

The coach was **irritated** by reduced time for practice, which **aggravated** the team's difficulties with concentration.

**ain't** *Ain't* is a nonstandard contraction. Use *am not, is not,* or *are not* for standard spoken and written English.

**all ready, already** *All ready* means "completely prepared." *Already* means "before; by this time."

The team was **all ready** to play, but it had **already** begun to rain.

**all right** *All right* is always written as two words, never one (never *alright*).

**allude, elude** *Allude* means "refer to indirectly." *Elude* means "escape notice."

The detectives **alluded** to budget cuts by saying, "Conditions beyond our control allowed the suspect to **elude** us."

**allusion, illusion** An *allusion* is an indirect reference to something. An *illusion* is a false impression or idea.

The couple's casual **allusions** to European tourist sites created the **illusion** that they had visited them.

**a lot** *A lot* is informal for *a great deal* or *a great many.* Avoid using it in academic writing. If you must use it, write it as two words (never *alot*).

**among, amongst, between**   Use *among* for three or more items. Use *between* for two items. American English prefers *among* to *amongst.*

> My three housemates discussed **among** [not *between* or *amongst*] themselves the choice **between** staying in college and getting full-time jobs.

**amount, number**   Use *amount* for noncountable things (wealth, work, happiness). Use *number* for countable items.

> The **amount** of rice to cook depends on the **number** of guests.

**an**   See *a, an.*

**and/or**   This term is appropriate in business and legal writing when either or both of the two items can apply: *We are planning to open additional offices in California **and/or** New York.* In the humanities, writers usually express the alternatives in words: *We are planning to open additional offices in California, New York, or both.*

**anyone, any one**   *Anyone* is a singular indefinite pronoun meaning "any person at all." *Any one* (two words), an adjective that modifies a pronoun, means "a member of a group."

> **Anyone** could test-drive **any one** of the display vehicles.

**anyways, anywheres**   *Anyways* and *anywheres* are nonstandard for *anyway* and *anywhere.*

**as, as if, as though, like**   Use *as, as if,* or *as though,* but not *like,* when the words coming after include a verb.

> This hamburger tastes good, **as** [not *like*] a hamburger should. It tastes **as if** [or *as though,* not *like*] it were barbequed over charcoal, not gas.

Both *as* and *like* can function as prepositions in comparisons. However, use *as* to indicate equivalence between two nouns or pronouns, and use *like* to indicate similarity but not equivalence.

> My friend Roger served **as** [not *like*] mediator in a dispute about my neighbor's tree that dripped sap on my driveway **like** [not *as*] a leaky water faucet.

**assure, ensure, insure**   *Assure* means "promise; convince." *Ensure* and *insure* both mean "make certain or secure," but *insure* is reserved for financial or legal matters.

> The insurance agent **assured** me that he could **insure** my car, but only I could **ensure** that I would drive safely.

**as to**   *As to* is nonstandard for *about.*

**awful, awfully**   *Awful* is an adjective meaning "inspiring awe" and "creating fear." *Awfully* is an adverb meaning "in a way to inspire awe" and "terrifying." Only colloquially are *awful* and *awfully* used to mean "very" or "extremely."

I was **extremely** [not awfully] tired yesterday.

**a while, awhile**   As two words, *a while* (an article and a noun) can function as a subject or object. As one word, *awhile* is an adverb. In a prepositional phrase, the correct form is *for a while, in a while,* or *after a while.*

It took **a while** [article and noun] to drive to the zoo, where we saw the seals bask **awhile** [adverb modifying verb bask] in the sun after romping **for a while** [prepositional phrase] in the water.

**bad, badly**   *Bad* is an adjective only after linking verbs (*look, feel, smell, taste, sound;* these verbs can function as either linking verbs or action verbs depending on the context). *Badly* is an adverb; it's nonstandard after linking verbs.

Farmers feel **bad** [feel is a linking verb, so bad is the adjective] because a **bad** [adjective] drought is **badly** [adverb] damaging their crops.

**being as, being that**   *Being as* and *being that* are nonstandard for *because* or *since.*

We had to forfeit the game **because** [not being as or being that] our goalie was badly injured.

**beside, besides**   As prepositions, *beside* means "next to, by the side of," and *besides* means "other than, in addition to." As an adverb, *besides* means "also, moreover."

She stood **beside** the new car, insisting that she would drive. No one **besides** her had a driver's license. **Besides,** she owned the car.

**better, had better**   *Better* is informal for *had better.*

We **had better** [not better alone] be careful of the ice.

**between**   See *among, amongst, between.*

**can, may**   *Can* signifies ability or capacity. *May* requests or grants permission. In negative expressions, *can* is acceptable for *may.*

When you **can** [not may] get here on time, you **may** [not can] be excused early. However, if you are *not* on time, you **cannot** [or may not] expect privileges.

**capitol, capital**   *Capitol* means "a building in which legislators meet." *Capital* means a city (Denver, the *capital* of Colorado), wealth, or "most important" (a *capital* offense).

If the governor can find enough **capital,** the state legislature will agree to build a new **capitol** for our state.

**censor, censure** The verb *censor* means "delete objectionable material; judge." The verb *censure* means "condemn or reprimand officially."

The town council **censured** the mayor for trying to **censor** a report.

**cite, site** The verb *cite* means "quote by way of example, authority, or proof." The noun *site* means "a particular place or location."

The private investigator **cited** evidence from the crime **site** and the defendant's Web **site.**

**complement, compliment** As a noun, *complement* means "something that goes well with or completes." As a noun, *compliment* means "praise, flattery." As a verb, *complement* means "brings to perfection; goes well with, completes." As a verb, *compliment* means "praise, flatter."

The dean's **compliment** was a perfect **complement** to the thrill of my graduating. My parents felt proud when she **complimented** me publicly, an honor that **complemented** their joy.

**comprise, include** See *include, comprise.*

**criteria, criterion** A *criterion* is "a standard of judgment." *Criteria* is the plural of *criterion.*

A sense of history is an important **criterion** for judging political candidates, but voters must consider other **criteria** as well.

**data** *Data* is the plural of *datum,* a word rarely used today. Informally, *data* is used as a singular noun that takes a singular verb. In academic or professional writing, *data* is considered plural and takes a plural verb (although this usage is currently viewed as overly formal by some).

The **data** suggest [not *suggests*] some people are addicted to e-mail.

**different from, different than** In academic and professional writing, use *different from* even though *different than* is common in informal speech.

Please advise us if your research yields data **different from** past results.

**disinterested, uninterested** The preferred use of *disinterested* means "impartial, unbiased." Colloquially, *disinterested* can mean "not interested, indifferent," but in more formal contexts, *uninterested* is preferred for "not interested, indifferent."

Jurors need to be **disinterested** in hearing evidence, but never **uninterested.**

**effect** See *affect, effect.*

**elicit, illicit**   The verb *elicit* means "draw forth or bring out." The adjective *illicit* means "illegal."

> The senator's **illicit** conduct **elicited** a mass outcry from her constituents.

**elude**   See *allude, elude.*

**ensure**   See *assure, ensure, insure.*

**enthused**   *Enthused* is nonstandard for *enthusiastic.*

> Adam was **enthusiastic** [not *enthused*] about the college he chose.

**etc.**   *Etc.* is the abbreviation for the Latin *et cetera,* meaning "and the rest." For writing in the humanities, avoid using *etc.* Acceptable substitutes are *and the like, and so on,* or *and so forth.*

**everyone, every one**   *Everyone* is a singular, indefinite pronoun. *Every one* (two words) is an adjective and a pronoun, meaning "each member in a group."

> **Everyone** enjoyed **every one** of the comedy skits.

**except**   See *accept, except.*

**farther, further**   Although many writers reserve *farther* for geographical distances and *further* for all other cases, current usage treats them as interchangeable.

**fewer, less**   Use *fewer* for anything that can be counted (that is, with count nouns): *fewer* dollars, *fewer* fleas, *fewer* haircuts. Use *less* with collective nouns (or other noncount nouns): *less* money, *less* scratching, *less* hair.

**good, well**   *Good* is an adjective. As an adverb, *good* is nonstandard. Instead, use *well.*

> **Good** [adjective] maintenance helps cars run **well** [adverb; not *good*].

**got, have**   *Got* is nonstandard for *have.*

> What do we **have** [not *got*] for supper?

**have, of**   Use *have,* not *of,* after such verbs as *could, should, would, might,* and *must.*

> You ***should*** **have** [not *should of* ] called first.

**he/she, s/he, his/her**   When using gender-neutral language, write out *he or she* or *his or her* instead of using and/or constructions. To be more concise, switch to plural pronouns and antecedents. (For more about gender-neutral language, see 12f.)

> **Everyone** bowed ***his or her*** head. [*Everyone bowed his head* is considered sexist language if women were present when the heads were bowed.]

> The **people** bowed **their** heads.

**hopefully**    *Hopefully* is an adverb meaning "with hope, in a hopeful manner," so as an adverb, it can modify a verb, an adjective, or another adverb. However, *hopefully* is nonstandard as a sentence modifier meaning "we hope"; therefore, in academic writing, avoid this usage.

> They waited **hopefully** [adverb] for the crippled airplane to land. **We hope** [not *Hopefully,*] it will land safely.

**humanity, humankind, humans, mankind**    To use gender-neutral language, choose *humanity, humankind,* or *humans* instead of *mankind.*

> Some think that the computer has helped **humanity** more than any other twentieth-century invention.

**i.e.**    This abbreviation refers to the Latin term *id est.* In academic writing, use the English translation "that is."

**if, whether**    At the start of a noun clause that expresses speculation or unknown conditions, you can use either *if* or *whether.* However, in such conditional clauses use only *whether* (or *whether or not*) when alternatives are expressed or implied. In a conditional clause that does not express or imply alternatives, use only *if.*

> **If** [not *whether*] you promise not to step on my feet, I might dance with you. Still, I'm not sure **if** [or *whether*] I want to dance with you. Once I decide, I'll dance with you **whether** [not *if*] I like the music or **whether** [not *if*] the next song is fast or slow.

**imply, infer**    *Imply* means "hint at or suggest." *Infer* means "draw a conclusion." A writer or speaker *implies;* a reader or listener *infers.*

> When the governor **implied** that she wouldn't seek reelection, reporters **inferred** that she was planning to run for vice president.

**include, comprise**    The verb *include* means "contain or regard as part of a whole." The verb *comprise* means "consist of or be composed of."

**in regard to, with regard to, as regards, regarding**    Use *about, concerning,* and *for* in place of these wordy phrases. Also, avoid the nonstandard *as regards to.*

> **Concerning** [not *in regard to, with regard to, as regards,* or *regarding*] your question, we can now confirm that your payment was received.

**irregardless**   *Irregardless* is nonstandard for *regardless.*

**is when, is where**   Never use these constructions when you define something. Instead, use active verbs.

> Defensive driving **involves staying** [not *is when you stay*] alert.

**its, it's**   *Its* is a personal pronoun in the possessive case. *It's* is a contraction of *it is.*

> The dog buried **its** bone today. **It's** hot today, which makes the dog restless.

**kind of, sort of**   These phrases are colloquial adverbs. In academic writing, use *somewhat.*

> The campers were **somewhat** [not *kind of* ] dehydrated after the hike.

**lay, lie**   The verb *lay* (***lay***, *laid, laid, laying*) means "place or put something, usually on something else" and needs a direct object. The verb *lie* (***lie***, *lay, lain, lying*), meaning "recline," doesn't need a direct object. Substituting *lay* for *lie,* or the opposite, is nonstandard. *Layed* is not a word.

> **Lay** [not *lie*] down the blanket [direct object], and then place the baby to **lie** [not *lay*] in the shade.

**like**   See *as, as if, as though, like.*

**lots, lots of, a lot of**   These are colloquial constructions. Instead, use *many, much,* or *a great deal.*

**mankind**   See *humanity, humankind, humans, mankind.*

**maybe, may be**   *Maybe* is an adverb; *may be* (two words) is a verb phrase.

> **Maybe** [adverb] we can win, but our team **may be** [verb phrase] too tired.

**may of, might of**   *May of* and *might of* are nonstandard for *may have* and *might have.*

**media**   *Media* is the plural of *medium,* yet colloquial usage now pairs it with a singular verb (for example, *The **media saturates** us with information about every fire*).

**must of**   *Must of* is nonstandard for *must have.*

**nowheres**   *Nowheres* is nonstandard for *nowhere.*

**of**    Use *have,* not *of,* after modal auxiliary verbs (*could, may, might, must, should, would* ). See also *could of; may of; might of; must of; should of; would of.*

**off of**    *Off of* is nonstandard for *off.*

> Don't fall **off** [not *off of* ] the stage.

**OK, O.K., okay**    These three forms are informal. In academic writing, choose words that express more specific meanings. If you must use the term, choose the full word *okay.*

> The weather was **suitable** [not *okay*] for a picnic.

**oral, verbal**    The adjective *oral* means "spoken or being done by the mouth." The adjective *verbal* means "relating to language" (*verbal* skill) or to words rather than actions, facts, or ideas.

**plus**    *Plus* is nonstandard for *and, also, in addition,* and *moreover.*

> The band booked three concerts in Hungary, **and** [not *plus*] it will tour Poland for a month. **In addition,** [not *Plus,*] it may perform once in Austria.

**precede, proceed**    *Precede* is a verb that means "go before." *Proceed* is a verb that means "to advance, go on, undertake, carry on."

> **Preceded** by elephants and music, the ringmaster **proceeded** into the main tent.

**principal, principle**    As a noun, *principal* means "chief person; main or original amount." As an adjective, *principal* means "most important." *Principle* is a noun that means "a basic truth or rule."

> During the assembly, the **principal** [noun] said, "A **principal** [adjective] value in our democracy is the **principle** [noun] of free speech."

**quotation, quote**    *Quotation* is a noun, and *quote* is a verb. Don't use *quote* as a noun.

> One newspaper reporter **quoted** [verb] the US president, and soon the **quotations** [noun—not *quotes,* which is a verb] were widely broadcast.

**real, really**    These words are nonstandard for *very* and *extremely.*

**reason is because**   This phrase is redundant. To be concise and correct, use *reason is that.*

One **reason** we moved **is that** [not *is because*] our factory was relocated.

**reason why**   This phrase is redundant. To be concise and correct, use *reason* or *why.*

I don't know **why** [not *the reason why*] they left home.

**regarding**   See *in regard to, with regard to, as regards, regarding.*

**regardless**   See *irregardless.*

**respective, respectively**   *Respective,* a noun, refers to two or more individual persons or things. *Respectively,* an adverb, refers back to two or more individuals or things in the same sequence in which they were originally mentioned.

After the fire drill, Dr. Daniel Eagle and Dr. Jessica Chess returned to their **respective** offices [that is, he returned to his office, and she returned to her office] on the second and third floors, **respectively** [his office is on the second floor, and her office is on the third floor].

**set, sit**   The verb *set* (***set**, set, setting*) means "put in place, position, put down" and needs a direct object. The verb *sit* (***sit**, sat, sitting*) means "be seated" and doesn't need a direct object. Substituting *set* for *sit,* or the opposite, is nonstandard.

Susan **set** [not *sat*] the sandwiches beside the salad, made Spot **sit** [not *set*] down, and then **sat** [not *set*] on the sofa.

**should of**   *Should of* is nonstandard for *should have.*

**sometime, sometimes, some time**   The adverb *sometime* means "at an unspecified time." The adverb *sometimes* means "now and then." *Some time* (two words) is an adjective with a noun that means "an amount or span of time."

**Sometime** [adverb for "at an unspecified time"] next year, I must take my qualifying exams. I **sometimes** [adverb for "now and then"] worry whether I'll find **some time** [adjective with a noun] to study for them.

**supposed to, used to**   The final *-d* is essential in both phrases.

We were **suppose*d*** to [not *suppose to*] leave early. I **use*d*** to [not *use to*] wake up before the alarm rang.

**than, then**    *Than* indicates comparison; *then* relates to time.

> Please put on your gloves, and **then** your hat. It's colder outside **than** you think.

**that, which**    Use *that* with restrictive (essential) clauses only. You can use *which* with both restrictive and nonrestrictive (nonessential) clauses; however, many people reserve *which* to use only with nonrestrictive clauses.

> The house **that** [or which] Jack built is on Beanstalk Street, **which** [not that] runs past the reservoir.

**that there, them there, this here, these here**    These phrases are nonstandard for *that, them, this, these,* respectively.

**their, there, they're**    *Their* is a possessive pronoun. *There* means "in that place" or is part of an expletive construction. *They're* is a contraction of *they are.*

> **They're** going to **their** accounting class in the building over **there** near the library. Do you know that **there** are twelve sections of Accounting 101?

**theirself, theirselves, themself**    These words are nonstandard for *themselves.*

**then**    See *than, then.*

**to, too, two**    *To* is a preposition; it also is part of an infinitive verb. *Too* is an adverb meaning "also; more than enough." *Two* is a number.

> When you go **to** Chicago, visit the Art Institute. Try **to** visit Harry Caray's for dinner, **too.** It won't be **too** expensive because **two** people can share a meal.

**type**    *Type* is nonstandard when used to mean *type of.*

> I recommend that you use only that **type of** [not type] glue on plastic.

**uninterested**    See *disinterested, uninterested.*

**utilize**    *Utilize* is considered an overblown word for *use* in academic writing.

> The team **used** [not utilized] all its players to win the game.

**way, ways**    When referring to distance, use *way* rather than *ways.*

> He is a long **way** [not ways] from home.

**Web site, website**   Usage at the time of this book's publication calls for two words and a capital *W.* Increasingly, the informal *website* is being used.

**well**   See *good, well.*

**where**   *Where* is nonstandard for *that* when *where* is used as a subordinating conjunction.

   I read **that** [not *where*] salt raises blood pressure.

**which**   See *that, which.*

**who, whom**   Use *who* as a subject or a subject complement; use *whom* as an object (see 16g).

**who's, whose**   *Who's* is the contraction of *who is. Whose* is a possessive pronoun.

   **Who's** willing to drive? **Whose** truck should we take?

**World Wide Web**   Written out, the three words start with a capital *W.* Its abbreviation only in URLs is *www.* When you use only the word *Web,* start it with a capital *W.*

**would of**   *Would of* is nonstandard for *would have.*

**your, you're**   *Your* is a possessive pronoun. *You're* is the contraction of *you are.*

   **You're** kind to volunteer **your** time at the senior center.

# 14 ■ ■ ■

# Parts of Speech and Sentence Structures

## PARTS OF SPEECH

## 14a What is a noun?

A **noun** names a person, place, thing, or idea: *student, college, textbook, education.* Quick Reference 14.1 lists different kinds of nouns.

| Quick Reference 14.1 ■ ■ ■ ■ ■ |
| --- |

| Nouns | | |
| --- | --- | --- |
| PROPER | names specific people, places, or things (first letter is always capitalized) | *Dave Matthews, Paris, Toyota* |
| COMMON | names general groups, places, people, or things | *singer, city, automobile* |
| CONCRETE | names things experienced through the senses: sight, hearing, taste, smell, and touch | *landscape, pizza, thunder* |
| ABSTRACT | names things not knowable through the senses | *freedom, shyness* |
| COLLECTIVE | names groups | *family, team* |
| NONCOUNT OR MASS | names "uncountable" things | *water, time* |
| COUNT | names countable items | *lake, minute* |

⊕ **ESOL Tips:** Here are some useful tips for working with nouns.

- Nouns often appear with words that tell how much or how many, whose, which one, and similar information. These words include ARTICLES (*a, an, the*) and other determiners or limiting adjectives; see section 14e and Chapter 51.

- Nouns sometimes serve as ADJECTIVES. For example, in the term *police officer,* the word *police* serves as an adjective to describe *officer.*

- Nouns in many languages other than English are *inflected.* This means they change form, usually with a special ending, to communicate gender (male, female, neuter); number (singular, plural); and case (see 16a through 16k).

- Words with these suffixes (word endings) are usually nouns: *-ness, -ence, -ance, -ty,* and *-ment.* ●

# 14b   What is a pronoun?

A **pronoun** takes the place of a NOUN. The words or word that a pronoun replaces is called the pronoun's ANTECEDENT. See Quick Reference 14.2 for a list of different kinds of pronouns. For information on how to use pronouns correctly, see Chapters 16 and 17.

**David** is an accountant. [The noun *David* names a person.]

**He** is an accountant. [The pronoun *he* refers to its antecedent, *David.*]

The finance committee needs to consult **him.** [The pronoun *him* refers to its antecedent, *David.*]

---

## Quick Reference 14.2    ■ ■ ■ ■ ■

### Pronouns

| | | |
|---|---|---|
| **PERSONAL** <br> *I, you, its, her, they, ours,* and others | refers to people or things | *I saw **her** take a book to **them**.* |
| **RELATIVE** <br> *who, which, that* | introduces certain NOUN CLAUSES and ADJECTIVE CLAUSES | *The book **that** I lost was valuable.* |
| **INTERROGATIVE** <br> *which, who, whose,* and others | introduces a question | ***Who** called?* |
| **DEMONSTRATIVE** <br> *this, that, these, those* | points out the antecedent | *Whose books are **these**?* |
| **REFLEXIVE OR INTENSIVE** <br> *myself, themselves,* and other *-self* or *-selves* words | reflects back to the antecedent; intensifies the antecedent | *They claim to support **themselves**. **I myself** doubt it.* |
| **RECIPROCAL** <br> *each other, one another* | refers to individual parts of a plural antecedent | *We respect **each other**.* |
| **INDEFINITE** <br> *all, anyone, each,* and others | refers to nonspecific persons or things | ***Everyone** is welcome here.* |

**EXERCISE 14-1**    Underline and label all nouns (N) and pronouns (P). Refer to 14a through 14b for help.

EXAMPLE    My mother celebrated her eightieth birthday this summer with
P    N                    P              N              N

her family and friends; she greatly enjoyed the festivities.
P    N              N    P                              N

1. More and more people live into their eighties and nineties because they get better health benefits and they take better care of themselves.

2. Many elderly people now live busy lives, continuing in businesses or volunteering at various agencies.

3. My mother, Elizabeth, for example, spends four hours each morning as a volunteer for the Red Cross, where she takes histories from blood donors.

4. My neighbors, George and Sandra, who are eighty-six years old, still own and run a card and candy shop.

5. Age has become no obstacle for active seniors as evidenced by the activities they pursue today.

# 14c   What is a verb?

**Main verbs** express action, occurrence, or state of being. For information on how to use verbs correctly, see Chapter 15.

> I **dance.** [action]
>
> The audience **became** silent. [occurrence]
>
> Your dancing **was** excellent. [state of being]

🛇 Alert:  If you're not sure whether a word is a verb, try substituting a different TENSE for the word. If the sentence still makes sense, the word is a verb.

**NO**    He is a **changed** man. He is a **will change** man. [*Changed* isn't a verb because the sentence doesn't make sense when *will change* is substituted.]

**YES**    The man **changed** his profession. The man **will change** his profession. [*Changed* is a verb because the sentence makes sense when the verb *will change* is substituted.] ●

# 14d   What is a verbal?

**Verbals** are verb parts functioning as NOUNS, ADJECTIVES, or ADVERBS. Quick Reference 14.3 lists the three different kinds of verbals.

---

### Quick Reference 14.3

■ ■ ■ ■ ■

#### Verbals and their functions

| | | |
|---|---|---|
| **INFINITIVE** *to* + verb | 1. noun<br>2. adjective or adverb | *To eat* now is inconvenient.<br>Still, we have far *to go.* |
| **PAST PARTICIPLE** *-ed* form of REGULAR VERB or equivalent in IRREGULAR VERB | adjective | *Boiled, filtered* water is safe. |
| **PRESENT PARTICIPLE** *-ing* form of verb | 1. noun (called a GERUND)<br>2. adjective | *Eating* in diners on the road is an adventure.<br>*Running* water may not be safe. |

---

⊕ **ESOL Tip:** For information about correctly using the verbals called *infinitives* and *gerunds* as objects, see Chapter 46. ●

## 14e What is an adjective?

**Adjectives** modify—that is, they describe or limit—NOUNS, PRONOUNS, and word groups that function as nouns. For information on how to use adjectives correctly, see Chapter 18.

> I saw a **green** tree. [*Green* modifies the noun *tree.*]

> It was **leafy.** [*Leafy* modifies the pronoun *it.*]

> The flowering trees were **beautiful.** [*Beautiful* modifies the noun phrase *the flowering trees.*]

⊕ **ESOL Tip:** You can identify some kinds of adjectives by looking at their endings. Usually, words with the SUFFIXES *-ful, -ish, -less,* and *-like* are adjectives. ●

**Determiners,** frequently called **limiting adjectives,** tell whether a noun is general (*a* tree) or specific (*the* tree). Determiners also tell which one (*this* tree), how many (*twelve* trees), whose (*our* tree), and similar information.

The determiners *a, an,* and *the* are almost always called **articles.** *The* is a **definite article.** Before a noun, *the* conveys that the noun refers to a specific item (*the* plan). *A* and *an* are **indefinite articles.** They convey that a noun refers to an item in a nonspecific or general way (*a* plan).

🔴 **Alert:** Use *a* when the word following it starts with a consonant: *a carrot, a broken egg, a hip.* Also, use *a* when the word following starts with an *h* that is sounded: *a historical event, a home.* Use *an* when the word following starts with a vowel sound: *an honor, an old bag, an egg.* ●

🌐 **ESOL Tip:** For information about using articles with COUNT and NONCOUNT NOUNS, and about articles with PROPER NOUNS and GERUNDS, see Chapter 46. ●

Quick Reference 14.4 lists kinds of determiners. Notice, however, that some words in Quick Reference 14.4 function also as pronouns. To identify a word's part of speech, always check to see how it functions in each particular sentence.

**That** car belongs to Harold. [*That* is a limiting adjective.]

**That** is Harold's car. [*That* is a demonstrative pronoun.]

---

### Quick Reference 14.4   ■ ■ ■ ■ ■

#### Determiners (or limiting adjectives)

| | |
|---|---|
| **ARTICLES** <br> *a, an, the* | *The news reporter used **a** cell phone to report **an** assignment.* |
| **DEMONSTRATIVE** <br> *this, these, that, those* | *Those students rent **that** house.* |
| **INDEFINITE** <br> *any, each, few, other, some,* and others | *Few films today have complex plots.* |
| **INTERROGATIVE** <br> *what, which, whose* | *What answer did you give?* |
| **NUMERICAL** <br> *one, first, two, second,* and others | *The **fifth** question was tricky.* |
| **POSSESSIVE** <br> *my, your, their,* and others | *My violin is older than **your** cello.* |
| **RELATIVE** <br> *what, which, whose, whatever,* and others | *We do not know **which** road to take.* |

---

## 14f   What is an adverb?

**Adverbs** modify—that is, adverbs describe or limit—VERBS, ADJECTIVES, other adverbs, and CLAUSES. For information on how to use adverbs correctly, see Chapter 18.

Chefs plan meals **carefully.** [*Carefully* modifies the verb *plan.*]

Vegetables provide **very** important vitamins. [*Very* modifies the adjective *important.*]

Those potato chips are **too** heavily salted. [*Too* modifies the adverb *heavily.*]

**Fortunately,** people are learning that overuse of salt is harmful. [*Fortunately* modifies the rest of the sentence, an independent clause.]

**Descriptive adverbs** show levels of intensity, usually by adding *more* (or *less*) and *most* (or *least*): *more* happily, *least* clearly (18e). Many descriptive adverbs are formed by adding *-ly* to adjectives: *sadly, loudly, normally*. But many adverbs do not end in *-ly: very, always, not, yesterday,* and *well* are a few. Some adjectives look like adverbs but are not: *brotherly, lonely, lovely*.

**Relative adverbs** are words such as *where, why,* and *when*. They are used to introduce ADJECTIVE CLAUSES.

**Conjunctive adverbs** modify—that is, conjunctive adverbs describe or limit—by creating logical connections to give words meaning. Conjunctive adverbs can appear anywhere in a sentence: at the start, in the middle, or at the end. Quick Reference 14.5 lists the kinds of relationships that conjunctive adverbs can show.

---

**Quick Reference 14.5** ■ ■ ■ ■ ■

### Conjunctive adverbs and relationships they express

| Relationship | Words |
|---|---|
| ADDITION | *also, furthermore, moreover, besides* |
| CONTRAST | *however, still, nevertheless, conversely, nonetheless, instead, otherwise* |
| COMPARISON | *similarly, likewise* |
| RESULT OR SUMMARY | *therefore, thus, consequently, accordingly, hence, then* |
| TIME | *next, then, meanwhile, finally, subsequently* |
| EMPHASIS | *indeed, certainly* |

---

# 14g What is a preposition?

**Prepositions** are words that convey relationships, usually in time or space. Common prepositions include *in, under, by, after, to, on, over,* and *since*. A PREPOSITIONAL PHRASE consists of a preposition and the words it modifies. For information about prepositions and commas, see 24k.

**In the fall,** we will hear a concert **by our favorite tenor.**

**After the concert,** he will fly **to San Francisco.**

⊕ **ESOL Tip:** For a list of prepositions and the IDIOMS they create, see Chapter 53. ●

## 14h What is a conjunction?

A **conjunction** connects words, PHRASES, or CLAUSES. **Coordinating conjunctions** join two or more grammatically equal words, phrases, or clauses. Quick Reference 14.6 lists the coordinating conjunctions and the relationships they express.

> We hike **and** camp every summer. [*And* joins two words.]
>
> We hike along scenic trails **or** in the wilderness. [*Or* joins two phrases.]
>
> I love the outdoors, **but** my family does not. [*But* joins two independent clauses.]

### Quick Reference 14.6 ■ ■ ■ ■ ■

#### Coordinating conjunctions and relationships they express

| Relationship | Words |
|---|---|
| ADDITION | *and* |
| CONTRAST | *but, yet* |
| RESULT OR EFFECT | *so* |
| REASON OR CAUSE | *for* |
| CHOICE | *or* |
| NEGATIVE CHOICE | *nor* |

**Correlative conjunctions** are two conjunctions that work as a pair: *both . . . and; either . . . or; neither . . . nor; not only . . . but (also); whether . . . or;* and *not . . . so much as.* For example, ***Not only*** *students* ***but also*** *businesspeople should study a second language.* **Subordinating conjunctions** introduce DEPENDENT CLAUSES. Subordinating conjunctions express relationships making the dependent clause in a sentence grammatically less important than the INDEPENDENT CLAUSE in the sentence. Quick Reference 14.7 lists the most common subordinating conjunctions. For information about how to use them correctly, see 9d through 9m.

## 14i What is an interjection?

An **interjection** is a word or expression that conveys surprise or a strong emotion. Alone, an interjection is usually punctuated with an exclamation

## Quick Reference 14.7

■ ■ ■ ■ ■

### Subordinating conjunctions and relationships they express

| Relationship | Words |
|---|---|
| TIME | *after, before, once, since, until, when, whenever, while* |
| REASON OR CAUSE | *as, because, since* |
| RESULT OR EFFECT | *in order that, so, so that, that* |
| CONDITION | *if, even if, provided that, unless* |
| CONTRAST | *although, even though, though, whereas* |
| LOCATION | *where, wherever* |
| CHOICE | *than, whether* |

point (!). As part of a sentence, an interjection is usually set off by one or more commas.

**Hooray!** I won the race.

**Oh,** my friends missed seeing the finish.

**EXERCISE 14-2** Identify the part of speech of each numbered and underlined word. Choose from noun, pronoun, verb, adjective, adverb, preposition, coordinating conjunction, correlative conjunction, and subordinating conjunction. For help, consult 14a through 14h.

The Mason-Dixon line <u>primarily</u>¹ marks the <u>boundary</u>² between Pennsylvania and Maryland. It was surveyed in the <u>eighteenth</u>³ century by Charles Mason and Jeremiah Dixon, who had <u>previously</u>⁴ worked together on a <u>scientific</u>⁵ expedition to South Africa.

In 1760, the Calverts of Maryland and the Penns of Pennsylvania <u>hired</u>⁶ Mason and Dixon to settle a <u>boundary</u>⁷ dispute between their parcels <u>of</u>⁸ land. Mason and Dixon <u>marked</u>⁹ their line every <u>five</u>¹⁰ miles using <u>stones</u>¹¹ shipped from England, which are called crownstones. These markers were decorated with two coats-of-arms and can still be found scattered <u>throughout</u>¹² this part of the country.

          13              14                      15

Even though Mason and Dixon were British, they had very different

backgrounds. Mason was the son of a baker and trained in astronomy. Dixon

               16

was a Quaker, and he specialized in surveying.

                                17         18

    The line they drew in America eventually became a symbolic division

19                          20                                21

between free states and slave states until the end of the Civil War. Because of

                22                          23

the line's importance, it has been the focus of both literature and music, such

          24

as the song "Sailing to Philadelphia" by Mark Knopfler.

## SENTENCE STRUCTURES

## 14j  What are a subject and a predicate in a sentence?

The **subject** and **predicate** of a sentence are its two essential parts. Without both, a group of words isn't a sentence. Quick Reference 14.8 shows the sentence pattern with both. Terms used in the Quick Reference are defined after it.

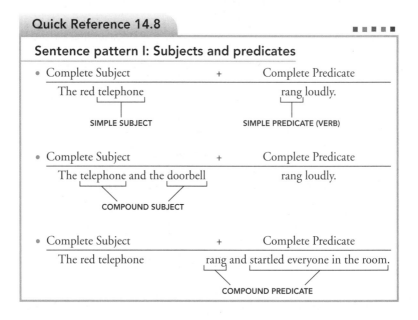

**Quick Reference 14.8**    ■ ■ ■ ■ ■

| Sentence pattern I: Subjects and predicates |
| --- |

- Complete Subject    +    Complete Predicate

    The red telephone        rang loudly.
    SIMPLE SUBJECT        SIMPLE PREDICATE (VERB)

- Complete Subject    +    Complete Predicate

    The telephone and the doorbell    rang loudly.
    COMPOUND SUBJECT

- Complete Subject    +    Complete Predicate

    The red telephone    rang and startled everyone in the room.
    COMPOUND PREDICATE

The **simple subject** is the word or group of words that acts, is described, or is acted upon.

The **telephone** rang. [Simple subject, *telephone*, acts.]

The **telephone** is red. [Simple subject, *telephone*, is described.]

The **telephone** was being connected. [Simple subject, *telephone*, is acted upon.]

The **complete subject** is the simple subject and its MODIFIERS.

**The red telephone** rang.

A **complete compound subject** consists of two or more NOUNS or PRONOUNS and their modifiers.

**The telephone and the doorbell** rang.

The **predicate** contains the VERB in the sentence. The predicate tells what the subject is doing or experiencing or what is being done to the subject.

The telephone **rang.** [*Rang* tells what the subject, *telephone*, did.]

The telephone **is** red. [*Is* tells what the subject, *telephone*, experiences.]

The telephone **was being connected.** [*Was being connected* tells what was being done to the subject, *telephone*.]

A **simple predicate** contains only the verb.

The lawyer **listened.**

A **complete predicate** contains the verb and its modifiers.

The lawyer **listened carefully.**

A **compound predicate** contains two or more verbs.

The lawyer **listened and waited.**

**ESOL Tips:** (1) The subject of a declarative sentence usually comes before the predicate, but there are exceptions (9o). In sentences that ask a question, part of the predicate usually comes before the subject. For more information about word order in English sentences, see Chapter 44. (2) In English, don't add a PERSONAL PRONOUN to repeat the stated noun.

**NO**   My **grandfather he** lived to be eighty-seven. [The personal pronoun, *he*, mistakenly repeats the stated noun, *grandfather*.]

**YES**   My **grandfather** lived to be eighty-seven.

**NO**     **Winter storms** that bring ice, sleet, and snow **they** can cause traffic problems. [The personal pronoun, *they,* mistakenly repeats the stated noun, *winter storms.*]

**YES**    **Winter storms** that bring ice, sleet, and snow can cause traffic problems. ●

# 14k   What are direct and indirect objects?

A **direct object** is a noun, pronoun, or group of words acting as a noun that receives the action of a TRANSITIVE VERB. To check for a direct object, make up a *whom?* or *what?* question about the verb.

An **indirect object** is a noun, pronoun, or group of words acting as a noun that tells *to whom* or *for whom* the action expressed by a transitive verb was done. To check for an indirect object, make up a ***to whom? for whom? to what?*** or ***for*** *what?* question about the verb.

Direct objects and indirect objects always fall in the PREDICATE of a sentence. Quick Reference 14.9 shows how direct and indirect objects function in sentences.

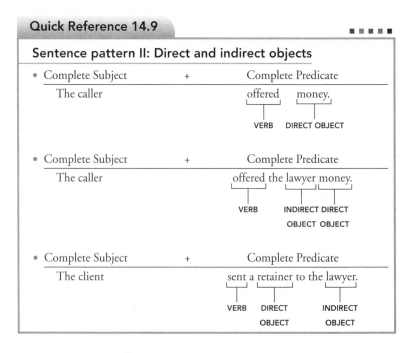

## Quick Reference 14.9     ■ ■ ■ ■ ■

### Sentence pattern II: Direct and indirect objects

- Complete Subject     +     Complete Predicate

  The caller                    offered    money.

                              VERB    DIRECT OBJECT

- Complete Subject     +     Complete Predicate

  The caller                    offered the lawyer money.

                         VERB     INDIRECT DIRECT

                                    OBJECT OBJECT

- Complete Subject     +     Complete Predicate

  The client                  sent a retainer to the lawyer.

                       VERB    DIRECT        INDIRECT

                                OBJECT       OBJECT

**EXERCISE 14-3**    Draw a single line under all direct objects and a double line under all indirect objects. For help, consult 14k.

EXAMPLE    Toni Morrison's award-winning novels give <u>readers</u> the <u>gifts</u> of wisdom, inspiration, and pleasure.

1. Literary critics gave high praise to Toni Morrison for her first novel, *The Bluest Eye,* but the general public showed little interest.

2. *Song of Solomon* won Morrison the National Book Critics Circle Award in 1977, and *Beloved* won her the Pulitzer Prize in 1988.

3. A literary panel awarded Toni Morrison the 1993 Nobel Prize in Literature, the highest honor a writer can receive.

4. Her 1998 novel, *Paradise,* traces for readers the tragic lives of a rejected group of former slaves.

5. Twenty-five years after *The Bluest Eye* was published, Oprah Winfrey selected it for her reader's list, and it immediately became a bestseller.

# 14l    What are complements, modifiers, and appositives?

A **complement** renames or describes a subject or an object. It appears in the predicate of a sentence.

A **subject complement** is a NOUN, PRONOUN, or ADJECTIVE that follows a LINKING VERB. **Predicate nominative** is another term for a noun used as a subject complement, and **predicate adjective** is another term for an adjective used as a subject complement.

An **object complement** follows a DIRECT OBJECT and either describes or renames the direct object. Quick Reference 14.10 shows how subject and object complements function in a sentence.

## Quick Reference 14.10    ■ ■ ■ ■ ■

### Sentence pattern III: Complements

- Complete Subject         +         Complete Predicate

  The caller                          was a student.

  LINKING    SUBJECT
  VERB    COMPLEMENT

- Complete Subject         +         Complete Predicate

  The student                         called himself a victim.

  VERB    DIRECT    OBJECT
  OBJECT    COMPLEMENT

A **modifier** is a word or group of words that describes or limits other words. Modifiers appear in the subject or the predicate of a sentence.

> The **large red** telephone rang. [The adjectives *large* and *red* modify the noun *telephone*.]

> The lawyer answered **quickly.** [The adverb *quickly* modifies the verb *answered.*]

> The person **on the telephone** was **extremely** upset. [The prepositional phrase *on the telephone* modifies the noun *person;* the adverb *extremely* modifies the adjective *upset.*]

> **Therefore,** the lawyer spoke **gently.** [The adverb *therefore* modifies the independent clause *the lawyer spoke gently;* the adverb *gently* modifies the verb *spoke.*]

> **Because the lawyer's voice was calm,** the caller felt reassured. [The adverb clause *because the lawyer's voice was calm* modifies the independent clause *the caller felt reassured.*]

An **appositive** is a word or group of words that renames the noun or pronoun preceding it.

> The student's story, **a tale of broken promises,** was complicated. [The appositive *a tale of broken promises* renames the noun *story.*]

> The lawyer consulted an expert, **her law professor.** [The appositive *her law professor* renames the noun *expert.*]

> The student, **Joe Jones,** asked to speak to his lawyer. [The appositive *Joe Jones* renames the noun *student.*]

🛈 **Alert:** When an appositive is not essential for identifying what it renames (that is, when it is NONRESTRICTIVE), use a comma or commas to set off the appositive from the rest of the sentence; see 24f. ●

# **14m** What is a phrase?

A **phrase** is a group of words that does not contain both a SUBJECT and a PREDICATE and therefore cannot stand alone as an independent unit.

A **noun phrase** functions as a noun in a sentence: *The **modern census** dates back to the seventeenth century.*

A **verb phrase** functions as a verb in a sentence: *Two military censuses **are mentioned** in the Bible.*

A **prepositional phrase** always starts with a preposition and functions as a modifier: *William the Conqueror conducted a census **of landowners in newly conquered England in 1086.***

An **absolute phrase** usually contains a noun or pronoun and a present or past participle. An absolute phrase modifies the entire sentence that it's in: ***Censuses being the fashion,*** *Quebec and Nova Scotia took sixteen counts between 1665 and 1754.*

A **verbal phrase** contains a verb part that functions not as a verb, but as a noun or an adjective. Such cases are infinitives, present participles, and past participles.

In 1624, Virginia began **to count its citizens** in a census. [*To count its citizens* is an infinitive phrase.]

**Going from door to door,** census takers interview millions of people. [*Going from door to door* is a present participial phrase.]

**Amazed by some people's answers,** census takers always listen carefully. [*Amazed by some people's answers* is a past participial phrase.]

A **gerund phrase** functions as a noun. Telling the difference between a gerund phrase and a present participial phrase can be tricky because both use the *-ing* verb form. The key is to determine how the phrase functions in the sentence: A gerund phrase functions only as a noun, and a participial phrase functions only as a modifier.

**Including each person in the census** was important. [This is a gerund phrase because it functions as a noun, which is the subject of the sentence.]

**Including each person in the census,** Abby spent many hours on the crowded city block. [This is a present participial phrase because it functions as a modifier, namely, an adjective describing Abby.]

**EXERCISE 14-4**   Combine each set of sentences into a single sentence by converting one sentence into a phrase—a noun phrase, verb phrase, prepositional phrase, absolute phrase, verbal phrase, or gerund phrase. You can omit, add, or change words. Identify which type of phrase you created.

You can combine most sets in several correct ways, but make sure the meaning of your finished sentence is clear. For help, consult 14m.

EXAMPLE   Large chain stores often pose threats to local independent retailers. Smaller store owners must find innovative ways to stay in business.

*With large chains posing threats to local independent retailers, smaller store owners must find innovative ways to stay in business.* (prepositional phrase)

1. Independent stores develop creative marketing strategies to compete with chain stores. Independent stores figure out ways to offer special features.

2. One independent children's bookstore attracted new customers. It did that by bringing live animals into the store.

3. Animals are popular with children. The store purchased two pet chickens, plus tarantulas, rats, cats, and fish.

4. This children's bookstore did not need to lower prices to draw customers. The store could survive by owning animals that appeal to youngsters.

5. Other sorts of independent stores sometimes take a slightly different approach. They compete by offering better service than the large chain stores can.

# 14n   What is a clause?

A **clause** is a group of words with both a SUBJECT and a PREDICATE. Clauses can be either *independent clauses,* also called *main clauses,* or *dependent clauses,* also called *subordinate clauses.*

An **independent clause** contains a subject and a predicate and can stand alone as a sentence. Quick Reference 14.11 shows the basic pattern.

| Quick Reference 14.11 | | ▪ ▪ ▪ ▪ ▪ |
| --- | --- | --- |
| **Sentence pattern IV: Independent clauses** | | |
| | Independent Clause | |
| • Complete Subject | + | Complete Predicate |
| The telephone | | rang. |

A **dependent clause** contains a subject and a predicate but can't stand alone as a sentence. To be part of a complete sentence, a dependent clause must be joined to an independent clause. Dependent clauses are either *adverb clauses* or *adjective clauses.*

An **adverb clause,** also called a *subordinate clause,* starts with a subordinating conjunction, such as *although, because, when,* or *until.* A subordinating conjunction expresses a relationship between a dependent clause and an independent clause; see Quick Reference 14.7 in section 14h. Adverb clauses usually answer some question about the independent clause: How? Why? When? Under what circumstances?

> **If the bond issue passes,** the city will install sewers. [The adverb clause modifies the verb phrase *will install;* it explains under what circumstances.]

> They are drawing up plans **as quickly as they can.** [The adverb clause modifies the verb phrase *drawing up;* it explains how.]

The homeowners feel happier **because they know the flooding will soon be better controlled.** [The adverb clause modifies the entire independent clause; it explains why.]

❗**Alert:** When you write an adverb clause before an independent clause, separate the clauses with a comma; see 24c. ●

An **adjective clause,** also called a *relative clause,* starts with a relative pronoun, such as *who, which,* or *that.* Or an adjective clause can start with a relative adverb, such as *when* or *where.* An adjective clause modifies the noun or pronoun that it follows. Quick Reference 14.12 shows how adverb and adjective clauses function in sentences.

---

## Quick Reference 14.12 ■ ■ ■ ■ ■

### Sentence pattern V: Dependent clauses

• Dependent (Adverb) Clause     +     Independent Clause

  Although    the hour    was quite late,    the telephone rang.

  SUBORDINATING   COMPLETE    COMPLETE         COMPLETE   COMPLETE
  CONJUNCTION     SUBJECT     PREDICATE        SUBJECT    PREDICATE

• First Part of              Dependent              Second Part of
  Independent Clause  +   (Adjective) Clause  +  Independent Clause

  The red telephone,  which belonged to Ms. Smythe,  rang loudly.

  COMPLETE            RELATIVE                        COMPLETE
  SUBJECT            PRONOUN                          PREDICATE

---

The car **that Jack bought** is practical. [The adjective clause describes the noun *car; that* is a relative pronoun referring to *car.*]

The day **when I can buy my own car** is getting closer. [The adjective clause modifies the noun *day; when* is a relative adverb referring to *day.*]

Use *who, whom, whoever, whomever,* and *whose* when an adjective clause refers to a person or to an animal with a name.

The Smythes, **who collect cars,** are wealthy.

Their dog Bowser, **who is large and loud,** has been spoiled.

Use *which* or *that* when an adjective clause refers to a thing or to an animal that isn't a pet. Sometimes, writers omit *that* from an adjective clause. For grammatical analysis, however, consider the omitted *that* to be implied and, therefore, present.

For help in deciding whether to use *that* or *which*, see Quick Reference 16.4 in section 16s.

⚠ **Alert:** When an adjective clause is NONRESTRICTIVE, use *which* and set it off from the independent clause with commas. Don't use commas with *that* in a RESTRICTIVE CLAUSE.

> My car, **which** I bought used, needs major repairs. [The adjective clause is nonrestrictive, so it begins with *which* and is set off with commas.]

> The car **that** I want to buy has a CD player. [The adjective clause uses *that* and is restrictive, so it is not set off with commas.] ●

**Noun clauses** function as nouns. Noun clauses can begin with many of the same words that begin adjective clauses: *that, who, which,* and their derivatives, as well as *when, where, whether, why,* and *how.*

> **Promises** are not always dependable. [noun]

> **What politicians promise** is not always dependable. [noun clause]

> The electorate often cannot figure out the **truth.** [noun]

> The electorate often cannot know **that the truth is being manipulated.** [noun clause]

Because they start with similar words, noun clauses and adjective clauses are sometimes confused with each other. The way to tell them apart is that the word starting an adjective clause has an ANTECEDENT, while the word starting a noun clause doesn't.

> Good politicians understand **whom they must please.** [Noun clause; *whom* does not have an antecedent.]

> Good politicians **who make promises** know all cannot be kept. [Adjective clause modifies *politicians*, which is the antecedent of *who*.]

🌐 **ESOL Tip:** Noun clauses in INDIRECT QUESTIONS are phrased as statements, not questions: *Kara asked why we needed the purple dye.* Don't phrase a noun clause this way: *Kara asked why **did** [or **do**] we need the purple dye?* If you prefer to change to a DIRECT QUESTION, usually VERB TENSE, PRONOUN, and other changes are necessary; see 22e. ●

In an **elliptical clause,** one or more words are deliberately left out for conciseness. For an elliptical clause to be correct, the one or more words you leave out need to be identical to those already appearing in the clause.

Engineering is one of the majors **[that] she considered.** [*that*, functioning as a relative pronoun, omitted from adjective clause]

She decided **[that] she would rather major in management.** [*that*, functioning as a conjunction, omitted between clauses]

**After [he takes] a refresher course,** he will be eligible for a raise. [subject and verb omitted from adverb clause]

Broiled fish tastes better **than boiled fish [tastes].** [second half of the comparison omitted]

**EXERCISE 14-5**   Use subordinate conjunctions and relative pronouns from the list below to combine each pair of sentences. You may use words more than once, but try to use as many different ones as possible. Some sentence pairs may be combined in several ways. Create at least one elliptical construction.

| since | which | if | after | when | as |
|---|---|---|---|---|---|
| although | so that | unless | because | even though | that |

EXAMPLE    Bluegrass music is associated with American South. It has roots in Irish and Scottish folk music.

*Even though it has roots in Irish and Scottish folk music,* bluegrass is associated with the American South.

1. Certain aspects of jazz seem to have influenced bluegrass. It involves players of an instrumental ensemble improvising around a standard melody.

2. However, the instruments used in jazz are very different than those played in bluegrass. This style of music usually uses a banjo, fiddle, mandolin, and a dobro.

3. The singing in bluegrass involves tight harmonies and a tenor lead singer. People who listen closely to the vocal arrangements can hear this.

4. Bill Monroe, the founder of bluegrass, added banjo player Earl Scruggs to his band, the Blue Grass Boys. This allowed him to produce a fuller sound.

5. The Blue Grass Boys went into the studio in 1945 to record some songs for Columbia Records. They hit the charts with "Kentucky Waltz" and "Footprints in the Snow."

# 14o   What are the four sentence types?

English uses four **sentence types:** simple, compound, complex, and compound complex. A **simple sentence** is composed of a single INDEPENDENT CLAUSE and no DEPENDENT CLAUSES.

Charlie Chaplin was born in London on April 16, 1889.

A **compound sentence** is composed of two or more independent clauses. These clauses may be connected by a COORDINATING CONJUNCTION (*and, but, for, or, nor, yet, so*), a semicolon alone, or a semicolon and a CONJUNCTIVE ADVERB.

His father died early, **and** his mother spent time in mental hospitals.

Many people enjoy Chaplin films; others do not.

Many people enjoy Chaplin films; **however,** others do not.

A **complex sentence** is composed of one independent clause and one or more dependent clauses.

**When times were bad,** Chaplin lived in the streets. [dependent clause starting *when*; independent clause starting *Chaplin*]

**When Chaplin was performing with a troupe that was touring the United States,** he was hired by Mack Sennett, **who owned the Keystone Company.** [dependent clause starting *when*; dependent clause starting *that*; independent clause starting *he*; dependent clause starting *who*]

A **compound-complex sentence** integrates a compound sentence and a complex sentence. It contains two or more independent clauses and one or more dependent clauses.

Chaplin's comedies were immediately successful, and he became rich **because he was enormously popular for playing the Little Tramp, who was loved for his tiny mustache, baggy trousers, big shoes, and trick derby.** [independent clause starting *Chaplin's*; independent clause starting *he*; dependent clause starting *because*; dependent clause starting *who*]

**When studios could no longer afford him,** Chaplin co-founded United Artists, and then he produced and distributed his own films. [dependent clause starting *when*; independent clause starting *Chaplin*; independent clause starting *then*]

🎯 **Alerts:** (1) Use a comma before a coordinating conjunction connecting two independent clauses; see 24b. (2) When independent clauses are long or contain commas, use a subordinating conjunction—or use a semicolon to connect the sentences; see 25d. ●

**EXERCISE 14-6**  Decide whether each of the following sentences is simple, compound, complex, or compound-complex. For help, consult 14o.

EXAMPLE  Many people would love to eat a healthy meal at a fast-food restaurant or a food concession at the movies. (*simple*)

1. Fast-food restaurants and healthy meals rarely go together.

2. A fried-chicken sandwich packs an enormous number of calories and fat, and a fried-fish sandwich is no better.

3. A double cheeseburger with bacon at a fast-food restaurant can contain over 1,000 calories and 80 grams of fat, but a plain burger reduces the unhealthy overload considerably.

4. You can purchase other relatively healthy meals at a fast-food restaurant, if you first get to know the chart of nutritional values provided for customers.

5. Even though US government regulations require that nutritional charts be posted on the wall in the public areas of every fast-food restaurant, consumers often ignore the information, and they choose main meals and side dishes with the most flavor, calories, and fat.

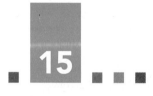

# Verbs

## 15a What do verbs do?

A **verb** expresses an action, an occurrence, or a state of being.

Many people **overeat** on Thanksgiving. [action]

Mother's Day **fell** early this year. [occurrence]

Memorial Day **is** tomorrow. [state of being]

Verbs also reveal when something occurs—in the present, the past, or the future. Verbs convey other information as well; see Quick Reference 15.1. For types of verbs, see Quick Reference 15.2.

## Quick Reference 15.1 ▪ ▪ ▪ ▪ ▪

### Information that verbs convey

| | |
|---|---|
| **PERSON** | First person (the speaker: *I dance*), second person (the one spoken to: ***you** dance*), or third person (the one spoken about: ***the man** dances*). |
| **NUMBER** | Singular (one) or plural (more than one). |
| **TENSE** | Past (*we **danced***), present (*we **dance***), or future (*we **will dance***); see 15g through 15k. |
| **MOOD** | Moods are indicative (*we dance*), imperative (commands and polite requests: *Dance*), or conditional (speculation, wishes: *if we were dancing . . .*); see 15l and 15m. |
| **VOICE** | Active voice or passive voice; see 15n through 15p. |

## Quick Reference 15.2 ▪ ▪ ▪ ▪ ▪

### Types of verbs

| | |
|---|---|
| **MAIN VERB** | The word in a PREDICATE that says something about the SUBJECT: *She **danced** for the group.* |
| **AUXILIARY VERB** | A verb that combines with a main verb to convey information about TENSE, MOOD, or VOICE (15e). The verbs *be, do,* and *have* can be auxiliary verbs or main verbs. The verbs *can, could, may, might, should, would, must,* and others are MODAL AUXILIARY VERBS. They add shades of meaning such as ability or possibility to verbs: *She **might dance** again.* |
| **LINKING VERB** | The verb that links a subject to a COMPLEMENT, a word or words that rename or describe the subject: *She **was** happy dancing. Be* is the most common linking verb; sometimes sense verbs (*smell, taste*) or verbs of perception (*seem, feel*) function as linking verbs. See also Quick Reference 15.3. |
| **TRANSITIVE VERB** | The verb followed by a DIRECT OBJECT that completes the verb's message: *They **sent** her a fan letter.* |
| **INTRANSITIVE VERB** | A verb that does not require a direct object: *Yesterday she **danced**.* |

Linking verbs are main verbs that indicate a state of being or a condition. They link a SUBJECT with one or more words that rename or describe the subject, called a SUBJECT COMPLEMENT. A linking verb is like an equal sign between a subject and its complement. Quick Reference 15.3 shows how linking verbs function in sentences.

---

### Quick Reference 15.3    ■ ■ ■ ■ ■

**Linking verbs**

- Linking verbs may be forms of the verb *be* (*am, is, was, were;* see 15e for a complete list).

  | George Washington | *was* | president. |
  |---|---|---|
  | SUBJECT | LINKING VERB | COMPLEMENT (PREDICATE NOMINATIVE: RENAMES SUBJECT) |

- Linking verbs may deal with the senses (*look, smell, taste, sound, feel*).

  | George Washington | *sounded* | confident. |
  |---|---|---|
  | SUBJECT | LINKING VERB | COMPLEMENT (PREDICATE ADJECTIVE DESCRIBES SUBJECT) |

- Linking verbs can be verbs that convey a sense of existing or becoming—*appear, seem, become, get, grow, turn, remain, stay,* and *prove,* for example.

  | George Washington | *grew* | old. |
  |---|---|---|
  | SUBJECT | LINKING VERB | COMPLEMENT (PREDICATE ADJECTIVE DESCRIBES SUBJECT) |

- To test whether a verb other than a form of *be* is functioning as a linking verb, substitute *was* (for a singular subject) or *were* (for a plural subject) for the original verb. If the sentence makes sense, the original verb is functioning as a linking verb.

  **NO**  George Washington *grew* a beard → George Washington *was* a beard. [*Grew* is not functioning as a linking verb.]

  **YES**  George Washington *grew* old → George Washington *was* old. [*Grew* is functioning as a linking verb.]

---

## VERB FORMS

# 15b  What are the forms of main verbs?

A **main verb** names an action (*People **dance***), an occurrence (*Christmas **comes** once a year*), or a state of being (*It **will be** warm tomorrow*). Every main verb has five forms.

- The **simple form** conveys an action, occurrence, or state of being taking place in the present (*I laugh*) or, with an AUXILIARY VERB, in the future (*I will laugh*).

- The **past-tense form** conveys an action, occurrence, or state completed in the past (*I laughed*). REGULAR VERBS add *-ed* or *-d* to the simple form. IRREGULAR VERBS vary (see Quick Reference 15.4 for a list of common irregular verbs).

- The **past participle form** in regular verbs uses the same form as the past tense. Irregular verbs vary; see Quick Reference 15.4. To function as a verb, a past participle must combine with a SUBJECT and one or more auxiliary verbs (*I have laughed*). Otherwise, past participles function as ADJECTIVES (*crumbled cookies*).

- The **present participle form** adds *-ing* to the simple form (*laughing*). To function as a verb, a present participle combines with a subject and one or more auxiliary verbs (*I was laughing*). Otherwise, present participles function as adjectives (*my laughing friends*) or as NOUNS (*Laughing is healthy*).

- The **infinitive** usually consists of *to* and the simple form following *to* (*I started to laugh at his joke*); see 16i. The infinitive functions as a noun or an adjective, not a verb.

**ESOL Tip:** When verbs function as other parts of speech, they're called VERBALS. Verbals are INFINITIVES, PRESENT PARTICIPLES, and PAST PARTICIPLES. When present participles function as nouns, they're called GERUNDS. For information about using gerunds and infinitives as OBJECTS after certain verbs, see Chapter 46. ●

## 15c  What is the -s, or -es, form of a verb?

The *-s* **form of a verb** is the third-person singular in the PRESENT TENSE. The ending *-s* (or *-es*) is added to the verb's SIMPLE FORM (*smell* becomes *smells,* as in *The bread smells delicious*).

*Be* and *have* are irregular verbs. For the third-person singular, present tense, *be* uses *is* and *have* uses *has.*

The cheesecake **is** popular.

The éclair **has** chocolate icing.

Even if you tend to drop the *-s* or *-es* ending when you speak, always use it when you write. Proofread carefully to make sure you haven't omitted any *-s* forms.

⚠ **Alert:** In informal speech, the LINKING, or *copula,* VERB *to be* sometimes doesn't change forms in the present tense. However, ACADEMIC WRITING requires you to use standard third-person singular forms in the present tense.

He **is** [not *be*] hungry.

The bakery **has** [not *have*] fresh bread. ●

**EXERCISE 15-1**    Rewrite each sentence, changing the subjects to the word or words given in parentheses. Change the form of the verbs shown in italics to match the new subject. Keep all sentences in the present tense. For help, consult 15c.

EXAMPLE    The Oregon giant earthworm *escapes* all attempts at detection. (Oregon giant earthworms)

*Oregon giant earthworms escape* all attempts at detection.

1. Before declaring the Oregon giant earthworm a protected species, US government agencies *require* concrete proof that it *is* not extinct. (a government agency) (they)

2. A scientist who *finds* one alive will demonstrate that Oregon giant earthworms *do* still exist, in spite of no one's having seen any for over twenty years. (Scientists) (the Oregon giant earthworm)

3. Last seen in the Willamette Valley near Portland, Oregon, the earthworms *are* white, and they *smell* like lilies. (the earthworm) (it)

4. Oregon giant earthworms *grow* up to three feet long. (The Oregon giant earthworm)

5. A clump of soil with a strange shape *indicates* that the giant creatures *continue* to live, but to demonstrate that they *are* not extinct, only a real specimen will do. (clumps of soil) (creature) (it)

## 15d    What is the difference between regular and irregular verbs?

A **regular verb** forms its PAST TENSE and PAST PARTICIPLE by adding *-ed* or *-d* to the SIMPLE FORM: *type, typed; cook, cooked; work, worked.* Most verbs in English are regular.

In informal speech, some people skip over the *-ed* sound, pronouncing it softly or not at all. In ACADEMIC WRITING, however, you're required to use it. If you're not used to hearing or pronouncing this sound, proofread carefully to see that you have all the needed *-ed* endings in your writing.

**Irregular verbs,** in contrast, don't consistently add *-ed* or *-d* to form the past tense and past participle. Some irregular verbs change an internal vowel to make the past tense and past participle: *sing, sang, sung.* Some change an internal vowel and add an ending other than *-ed* or *-d: grow, grew, grown.* Some use the simple form throughout: *cost, cost, cost.* Unfortunately, a verb's simple form doesn't provide a clue about whether the verb is irregular or regular. Quick Reference 15.4 lists frequently used irregular verbs.

🛇 **Alert:** For information about changing *y* to *i,* or doubling a final consonant before adding the *-ed* ending, see 31d. ●

---

### Quick Reference 15.4   ■ ■ ■ ■ ■

#### Common irregular verbs

| Simple Form | Past Tense | Past Participle |
|---|---|---|
| arise | arose | arisen |
| awake | awoke *or* awaked | awaked *or* awoken |
| be (is, am, are) | was, were | been |
| beat | beat | beaten |
| become | became | become |
| begin | began | begun |
| bend | bent | bent |
| bite | bit | bitten *or* bit |
| blow | blew | blown |
| break | broke | broken |
| bring | brought | brought |
| build | built | built |
| burst | burst | burst |
| buy | bought | bought |
| catch | caught | caught |
| choose | chose | chosen |
| cling | clung | clung |
| come | came | come |
| cost | cost | cost |
| cut | cut | cut |
| deal | dealt | dealt |
| dig | dug | dug |
| dive | dived *or* dove | dived |
| do | did | done |
| draw | drew | drawn |
| drink | drank | drunk |
| drive | drove | driven |
| eat | ate | eaten |
| fall | fell | fallen |
| fight | fought | fought |
| find | found | found |

continued >>

## Quick Reference 15.4 (continued) ▪ ▪ ▪ ▪ ▪

| Simple Form | Past Tense | Past Participle |
|---|---|---|
| fly | flew | flown |
| forget | forgot | forgotten *or* forgot |
| freeze | froze | frozen |
| get | got | got *or* gotten |
| give | gave | given |
| go | went | gone |
| grow | grew | grown |
| hang ("to suspend")* | hung | hung |
| have | had | had |
| hear | heard | heard |
| hide | hid | hidden |
| hurt | hurt | hurt |
| keep | kept | kept |
| know | knew | known |
| lay | laid | laid |
| lead | led | led |
| lend | lent | lent |
| let | let | let |
| lie | lay | lain |
| light | lighted *or* lit | lighted *or* lit |
| lose | lost | lost |
| make | made | made |
| mean | meant | meant |
| prove | proved | proved *or* proven |
| read | read | read |
| ride | rode | ridden |
| ring | rang | rung |
| rise | rose | risen |
| run | ran | run |
| say | said | said |
| see | saw | seen |
| seek | sought | sought |
| send | sent | sent |
| set | set | set |
| shake | shook | shaken |
| shoot | shot | shot |
| show | showed | shown *or* showed |
| shrink | shrank | shrunk |
| sing | sang | sung |
| sink | sank *or* sunk | sunk |
| sit | sat | sat |
| slay | slew | slain |

continued >>

## Quick Reference 15.4    (continued)    ■ ■ ■ ■ ■

| Simple Form | Past Tense | Past Participle |
| --- | --- | --- |
| sleep | slept | slept |
| speak | spoke | spoken |
| spin | spun | spun |
| spring | sprang *or* sprung | sprung |
| stand | stood | stood |
| steal | stole | stolen |
| sting | stung | stung |
| stink | stank *or* stunk | stunk |
| strike | struck | struck |
| swear | swore | sworn |
| swim | swam | swum |
| swing | swung | swung |
| take | took | taken |
| teach | taught | taught |
| throw | threw | thrown |
| wake | woke *or* waked | waked *or* woken |
| wear | wore | worn |
| wring | wrung | wrung |
| write | wrote | written |

*When it means "to execute by hanging," *hang* is a regular verb: *In wartime, some armies routinely **hanged** deserters.*

**EXERCISE 15-2**    Write the correct past-tense form of the regular verbs given in parentheses. For help, consult 15d.

EXAMPLE    Native North Americans (invent) <u>invented</u> the game of lacrosse.

(1) Ancient lacrosse games (involve) _____ up to 1,000 men and (last) _____ the entire day. (2) Native Americans (play) _____ the game using balls they (create) _____ out of deerskin and wood. (3) Lacrosse (serve) _____ many purposes in tribal life as warriors (train) _____ for battle and (resolve) _____ conflicts. (4) French missionaries eventually (name) _____ the game "la crosse," perhaps referring to the staffs Jesuit bishops (use) _____. (5) Lacrosse (resemble) _____ the Irish sport hurling, so when Irish immigrants (arrive) _____ in America in the 19th century, they (help) _____ to make the game more popular.

**EXERCISE 15-3** Write the correct past-tense form of the irregular verbs given in parentheses. For help, consult Quick Reference 15.4 in 15d.

EXAMPLE In August, 1969, the Woodstock music festival (begin) <u>began</u> as thousands of fans (drive) <u>drove</u> to upstate New York for three days of music.

(1) The official name of the festival (is) _____ the Woodstock Music and Art Fair. (2) It (draw) _____ nearly half a million people to Max Yasgur's farm, which (stand) _____ in the small town of Bethel, New York. (3) The concert (have) _____ to move to Bethel at the last minute after residents of the town of Woodstock (forbid) _____ organizers to hold the festival in their town. (4) Those who (come) _____ to hear music were not disappointed, since several well known artists (sing) _____ to the large crowd. (5) Performers such as Jimi Hendrix, Santana, and Janis Joplin (lend) _____ their talents to the festival.

# 15e  What are auxiliary verbs?

**Auxiliary verbs,** also called *helping verbs,* combine with MAIN VERBS to make VERB PHRASES. Quick Reference 15.5 shows how auxiliary verbs work.

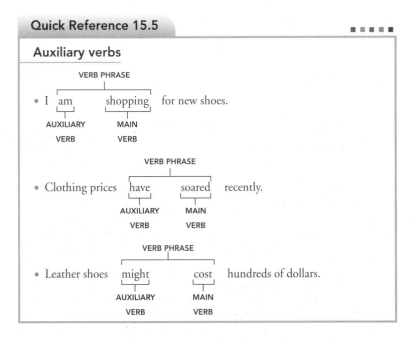

**Quick Reference 15.5**

**Auxiliary verbs**

- I am shopping for new shoes.
  - am = AUXILIARY VERB
  - shopping = MAIN VERB

- Clothing prices have soared recently.
  - have = AUXILIARY VERB
  - soared = MAIN VERB

- Leather shoes might cost hundreds of dollars.
  - might = AUXILIARY VERB
  - cost = MAIN VERB

## USING *BE, DO, HAVE*

The three most common auxiliary verbs are *be, do,* and *have*. These three verbs can also be main verbs. Their forms vary more than most irregular verbs, as Quick References 15.6 and 15.7 show.

---

### Quick Reference 15.6 ■ ■ ■ ■ ■

#### Forms of the verb *be*

| | |
|---|---|
| SIMPLE FORM | be |
| -*S* FORM | is |
| PAST TENSE | was, were |
| PRESENT PARTICIPLE | being |
| PAST PARTICIPLE | been |

| Person | Present Tense | Past Tense |
|---|---|---|
| I | am | was |
| you (singular) | are | were |
| he, she, it | is | was |
| we | are | were |
| you (plural) | are | were |
| they | are | were |

---

### Quick Reference 15.7 ■ ■ ■ ■ ■

#### Forms of the verbs *do* and *have*

| | | |
|---|---|---|
| SIMPLE FORM | do | have |
| -*S* FORM | does | has |
| PAST TENSE | did | had |
| PRESENT PARTICIPLE | doing | having |
| PAST PARTICIPLE | done | had |

---

🛈 **Alert:** In ACADEMIC WRITING, always use the standard forms for *be, do,* and *have,* as shown in Quick References 15.6 and 15.7.

The gym **is** [not *be*] a busy place.

The gym **is** [not *be*] filling with spectators. ●

🌐 **ESOL Tip:** When *be, do,* and *have* function as auxiliary verbs, change their form to agree with a third-person singular subject—and don't add *-s* to the main verb.

> **NO**  **Does** the library **closes** at 6:00?
>
> **YES**  **Does** the library **close** at 6:00? ●

#### MODAL AUXILIARY VERBS

*Can, could, shall, should, will, would, may, might,* and *must* are the nine modal auxiliary verbs. **Modal auxiliary verbs** communicate ability, permission, obligation, advisability, necessity, or possibility. They never change form.

> Exercise **can lengthen** lives. [possibility]
>
> She **can jog** for five miles. [ability]

🌐 **ESOL Tip:** For more about modal auxiliary verbs and the meanings they communicate, see Chapter 47. ●

## 15f What are intransitive and transitive verbs?

A verb is **intransitive** when an OBJECT isn't required to complete the verb's meaning: *I sing.* A verb is **transitive** when an object is necessary to complete the verb's meaning: *I need a guitar.* Many verbs have both transitive and intransitive meanings. Some verbs are only transitive: *need, have, like, owe, remember.* Only transitive verbs function in the PASSIVE VOICE. Dictionaries label verbs as transitive (*vt*) or intransitive (*vi*).

The verbs *lie* and *lay* are particularly confusing. *Lie* means "to recline, to place oneself down, or to remain." *Lie* is intransitive (it cannot be followed by an object). *Lay* means "to put something down." *Lay* is transitive (it must be followed by an object). As you can see in Quick Reference 15.8, the word *lay* is both the past tense of *lie* and the present-tense simple form of *lay.* That makes things difficult. Our best advice is memorize them. Yet truthfully, each time we use *lie* and *lay,* we need to pause, think, and recite the list to ourselves.

Two other verb pairs tend to confuse people because of their intransitive and transitive forms: *raise* and *rise* and *set* and *sit.*

*Raise* and *set* are transitive (they must be followed by an object). *Rise* and *sit* are intransitive (they cannot be followed by an object). Fortunately, although each word has a meaning different from the other words, they don't share forms: *raise, raised, raised; rise, rose, risen;* and *set, set, set; sit, sat, sat.*

---

**Quick Reference 15.8**   ▪ ▪ ▪ ▪ ▪

### Using *lie* and *lay*

|  | lie | lay |
|---|---|---|
| SIMPLE FORM | lie | lay |
| -S FORM | lies | lays |
| PAST TENSE | lay | laid |
| PRESENT PARTICIPLE | lying | laying |
| PAST PARTICIPLE | lain | laid |

**INTRANSITIVE FORMS**

| PRESENT TENSE | The hikers **lie** down to rest. |
|---|---|
| PAST TENSE | The hikers **lay** down to rest. |

**TRANSITIVE FORMS**

| PRESENT TENSE | The hikers **lay** their backpacks on a rock. [*Backpacks* is a direct object.] |
|---|---|
| PAST TENSE | The hikers **laid** their backpacks on a rock. [*Backpacks* is a direct object.] |

---

**EXERCISE 15-4**   Underline the correct word of each pair in parentheses. For help, consult 15f.

EXAMPLE   During the summer, Caroline enjoys (<u>lying</u>/laying) on the beach.

(1) One day, after (setting/sitting) her chair on the sand, Caroline (lay/laid) her blanket near her umbrella. (2) Worried about getting a sunburn, she (raised/rose) her umbrella and (lay/laid) under it. (3) After a brief nap, Caroline began (rising/raising) to her feet when she realized she had forgotten where she had (lain/laid) her cooler. (4) She soon found it (lying/laying) near her car, just where she had (sat/set) it earlier. (5) She decided to pick it up and (lie/lay) it down near where her blanket (lies/lays).

## VERB TENSE

# 15g   What is verb tense?

**Verb tense** conveys time. Verbs show tense (time) by changing form. English has six verb tenses, divided into simple and perfect groups. The three **simple tenses** divide time into present, past, and future. The simple **present tense**

describes what happens regularly, what takes place in the present, and what is consistently or generally true. The simple **past tense** tells of an action completed or a condition ended. The simple **future tense** indicates action yet to be taken or a condition not yet experienced.

Rick **wants** to speak Spanish fluently. [simple present tense]

Rick **wanted** to improve rapidly. [simple past tense]

Rick **will want** to progress even further next year. [simple future tense]

The three **perfect tenses** also divide time into present, past, and future. They show more complex time relationships than the simple tenses. For information on using the perfect tenses, see section 15i.

The three simple tenses and the three perfect tenses also have **progressive forms.** These forms indicate that the verb describes what is ongoing or continuing. For information on using progressive forms, see section 15j. Quick Reference 15.9 summarizes verb tenses and progressive forms.

## Quick Reference 15.9 ■ ■ ■ ■ ■

### Simple, perfect, and progressive tenses

**SIMPLE TENSES**

|  | Regular Verb | Irregular Verb | Progressive Form |
|---|---|---|---|
| **PRESENT** | I talk | I eat | I am talking; I am eating |
| **PAST** | I talked | I ate | I was talking; I was eating |
| **FUTURE** | I will talk | I will eat | I will be talking; I will be eating |

**PERFECT TENSES**

|  | Regular Verb | Irregular Verb | Progressive Form |
|---|---|---|---|
| **PRESENT PERFECT** | I have talked | I have eaten | I have been talking; I have been eating |
| **PAST PERFECT** | I had talked | I had eaten | I had been talking; I had been eating |
| **FUTURE PERFECT** | I will have talked | I will have eaten | I will have been talking; I will have been eating |

⊕ **ESOL Tip:** Quick Reference 15.9 shows that most verb tenses are formed by combining one or more AUXILIARY VERBS with the SIMPLE FORM, the PRESENT PARTICIPLE, or the PAST PARTICIPLE of a MAIN VERB. Auxiliary verbs are necessary in the formation of most tenses, so never omit them.

> **NO**  I **talking** to you.
>
> **YES**  I **am talking** to you. ●

## 15h How do I use the simple present tense?

The **simple present tense** uses the SIMPLE FORM of the verb (15b). It describes what happens regularly, what takes place in the present, and what is generally or consistently true. Also, it can convey a future occurrence with verbs like *start, stop, begin, end, arrive,* and *depart.*

> Calculus class **meets** every morning. [regularly occurring action]
>
> Mastering calculus **takes** time. [general truth]
>
> The course **ends** in eight weeks. [specific future event]

❗**Alert:** For a work of literature, always describe or discuss the action in the present tense. This holds true no matter how old the work.

> In Shakespeare's *Romeo and Juliet,* Juliet's father **wants** her to marry Paris, but Juliet **loves** Romeo. ●

## 15i How do I form and use the perfect tenses?

The **perfect tenses** generally describe actions or occurrences that are still having an effect at the present time or are having an effect until a specified time. The perfect tenses are composed of an AUXILIARY VERB and a main verb's PAST PARTICIPLE (15b).

For the **present perfect tense** (see Quick Reference 15.9), use *has* only for the third-person singular subjects and *have* for all other subjects. For the **past perfect,** use *had* with the past participle. For the **future perfect,** use *will have* with the past participle.

> **PRESENT PERFECT**  The drought **has created** terrible hardship. [having effect until a specified time—when the rains come]
>
> **PAST PERFECT**  As soon as the tornado **had passed,** the heavy rain started. [Both events occurred in the past; the tornado occurred before the rain, so the earlier event uses *had.*]

| | |
|---|---|
| **FUTURE PERFECT** | Our chickens' egg production **will have reached** five hundred per day by next year. [The event will occur before a specified time.] |

## 15j How do I form and use progressive forms?

**Progressive forms** describe an ongoing event, action, or condition. They also express habitual or recurring actions or conditions. The **present progressive** uses the present-tense form of *be* that agrees with the subject in PERSON and NUMBER, plus the *-ing* form (PRESENT PARTICIPLE) of the main verb. The **past progressive** uses *was* or *were* to agree with the subject in person and number, and it uses the present participle of the main verb. The **future progressive** uses *will be* and the present participle. The **present perfect progressive** uses *have been* or *has been* to agree with the subject, plus the *-ing* form of the main verb. The **past perfect progressive** uses *had been* and the *-ing* form of the main verb. The **future perfect progressive** uses *will have been* plus the PRESENT PARTICIPLE.

| | |
|---|---|
| **PRESENT PROGRESSIVE** | The smog **is stinging** everyone's eyes. [event taking place now] |
| **PAST PROGRESSIVE** | Eye drops **were selling** well last week. [event ongoing in the past within stated limits] |
| **FUTURE PROGRESSIVE** | We **will be ordering** more eye drops than usual this month. [recurring event that will take place in the future] |
| **PRESENT PERFECT PROGRESSIVE** | Scientists **have been warning** us about air pollution for years. [recurring event that took place in the past and may still take place] |
| **PAST PERFECT PROGRESSIVE** | We **had been ordering** three cases of eye drops a month until the smog worsened. [recurring past event that has now ended] |
| **FUTURE PERFECT PROGRESSIVE** | By May, we **will have been selling** eye drops for eight months. [ongoing condition to be completed at a specific time in the future] |

**EXERCISE 15-5** Underline the correct verb in each pair of parentheses. If more than one answer is possible, be prepared to explain the differences in meaning between the two choices. For help, consult 15g through 15j.

EXAMPLE    According to an article in *National Geographic News*, weird plants (are taking root, would have taken root) in ordinary backyards.

1. Some, smelling like spoiled meat, (will have ruined, are ruining) people's appetites.

2. Stalks similar to male anatomy (typify, are typifying) other examples.

3. *Shockingly large, black, carnivorous,* and *volatile* (describe, is describing) additional unusual plants.

4. Indeed, many unusual plants (live, lived) in places the world over today.

5. Many people now (are planting, planted) these weird items in their backyards.

# 15k   How do I use tense sequences accurately?

Verb **tense sequences** communicate time relationships. They help deliver messages about actions, occurrences, or states that take place at different times. Quick Reference 15.10 shows how tenses in the same sentence can vary depending on the timing of actions (or occurrences or states).

---

### Quick Reference 15.10    ■ ■ ■ ■ ■

#### Tense sequences

If your independent clause contains a simple-present-tense verb, then in your dependent clause you can

- use PRESENT TENSE to show same-time action:

    I **avoid** shellfish because I **am** allergic to it.

- use PAST TENSE to show earlier action:

    I **am** sure that I **deposited** the check.

- use the PRESENT PERFECT TENSE to show (1) a period of time extending from some point in the past to the present or (2) an indefinite past time:

    They **claim** that they **have visited** the planet Venus.

    I **believe** that I **have seen** that movie before.

- use the FUTURE TENSE for action to come:

    The book **is** open because I **will be reading** it later.

If your independent clause contains a past-tense verb, then in your dependent clause you can

- use the past tense to show another completed past action:

    I **closed** the door because you **told** me to.

continued >>

## Quick Reference 15.10 *(continued)* ▪ ▪ ▪ ▪ ▪

- use the PAST PERFECT TENSE to show earlier action:

   The sprinter **knew** that she **had broken** the record.

- use the present tense to state a general truth:

   Christopher Columbus **determined** that the world **is** round.

If your independent clause contains a present-perfect-tense or past-perfect-tense verb, then in your dependent clause you can

- use the past tense:

   The bread **has become** moldy since I **purchased** it.

   Sugar prices **had** already **declined** when artificial sweeteners first appeared.

If your independent clause contains a future-tense verb, then in your dependent clause you can

- use the present tense to show action happening at the same time:

   You **will be** rich if you **win** the prize.

- use the past tense to show earlier action:

   You **will** surely **win** the prize if you **remembered** to mail the entry form.

### TENSE SEQUENCES

- use the present perfect tense to show future action earlier than the action of the independent-clause verb:

   The river **will flood** again next year unless we **have built** a better dam by then.

If your independent clause contains a future-perfect-tense verb, then in your dependent clause you can

- use either the present tense or the present perfect tense:

   Dr. Chang **will have delivered** five thousand babies by the time she **retires**.

   Dr. Chang **will have delivered** five thousand baies by the time she **has retired**.

🚫 Alert: Never use a future-tense verb in a dependent clause when the verb in the independent clause is in the future tense. Instead, use a present-tense verb or present-perfect-tense verb in the dependent clause.

**NO**   The river **will flood** us unless we **will prepare** our defense.

**YES**   The river **will flood** us unless we **prepare** our defense. [*Prepare* is a present-tense verb.]

**YES**   The river **will flood** us unless we **have prepared** our defense. [*Have prepared* is a present-perfect-tense verb.] ●

Tense sequences may include INFINITIVES and PARTICIPLES. To name or describe an activity or occurrence coming either at the same time as the time expressed in the MAIN VERB or after, use the **present infinitive.**

> I **hope to buy** a used car. [*To buy* comes at a future time. *Hope* is the main verb, and its action is now.]

> I **hoped to buy** a used car. [*Hoped* is the main verb, and its action is over.]

> I **had hoped to buy** a used car. [*Had hoped* is the main verb, and its action is over.]

The PRESENT PARTICIPLE (a verb's -*ing* form) can describe action happening at the same time.

> **Driving** his new car, the man **smiled.** [The driving and the smiling happened at the same time.]

To describe an action that occurs before the action in the main verb, use the **perfect infinitive** (*to have gone, to have smiled*), the PAST PARTICIPLE, or the **present perfect participle** (*having gone, having smiled*).

> Candida **claimed to have written** fifty short stories in college. [*Claimed* is the main verb, and *to have written* happened first.]

> **Pleased** with the short story, Candida **mailed** it to several magazines. [*Mailed* is the main verb, and *pleased* happened first.]

> **Having sold** one short story, Candida **invested** in a computer. [*Invested* is the main verb, and *having sold* happened first.]

**EXERCISE 15-6**    Underline the correct verb in each pair of parentheses that best suits the sequence of tenses. Be ready to explain your choices. For help, consult 15k.

EXAMPLE    When he (is, <u>was</u>) seven years old, Yo-Yo Ma, possibly the world's greatest living cellist, (moves, <u>moved</u>) to the United States with his family.

1. Yo-Yo Ma, who (had been born, was born) in France to Chinese parents, (lived, lives) in Boston, Massachusetts, today and (toured, tours) as one of the world's greatest cellists.

2. Years from now, after Mr. Ma has given his last concert, music lovers still (treasure, will treasure) his many fine recordings.

3. Mr. Ma's older sister, Dr. Yeou-Cheng Ma, was nearly the person with the concert career. She had been training to become a concert violinist when her brother's musical genius (began, had begun) to be noticed.

4. Even though Dr. Ma eventually (becomes, became) a physician, she still (had been playing, plays) the violin.

5. The family interest in music (continues, was continuing), for Mr. Ma's children (take, had taken) piano lessons.

## MOOD

# 15l  What is "mood" in verbs?

**Mood** in verbs conveys an attitude toward the action in a sentence. English has three moods: *indicative, imperative,* and *subjunctive.* Use the **indicative mood** to make statements about real things, about highly likely things, and for questions about fact.

> **INDICATIVE**  The door to the tutoring center opened. [real]
>
> She seemed to be looking for someone. [highly likely]

The **imperative mood** expresses commands and direct requests. Often, the subject is omitted in an imperative sentence, but nevertheless the subject is implied to be either *you* or one of the indefinite pronouns such as *anybody, somebody,* or *everybody.*

🛑 **Alert:**  Use an exclamation point after a strong command; use a period after a mild command or a request (23e, 23a). ●

> **IMPERATIVE**  Please shut the door.
>
> Watch out! That screw is loose.

The **subjunctive mood** expresses speculation, other unreal conditions, conjectures, wishes, recommendations, indirect requests, and demands. Often, the words that signal the subjunctive mood are *if, as if, as though,* and *unless.* In speaking, subjunctive verb forms were once used frequently in English, but they're heard far less today. Nevertheless, in ACADEMIC WRITING, you need to use the subjunctive mood.

> **SUBJUNCTIVE**  If I **were** you, I would ask for a tutor.

# 15m  What are subjunctive forms?

For the **present subjunctive,** always use the SIMPLE FORM of the verb for all PERSONS and NUMBERS.

> The prosecutor asks that she **testify** [not *testifies*] again.
>
> It is important that they **be** [not *are*] allowed to testify.

For the **past subjunctive,** use the simple past tense: *I wish that I **had** a car.* The one exception is for the past subjunctive of *be:* Use *were* for all forms.

> I wish that I **were** [not *was*] leaving on vacation today.
>
> They asked if she **were** [not *was*] leaving on vacation today.

## USING THE SUBJUNCTIVE IN *IF, AS IF, AS THOUGH,* AND *UNLESS* CLAUSES

In dependent clauses introduced by *if, as if, as though,* and sometimes *unless,* the subjunctive describes speculations or conditions contrary to fact.

> If it **were** [not *was*] to rain, attendance at the race would be disappointing. [speculation]
>
> The runner looked as if he **were** [not *was*] winded, but he said he wasn't. [a condition contrary to fact]

In an *unless* clause, the subjunctive signals that what the clause says is highly unlikely.

> Unless rain **were** [not *was*] to create floods, the race will be held this Sunday. [Floods are highly unlikely.]

Not every clause introduced by *if, unless, as if,* or *as though* requires the subjunctive. Use the subjunctive only when the dependent clause describes speculation or a condition contrary to fact.

> **INDICATIVE**    If she **is** going to leave late, I will drive her to the race. [Her leaving late is highly likely.]
>
> **SUBJUNCTIVE**    If she **were** going to leave late, I would drive her to the race. [Her leaving late is a speculation.]

## USING THE SUBJUNCTIVE IN *THAT* CLAUSES

When *that* clauses describe wishes, requests, demands, or recommendations, the subjunctive can convey the message.

> I wish that this race **were** [not *was*] over. [a wish about something happening now]
>
> He wishes that he **had seen** [not *saw*] the race. [a wish about something that is past]
>
> The judges are demanding that the doctor **examine** [not *examines*] the runners. [a demand for something to happen in the future]

Also, MODAL AUXILIARY VERBS *would, could, might,* and *should* can convey speculations and conditions contrary to fact.

> If the runner **were** [not *was*] faster, we **would** see a better race. [*Would* is a modal auxiliary verb.]

The issue here is that when an INDEPENDENT CLAUSE expresses a conditional statement using a modal auxiliary verb, you want to be sure that in the DEPENDENT CLAUSE you don't use another modal auxiliary verb.

| NO | If I **would have trained** for the race, I **might have** won. |
|----|----|
| YES | If I **had trained** for the race, I **might have** won. |

**EXERCISE 15-7**   Fill in each blank with the correct form of the verb given in parentheses. For help, consult 15l and 15m.

EXAMPLE   Imagining the possibility of brain transplants requires that we (to be) be open-minded.

(1) If almost any organ other than the brain (to be) _____ the candidate for a swap, we would probably give our consent. (2) If the brain (to be) _____ to hold whatever impulses form our personalities, few people would want to risk a transplant. (3) Many popular movies have asked that we (to suspend) _____ disbelief and imagine the consequences should a personality actually (to be) _____ transferred to another body. (4) In real life, however, the complexities of a successful brain transplant require that not-yet-developed surgical techniques (to be) _____ used. (5) For example, it would be essential that during the actual transplant each one of the 500 trillion nerve connections within the brain (to continue) _____ to function as though the brain (to be) _____ lying undisturbed in a living human body.

## VOICE

# 15n   What is "voice" in verbs?

**Voice** in a verb tells whether a SUBJECT acts or is acted upon. English has two voices, *active* and *passive*. A subject in the **active voice** performs the action.

Most clams **live** in salt water. [The subject *clams* does the acting: Clams *live*.]

They **burrow** into the sandy bottoms of shallow waters. [The subject *they* does the acting: They *burrow*.]

A subject in the **passive voice** is acted upon. The person or thing doing the acting often appears in a PHRASE that starts with *by.* Verbs in the passive voice use forms of *be, have,* and *will* as AUXILIARY VERBS with the PAST PARTICIPLE of the MAIN VERB.

Clams **are considered** a delicacy by many people. [The subject *clams* is acted upon *by many people.*]

Some types of clams **are** highly **valued** by seashell collectors. [The subject *types* is acted upon *by seashell collectors.*]

# 15o   How do I write in the active, not passive, voice?

Because the ACTIVE VOICE emphasizes the doer of an action, active constructions are more direct and dramatic. Active constructions usually require fewer
words than passive constructions, which makes for greater conciseness (11c).
Most sentences in the PASSIVE VOICE can be converted to active voice.

> **PASSIVE**   African tribal masks are often imitated by Western sculptors.
>
> **ACTIVE**   Western sculptors often imitate African tribal masks.

# 15p   What are proper uses of the passive voice?

Although the active voice is usually best, in special circumstances you need to
use the passive voice.

   When no one knows who or what did something or when the doer of an
action isn't important, writers use the passive voice.

> The lock **was broken** sometime after four o'clock. [Who broke the lock
> is unknown.]

> In 1899, the year I was born, a peace conference **was held** at The Hague.
> [The doers of the action—holders of the conference—aren't important.]
> —E. B. White, "Unity"

   Sometimes the action in the sentence is more important than the doer of
the action. For example, if you want to focus on historical discoveries in a narrative, use the passive voice. Conversely, if you want to emphasize the people
making the discoveries, use the active voice.

> **ACTIVE**   The postal clerk **sent** the unsigned letter before I **could**
> **retrieve** it from the mailroom. [The emphasis is on the
> doers of the action, *the postal clerk* and *I*, rather than on
> the events, *sent* and *could retrieve*.]
>
> **PASSIVE**   The unsigned letter **was sent** before it **could be retrieved**
> from the postal clerk. [The emphasis is on the events, *was*
> *sent* and *could be retrieved*, not on the doers of the action,
> the unknown sender and *the postal clerk*.]

   In former years, the social sciences and natural sciences preferred the passive
voice. Recently, style manuals for these disciplines have been advising writers to
use the active voice whenever possible. "Verbs are vigorous, direct communica-
tors," point out the editors of the *Publication Manual of the American Psychological Association.* "Use the active rather than the passive voice," they say.*

---

*American Psychological Association, *Publication Manual of the American Psychological As-
sociation,* 5th ed. (Washington: APA, 2001) 41.

# 16

# Pronouns: Case and Reference

## PRONOUN CASE

## 16a  What does "case" mean?

**Case** applies in different ways to PRONOUNS and to NOUNS. For pronouns, case refers to three pronoun forms: the **subjective** (pronoun as a SUBJECT), the **objective** (pronoun as an OBJECT), and the **possessive** (pronouns used in possessive constructions). For nouns, case refers to only one noun form: the possessive. (For help in using apostrophes in the possessive case, see Chapter 27.)

## 16b  What are personal pronouns?

**Personal pronouns** refer to persons or things. Quick Reference 16.1 shows the case forms of personal pronouns (subjective, objective, and possessive), in both the singular and the plural.

### Quick Reference 16.1

#### Case forms of personal pronouns

|  | Subjective | Objective | Possessive |
|---|---|---|---|
| **SINGULAR** | I, you, he, she, it | me, you, him, her, it | my, mine, your, yours, his, her, hers, its |
| **PLURAL** | we, you, they | us, you, them | our, ours, your, yours, their, theirs |

Many of the most difficult questions about pronoun case concern *who/whom* and *whoever/whomever*. For a full discussion of how to choose between them, see 16g.

## **16c** How do pronouns work in case?

In the subjective case, pronouns function as SUBJECTS.

> **We** were going to get married. [*We* is the subject.]
>
> John and **I** wanted an inexpensive band for our wedding. [*I* is part of the compound subject *John and I.*]

In the objective case, pronouns function as OBJECTS.

> We saw **him** perform in a public park. [*Him* is the direct object.]
>
> We showed **him** our budget. [*Him* is the indirect object.]

In the possessive case, nouns and pronouns usually indicate ownership or imply a relationship.

> The **musician's contract** was very fair. [The possessive noun *musician's* implies a type of ownership.]
>
> **His contract** was very fair. [The possessive pronoun *his* implies a type of ownership.]

Sometimes, however, the notion of ownership or relationship calls for a major stretch of the imagination in possessive constructions. In such cases, look for the following pattern: noun + the *s* sound + noun. This means that two nouns work together, one of which does the possessing and the other of which is possessed.

> The **musician's arrival** was eagerly anticipated. [The musician neither owns the arrival nor has a relationship with the arrival. Instead, the pattern noun + the *s* sound + noun is operating.]

**Alert:** Never use an apostrophe in personal pronouns: *ours, yours, its, his, hers, theirs* (27c). ●

## **16d** Which case is correct when *and* connects pronouns?

When *and* connects pronouns, or nouns and pronouns, the result is a **compound construction.** Compounding, which means "putting parts together in a whole," has no effect on case. Always use pronouns in the subjective case when they serve as the subjects of a sentence; also, always use pronouns in the objective case when they serve as objects in a sentence. Never mix cases.

| | |
|---|---|
| **COMPOUND PRONOUN SUBJECT** | **He and I** saw the solar eclipse. [*He and I* is a compound subject.] |
| **COMPOUND PRONOUN OBJECT** | That eclipse astonished **him and me.** [*Him and me* is a compound object.] |

When you're unsure of the case of a pronoun, use the "Troyka test for case" in Quick Reference 16.2. In this four-step test, you drop some of the words from your sentence so that you can tell which case sounds correct.

---

## Quick Reference 16.2 ■ ■ ■ ■ ■

### Troyka test for case

**SUBJECTIVE CASE**

**STEP 1:** Write the sentence twice, once using the subjective case, and once using the objective case.

**STEP 2:** Cross out enough words to isolate the element you are questioning.

~~Janet and~~ **me**

~~Janet and~~ **I**

learned about the moon.

**STEP 3:** Omit the crossed-out words and read each sentence aloud to determine which one sounds right.

**NO**   **Me** learned about the moon. [This doesn't sound right.]

**YES**   **I** learned about the moon. [This sounds right, so the subjective case is correct.]

**STEP 4:** Select the correct version and restore the words you crossed out.

**Janet and I** learned about the moon.

**OBJECTIVE CASE**

**STEP 1:** Write the sentence twice, once using the subjective case, and once using the objective case.

**STEP 2:** Cross out enough words to isolate the element you are questioning.

The astronomer taught ~~Janet and~~ **I**

The astronomer taught ~~Janet and~~ **me**

about the moon.

**STEP 3:** Omit the crossed-out words and read each sentence aloud to determine which one sounds right.

**NO**   The astronomer taught **I** about the moon. [This doesn't sound right.]

**YES**   The astronomer taught **me** about the moon. [This sounds right, so the objective case is correct.]

**STEP 4:** Select the correct version and restore the words you crossed out.

The astronomer taught **Janet and me** about the moon.

When pronouns are in a PREPOSITIONAL PHRASE, they are always in the objective case. (That is, a pronoun is always the OBJECT of the preposition.) This rule holds whether the pronouns are singular or plural.

**NO** Ms. Lester gave an assignment *to* **Sam and I.** [The prepositional phrase, which starts with the preposition *to*, cannot use the subjective-case pronoun *I*.]

**YES** Ms. Lester gave an assignment *to* **Sam and me.** [The prepositional phrase, which starts with the preposition *to*, calls for the objective-case pronoun *me*.]

Be especially careful when one or more pronouns follow the preposition *between*.

**NO** The dispute is *between* **Thomas and I.** [The prepositional phrase, which starts with the preposition *between*, cannot use the subjective-case pronoun *I*.]

**YES** The dispute is *between* **Thomas and me.** [The prepositional phrase, which starts with the preposition *between*, calls for the objective-case pronoun *me*.]

**EXERCISE 16-1**   Underline the correct pronoun of each pair in parentheses. For help, consult 16c and 16d.

EXAMPLE   Bill and (I, me) noticed two young swimmers being pulled out to sea.

(1) The two teenagers caught in the rip current waved and hollered at Bill and (I, me). (2) The harder (they, them) both swam toward shore, the further away the undercurrent pulled them from the beach. (3) The yellow banners had warned Bill and (I, me) that a dangerous rip current ran beneath the water. (4) I yelled at Bill, "Between you and (I, me), (we, us) have to save them!" (5) (He and I, Him and me) both ran and dove into the crashing waves.

# 16e   How do I match cases with appositives?

You can match cases with APPOSITIVES by putting pronouns and nouns in the same case as the word or words the appositive is renaming. Whenever you're unsure about whether to use the subjective or objective case, use the "Troyka test for case" in Quick Reference 16.2 to get the answer.

**We** [not *Us*] tennis players practice hard. [Here, the subjective-case pronoun *we* matches the noun phrase *tennis players*, which is the subject of this sentence.]

The winners, **she and I** [not *her and me*], advanced to the finals. [The subjective-case pronoun phrase *she and I* matches the noun *winners*, which is the subject of this sentence.]

# 16f   How does case work after linking verbs?

A pronoun that comes after a LINKING VERB either renames the SUBJECT or shows possession. In both constructions, always use a pronoun in the subjective case. If you're unsure about how to identify a pronoun's case, use the "Troyka test for case" in Quick Reference 16.2.

> The contest winner was **I** [not *me*]. [*Was* is a linking verb. *I* renames the subject, which is the noun phrase *contest winner*, so the subjective-case pronoun *I* is correct.]

> The prize is **mine.** [*Is* is a linking verb. *Mine* shows possession, so the possessive-case pronoun *mine* is correct.]

# 16g   When should I use *who, whoever, whom,* and *whomever*?

The pronouns *who* and *whoever* are in the SUBJECTIVE CASE. The pronouns *whom* and *whomever* are in the OBJECTIVE CASE.

Informal spoken English tends to blur distinctions between *who* and *whom,* so with these words some people can't rely entirely on what "sounds right." Whenever you're unsure of whether to use *who* or *whoever* or to use *whom* or *whomever,* apply the "Troyka test for case" in Quick Reference 16.2. If you see *who* or *whoever,* test by temporarily substituting *he, she,* or *they.* If you see *whom* or *whomever,* test by temporarily substituting *him, her,* or *them.*

> My father tells the same story to **whoever/whomever** he meets.

> My father tells the same story to ~~she~~/**her.** [*Note:* When substituting, stop at *she/her.* The objective case *whomever* is correct because the sentence works when you substitute *her* for *whoever/whomever.* In contrast, the subjective case *whoever* is wrong because the sentence doesn't work when you substitute *she* for *whoever/whomever.*]

> My father tells the same story to **whomever** he meets.

The most reliable variation of the test for *who, whom, whoever, whomever* calls for you to add a word before the substituted word set. In this example, the word *if* is added:

> I wondered **who/whom** would vote for Ms. Wallace.

> I wondered **if he**/~~if him~~ would vote for Ms. Wallace. [The subjective case *who* is correct because the sentence works when you substitute *if he* for *who/whom.* In contrast, the objective case *whom* is wrong because the sentence doesn't work when you substitute *if him* for *who/whom.*]

> I wondered **who** would vote for Ms. Wallace.

Another variation of the test for *who, whom, whoever, whomever* calls for you to invert the word order in the test sentence.

Babies **who/whom** mothers cuddle grow faster and feel happier.

Mothers cuddle ~~they~~/**them.** [*Note:* When substituting, stop at *they/them.* By inverting the word order in the sentence—that is, by temporarily using *mothers* as the subject of the sentence—and substituting *they/them* for *who/whom,* you see that *them* is correct. Therefore, the objective case *whom* is correct.]

Babies **whom** mothers cuddle grow faster and feel happier.

At the beginning or end of a question, use *who* if the question is about the subject and *whom* if the question is about the object. To determine which case to use, recast the question into a statement, substituting *he* or *him* (or *she* or *her*).

**Who** watched the space shuttle liftoff? [*He* (not *Him*) *watched the space shuttle liftoff* uses the subjective case, so *who* is correct.]

Ted admires **whom?** [*Ted admires him* (not *he*) uses the objective case, so *whom* is correct.]

**Whom** does Ted admire? [*Ted admires him* (not *he*) uses the objective case, so *whom* is correct.]

## 16h   What pronoun case comes after *than* or *as*?

When *than* or *as* is part of a sentence of comparison, the sentence sometimes doesn't include words to complete the comparison outright. Rather, by omitting certain words, the sentence implies the comparison. For example, *My two-month-old Saint Bernard is larger **than** most full-grown dogs [are]* doesn't need the final word *are.*

When a pronoun follows *than* or *as,* the meaning of the sentence depends entirely on whether the pronoun is in the subjective case or the objective case. Here are two sentences that convey two very different messages, depending on whether the subjective case (*I*) or the objective case (*me*) is used.

1.  My sister loved that dog more *than* **I.**
2.  My sister loved that dog more *than* **me.**

In sentence 1, because *I* is in the subjective case, the sentence means *My sister loved that dog more than **I** [loved it].* In sentence 2, because *me* is in the objective case, the sentence means *My sister loved that dog more than [she loved]* **me.** In both situations, you can check whether you're using the correct case by supplying the implied words to see if they make sense.

# 16i  How do pronouns work before infinitives?

Most INFINITIVES consist of the SIMPLE FORMS of verbs that follow *to:* for example, *to laugh, to sing, to jump, to dance.* (A few exceptions occur when the *to* is optional: *My aunt helped the elderly man [to] cross the street;* and when the *to* is awkward: *My aunt watched the elderly man [to] get on the bus.*) For both the SUBJECTS of infinitives and the OBJECTS of infinitives, use the objective case.

> Our tennis coach expects **me** *to serve.* [Because the word *me* is the subject of the infinitive *to serve,* the objective-case pronoun is correct.]

> Our tennis coach expects **him** *to beat* **me.** [Because the word *him* is the subject of the infinitive *to beat,* and *me* is the object of the infinitive, the objective-case pronoun is correct.]

# 16j  How do pronouns work with -*ing* words?

When a verb's -*ing* form functions as a NOUN, it's called a GERUND: *Brisk **walking** is excellent exercise.* When a noun or PRONOUN comes before a gerund, the POSSESSIVE CASE is required: ***His** brisk **walking** built up his stamina.* In contrast, when a verb's -*ing* form functions as a MODIFIER, it requires the subjective case for the pronoun, not the possessive case: ***He, walking** briskly, caught up to me.*

Here are two sentences that convey different messages, depending entirely on whether a possessive comes before the -*ing* word.

1. The detective noticed the **man** *staggering.*
2. The detective noticed the **man's** *staggering.*

Sentence 1 means that the detective noticed the *man;* sentence 2 means that the detective noticed the *staggering.* The same distinction applies to pronouns: When *the man* is replaced by *him* or *the man's* by *his,* the meaning is the same as in sentences 1 and 2.

1. The detective noticed **him** *staggering.*
2. The detective noticed **his** *staggering.*

In conversation, such distinctions are often ignored, but use them in ACADEMIC WRITING.

# 16k  What case should I use for -*self* pronouns?

Two types of pronouns end in -*self:* reflexive pronouns and intensive pronouns.

A **reflexive pronoun** reflects back on the subject, so it needs a subject in the sentence to be reflected back on. Without a subject, the reflexive pronoun cannot operate correctly.

The **detective** disguised ***himself.*** [The reflexive pronoun *himself* reflects back on the subject *detective.*]

Never use a reflexive pronoun to replace a personal pronoun in the subjective case.

**NO**    My teammates and **myself** will vote for a team captain.

**YES**    My teammates and **I** will vote for a team captain.

Also, never use a reflexive pronoun to replace a personal pronoun in the objective case. The only exception is when the object restates the subject.

**NO**    That decision is up to my teammates and **myself.**

**YES**    That decision is up to my teammates and **me.**

**Intensive pronouns,** which reflect back in the same way as reflexive pronouns, provide emphasis by making the message of the sentence more intense in meaning.

The detective felt that **his career *itself*** was at risk. [*Itself* intensifies the idea that the detective's career was at risk.]

## PRONOUN REFERENCE

# 16l    What is pronoun reference?

The word or group of words that a pronoun replaces is called its **antecedent.** In order for your writing to communicate its message clearly, each pronoun must relate precisely to an antecedent.

> I knew a **woman,** lovely in **her** bones / When small **birds** sighed, **she** would sigh back at **them.**
>
> —Theodore Roethke, "I Knew a Woman"

# 16m    What makes pronoun reference clear?

**Pronoun reference** is clear when your readers know immediately to whom or what each pronoun refers. Quick Reference 16.3 lists guidelines for using pronouns clearly, and the section in parentheses is where each is explained.

# 16n    How can I avoid unclear pronoun reference?

Every pronoun needs to refer to a specific, nearby ANTECEDENT. If the same pronoun in your writing has to refer to more than one antecedent, replace some pronouns with nouns.

**NO** In 1911, **Roald Amundsen** reached the South Pole just thirty-five days before **Robert F. Scott** arrived. **He** [who? Amundsen or Scott?] had told people that **he** [who? Amundsen or Scott?] was going to sail for the Arctic, but **he** [who? Amundsen or Scott?] was concealing **his** [whose? Amundsen's or Scott's?] plan. Soon, **he** [who? Amundsen or Scott?] turned south for the Antarctic. On the journey home, **he** [who? Amundsen or Scott?] and **his** [whose? Amundsen's or Scott's?] party froze to death just a few miles from safety.

**YES** In 1911, **Roald Amundsen** reached the South Pole just thirty-five days before **Robert F. Scott** arrived. **Amundsen** had told people that **he** was going to sail for the Arctic, but **he** was concealing **his** plan. Soon, **Amundsen** turned south for the Antarctic. Meanwhile, on **their** journey home, **Scott** and **his party** froze to death just a few miles from safety.

## Quick Reference 16.3 ▪ ▪ ▪ ▪ ▪

### Guidelines for clear pronoun reference

- Place pronouns close to their ANTECEDENTS (16n).
- Make a pronoun refer to a specific antecedent (16n).
- Do not overuse *it* (16q).
- Reserve *you* only for DIRECT ADDRESS (16r).
- Use *that, which,* and *who* correctly (16s).

🛇 **Alert:** Be careful with the VERBS *said* and *told* in sentences that contain pronoun reference. To maintain clarity, use quotation marks and slightly reword each sentence to make the meaning clear.

**NO** **Her** mother told **her she** was going to visit **her** grandmother.

**YES** **Her** mother told **her**, "**You** are going to visit your grandmother."

**YES** **Her** mother told **her**, "**I** am going to visit your grandmother." ●

Further, if too much material comes between a pronoun and its antecedent, readers can lose track of the meaning.

Alfred Wegener, a German meteorologist and professor of geophysics

at the University of Graz in Austria, was the first to suggest that all the

continents on earth were originally part of one large landmass. According to this theory, the supercontinent broke up long ago and the fragments

drifted apart. ~~He~~ named this supercontinent Pangaea.
<sub>Wegener</sub>

[*He* can refer only to Wegener, but material about Wegener's theory intervenes, so using *Wegener* again instead of *he* jogs the reader's memory and makes reading easier.]

When you start a new paragraph, be cautious about beginning it with a pronoun whose antecedent is in a prior paragraph. You're better off repeating the word.

**ESOL Tip:** Many languages omit a pronoun as a subject because the verb delivers the needed information. English requires the use of the pronoun as a subject. For example, never omit *it* in the following: *Political science is an important academic subject. **It** is studied all over the world.* ●

**EXERCISE 16-2**   Revise so that each pronoun refers clearly to its antecedent. Either replace pronouns with nouns or restructure the material to clarify pronoun reference. For help, consult 16n.

> Most companies used to frown on employees who became involved in office romances. They often considered them to be using company time for their own enjoyment. Now, however, managers realize that happy employees are productive employees. With more women than ever before in the workforce and with people working longer hours, they have begun to see that male and female employees want and need to socialize. They are also dropping their opposition to having married couples on the payroll. They no longer automatically believe that they will bring family matters into the workplace or stick up for each other at the company's expense.

## 16o   How do pronouns work with *it, that, this,* and *which*?

When you use *it, that, this,* and *which,* be sure that your readers can easily understand what each word refers to.

> **NO**   Comets usually fly by the earth at 100,000 mph, whereas asteroids sometimes collide with the earth. This interests scientists.
> [Does *this* refer to the speed of the comets, to comets flying by the earth, or to asteroids colliding with the earth?]

> **YES**   Comets usually fly by the earth at 100,000 mph, whereas asteroids sometimes collide with the earth. **This difference** interests scientists. [Adding a noun after *this* or *that* clarifies the meaning.]

Also, the title of any piece of writing stands on its own. Therefore, in your introductory paragraph, never refer to your title with *this* or *that*. For example, if an essay's title is "Geophysics as a Major," the following holds for the first sentence:

NO   **This subject** unites the sciences of physics, biology, and paleontology.

YES   **Geophysics** unites the sciences of physics, biology, and paleontology.

## 16p   How do I use *they* and *it* precisely?

The expression *they say* can't take the place of stating precisely who is doing the saying. Your credibility as a writer depends on your mentioning a source precisely.

NO   **They say** that earthquakes are becoming more frequent. [*They doesn't identify the authority who made the statement.*]

YES   **Seismologists** say that earthquakes are becoming more frequent.

The expressions *it said* and *it is said that* reflect imprecise thinking. Also, they're wordy. Revising such expressions improves your writing.

NO   **It said** in the newspaper that California has minor earthquakes almost daily. [*It said in the newspaper that is wordy.*]

YES   **The newspaper reported** that California has minor earthquakes almost daily.

## 16q   How do I use *it* to suit the situation?

The word *it* has three different uses in English. Here are examples of correct uses of *it.*

1. PERSONAL PRONOUN: Ryan wants to visit the 18-inch Schmidt telescope, but **it** is on Mount Palomar.

2. EXPLETIVE (sometimes called a *subject filler,* it delays the subject): **It** is interesting to observe the stars.

3. IDIOMATIC EXPRESSION (words that depart from normal use, such as using *it* as the sentence subject when writing about weather, time, distance, and environmental conditions): **It** is sunny. **It** is midnight. **It** is not far to the hotel. **It** is very hilly.

All three uses listed above are correct, but avoid combining them in the same sentence. The result can be an unclear and confusing sentence.

**NO** Because our car was overheating, **it** came as no surprise that **it** broke down just as **it** began to rain. [*It* is overused here, even though all three uses—2, 1, and 3 on the above list, respectively—are acceptable.]

**YES** **It** came as no surprise that our overheating car broke down just as the rain began. [The word order is revised so that *it* is used once.]

**ESOL Tip:** In some languages, *it* is not used as an expletive. In English, it is.

**NO** Is a lovely day.

**YES** **It** is a lovely day. ●

## 16r When should I use *you* for direct address?

Reserve *you* for **direct address,** writing that addresses the reader directly. For example, we use *you* in this handbook to address you, the student. *You* is not a suitable substitute for specific words that refer to people, situations, or occurrences.

**NO** In Russia, **you** usually have to stand in long lines to buy groceries. [Are *you*, the reader, planning to do your grocery shopping in Russia?]

**YES** **Russian consumers** usually have to stand in long lines to buy groceries.

**EXERCISE 16-3** Revise these sentences so that all pronoun references are clear. If a sentence is correct, circle its number. For help, consult 16o through 16r.

EXAMPLE They say that reaching the summit of Mount Everest is easiest in the month of May.

*Experienced climbers say that reaching the summit of Mount Everest is easiest in the month of May.* [Revision eliminates imprecise use of *they*, see section 16p.]

1. Climbing Mount Everest is more expensive than you realize.

2. In addition to training, they need to raise as much as $60,000 for the expedition.

3. By contacting the Nepalese embassy in Washington, DC, you can secure the help of Sherpa guides.

4. The government of Nepal requires permits, copies of passports, and letters of recommendation for each climbing team.

5. Climbers will need to pack oxygen bottles, a first aid kit, medications, a satellite phone, walkie-talkies, and a laptop computer. This will ensure a climber's safety.

# 16s When should I use *that, which,* and *who?*

To use the pronouns *that* and *which* correctly, you want to check the context of the sentence you're writing. *Which* and *that* refer to animals and things. Only sometimes do they refer to anonymous or collective groups of people. Quick Reference 16.4 shows how to choose between *that* and *which*. For information about the role of commas with *that* and *which,* see 24f.

*Who* refers to people and to animals mentioned by name.

**John Polanyi, who** was awarded the Nobel Prize in Chemistry, speaks passionately in favor of nuclear disarmament. [*John Polanyi* is a person.]

**Lassie, who** was known for her intelligence and courage, was actually played by a series of male collies. [*Lassie* is the name of an animal.]

Many professional writers reserve *which* for nonrestrictive clauses and *that* for restrictive clauses. Other writers use *that* and *which* interchangeably for restrictive clauses. Current practice allows the use of either as long as you're consistent in each piece of writing. However, for ACADEMIC WRITING, your instructor might expect you to maintain the distinction.

---

### Quick Reference 16.4 ■ ■ ■ ■ ■

#### Choosing between *that* and *which*

**Choice:** Some instructors and style guides use either *that* or *which* to introduce a RESTRICTIVE CLAUSE (a DEPENDENT CLAUSE that is essential to the meaning of the sentence or part of the sentence). Others may advise you to use only *that* so that your writing distinguishes clearly between restrictive and NONRESTRICTIVE CLAUSES. Whichever style you use, be consistent in each piece of writing:

- The zoos **that** (or **which**) **most children like** display newborn and baby animals. [The point in this sentence concerns children's preferences. Therefore, the words *most children like* are essential for delivering the meaning and make up a restrictive clause.]

**No choice:** You are required to use *which* to introduce a nonrestrictive clause (a dependent clause that isn't essential to the meaning of the sentence or part of the sentence).

- Zoos, **which most children like,** attract more visitors if they display newborn and baby animals. [The point in this sentence concerns attracting more visitors to zoos. Therefore, the words *most children like* are not essential to the meaning of the sentence and make up a nonrestrictive clause.]

---

**Alert:** Use commas before and after a nonrestrictive clause. Don't use commas before and after a restrictive clause; see 24k. ●

# 17

# Agreement

## SUBJECT-VERB AGREEMENT

## 17a What is subject-verb agreement?

**Subject-verb agreement** means that a SUBJECT and its VERB match in NUMBER (singular or plural) and PERSON (first, second, or third person). Quick Reference 17.1 presents these major concepts in grammatical agreement.

> The **firefly glows.** [*Firefly* is a singular subject in the third person; *glows* is a singular verb in the third person.]
>
> **Fireflies glow.** [*Fireflies* is a plural subject in the third person; *glow* is a plural verb in the third person.]

---

### Quick Reference 17.1 ■ ■ ■ ■ ■

#### Grammatical agreement: first, second, and third person

- **Number,** as a concept in grammar, refers to *singular* (one) and *plural* (more than one).
- The **first person** is the speaker or writer. *I* (singular) and *we* (plural) are the only subjects that occur in the first person.

  **SINGULAR**    **I see** a field of fireflies.

  **PLURAL**    **We see** a field of fireflies.

- The **second person** is the person spoken or written to. *You* (for both singular and plural) is the only subject that occurs in the second person.

  **SINGULAR**    **You see** a shower of sparks.

  **PLURAL**    **You see** a shower of sparks.

- The **third person** is the person or thing being spoken or written about. *He, she, it* (singular) and *they* (plural) are the third-person subject forms. Most rules for subject-verb agreement involve the third person.

  **SINGULAR**    The **scientist sees** a cloud of cosmic dust.

  **PLURAL**    The **scientists see** a cloud of cosmic dust.

---

# 17b Why is a final -s or -es in a subject or verb so important?

SUBJECT-VERB AGREEMENT often involves one letter: *s* (or *es* for words that end in *-s*). For verbs in the present tense, you form the SIMPLE FORM of third-person singular by adding *-s* or *-es*: *laugh, laughs; kiss, kisses.* Major exceptions are the verbs *be* (*is*), *have* (*has*), and *do* (*does*), see 15c.

> That **student agrees** that **young teenagers watch** too much television.

> Those **young teenagers are** taking valuable time away from studying.

For a subject to become plural, you add *-s* or *-es* to its end: *lip, lips; princess, princesses.* Major exceptions include most pronouns (*they, it*) and a few nouns that for singular and plural either don't change (*deer, deer*) or change internally (*mouse, mice*). Quick Reference 17.2 shows you how to visualize the basic pattern for agreement using *-s* or *-es*.

Here's a device for remembering how agreement works for most subject-verb constructions. Note that the final *-s* or *-es* can take only one path at a time—to the end of the verb or to the end of the subject.

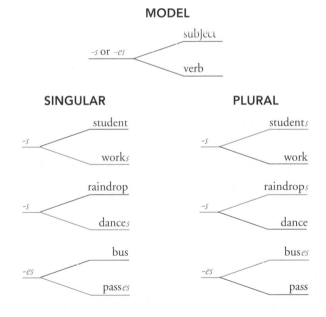

**MODEL**

*-s* or *-es* — subject / verb

**SINGULAR**

*-s* — student / work*s*

*-s* — raindrop / dance*s*

*-es* — bus / pass*es*

**PLURAL**

*-s* — student*s* / work

*-s* — raindrop*s* / dance

*-es* — bus*es* / pass

🛑 **Alert:** When you use an AUXILIARY VERB with a main verb, never add *-s* or *-es* to the main verb: *The coach **can walk*** [not can walks] *to campus. The coach **does like*** [not does likes] *his job.* ●

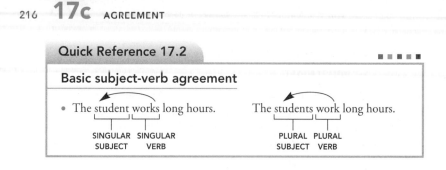

> ### Quick Reference 17.2  ▪ ▪ ▪ ▪ ▪
>
> #### Basic subject-verb agreement
>
> • The student works long hours.  The students work long hours.
>
> SINGULAR SINGULAR  PLURAL PLURAL
> SUBJECT VERB  SUBJECT VERB

**EXERCISE 17-1**  Use the subject and verb in each set to write two complete sentences—one with a singular subject and one with a plural subject. Keep all verbs in the present tense. For help, consult 17b.

EXAMPLE  bird, sing

SINGULAR SUBJECT:  When a *bird sings*, you will know spring is here.
PLURAL SUBJECT:  When *birds sing*, you will know spring is here.

1. chair, rock
2. leaf, fall
3. river, flow
4. clock, tick

5. singer, sing
6. girl, laugh
7. hand, grab
8. loaf, rise

## 17c  Can I ignore words between a subject and its verb?

You can ignore all words between a subject and its verb. Focus strictly on the subject and its verb. Quick Reference 17.3 shows you this pattern.

NO  **Winners** of the state contest **goes** to the national finals. [*Winners* is the subject; the verb must agree with it. Ignore the words *of the state contest.*]

YES  **Winners** of the state contest **go** to the national finals.

The words *one of the . . .* often require a second look. Use a singular verb to agree with the word *one*. Don't be distracted by the plural noun that comes after *of the*. (For information on the phrase *one of the . . . who*, see 17l.)

NO  **One** of the problems **are** the funds needed for traveling to the national finals.

YES  **One** of the problems **is** the funds needed for traveling to the national finals.

---

**Quick Reference 17.3**    ■ ■ ■ ■ ■

**When words separate subject and verb**

- The student  ~~in my college class~~ / ~~in my college classes~~  works long hours.

  SINGULAR SUBJECT · INTERVENING WORDS · SINGULAR VERB

- The students  ~~in my college class~~ / ~~in my college classes~~  work long hours.

  PLURAL SUBJECT · INTERVENING WORDS · PLURAL VERB

---

Similarly, eliminate all word groups between the subject and the verb, starting with *including, together with, along with, accompanied by, in addition to, except,* and *as well as.*

**NO**  The **moon,** *as well as* the planet Venus, **are** visible in the night sky. [*Moon* is the subject. The verb must agree with it. Ignore the words *as well as the planet Venus.*]

**YES**  The **moon,** as well as the planet Venus, **is** visible in the night sky.

## 17d How do verbs work when subjects are connected by *and*?

When two SUBJECTS are connected by *and,* they create a single COMPOUND SUBJECT. A compound subject calls for a plural verb. Quick Reference 17.4

---

**Quick Reference 17.4**    ■ ■ ■ ■ ■

**When subjects are joined by *and***

- The student and the instructor work long hours.

  COMPOUND SUBJECT (uses *and*) · PLURAL VERB

---

shows you this pattern. (For related material on PRONOUNS and ANTECEDENTS, see 17o.)

> **The Cascade Diner *and* the Wayside Diner *have*** [not *has*] fried catfish today. [These are two different diners.]

One exception occurs when *and* joins subjects that refer to a single thing or person.

> **My friend *and* neighbor *makes*** [not *make*] excellent chili. [In this sentence, the friend is the same person as the neighbor. If they were two different people, *makes* would become *make*.]

> **Macaroni *and* cheese *contains*** [not *contain*] carbohydrates, protein, and many calories. [*Macaroni and cheese* is one dish, not two separate dishes, so it requires a singular verb.]

## 17e How do verbs work with *each* and *every*?

The words *each* and *every* are singular even if they refer to a compound subject. Therefore, they take a singular verb.

> ***Each* human hand and foot *makes*** [not *make*] a distinctive print.

> To identify lawbreakers, ***every* police chief, sheriff, and federal marshal *depends*** [not *depend*] on such prints.

**⓵ Alert:** Use one word, either *each* or *every,* not both at the same time: ***Each*** [not *Each and every*] *robber has been caught.* (For more information about pronoun agreement for *each* and *every,* see 17h, 17o, and 17q.) ●

## 17f How do verbs work when subjects are connected by *or*?

As Quick Reference 17.5 shows, when SUBJECTS are joined by *or*—or by the sets *either . . . or, neither . . . nor, not only . . . but (also)*—the verb agrees with the subject closest to it. Ignore everything before the last-mentioned noun or pronoun. Quick Reference 17.5 shows this pattern with *either . . . or.* (For related material on pronouns and antecedents, see 17p.)

> ~~Neither~~ spiders ~~nor~~ **flies upset** *me.*

> ~~Not only~~ spiders ~~but also~~ ~~all other~~ **arachnids have** four pairs of legs.

> ~~A dinner of six clam fritters, four blue crabs,~~ *or* ~~one steamed~~ **lobster sounds** good.

## Quick Reference 17.5

### When subjects are joined by *or*

- ~~Either the instructor or~~
  ~~Either the instructors or~~  >  the student knows the answer.

  SINGULAR  SINGULAR
  SUBJECT  VERB

- ~~Either the instructor or~~
  ~~Either the instructors or~~  >  the students know the answer.

  PLURAL  PLURAL
  SUBJECT  VERB

## 17g  How do verbs work with inverted word order?

In English sentences, the SUBJECT normally comes before its VERB: *Astronomy is interesting.* **Inverted word order** reverses the typical subject-verb pattern by putting the verb first. Most questions use inverted word order: *Is astronomy interesting?* In inverted word order, find the subject first and then check whether the verb agrees with it.

> Into deep space **shoot** probing **satellites.** [The plural verb *shoot* agrees with the inverted plural subject *satellites.*]
>
> On the television screen **appears** an **image** of Saturn. [The singular verb *appears* agrees with the inverted singular subject *image.*]

## 17h  How do verbs work with indefinite pronouns?

**Indefinite pronouns** usually refer to nonspecific persons, things, quantities, or ideas. The nonspecific aspect is the reason these pronouns are labeled "indefinite." As part of a sentence, however, the indefinite pronoun is usually clear from the meaning.

Most indefinite pronouns are singular and require a singular verb for agreement. Yet others are always plural, and a few can be singular *or* plural. Quick Reference 17.6 clarifies this situation by listing indefinite pronouns according to what verb form they require. (For related material on pronouns and antecedents, see 17n–17q.)

### Quick Reference 17.6

■ ■ ■ ■ ■

#### Common indefinite pronouns

**ALWAYS PLURAL**

| | |
|---|---|
| both | many |

**ALWAYS SINGULAR**

| | | |
|---|---|---|
| another | every | no one |
| anybody | everybody | nothing |
| anyone | everyone | one |
| anything | everything | somebody |
| each | neither | someone |
| either | nobody | something |

**SINGULAR *OR* PLURAL, DEPENDING ON CONTEXT**

| | | |
|---|---|---|
| all | more | none |
| any | most | some |

Here are sample sentences:

**SINGULAR INDEFINITE PRONOUNS**

**Each** of us **has** [not *have*] to shovel snow; **each is** [not *are*] expected to help.

**Every** snowstorm of the past two years **has** [not *have*] been severe.

**Every** one of them **has** [not *have*] caused massive traffic jams.

**SINGULAR OR PLURAL INDEFINITE PRONOUNS (DEPENDING ON MEANING)**

**Some** of our streams **are** polluted. [*Some* refers to the plural noun *streams*, so the plural verb *are* is correct.]

**Some** pollution **is** reversible, but **all** pollution **threatens** the balance of nature. [*Some* and *all* refer to the singular noun *pollution*, so the singular verbs *is* and *threatens* are correct.]

**All** that environmentalists ask **is** to give nature a chance. [*All* has the meaning here of "everything" or "the only thing," so the singular verb *is* is correct.]

## 17i   How do verbs work with collective nouns?

A **collective noun** names a group of people or things: *family, audience, class, number, committee, team, group,* and the like. When the group of people or things is acting as one unit, use a singular verb. When members of the group are acting individually, use a plural verb. As you're writing, be careful not to shift back and forth between a singular and a plural verb for the same noun.

The senior **class** nervously *awaits* final exams. [The *class* is acting as a single unit, so the verb is singular.]

The senior **class** *were fitted* for their graduation robes today. [The members (of the class) were fitted as individuals, so the verb is plural.]

## 17j Why does the linking verb agree with the subject, not the subject complement?

Even though a LINKING VERB connects a sentence's SUBJECT to its SUBJECT COMPLEMENT, the linking verb agrees with the subject. It does not agree with the subject complement.

**NO** The worst **part** of owning a car *are* the bills. [The subject is the singular *part,* so the plural verb *are* is wrong. The subject complement is the plural *bills* and doesn't affect agreement.]

**YES** The worst **part** of owning a car *is* the bills. [The singular subject *part* agrees with the singular verb *is*. The subject complement doesn't affect agreement.]

## 17k What verbs agree with *who, which,* and *that?*

If the ANTECEDENT of *who, which,* or *that* is singular, use a singular verb. If the antecedent is plural, use a plural verb.

The scientist will share the prize with the **researchers** *who* **work** with her. [*Who* refers to *researchers,* so the plural verb *work* is used.]

George Jones is the **student** *who* **works** in the science lab. [*Who* refers to *student,* so the singular verb *works* is used.]

If you use phrases including *one of the* or *the only one of the* immediately before *who, which,* or *that* in a sentence, be careful about the verb you use. *Who, which,* or *that* always refers to the plural word immediately following *one of the,* so the verb must be plural. Although *the only one of* is also always followed by a plural word, *who, which,* or *that* must be singular to agree with the singular *one.*

Tracy is *one of the* students *who* **talk** in class. [*Who* refers to *students,* so the verb *talk* is plural. *Tracy* is pointed out, but the talking is still done by all of the students.]

Jim is *the only one of the* students *who* **talks** in class. [*Who* refers to *one,* so the verb *talks* is singular. *Jim* is the single person who is talking.]

## 171  How do verbs work with amounts, fields of study, and other special nouns?

### AMOUNTS

Subjects that refer to time, sums of money, distance, or measurement are singular. They take singular verbs.

> **Two hours *is*** not enough time to finish. [time]
>
> **Three hundred dollars *is*** what we must pay. [sum of money]

### FIELDS OF STUDY

The name for a field of study is singular even if it appears to be plural: *economics, mathematics, physics,* and *statistics.*

> ***Statistics* is** required of science majors. [*Statistics* is a course of study, so the singular verb *is* is correct.]
>
> ***Statistics* show** that a teacher shortage is coming. [*Statistics* isn't used here as a field of study, so the plural verb *show* is correct.]

### SPECIAL NOUNS

*Athletics, news, ethics,* and *measles* are singular despite their plural appearance. Also, *United States of America* is singular: It is one nation. However, *politics* and *sports* take singular or plural verbs, depending on the meaning of the sentence.

> The ***news* gets** better each day. [*News* is a singular noun, so the singular verb *gets* is correct.]
>
> ***Sports* is** a good way to build physical stamina. [*Sports* is one general activity, so the singular verb *is* is correct.]
>
> Three ***sports* are** offered at the recreation center. [*Sports* are separate activities, so the plural verb *are* is correct.]

*Jeans, pants, scissors, clippers, tweezers, eyeglasses, thanks,* and *riches* are some of the words that require a plural verb, even though they refer to one thing. However, if you use *pair* with *jeans, pants, scissors, clippers, tweezers,* or *eyeglasses,* use a singular verb for agreement.

> Those ***slacks* need** pressing. [plural]
>
> That ***pair*** of slacks **needs** pressing. [singular]

*Series* and *means* can be singular or plural, according to the meaning you intend.

> Two new TV ***series* are** big hits. [*Series* refers to individual items (two different series), so the plural verb *are* is correct.]
>
> A ***series*** of disasters **is** plaguing our production. [*Series* refers to a whole group (the whole series of disasters), so the singular verb *is* is correct.]

# 17m How do verbs work with titles, company names, and words as themselves?

## TITLES

A title itself refers to one work or entity (even when plural and compound NOUNS are in the title), so a singular verb is correct.

**Breathing Lessons** by Anne Tyler **is** a prize-winning novel.

## COMPANY NAMES

Many companies have plural words in their names. However, a company should always be treated as a singular unit, requiring a singular verb.

**Cohn Brothers boxes** and **delivers** fine art.

## WORDS AS THEMSELVES

Whenever you write about words as themselves to call attention to those words, use a singular verb, even if more than one word is involved.

**We implies** that everyone is included.

During the Vietnam War, **protective reaction strikes was** a euphemism for *bombing.*

**EXERCISE 17-2** Supply the correct present-tense form of the verb in parentheses. For help, consult 17h through 17m.

EXAMPLE  The movie *Wordplay* is about those who (to enjoy) <u>enjoy</u> solving crossword puzzles.

1. When the movie plays at theaters, the audience often (to consist) _____ of different ages and types of people.

2. For fans of crossword puzzles, the major attraction (to be) _____ the challenges they present.

3. Every creator of puzzles (to know) _____ that in the most successful puzzles all of the clues (to be) _____ interesting.

4. *Setters* (to be) _____ a term used by crossword puzzle fans to describe someone who creates puzzles.

5. These fans, which (to include) _____ celebrities like Jon Stewart, consider the Sunday puzzle in the *New York Times* one of the most difficult.

**EXERCISE 17-3** This exercise covers all of subject-verb agreement (17a through 17m). Supply the correct form of the verb in parentheses.

EXAMPLE  Of the thirty thousand plant species on earth, the rose (to be) <u>is</u> the most universally known.

1. Each plant species (to invite) _____ much discussion about origins and meanings, and when talk turns to flowers, the rose is usually the first mentioned.

2. More fragrant and colorful (to be) _____ other types of flowers, yet roses (to remain) _____ the most popular worldwide.

3. Each of the types of roses (to symbolize) _____ beauty, love, romance, and secrecy.

4. There (to be) _____ more than two hundred pure species of roses and thousands of mixed species, thirty-five of which (to flourish) _____ in the soil of North America.

5. It's impossible to determine exactly where or when the first rose (to be) _____ domesticated, because roses have existed for so many centuries; one of the earliest references dates back to 3000 BC.

## PRONOUN-ANTECEDENT AGREEMENT

# 17n What is pronoun-antecedent agreement?

**Pronoun-antecedent agreement** means that a PRONOUN matches its ANTECEDENT in NUMBER (singular or plural) and PERSON (first, second, or third person). Quick Reference 17.7 shows you how to visualize this pattern of grammatical agreement. You might also want to consult Quick Reference 17.1 in 17a for explanations and examples of the concepts *number* and *person*.

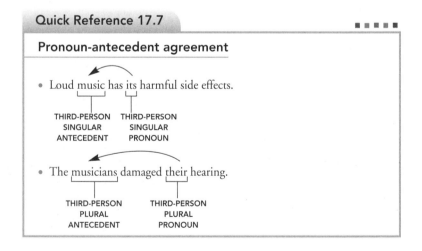

> Quick Reference 17.7　　　　　■ ■ ■ ■ ■
>
> ### Pronoun-antecedent agreement
>
> • Loud music has its harmful side effects.
>
>   THIRD-PERSON　　THIRD-PERSON
>   SINGULAR　　　　SINGULAR
>   ANTECEDENT　　　PRONOUN
>
> • The musicians damaged their hearing.
>
>   THIRD-PERSON　　THIRD-PERSON
>   PLURAL　　　　　PLURAL
>   ANTECEDENT　　　PRONOUN

The **firefly** glows when **it** emerges from **its** nest at night. [The singular pronouns *it* and *its* match their singular antecedent, *firefly.*]

**Fireflies** glow when **they** emerge from **their** nests at night. [The plural pronouns *they* and *their* match their plural antecedent, *fireflies*.]

## 17o How do pronouns work when *and* connects antecedents?

When *and* connects two or more ANTECEDENTS, they require a plural pronoun. This rule applies even if each separate antecedent is singular. (For related material on subjects and verbs, see 17d.)

**The Cascade Diner *and* the Wayside Diner** closed for New Year's Eve to give **their** [not *its*] employees the night off. [Two separate diners require a plural pronoun.]

When *and* joins singular nouns that nevertheless refer to a single person or thing, use a singular pronoun.

**My friend *and* neighbor** makes **his** [not *their*] excellent chili every Saturday. [The friend is the same person as the neighbor, so the singular *his* (or *her*) is correct. If two different people were involved, the correct pronoun would be *their*, and *make* would be the correct verb.]

### EACH, EVERY

The words *each* and *every* are singular, even when they refer to two or more antecedents joined by *and*. The same rule applies when *each* or *every* is used alone (17h). (For related material on subjects and verbs, see 17e.)

**Each** human hand *and* foot leaves **its** [not *their*] distinctive print.

The rule still applies when the construction *one of the* follows *each* or *every.*

**Each one of the** robbers left **her** [not *their*] fingerprints at the scene.

## 17p How do pronouns work when *or* connects antecedents?

When ANTECEDENTS are joined by *or*—or by CORRELATIVE CONJUNCTIONS such as *either . . . or, neither . . . nor,* or *not only . . . but (also)*—the antecedents might mix singulars and plurals. For the purposes of agreement, ignore everything before the final antecedent. Quick Reference 17.8 shows you how to visualize this pattern. (For related material on subjects and verbs, see 17f.)

After the restaurant closes, *either* the resident mice *or* **the owner's cat** gets **itself** a meal.

After the restaurant closes, *either* the owner's cat *or* **the resident mice** get **themselves** a meal.

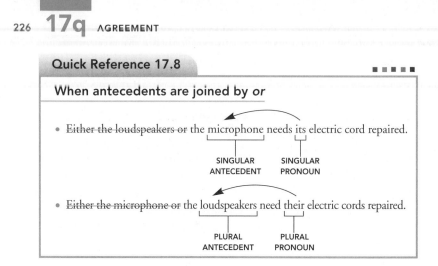

**When antecedents are joined by *or***

- ~~Either the loudspeakers or~~ the microphone needs its electric cord repaired.

  SINGULAR ANTECEDENT     SINGULAR PRONOUN

- ~~Either the microphone or~~ the loudspeakers need their electric cords repaired.

  PLURAL ANTECEDENT     PLURAL PRONOUN

## 17q How do pronouns work when antecedents are indefinite pronouns?

INDEFINITE PRONOUNS usually refer to unknown persons, things, quantities, or ideas. The unknown aspect is the reason these pronouns are labeled "indefinite." But in a sentence, context gives an indefinite pronoun a clear meaning, even if the pronoun doesn't have a specific antecedent. Most indefinite pronouns are singular. Two indefinite pronouns, *both* and *many,* are plural. A few indefinite pronouns can be singular or plural, depending on the meaning of the sentence.

For a list of indefinite pronouns, grouped as singular or plural, see Quick Reference 17.6 in 17h. For more information about avoiding sexist language, especially when using indefinite pronouns, see 17r and 12f. (For related material on subjects and verbs, see 17h.)

### SINGULAR INDEFINITE PRONOUNS

**Everyone** taking this course hopes to get **his or her** [not *their*] college degree within a year.

**Anybody** wanting to wear a cap and gown at graduation must have **his or her** [not *their*] measurements taken.

**Each** of the students handed in **his or her** [not *their*] final term paper.

### SINGULAR *OR* PLURAL INDEFINITE PRONOUNS

When winter break arrives for students, **most** leave **their** dormitories for home. [*Most* refers to *students,* so the plural pronoun *their* is correct.]

As for the luggage, **most** is already on **its** way to the airport. [*Most* refers to *luggage,* so the singular pronoun *its* is correct.]

**None** thinks that **he or she** will miss graduation. [*None* is singular as used in this sentence, so the singular pronoun phrase *he or she* is correct.]

# 17r  How do I use nonsexist pronouns?

A word is **nonsexist** when it carries neither male nor female gender. Each PRONOUN in English carries one of three genders: male (*he, him, his*); female (*she, her, hers*); or neutral (*you, your, yours, we, our, ours, them, they, their, theirs, it, its*). Usage today favors nonsexist terms in all word choices. You therefore want to use gender-free pronouns whenever possible. In the past, it was grammatically correct to use only masculine pronouns to refer to INDEFINITE PRONOUNS: "*Everyone open **his** book.*" Today, however, people feel that the pronouns *he, his, him,* and *himself* exclude women, who make up over half the population. Quick Reference 17.9 shows three ways to avoid using masculine pronouns when referring to males and females together. For more information on gender-neutral language, see 12f.

Questions often arise concerning the use of *he or she* and *his or her*. In general, writers find these gender-free pronoun constructions awkward. To avoid them, many writers make the antecedents plural. Doing this becomes problematic when the subject is a SINGULAR INDEFINITE PRONOUN (Quick Reference 17.6 in section 17h). In the popular press (such as newspapers and magazines), the use of the plural pronoun *they* or *them* with a singular antecedent has been gaining favor. Indeed, some experts find that the history of English supports

---

**Quick Reference 17.9**  ▪ ▪ ▪ ▪ ▪

### Avoiding the masculine pronoun when referring to males and females together

- **Solution 1:** Use a pair of pronouns—as in the phrase *he or she*. However, avoid using a pair more than once in a sentence or in many sentences in a row. A *he or she* construction acts as a singular pronoun.

  **Everyone** hopes that **he or she** will win a scholarship.

  A **doctor** usually has time to keep up to date only in **his or her** specialty.

- **Solution 2:** Revise into the plural.

  **Many students** hope that **they** will win a scholarship.

  **Most doctors** have time to keep up to date only in **their** specialties.

- **Solution 3:** Recast the sentence.

  Everyone hopes to win a scholarship.

  Few specialists have time for general reading.

this use. In ACADEMIC WRITING, however, it is better for you not to follow the practice of the popular press. Language practice changes, however, so what we say here is our best advice as we write this book.

## 17s  How do pronouns work when antecedents are collective nouns?

A COLLECTIVE NOUN names a group of people or things, such as *family, group, audience, class, number, committee,* and *team.* When the group acts as one unit, use a singular pronoun to refer to it. When the members of the group act individually, use a plural pronoun. In the latter case, if the sentence is awkward, substitute a plural noun for the collective noun. (For related material on subjects and verbs, see 17i.)

> The **audience** was cheering as **it** stood to applaud the performers. [The *audience* was acting as one unit, so the singular pronoun *it* is correct.]
>
> The **audience** put on **their** coats and walked out. [The members of the audience were acting as individuals, so all actions become plural; therefore, the plural pronoun *their* is correct.]
>
> The **family** is spending **its** vacation in Rockport, Maine. [All the family members went to one place together.]

The parallel sentence to the last example above would be *The **family** are spending **their** vacations in Maine, Hawaii, and Rome,* which might mean that each family member is going to a different place. But such a sentence is awkward. Therefore, revise the sentence.

> The **family members** are spending **their** vacations in Maine, Hawaii, and Rome. [Substituting a plural noun phrase *family members* for the collective noun *family* sounds more natural.]

**EXERCISE 17-4**   Underline the correct pronoun in parentheses. For help, consult 17n through 17s.

EXAMPLE   Many wonder where inventors like Benjamin Franklin get (his or her, <u>their</u>) creative energy.

1. Many so-called Founding Fathers are famous one or two of (his, his or her, their) accomplishments, but anyone who knows (his, her, his or her, their) history knows that Franklin is known for many things, including (his, her, his or her, their) inventions.

2. The armonica is not one of his well known inventions, but (its, their) design is ingenious.

3. Also called the glass harmonica, the armonica required a person to place (himself, herself, himself or herself) in front of the instrument and to rotate (its, their) glass bowls.

4. The lightning rod and the Franklin stove established his reputation as an inventor, but (it, they) remained in public domain because Franklin refused to secure patents for his inventions.

5. An inventor like Franklin does not limit (his, her, his or her, their) imagination to one field of science.

# 18

# Adjectives and Adverbs

## 18a What are the differences between adjectives and adverbs?

The differences between adjectives and adverbs relate to how they function. **Adjectives** modify NOUNS and PRONOUNS. **Adverbs** modify VERBS, adjectives, and other adverbs. What's the same about adjectives and adverbs is that they're both MODIFIERS—that is, words or groups of words that describe other words.

| | |
|---|---|
| **ADJECTIVE** | The **brisk** *wind* blew. [Adjective *brisk* modifies noun *wind*.] |
| **ADVERB** | The wind *blew* **briskly.** [Adverb *briskly* modifies verb *blew*.] |

⊕ **ESOL Tips:** (1) In English, the adjective is always singular, even if its noun is plural: *The **hot** [not *hots*] drinks warmed us up.* (2) Word order in English calls for special attention to the placement of adjectives and adverbs. Here is an example using the adverb *carefully: Thomas closed* [don't place *carefully* here] *the window **carefully*** (see 44b and 44c). ●

**EXERCISE 18-1** Underline and label all adjectives (ADJ) and adverbs (ADV). Then, draw an arrow from each adjective and adverb to the word or words it modifies. Ignore *a, an,* and *the* as adjectives. For help, consult 18a.

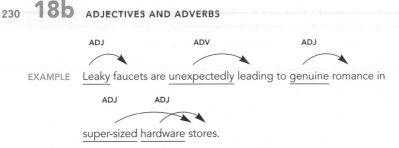

EXAMPLE   Leaky faucets are unexpectedly leading to genuine romance in

super-sized hardware stores.

1. Today's singles carefully look for possible mates at discount home improvement stores across the country.

2. Understandably, many people find these stores a healthy alternative to dark bars and blind dates.

3. Recently, an employee in the flooring department quietly confided that the best nights for singles are Wednesdays and Thursdays, while weekends generally attract families.

4. A young single mom returns home excitedly because a quick trip to the lumber department for a new door resulted in a date for Saturday night.

5. A lonely widower in his fifties jokingly says he wishes he had developed earlier an interest in wallpapering and gardening.

# 18b  When do I use adverbs—not adjectives—as modifiers?

Adverbs MODIFY verbs, adjectives, and other adverbs. Don't use adjectives as adverbs.

> **NO**   The candidate inspired us **great.** [Adjective *great* cannot modify verb *inspired*.]
>
> **YES**   The candidate inspired us **greatly.** [Adverb *greatly* can modify verb *inspired*.]
>
> **NO**   The candidate felt **unusual** energetic. [Adjective *unusual* cannot modify adjective *energetic*.]
>
> **YES**   The candidate felt **unusually** energetic. [Adverb *unusually* can modify adjective *energetic*.]

# 18c  What is wrong with double negatives?

A **double negative** is a nonstandard form. It is a statement with two negative MODIFIERS, the second of which repeats the message of the first. Negative modifiers include *no, never, not, none, nothing, hardly, scarcely,* and *barely.*

> **NO**   The factory workers will **never** vote for **no** strike.
>
> **YES**   The factory workers will **never** vote for **a** strike.

# 18d   Do adjectives or adverbs come after linking verbs?

LINKING VERBS connect a SUBJECT to a COMPLEMENT. Always use an adjective, not an adverb, as the complement.

> The *guests looked* **happy.** [Verb *looked* links subject *guests* to adjective *happy*.]

The words *look, feel, smell, taste, sound,* and *grow* are usually linking verbs, but sometimes they're simply verbs. Check how any of these verbs is functioning in a sentence.

> Zora *looks* **happy.** [*Looks* functions as a linking verb, so the adjective *happy* is correct.]
>
> Zora *looks* **happily** at the sunset. [*Looks* doesn't function as a linking verb, so the adverb *happily* is correct.]

## BAD, BADLY

The words *bad* (adjective) and *badly* (adverb) are particularly prone to misuse with linking verbs.

> **NO**   The students felt **badly.** [This means the students used their sense of touch badly.]
>
> **YES**   The student felt **bad.** [This means the student had a bad feeling about something.]

## GOOD, WELL

When the word *well* refers to health, it is an adjective; at all other times, *well* is an adverb. The word *good* is always an adjective.

> Evander looks **well.** [This means that Evander seems to be in good health, so the adjective *well* is correct.]
>
> Evander writes **well.** [This means that Evander writes skillfully, so the adverb *well* is correct.]

# 18e   What are comparative and superlative forms?

When you write about comparisons, ADJECTIVES and ADVERBS often carry the message. The adjectives and adverbs also communicate degrees of intensity. When a comparison is made between two things, a **comparative** form is used. When a comparison is made about three or more things, a **superlative** form is used.

**REGULAR FORMS OF COMPARISON**

Most adjectives and adverbs are regular. They communicate degrees of intensity in one of two ways: either by adding *-er* and *-est* endings or by adding the words *more, most, less,* and *least* (see Quick Reference 18.1).

The number of syllables in the adjective or adverb usually determines whether to use *-er, -est* or *more, most* and *less, least.*

- **One-syllable words** usually take *-er* and *-est* endings: *large, larger, largest* (adjectives); *far, farther, farthest* (adverbs).

- **Adjectives of two syllables** vary. If the word ends in *-y,* change the *y* to *i* and add *-er, -est* endings: *pretty, prettier, prettiest.* Otherwise, some two-syllable adjectives take *-er, -est* endings: *yellow, yellower, yellowest.* Others take *more, most* and *less, least: tangled, more tangled, most tangled; less tangled, least tangled.*

- **Adverbs of two syllables** take *more, most* and *less, least: quickly, more quickly, most quickly; less quickly, least quickly.*

- **Three-syllable words** take *more, most* and *less, least: dignified, more/most dignified, less/least dignified* (adjective); *carefully, more/most carefully, less/least carefully* (adverb).

---

### Quick Reference 18.1 ■ ■ ■ ■ ■

#### Regular forms of comparison for adjectives and adverbs

| | |
|---|---|
| POSITIVE | Use when nothing is being compared. |
| COMPARATIVE | Use when two things are being compared. Add the ending *-er* or the word *more* or *less.* |
| SUPERLATIVE | Use to compare three or more things. Add the ending *-est* or the word *most* or *least.* |

| Positive [1] | Comparative [2] | Superlative [3+] |
|---|---|---|
| green | greener | greenest |
| happy | happier | happiest |
| selfish | less selfish | least selfish |
| beautiful | more beautiful | most beautiful |

---

🔵 **Alert:** Be careful not to use a double comparative or double superlative. Use either the *-er* and *-est* endings or *more, most* or *less, least.*

He was **younger** [not more younger] than his brother.

Her music was the **loudest** [not most loudest] on the stereo. ●

## IRREGULAR FORMS OF COMPARISON

A few comparative and superlative forms are irregular. Quick Reference 18.2 gives you the list. We suggest that you memorize them so they come to mind easily.

### Quick Reference 18.2 ■ ■ ■ ■ ■

#### Irregular forms of comparison for adjectives and adverbs

| Positive [1] | Comparative [2] | Superlative [3+] |
|---|---|---|
| good (*adjective*) | better | best |
| well (*adjective* and *adverb*) | better | best |
| bad (*adjective*) | worse | worst |
| badly (*adverb*) | worse | worst |
| many | more | most |
| much | more | most |
| some | more | most |
| little* | less | least |

*When you're using *little* for items that can be counted (e.g., pickles), use the regular forms *little, littler, littlest*.

# 18f Why avoid a long string of nouns as modifiers?

NOUNS sometimes MODIFY other nouns: *truck driver, train track, security system.* Usually, these terms create no problems. However, avoid using several nouns in a row as modifiers. A string of too many nouns makes it difficult for your reader to figure out which nouns are being modified and which nouns are doing the modifying. You can revise such sentences in several ways.

> REWRITE THE SENTENCE
>
> **NO** I asked my adviser to write **two college recommendation letters** for me.
>
> **YES** I asked my adviser to write ***letters of recommendation to two colleges*** for me.

> CHANGE ONE NOUN TO A POSSESSIVE AND ANOTHER TO AN ADJECTIVE
>
> **NO** He will take the **United States Navy examination** for **navy engineer training.**
>
> **YES** He will take the *United States **Navy's** examination* for ***naval engineer training.***

CHANGE ONE NOUN TO A PREPOSITIONAL PHRASE

**NO**   Our **student adviser training program** has won many awards.

**YES**   Our *training program* **for student advisers** has won many
awards. [This change requires a change from the singular *adviser*
to the plural *advisers*.]

**EXERCISE 18-2**   Underline the better choice in parentheses. For help,
consult this entire chapter.

EXAMPLE   Alexis, a huge and powerful six-year-old Siberian tiger, (curious,
<u>curiously</u>) explores her new zoo home together with five other tigers.

1. The new tiger home at the world-famous Bronx Zoo is a (special, specially)
designed habitat, planted with (dense, denser) undergrowth so that it
(close, closely) imitates the tigers' natural wilderness.

2. Like tigers in the wild, the six tigers in this habitat, which (more, many) experts consider the (more authentic, most authentic) of all artificial tiger environments in the world, will face some of the physical challenges and
sensory experiences that keep them happy and (healthy, healthier).

3. Research shows that tigers feel (bad, badly) and fail to thrive in zoos without enrichment features placed in (good, well) locations to inspire tigers to
stalk (stealthy, stealthily) through underbrush, loll (lazy, lazily) on heated
rocks, or tug (vigorous, vigorously) on massive pull toys.

4. Wildlife zoologists think that the new Tiger Mountain exhibit will also serve
zoo visitors (good, well) by allowing them to observe and admire the amaz-
ing strength, agility, and intelligence of a (rapid, rapidly) dwindling species.

5. Today, (fewer, less) than 5,000 Siberian tigers remain in the wild, which
makes it imperative for zoos to raise people's awareness of the (great,
greatest) need to prevent the extinction of these big cats that are considered among the (more, most) powerful, beautiful animals in the world.

# 19

# Sentence Fragments

## 19a What is a sentence fragment?

A **sentence fragment** looks like a sentence, but it's actually only part of a sentence. That is, even though a sentence fragment begins with a capital letter and ends with a period (or question mark or exclamation point), it doesn't contain an INDEPENDENT CLAUSE. Fragments are merely unattached PHRASES or DEPENDENT CLAUSES.

| | |
|---|---|
| **FRAGMENT** | The telephone with redial capacity. [no verb] |
| **CORRECT** | The telephone has redial capacity. |
| **FRAGMENT** | Rang loudly for ten minutes. [no subject] |
| **CORRECT** | The telephone rang loudly for ten minutes. |
| **FRAGMENT** | Because the telephone rang loudly. [dependent clause starting with subordinating conjunction *because*] |
| **CORRECT** | Because the telephone rang loudly, the family was awakened in the middle of the night. |

## 19b How can I recognize a sentence fragment?

If you tend to write SENTENCE FRAGMENTS, you want a system for recognizing them. Quick Reference 19.1 shows you a Sentence Test for checking that you haven't written a sentence fragment.

**EXERCISE 19-1**   Identify each word group as either a complete sentence or a fragment. If the word group is a sentence, circle its number. If it's a fragment, tell why it's incomplete. For help, see Quick Reference 19.1.

EXAMPLE   Although antibacterial soaps have become popular. [Starts with a subordinating conjunction (*although*), which creates dependence, and lacks an independent clause to complete the thought; see Quick Reference 19.1]

1. Because antibacterial soaps do not provide protection against viruses.

2. Viruses responsible for a variety of common health problems.

3. Regular soap often successfully eliminates bacteria, viruses, and dirt.

4. Indicate that antibacterial soaps may wash away useful bacteria.

5. Eliminates most of the harmful bacteria as effectively as regular soap.

---

### Quick Reference 19.1  ■ ■ ■ ■ ■

#### Sentence test to identify sentence fragments

**QUESTION 1: IS THE WORD GROUP A DEPENDENT CLAUSE?**

A DEPENDENT CLAUSE is a word group that has a subject and a verb but starts with a word that creates dependence—either a SUBORDINATING CONJUNCTION or a RELATIVE PRONOUN.

| | |
|---|---|
| **FRAGMENT** | **When** winter comes early. [starts with *when,* a word that creates dependence] |
| **CORRECT** | **When** winter comes early, **ships often rescue the stranded whales.** [adds an independent clause to create a sentence] |
| **FRAGMENT** | **Which** can happen quickly. [starts with *which,* a word that creates dependence] |
| **CORRECT** | **Whales cannot breathe through the ice and will drown, which** can happen quickly. [adds an independent clause to create a sentence] |

**QUESTION 2: IS THERE A VERB?**

| | |
|---|---|
| **FRAGMENT** | Thousands of whales in the Arctic Ocean. [Because a verb is missing, this is a phrase, not a sentence.] |
| **CORRECT** | Thousands of whales **live** in the Arctic Ocean. [adds a verb to create a sentence] |

**QUESTION 3: IS THERE A SUBJECT?**

| | |
|---|---|
| **FRAGMENT** | Stranded in the Arctic Ocean. [Because a subject is missing, this is a phrase, not a sentence.] |
| **CORRECT** | **Many whales** *were* stranded in the Arctic Ocean. [adds a subject (and the verb *were* to *stranded*) to create a sentence] |

---

# 19c  What are major ways of correcting fragments?

Once you've identified a SENTENCE FRAGMENT (19b), you're ready to correct it. You can do this in one of two ways: by joining it to an independent clause or by rewriting it.

■ **Correcting a sentence fragment by joining it to an independent clause**

One way you can correct a sentence fragment is by joining it to an INDEPENDENT CLAUSE—that is, to a complete sentence. The example that follows deals with dependent-clause fragments; the examples following the ALERT examine fragments with missing subjects and/or verbs.

| | |
|---|---|
| FRAGMENT | **Because** the ice was thick. [Although this word group has a subject (*ice*) and verb (*was*), it starts with the subordinating conjunction *because*.] |
| CORRECT | **Because** the ice was thick, *icebreakers were required to serve as rescue ships.* [Adding a comma and joining the fragment to the independent clause *icebreakers were required to serve as rescue ships* creates a complete sentence.] |
| CORRECT | *Icebreakers were required to serve as rescue ships* **because** the ice was thick. [Joining the fragment to the independent clause *Icebreakers were required to serve as rescue ships* creates a complete sentence.] |

🚫 **Alert:** Be careful with all words that indicate time, such as *after, before, since,* and *until.* They aren't always subordinating conjunctions. Sometimes they function as ADVERBS—especially if they begin a complete sentence. At other times, they function as PREPOSITIONS. When you see one of these words that indicate time, realize that you aren't necessarily looking at a dependent-clause fragment.

**Before,** the whales had responded to classical music. [This is a complete sentence in which *Before* is an adverb that modifies the independent clause *the whales had responded to classical music.*]

**Before the whales had responded to classical music,** some crew members tried rock and roll music. [If the word group before the comma stood on its own, it would be a sentence fragment because it starts with *Before* functioning as a subordinating conjunction.] ●

| | |
|---|---|
| FRAGMENT | **To announce new programs for crime prevention.** [*To announce* starts an infinitive phrase, not a sentence.] |
| CORRECT | *The mayor called a news conference last week* **to announce** new programs for crime prevention. [The infinitive phrase starting with *to announce* is joined with an independent clause.] |

FRAGMENT  **Hoping for strong public support.** [*Hoping* starts a present-participle phrase, not a sentence.]

CORRECT  **Hoping** for strong public support, ***she gave examples of problems throughout the city.*** [The present-participle phrase starting with *Hoping* is joined with an independent clause.]

FRAGMENT  **Introduced by her assistant.** [*Introduced* starts a past-participle phrase, not a sentence.]

CORRECT  **Introduced** by her assistant, ***the mayor began with an opening statement.*** [The past-participle phrase starting with *Introduced* is joined with an independent clause.]

**EXERCISE 19-2**  Find and correct any sentence fragments. If a sentence is correct, circle its number. For help, consult 19a through 19c.

EXAMPLE  Even though lice are a common problem for young children.

Correct: Lice are a common problem for young children.

1. Even though lice are not dangerous and do not spread disease, parents tend to worry about their children. Who have been infected with this parasite.

2. Although good hygiene is important, it does not prevent lice infestation. Which can occur on clean, healthy scalps.

3. Spread only through direct contact. Lice are unable to fly or jump.

4. Evidence of lice has been found on ancient Egyptian mummies, which suggests that lice have been annoying humans for a long time.

5. While lice can spread among humans who share combs or pillows or hats. Lice cannot be spread from pets to humans.

## ■ Correcting a sentence fragment by rewriting it

A second way you can correct a sentence fragment is by rewriting it as an INDEPENDENT CLAUSE—that is, as a complete sentence. The first two examples below deal with dependent-clause fragments; the others examine fragments with missing subjects and/or verbs.

FRAGMENT  **Because** the ice was thick. [Although this word group has a subject (*ice*) and verb (*was*), it starts with the subordinating conjunction *because*.]

CORRECT  The ice was thick. [The fragment starting with *Because* is rewritten to become a complete sentence.]

FRAGMENT  **Who** feared the whales would panic. [This fragment starts with the relative pronoun *who*.]

CORRECT  *The crew* feared the whales would panic. [The fragment starting with *Who* is rewritten to become a complete sentence.]

FRAGMENT  **To announce** new programs for crime prevention. [*To announce* starts an infinitive phrase, not a sentence.]

CORRECT  *The mayor called a news conference last week because she wanted* **to announce** new programs for crime prevention. [The infinitive phrase starting with *To announce* is rewritten to become a complete sentence.]

FRAGMENT  **Hoping** for strong public support. [*Hoping* starts a present-participle phrase, not a sentence.]

CORRECT  *She was* **hoping** for strong public support. [The present-participle phrase starting with *Hoping* is rewritten to become a complete sentence.]

## 19d How can I fix a fragment that is part of a compound predicate?

A COMPOUND PREDICATE contains two or more VERBS. When the second part of a compound predicate is punctuated as a separate sentence, it becomes a sentence fragment.

FRAGMENT  The reporters asked the mayor many questions about the new program. **And then discussed her answers among themselves.** [*And then discussed* starts a compound predicate fragment, not a sentence.]

CORRECT  The reporters asked the mayor many questions about the new program and then discussed her answers among themselves. [The compound predicate fragment starting with *And then discussed* is joined to the independent clause.]

CORRECT  The reporters asked the mayor many questions about the new program. *Then the reporters* discussed her answers among themselves. [The compound predicate fragment starting with *And then discussed* is rewritten as a complete sentence.]

## 19e What are the two special fragment problems?

Two special fragment problems sometimes involve lists and examples. Lists and examples must be part of a complete sentence, unless they are formatted as a column.

You can connect a list fragment by attaching it to the preceding independent clause using a colon or a dash. You can correct an example fragment by attaching it to an independent clause (with or without punctuation, depending on the meaning) or by rewriting it as a complete sentence.

FRAGMENT    You have a choice of desserts. **Carrot cake, chocolate silk pie, apple pie, or peppermint ice cream.** [The list cannot stand on its own as a sentence.]

CORRECT    You have a choice of desserts: carrot cake, chocolate silk pie, apple pie, or peppermint ice cream. [A colon joins the sentence and the list.]

CORRECT    You have a choice of desserts—carrot cake, chocolate silk pie, apple pie, or peppermint ice cream. [A dash joins the sentence and the list.]

## 19f    How can I recognize intentional fragments?

Professional writers sometimes intentionally use fragments for emphasis and effect.

> But in the main, I feel like a brown bag of miscellany propped against a wall. Pour out the contents, and there is discovered a jumble of small things priceless and worthless. **A first-water diamond, an empty spool, bits of broken glass, lengths of string, a key to a door long since crumbled away, a rusty knife-blade, old shoes saved for a road that never was and never will be, a nail bent under the weight of things too heavy for any nail, a dried flower or two still a little fragrant.**
>
> —Zora Neale Hurston, *How It Feels to Be Colored Me*

Being able to judge the difference between an acceptable and unacceptable sentence fragment comes from years of reading the work of skilled writers. For ACADEMIC WRITING, most instructors don't accept sentence fragments in student writing until a student demonstrates a consistent ability to write well-constructed, complete sentences. As a rule, avoid sentence fragments in academic writing.

**EXERCISE 19-3**    Revise this paragraph to eliminate all sentence fragments. In some cases, you can combine word groups to create complete sentences; in other cases, you must supply missing elements to rewrite. Some sentences may not require revision. In your final version, check not only the individual sentences but also the clarity of the whole paragraph. For help, consult 19a through 19d.

(1) Throughout his career as a philosopher and Cynic, Diogenes cultivated a following. That included the likes of Aristotle and Alexander the Great. (2) Diogenes was an important member of the Cynics, a group of people who rejected conventional life. The word *Cynic* comes from the

Greek word for dog. (3) Diogenes lived like a beggar and slept in a tub. Which he carried around with him wherever he went. (4) He rejected the pursuit of wealth and once destroyed his wooden bowl. Because he saw a peasant boy drinking water with his hands. (5) Although none of his writings have survived, Diogenes produced dialogues and a play. That allegedly describes a social utopia in which people live unconventional lives. (6) Since he often walked around Athens in broad daylight with a lamp looking for an honest man. (7) When Plato defined *man* as a featherless biped, Diogenes plucked a chicken and said, "Here is Plato's man." (8) According to legend, Diogenes was once sunbathing when he was approached by Alexander the Great. Who was a fan of the eccentric Cynic. (9) Alexander asked if he could do anything for Diogenes. Which the philosopher answered by saying, "Don't block my sunlight." (10) Because Diogenes is a strange and interesting character. He has inspired works by such writers and artists as William Blake, Anton Chekhov, and Rabelais.

# 20

# Comma Splices and Run-On Sentences

## 20a What are comma splices and run-on sentences?

Comma splices and run-on sentences are somewhat similar errors: One has a comma by itself between two complete sentences, and one has no punctuation at all between two complete sentences.

A **comma splice,** also called a *comma fault,* occurs when a comma, rather than a period, is used incorrectly between complete sentences. The word *splice* means "to fasten ends together," which is a handy procedure, except when splicing has anything to do with sentences.

A **run-on sentence,** also called a *fused sentence* and a *run-together sentence,* occurs when two complete sentences run into each other without any punctuation. Comma splices and run-on sentences create confusion because readers can't tell where one thought ends and another begins.

| COMMA SPLICE | The icebergs broke off from the **glacier, they** drifted into the sea. |
|---|---|
| RUN-ON SENTENCE | The icebergs broke off from the **glacier they** drifted into the sea. |
| CORRECT | The icebergs broke off from the **glacier. They** drifted into the sea. |

There is one exception. You can use a comma between two independent clauses, but only if the comma is followed by one of the seven coordinating conjunctions: *and, but, for, or, nor, yet, so.* A comma in such a construction is correct; see Chapter 24.

| CORRECT | The icebergs broke off from the glacier**, and** they drifted into the sea. |
|---|---|

🛑 **Alert:** Occasionally, when your meaning allows it, you can use a colon or a dash to join two independent clauses. ●

## 20b How can I recognize comma splices and run-on sentences?

When you know how to recognize an INDEPENDENT CLAUSE, you'll know how to recognize COMMA SPLICES and RUN-ON SENTENCES. An independent clause can stand alone as a complete sentence. An independent clause contains a SUBJECT and a PREDICATE. Also, an independent clause doesn't begin with a word that creates dependence—that is, it doesn't begin with a SUBORDINATING CONJUNCTION or a RELATIVE PRONOUN.

Interestingly, almost all comma splices and run-on sentences are caused by only four patterns. If you become familiar with these four patterns, listed in Quick Reference 20.1, you'll more easily locate them in your writing.

---

**Quick Reference 20.1** ■ ■ ■ ■ ■

### Detecting comma splices and run-on sentences

• Watch out for a PRONOUN starting the second independent clause.

| NO | The physicist Marie Curie discovered **radium, she** won two Nobel Prizes. |
|---|---|
| YES | The physicist Marie Curie discovered **radium. She** won two Nobel Prizes. |

continued >>

---

## Quick Reference 20.1   (continued)   ■ ■ ■ ■ ■

- Watch out for a CONJUNCTIVE ADVERB (such as *furthermore, however, similarly, therefore,* and *then;* see Quick Reference 14.5, section 14f, for a complete list) starting the second independent clause.

  **NO**   Marie Curie and her husband, Pierre, worked together at **first, however**, he died tragically at age forty-seven.

  **YES**   Marie Curie and her husband, Pierre, worked together at **first. However,** he died tragically at age forty-seven.

- Watch out for a TRANSITIONAL EXPRESSION (such as *in addition, for example, in contrast, of course,* and *meanwhile;* see Quick Reference 3.5, section 3g, for a reference list) starting the second independent clause.

  **NO**   Marie Curie and her husband won a Nobel Prize for the discovery of **radium, in addition, Marie** herself won another Nobel Prize for her work on the atomic weight of radium.

  **YES**   Marie Curie and her husband won a Nobel Prize for the discovery of **radium; in addition, Marie** herself won another Nobel Prize for her work on the atomic weight of radium.

- Watch out for a second independent clause that explains, says more about, contrasts with, or gives an example of what's said in the first independent clause.

  **NO**   Marie Curie died of leukemia in **1934, exposure** to radioactivity killed her.

  **YES**   Marie Curie died of leukemia in **1934. Exposure** to radioactivity killed her.

🛇 **Alert:** To proofread for comma splices, cover all words on one side of the comma and see if the words remaining form an independent clause. If they do, next cover all words you left uncovered, on the other side of the comma. If the second side of the comma is also an independent clause, you're looking at a comma splice. (This technique doesn't work for run-on sentences because a comma isn't present.) ●

Experienced writers sometimes use a comma to join very short independent clauses, especially if one independent clause is negative and the other is positive: *Mosquitoes don't **bite, they** stab.* In ACADEMIC WRITING, however, many instructors consider this an error, so you'll be safe if you use a period. (Another option is a semicolon, if the two independent clauses are closely related in meaning: *Mosquitoes don't **bite; they** stab.*)

## **20c** How can I correct comma splices and run-on sentences?

Once you have identified a COMMA SPLICE or a RUN-ON SENTENCE, you're ready to correct it. You can do this in one of four ways, as shown in Quick Reference 20.2.

### ■ Using a period to correct comma splices and run-on sentences

You can use a period to correct comma splices and run-on sentences by placing the period between the two sentences. For the sake of sentence variety and emphasis (Chapter 9), however, you want to choose other options as well, such as those shown on the next few pages. Strings of short sentences rarely establish relationships and levels of importance among ideas.

---

### Quick Reference 20.2                        ■ ■ ■ ■ ■

#### Ways to correct comma splices and run-on sentences

- Use a period between the INDEPENDENT CLAUSES.
- Use a semicolon between the INDEPENDENT CLAUSES.
- Use a comma together with a COORDINATING CONJUNCTION.
- Revise one independent clause into a DEPENDENT CLAUSE.

---

| | |
|---|---|
| **COMMA SPLICE** | A shark is all **cartilage, it** doesn't have a bone in its body. |
| **RUN-ON SENTENCE** | A shark is all **cartilage it** doesn't have a bone in its body. |
| **CORRECT** | A shark is all **cartilage. It** doesn't have a bone in its body. [A period separates the independent clauses.] |

### ■ Using a semicolon to correct comma splices and run-on sentences

You can use a semicolon to correct comma splices and run-on sentences by placing the semicolon between the two sentences. Use a semicolon only when the separate sentences are closely related in meaning. For the sake of sentence variety and emphasis, however, you'll want to choose other options; for correct semicolon use, see Chapter 25.

| | |
|---|---|
| **COMMA SPLICE** | The great white shark supposedly eats **humans, research** shows that most white sharks spit them out after the first bite. |

| | |
|---|---|
| **RUN-ON SENTENCE** | The great white shark supposedly eats **humans research** shows that most white sharks spit them out after the first bite. |
| **CORRECT** | The great white shark supposedly eats **humans; research** shows that most white sharks spit them out after the first bite. [A semicolon separates two independent clauses that are close in meaning.] |

## ▪ Using a comma together with a coordinating conjunction to correct comma splices and run-on sentences

You can connect independent clauses with a comma together with a coordinating conjunction (*and, but, for, or, nor, yet, so*) to correct a comma splice. You can also correct a run-on sentence by inserting a comma followed by a coordinating conjunction.

🛑 **Alert:** Use a comma before a coordinating conjunction that links independent clauses (24b). ●

When you use a coordinating conjunction, be sure that your choice fits the meaning of the material. *And* signals addition; *but* and *yet* signal contrast; *for* and *so* signal cause; and *or* and *nor* signal alternatives.

| | |
|---|---|
| **COMMA SPLICE** | All living creatures give off weak electrical charges in the **water, special** pores on a shark's skin can detect these signals. |
| **RUN-ON SENTENCE** | All living creatures give off weak electrical charges in the **water special** pores on a shark's skin can detect these signals. |
| **CORRECT** | All living creatures give off weak electrical charges in the **water, and special** pores on a shark's skin can detect these signals. |

**EXERCISE 20-1**   Revise the comma splices and run-on sentences by using a period, a semicolon, or a comma and coordinating conjunction. For help, consult section 20c.

1. During the "Celebration of Books," aspiring writers can ask published authors questions about writing, for example, many people wish to know how to find an agent.

2. Besides asking about agents, would-be writers also query published authors about writing techniques many questions deal with whether to write using a computer or by longhand.

3. The "Celebration of Books" offers panel discussions on a variety of topics, including memoir writing, poetry development, and techniques of plotting short stories other panels cover writing the western novel and true crime stories.

4. The "Celebration of Books" appeals to readers, many of whom can see their favorite authors in person speaking on panels and in more informal settings such as receptions and book signings fans of authors greatly enjoy such opportunities.

5. In addition to writers, many well-known artists and musicians are honored at the "Celebration of Books," its Advisory Board recommended this expansion years ago to widen the conference's appeal.

### ■ Revising one independent clause into a dependent clause to correct comma splices and run-on sentences

You can correct a comma splice or run-on sentence by revising one of the two independent clauses into a dependent clause. This method is suitable only when one idea can logically be subordinated to the other. Also, be careful never to end the dependent clause with a period or semicolon. If you do, you've created the error of a SENTENCE FRAGMENT.

#### CREATE DEPENDENT CLAUSES
#### WITH SUBORDINATING CONJUNCTIONS

One way to create a dependent clause is to insert a SUBORDINATING CONJUNCTION (such as *because, although, when,* and *if*—see Quick Reference 14.7, section 14h, for a complete list). Always choose a subordinating conjunction that fits the meaning of each particular sentence: *because* and *since* signal cause; *although* signals contrast; *when* signals time; and *if* signals condition. Dependent clauses that begin with a subordinating conjunction are called ADVERB CLAUSES.

| | |
|---|---|
| **COMMA SPLICE** | Homer and Langley Collyer had packed their house from top to bottom with **junk, police** could not open the front door to investigate a reported smell. |
| **RUN-ON SENTENCE** | Homer and Langley Collyer had packed their house from top to bottom with **junk police** could not open the front door to investigate a reported smell. |
| **CORRECT** | **Because** Homer and Langley Collyer had packed their house from top to bottom with **junk, police** could not open the front door to investigate a reported smell. |
| | [*Because* starts a dependent clause that is joined by a comma with the independent clause starting with *police.*] |

🛈 **Alert:** Place a comma between an introductory dependent clause and the independent clause that follows (24c). ●

## CREATE DEPENDENT CLAUSES WITH RELATIVE PRONOUNS

You can create a dependent clause with a RELATIVE PRONOUN (*who, whom, whose, which, that*). Dependent clauses with a relative pronoun are called ADJECTIVE CLAUSES.

| | |
|---|---|
| **COMMA SPLICE** | The Collyers had been crushed under a pile of **newspapers, the newspapers** had toppled onto the brothers. |
| **RUN-ON SENTENCE** | The Collyers had been crushed under a pile of **newspapers the newspapers** had toppled onto the brothers. |
| **CORRECT** | The Collyers had been crushed under a pile of **newspapers *that* had toppled** onto the brothers. [The relative pronoun *that* starts a dependent clause and is joined with the independent clause starting with *The Collyers,* after deletion of *the newspapers.*] |

🛈 **Alert:** Sometimes you need commas to set off an adjective clause from the rest of the sentence. This happens only when the adjective is NONRESTRICTIVE (nonessential), so check carefully (24f). ●

## 20d How can I correctly use a conjunctive adverb or other transitional expression between independent clauses?

CONJUNCTIVE ADVERBS and other TRANSITIONAL EXPRESSIONS link ideas between sentences. When these words fall between sentences, a period or semicolon must immediately precede them—and a comma usually immediately follows them.

Conjunctive adverbs include such words as *however, therefore, also, next, then, thus, furthermore,* and *nevertheless* (see Quick Reference 14.5, section 14f, for a complete list). Be careful to remember that conjunctive adverbs are not COORDINATING CONJUNCTIONS (*and, but,* and so on; see 20c).

| | |
|---|---|
| **COMMA SPLICE** | Buying or leasing a car is a matter of individual preference, **however,** it's wise to consider several points before making a decision. |
| **RUN-ON SENTENCE** | Buying or leasing a car is a matter of individual preference **however** it's wise to consider several points before making a decision. |
| **CORRECT** | Buying or leasing a car is a matter of individual preference. **However,** it's wise to consider several points before making a decision. |

| CORRECT | Buying or leasing a car is a matter of individual preference**; however,** it's wise to consider several points before making a decision. |
|---|---|

Transitional expressions include *for example, for instance, in addition, in fact, of course,* and *on the one hand/on the other hand* (see Quick Reference 3.5, section 3g, for a complete list).

| COMMA SPLICE | Car leasing requires a smaller down payment**, for example,** in many cases, you need only $1,000 or $2,000 and the first monthly payment. |
|---|---|
| RUN-ON SENTENCE | Car leasing requires a smaller down payment **for example** in many cases, you need only $1,000 or $2,000 and the first monthly payment. |
| CORRECT | Car leasing requires a smaller down payment**. For example,** in many cases, you need only $1,000 or $2,000 and the first monthly payment. |
| CORRECT | Car leasing requires a smaller down payment**; for example,** in many cases, you need only $1,000 or $2,000 and the first monthly payment. |

🛑 **Alert:** A conjunctive adverb or a transitional expression is usually followed by a comma when it starts a sentence (24c). ●

**EXERCISE 20-2**    Revise comma splices or run-on sentences caused by incorrectly punctuated conjunctive adverbs or other transitional expressions. If a sentence is correct, circle its number. For help, consult 20d.

EXAMPLE    Yearly, the US National Aeronautics and Space Administration (NASA) requests federal funding for space exploration, however, many US citizens wonder what practical value the space program offers.

Corrected: Yearly, the US National Aeronautics and Space Administration (NASA) requests federal funding for space *exploration. However,* many US citizens wonder what practical value the space program offers. [comma splice; corrected by inserting a period before a conjunctive adverb]

1. US citizens may not realize products developed by NASA directly affect their lives. For example, NASA has developed or improved a number of goods and services now available to the general public.

2. People may be surprised to learn that bar coding on products grew out of NASA's need to keep track of thousands of spacecraft components, indeed, bar codes allow merchants to track what they sell and to record items for reordering.

3. Methods of medical imaging today are based on NASA's developing ways to process signals for sending images from space, in addition, the ear thermometer, popular for use with adults and children, developed out of NASA technology to identify the birth of stars.

4. Firefighters now wear fire-resistant suits because of space technology furthermore, NASA research created protective lenses that now save welders' eyes from harmful radiation.

5. Not all items coming from NASA's experiments result in medical advances or safety for workers, for instance, thermal gloves, ski boots, and failsafe flashlights are now available to the general public as a direct result of NASA's work.

# Misplaced and Dangling Modifiers

## MISPLACED MODIFIERS

## 21a  What is a misplaced modifier?

A **modifier** is a word or group of words that describes or limits another word or group of words. A **misplaced modifier** is positioned incorrectly in a sentence, which means, therefore, that it describes the wrong word and changes the writer's meaning. Always place a modifier as close as possible to what it describes.

### AVOIDING SQUINTING MODIFIERS

A **squinting modifier** is misplaced because it modifies both the word that comes before it and the word that follows it. Check that your modifiers are placed so that they communicate the meaning you intend.

| NO | The football player being recruited **eagerly** believed each successive offer would be better. [What was *eager*? The recruitment or the player's belief?] |
|---|---|
| YES | The football player being recruited believed **eagerly** that each successive offer would be better. |

## PLACING LIMITING WORDS CAREFULLY

Words such as *only, not only, just, not just, almost, hardly, nearly, even, exactly, merely, scarcely,* and *simply* serve to limit the meaning of a word according to where they are placed. When you use such words, position them precisely.

# 21b How can I avoid split infinitives?

An INFINITIVE is a VERB form that starts with *to: to motivate, to convince, to create* are examples (14d). A **split infinitive** occurs when words are placed between the word *to* and its verb. The effect is awkward.

| NO | Orson Welles's radio drama "War of the Worlds" managed ***to,* in October 1938, *convince*** listeners that they were hearing an invasion by Martians. [*In October 1938* is misplaced because the words come between *to* and *convince.*] |
|---|---|
| YES | **In October 1938,** Orson Welles's radio drama "War of the Worlds" managed ***to convince*** listeners that they were hearing an invasion by Martians. |

Often, the word that splits an infinitive is an ADVERB ending in *-ly*. In general, place adverbs either before or after the infinitive.

| NO | People feared that they would no longer be able **to *happily* live** in peace. |
|---|---|
| YES | People feared that they would no longer be able **to live *happily*** in peace. |

The rule about split infinitives has changed recently. Current usage says that when the best placement for a single adverb is actually between *to* and the verb, use that structure freely.

Welles wanted **to *realistically* portray** a Martian invasion for the radio audience.

If you want to avoid splitting infinitives in your ACADEMIC WRITING, revise to avoid the split:

Welles wanted his "Martian invasion" **to sound *realistic*** for the radio audience. [The adverb *realistically* was changed to the adjective *realistic*.]

## 21c  How can I avoid other splits in my sentences?

When too many words split—that is, come between—a SUBJECT and its VERB or between a verb and its OBJECT, the result is a sentence that lurches rather than flows from beginning to end.

> **NO** The **announcer,** because the script, which Welles himself wrote, called for perfect imitations of emergency announcements, **opened** with a warning that included a description of the "invasion." [The subject *announcer* is placed too far away from the verb *opened*, so this split is too large.]

> **YES** Because the script, which Welles himself wrote, called for perfect imitations of emergency announcements, the **announcer opened** with a warning that included a description of the "invasion." [The subject and verb, *announcer opened*, aren't split.]

**EXERCISE 21-1**   Revise these five sentences to correct misplaced modifiers, split infinitives, and other splits. If a sentence is correct, circle its number. For help, consult 21a through 21c.

EXAMPLE   The city of Deadwood is known for its many notorious residents made popular by a TV show including Wild Bill Hickok and Calamity Jane.

Made popular by a TV show, the city of Deadwood is known for its many notorious residents, including Wild Bill Hickok and Calamity Jane.

1. Deadwood, because of its location near the Deadwood Gulch and the Black Hills of South Dakota, was named for the dead trees found in that canyon.

2. The city's founding, during a gold rush that attracted a quarter of a million miners to the area, was in 1876.

3. The main source of revenue for the city was gambling, which was outlawed in 1905 but reinstated in 1989.

4. Today, tourists who visit Deadwood often gamble and enjoy the historical reenacts of the town's famous events.

5. Deadwood nearly was the home to a dozen of famous characters from the Old West.

## DANGLING MODIFIERS

## 21d  How can I avoid dangling modifiers?

A **dangling modifier** describes or limits a word or words that never actually appear in the sentence. Aware of the intended meaning, the writer unconsciously supplies the missing words, but the reader gets confused. To correct a dangling modifier, state clearly your intended SUBJECT in the sentence.

> **NO** **Having read Faulkner's short story "A Rose for Emily," *the ending*** surprised us. [This sentence says *the ending* was reading the story, which is impossible.]

> **YES** Having read Faulkner's short story "A Rose for Emily," **we were surprised by the ending.** [Second half of sentence is rewritten to include the subject *we*.]

> **YES** **We** read Faulkner's short story "A Rose for Emily" **and were surprised by the ending.** [Sentence is rewritten to include the subject *We*.]

A major cause of dangling modifiers is the unnecessary use of the PASSIVE VOICE. Whenever possible, use the ACTIVE VOICE.

> **NO** **To earn money, china painting lessons** were offered by Emily to wealthy young women. [*China painting lessons* cannot *earn money*. *Were offered by Emily* is in the passive voice.]

> **YES** **To earn money, Emily** offered china painting lessons to wealthy young women. [Change to the active voice; *Emily offered* corrects the problem.]

**EXERCISE 21-2**  Identify and correct any dangling modifiers in these sentences. If a sentence is correct, circle its number. For help, consult 21d.

EXAMPLE  To understand what happened to Krakatoa, the volcano and its history must be studied.

Corrected: To understand what happened to Krakatoa, one must study the volcano and its history.

1. In 1883, massive destruction was caused by the eruption of the volcano Krakatoa, an event recently examined in the book *Krakatoa: The Day the World Exploded.*

2. Exploding with a force 13,000 times stronger than the bomb dropped on Hiroshima, people thousands of miles away heard the eruption.

3. The loudest sound historically reported was generated by the explosion, with devastating tsunamis soon following.

4. Ejecting tons of debris into the air, the volcano destroyed or damaged hundreds of nearby villages.

5. Darkening the sky for days afterwards and producing unusual sunsets, the ash and gases from the volcano temporarily lowered the average temperature of the earth.

# 22

# Shifting and Mixed Sentences

## SHIFTING SENTENCES

## 22a What is a shifting sentence?

A **shift** within a sentence is an unnecessary, abrupt change in PERSON, NUMBER, SUBJECT, VOICE, TENSE, MOOD, or DIRECT or INDIRECT DISCOURSE. These shifts blur meaning. Sometimes a shift occurs between two or more sentences in a paragraph. If you set out on one track (writing in FIRST PERSON, for example), your readers expect you to stay on that same track (and not unnecessarily shift to THIRD PERSON, for example). When you go off track, you have written a shifting sentence or paragraph.

## 22b How can I avoid shifts in person and number?

Who or what performs or receives an action is defined by the term *person*. FIRST PERSON (*I, we*) is the speaker or writer; SECOND PERSON (*you*) is the one being spoken or written *to;* and THIRD PERSON (*he, she, it, they*) is the person or thing being spoken or written *about.*

The essential point is that shifts are incorrect unless the meaning in a particular context makes them necessary.

NO    I enjoy reading financial forecasts of the future, but **you** wonder which will turn out to be correct. [The first person *I* shifts to the second person *you.*]

YES    I enjoy reading financial forecasts of the future, but **I** wonder which will turn out to be correct.

NUMBER refers to whether words are *singular* (one) or *plural* (more than one) in meaning. Do not start to write in one number and then shift for no reason to the other number.

NO    Because **people** are living longer, **an employee** now retires later. [The plural *people* shifts to the singular *employee.*]

YES    Because **people** are living longer, **employees** now retire later.

In ACADEMIC WRITING, reserve *you* for addressing the reader directly. Use the third person for general statements.

> **NO**  **People** enjoy feeling productive, so when a job is unsatisfying, **you** usually become depressed. [*People* is in the third person, so a shift to the second person *you* is incorrect.]

> **YES**  **People** enjoy feeling productive, so when a job is unsatisfying, **they** usually become depressed.

Be careful with words in the singular (usually NOUNS) used in a general sense, such as *employee, student, consumer, neighbor,* and *someone*. These words are always third-person singular. The only pronouns for these ANTECEDENTS in the third-person singular are *he, she,* and *it*. Remember that *they* is plural, so the word *they* can't be used with singular nouns.

> **NO**  When **an employee** is treated with respect, **they** are more motivated to do a good job. [*Employee* is third-person singular, so the shift to the third-person plural *they* is incorrect.]

> **YES**  When **an employee** is treated with respect, **he or she** is more motivated to do a good job.

🛑 **Alert:**  When you use INDEFINITE PRONOUNS (such as *someone, everyone,* or *anyone*), you want to use GENDER-NEUTRAL LANGUAGE. For advice, see 17r and 12f. ●

**EXERCISE 22-1**    Eliminate shifts in person and number between, as well as within, sentences. Some sentences may not need revision. For help, consult 22b.

(1) First-time visitors to the Mall of America may be overwhelmed by its size, but you will also see its helpful design. (2) A shopper will notice that the mall is divided into architecturally distinct areas so they won't get lost. (3) The four sides of the mall have different themes and matching décor, so it is easy to navigate. (4) The architects named the four sides the North Garden, South Avenue, East Broadway, and West Market. (5) He or she also called the fourth floor's collection of nightclubs the Upper East Side to reflect an urban environment.

# 22c  How can I avoid shifts in subject and voice?

A SHIFT in SUBJECT is rarely justified when it is accompanied by a shift in VOICE. The voice of a sentence is either *active* (*People expect changes*) or *passive* (*Changes are expected*). Some subject shifts, however, are justified by the meaning of a passage: for example, *People look forward to the future, but the future holds many secrets.*

> **NO**  Most **people expect** major improvements in the future, but some **hardships are** also **anticipated.** [The subject shifts from *people* to *hardships,* and the voice shifts from active to passive.]

**YES** Most **people expect** major improvements in the future, but **they** also **anticipate** some hardships.

## 22d How can I avoid shifts in tense and mood?

TENSE refers to the time in which the action of a VERB takes place—past, present, or future: *We **will go** to the movies after we **finish** dinner.* An unnecessary tense SHIFT within or between sentences can make the statement confusing or illogical.

**NO** A campaign to clean up movies in the United States **began** in the 1920s as civic and religious groups **try** to ban sex and violence from the screen. [The tense incorrectly shifts from the past *began* to the present *try*.]

**YES** A campaign to clean up movies in the United States **began** in the 1920s as civic and religious groups **tried** to ban sex and violence from the screen.

MOOD indicates whether a sentence is a statement or a question (INDICATIVE MOOD), a command or request (IMPERATIVE MOOD), or a conditional or other-than-real statement (SUBJUNCTIVE MOOD). A shift in mood creates an awkward construction and can cause confusion.

**NO** The Production Code included two guidelines on violence: **Do not show** the details of brutal killings, and movies **should not be** explicit about how to commit crimes. [The verbs shift from the imperative mood *do not show* to the indicative mood *movies should not be*.]

**YES** The Production Code included two guidelines on violence: **Do not show** the details of brutal killings, and **do not show** explicitly how to commit crimes. [This revision uses the imperative mood for both guidelines.]

## 22e How can I avoid shifts between indirect and direct discourse?

**Indirect discourse** is not enclosed in quotation marks because it reports, rather than quotes, something that someone said. In contrast, **direct discourse** is enclosed in quotation marks because it quotes exactly the words that someone said. It's incorrect to write direct discourse and omit the quotation marks. Also, it's incorrect to write sentences that mix indirect and direct discourse. Such SHIFT errors confuse readers, who can't tell what was said and what is being merely reported.

**NO** A critic said that board members were acting as censors and **what you are doing is unconstitutional.** [*Said that* sets up indirect discourse, but *what you are doing is unconstitutional* is direct discourse; it also lacks quotation marks and the changes in language that distinguish spoken words from reported words.]

**YES** A critic said that board members were acting as censors and **that what they were doing was unconstitutional.** [This revision uses indirect discourse consistently.]

Whenever you change your writing from direct discourse to indirect discourse (when you decide to paraphrase rather than quote someone directly, for example), you need to make changes in VERB TENSE and other grammatical features for your writing to make sense. Simply removing the quotation marks is not enough.

**NO** He asked **did we enjoy the movie?** [This version has the verb form needed for direct discourse, but the pronoun *we* is wrong and quotation punctuation is missing.]

**YES** He asked **whether we enjoyed the movie.** [This version is entirely indirect discourse, and the verb has changed from *enjoy* to *enjoyed.*]

**YES** He asked, **"Did you enjoy the movie?"** [This version is direct discourse. It repeats the original speech exactly, with correct quotation punctuation.]

**EXERCISE 22-2** Revise these sentences to eliminate incorrect shifts within sentences. Some sentences can be revised in several ways. For help, consult 22b through 22e.

EXAMPLE In 1942, the US government is faced with arresting five million people for not paying their federal income taxes.

In 1942, the US government *was faced* with arresting five million people for not paying their federal income taxes.

1. Congress needed money to pay for US participation in World War II, so a new tax system was proposed.

2. Tax payments were due on March 15, not April 15 as it is today.

3. For the first time, Congress taxed millions of lower-income citizens. Most people do not save enough to pay the amount of taxes due.

4. When a scientific poll showed lawmakers that only one in seven Americans had saved enough money, he became worried.

## MIXED SENTENCES

### 22f What is a mixed sentence?

A mixed sentence has two or more parts, with the first part starting in one direction and the rest of the parts going off in another. This mixing of sentence parts leads to unclear meaning. To avoid this error, as you write each sentence, remember how you started it and make sure that whatever comes next in the sentence relates grammatically and logically to that beginning.

> **NO** Because our side lost the contest eventually motivated us to do better. [*Because our side lost the contest* starts the sentence in one direction, but *eventually motivated us to do better* goes off in another direction.]
>
> **YES** Because our side lost the contest, **we** eventually became motivated to do better.
>
> **YES** Our side lost the contest, **which** eventually motivated us to do better.

### 22g How can I correct a mixed sentence due to faulty predication?

**Faulty predication**, sometimes called *illogical predication,* occurs when a SUBJECT and its PREDICATE don't make sense together.

> **NO** The purpose of television was invented to entertain people. [A *purpose* cannot be *invented.*]
>
> **YES** The purpose of television was to entertain people.
>
> **YES** Television was invented to entertain people.

In ACADEMIC WRITING, avoid nonstandard constructions such as *is when* and *is where.* They should be avoided not only because they are nonstandard, but also because they usually lead to faulty predication.

> **NO** A disaster **is when** TV news shows get some of their highest ratings.
>
> **YES** TV news shows get some of their highest ratings during a disaster.

In academic writing, avoid constructions such as *the reason . . . is because.* Using both *reason* and *because* makes the construction redundant (it says the same thing twice). Instead, use either *the reason . . . is that* or *because* alone.

> **NO** One **reason** that TV news captured national attention in the 1960s **is because** it covered the Vietnam War thoroughly.

> **YES**   One **reason** TV news captured national attention in the 1960s **is that** it covered the Vietnam War thoroughly.

> **YES**   TV news captured national attention in the 1960s **because** it covered the Vietnam War thoroughly.

## 22h   What are correct elliptical constructions?

An **elliptical construction** deliberately leaves out one or more words in a sentence for CONCISENESS.

> Victor has his book and Joan's. [This means *Victor has his book and Joan's book.* The second *book* is left out deliberately.]

For an elliptical construction to be correct, the one or more words you leave out need to be identical to those already appearing in the sentence. For instance, the sample sentence above about Victor and Joan would have an incorrect elliptical construction if the writer's intended meaning were *Victor has his book, and Joan has her own book.*

> **NO**   During the 1920s in Chicago, the cornetist Manuel Perez **was leading** one outstanding jazz group, and Tommy and Jimmy Dorsey another. [The words *was leading* cannot take the place of *were leading,* which is required after *Tommy and Jimmy Dorsey.*]

> **YES**   During the 1920s in Chicago, the cornetist Manuel Perez **was leading** one outstanding jazz group, and Tommy and Jimmy Dorsey **were leading** another.

> **YES**   During the 1920s in Chicago, the cornetist Manuel Perez **led** one outstanding jazz group, and Tommy and Jimmy Dorsey another. [*Led* is correct with both *Manuel Perez* and *Tommy and Jimmy Dorsey,* so *led* can be omitted after *Dorsey.*]

## 22i   What are correct comparisons?

When you write a sentence in which you want to compare two or more things, make sure that no important words are omitted.

> **NO**   Individuals driven to achieve make **better** business executives. [*Better* is a word of comparison (18e), but no comparison is stated.]

> **YES**   Individuals driven to achieve make **better** business executives **than do people not interested in personal accomplishments.**

**EXERCISE 22-3**   Revise this paragraph to create correct elliptical constructions, to complete comparisons, and to insert any missing words. For help, see 22h through 22i.

(1) A giant tsunami is as destructive and even larger than a tidal wave. (2) The word *tsunami* is Japanese for "harbor wave," for this kind wave appears suddenly in harbor or bay. (3) A tsunami begins with rapid shift in ocean floor caused by an undersea earthquake or volcano. (4) The wave this produces in the open sea is less than three feet high, but it can grow to a height of a hundred feet as it rushes and strikes against the shore. (5) For this reason, tsunamis are much more dangerous to seaside towns than ships on the open sea.

# 23

# Periods, Question Marks, and Exclamation Points

## PERIODS

## 23a When does a period end a sentence?

A **period** ends a statement, a mild command, or an INDIRECT QUESTION. Never use a period to end a DIRECT QUESTION, a strong command, or an emphatic declaration.

**END OF A STATEMENT**

A journey of a thousand miles must begin with a single step.
—Lao-tsu, The Way of Lao-tsu

**MILD COMMAND**

Put a gram of boldness into everything you do.
—Baltasar Gracian

**INDIRECT QUESTION**

I asked if they wanted to climb Mt. Everest. [As an indirect question, this sentence reports that a question was asked. If it were a direct question, it would end with a question mark: *I asked, "Do you want to climb Mt. Everest?"*]

## 23b   How do I use periods with abbreviations?

Most **abbreviations**, though not all, call for periods. Typical abbreviations with periods include *Mt., St., Dr., Mr., Ms., Mrs., Jr., Fri., Feb., a.m.,* and *p.m.* (For more about *a.m.* and *p.m.,* see Chapter 13, "Usage Glossary," and section 30j; for more about abbreviations in general, see 30i through 30l.)

**❗ Alert:**  Spell out the word *professor* in ACADEMIC WRITING; never abbreviate it. ●

Abbreviations without periods include the postal codes for states (for example, IL, CO) and the names of some organizations and government agencies (for example, CBS and NASA).

> **Ms.** Yuan, who works at **NASA,** lectured to **Dr.** Garcia's physics class at 9:30 **a.m.**

**❗ Alert:**  When the period of an abbreviation falls at the end of a sentence that calls for a period, the period of the abbreviation serves also to end the sentence. If, however, your sentence ends in a question mark or an exclamation point, put it after the period of the abbreviation.

> The phone rang at 4:00 **a.m.**
> It's upsetting to answer a wrong-number call at 4:00 **a.m.!**
> Who would call at 4:00 **a.m.?** ●

## QUESTION MARKS

## 23c   When do I use a question mark?

A **question mark** ends a **direct question,** one that quotes the exact words the speaker used. (In contrast, an **indirect question** reports a question and ends with a period.)

> How many attempts have been made to climb Mt. Everest? [An indirect question would end with a period: *She wants to know how many attempts have been made to climb Mt. Everest.*]

Questions in a series are each followed by a question mark, whether or not each question is a complete sentence.

> After the fierce storm, the mountain climbers debated what to do next. Turn back**?** Move on**?** Rest for a while**?**

❗ **Alert:** When questions in a series are not complete sentences (as in the preceding example), you can choose whether to capitalize the first letter, but be consistent within each piece of writing. ●

Sometimes a statement or mild command is phrased as a question to be polite. In such cases, a question mark is optional, but be consistent in each piece of writing.

Would you please send me a copy.

## 23d  When can I use a question mark in parentheses?

The only time to use a question mark in parentheses (?) is if a date or other number is unknown or doubtful. Never use (?) to communicate that you're unsure of information.

Mary Astell, a British writer of pamphlets on women's rights, was born in 1666 **(?)** and died in 1731.

The word *about* is often a more graceful substitute for (?): *Mary Astell was born about 1666.*

Also, never use (?) to communicate IRONY or sarcasm. Choose words to deliver your message.

NO  Having altitude sickness is a pleasant **(?)** experience.

YES  Having altitude sickness is **as** pleasant **as having a bad case of the flu.**

## EXCLAMATION POINTS

## 23e  When do I use an exclamation point?

An **exclamation point** ends a strong command or an emphatic declaration. A strong command is a firm and direct order: *Look out behind you!* An emphatic declaration is a shocking or surprising statement: *There's been an accident!*

## 23f  What is considered overuse of exclamation points?

In ACADEMIC WRITING, words, not exclamation points, need to communicate the intensity of your message. Reserve exclamation points for an emphatic declaration within a longer passage.

When we were in Nepal, we tried each day to see Mt. Everest. But each day we failed. **Clouds defeated us!** The summit never emerged from a heavy overcast.

Also, using exclamation points too frequently suggests an exaggerated sense of urgency.

**NO**  Mountain climbing can be dangerous. You must know correct procedures! You must have the proper equipment! Otherwise, you could die!

**YES**  Mountain climbing can be dangerous. You must know correct procedures. You must have the proper equipment. Otherwise, you could die!

Never use (!) to communicate amazement or sarcasm. Choose words to deliver your message.

**NO**  At 29,035 feet (!), Mt. Everest is the world's highest mountain. Yet, Chris (!) wants to climb it.

**YES**  At **a majestic** 29,035 feet, Mt. Everest is the world's highest mountain. Yet, Chris, **amazingly,** wants to climb it.

**EXERCISE 23-1**  Insert any needed periods, question marks, and exclamation points and delete any unneeded ones. For help, consult all sections of this chapter.

EXAMPLE  Dr Madan Kataria, who calls himself the Giggling Guru (!), established the world's first laughter club in 1995.

Dr. Madan Kataria, who calls himself the Giggling Guru, established the world's first laughter club in 1995.

1. More than 1,000 (?) laughter clubs exist throughout the world, each seeking to promote health by reducing stress and strengthening the immune system!

2. Dr Madan Kataria, a physician in Mumbai, India, developed a yoga-like (!) strategy based on group (!) laughter and then set up laughter clubs.

3. Laughter clubs say, "Yes!" when asked, "Is laughter the best medicine."

4. The clubs' activities include breathing and stretching exercises and playful (?) behaviors, such as performing the opera laugh (!), the chicken laugh (!), and the "Ho-Ho, Ha-Ha" (?) exercise.

5. According to the German psychologist Dr Michael Titze, "In the 1950s people used to laugh eighteen minutes a day (!), but today we laugh not more than six (?) minutes per day, despite huge rises in the standard of living."

# 24

# Commas

## 24a What is the role of the comma?

Commas are the most frequently used marks of punctuation, occurring twice as often as all other punctuation marks combined. A comma must be used in certain places, it must not be used in other places, and it's optional in still other places. This chapter helps you sort through the various rules.

For quick access to most answers when you have a comma question, consult Quick Reference 24.1. The sections in parentheses indicate where you can find fuller explanations.

---

### Quick Reference 24.1

#### Key uses of commas

**COMMAS WITH COORDINATING CONJUNCTIONS LINKING INDEPENDENT CLAUSES (24b)**

Postcards are ideal for brief greetings**, and** they can also be miniature works of art. [*and* is a coordinating conjunction]

**COMMAS AFTER INTRODUCTORY ELEMENTS (24c)**

**Although most postcards cost only a quarter,** one recently sold for thousands of dollars. [clause]

**On postcard racks,** several designs are usually available. [phrase]

**For example,** animals are timeless favorites. [transitional expression]

**However,** most cards show local landmarks. [word]

**COMMAS WITH ITEMS IN A SERIES (24d)**

**Places, paintings, and people** appear on postcards. [*and* between last two items]

**Places, paintings, people, animals** occupy dozens of display racks. [no *and* between last two items]

**COMMAS WITH COORDINATE ADJECTIVES (24e)**

Some postcards feature **appealing, dramatic** scenes.

continued >>

---

**Quick Reference 24.1** (continued) ■ ■ ■ ■ ■

### NO COMMAS WITH CUMULATIVE ADJECTIVES (24e)

Other postcards feature **famous historical** scenes.

### COMMAS WITH NONRESTRICTIVE ELEMENTS (24f)

**Four years after the first postcard appeared,** the US government began to issue prestamped postcards. [nonrestrictive element introduces independent clause]

The Golden Age of postcards, **which lasted from about 1900 to 1929,** yielded many especially valuable cards. [nonrestrictive element interrupts independent clause]

Collectors attend postcard shows, **which are similar to baseball-card shows.** [nonrestrictive element ends independent clause]

### NO COMMAS WITH RESTRICTIVE ELEMENTS (24f)

Collectors **who attend these shows** may specialize in a particular kind of postcard. [restrictive clause]

### COMMAS WITH QUOTED WORDS (24h)

One collector told me, "Attending a show is like digging for buried treasure." [quoted words at end of sentence]

"I always expect to find a priceless postcard," he said. [quoted words at start of sentence]

"Everyone there," he joked, "believes a million-dollar card is hidden in the next stack." [quoted words interrupted mid-sentence]

## **24b** How do commas work with coordinating conjunctions?

Never use a comma when a coordinating conjunction links only two words, two PHRASES, or two DEPENDENT CLAUSES.

> **NO**  Habitat for Humanity depends on volunteers for **labor, and donations** to help with its construction projects. [*Labor* and *donations* are two words; the conjunction explains their relationship. No comma is needed.]

> **YES**  Habitat for Humanity depends on volunteers for **labor and donations** to help with its construction projects.

Do use a comma when a coordinating conjunction links two or more INDEPENDENT CLAUSES. Place the comma before the coordinating conjunction.

The sky turned dark gray, **and** the wind died suddenly.

The November morning had just begu**n,** **but** it looked like dusk.

## Exceptions

- When two independent clauses are very short and they contrast with each other, you can link them with a comma without using a coordinating conjunction: *Mosquitoes don't bite, they stab.* Some instructors consider this an error, so in ACADEMIC WRITING, you'll never be wrong if you use a period or semicolon (Chapter 25) instead of a comma.

- When one or both independent clauses linked by a coordinating conjunction happen to contain other commas, dropping the coordinating conjunction and using a semicolon instead of the comma can help clarify meaning.

  > With temperatures below freezing, the snow did not melt; and **people** wondered, gazing at the white landscape, when they would see grass again.

**EXERCISE 24-1** Combine each pair of sentences using the coordinating conjunction shown in parentheses. Rearrange words when necessary. For help, consult 24b.

EXAMPLE Children spend less time playing outdoors than ever before. That has been found to be a significant problem. (and)

Children spend less time playing outdoors than ever before, **and** that has been found to be a significant problem.

1. If your parents ever said to you, "Go outside and burn off some energy," you should thank them. They did you a big favor. (for)

2. Spending time outside as children is good for people. Now there is scientific proof. (and)

3. As children play outside, their senses are stimulated. That helps them learn in numerous ways. (and)

4. For example, children's vision is fully stimulated by being outside. They should spend more time playing outdoors than reading or watching TV, which stimulates only a narrow part of their vision. (so)

5. When children spend time playing outside, they may engage in intense physical activity. They may be less active but still discover the magic of the natural world. (or)

## **24c** How do commas work with introductory clauses, phrases, and words?

A comma follows any introductory element that comes before an INDEPENDENT CLAUSE. An introductory element can be a CLAUSE, PHRASE, or words. Because these elements are not sentences by themselves, you need to join them to independent clauses.

> **When the topic is dieting,** many people say sugar craving is their worst problem. [introductory dependent clause]

> **Sweets being a temptation for many adults,** most parents avoid commercial baby foods that contain sugar. [introductory absolute phrase]

> **For example,** fructose comes from fruit, but it's still sugar. [introductory transitional expression]

### EXCEPTION

When an introductory element is short, and the sentence can be understood easily, some writers omit the comma. However, in ACADEMIC WRITING, you'll never be wrong if you use the comma.

> **YES** In 1992, the Americans with Disabilities Act was passed. [preferred]

> **YES** In 1992 the Americans with Disabilities Act was passed.

An **interjection** is an introductory word that conveys surprise or other emotions. Use a comma after an interjection at the beginning of a sentence: ***Oh,*** *we didn't realize that you're allergic to cats.* ***Yes,*** *your sneezing worries me.*

**Alert:** Use a comma before and after a transitional expression that falls in the middle of a sentence. When the transitional expression starts a sentence, follow it with a comma. When the transitional expression ends a sentence, put a comma before it.

> **By the way,** the parade begins at noon. [introductory transitional expression with comma after it]

> The parade, **by the way,** begins at noon. [transitional expression with comma before and after it, in middle of sentence]

> The parade begins at noon, **by the way.** [transitional expression with comma before it, at end of sentence] ●

**EXERCISE 24-2**   Combine each set of sentences into one sentence according to the direction in parentheses. Use a comma after the introductory element. You can add, delete, and rearrange words as needed. For help, consult 24c.

EXAMPLE    People have known that humor is good for them. They have
known this for a long time. (Begin with *for a long time*.)

**For a long time,** people have known that humor is good for them.

1. People laugh. Scientists study them to find out what actually happens.
(Begin with *when*.)

2. Scientists track our physiological reactions. They discover the chemicals we
produce while we are laughing. (Begin with *in fact*.)

3. Our brains use dopamine when we laugh. Dopamine is a chemical we
produce that makes us feel good. (Begin with *produced*.)

4. We sometimes activate our tear ducts by laughing. That reduces stress.
(Begin with *interestingly*.)

5. Scientists tested people's saliva immediately after they laughed. Scientists
concluded that immune systems may benefit from laughter. (Begin with
*immediately*.)

## 24d   How do commas work with items in a series?

A **series** is a group of three or more elements—words, PHRASES, or CLAUSES—
that match in grammatical form and are of equal importance in a sentence.

My love of flying goes back to those early days **of roller skates, of
swings, and of bicycles.**

—Tresa Wiggins, student

Many general publications omit the comma between the next to last item
of a series and the coordinating conjunction. Recently, practice is changing
even in ACADEMIC WRITING, which means that some instructors require the
use of a comma here and others consider it an error. Check with your instructor.

NO    The sweater comes in **blue, green, pink and black.** [Do the
sweaters come in three or four colors?]

YES    The sweater comes in **blue, green, pink, and black.** [The comma
before *and* clarifies that the sweaters come in four colors.]

At all times, however, follow the "toast, juice, and ham and eggs" rule. That is,
when one of the items in a series contains *and,* don't use a comma in that item.

When items in a series contain commas or other punctuation, separate
them with SEMICOLONS instead of commas (25e).

If it's a bakery, they have to sell cake; if it's a photography shop, they
have to develop film; and if it's a dry-goods store, they have to sell warm
underwear.

—Art Buchwald, "Birth Control for Banks"

Numbered or lettered lists within a sentence are considered items in a series. With three or more items, use commas (or semicolons if the items themselves contain commas) to separate them.

> To file your insurance claim, please enclose (1) a letter requesting payment, (2) a police report about the robbery, **and** (3) proof of purchase of the items you say are missing.

**!** **Alert:** In a series, never use a comma before the first item or after the last item, unless a different rule makes it necessary.

**NO**　　Such dreamers include, Miró, Debussy, Dostoevsky, and Dickinson.

**YES**　　Such dreamers include Miró, Debussy, Dostoevsky, and Dickinson.

**YES**　　Such dreamers include, of course, Miró, Debussy, Dostoevsky, and Dickinson. [As a transitional expression, *of course* is set off from the rest of the sentence by commas before and after it (24c).] ●

# 24e　How do commas work with coordinate adjectives?

**Coordinate adjectives** are two or more ADJECTIVES of equal weight that describe—that is, modify—a NOUN. In contrast, **cumulative adjectives** build meaning from word to word, as they move toward the noun. The key to applying this rule is recognizing when adjectives are coordinate and when they aren't. Quick Reference 24.2 tells you how.

---

**Quick Reference 24.2**　　■ ■ ■ ■ ■

### Tests for coordinate and cumulative adjectives

If either one of these tests works, the adjectives are coordinate and require a comma between them.

- Can the order of the adjectives be reversed without changing the meaning or creating nonsense? If yes, use a comma.

  **NO**　　The concert featured **new several** bands. [*New several* makes no sense.]

  **YES**　　The **huge, restless** crowd waited for the concert to begin. [*Restless, huge* still carries the same meaning, so these are coordinate adjectives.]

- Can *and* be sensibly inserted between the adjectives? If yes, use a comma.

  **NO**　　The concert featured **several and new** bands. [*Several and new* makes no sense.]

  **YES**　　The **huge and restless** crowd waited. [Modifier *huge and restless* makes sense, so these are coordinate adjectives.]

---

The audience cheered when the **pulsating, rhythmic** music filled the stadium. [*Pulsating* and *rhythmic* are coordinate adjectives.]

Each band had a **distinctive musical** style. [*Distinctive* and *musical* aren't coordinate adjectives.]

❗ **Alert:** Don't put a comma between a final coordinate adjective and the noun it modifies.

**NO**    Hundreds of **roaring, cheering, yelling, fans** filled the stadium.

**YES**    Hundreds of **roaring, cheering, yelling fans** filled the stadium. ●

**EXERCISE 24-3**   Insert commas to separate coordinate adjectives. If a sentence needs no commas, explain why. For help, consult 24e.

EXAMPLE   Only corn grown for popcorn pops consistently because all other kinds of corn lack tough enamel-like shells.

                Only corn grown for popcorn pops consistently because all other kinds of corn lack *tough, enamel-like* shells.

1. The outside of an unpopped popcorn kernel is a hard plastic-like coating.
2. Inside an unpopped kernel is a soft starchy substance combined with water.
3. Applying heat causes the water molecules to expand until the pressure pops the dark yellow kernel.
4. The popped kernel turns itself inside out and absorbs air into its white pulpy matter.
5. The thinner softer shells of nonpopcorn corn don't allow water to heat to the high popping temperature.

## 24f  How do commas work with nonrestrictive elements?

A **restrictive element** contains information (a descriptive word, clause, or phrase) that's essential for a sentence to deliver its message; thus, it is often called an *essential element.* A **nonrestrictive element** contains information that's not essential for a sentence to deliver its meaning, and therefore, it is often called a *nonessential element.* The key is in recognizing what's essential (restrictive) and what's nonessential (nonrestrictive) in a sentence. Quick Reference 24.3 defines and explains the differences in the meanings of these terms.

Quick Reference 24.4 shows the pattern for comma use with nonrestrictive elements. The pattern for restrictive elements calls for no commas.

Restrictive and nonrestrictive elements can fall at the beginning, in the middle, or at the end of a sentence. To test whether an element is nonrestrictive, read the sentence without the element. If the meaning of the sentence does not change, the element is nonrestrictive.

### Quick Reference 24.3

■ ■ ■ ■ ■

#### Restrictive and nonrestrictive defined

**RESTRICTIVE**

A restrictive element contains information essential for the sentence to deliver its message. By being essential, the words in the element limit—that is, "restrict"—the meaning in some way. Don't use commas with restrictive elements.

> Many US states retest drivers **who are over sixty-five** to check their driving competency.

The information *who are over sixty-five* is essential to understanding the sentence because it limits or restricts the meaning of *drivers* to only those over the age of sixty-five. Drivers *under* sixty-five are not included. To check whether an element is essential, drop it and read the sentence. If the meaning of the sentence changes, then the information element is essential in delivering the message intended in the sentence. This means the element is restrictive (essential), and commas are not used.

**NONRESTRICTIVE**

A nonrestrictive element contains information that's *not* essential for the sentence to deliver its message. By being nonessential, the words in the element don't limit—or "restrict"—the meaning. Use commas with nonrestrictive (nonessential) elements.

> My parents**,** **who are both over sixty-five,** took a defensive-driving course.

The information *who are both over sixty-five* is not essential because the words *my parents* carry the sentence's message so that we know who took a defensive driving course. (Information about their age is "extra" to this message, so commas are required.)

### Quick Reference 24.4

■ ■ ■ ■ ■

#### Commas with nonrestrictive elements

**Nonrestrictive element,** independent clause.

Beginning of independent clause**, nonrestrictive element,** end of independent clause.

Independent clause**, nonrestrictive element.**

---

**EXERCISE 24-4**   Using your knowledge of restrictive and nonrestrictive elements, insert commas as needed. If a sentence is correct, explain why. For help, consult 24f.

EXAMPLE   During the summer when butterflies are most active gardeners can attract them by planting the right flowers.

> During the summer, when butterflies are most active, gardeners can attract them by planting the right flowers.

1. In spring as birds and bees look for water and food certain plants and trees provide those needs and thus attract the greatest number of airborne visitors.
2. Gardeners who learn to attract birds may find they have fewer problems with insects and other unwelcome pests.
3. During suburban sprawl when cities eat up more and more land birds have to adapt by putting their nests in buildings.
4. Birds are attracted to pines and evergreens where they can find food and shelter.
5. Hungry birds who are not picky will enjoy a feeder stocked with black oil sunflower seeds.

## 24g How do commas set off parenthetical expressions, contrasts, words of direct address, and tag sentences?

**Parenthetical expressions** are "asides." They add information but aren't necessary for understanding the message of a sentence. Set them off with parentheses or commas.

> American farmers **(according to US government figures)** export more wheat than they sell at home.

> A major drought**, sad to say,** wiped out this year's wheat crop.

Expressions of **contrast** state what is *not* the case. Set them off with commas.

> Feeding the world's population is a serious**, though not impossible,** problem.

> We must work against world hunger continuously**, not only when famines strike.**

Words of **direct address** name the person or group being spoken to (addressed). Set them off with commas.

> Join me**, brothers and sisters,** to end hunger.

> Your contribution to the Relief Fund**, Steve,** will help us greatly.

A **tag sentence** is a normal sentence that ends with a "tag," an attached phrase or question. Set off a tag with a comma. When the tag is a question, the sentence ends with a question mark. This holds whether or not the **tag question** is formed with a CONTRACTION.

> People will give blood regularly**, I hope.**

> The response to the blood drive was impressive**, wasn't it?**

## **24h** How do commas work with quoted words?

Explanatory words are *said, stated, declared,* and other words that introduce DIRECT DISCOURSE. When they fall in the same sentence, quoted words are set off from explanatory words.

> Speaking of ideal love, the poet William Blake wrote, "Love seeketh not itself to please."

> "My love is a fever," said William Shakespeare about love's passion.

> "I love no love," proclaimed the poet Mary Coleridge, "but thee."

### EXCEPTION

When the quoted words are blended into the grammatical structure of your sentence, don't use commas to set them off. These are instances of INDIRECT DISCOURSE, usually occurring with *as* and *that.*

> The duke describes the duchess **as** "too soon made glad."

> The duchess insists **that** "appearing glad often is but a deception."

## **24i** How do commas work in dates, names, addresses, correspondence, and numbers?

When you write dates, names, addresses, correspondence, and numbers, use commas according to accepted practice. Quick References 24.5 through 24.8 provide some guidelines.

---

### Quick Reference 24.5    ■ ■ ■ ■ ■

#### Commas with dates

- Use a comma between the date and the year: *July 20, 1969.*
- Use a comma between the day and the date: *Sunday, July 20.*
- Within a sentence, use a comma on both sides of the year in a full date: *Everyone planned to be near a TV set on July 20, 1969, to watch the lunar landing.*
- Never use a comma when only the month and year, or the month and day, are given. Also, never use a comma between the season and year.

    **YES**  People knew that one day in **July 1969** would change the world.

    **YES**  News coverage was especially heavy on **July 21.**

    **YES**  In **summer 1969** a man walked on the moon.

- Never use a comma in an inverted date, a form used in the US military and throughout the world except in the United States.

    **YES**  People stayed near their televisions on **20 July 1969** to watch the lunar landing.

## Quick Reference 24.6

### Commas with names, places, and addresses

- When an abbreviated academic degree (*MD, PhD*) comes after a person's name, use a comma between the name and the title (*Angie Eng, MD*), and also after the title if other words follow in the sentence: *The jury listened closely to the expert testimony of* **Angie Eng, MD, last week.**

- When an indicator of birth order or succession (*Jr., Sr., III, IV*) follows a name, never use a comma: *Martin Luther* **King Jr.** or *Henry* **Ford II**

- When you invert a person's name, use a comma to separate the last name from the first: **Troyka, David**

- When city and state names are written together, use a comma to separate them: **Philadelphia, Pennsylvania.** If the city and state fall within a sentence, use a comma after the state as well: *My family settled in* **Philadelphia, Pennsylvania,** *before I was born.*

- When a complete address is part of a sentence, use a comma to separate all the items, except the state and ZIP code: *I wrote to* **Shelly Kupperman, 1001 Rule Road, Upper Saddle River, NJ 07458,** *for more information about the comma.*

## Quick Reference 24.7

### Commas in correspondence

- For the opening of an informal letter, use a comma: **Dear Betty,**

- For the opening of a business or formal letter, use a colon:

  **Dear Ms. Kiviat:**

- For the close of a letter, use a comma:

  **Sincerely yours,**     **Best regards,**     **Love,**

## Quick Reference 24.8

### Commas with numbers

- Counting from right to left, put a comma after every three digits in numbers with more than four digits.

  72,867                    156,567,066

- A comma is optional in most four-digit numbers. Be consistent within each piece of writing.

  $1776                     $1,776

  1776 miles                1,776 miles

  1776 potatoes             1,776 potatoes

continued >>

---

**Quick Reference 24.8** (continued) ■ ■ ■ ■ ■

- Never use a comma in a four-digit year: **1990** (*Note:* If the year has five digits or more, do use a comma: **25,000 BC.**)
- Never use a comma in an address of four digits or more: ***12161 Dean Drive***
- Never use a comma in a page number of four digits or more: ***see page 1338***
- Use a comma to separate related measurements written as words: ***five feet, four inches***
- Use a comma to separate a scene from an act in a play: ***act II, scene iv*** (or ***act 2, scene 4***)
- Use a comma to separate references to a page and a line: ***page 10, line 6***

---

**EXERCISE 24-5** Insert commas where they are needed. For help, consult 24i.

EXAMPLE On June 1 1984 the small German-French production company released a feature film called *Paris Texas*.

On June 1, 1984, the small German-French production company released a feature film called *Paris, Texas*.

1. Made by the noted German director Wim Wenders, *Paris Texas* was set in an actual town in Lamar County Texas with a population of 24699.

2. The movie's title was clearly intended to play off the slightly more famous Paris in France.

3. The custom of naming little towns in the United States after cosmopolitan urban centers in the Old World has resulted in such places as Athens Georgia and St. Petersburg Florida.

4. As of December 1 2005 the American St. Petersburg was estimated to have nearly 250000 citizens and the American Athens nearly 109000.

5. By comparison, St. Petersburg Russia and Athens Greece were estimated to have populations of 4 million and 1 million, respectively.

# 24j How do commas clarify meaning?

A comma is sometimes needed to clarify the meaning of a sentence, even though no rule calls for one. The best solution is to revise the sentence.

NO Of the gymnastic team's twenty five were injured.

YES Of the gymnastic team's **twenty, five** were injured.

YES Of **twenty on** the gymnastic team, five were injured. [preferred]

**EXERCISE 24-6**   Insert commas to prevent misreading. For help, consult 24j.

EXAMPLE   For scientists tracking and measuring hurricanes is still an inexact science.

For scientists, tracking and measuring hurricanes is still an inexact science.

1. Lasting for thirteen days in August 1992 Hurricane Andrew after 2005's Katrina was the second most expensive hurricane.

2. Andrew was rated a category four smaller than 2005's Katrina when it made landfall in south Florida.

3. The highest gust officially recorded 164 miles per hour at 130 feet above the ground occurred before Andrew shut down the National Hurricane Center's measuring devices.

4. The thousands of vortexes within Andrew as with many high-intensity storms are what caused the worst damage.

5. Andrew difficult to measure accurately was upgraded from a category four to a category five hurricane ten years after it occurred.

## 24k   How can I avoid misusing commas?

Throughout this chapter, Alert notes remind you about comma misuses as they relate to each comma rule. Most of these misuses are overuses—inserting a comma where one is unnecessary. This section summarizes the Alert notes and lists other frequent misuses of the comma.

When advice against overusing a comma clashes with a rule requiring one, follow the rule that requires the comma.

> The town of Kitty Hawk, North Carolina, attracts thousands of tourists each year. [Even though the comma after *North Carolina* separates the subject and its verb (which it normally shouldn't), the comma is required here because of the rule that calls for a comma when the name of a state follows the name of a city within a sentence (24i).]

### ■ Commas with coordinating conjunctions

Never use a comma after a COORDINATING CONJUNCTION that joins two INDEPENDENT CLAUSES, unless another rule makes it necessary (24b). Also, don't use a comma to separate two items joined with a coordinating conjunction—there must be at least three (24d).

NO   The sky was dark gray **and,** it looked like dusk.

YES   The sky was dark gray**,** and it looked like dusk.

### ■ Commas with subordinating conjunctions and prepositions

Never put a comma after a SUBORDINATING CONJUNCTION or a PREPOSITION, unless another rule makes it necessary.

  **NO**   **Although,** the storm brought high winds, it did no damage.

  **YES**   **Although the storm brought high winds,** it did no damage.
  [comma follows full subordinated dependent clause, not the subordinate conjunction that begins it]

  **NO**   The storm did no damage **although,** it brought high winds.

  **YES**   The storm did no damage **although it brought high winds.**
  [no comma after a subordinating conjunction]

### ■ Commas in a series

Never use a comma before the first, or after the last, item in a series, unless another rule makes it necessary (24d).

  **NO**   The gymnasium was decorated with **red, white, and blue,
  ribbons** for the Fourth of July.

  **YES**   The gymnasium was decorated with **red, white, and blue** ribbons for the Fourth of July.

Never put a comma between a final COORDINATE ADJECTIVE and the NOUN that the adjectives modify. Also, don't use a comma between adjectives that are not coordinate (24e).

  **NO**   He wore an **old, baggy, sweater.**

  **YES**   He wore an **old, baggy sweater.** [coordinate adjectives]

### ■ Commas with restrictive elements

Never use a comma to set off a RESTRICTIVE (essential) element from the rest of a sentence (24f).

  **NO**   **Vegetables, stir-fried in a wok,** are crisp and flavorful. [The words *stir-fried in a wok* are essential, so they are not set off with commas.]

  **YES**   **Vegetables stir-fried in a wok** are crisp and flavorful.

### ■ Commas with quotations

Never use a comma to set off INDIRECT DISCOURSE; use a comma only with DIRECT DISCOURSE (24h).

**NO**    Jon said **that, he likes** stir-fried vegetables.

**YES**    Jon said **that he likes** stir-fried vegetables.

**YES**    **Jon said, "I like** stir-fried vegetables."

## ■ Commas that separate a subject from its verb, a verb from its object, or a preposition from its object

A comma does not make sense between these elements, though in some cases another comma rule might supersede this guideline (as in the first example in section 24k).

**NO**    **The brothers Wright, made** their first successful airplane flights on December 17, 1903. [As a rule, a comma doesn't separate a subject from its verb.]

**YES**    **The brothers Wright made** their first successful airplane flights on December 17, 1903.

**NO**    These inventors enthusiastically **tackled, the problems** of powered flight and aerodynamics. [As a rule, a comma doesn't separate a verb from its object.]

**YES**    These inventors enthusiastically **tackled the problems** of powered flight and aerodynamics.

**NO**    Airplane hobbyists **from, all over the world** visit Kitty Hawk's flight museum. [As a rule, a comma doesn't separate a preposition from its object.]

**YES**    Airplane hobbyists **from all over the world** visit Kitty Hawk's flight museum.

## 24l   How can I avoid comma errors?

You can avoid most comma errors with these two bits of advice:

- As you write or reread what you've written, never insert a comma simply because you happen to pause to think or take a breath before moving on. Pausing isn't a reliable guide for writers, although that myth continues to thrive. Throughout the United States, and indeed the world, people's breathing rhythms, accents, and thinking patterns vary greatly.

- As you're writing, if you're unsure about a comma, insert it and circle the spot. Later, when you're EDITING, **check this handbook for the rule that applies.**

# 25

## Semicolons

### 25a What are the uses of a semicolon?

While a period signals the complete separation of INDEPENDENT CLAUSES, a **semicolon** indicates only a partial ("semi") separation. Use a semicolon in only two situations. A semicolon can replace a period between sentences that are closely related in meaning (25b and 25c). Also, a semicolon belongs between sentence structures that already contain one or more commas (25d) and with certain lists (25e). Quick Reference 25.1 shows different patterns for using semicolons.

### 25b When can I use a semicolon, instead of a period, between independent clauses?

The choice between a period and a semicolon for separating independent clauses depends on whether your meaning is better communicated by a complete separation (period) or a partial separation (semicolon).

> This is my husband's second marriage; it's the first for me.
> —Ruth Sidel, "Marion Deluca"

---

**Quick Reference 25.1**

**Semicolon patterns**

- Independent clause; independent clause. [25b]
- Independent clause; conjunctive adverb, independent clause. [25c]
- Independent clause; transitional expression,independent clause. [25c]
- Independent clause, one that contains a comma; coordinating conjunction followed by independent clause. [25d]
- Independent clause; coordinating conjunction followed by independent clause, one that contains a comma. [25d]
- Independent clause, one that contains a comma; coordinating conjunction followed by independent clause, one that contains a comma. [25d]
- Independent clause containing a series of items, any of which contains a comma; another item in the series; and another item in the series. [25e]

---

**Alert:** Never use a comma alone between independent clauses—this rule will prevent you from creating the error known as a COMMA SPLICE (Chapter 20). ●

## 25c When else can I use a semicolon between independent clauses?

When the second of a set of independent clauses closely related in meaning starts with a CONJUNCTIVE ADVERB or with a TRANSITIONAL EXPRESSION, you can choose to separate the clauses with a semicolon instead of a period. Also, insert a comma following a conjunctive adverb or transitional expression that starts an independent clause. Although some professional writers today omit the comma after short words (*then, next, soon*), the rule remains for most ACADEMIC WRITING. Quick Reference 25.1 shows this pattern for using semicolons.

The average annual rainfall in Death Valley is about two inches**; nevertheless,** hundreds of plant and animal species survive and even thrive there. [conjunctive adverb]

Photographers have spent years recording desert life cycles**; as a result,** we can watch bare sand flower after a spring storm. [transitional expression]

**Alert:** Never use only a comma between independent clauses that are connected by a conjunctive adverb or word of transition—this rule will prevent you from creating the error known as a COMMA SPLICE. ●

## 25d How do semicolons work with coordinating conjunctions?

As a general rule, when INDEPENDENT CLAUSES are linked by a COORDINATING CONJUNCTION, good practice calls for a comma, not a period or semicolon, before the coordinating conjunction (24b). However, when one or more of the independent clauses already contain a comma, link the independent clauses by substituting a semicolon for the period. This can help your reader see the relationship between the ideas more clearly. Quick Reference 25.1 shows the various combinations of this pattern.

For anything worth having, one must pay the price**; and** the price is always work, patience, love, self-sacrifice.

—John Burroughs

## 25e   When should I use semicolons between items in a series?

When a sentence contains a series of items that are long or that already contain one or more commas, separate the items with semicolons. Punctuating this way groups the elements so that your reader can see where one item ends and the next begins. Quick Reference 25.1 shows this pattern.

## 25f   How do I avoid misusing the semicolon?

### NOT USING A SEMICOLON AFTER AN INTRODUCTORY PHRASE

If you use a semicolon after an introductory phrase, you create the error known as a sentence fragment (Chapter 19).

> **NO**   **Open until midnight;** the computer lab is well used. [Using a semicolon turns an introductory phrase into a sentence fragment.]
>
> **YES**   **Open until midnight,** the computer lab is well used.

### NOT USING A SEMICOLON WITH A DEPENDENT CLAUSE

If you use a semicolon with a DEPENDENT CLAUSE, you create the error known as a sentence fragment.

> **NO**   **Although the new dorms have computer facilities;** many students still prefer to go to the computer lab. [Using a semicolon turns a dependent clause into a sentence fragment.]
>
> **YES**   **Although the new dorms have computer facilities,** many students still prefer to go to the computer lab.

### NOT USING A SEMICOLON TO INTRODUCE A LIST

When the words that introduce a list form an independent clause, use a colon, never a semicolon (26b).

> **NO**   **The newscast featured three major stories;** the latest pictures of Uranus, a speech by the president, and dangerous brush fires in Nevada. [*The newscast featured three major stories* is an independent clause, so the punctuation before the list should be a colon, not a semicolon.]
>
> **YES**   **The newscast featured three major stories:** the latest pictures of Uranus, a speech by the president, and dangerous brush fires in Nevada.

**EXERCISE 25-1** Insert semicolons as needed in these items. Also, fix any incorrectly used semicolons. If a sentence is correct, explain why. For help, consult all sections of this chapter.

EXAMPLE Bicycle racing is as popular in Europe as baseball or basketball is in the United States, it is even more heavily commercialized.

Bicycle racing is as popular in Europe as baseball or basketball is in the United States; it is even more heavily commercialized.

1. The Tour de France is the world's best-known bicycle race, the 94-year-old Giro d'Italia runs a close second.

2. Both are grueling, three-week-long events that require cyclists to cover over 2,000 miles of difficult, mountainous terrain, and both are eagerly anticipated, draw enormous crowds along their routes, and receive extensive media coverage.

3. That media attention leads to marketing opportunities for the events' sponsors; which place ads along the race's route, in the nearby towns, and on the cyclists themselves.

4. Martin Hvastija, a participant in the 2003 Giro d'Italia, had no chance of winning the race, nevertheless, he drew extensive media attention for his sponsors.

5. His method was simple; he managed to ride out in front of the field for a few brief miles.

# 26

# Colons

## 26a What are the uses of a colon?

A **colon** is a full stop that draws attention to the words that follow. It can be placed only at the end of an INDEPENDENT CLAUSE. A colon introduces a list, an APPOSITIVE, or a QUOTATION. Quick Reference 26.1 shows different patterns for using a colon.

> **Quick Reference 26.1** ■ ■ ■ ■ ■
>
> ## Colon patterns
>
> - Independent clause: list. [26b]
> - Independent clause: appositive. [26b]
> - Independent clause: "Quoted words." [26b]
> - Independent clause: Independent clause that explains or summarizes the prior independent clause. [26c]

## 26b When can a colon introduce a list, an appositive, or a quotation?

When a complete sentence—that is, an INDEPENDENT CLAUSE—introduces a list, an APPOSITIVE, or a QUOTATION, place a colon before the words being introduced. These words don't have to form an independent clause themselves, but a complete sentence before the colon is essential.

### INTRODUCING LISTED ITEMS

When a complete sentence introduces a list, a colon is required, as demonstrated in the following example.

> **If you really want to lose weight, you must do three things:** eat smaller portions, exercise, and drink lots of water. [The required independent clause comes before the listed items, so a colon is correct.]

When the lead-in words at the end of an independent clause are *such as, including, like,* or *consists of,* never use a colon. In contrast, if the lead-in words at the end of an independent clause are *the following* or *as follows,* do use a colon.

> **The students demanded improvements** *such as* an expanded menu in the cafeteria, improved janitorial services, and more up-to-date textbooks.

> **The students demanded** *the following:* an expanded menu in the cafeteria, improved janitorial services, and more up-to-date textbooks.

### INTRODUCING APPOSITIVES

An APPOSITIVE is a word or words that rename a NOUN or PRONOUN. When an appositive is introduced by an independent clause, use a colon.

> **Only cats are likely to approve of one old-fashioned remedy for cuts:** a lotion of catnip, butter, and sugar. [The required independent clause comes before the appositive: *a lotion of catnip, butter, and sugar* renames *old-fashioned remedy.*]

**INTRODUCING QUOTATIONS**

When an independent clause introduces a quotation, use a colon after it. (If the words introducing a quotation don't form an independent clause, use a comma.)

> **The little boy in *E.T.* did say something neat:** "How do you explain school to a higher intelligence?" [The required independent clause comes before the quotation.]
>
> —George F. Will, "Well, I Don't Love You, E.T."

## 26c   When can I use a colon between two independent clauses?

When a second INDEPENDENT CLAUSE explains or summarizes a first independent clause, you can use a colon to separate them. Quick Reference 26.1 shows this pattern for using a colon.

🚫 **Alert:** You can choose to use a capital letter or a lowercase letter for the first word of an independent clause that follows a colon. Whichever you choose, be consistent within a piece of writing. We use a capital letter in this handbook.

> We will never forget the first time we made dinner together: He got stomach poisoning and was too sick to go to work for four days.
>
> —Lisa Baladendrum, student ●

## 26d   What standard formats require a colon?

A variety of standard formats in American English require a colon. Also, colons are used in many DOCUMENTATION STYLES, as shown in Chapters 35 and 36.

**TITLE AND SUBTITLE**

*A Brief History of Time: From the Big Bang to Black Holes*

**HOURS, MINUTES, AND SECONDS**

The plane took off at 7:15 p.m.

The runner passed the halfway point at 1:23:02.

**REFERENCES TO BIBLE CHAPTERS AND VERSES**

Psalms 23:1–3

Luke 3:13

**MEMOS**

Date:     January 9, 2009

To:     Dean Kristen Olivero

From:     Professor Daniel Black

Re:     Student Work-Study Program

SALUTATION IN A BUSINESS LETTER

Dear Dr. Jewell:

# 26e When is a colon wrong?

## INDEPENDENT CLAUSES

A colon can introduce a list, an APPOSITIVE, or a QUOTATION, but only when an INDEPENDENT CLAUSE does the introducing. Similarly, a colon can be used between two independent clauses when the second summarizes or explains the first. In following these rules, be sure that you're dealing with independent clauses, not other word groups.

> **NO** The cook bought: eggs, milk, cheese, and bread. [*The cook bought* isn't an independent clause.]
>
> **YES** The cook bought eggs, milk, cheese, and bread.

Never use a colon to separate a PHRASE or DEPENDENT CLAUSE from an independent clause. Otherwise, you'll create the error known as a SENTENCE FRAGMENT.

> **NO** Day after day: the drought dragged on. [*Day after day* is a phrase, not an independent clause.]
>
> **YES** Day after day, the drought dragged on.

## LEAD-IN WORDS

Never use a colon after the lead-in words *such as, including, like,* and *consists of.*

> **NO** The health board discussed many problems **such as:** poor water quality, aging sewage treatment systems, and the lack of alternative water supplies. [A colon is incorrect after *such as.*]
>
> **YES** The health board discussed poor water quality, aging sewage treatment systems, and the lack of alternative water supplies. [*Such as* is dropped and the sentence slightly revised so that the colon is not needed.]

**EXERCISE 26-1** Insert colons where needed and delete any not needed. If a sentence is correct, explain why. For help, consult all sections of this chapter.

1. People who work the night shift are typically deprived of essential sleep, an average of nine hours a week.

2. The Iroquois of the Great Lakes region lived in fortified villages and cultivated: corn, beans, and squash.

3. Five nations originally formed the Iroquois Confederacy: the Mohawk, the Oneida, the Onondaga, the Cayuga, and the Seneca.

4. Later, these five Iroquois nations were joined by: the Tuscarora.

5. Shouting: "Come back!" Adam watched the vehicle speed down the highway.

# Apostrophes

## 27a What is the role of the apostrophe?

The **apostrophe** plays four roles in writing: It creates the POSSESSIVE CASE of NOUNS, forms the possessive case of INDEFINITE PRONOUNS, stands for one or more omitted letters in a word (a CONTRACTION), and can help form plurals of letters and numerals.

In contrast, here are two roles the apostrophe doesn't play: It doesn't belong with plurals of nouns, and it doesn't form the plural of PERSONAL PRONOUNS in the possessive case.

## 27b How do I use an apostrophe to show a possessive noun?

An apostrophe works with a NOUN to form the POSSESSIVE CASE, which shows ownership or a close relationship.

| | |
|---|---|
| **OWNERSHIP** | The **writer's** pen ran out of ink. |
| **CLOSE RELATIONSHIP** | The **novel's** plot is complicated. |

Possession in nouns can be communicated in two ways: by a PHRASE starting with *of* (*comments **of** the instructor; comments **of** Professor Furman*) or by an apostrophe and the letter *s* (*the instructor's comments; Professor Furman's comments*). Here's a list of specific rules governing the usage of *'s*.

* **Add *'s* to nouns not ending in *-s*:**

   She felt a **parent's** joy. [*Parent* is a singular noun not ending in -s.]

They care about their **children's** education. [*Children* is a plural noun not ending in -s.]

- **Add 's to singular nouns ending in -s:** You can add 's or the apostrophe alone to show possession when a singular noun ends in -s. In this handbook, we use 's to clearly mark singular-noun possessives, no matter what letter ends the noun. Whichever rule variation you choose, be consistent within each piece of writing.

  The **bus's** (or **bus'**) air conditioning is out of order.

  **Chris's** (or **Chris'**) ordeal ended.

  If you encounter a tongue-twisting pronunciation (*Charles **Dickens's** novel*), you may decide not to add the additional -s (*Charles **Dickens'** novel*). You must, however, be consistent in each piece of writing.

- **Add only an apostrophe to a plural noun ending in -s:**

  The **boys'** statements were taken seriously.

  Three **months'** maternity leave is in the **workers'** contract.

- **Add 's to the last word in compound words and phrases:**

  His **mother-in-law's** corporation has bought out a competitor.

  The **tennis player's** strategy was brilliant.

  We want to hear the **caseworker's** recommendation.

- **Add 's to each noun in individual possession:**

  **Shirley's** and **Kayla's** houses are next to each other. [Shirley and Kayla each own a house; they don't own the houses jointly.]

- **Add 's to only the last noun in joint or group possession:**

  **Kareem and Brina's** house has a screened porch. [Kareem and Brina own one house.]

  **Avram and Justin's** houses always have nice lawns. [Avram and Justin jointly own more than one house.]

## 27c   How do I use an apostrophe with possessive pronouns?

When a POSSESSIVE PRONOUN ends with -s (*hers, his, its, ours, yours,* and *theirs*), never add an apostrophe. Below is a list of PERSONAL PRONOUNS and their possessive forms.

| Personal Pronouns | Possessive Forms |
| --- | --- |
| I | my, mine |
| you | your, yours |

| | |
|---|---|
| he | his |
| she | her, hers |
| it | its |
| we | our, ours |
| they | their, theirs |
| who | whose |

## 27d How do I use an apostrophe with contractions?

In a **contraction,** an apostrophe takes the place of one or more omitted letters. Be careful not to confuse a contraction with a POSSESSIVE PRONOUN. Doing so is a common spelling error, one that many people—including employers—consider evidence of a poor education. Whether or not that's fair, it's usually true.

| | |
|---|---|
| **it's** (contraction for *it is*) | **its** (possessive pronoun) |
| **they're** (contraction for *they are*) | **their** (possessive pronoun) |
| **who's** (contraction for *who is*) | **whose** (possessive form of *who*) |
| **you're** (contraction for *you are*) | **your** (possessive pronoun) |

In choosing whether or not to use a contraction, consider that many instructors think contractions aren't appropriate in ACADEMIC WRITING. Nevertheless, the *MLA Handbook* accepts contractions, including *'90s* for *the 1990s.*

🚫 Alert: One contraction required in all writing is *o'clock* (which stands for *of the clock,* an expression used long ago). ●

## 27e How do I use an apostrophe with possessive indefinite pronouns?

An apostrophe works with an INDEFINITE PRONOUN (see list in Quick Reference 17.6 in 17h) to form the POSSESSIVE CASE, which shows ownership or a close relationship.

| | |
|---|---|
| OWNERSHIP | **Everyone's** dinner is ready. |
| CLOSE RELATIONSHIP | **Something's** aroma is appealing. |

Possession in indefinite pronouns can be communicated in two ways: by a PHRASE starting with *of* (*comments of everyone*) or by an apostrophe and the letter *s* (*everyone's comments*).

## **27f**  How do I form the plural of miscellaneous elements?

Until recently, the plural of elements such as letters meant as letters, words meant as words, numerals, and symbols could be formed by adding either *'s* or *s*. The most current MLA guidelines endorse the use of *s* only, with the exception of adding *'s* to letters meant as letters. MLA recommends using italics for letters meant as letters and words meant as words. The examples below reflect MLA practices.

| | |
|---|---|
| **PLURAL OF LETTERS MEANT AS LETTERS** | Printing *M's* and *N's* confuses young children. |
| | Printing *m's* and *n's* confuses young children. |
| **PLURAL OF LETTERS MEANT AS WORDS** | He was surprised to get all **Bs** in his courses. |
| **PLURAL OF WORDS MEANT AS WORDS** | Too many *ifs* in a contract make me suspicious. |
| **PLURAL OF NUMBERS** | Her e-mail address contains many **7s.** |
| **PLURAL OF YEARS** | I remember the **1990s** well. |
| **PLURAL OF SYMBOLS** | What do those **&s** mean? |

## **27g**  When is an apostrophe wrong?

If you're a writer who makes the same apostrophe errors repeatedly, memorize the rules you need (some you're likely to know almost without thought). Then you won't be annoyed by "that crooked little mark," a nickname popular with students who wish the apostrophe would go away. Quick Reference 27.1 lists the major apostrophe errors.

### Quick Reference 27.1   ■ ■ ■ ■ ■

#### Leading apostrophe errors

- Never use an apostrophe with the PRESENT-TENSE VERB.
  Cholesterol **plays** [not play's] an important role in how long we live.
- Always use an apostrophe after the *-s* in a POSSESSIVE plural of a noun.
  **Patients'** [not Patients] questions seek detailed answers.
- Never add an apostrophe at the end of a nonpossessive noun ending in *-s*.
  Medical **studies** [not studies' or study's] show this to be true.
- Never use an apostrophe to form a nonpossessive plural.
  **Teams** [not Team's] of doctors have studied the effects of cholesterol.

**EXERCISE 27-1**   Rewrite these sentences to insert 's or an apostrophe alone to make the words in parentheses show possession. (Delete the parentheses.) For help, consult 27b and 27e.

EXAMPLE   All boxes, cans, and bottles on a (supermarket) shelves are designed to appeal to (people) emotions.

All boxes, cans, and bottles on a *supermarket's* shelves are designed to appeal to *people's* emotions.

1. A (product) manufacturer designs packaging to appeal to (consumers) emotions through color and design.

2. Marketing specialists know that (people) beliefs about a (product) quality are influenced by their emotional response to the design of its package.

3. Circles and ovals appearing on a (box) design supposedly increase a (product user) feelings of comfort, while bold patterns and colors attract a (shopper) attention.

4. Using both circles and bold designs in (Arm & Hammer) and (Tide) packaging produces both effects in consumers.

5. (Heinz) ketchup bottle and (Coca-Cola) famous logo achieve the same effects by combining a bright color with an old-fashioned, "comfortable" design.

# 28

# Quotation Marks

## 28a  What is the role of quotation marks?

**Quotation marks** are used most often to enclose **direct quotations**—the exact spoken or written words of a speaker or writer. Quotation marks also set off some titles, and quotation marks can call attention to words used in a special sense.

Double quotation marks (" ") are standard. In most computer fonts, the opening marks differ slightly in appearance from the closing marks. The opening marks look like tiny 6s, the closing marks like tiny 9s. In some computer fonts, the opening and closing marks look the same (" " or " "). Single quotation marks (' or ' ') are used for quotations within quotations: *Gregory said,*

*"I heard the man shout 'Help me' but could not reach him in time."* Quotation marks operate only in pairs: to open and to close. When you proofread your writing, check carefully that you've inserted the closing mark.

Please note, before you continue reading this chapter, that we use MLA STYLE to format the examples here and in other chapters. This affects the documentation features and the lengths of "short" and "long" quotations. These factors vary with different documentation styles. For MLA STYLE, used in most English courses, see Chapter 35. For APA STYLE, see Chapter 36.

## 28b How do I use quotation marks with short direct quotations?

DIRECT QUOTATIONS are exact words from print or nonprint sources. In MLA STYLE, a quotation is considered *short* if it occupies no more than four typed lines. Use double quotation marks at the start and finish of a short quotation. Give DOCUMENTATION information after a short quotation, before the sentence's ending period.

## 28c Are quotation marks used with long quotations?

No. With a long DIRECT QUOTATION, don't use quotation marks. In MLA STYLE, a quotation is *long* if it occupies more than four typed lines. Instead of using quotation marks with a long quotation, indent all its lines as a block (that is, the quotation is "set off" or "displayed"). This format makes quotation marks unnecessary. Give DOCUMENTATION information after the period that ends the quotation.

⊘ **Alert:** Whether a quotation is one word or occupies many lines, always document its SOURCE. Also, when you quote material, be very careful to record the words exactly as they appear in the original. ●

## 28d How do I use quotation marks for quotations within quotations?

In MLA STYLE, practice varies between short and long quotations when a quotation contains internal quotation marks. In short quotations of prose, use single quotation marks for any internal quotation marks, and use double quotation marks for the entire quotation. Give DOCUMENTATION information after the entire quotation, before the sentence's ending period. For other documentation styles, check each style's manual.

In long quotations of prose—those that are displayed (set off in a block) and not enclosed in quotation marks—keep the double quotation marks as they appear in the original. Give DOCUMENTATION information after the long quotation following any closing punctuation, and before the period that ends a short quotation.

## SHORT QUOTATIONS: USE SINGLE WITHIN DOUBLE QUOTATION MARKS (MLA STYLE)

With short quotations, the double quotation marks show the beginning and end of words taken from the source; the single quotation marks replace double marks used in the source.

### ORIGINAL SOURCE

Most scientists concede that they don't really know what "intelligence" is. Whatever it might be, paper and pencil tests aren't the tenth of it.

—Brent Staples, "The IQ Cult," p. 293

### STUDENT'S USE OF THE SOURCE

Brent Staples argues in his essay about IQ as an object of reverence: "Most scientists concede that they don't really know what 'intelligence' is. Whatever it might be, paper and pencil tests aren't the tenth of it" (293).

## LONG QUOTATIONS: USE QUOTATION MARKS AS IN SOURCE

All long quotations must be set off (displayed) without being enclosed in quotation marks. Therefore, show any double and single quotation marks exactly as the source does.

## 28e How do I use quotation marks for quotations of poetry and dialogue?

### POETRY (MLA STYLE)

A quotation of poetry is *short* if it includes three lines or fewer of the poem. As with prose quotations (28d), use double quotation marks to enclose the material. If the poetry lines have internal double quotation marks, change them to single quotation marks. To show when a line of poetry breaks to the next line, use a slash (/) with one space on each side. Give DOCUMENTATION information after a short poetry quotation, before the period that ends the sentence (see also 29c).

As Auden wittily defined personal space, "some thirty inches from my nose / The frontier of my person goes" (*Complete* 205).

A quotation of poetry is *long* if it includes more than three lines of the poem. As with prose quotations (28d), indent all lines as a block, without quotation marks to enclose the material. Start new lines exactly as they appear in your source. Give documentation information for a long quotation after the period that ends the quotation.

🛑 **Alert:** When you quote lines of poetry, follow·the capitalization of your source. ●

### DIALOGUE (MLA AND APA STYLES)

Dialogue, also called DIRECT DISCOURSE, presents a speaker's exact words. Enclose direct discourse in quotation marks. In contrast, INDIRECT DISCOURSE reports what a speaker said. Don't enclose indirect discourse in quotation marks. In addition to these differences in punctuation, PRONOUN use and VERB TENSES also differ for these two types of discourse.

> **DIRECT DISCOURSE**      The mayor said, "I intend to veto that bill."
>
> **INDIRECT DISCOURSE**    The mayor said that he intended to veto
>                          that bill.

Whether you're reporting the words of a real speaker or making up dialogue in a short story, use double quotation marks at the beginning and end of a speaker's words. This tells your reader which words are the speaker's. Also, start a new paragraph each time the speaker changes.

In American English, if two or more paragraphs present a single speaker's words, use double opening quotation marks at the start of each paragraph, but save the closing double quotation marks until the end of the last quoted paragraph.

## 28f How do I use quotation marks with titles of short works?

When you refer to certain short works by their titles, enclose the titles in quotation marks (other works, usually longer, need to be in italics; see 30g). Short works include short stories, essays, poems, articles from periodicals, pamphlets, brochures, songs, and individual episodes of a series on television or radio.

> The best source I found is "The Myth of Political Consultants."
> [magazine article]
>
> "Shooting an Elephant" describes George Orwell's experiences in
> Burma. [essay]

Titles of some other works are neither enclosed in quotation marks nor written in italics. For guidelines, see Quick Reference 30.1 in 30e and Quick Reference 30.2 in 30g.

🛑 **Alert:** When placing the title of your own piece of writing on a title page or at the top of a page, never use quotation marks. ●

## 28g How do I use quotation marks for words used as words?

When you refer to a word as a word, you can choose to either enclose it in quotation marks or put it in italics. Whichever you choose, be consistent throughout each piece of writing.

> **NO** Many people confuse affect and effect.
>
> **YES** Many people confuse "affect" and "effect."

Always put quotation marks around the English translation of a word or PHRASE. Also, use italics for the word or phrase in the other language.

> My grandfather usually ended arguments with *de gustibus non disputandum est* ("there is no disputing about tastes").

Many writers use quotation marks around words or phrases meant ironically or in other nonliteral ways.

> The proposed tax "reform" is actually a tax increase.

Some writers put technical terms in quotation marks and define them—but only the first time they appear. Never reuse quotation marks after a term has been introduced and defined.

> "Plagiarism"—the undocumented use of another person's words or ideas—can result in expulsion. Plagiarism is a serious offense.

Some student writers put quotation marks around words that they sense might be inappropriate for ACADEMIC WRITING, such as a SLANG term or a CLICHÉ used intentionally to make a point. However, when possible, use different language—not quotation marks. Take time to think of accurate, appropriate, and fresh words instead. If you prefer to stick with the slang or cliché, use quotation marks.

> They "eat like birds" in public, but they "stuff their faces" in private.

## 28h How do I use quotation marks with other punctuation?

### COMMAS AND PERIODS WITH QUOTATION MARKS

A comma or period that is grammatically necessary is always placed inside the closing quotation mark.

> Jessica enjoyed F. Scott Fitzgerald's story "The Freshest Boy," so she was eager to read his novels. [comma before closing quotation mark]
>
> Max said, "Don't stand so far away from me." [comma before opening quotation mark (24k); period before closing quotation mark]

## SEMICOLONS AND COLONS WITH QUOTATION MARKS

A semicolon or colon is placed outside the closing quotation mark, unless it is part of the quotation.

> Computers offer businesses "opportunities that never existed before"; some workers disagree. [semicolon after closing quotation mark]

> We have to know each culture's standard for "how close is close": No one wants to offend. [colon after closing quotation mark]

## QUESTION MARKS, EXCLAMATION POINTS, AND DASHES WITH QUOTATION MARKS

If the punctuation marks belong to the words enclosed in quotation marks, put them inside the quotation marks.

> "Did I Hear You Call My Name?" was the winning song.

> "I've won the lottery!" Arielle shouted.

If a question mark, an exclamation point, or a dash doesn't belong to the material being quoted, put the punctuation outside the quotation marks.

> Have you read Nikki Giovanni's poem "Knoxville, Tennessee"?

> If only I could write a story like David Wallace's "Girl with Curious Hair"!

When you use quotation marks and want to know how they work with capital letters, see 30d; with brackets, 29c; with ellipsis points, 29d; and with the slash, 29e.

# 28i   When are quotation marks wrong?

Never enclose a word in quotation marks to call attention to it, to intensify it, or to be sarcastic.

> **NO**   I'm "very" happy about the news.
> **YES**   I'm very happy about the news.

Never enclose the title of your paper in quotation marks (or underline it). However, if the title of your paper contains another title that requires quotation marks, use those marks only for the included title.

> **NO**   Character Development in Shirley Jackson's Story The Lottery
> **YES**   Character Development in Shirley Jackson's Story "The Lottery"

**EXERCISE 28-1**  Correct any errors in the use of quotation marks and other punctuation with quotation marks. If you think a sentence is correct, explain why. For help, consult 28e through 28i.

1. Dying in a shabby hotel room, the witty writer Oscar Wilde supposedly said, "Either that wallpaper goes, or I do".

2. Was it the Russian novelist Tolstoy who wrote, "All happy families resemble one another, but each unhappy family is unhappy in its own way?"

3. In his poem A Supermarket in California, Allen Ginsberg addresses the dead poet Walt Whitman, asking, Where are we going, Walt Whitman? The doors close / in an hour. Which way does your beard point tonight?

4. Toni Morrison made this reply to the claim that "art that has a political message cannot be good art:" She said that "the best art is political" and that her aim was to create art that was "unquestionably political" and beautiful at the same time.

5. Benjamin Franklin's strange question—"What is the use of a newborn child?—" was his response to someone who doubted the usefulness of new inventions.

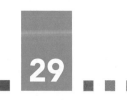

# 29

# Other Punctuation Marks

This chapter explains the uses of **dashes, parentheses, brackets, ellipsis points, slashes,** and **hyphens.** These punctuation marks aren't used often, but each serves a purpose and gives you options with your writing style.

## DASH

## 29a  When can I use a dash in my writing?

The **dash,** or a pair of dashes, lets you interrupt a sentence to add information. Such interruptions can fall in the middle or at the end of a sentence. To make a dash, hit the hyphen key twice (--). Do not put a space before, between, or after the hyphens. Some word processing programs automatically convert two hyphens into a dash; either form is correct. In print, the dash appears as an unbroken line approximately the length of two hyphens joined together (—). If you handwrite, make the dash at least twice as long as a hyphen.

## USING DASHES FOR SPECIAL EMPHASIS

If you want to emphasize an example, a definition, an appositive, or a contrast, you can use a dash or dashes. Some call a dash "a pregnant pause"—that is, take note, something special is coming. Use dashes sparingly so that you don't dilute their impact.

#### EXAMPLE
The caretakers—those who are helpers, nurturers, teachers, mothers—are still systematically devalued.

> —Ellen Goodman, "Just Woman's Work?"

#### DEFINITION
Although the emphasis at the school was mainly language—speaking, reading, writing—the lessons always began with an exercise in politeness.

> —Elizabeth Wong, *Fifth Chinese Daughter*

#### APPOSITIVE
Two of the strongest animals in the jungle are vegetarians—the elephant and the gorilla.

> —Dick Gregory, *The Shadow That Scares Me*

#### CONTRAST
Fire cooks food—and burns down forests.

> —Smokey the Bear

Place what you emphasize with dashes next to or nearby the material it refers to so that what you want to accomplish with your emphasis is not lost.

**NO** The current **argument is**—one that faculty, students, and coaches debate fiercely—whether to hold athletes to the same academic standards as others face.

**YES** The current **argument**—one that faculty, students, and coaches debate fiercely—**is** whether to hold athletes to the same academic standards as others face.

## USING DASHES TO EMPHASIZE AN ASIDE

An **aside** is a writer's comment, often the writer's personal views, on what's been written. Generally, this technique isn't appropriate for academic writing, so before you insert an aside, carefully consider your writing purpose and your audience.

Television showed us the war. It showed us the war in a way that was—if you chose to watch television, at least—unavoidable.

—Nora Ephron, *Scribble Scribble*

**Alerts:** (1) If the words within a pair of dashes require a question mark or an exclamation point, place it before the second dash.

A first date—do you remember?—stays in the memory forever.

(2) Never use commas, semicolons, or periods next to dashes. If such a need arises, revise your writing.

(3) Never enclose quotation marks in dashes except when the meaning requires them. These two examples show that, when required, the dash stops before or after the quotation marks; the two punctuation marks do not overlap.

Many of George Orwell's essays—"A Hanging," for example—draw on his experiences as a civil servant.

"Shooting an Elephant"—another Orwell essay—appears in many anthologies. ●

## PARENTHESES

## 29b When can I use parentheses in my writing?

**Parentheses** let you interrupt a sentence to add various kinds of information. Parentheses are like dashes (29a) in that they set off extra or interrupting words—but unlike dashes, which emphasize material, parentheses de-emphasize what they enclose. Use parentheses sparingly because overusing them can make your writing lurch, not flow.

### USING PARENTHESES TO ENCLOSE INTERRUPTING WORDS

#### EXPLANATION
After they've finished with the pantry, the medicine cabinet, and the attic, they will throw out the red geranium (too many leaves), sell the dog (too many fleas), and send the children off to boarding school (too many scuffmarks on the hardwood floors).

—Suzanne Britt, "Neat People vs. Sloppy People"

#### EXAMPLE
Though other cities (Dresden, for instance) had been utterly destroyed in World War II, never before had a single weapon been responsible for such destruction.

—Laurence Behrens and Leonard J. Rosen,
*Writing and Reading Across the Curriculum*

**ASIDE**

The older girls (non-graduates, of course) were assigned the task of making refreshments for the night's festivities.

—Maya Angelou, *I Know Why the Caged Bird Sings*

## USING PARENTHESES FOR LISTED ITEMS AND ALTERNATIVE NUMBERS

When you number listed items within a sentence, enclose the numbers (or letters) in parentheses. Never use closing parentheses to set off numbers in a displayed list; use periods.

Four items are on the agenda for tonight's meeting: (1) current treasury figures, (2) current membership figures, (3) the budget for renovations, and (4) the campaign for soliciting additional public contributions.

**! Alerts:** For listed items that fall within a sentence, (1) use a colon before a list only if an INDEPENDENT CLAUSE comes before the list, and (2) use commas or semicolons to separate three or more items, but be consistent within a piece of writing. If, however, any item contains punctuation itself, use a semicolon to separate the items. ●

In legal writing and in some BUSINESS WRITING, you can use parentheses to enclose a numeral that repeats a spelled-out number.

The monthly rent is three hundred fifty dollars ($350).

Your order of fifteen (15) gross was shipped today.

In ACADEMIC WRITING, especially in subjects in which the use of figures or measurements is frequent, enclose alternative or comparative forms of the same number in parentheses: *2 mi (3.2 km).*

## USING OTHER PUNCTUATION WITH PARENTHESES

When a complete sentence enclosed in parentheses stands alone, start it with a capital letter and end it with a period. When a sentence in parentheses falls within another sentence, never start with a capital or end with a period.

**NO** Looking for his car keys (He had left them at my sister's house.) wasted an entire hour.

**YES** Looking for his car keys (he had left them at my sister's house) wasted an entire hour.

If the material before the parenthetical material requires a comma, place that comma after the closing parenthesis unless you're using commas to set off numbers in a list.

| NO | Although clearly different from my favorite film, (*The Wizard of Oz*) *Gone With the Wind* is also outstanding. |
|---|---|
| YES | Although clearly different from my favorite film (*The Wizard of Oz*), *Gone With the Wind* is also outstanding. |

You can use a question mark or an exclamation point within parentheses that occur in a sentence.

Looking for clues (what did we expect to find?) wasted four days.

Place parentheses around quotation marks that come before or after any quoted words.

| NO | Alberta Hunter "(Down Hearted Blues)" is known for singing jazz. |
|---|---|
| YES | Alberta Hunter ("Down Hearted Blues") is known for singing jazz. |

# BRACKETS

## 29c When do I need to use brackets in my writing?

**Brackets** allow you to enclose words that you want to insert into quotations, but only in the specific cases discussed below.

### ADJUSTING A QUOTATION WITH BRACKETS

When you use a quotation, you might need to change the form of a word (a verb's tense, for example), add a brief definition, or fit the quotation into the grammatical structure of your sentence. In such cases, enclose the material you have inserted into the quotation in brackets. (These examples use MLA style for parenthetical references; see 35b.)

#### ORIGINAL SOURCE
Current research shows that successful learning takes place in an active environment.

—Deborah Moore, "Facilities and Learning Styles," p. 22

#### QUOTATION WITH BRACKETS

Deborah Moore supports a student-centered curriculum and agrees with "current research [which] shows that successful learning takes place in an active environment" (22).

### USING BRACKETS TO POINT OUT AN ERROR IN A SOURCE OR TO ADD INFORMATION WITHIN PARENTHESES

In words you want to quote, sometimes page-makeup technicians or authors make a mistake without realizing it—a wrong date, a misspelled word, or an error of fact. You fix that mistake by putting your correction in brackets, without changing the words you want to quote. This tells your readers that the error was in the original work and not made by you.

### USING [SIC] TO SHOW A SOURCE'S ERROR

Insert *sic* (without italics), enclosed in brackets, in your MLA-style essays and research papers to show your readers that you've quoted an error accurately. *Sic* is a Latin word that means "so," or "thus," which says "It is so (or thus) in the original."

#### USE FOR ERROR
A journalist wrote, "The judge accepted an [sic] plea of not guilty."

#### USE FOR MISSPELLING
The building inspector wrote about the consequence of doubling the apartment's floor space: "With that much extra room per person, the tennants [sic] would sublet."

### USING BRACKETS WITHIN PARENTHESES

Use brackets to insert information within parentheses.

That expression **(first used in *A Fable for Critics* [1848] by James R. Lowell)** was popularized in the early twentieth century by Ella Wheeler Wilcox.

## ELLIPSIS POINTS

# 29d   How do I use ellipsis points in my writing?

The word *ellipsis* means "omission." **Ellipsis points** in writing are a series of three spaced dots (use the period key on the keyboard). You're required to use ellipsis points to indicate you've intentionally omitted words—perhaps even a sentence or more—from the source you're quoting. These rules apply to both prose and poetry.

The *MLA Handbook* no longer recommends that ellipsis points you have inserted be enclosed in brackets to make it clear to your reader that the omission is yours. See Chapter 35 for more information.

## ■ Using ellipsis points with prose

ORIGINAL SOURCE

These two minds, the emotional and the rational, operate in tight harmony for the most part, intertwining their very different ways of knowing to guide us through the world. Ordinarily, there is a balance between emotional and rational minds, with emotion feeding into and informing the operations of the rational mind, and the rational mind refining and sometimes vetoing the inputs of the emotions. Still, the emotional and rational minds are semi-independent faculties, each, as we shall see, reflecting the operation of distinct, but interconnected, circuitry in the brain.

—Daniel Goleman, *Emotional Intelligence,* p. 9

QUOTATION OF SELECTED WORDS, NO ELLIPSIS NEEDED

Goleman explains that the "two minds, the emotional and the rational" usually provide "a balance" in our daily observations and decision making (9).

QUOTATION WITH ELLIPSIS MID-SENTENCE

Goleman emphasizes the connections between parts of the mind: "Still, the emotional and rational minds are semi-independent faculties, each . . . reflecting the operation of distinct, but interconnected, circuitry in the brain" (9).

QUOTATION WITH ELLIPSIS AND PARENTHETICAL REFERENCE

Goleman emphasizes that the "two minds, the emotional and the rational, operate in tight harmony for the most part . . ." (9). [Note: In MLA style, place a sentence-ending period after the parenthetical reference.]

QUOTATION WITH ELLIPSIS ENDING THE SENTENCE

On page 9, Goleman states: "These two minds, the emotional and the rational, operate in tight harmony for the most part. . . ." [*Note:* In MLA style, when all needed documentation information is written into a sentence—that is, not placed in parentheses at the end of the sentence—there's no space between the sentence-ending period and an ellipsis.]

QUOTATION WITH SENTENCE OMITTED

Goleman explains: "These two minds, the emotional and the rational, operate in tight harmony for the most part, intertwining their very different ways of knowing to guide us through the world. . . . Still, the emotional and rational minds are semi-independent faculties" (9).

QUOTATION WITH WORDS OMITTED FROM THE MIDDLE OF ONE SENTENCE
TO THE MIDDLE OF ANOTHER

Goleman states: "Ordinarily, there is a balance between emotional and
rational minds . . . reflecting the operation of distinct, but interconnected,
circuitry in the brain" (9).

QUOTATION WITH WORDS OMITTED FROM THE BEGINNING
OF A SENTENCE AND FROM THE MIDDLE OF ONE SENTENCE
TO A COMPLETE OTHER SENTENCE

Goleman explains: ". . . there is a balance between emotional and
rational minds. . . . Still, the emotional and rational minds are semi-
independent faculties, each, as we shall see, reflecting the operation of
distinct, but interconnected, circuitry in the brain" (9).

When you omit words from a quotation, you also omit punctuation related to
those words, unless it's needed for the sentence to be correct.

Goleman explains: "These two minds . . . operate in tight harmony" (9).
[comma in original source omitted after *minds*]

Goleman explains that the emotional and rational minds work together
while, "still, . . . each, as we shall see, [reflects] the operation of distinct,
but interconnected, circuitry in the brain" (9). [comma kept after *still*
because it's an introductory word; *still* changed to begin with lowercase
letter because it's now in the middle of the sentence; form of *reflecting*
changed to improve the sense of sentence]

## ■ Using ellipsis points with poetry

When you omit one or more words from a line of poetry, follow the rules stated
above for prose. However, when you omit a full line or more from poetry, use
a full line of spaced dots.

ORIGINAL SOURCE

**Little Boy Blue**
Little boy blue, come blow your horn,
The sheep's in the meadow, the cow's in the corn
Where is the little boy who looks after the sheep?
He's under the haystack, fast asleep.

QUOTATION WITH LINES OMITTED

**Little Boy Blue**

Little boy blue, come blow your horn,

. . . . . . . . . . . . . . . . . . . . . . . . . . . . . . . . . . .

Where is the little boy who looks after the sheep?

He's under the haystack, fast asleep.

# SLASH

## 29e When can I use a slash in my writing?

The **slash** (/), also called a *virgule* or *solidus,* is a diagonal line that separates or joins words in special circumstances.

### USING A SLASH TO SEPARATE QUOTED LINES OF POETRY

When you quote more than three lines of a poem, no slash is involved; you merely follow the rules in 28e. When you quote three lines or fewer, enclose them in quotation marks and run them into your sentence—and use a slash to divide one line from the next. Leave a space on each side of the slash.

> One of my mottoes comes from the beginning of Anne Sexton's poem "Words": "Be careful of words, / even the miraculous ones."

Capitalize and punctuate each line of poetry as in the original—but even if the quoted line of poetry doesn't have a period, use one to end your sentence. If your quotation ends before the line of poetry ends, use ellipsis points (29d).

### USING A SLASH FOR NUMERICAL FRACTIONS IN MANUSCRIPTS

To type numerical fractions, use a slash (with no space before or after the slash) to separate the numerator and denominator. In mixed numbers—that is, whole numbers with fractions—leave a space between the whole number and its fraction: 1 2/3, 3 7/8. Do not use a hyphen. (For information about using spelled-out and numerical forms of numbers, see 30m through 30o.)

### USING A SLASH FOR *AND/OR*

When writing in the humanities, try not to use word combinations connected with a slash, such as *and/or.* In academic disciplines in which such combinations are acceptable, separate the words with a slash. Leave no space before or after the slash. In the humanities, listing both alternatives in normal sentence structure is usually better than separating choices with a slash.

> **NO** The best quality of reproduction comes from 35 mm slides/direct-positive films.
>
> **YES** The best quality of reproduction comes from 35 mm slides **or** direct-positive films.

**EXERCISE 29-1**  Supply needed dashes, parentheses, brackets, ellipsis points, and slashes. If a sentence is correct as written, circle its number. In some sentences, when you can use either dashes or parentheses, explain your choice. For help, consult all sections of this chapter.

EXAMPLE  Two tiny islands in the English Channel Jersey and Guernsey have breeds of cows named after them.

Two tiny islands in the English Channel—Jersey and Guernsey— have breeds of cows named after them.

1. In *The Color Purple* a successful movie as well as a novel, Alice Walker explores the relationships between women and men in traditional African American culture.

2. W. C. Fields offered two pieces of advice on job hunting: 1 never show up for an interview in bare feet, and 2 don't read your prospective employer's mail while he is questioning you about your qualifications.

3. A series of resolutions was passed 11–0 with one council member abstaining calling on the mayor and the district attorney to improve safety conditions and step up law enforcement on city buses.

4. All the interesting desserts ice cream, chocolate fudge cake, pumpkin pie with whipped cream are fattening, unfortunately.

5. Thunder is caused when the flash of lightning heats the air around it to temperatures up to 30,000°F 16,666°C.

## HYPHEN

# 29f When do I need a hyphen in my writing?

A **hyphen** serves to divide words at the end of a line, to combine words into compounds, and to communicate numbers.

# 29g When do I use a hyphen at the end of a line?

Generally, try not to divide a word with a hyphen at the end of a line. (In printed books, hyphens are acceptable because of the limits on line length.) Word processing programs can be set either to space the words in a line (in order to avoid dividing words at the end of a line) or to hyphenate words automatically. If you must divide a word, or if the computer divides one automatically, try hard not to divide the last word on the first line of a paper, the last word in a paragraph, or the last word on a page.

When you can't avoid using a hyphen at the end of a line, break the word only between syllables. If you aren't sure about the syllables in a word, consult a dictionary. Never divide words that are short, contain only one syllable, or are pronounced as one syllable.

# 29h   How do I use a hyphen with prefixes and suffixes?

**Prefixes** are syllables in front of a **root**—a word's core, which carries the origin or meaning. Prefixes modify meanings. **Suffixes** also have modifying power, but they follow roots. Some prefixes and suffixes are attached to root words with hyphens, but others are not. Quick Reference 29.1 shows you how to decide.

## Quick Reference 29.1   ■ ■ ■ ■ ■

### Hyphens with prefixes and suffixes

- Use hyphens after the prefixes *all-, ex-, quasi-,* and *self-.*

  **YES**   all-inclusive    self-reliant

- Never use a hyphen when *self* is a root word, not a prefix.

  **NO**   self-ishness    self-less

  **YES**   selfishness    selfless

- Use a hyphen to avoid a distracting string of letters.

  **NO**   anti**i**ntellectual    bel**ll**ike    pro**o**utsourcing

  **YES**   anti-**i**ntellectual    bell-**l**ike    pro-**o**utsourcing

- Use a hyphen to add a prefix or suffix to a numeral or a word that starts with a capital letter.

  **NO**   post1950    proAmerican    Rembrandtlike

  **YES**   post-1950    pro-American    Rembrandt-like

- Use a hyphen before the suffix *-elect.*

  **NO**   presidentelect

  **YES**   president-elect

- Use a hyphen to prevent confusion in meaning or pronunciation.

  **YES**   re-dress (means *dress again*)    redress (means *set right*)

  **YES**   un-ionize (means *remove the ions*)    unionize (means *form a union*)

- Use a hyphen when two or more prefixes apply to one root word.

  **YES**   pre- and post-Renaissance

## 29i How do I use hyphens with compound words?

A **compound word** puts two or more words together to express one concept. Compound words come in three forms: an open-compound word, as in *night shift;* hyphenated words, as in *tractor-trailer;* and a closed-compound word, as in *handbook.* Quick Reference 29.2 lists basic guidelines for positioning hyphens in compound words.

### Quick Reference 29.2 ■ ■ ■ ■ ■

#### Hyphens with compound words

- Divide a compound word already containing a hyphen only after that hyphen, if possible. Also, divide a closed-compound word only between the two complete words, if possible.

  **NO**   self-con-scious   sis-ter-in-law   mas-terpiece
  **YES**   self-conscious   sister-in-law   master-piece

- Use a hyphen between a prefix and an open-compound word.

  **NO**   antigun control [*gun control* is an open-compound word]
  **YES**   anti-gun control

- Use a hyphen for most compound words that precede a noun but not for most compound words that follow a noun.

  **YES**   well-researched report   report is well researched

- Use hyphens when a compound modifier includes a series.

  **YES**   two-, three-, or four-year program

- Never use a hyphen when a compound modifier starts with an *-ly* adverb.

  **NO**   happily-married couple   loosely-tied package
  **YES**   happily married couple   loosely tied package

- Use a hyphen with most COMPARATIVE (*-er*) and SUPERLATIVE (*-est*) compound forms, but not when the compound modifier includes *more/most* or *less/least.*

  **NO**   better fitting shoe
  **YES**   better-fitting shoe

  **NO**   least-significant factors
  **YES**   least significant factors

- Never use a hyphen when a compound modifier is a foreign phrase.

  **YES**   *post hoc* fallacies

- Never use a hyphen with a possessive compound.

  **NO**   a full-week's work   eight-hours' pay
  **YES**   a full week's work   eight hours' pay

**EXERCISE 29-2** Provide the correct form of the words in parentheses, according to the rules in 29f through 29i. Explain your reasoning for each.

1. The tiger is (all powerful) _____ in the cat family.

2. (Comparison and contrast) _____ studies of tigers and lions show that the tiger is the (more agile) _____ and powerful.

3. Male tigers and lions look similar except for their hair length: Tigers have (ultra short) _____ hair and male lions have (extra long) _____ hair in their manes.

4. The tiger's body is a (boldly striped) _____ yellow, with a white (under body) _____.

5. The Bengal tiger, the largest of the family, is aggressive and (self confident) _____.

# 30

# Capitals, Italics, Abbreviations, and Numbers

## CAPITALS

## 30a When do I capitalize a "first" word?

### FIRST WORD IN A SENTENCE

Always capitalize the first letter of the first word in a sentence.

Four inches of snow fell last winter.

### A SERIES OF QUESTIONS

If questions in a series are complete sentences, start each with a capital letter. If, however, the questions aren't complete sentences, you can choose to capitalize or not. Whatever your choice, be consistent in each piece of writing. In this handbook, we use capitals for a series of questions.

What facial feature would most people like to change? Eyes? Ears? Nose?

What facial feature would most people like to change? eyes? ears? nose?

## SMALL WORDS IN TITLES OR HEADINGS

Capitalize small words (*the, a, an,* and short PREPOSITIONS such as *of, to*) in a title or heading only when they begin the title or when the source capitalizes these small words. Always capitalize *I,* no matter where it falls in a sentence or group of words.

## AFTER A COLON

When a complete sentence follows a colon, you can choose to start that sentence with either a capital or a lowercase letter, but be consistent in each piece of writing. When the words after a colon are not a complete sentence, do not capitalize.

> She reacted instantly: **S**he picked up the ice cream and pushed it back into her cone.

> She reacted instantly: **s**he picked up the ice cream and pushed it back into her cone.

**!** **Alert:** A colon can follow only a complete sentence (an INDEPENDENT CLAUSE; see 26a). ●

## FORMAL OUTLINE

In a formal outline, start each item with a capital letter. Use a period only when the item is a complete sentence.

# 30b When do I use capitals with listed items?

## A LIST RUN INTO A SENTENCE

If run-in listed items are complete sentences, start each with a capital and end each with a period (or question mark or exclamation point). If the run-in listed items are incomplete sentences, start each with a lowercase letter and end each with a comma—unless the items already contain commas, in which case use semicolons. If you list three or more items that are incomplete sentences, use *and* before the last item.

> **YES** We found three reasons for the delay: (1) **B**ad weather held up delivery of materials. (2) **P**oor scheduling created confusion. (3) **I**mproper machine maintenance caused an equipment failure.

> **YES** The reasons for the delay were (1) **b**ad weather**,** (2) **p**oor scheduling**, and** (3) **e**quipment failure.

> **YES** The reasons for the delay were (1) **b**ad weather, which had been predicted**;** (2) **p**oor scheduling, which is the airline's responsibility**; and** (3) **e**quipment failure, which no one can predict.

## A DISPLAYED LIST

In a displayed list, each item starts on a new line. If the items are sentences, capitalize the first letter and end with a period (or question mark or exclamation point). If the items are not sentences, you can use a capital letter or not. Whichever you choose, be consistent in each piece of writing. Punctuate a displayed list as you would a run-in list.

**YES** We found three reasons for the delay:
1. Bad weather held up delivery of materials.
2. Poor scheduling created confusion.
3. Improper machine maintenance caused an equipment failure.

**YES** The reasons for the delay were
1. bad weather,
2. poor scheduling, **and**
3. equipment failure.

**Alerts:** (1) If a complete sentence leads into a displayed list, you can end the sentence with a colon. However, if an incomplete sentence leads into a displayed list, use no punctuation. (2) Use PARALLELISM for items in a list. For example, if one item is a sentence, use sentences for all the items (10e); or if one item starts with a VERB, start all items with a verb in the same TENSE; and so on. ●

## 30c When do I use capitals with sentences in parentheses?

When you write a complete sentence within parentheses that falls within another sentence, don't start with a capital or end with a period—but do use a question mark or exclamation point, if needed. When you write a sentence within parentheses that doesn't fall within another sentence, capitalize the first word and end with a period (or question mark or exclamation point).

> I did not know till years later that they called it the Cuban Missile Crisis. But I remember Castro. (We called him Castor Oil and were awed by his beard.) We might not have worried so much (what would the communists want with our small New Hampshire town?) except we lived 10 miles from a U.S. air base.
>
> —Joyce Maynard, "An 18-Year-Old Looks Back on Life"

## 30d When do I use capitals with quotations?

If a quotation within your sentence is itself less than a complete sentence, never capitalize the first quoted word. If the quotation you have used in your sentence is itself a complete sentence, capitalize the first word.

Mrs. Enriquez says that students who are learning a new language should visit that country and "absorb a good accent with the food."

Talking about students who live in a new country Mrs. Enriquez says, "They'll absorb a good accent with the food."

When you write DIRECT DISCOURSE—which you introduce with verbs such as *said, stated, reported,* and others followed by a comma, capitalize the first letter of the quoted words. However, never capitalize a partial quotation, and never capitalize the continuation of a one-sentence quotation within your sentence.

Mrs. Enriquez said, "Students who are learning a new language should visit that country. They'll absorb a good accent with the food."
[complete sentence]

Mrs. Enriquez told me that the best way to "absorb a good accent" in a language is to visit the country and eat its food. [part of a quotation integrated in a sentence]

## 30e When do I capitalize nouns and adjectives?

Capitalize PROPER NOUNS (nouns that name specific people, places, and things): *Abraham Lincoln, Mexico, World Wide Web.* Also, capitalize **proper adjectives** (adjectives formed from proper nouns): *a Mexican entrepreneur, a Web address.* Don't capitalize ARTICLES (*the, a, an*) that accompany proper nouns and proper adjectives, unless they start a sentence.

When a proper noun or adjective loses its very specific "proper" association, it also loses its capital letter: *french fries, pasteurized.* When you turn a common noun (*lake*) into a proper noun (*Lake Mead*), capitalize all words.

Quick Reference 30.1 is a capitalization guide. If you don't find what you need, locate an item in it (or in Quick Reference 30.2 on page 315) that's close to what you want, and use it as a model.

### Quick Reference 30.1 ■ ■ ■ ■ ■

#### Capitalization

|  | Capitals | Lowercase Letters |
|---|---|---|
| **NAMES** | Mother Teresa (*also, used as names:* Mother, Dad, Mom, Pa) | my mother [relationship] |
|  | Doc Holliday | the doctor [role] |

continued >>

## Quick Reference 30.1    (continued)    ■ ■ ■ ■ ■

| | Capitals | Lowercase Letters |
|---|---|---|
| **TITLES** | President Truman | the president |
| | Democrat [party member] | a democrat [believer in democracy] |
| | Representative Harold Ford | the congressional representative |
| | Senator Edward M. Kennedy | a senator |
| | Queen Elizabeth II | the queen |
| **GROUPS OF PEOPLE** | Caucasian [race] | white, black [*also* White, Black] |
| | African American, Hispanic [ethnic group] | |
| | Irish, Korean, Canadian [nationality] | |
| | Jewish, Catholic, Protestant, Buddhist [religious affiliation] | |
| **ORGANIZATIONS** | Congress | the legislative branch of the US government |
| | the Ohio State Supreme Court | the state supreme court |
| | the Republican Party | the party |
| | National Gypsum Company | the company |
| | Chicago Cubs | a baseball team |
| | American Medical Association | a professional group |
| | Sigma Chi | a fraternity |
| | Alcoholics Anonymous | a self-help group |
| **PLACES** | Los Angeles | the city |
| | the South [region] | turn south [direction] |
| | the West Coast | the US states along the western seaboard |
| | Main Street | the street |
| | Atlantic Ocean | the ocean |
| | the Black Hills | the hills |
| **BUILDINGS** | the Capitol [in Washington, DC] | the state capitol |
| | Ace High School | a high school |
| | Front Road Café | a restaurant |
| | Highland Hospital | a hospital |

continued >>

**Quick Reference 30.1**   (continued)   ■ ■ ■ ■ ■

| | Capitals | Lowercase Letters |
|---|---|---|
| **SCIENTIFIC TERMS** | Earth [as one of nine planets] | the earth [otherwise] |
| | the Milky Way, the Galaxy [as name] | our galaxy, the moon, the sun |
| | *Streptococcus aureus* | a streptococcal infection |
| | Gresham's law | the theory of relativity |
| **LANGUAGES, SCHOOL COURSES** | Spanish, Chinese | |
| | Chemistry 342 | a chemistry course |
| | History 111 | my history class |
| | Introduction to Photography | a photography course |
| **NAMES OF SPECIFIC THINGS** | Black Parrot tulip | a climbing rose |
| | Purdue University | the university |
| | Heinz ketchup | ketchup, sauce |
| | a Toyota Camry | a car |
| | Twelfth Dynasty | the dynasty |
| | the *Boston Globe* | a newspaper |
| **TIMES, SEASONS, HOLIDAYS** | Monday, Fri. | today |
| | September, February | a month |
| | the Roaring Twenties | the decade |
| | the Christmas season | spring, summer, autumn, winter, the fall semester |
| | Kwanzaa, New Year's Day | a feast day, the holiday |
| | Passover, Ramadan | a religious holiday or observance |
| **HISTORICAL EVENTS AND DOCUMENTS** | World War II | the war |
| | Battle of the Bulge | the battle |
| | the Great Depression (of the 1930s) | the depression [any serious economic downturn] |
| | the Reformation | the eighteenth century |
| | Paleozoic | an era or age, prehistory |
| | the Bill of Rights | fifth-century manuscripts |
| **RELIGIOUS TERMS** | Athena, God | a goddess, a god |
| | Islam | a religion |
| | the Torah, the Koran (or Qur'an) | a holy book |
| | the Bible | biblical |
| **LETTER PARTS** | Dear Ms. Schultz: | |
| | Sincerely, | |
| | Yours truly, | |

continued >>

## Quick Reference 30.1   (continued)   ■ ■ ■ ■ ■

| | Capitals | Lowercase Letters |
|---|---|---|
| **PUBLISHED AND RELEASED MATERIAL** | "The Lottery" <br> *A History of the United States to 1877* <br> *Jazz on Ice* <br> Nixon Papers <br> Mass in B Minor | [Capitalize first letter of first word and all other major words] <br> the show, a performance <br> the archives <br> the B minor mass |
| **ACRONYMS AND INITIALISMS** | NASA, NATO, UCLA, AFL-CIO, DNA | |
| **COMPUTER TERMS** | Gateway, Dell <br> Microsoft Word, WordPerfect <br> Netscape Navigator <br> the Internet <br> World Wide Web, the Web <br> Web site, Web page | a computer company <br> computer software <br><br> a browser <br> a computer network <br> www <br> a home page, a link |
| **PROPER ADJECTIVES** | Victorian <br> Midwestern <br> Indo-European | southern <br> transatlantic <br> alpine |

**EXERCISE 30-1**   Add capital letters as needed. See 30a through 30e for help.

1. The state of california is best known as the golden state, but other nicknames include the land of milk and honey, the el dorado state, and the grape state.

2. Most people think of san Francisco as northern california, but the city of Eureka, from the greek word meaning "I have found it," is 280 miles north of san Francisco, and the state line is another 90 miles north of eureka.

3. South of san Francisco on the california coast is santa Barbara, which hosts the annual Dickens Universe, a weeklong series of studies and celebrations of the famous writer charles dickens.

4. The highest point in the contiguous United States is mt. Whitney at 14,495 feet high, and the lowest place in the contiguous United States is bad Water in death valley at 282 feet below sea level, both located in california.

5. Having approximately 500,000 detectable seismic tremors per year, california rocks, literally.

## ITALICS

## 30f What are italics?

**Italic typeface** slants to the right (*like this*); **roman typeface** does not (like this). MLA STYLE requires italics, not underlining, in all documents.

ROMAN    your writing

ITALICS    *your writing*

## 30g How do I choose between using italics and quotation marks?

As a rule, use italics for titles of long works (*Juno,* a movie) or for works that contain subsections (*Masterpiece Theater,* a television show). Generally, use quotation marks for titles of shorter works ("Smells like Teen Spirit," a song) and for titles of subsections within longer works such as books (Chapter 1, "Loomings").

Quick Reference 30.2 is a guide for using italics, quotation marks, or nothing. If you don't find what you need, locate an item that is as much like what you want as possible and use it as a model.

## 30h Can I use italics for special emphasis?

Some professional writers, especially writers of nonfiction and self-help material, occasionally use italics to clarify a meaning or stress a point. In ACADEMIC WRITING, however, you're expected to convey special emphasis through your choice of words and sentence structure, not with italics (or underlining). If your message absolutely calls for it, use italics sparingly—and only after you're sure nothing else will do.

Many people we *think* are powerful turn out on closer examination to be merely frightened and anxious.

—Michael Korda, *Power!*

## ABBREVIATIONS

## 30i What are standard practices for using abbreviations?

Some abbreviations are standard in all writing circumstances (*Mr.,* not *Mister,* in a name; *St.* Louis, the city, not *Saint* Louis). In some situations, you may have a choice whether to abbreviate or spell out a word. Choose what seems suited to your PURPOSE for writing and your AUDIENCE, and be consistent within each piece of writing.

## Quick Reference 30.2

■ ■ ■ ■ ■

### Italics, quotation marks, or nothing

| Italics | Quotation Marks or Nothing |
|---|---|
| **TITLES AND NAMES** | |
| *Sense and Sensibility* [a novel] | title of student essay |
| *Death of a Salesman* [a play] | act 2 [part of a play] |
| *A Beautiful Mind* [a film] | the Epilogue [a part of a film or book] |
| *Collected Works of O. Henry* [a book] | "The Last Leaf" [a story in a book] |
| *Simon & Schuster Handbook for Writers* [a textbook] | "Agreement" [a chapter in a book] |
| *The Prose Reader* [a collection of essays] | "Putting in a Good Word for Guilt" [an essay] |
| *Iliad* [a book-length poem] | "Nothing Gold Can Stay" [a short poem] |
| *Scientific American* [a magazine] | "The Molecules of Life" [an article in a magazine] |
| *Symphonie Fantastique* [a long musical work] | Violin Concerto No. 2 in B-flat Minor [a musical work identified by form, number, and key—neither quotation marks nor italics] |
| *U2 18 Singles* [an album] | "With or Without You" [a song] |
| *Lost* [a television series] | "Something Nice Back Home" [an episode of a television series] |
| *Kids Count* [a Web site title] | Excel [a software program] |
| the *Los Angeles Times* [a newspaper]* | |
| **OTHER WORDS** | |
| *semper fidelis* [words in a language other than English] | burrito, chutzpah [widely understood non-English words] |
| What does *our* imply? [a word meant as a word] | |
| the *abc*'s; the letter *x* [letters meant as letters] | 6s and 7s; & [numerals and symbols] |

*When *The* is part of a newspaper's title, don't capitalize or italicize it in MLA-style or CM-style documentation. In APA-style and CSE-style documentation, capitalize and italicize *The*.

> **NO**   Our field hockey team left after Casey's **psych** class on **Tues., Oct.** 10, but the flight had to make an unexpected stop (in **Chi.**) before reaching **L.A.**

> **YES**   Our field hockey team left after Casey's **psychology** class on **Tuesday, October** 10, but the flight had to make an unexpected stop (in **Chicago**) before reaching **Los Angeles.**

❗ **Alerts:** (1) Many abbreviations call for periods (*Mrs., Ms., Dr.*), but the practice is changing. The trend today is to drop the periods (*PS,* not *P.S.; MD,* not *M.D.; US,* not *U.S.*), yet firm rules are still evolving.

(2) **Acronyms** (pronounceable words formed from the initials of a name) generally have no periods: *NASA* (National Aeronautics and Space Administration) and *AIDS* (*a*cquired *i*mmune *d*eficiency *s*yndrome).

(3) **Initialisms** (names spoken as separate letters) usually have no periods (*IBM, ASPCA, UN*).

(4) US Postal abbreviations for states have no periods (30k).

(5) When the final period of an abbreviation falls at the end of a sentence, that period serves also to end the sentence. ●

## 30j   How do I use abbreviations with months, time, eras, and symbols?

### MONTHS

According to MLA STYLE, abbreviations for months belong only in "Works Cited" lists, tables, charts, and the like. Write out the full spelling, never the abbreviation, in your ACADEMIC WRITING.

### TIMES

Use the abbreviations *a.m.* and *p.m.* only with exact times: *7:15 a.m.; 3:47 p.m.* Although some publication styles use the capitalized versions, *A.M.* and *P.M.,* MLA style calls for the use of lowercase letters.

❗ **Alert:** Never use *a.m.* and *p.m.* in place of the words *morning, evening,* and *night.*

> **NO**   My hardest final exam is in the **a.m.** tomorrow, but by early **p.m.,** I'll be ready to study for the rest of my finals.

> **YES**   My hardest final exam is in the **morning** tomorrow, but by early **evening,** I'll be ready to study for the rest of my finals. ●

## ERAS

In MLA style, use capital letters, without periods, in abbreviations for eras. Some writers prefer using *CE* ("common era") in place of *AD* (Latin for *anno Domini,* "in the year of our Lord") as the more inclusive term. In addition, many writers prefer using *BCE* ("before the common era") in place of *BC* ("before Christ").

When writing the abbreviations for eras, place *AD* before the year (*AD 476*) and all the others after the year (*29 BC; 165 BCE; 1100 CE*).

## SYMBOLS

In MLA style, decide whether to use symbols or spelled-out words according to your topic and the focus of your document (see also 30m). However, never use a freestanding symbol, such as *$, %,* or *¢* in your sentences; always use it with a numeral. With many exceptions, spell out both the symbol and the numeral accompanying it (*twenty centimeters*), unless the number is more than one or two words (*345 centimeters,* not *three hundred forty-five centimeters*).

The exceptions include *$18; 7 lbs.; 24 KB; 6:34 a.m.; 5"; 32°;* and numbers in addresses, dates, page references, and decimal fractions (*8.3*). In writing about money, the form *$25 million* is an acceptable combination of symbol, numeral, and spelled-out word.

In confined spaces, such as charts and tables, use symbols with numerals (*20¢*). In documents that focus on technical matters, use numerals but spell out the unit of measurement (*2,500 pounds*), in MLA style. In other documentation styles, such as APA, CM, and CSE, the guidelines differ somewhat, so you need to check each style's manual.

# 30k   How do I use abbreviations for other elements?

## TITLES

Use either a title of address before a name (***Dr.** Daniel Klausner*) or an academic degree after a name (*Daniel Klausner, **PhD***), not both. However, because *Jr., Sr., II, III,* and so forth are part of a given name, you can use both titles of address and academic degree abbreviations: ***Dr.** Martin Luther King **Jr.**; Gavin Alexander **II, MD.***

⦸ **Alerts:**  (1) Insert a comma both before and after an academic degree that follows a person's name, unless it falls at the end of a sentence: *Joshua Coleman**, LLD,** is our guest speaker,* or *Our guest speaker is Joshua Coleman**, LLD.*** (2) Never put a comma before an abbreviation that is part of a given name: *Steven Elliott **Sr.**, Douglas Young **III.*** ●

## NAMES AND TERMS

If you use a term frequently in a piece of writing, follow these guidelines: The first time you use the term, spell it out completely and then put its abbreviation in parentheses immediately after. In later references, use the abbreviation alone.

> Spain voted to continue as a member of the **North Atlantic Treaty Organization** (**NATO**), to the surprise of other **NATO** members.

> When referring to the United States, use the abbreviation *US* as a modifier before a noun (*the **US** ski team*), but spell out *United States* when you use it as a noun (*the ski team from the **United States***).

## ADDRESSES

If you include a full address in a piece of writing, use the two-letter postal abbreviation for the state name. For any other combination of a city and a state, or a state by itself, spell out the state name; never abbreviate it.

**❗ Alert:**  When you write the names of a US city and state within a sentence, use a comma before and after the state.

> **NO**   Portland, Oregon is much larger than Portland, Maine.
>
> **YES**   Portland, Oregon, is much larger than Portland, Maine.

If you include a ZIP code, however, don't use a comma after the state. Do place the comma after the ZIP code. ●

## SCHOLARLY WRITING (MLA STYLE)

MLA style permits abbreviations for a selection of scholarly terms. These are listed in Quick Reference 30.3. Never use them in the body of your ACADEMIC WRITING. Reserve them for your "Works Cited" lists and for any notes you might write in a separate list at the end of your research paper.

# 30I   When can I use *etc.*?

The abbreviation *etc.* comes from the Latin *et cetera*, meaning "and the rest." In ACADEMIC WRITING, don't use *etc.* Accepted substitutes include *and the like, and so on, and so forth,* among others. Even better is a more concrete description. An acceptable use of *etc.* is in tables and charts.

> **NO**   We took paper plates, plastic forks, **etc.,** to the picnic.
>
> **YES**   We took paper plates, plastic forks, **and other disposable items** to the picnic.

## Quick Reference 30.3

■ ■ ■ ■ ■

### Major scholarly abbreviations—MLA style

| | | | |
|---|---|---|---|
| **anon.** | anonymous | **i.e.** | that is |
| **b.** | born | **ms., mss.** | manuscript, manuscripts |
| **c.** *or* © | copyright | | |
| **c.** *or* **ca.** | circa *or* about [with dates] | **NB** | note well (*nota bene*) |
| **cf.** | compare | **n.d.** | no date (of publication) |
| **col., cols.** | column, columns | **p., pp.** | page, pages |
| **d.** | died | **par.** | paragraph |
| **ed., eds.** | edition, edited by, editor(s) | **pref.** | preface, prefaced by |
| | | **rept.** | report, reported by |
| **e.g.** | for example | **rev.** | review, reviewed by; revised, revised by |
| **esp.** | especially | | |
| **et al.** | and others | **sec., secs.** | section, sections |
| **ff.** | following pages, following lines, folios | **v.** *or* **vs.** | versus [*v.* in legal cases] |
| | | **vol., vols.** | volume, volumes |

**Alert:** If you do write *etc.*, always put a comma after the period if the abbreviation falls in the middle of a sentence. ●

**EXERCISE 30-2**   Revise these sentences for correct use of abbreviations. For help, consult 30i through 30l.

1. Originally named the Geo. S. Parker Company, located in Salem, Mass., the toy co. changed its name to Parker Bros. when Chas. joined the business in 1888.

2. Sev. of their games have become quite famous, esp. Monopoly and Clue, both of which were released in the 20th cent.

3. The obj. of the game Monopoly (meaning "dominating the mkt.") is to get the most $ by purchasing, renting, & selling real est.

4. Clue, another pop. brd. game, is a murder mys. in which players move from 1 rm. to another, making accusations to reveal the i.d. of the murderer, the weapon used, and the room where the crime took place.

5. On a cold day in Jan., when the snow is 3 ft. deep and it's dark by early eve., passing the hrs. with your fam. and friends playing a board game is great fun.

## NUMBERS

## 30m When do I use spelled-out numbers?

Your decision to write a number as a word or as a figure depends on what you're referring to and how often numbers occur in your piece of writing. The guidelines we give in this handbook are for MLA STYLE, which focuses on writing in the humanities. For other disciplines, follow the guidelines in their style manuals.

When you write numbers for more than one category in a piece of writing, reserve figures for some categories of numbers and spelled-out words for other categories. Never mix spelled-out numbers and figures for a particular category.

> NO    In **four** days, our volunteers increased from **five** to **eight** to **17** to **233.**

> YES   In **four** days, our volunteers increased from **5** to **8** to **17** to **233.**
> [Numbers referring to volunteers are in numerals, while *four* is spelled out because it refers to a different category: days.]

🛑 **Alert:** When you write a two-word number, use a hyphen between the spelled-out words, starting with *twenty-one* and continuing through *ninety-nine.* ●

If you use numbers infrequently in a document, spell out all numbers that call for no more than two words: *fifty-two cards, twelve hundred students.* If you use specific numbers often in a document (temperatures when writing about climate, percentages in an economics essay, or other specific measurements of time, distance, and other quantities), use figures: *36 inches, 11 nanoseconds.* If you give only an approximation, spell out the numbers: *About twelve inches of snow fell.*

In the humanities, the names of centuries are always spelled out: *the eighteenth century.*

When you write for courses in the humanities, never start a sentence with a figure. Spell out the number—or better still, revise the sentence so that the number doesn't need to fall at the beginning. For practices in other disciplines, consult their manuals.

> NO    **$375 dollars** for each credit is the tuition rate for nonresidents.

> YES   **Three hundred seventy-five dollars** for each credit is the tuition rate for nonresidents.

## 30n What are standard practices for writing numbers?

Quick Reference 30.4 shows standard practices for writing numbers. Consider it a basic guide, and rely on the manual of each documentation style for answers to other questions you may have.

## Quick Reference 30.4  ▪ ▪ ▪ ▪ ▪

### Specific numbers in writing

| | |
|---|---|
| **DATES** | August 6, 1941<br>1732–1845<br>from 34 BC to AD 230 (*or* 34 BCE to 230 CE) |
| **ADDRESSES** | 10 Downing Street<br>237 North 8th Street<br>Export Falls, MN 92025 |
| **TIMES** | 8:09 a.m., 6:00 p.m.<br>six o'clock (*not* 6 o'clock)<br>four in the afternoon *or* 4 p.m. (*not* four p.m.) |
| **DECIMALS AND FRACTIONS** | 0.01<br>98.6<br>3.1416<br>7/8<br>12 1/4<br>a sixth<br>three-quarters (*not* 3-quarters)<br>one-half |
| **CHAPTERS AND PAGES** | Chapter 27, page 2<br>p. 1023 *or* pp. 660–62 (MLA style) |
| **SCORES AND STATISTICS** | a 6–0 score<br>29% (or twenty-nine percent)<br>a 5 to 1 ratio (*and* a ratio of 5:1)<br>a one percent change (*and* at the 1 percent level) |
| **IDENTIFICATION NUMBERS** | 94.4 on the FM dial<br>please call (012) 345–6789 |
| **MEASUREMENTS** | 67.8 miles per hour<br>2 level teaspoons<br>a 700-word essay<br>8-by-10-inch photograph<br>2 feet<br>1.5 gallons<br>14 liters |
| **ACT, SCENE, AND LINE** | act 2, scene 2 (*or* act II, scene ii)<br>lines 75–79 |
| **TEMPERATURES** | 40°F *or* −5°F<br>20° Celsius |
| **MONEY** | $1.2 billion<br>$3.41<br>25¢ (*or* twenty-five cents)<br>$10,000 |

## **30o** How do I use hyphens with spelled-out numbers?

A spelled-out number uses words, not figures. Quick Reference 30.5 gives you guidelines.

---

### Quick Reference 30.5

■ ■ ■ ■ ■

#### Hyphens with spelled-out numbers

- Use a hyphen between two-word numbers from *twenty-one* through *ninety-nine,* whether they stand alone or are part of a larger number.

  **YES**      thirty-five      two hundred thirty-five

- Use a hyphen in a COMPOUND-WORD modifier formed from a number and a word, whether the number is in words or figures.

  **YES**      fifty-minute class [*also* 50-minute class]

  **YES**      three-to-one odds [*also* 3-to-1 odds]

- Use a hyphen between the numerator and the denominator of two-word fractions.

  **YES**      one-half      two-fifths      seven-tenths

- Use a hyphen between compound nouns joining two units of measure.

  **YES**      light-years      kilowatt-hours

---

🛈 **Alert:** Use figures rather than words for a fraction written in more than two words. If your context calls for figures, use hyphens only between the words of the numerator and only between the words of the denominator—but never between the numerator and the denominator: two one-hundredths (*2/100*), thirty-three ten-thousandths (*33/10,000*). ●

# 31

# Spelling

## 31a  What makes a good speller?

You might be surprised to hear that good spellers don't know how to spell and hyphenate every word they write. What they do know, however, is to check if they're not sure of a word's spelling. If your inner voice questions a spelling, do what good spellers do—consult a dictionary.

**!Alert:**  Word-processing software usually includes a spell-check program, which claims to spot spelling errors because the words typed in don't match the spellings in the software's dictionary. Such programs have one major drawback. The programs can't detect that you've spelled a word incorrectly if what you've typed is a legitimate spelling of a legitimate word. ●

## 31b  How can I proofread for errors in spelling and hyphen use?

Many spelling errors are the result of illegible handwriting, slips of the pen, or typographical mistakes. Catching these "typos" requires especially careful proofreading, using the techniques in Quick Reference 31.1.

---

**Quick Reference 31.1**   ■ ■ ■ ■ ■

### Proofreading for errors in spelling

- Slow down your reading speed to allow yourself to concentrate on the individual letters of words rather than on the meaning of the words.

- Stay within your "visual span," the number of letters you can identify with a single glance (for most people, about six letters).

- Put a ruler or large index card under each line as you proofread, to focus your vision and concentration.

- Read each paragraph in reverse, from the last sentence to the first. This method can keep you from being distracted by the meaning of the material.

---

# 31c How are plurals spelled?

In American English, plurals take many forms. The most common form adds -*s* or -*es* at the end of the word. The following list covers all variations of creating plurals.

- **Adding -s or -es:** Plurals of most words are formed by adding -*s*, including words that end in "hard" -*ch* (sounding like *k*): *leg, legs; shoe, shoes; stomach, stomachs.* Words ending in -*s*, -*sh*, -*x*, -*z*, or "soft" -*ch* (as in *beach*) are formed by adding -*es* to the singular: *lens, lenses; tax, taxes; beach, beaches.*

- **Words ending in -o:** Add -*s* if the -*o* is preceded by a vowel: *radio, radios; cameo, cameos.* Add -*es* if the -*o* is preceded by a consonant: *potato, potatoes.* With a few words, you can choose the -*s* or -*es* plural form, but current practice generally supports adding -*es*: *cargo, cargoes; tornado, tornadoes; zero, zeros* or *zeroes.*

- **Words ending in -f or -fe:** Some words ending in -*f* and -*fe* are made plural by adding -*s*: *belief, beliefs.* Others require changing -*f* or -*fe* to -*ves*: *life, lives; leaf, leaves.* Words ending in -*ff* or -*ffe* simply add -*s*: *staff, staffs; giraffe, giraffes.*

- **Compound words:** For most compound words, add -*s* or -*es* at the end of the last word: *checkbooks, player-coaches.* In a few cases, the first word is made plural: *sister-in-law, sisters-in-law; miles per hour.* (For information about hyphens in compound words, see 31g.)

- **Internal changes and endings other than -s:** A few words change internally or add endings other than -*s* to become plural: *foot, feet; man, men; crisis, crises; child, children.*

- **Foreign words:** The best advice is to check your dictionary. In general, many Latin words ending in -*um* form the plural by changing -*um* to -*a*: *curriculum, curricula; datum, data; medium, media.* Also, Latin words that end in -*us* usually form the plural by changing -*us* to -*i*: *alumnus, alumni; syllabus, syllabi.* Additionally, Greek words that end in -*on* usually form the plural by changing -*on* to -*a*: *criterion, criteria; phenomenon, phenomena.*

- **One-form words:** Some words have the same form in both the singular and the plural: *deer, elk, fish.* You need to use modifiers, as necessary, to indicate which form you mean: *one deer, nine deer.*

# 31d How are suffixes spelled?

A **suffix** is an ending added to a word that changes the word's meaning or its grammatical function. For example, adding the suffix -*able* to the VERB *depend* creates the ADJECTIVE *dependable.*

- **-y words:** If the letter before a final *-y* is a consonant, change the *-y* to *-i* and add the suffix: *try, tries, tried.* In the case of *trying* and similar words, the following rule applies: Keep the *-y* when the suffix begins with *-i* (*apply, applying*). If the letter before the final *-y* is a vowel, keep the final *-y: employ, employed, employing.* These rules don't apply to IRREGULAR VERBS (see Quick Reference 15.4 in section 15d).

- **-e words:** Drop a final *-e* when the suffix begins with a vowel, unless doing this would cause confusion: for example, *be + ing* can't be written *bing,* but *require* does become *requiring; like* does become *liking.* Keep the final *-e* when the suffix begins with a consonant: *require, requirement; like, likely.* Exceptions include *argue, argument; judge, judgment; true, truly.*

- **Words that double a final letter:** If the final letter is a consonant, double it *only* if it passes three tests: (1) Its last two letters are a vowel followed by a consonant; (2) it has one syllable or is accented on the last syllable; (3) the suffix begins with a vowel: *drop, dropped; begin, beginning; forget, forgettable.*

- **-cede, -ceed, -sede words:** Only one word in the English language ends in *-sede: supersede.* Only three words end in *-ceed: exceed, proceed, succeed.* All other words with endings that sound like "seed" end in *-cede: concede, intercede, precede.*

- **-ally and -ly words:** The suffixes *-ally* and *-ly* turn words into adverbs. For words ending in *-ic,* add *-ally: logically, statistically.* Otherwise, add *-ly: quickly, sharply.*

- **-ance, -ence, and -ible, -able:** No consistent rules govern words with these suffixes. When in doubt, look up the word.

# 31e  What is the *ie, ei* rule?

The famous rhymed rule for using *ie* and *ei* is usually true:

> *I* before *e* [believe, field, grief],
> Except after *c* [ceiling, conceit],
> Or when sounded like "ay"—
> As in neighbor and weigh [eight, vein].

There are major exceptions (sorry!) to the *ie, ei* rule, listed here. Our best advice is that you memorize them.

- **ie:** conscience, financier, science, species
- **ei:** either, neither, leisure, seize, counterfeit, foreign, forfeit, sleight (as in *sleight of hand*), weird

# 31f  How are homonyms and other frequently confused words spelled?

**Homonyms** are words that sound exactly like other words: *to, too, two; no, know.* The different spellings of homonyms tend to confuse many writers. The same holds for words that sound almost alike (*accept, except; conscience, conscious*).

Another reason for spelling problems is so-called swallowed pronunciation, which means one or more letters at the end of a word aren't pronounced clearly. For example, the *-d* ending in *use**d** to* or *prejudice**d*** or the *-ten* ending in *wri**tten*** are often swallowed rather than pronounced. When writers spell as they mispronounce, spelling errors result.

For more information about word usage that affects spelling, see Chapter 13, "Usage Glossary." Quick Reference 31.2 lists homonyms and other words that can be confused and lead to misspellings.

---

### Quick Reference 31.2  ▪ ▪ ▪ ▪ ▪

#### Homonyms and other frequently confused words

| | |
|---|---|
| • ACCEPT | to receive |
| EXCEPT | with the exclusion of |
| • ADVICE | recommendation |
| ADVISE | to recommend |
| • AFFECT | to influence [verb]; emotion [noun] |
| EFFECT | result [noun]; to bring about or cause [verb] |
| • ALLUDE | to make indirect reference to |
| ELUDE | to avoid |
| • ALREADY | by this time |
| ALL READY | fully prepared |
| • ALTOGETHER | thoroughly |
| ALL TOGETHER | everyone or everything in one place |
| • ASCENT | the act of rising or climbing |
| ASSENT | consent [noun]; to consent [verb] |
| • BREATH | air taken in |
| BREATHE | to take in air |
| • CAPITAL | major city; money |
| CAPITOL | government building |
| • CHOOSE | to pick |
| CHOSE | PAST TENSE of *choose* |

continued >>

## Quick Reference 31.2    (continued)    ▪ ▪ ▪ ▪ ▪

- CITE    to point out
  SIGHT    vision
  SITE    a place

- COARSE    rough
  COURSE    path; series of lectures

- COMPLEMENT    something that completes
  COMPLIMENT    praise, flattery

- CONSCIENCE    sense of morality
  CONSCIOUS    awake, aware

- COUNCIL    governing body
  COUNSEL    advice [noun]; to advise [verb]

- DESERT    to abandon [verb]; dry, usually sandy area [noun]
  DESSERT    final, sweet course in a meal

- DIE    to lose life (dying) [verb]; one of a pair of dice [noun]
  DYE    to change the color of something (dyeing)

- ELICIT    to draw out
  ILLICIT    illegal

- EMINENT    prominent
  IMMANENT    living within; inherent
  IMMINENT    about to happen

- FAIR    light-skinned; just, honest
  FARE    money for transportation; food

- FORTH    forward
  FOURTH    number four in a series

- GORILLA    animal in ape family
  GUERRILLA    fighter conducting surprise attacks

- HEAR    to sense sound by ear
  HERE    in this place

- INSURE    to buy or give insurance
  ENSURE    to guarantee, protect

- ITS    POSSESSIVE form of *it*
  IT'S    CONTRACTION for *it is*

- LEAD    a heavy metal [noun]; to guide [verb]
  LED    past tense of *lead*

- LOOSE    unbound, not tightly fastened
  LOSE    to misplace

continued >>

## Quick Reference 31.2 (continued)  ■ ■ ■ ■ ■

| | |
|---|---|
| • MAYBE | perhaps [adverb] |
| MAY BE | might be [verb] |
| • MORAL | distinguishing right from wrong; the lesson of a fable, story, or event |
| MORALE | attitude or outlook, usually of a group |
| • PASSED | past tense of *pass* |
| PAST | at a previous time |
| • PATIENCE | forbearance |
| PATIENTS | people under medical care |
| • PRECEDE | to come before |
| PROCEED | to continue |
| • PRESENCE | being at hand; attendance at a place or in something |
| PRESENTS | gifts |
| • PRINCIPAL | foremost [adjective]; school head [noun] |
| PRINCIPLE | moral conviction, basic truth |
| • RIGHT | correct; opposite of *left* |
| RITE | ritual |
| WRITE | to put words on paper |
| • SCENE | place of an action; segment of a play |
| SEEN | viewed |
| • SENSE | perception, understanding |
| SINCE | measurement of past time; because |
| • STATIONARY | standing still |
| STATIONERY | writing paper |
| • THAN | in comparison with; besides |
| THEN | at that time; next; therefore |
| • THEIR | possessive form of *they* |
| THERE | in that place |
| THEY'RE | contraction of *they are* |
| • TO | toward |
| TOO | also; indicates degree (*too much*) |
| TWO | number following *one* |
| • WAIST | midsection of the body |
| WASTE | discarded material [noun]; to squander, to fail to use up [verb] |

continued >>

| Quick Reference 31.2 | (continued) ■ ■ ■ ■ ■ |
|---|---|

| | | |
|---|---|---|
| • | WHERE | in which place |
| | WERE | past tense of *be* |
| • | WHOSE | possessive form of *who* |
| | WHO'S | contraction for *who is* |
| • | YOUR | possessive form of *you* |
| | YOU'RE | contraction for *you are* |
| | YORE | long past |

# 31g   What are compound words?

A **compound word** puts together two or more words to express one concept.

**Open compound words** remain as separate words, such as *decision making, problem solving,* and *editor in chief.*

**Hyphenated compound words** use a hyphen between the words, such as *trade-in, fuel-efficient,* and *tax-sheltered.* For punctuation advice about hyphens, see 29i.

**Closed compound words** appear as one word, such as *proofread, city-wide,* and *workweek.*

Single-word compounds usually start as open (two-word) compounds and then become hyphenated compounds before ending up as closed compounds. To check whether a compound term consists of closed, hyphenated, or open words, consult an up-to-date dictionary.

# 32

# Writing Research Papers

## 32a  What is the role of research in writing?

**Research** is a systematic process of gathering information to answer a question. The amount of research in a piece of writing can vary, depending on your audience, purpose, and type of writing (see 1b; 7a). You might be familiar with RESEARCH PAPERS or TERM PAPERS, which are dense with sources, synthesizing information to support a thesis. This chapter will help you with extended formal research projects. However, any essay might potentially benefit from even a little research.

Writers do research for several reasons and at different points in the writing process, from generating and planning to revising.

1. **To find a fact or piece of information.** Sometimes you simply need to answer a direct question of "how much?" or "when?" or "where?" or "who?" In each case, you need to find a credible source and extract only the specific information necessary to answer the question.

2. **To understand an issue or situation more fully.** Sometimes you need to learn basic information about a topic, even before writing. You're trying to learn not only information new to you but also the range of viewpoints or opinions on a particular topic.

3. **To synthesize current information.** Even if you know a good deal about a topic, you may need to bring together the most current information.

4. **To identify a specific opinion or point of view.** A good strategy in argumentative writing is to state and refute counter arguments. You might research in order to find out what people who disagree with you believe and, more important, why. You can then explain the shortcomings of their views or explain why your position is better. You might also look for expert viewpoints that support your own.

5. **To create new knowledge.** Writers often do kinds of research that make new knowledge rather than find knowledge others have already created. This is the kind of research that chemists and biologists do, but so do psychologists, sociologists, journalists and so on. This kind of research includes experiments, surveys, interviews, ethnographies, and observations.

# 32b What is the process of doing research?

Although the research process varies according to the specific reason you're doing research and to your writing situation (1a), a few general steps are common to most projects involving research.

1. **Develop a research question.** What is the question that you need to answer by conducting research? Some questions might be very specific, such as when you're looking for a piece of data. With substantial projects, however, your research question involves more than looking for a single fact. Section 32f has more advice about developing effective research questions.

2. **Decide what kinds of sources will best answer your question.** Some research questions are best answered by finding appropriate PUBLISHED SOURCES, generally through the library (Chapter 33). Others might require **field research,** gathering data firsthand through surveying, interviewing, or observing.

3. **Develop a search strategy.** Once you determine the sources you need, develop a plan for finding them. How will you search the library, for example? Whom will you contact to interview? When will you visit a location for direct observations, and how will you take notes once you're there? Be purposeful in designing your strategy so you'll be effective and efficient.

4. **Gather your sources.** This is the stage where you not only find appropriate books and articles, for example, but also take notes. Your goal is to accumulate more than enough materials so that you feel confident you can answer your research question.

5. **Interpret your source materials.** Having a bunch of reading notes, a lot of survey answers, a transcript of an interview, or a list of direct observations is only part of the process. Organizing and interpreting them to understand how they answer your research question is just as vital. This stage can also tell you whether your search strategy has been successful or whether you need to gather even more sources. Look for themes or patterns. Look not only for information and ideas that seem to fit together but also for conflicts or tensions.

6. **Draft, revise, edit, and proofread your paper.** The general writing processes that we explained in Chapter 2 also apply to researched writing.

A **source** is any form of information that provides ideas, examples, information, or evidence, and different kinds of college writing require different kinds of sources (7b). You're probably most familiar with PUBLISHED SOURCES:

books, magazine or journal articles, sources from organizational Web sites, and so on.

However, writers use other sources, too. As we discussed in Chapter 7, these include interviews; surveys; direct observations of situations, places, or people; performances or lectures; museums; and so on.

⊕ **ESOL Tip:** In the United States, PLAGIARISM is a major offense in academic writing. In some cultures, it's customary to take material from scholarly authorities on your topic. However, this practice is forbidden in the United States unless you use quotation marks around the exact words and then state the place where you found those words. For detailed information about how to avoid plagiarism, see Chapter 34. ●

A source is either primary or secondary. **Primary sources** are firsthand evidence based on your own or someone else's original work or direct observation. Primary sources can take the form of experiments, surveys, interviews, memoirs, FIELD RESEARCH, or original creative works (for example, poems, novels, paintings and other art, plays, films, or musical compositions). **Secondary sources** report, describe, comment on, or analyze the experiences or work of others.

**Field research** involves going into real-life situations to observe, survey, interview, or join some activity firsthand. A field researcher might, for example, go to a factory, a lecture, a day-care center, or a mall—anywhere that people engage in everyday activities. A field researcher might also interview experts and other identified individuals. Because field research yields original data, it's a PRIMARY SOURCE.

### ▓ Surveying

Surveys use several questions to gather information from a number of people, asking about experiences, situations, opinions, or attitudes. Responses to multiple choice or true/false questions are easy for people to complete and for researchers to summarize and report, as totals or averages. Open-ended questions, in which people are asked to respond in writing to a question, require more effort on the part of researchers and people completing the survey. However, they sometimes have the advantage of providing more complete or accurate information.

### ▓ Observing people and situations

CASE STUDIES and ETHNOGRAPHIES (7d) are examples of researching people in specific situations. For observations of behavior (for example, the audience at a sporting event or elementary school children at play during recess), you can take notes during the activity. Try to remain objective so that you can see things clearly. One strategy is to take notes in a two-column format. On the left, record only objective observations; on the right, record comments or possible interpretations.

## Interviewing

An expert can offer valuable information, a new point of view, and firsthand facts, statistics, and examples. Probably the best place to start is with the faculty at your college. Your instructors are also scholars and researchers with expertise in many areas. They may suggest good additional sources, as well as other experts to contact. Indeed, your family and friends might qualify as experts, if they've been involved with an issue you're researching. Corporations, institutions, and professional organizations often have public relations offices that can answer questions or put you in contact with experts.

## Gathering data about things or practices

Some kinds of primary research involve looking at objects, artifacts, or practices, describing or counting what you observe, and reporting what you find. Consider three research questions:

1. How are women portrayed on the covers of national magazines?

2. What are the most popular colors to paint houses in middle-class neighborhoods and in wealthy neighborhoods?

3. Are characters with foreign-sounding names or accents in current movies more likely to be heroes or villains?

You might be able to answer these questions by finding published sources, interviewing experts, or using existing means. However, it is more likely that you'd need to collect this information yourself, by directly and systematically looking at examples.

## 32c  What is a research paper?

A **research paper** (sometimes called a *term paper*) is a specific kind of researched writing common in many college courses. Research paper assignments usually require the use of several published sources throughout. Your mission is to synthesize those sources into a project of fairly significant length.

Every research activity, formal or informal, involves two processes:

1. Gathering information

2. Analyzing, synthesizing, and evaluating what you've gathered

Academic research writing (and many business and public reports) involves a third process:

3. Writing an accurately documented paper based on your ANALYSIS, SYNTHESIS, and EVALUATION of what you've gathered

Some research papers use information from PRIMARY SOURCES and FIELD RESEARCH. However, most use information from SECONDARY and PUBLISHED SOURCES.

## 32d  What is a research log?

A **research log** is your diary of your research process. Use a separate notebook for the log, or create a new folder or file on the computer. Whichever format you rely on, make your research schedule one of the first entries.

Although much of your research log will never find its way into your research paper itself, what you write in it greatly increases your efficiency. A well-kept log traces your line of reasoning as your project evolves, tells where you've ended each work session, and suggests what your next steps might be. It can also provide information about your process in a way that helps your instructor note your effort and determine how best to help you. In your log, always record the date as well as the following elements:

- Your **current step** in your search for information.
- The **search strategy** you used to find that information.
- The **name, location,** and other details of exactly where you found the information.
- The **main point** of the information you found.
- The exact **file or folder name** in which you've stored your detailed content notes.
- Your suggested **next step** for when you return to your research.
- Your evolving **overall thoughts** and insights as you move through the research and writing processes; particularly pay attention to the movements away from gathering material to organizing it, from organizing to drafting, and from drafting to revising.

## 32e  How do I choose and narrow a research topic?

Some instructors assign a specific topic for research (for example, "What are the most compelling scientific theories to explain false memory?"). Others leave more choice to you, assigning a general subject area appropriate to a specific course (for example, "memory" in a psychology course) and expecting you to narrow it to a manageable topic. Still other instructors expect you to choose a topic on your own (for example, "Write a research paper on a topic of current interest or importance").

### ■ Choosing a topic on your own

The freedom to choose any topic you want can sometimes be overwhelming. Don't panic. Instead, use some of the strategies for generating ideas in Quick Reference 32.1.

### ■ Narrowing a general topic into a workable one

Whether you're working with a topic of your choice or an assigned one, you want to check that it's sufficiently narrow for the time frame and other requirements of your research paper. Also, you want to be sure that the narrowed topic is worthy of a college research project.

---

### Quick Reference 32.1    ■ ■ ■ ■ ■

#### Finding general ideas for research

- **Talk with others.** Ask instructors or other experts in your area of interest what issues currently seem "hot" to them. Ask them to recommend readings or the names of authorities on those issues.

- **Browse some textbooks.** Read the table of contents and major headings of textbooks for subjects that interest you. As you narrow your focus, note the names of important books and experts, often mentioned in reference lists at the end of chapters or in the final pages of the book.

- **Browse the library or a well-stocked bookstore.** Stroll through the **stacks** (the rows of bookshelves) to find subjects that interest you. Look at books as well as periodicals. Thumb through popular magazines, and browse academic journals in fields that interest you.

- **Browse the Internet.** Many search engines provide topic directories. Click on some general categories and review subcategories until you locate specific topics that interest you. Then try further subject searches or KEYWORD searches (33b) to see where they lead.

- **Read encyclopedia articles about your interests.** General encyclopedias survey a wide range of topics, while specialized encyclopedias concentrate on a specific area. Never, however, stop with encyclopedias—they are too basic for college-level research.

- **Get ready.** Carry a small notebook and a pen, a laptop, or a PDA. Ideas have a way of popping into your mind when you least expect them. Jot down your thoughts on the spot so that they don't slip away.

- **Expect to consider various topics before making your final choice.** Give yourself time to think. Keep your mind open to flashes of insight and to alternative ideas. At the same time, be careful not to let indecision paralyze you.

- **Select a topic that interests you.** Your topic will be a companion for a while, sometimes for most of a semester. Select a topic that arouses your interest and allows you the pleasure of satisfying your intellectual curiosity.

- **Choose a sufficiently narrow topic.** You want to be successful within the time and length given by the assignment. Avoid topics that are too broad, such as "emotions." A better choice would be "how people perceive and respond to anger in others."

- **Choose a topic worth researching.** Avoid trivial topics that prevent you from doing what instructors and others expect of a student researcher.

  NO     The colors of MP3 players.

  YES    The legal issues of sharing downloaded music.

- **Choose a topic that has a sufficient number of appropriate sources available.** If you can't find useful sources—ones that relate directly to your topic and ones that are credible, not simply plentiful—drop the topic.

- **Talk with a professor in your field of interest, if possible.** Before the meeting, read a little about your topic so that you can ask informed questions. Ask whether you've narrowed your topic sufficiently and productively. Also, ask for the titles of major books and the names of major authorities on your topic.

A good academic topic allows you to demonstrate your critical thinking abilities. There are two broad ways of doing this. First, you might choose a topic on which intelligent people have formed different opinions. Then, you might analyze your sources and draw on your own experiences to decide which position appears best. The purpose of such a paper would be to attempt to PERSUADE readers that you've considered the various positions and reached a reasonable conclusion.

Alternatively, you might choose to INFORM readers in a paper that synthesizes several sources related to a complex subject. Writing a SYNTHESIS means pulling together extensive information from varied sources to examine essential points that relate to a topic. For example, imagine you've been assigned to write the sample research paper about déjà vu in section 35e. After you've read a dozen articles on the topic of déjà vu, you might try to identify three or four key points and then organize information from your reading around those points. Your goal is to clarify complicated or scattered information for your readers.

## 32f  What is a research question?

A **research question** about your topic is the controlling question that drives your research. Few research paper assignments are phrased as questions. Therefore, most research writing calls on you to ask a thought-provoking, underlying question and then to search for answers to it. Regarding research as a quest for an answer gives your work a specific focus: You can't know whether you've found useful source material unless you know what you're looking for.

Research questions, whether stated or implied, and the strategies needed to answer them vary widely. Your purpose might be to present and explain information: "How does penicillin destroy bacteria?" Or your purpose might be to argue one side of an issue: "Is Congress more important than the Supreme Court in setting social policy?" You can then consult various sources in an attempt to work toward an answer.

*Attempt* is an important word in relation to research. Some research questions lead to a final, definitive answer, but some do not. The previous question about penicillin leads to a reasonably definitive answer (you describe how the antibiotic penicillin destroys the cell walls of some bacteria); this means your writing has an informative purpose. The other question about social policy has no definitive answer, so you're asked to offer an informed opinion based on facts and authoritative viewpoints gathered from your research; this means your writing has a persuasive purpose.

To formulate a research question, begin by BRAINSTORMING a list of questions that come to mind about your topic. Write your list of ideas in your research log (32d).

Suppose, for example, the topic you want to write about is "homelessness." Here are some typical questions you might ask.

- Why can't a rich country like the United States eliminate homelessness?
- Who is homeless?
- How do people become homeless?
- Is it true that many families—not just adults—are homeless?
- Is the homelessness problem getting better or worse?
- What are we doing to solve the problem of homelessness?
- What is it like to be homeless?

Some questions will interest you more than others, so begin with one of those. If a question leads to a dead end, pursue another. Only when you find yourself accumulating answers—or in the case of questions without definitive answers, accumulating viewpoints—is it likely you're dealing with a usable research question. Once you have an explicitly stated research question, you can streamline your research by taking notes from those sources that help you answer your research question. If your research paper requires you to state an informed opinion, keep in mind that dealing with opposing positions is crucial to writing an effective argument (see section 5i).

Stay flexible as you work. The results of your research may lead you to modify the research question slightly. Actually, such modifying is part of the "moving ahead and circling back" that characterizes research writing. When you've finished researching and notetaking in response to your final research question, you have a starting place for formulating your preliminary THESIS STATEMENT (see 2d).

## 32g What documentation style should I use?

A **documentation style** is a system for providing information about each source you've used in your research paper. Documentation styles vary from one academic discipline to another. The humanities often use MLA (Modern Language Association) style (Chapter 35). The social sciences frequently use APA (American Psychological Association) style (Chapter 36). Instructors almost always have precise expectations about which style they want you to use. Find it out, and follow it to the letter! You don't want an instructor to minimize your research and writing effort because he or she is distracted by careless documentation.

## 32h What is a working bibliography?

A **working bibliography** is a preliminary list of the PRIMARY and SECONDARY SOURCES you gather in your research. It contains information about the source and where others might find it. The following is a list of basic elements to include.

| Books | Periodical Articles | Online Sources |
|---|---|---|
| Author(s) | Author(s) | Author (if available); editor or sponsor of site |
| Title | Title | Title of document and title of site |
| Publisher and place of publication | Name of periodical, volume number, issue number | Name of database or sponsor of online source |
| Year of publication | Date of issue | Date of electronic publication |
| Call number | Page numbers of article | Electronic address (URL) Date you accessed the source |

Begin your working bibliography as soon as you start identifying sources. Compiling a working bibliography will help you find out what is available on a particular subject before you do extensive reading and notetaking. If your search turns up very few sources, you may want to change your topic. If it reveals a vast number of sources, you definitely want to narrow your topic or even choose a different one. At the outset, don't leave anything out; even an unpromising source may later prove useful. Expect to add and drop sources throughout the research writing process. As a rough estimate, your working bibliography needs to be about twice as long as the list of sources you end up using. You can record your working bibliography on note cards or on a computer.

On the one hand, note cards have the advantage of being easy to sift through and rearrange. You can also carry them with you when you do library research. At the end of your writing process, you can easily sort and alphabetize them to prepare your final bibliography. Write only one source on each card.

On the other hand, putting your working bibliography on a computer saves you from having to type your list of sources later. If you use a computer for this purpose, clearly separate one entry from another. You can organize the list alphabetically, by author, or according to your subtopics.

Your library may even have a program like RefWorks or EndNote that allows you to download bibliographic information directly onto your computer, and then easily reformat it to the appropriate documentation style.

Whichever method you use, when you come across a potential source, immediately record the information exactly as you need it to fulfill the requirements of the DOCUMENTATION STYLE you need to use for your assignment. Spending a few extra moments at this stage can save you hours of work and frustration later on.

When you write **content notes,** you record information from your sources. As with your working bibliography, you can make content notes either in a computer file or on index cards.

## 32i How do I draft a thesis statement for a research paper?

Drafting a THESIS STATEMENT for a research paper marks the transition from the research process to the writing process. A thesis statement in a research paper sets out the central theme, which you need to sustain throughout the paper (see section 2d, especially Quick Reference 2.3). As with any piece of writing, your research paper must fulfill the promise of its thesis statement.

You might begin thinking of a preliminary thesis statement at some middle point in the research process, although it's perfectly acceptable to wait until you've completely finished researching. To start your thesis statement, you might try to convert your RESEARCH QUESTION into a preliminary thesis statement. Remember that a good thesis statement makes an assertion that conveys your point of view about your topic and foreshadows the content of your paper (see Quick Reference 2.3 in 2d). And not least, remember that your research needs to support your thesis statement. Ask yourself whether the material you've gathered from sources can effectively give support. If not, revise your thesis statement, conduct further research, or do both.

Here are examples of subjects narrowed to topics, focused into research questions, and then cast as thesis statements.

| | |
|---|---|
| SUBJECT | *nonverbal communication* |
| TOPIC | Personal space |
| RESEARCH QUESTION | How do standards for personal space differ among cultures? |
| INFORMATIVE THESIS STATEMENT | Everyone has expectations concerning the use of personal space, but accepted distances for that space are determined by each person's culture. |
| PERSUASIVE THESIS STATEMENT | To prevent intercultural misunderstandings, people must be aware of cultural differences in standards for personal space. |
| SUBJECT | *computers* |
| TOPIC | artificial intelligence |
| RESEARCH QUESTION | How close are researchers to developing artificial intelligence in computers? |
| INFORMATIVE THESIS STATEMENT | Scientists disagree about whether computers need emotions to have artificial intelligence. |
| PERSUASIVE THESIS STATEMENT | Because emotions play a strong role in human intelligence, computers must have emotions before they can truly have artificial intelligence. |

# 32j How do I outline a research paper?

Some instructors require an OUTLINE of your research paper, either before you hand in the paper or along with the paper. In such cases, your instructor is probably expecting you to be working from an outline as you write your drafts. Your research log often comes in handy when you group ideas, especially for a first draft of your paper—and as you make an *informal outline* for it. An outline can serve as a guide as you plan and write your paper. For directions on composing a *formal outline,* see section 2f.

## 32k How do I draft and revise a research paper?

DRAFTING and REVISING a research paper is like drafting and revising any other piece of writing (Chapter 2). Yet to write a research paper, you need extra time for planning, drafting, thinking, redrafting, rethinking, and creating a final draft because you need to demonstrate all of the following:

- You've followed the steps of the research processes presented in this chapter.
- You understand the information that you've located during your research.
- You've evaluated the SOURCES you've used in your research.
- You haven't PLAGIARIZED your material from someone else (34b).
- You've used sources well in your writing, correctly employing QUOTATIONS, PARAPHRASES, and SUMMARIES (34h–34j).
- You've moved beyond SUMMARY to SYNTHESIS so that your sources are interwoven with each other and with your own thinking, not merely listed one by one (4f).
- You've used DOCUMENTATION accurately. (For MLA STYLE, see Chapter 35; for APA STYLE, see Chapter 36.)

Expect to write a number of drafts of your research paper. Successive drafts help you master the information you've learned and add it authoritatively to the knowledge you already had about the topic. In the first draft, organize the broad categories of your paper. Quick Reference 32.2 suggests some ways to write your first draft.

Before you write each new draft, read your previous draft with a sharp eye. For best results, take a break of a few days (or at least a few hours) before beginning this process. This gives you distance from your material, and a clearer vision of what you need to revise. For a more objective point of view, consider asking a few people you respect to read and react to your first, or perhaps your second, draft.

One key to REVISING any research paper is to examine carefully the evidence you have included. **Evidence** consists of facts, statistics, expert studies and opinions, examples, and stories. As a reader, you expect writers to provide solid evidence to back up their claims and conclusions. Similarly, when you write, readers expect you to provide evidence that clearly supports your claims and conclusions. Use RENNS (3f) to see if you can develop paragraphs more

## Quick Reference 32.2 ■ ■ ■ ■ ■

### Suggestions for drafting a research paper

- Some writers categorize their notes and write a section at a time. They organize the notes into broad categories by making a separate group for each topic. As patterns begin to emerge, these writers might move material from one category to another. Each category becomes a section of the first draft. This method not only assures writers that their first draft will include all of the material from their research, but reveals any gaps in information that call for additional research. Of course, you may discover that some of your research doesn't fit your topic and thesis. Put it aside; it might be useful in a later draft.

- Some writers generate a list of questions that their paper needs to address, then answer each question, one at a time, looking for the content notes that will help them. For example, writing on the topic of organic foods, some possible questions might be, "What are organic foods? What benefits do people see for eating them? Why do they cost more than regular foods? Does everyone agree that they are beneficial?" Generating and answering questions can be a way of turning a mass of information into manageable groupings.

- Some writers finish their research and then slowly review half of the information they've gathered. Next, setting aside that information, they write a partial first draft by drawing on the information they remember from their reading. Then, they use the same process with the second half of the information that they've gathered. Finally, with their two partial drafts and all of their research notes in front of them, they write a complete first draft. Writers who use this method say it gives them a broad overview of their material quickly and identifies any gaps in information that they need to fill in with further research.

- Some writers stop at various points during their research and use FREEWRITING to get their ideas into words. Writers who use this method say that it helps them recognize when they need to adjust their RESEARCH QUESTION or change the emphasis of their search. After a number of rounds of researching and freewriting, these writers find that they can complete their first draft relatively easily.

- Some writers review their sources and create an OUTLINE before drafting (2f). Some find a formal outline helpful, while others use a less formal approach.

fully. Identify each of the points you have made in your paper, including your thesis and all your subpoints. Then ask the questions in Quick Reference 32.3.

Experienced writers know that writing is really *rewriting*. Research papers are among the most demanding composing assignments, and most writers revise several times. Once you've produced a *final draft,* you're ready to edit (2j), proofread (2k), and format your work. Check for correct grammar, punctuation, capitalization, and spelling. (No amount of careful research and good writing can make up for an incorrectly presented, sloppy, error-laden document.)

Consult Quick References 2.8 and 2.9 to remind yourself of the general principles of revising, and consult the research paper revision checklist in Quick Reference 32.4.

To see one example of the research writing process in action, turn to section 35e. There you'll see the final draft of an MLA-style research paper.

For an APA-style research paper, turn to section 36h.

---

## Quick Reference 32.3   ■ ■ ■ ■ ■

### Questions for evaluating your evidence

- **Is the evidence sufficient?** To be sufficient, evidence can't be thin or trivial. As a rule, the more evidence you present, the more convincing your thesis will be to readers.

- **Is the evidence representative?** Representative evidence is customary and normal, not based on exceptions. When evidence is representative, it provides a view of the issue that reflects the usual circumstances rather than rare ones.

- **Is the evidence relevant?** Relevant evidence relates directly to your thesis or topic sentences. It illustrates your reasons straightforwardly and never introduces unrelated material.

- **Is the evidence accurate?** Accurate evidence is correct, complete, and up to date. It comes from a reliable SOURCE. Equally important, you present it honestly, without distorting or misrepresenting it.

- **Is the evidence reasonable?** Reasonable evidence is not phrased in extreme language, such as *all, never,* or *certainly.* Reasonable evidence is well thought out and free of logical fallacies (4i).

## Quick Reference 32.4 ■ ■ ■ ■ ■

### Revising a research paper

If the answer to any of the following questions is no, you need to revise. The section numbers in parentheses tell you where to find useful information.

**WRITING**

- Does your introductory paragraph lead effectively into the material? (3c)
- Have you met the basic requirements for a written thesis statement? (2d)
- Do your thesis statement and the content of your paper address your research question(s)? (32f)
- Have you developed effective body paragraphs? (3d, 3f, Quick Reference 3.3)
- Does the concluding paragraph end your paper effectively? (3k)
- Does your paper satisfy a critical thinker? (Chapter 4)

**RESEARCH**

- Have you included appropriate and effective evidence? (3d and Quick Reference 32.3)
- Have you deleted irrelevant or insignificant information? (3g)
- Have you used quotations, paraphrases, and summaries well? (34h–34j)
- Have you integrated your source material well without plagiarizing? (34c)

**FORMAT AND DOCUMENTATION**

- Have you used the correct format for your parenthetical citations or other documentation style? (Chapters 35–36)
- Does each citation tie into an item in your WORKS CITED (MLA STYLE) or REFERENCES (APA STYLE) list of sources at the end of your paper? (35d and 36f)
- Does the paper exactly match the format you've been assigned to follow? Check margins, spacing, title, headings, page number, font, and so on.

# 33

# Finding and Evaluating
# Published Sources

## 33a  What is a published source?

A **published source** is a book, article, Web page, or other type of writing that appears in print or in electronic format. While the kinds of field research we discuss in section 32b require you to gather information and turn it into words, in published sources other writers have already done that work. However, it's up to you to decide whether they have done it accurately, fairly, and well. Your goal is to find sources needed to answer your research question, evaluate their quality, and SYNTHESIZE them into your own writing, using QUOTATION, SUMMARY, or PARAPHRASE. Published sources are PRIMARY if they are firsthand reports of experiments, observations, and so on, or if they are creative works like poems, letters, or stories. A SECONDARY published source is one that reports, describes, or comments on someone else's work.

## 33b  What is a search strategy?

A **search strategy** is an organized procedure for locating and gathering information to answer your specific RESEARCH QUESTION. Some research, such as finding one particular fact or piece of information, doesn't require an extensive strategy. Others, such as fully understanding an issue or synthesizing current knowledge, require care and planning. Using a search strategy means working systematically rather than haphazardly.

Following are three frequently used search strategies. If no single one meets your requirements, create your own.

The **expert method** is useful when you know your topic well enough to begin "at the top," with the best current thinking by experts on that subject. You'll begin by reading their books and articles to identify the main subtopics, positions, or issues. You'll ask yourself: What is in agreement? What is in dispute? What are the main questions under investigation?

Of course, the expert method means that you have to know who the experts are, and sometimes that's difficult. Talk with people who are generally knowledgeable about your topic, learn what you can from them, and ask them to refer you to works by experts on the topic. Your professors are an obvious place to start.

The **chaining method** is useful when you know only general things about your topic or can't tell who the experts are. Start by reading or skimming reference books or some current articles in scholarly journals, popular magazines, or newspapers. As you do, pay close attention to people who are cited in those readings or in any bibliographies at the end. Then search for works by those people or look for the specific books or articles mentioned.

The **questioning method** means breaking your overall research question into several smaller questions, then finding sources to answer each of them. This method has the advantage of allowing you to see if your sources cover all the areas important to your research question. Suppose your research question is, "How successful are relationships that begin on the Internet?" The list of questions you brainstorm might include, "Who participates in Internet dating? Are there typical ways Internet relationships develop? How may Internet contacts result in actual meetings?" Generating a list of questions like this can give your search a direction and purpose.

You may find yourself switching or combining methods. That's fine. "Flexibility with focus" is the guiding principle for experienced researchers. Discovering early in the process what sources are available allows you time to find those that are harder to locate; to use interlibrary loan if an item isn't available in your library or online; to wait for someone to return checked-out books you need; or to schedule interviews, arrange visits, or conduct surveys.

As you locate, assemble, and evaluate sources, expect to accumulate much more information than you'll actually use. Indeed, the quality of a research paper depends partly on your ability to eliminate inadequate or repetitive sources and to recognize what is valuable material. Turn to section 33g for detailed guidelines for evaluating sources.

One more piece of advice: Avoid getting too far along in your search until you're reasonably certain you're going in a useful direction. Rather than spend endless hours simply gathering sources, read and analyze some of your materials to make sure your topic is a good one. Your RESEARCH LOG can be useful for this purpose.

### ■ Using library-based sources

In an age when the Internet contains billions of pages of information, it might seem almost prehistoric to talk about libraries. After all, the **library** is where generations of college students have traditionally gone to find sources: books and periodicals organized by catalogs and indexes. However, notice that we've referred to "library-based" sources and not necessarily to the library itself. Many libraries give you online access to their holdings, so you might use library-based sources without ever setting foot in the building itself.

Still, the building itself continues to be a vital place for all research. One key advantage of going to the library is your chance to consult face-to-face with librarians. They train for their profession by learning how to advise students and other researchers about using library resources to the greatest advantage. Never hesitate to ask questions about how to proceed or where to find a resource.

**Catalogs** list sources—usually books, but also films, recordings, and documents—that the library owns. **Databases** contain extensive lists of articles, reports, and books, organized and searchable in many ways. Your library will own or provide access to many sources included in a database, but it almost certainly won't have all of them. Catalogs and databases exist in electronic formats that you can access and search from computers in the library or, often, by connecting to the library online. Both college and public libraries subscribe to database services, although they may be limited depending on the library's size. Many businesses and corporations also subscribe to databases, making them available to people associated with the company. A law firm, for example, likely subscribes to Lexis-Nexis, which provides searchable access to legal cases and decisions.

If you're accessing a database by connecting to the library online, you need to use a **browser** (such as Firefox or Internet Explorer), a software program that gives you access to the Web.

### ■ Using catalogs, databases, and the Web

Sources that you identify through catalogs and scholarly databases are almost always more reliable and appropriate than sources you find by simply browsing the Web. The reliability of scholarly databases stems from their origins: Only experts and professionals who judge works to have merit compile them.

The best way to access a database at your library is to go to your college library's Web site, whether you're online in the library, at home, or in a dormitory.

Each home page of a library shows the resources available through that Web site, although more might be available in the library itself. Most college libraries subscribe to one or more database services, such as EBSCO, ProQuest, or FirstSearch.

Each entry in a database contains bibliographic information, including a title, author, date of publication, and publisher (in the case of books or reports) or periodical (in the case of articles). The entry might also provide an abstract, or summary, of the material. Once you locate an entry that seems promising, you need to find the actual book or complete article itself.

#### USING KEYWORDS

When you search library databases, **keywords,** also called *descriptors* or *identifiers,* are your lifeline to success. Keywords are the main words in a source's title or the words that the author or editor has identified as central. Without keywords, you'd have great difficulty accessing sources listed in electronic databases.

When you search using keywords, chances are you'll come up with a large or even overwhelming number of sources. Much of what turns up won't be relevant to your topic. Two main ways to make keyword searches more efficient are using guided searches (answers to prompts) and using Boolean expressions (keyword combinations).

## USING GUIDED SEARCHES

**Guided searches,** also called *advanced searches,* allow you to look through a database or search engine by answering prompts provided in an onscreen form. A typical search involves selecting a range of dates of publication (for example, after 2006 or between 1990 and 1995) and specifying only a certain language (such as English) or a certain format (such as books).

## USING BOOLEAN EXPRESSIONS

Using **Boolean expressions** means that you search a database or search engine by typing keyword combinations that narrow and refine your search. To combine keywords, use the words *AND, OR,* and *NOT,* or the symbols that represent those words. Boolean expressions, generally placed between keywords, instruct the search engine to list only those Web sites in which your keywords appear in certain combinations and to ignore others. Quick Reference 33.1

---

### Quick Reference 33.1　　　　　■ ■ ■ ■ ■

#### Refining keyword searches with Boolean expressions

**AND or the + ("plus") symbol:** Narrows the focus of your search because both keywords must be found. For example, if you were researching the role of physical attractiveness in new relationships over the Internet, you would search for *relationships AND attractiveness AND Internet.* Many search engines, such as Google.com, don't require the word *AND* between terms.

**NOT or the – ("minus") symbol:** Narrows a search by excluding texts containing the specified word or phrase. If you want to eliminate instant messaging from your search, type *relationships AND attractiveness AND Internet NOT instant messaging.*

**OR:** Expands a search's boundaries by including more than one keyword. If you want to expand your search to include sources about relationships begun through either instant messaging or chat rooms, try the expression *relationships AND attractiveness AND Internet AND instant messaging OR chat rooms.* You'll get pages mentioning relationships and attractiveness only if they also mention instant messaging or chat rooms.

**" ":** Quotation marks direct a search engine to match your exact word order on a Web page. For example, a search for "online relationships" will find pages that contain the exact phrase *online relationships.* However, it won't return pages with the phrase *relationships online.*

explains a few ways to search with keywords more effectively, using the subject "relationships" as an example.

## 33c How do I find books?

A library's **book catalog,** which lists its entire collection, exists as a computer database in almost every modern library. You can find a book by searching by **author,** by **title,** by **subject,** and by KEYWORD.

Suppose you're using the EXPERT SEARCH STRATEGY and a source recommends that you find a book by the AUTHOR Thomas L. Friedman, but you don't know its title. You can search the catalog for books by this author. A screen on your library's computer will have a place for you to type "Friedman, Thomas" in a space for "author." (Usually, you enter last name, then first name, but check which system your library uses.) If your library owns any books by Thomas Friedman, the computer will display their titles and other bibliographic information, such as the library call number. Then you can use the call number to request the book or to find it yourself.

Among the books you might find when searching for "Friedman, Thomas" is *The World Is Flat: A Brief History of the Twenty-first Century* (New York: Farrar, Straus and Giroux, 2005). Suppose you know that book's TITLE, but not its author, and want to see if your library owns a copy. Your library's online catalog will have a place for you to type in the title; some systems omit words like *the* or *a,* so that in this case, you would type in only "World Flat Brief History Twenty-first Century."

Suppose, however, you don't know an author's name or a book title. You have only a research topic, and you need to find sources. In this case, you need to search by SUBJECT, using the terms listed in the *Library of Congress Subject Headings (LCSH).* The *LCSH* is a multivolume catalog available, primarily in book form, in the reference section of every library. A version of the information in the *LCSH* is online at http://authorities.loc.gov. The *LCSH* lists only **subject headings,** which are organized from most general to most narrow. Suppose you're researching the topic of "globalization." If you enter that term into a space for subject searches in your own library's "Search" screen, *The World Is Flat: A Brief History of the Twenty-first Century* by Thomas Friedman will be listed if the book is available.

Finally, you may wish to search by **keyword** in your library's holdings. If you were researching a paper on the future of jobs in the changing world economy, you could find Friedman's book using the keywords *economy, globalization, outsourcing, employment,* and so on.

An entry in the library's book catalog contains a great deal of useful information: a book's title, author, publisher, date and place of publication, and length, along with its location in the library. A full-record catalog entry (a complete set of information about the source rather than a brief listing that may have only author, title, and call number) lists additional subjects covered in that book. The list of additional subjects can provide valuable clues for further searching.

Many libraries allow you to print out this information, send it to your e-mail account, or download and save it. Whether you choose one of these options or copy the information yourself directly into your WORKING BIBLIOGRAPHY, it's crucial to record the **call number** exactly as it appears, with all numbers, letters, and decimal points. The call number tells where the book is located in the library's stacks (storage shelves). If you're researching in a library with *open stacks* (that is, you're permitted to go where books are shelved), the call number leads you to the area in the library where you can find all books on the same subject.

A call number is especially crucial in a library or special collection with *closed stacks* (that is, a library where you fill in a call slip, hand it in at the call desk, and wait for the book to arrive). Such libraries don't permit you to browse the stacks, so you have to rely entirely on the book catalog. If you fill in the wrong number or an incomplete number, your wait will be in vain.

# 33d How do I find periodicals?

**Periodicals** are newspapers, magazines, and journals published at set intervals. Different kinds of periodicals will meet different research purposes. To use periodicals efficiently, consult databases or **indexes** to periodicals, which allow you to search by subject, title, keyword, or author. Most exist as online databases that are updated frequently. Your library very likely subscribes to several of the ones that you'll need, and you can access them through the library's Web site.

## ▪ Using databases to find periodicals

Your library's home page generally provides different ways to access various databases. Users who know the name of a database can go directly to it. However, users who know only a general field can "Search by Category" and see an alphabetical list of subject areas. When you choose a category, you'll see a list of all the databases for that area. It's important to choose the right database for your search because the wrong one may miss some of the best sources for your paper.

**General databases** index articles in journals, magazines, and newspapers. Large libraries have many general databases. Among common ones are the following:

- *Academic Search Premier* covers thousands of general and scholarly publications in the social sciences, humanities, education, computer sciences, engineering, language and linguistics, arts and literature, medical sciences, and ethnic studies. Most of the sources in this database are available in full text. This database is suitable for academic research projects, as long as you take care to focus on journal articles and well-regarded general publications.

- *General Reference Center Gold* covers current events, popular culture, business and industry, the arts and sciences, and sports published in newspapers, reference books, and periodicals; it focuses on general interest periodicals.
- *LexisNexis Academic* provides abstracts of news, business, and legal information. Sources include foreign news publications; regional US news services; radio and television transcripts; federal and state case law; medical, legislative, and industry news; and so on.

**Specialized databases** are more appropriate than general ones for much college-level research. They list articles in journals published by and for expert, academic, or professional readers. Many specialized databases include the abstract, or summary, that is printed at the beginning of each scholarly article. Examples of specialized databases include *General Science Abstracts, Business Abstracts, Humanities Index, Social Sciences Abstracts, MLA International Bibliography,* and *PsycINFO.*

You search periodical indexes by using KEYWORDS.

### ▉ Locating the articles themselves

Periodical indexes help you locate the titles of specific articles on your topic. Once you have the listing, though, how do you get your hands on the article itself? Often you can find a full-text online version of the article to read, download, or print. A full-text version may be either in HTML format or PDF. The listing will tell you which one; if you have a choice, we recommend using the PDF version, which is easier to cite because it has the layout of a common article.

Sometimes, however, you need to find a printed copy of the periodical. Often the listing in the database will tell you whether your library owns a print copy and what its call number is. Otherwise, you'll need to check if the periodical is listed in the library's catalog. Search for the periodical name you want (for example, *American Literature* or *The Economist*), not for the article's author or title. If your library subscribes to that periodical, you can use its call number to find its location. You then need to find the specific article you want by looking for the issue in which the article you're looking for is printed.

Few libraries subscribe to all of the periodicals listed in specialized databases. However, many libraries are connected electronically to other libraries' book catalogs and can give you access to additional holdings. Often you or a librarian · can request materials from other libraries through interlibrary loan (generally free of charge). Alternatively, your college may have a different document delivery system (perhaps at a cost to you).

# 33e   How do I use reference works?

**Reference works** include encyclopedias, almanacs, yearbooks, fact books, atlases, dictionaries, biographical reference works, and bibliographies. Some references are *general,* providing information on a vast number of subjects, but without any depth. Others are *specialized,* providing information on selected topics, often for more expert or professional audiences.

## ■ General reference works

Reference works are the starting point for many college and other advanced researchers—but they're no more than a starting point. **General reference works** by themselves are insufficient for academic research. Still, they help researchers identify useful KEYWORDS, find examples, and verify facts. Most widely used reference works are available in electronic versions, usually online. Check your library's Web site to see if the reference work you want is available online through a subscription or license the library has purchased. You can also check your library's catalog. Finally, you can search the World Wide Web by entering the work's name to see if it's available there. (For example, *Encyclopaedia Britannica* is at http://www.britannica.com.) Be aware that often you have to pay a fee for works you don't access through the library.

### GENERAL ENCYCLOPEDIAS

Articles in multivolume general encyclopedias, such as the *Encyclopaedia Britannica,* summarize information on a wide variety of subjects. The articles can give you helpful background information and the names of major figures and experts in the field. Best of all, many articles end with a brief bibliography of major works on the subject. General encyclopedias aren't the place to look for information on recent events or current research, although sometimes they cover a field's ongoing controversies up until the date that the reference was published.

### ALMANACS, YEARBOOKS, FACT BOOKS

Almanacs, yearbooks, and fact books are huge compilations of facts in many subject areas. They're often available both in print and online. They're excellent for verifying information from other sources and, in some cases, for finding supporting facts and figures. Almanacs, such as *The World Almanac,* present capsule accounts of a year's events and data about government, politics, economics, science and technology, sports, and many other categories. *Facts on File,* which is indexed online by LexisNexis, covers world events in a weekly digest and in an annual one-volume yearbook. The annual *Statistical Abstract of the United*

*States* (accessed online through http://www.census.gov) contains a wealth of data on the United States. *Demographic Yearbook* and the *United Nations Statistical Yearbook* carry worldwide data.

### ATLASES AND GAZETTEERS

Atlases (such as *The Times Atlas of the World*) contain maps of our planet's continents, seas, and skies. Gazetteers (such as *The Columbia Gazetteer of the World,* available online for a fee at http://www.columbiagazetteer.org) provide comprehensive geographical information on topography, climates, populations, migrations, natural resources, crops, and so on.

### DICTIONARIES

Dictionaries define words and terms. In addition to general dictionaries, specialized dictionaries exist in many academic disciplines to define words and phrases specific to a field.

### BIOGRAPHICAL REFERENCE WORKS

Biographical reference books give brief factual information about famous people—their accomplishments along with pertinent events and dates in their lives. Biographical references include the *Who's Who* series, *The Dictionary of American Biography,* and many others. Specialized biographical references in various fields are also available.

### BIBLIOGRAPHIES

Bibliographies list books, articles, documents, films, and other resources and provide publication information so that you can find those sources. Some bibliographies are comprehensive and list sources on a wide range of topics. Others list only sources on a particular subject. Specialized bibliographies can be very helpful in your research process. Annotated or critical bibliographies describe and evaluate the works that they list. These resources are increasingly available online but require you either to access them through a library's paid subscription service or to pay a fee each time you use them.

### ■ Specialized reference works

**Specialized reference works** provide more authoritative and specific information than do general reference works. Specialized reference works are usually appropriate for college-level research because the information is more advanced and detailed. They can be invaluable for introducing you to the controversies and KEYWORDS in a subject area. In particular, finding authors' names in such books can help you begin to accumulate a list of credible authors.

There are hundreds of specialized references. Some examples include the *Encyclopedia of Banking and Finance,* the *Oxford Companion to American*

*Literature,* the *Encyclopedia of Chemistry,* the *Dictionary of American Biography,* and the *International Encyclopedia of Film.*

Because hundreds of one-volume works are highly specific, we haven't listed them here. Check what specialized reference books your college library has available that might help you in your search. They may be listed in the library's catalog or in a references database, such as the *Gale Virtual Reference Library,* which makes up to 1000 reference works available to users online.

## 33f How do I find government publications?

Government publications are available in astounding variety. You can find information on laws and legal decisions, regulations, population, weather patterns, agriculture, national parks, education, and health, to name just a few topics. Since the middle 1990s, most government documents have been available through the World Wide Web. The Government Printing Office maintains the *Catalog of U.S. Government Publications* at http://www.gpoaccess.gov.

The GPO site has a searchable database. Information about legislation is also available at the Web site THOMAS, a service of the Library of Congress, which you can access at http://thomas.loc.gov. A directory of all federal government sites that provide statistical information is at http://www.fedstats.gov.

The LexisNexis database service provides access to a huge number of other governmental reports and documents. For example, it includes the *Congressional Information Service (CIS),* which indexes all papers produced by US congressional panels and committees. These documents include the texts of hearings (for example, testimony about homelessness) and reports (for example, a comparative study of temporary shelters for homeless people).

## 33g How do I evaluate sources?

Finding a source is only part of your effort. Your next step is to evaluate the quality of each source. Your critical thinking skills (Chapter 4) will be important in this effort. First, decide whether the information in the source relates to your topic in more than a vague, general sense. Then, ask how a source might help you answer your research question (32f). Finally, using the criteria in Quick Reference 33.2, evaluate each source with a cold, critical eye.

## 33h What should I know about searching the Web?

Sources from the library or from library databases have the advantage of being selected by experts. While you still have to evaluate them, they have passed a screening process. On the other hand, anyone can put anything on the Web. This makes the Web a rich source of information, but it also makes finding what

## Quick Reference 33.2   ■ ■ ■ ■ ■

### Evaluating sources

1. **Is the source authoritative?** Generally, encyclopedias, textbooks, and academic journals (*The American Scholar, Journal of Counseling and Development*) are authoritative. Books published by university presses (Indiana University Press) and by publishers that specialize in scholarly books are also trustworthy. Material published in newspapers, in general-readership magazines (*Newsweek, U.S. News & World Report*), and by established commercial publishers (Prentice Hall) are usually reliable, but you want to apply the other criteria in this list with special care, cross-checking names and facts whenever possible. Web sites maintained by professional organizations, such as the National Council of Teachers of English at http://www.ncte.org, are authoritative.

2. **Is the author an expert?** Biographical material in the article or book may tell you if the author is an expert on the topic. Look up the author in a reputable, up-to-date biographical dictionary. Alternatively, enter the author's name in an Internet search engine. Look to see if the author has a degree in this field and whether he or she is affiliated with a reliable institution. Also, if an author is often cited by professionals in the field and published in journals, he or she is probably considered an expert.

3. **Is the source current?** Check the publication date. Research is ongoing in most fields, and information is often modified or replaced by new findings. Check databases and online subject directories to see if newer sources are available.

4. **Does the source support its information sufficiently?** Are its assertions or claims supported with sufficient evidence? Separate facts from opinions and see if the writer relies too much on opinion. If the author expresses a point of view, check what kind of evidence he or she offers to back up that position. If there are claims of cause and effect, ask yourself if they're justified (4d). If the writer resorts to logical fallacies, reject the source (4i). Use wise judgment and don't take chances.

5. **Is the author's tone balanced?** If the TONE is unbiased and the reasoning is logical, the source is probably useful (4d, 4e). Some warning signs of biased tone are name calling, sarcasm, stereotyping, or absolute assertions about matters that are open to interpretation (using *always, everyone,* and similar words).

you need difficult, and it opens the possibility of encountering inaccurate or biased materials. Therefore, searching library databases remains a crucial method of finding many scholarly sources.

Finding information on the Web has become so common that "google" has become a verb. The principles for searching the Web are much like those for searching databases (33b). Once you use a browser to get on the Web, you can search for sites by using a SEARCH ENGINE or by typing an address (called a **URL,** for "universal resource locator" or "uniform resource locator") into the search box. **Search engines** are programs designed to hunt the Internet for sources on specific topics that you identify by using keywords or through subject directories. Some commonly used search engines include Google (http://www.google.com) or Yahoo! (http://www.yahoo.com).

## ◼ Using keywords

In the same way you use KEYWORDS to find materials in library databases (33d), you can use them to find information on the Internet. Type a word or group of words in the search box on the opening page of the search engine, and click on the "Search" or "Enter" button. The engine scans for your word(s) in Web pages, and then lists sites that contain them.

## ◼ Using subject directories

**Subject directories** provide an alternative to keyword searches. These directories list topics (education, computing, entertainment, and so on) or resources and services (shopping, travel, and so on), with links to Web sites on those topics and resources. Most search engines' home pages have one or more subject directories. In addition, there are some independent subject directories. Some examples are *Educator's Reference Desk* (http://www.eduref.org), *Internet Public Library* (http://www.ipl.org), and *Refdesk.com* (http://www.refdesk.com).

Clicking on a general category within a subject directory will take you to lists of increasingly specific categories. Eventually, you'll get a list of Web pages on the most specific subtopic you select. These search engines also allow you to click on a category and enter keywords for a search. For example, suppose that you are using Google to search for information on organic food. You'll first go to Google's general category of "Health." Under "Health" you'll find the category of "Nutrition," and within "Nutrition," you'll find a link to "Organic Food," a page that lists dozens of additional categories and sources.

Quick Reference 33.3 summarizes some general guidelines for using search engines and directories with keywords.

## 33i How do I evaluate Web sources?

The same strategies for evaluating library sources, discussed in 33b, apply to evaluating Web sources. Ask yourself if the Web source is well supported with evidence and free from fallacies or bias. Use the strategies for critical thinking and analysis in Chapter 4.

## Quick Reference 33.3

■ ■ ■ ■ ■

### Tips on using search engines and directories

- Use keyword combinations or BOOLEAN EXPRESSIONS unless you have a very specific, narrow topic with unique keywords. A search for even a moderately common topic may produce thousands of hits, many of which won't be relevant to your topic. You might also switch to a subject directory.

- Most search engines attempt to search as much of the World Wide Web as possible. But because the Web is vast and unorganized, different search engines will give different results for the same search. Try using more than one search engine, or use a **metasearch engine** that searches several search engines at once, such as Dogpile (http://dogpile.com).

- Use the "Advanced Search" page, if one is available. It allows you to search or sort by date, language, file format, and domain type, as well as by various combinations of keywords.

- When you find a useful site, go to the toolbar at the top of the screen and click on "Bookmark" or "Favorites" and then click on "Add." This will make it easy for you to return to a good source.

- Use the "History" or "Go" function to track the sites you visit, in case you want to revisit one you previously thought was not helpful.

- Sources on the Web may come in various formats. Most common are Web pages in html (Hypertext Markup Language) format. However, you may also encounter Word or Excel documents, PowerPoint slides, or PDF (portable document format) files, each of which requires specific software.

However, you need to evaluate Web sources with additional care for two reasons. First, because anyone can post anything on the Web, some sources may very well be plagiarized. Second, many sources on the Web have been written by individuals posing as experts and, as a result, may offer false or misleading information.

You're always accountable for the sources you choose. Most sites also contain material that will help you assess their credibility, such as a bibliography, links to the author or editor, or a description of the sponsoring organization. You want to discard sites that do not contain such verifying information, however useful they may seem. Err on the side of caution.

An important question to ask about any Web site is why the information exists and why it was put on the Internet. What motives might the site's authors have? Are you asked to take action of any kind? If yes, take special care to judge the source's bias. For example, the World Wildlife Fund can ask for contributions and still maintain a Web site that contains reliable information. Conversely, a hate group or extreme political organization can't be trusted to be objective. Quick Reference 33.4 summarizes the questions to ask about Web sites.

### Quick Reference 33.4 ▪ ▪ ▪ ▪ ▪

#### Judging the reliability of Web sources

| Reliable sources are . . . | Questionable sources are . . . |
| --- | --- |
| **From educational, not-for-profit, or government organizations.** One sign is an Internet address ending in *.edu, .org, .gov,* or a country abbreviation such as *.us* or *.uk.* However, if any of these organizations fail to list their sources, don't use them. After all, many colleges and universities now host student Web sites, which also end in *.edu.* | **From commercial organizations advertising to sell a product (*.com*); Web sites that are advertisements or personal pages; junk mail.** These sites may or may not list sources. If they fail to, don't use them. If they do, check that the sources are legitimate, not a front for some commercial enterprise. |
| **From expert authors.** Experts have degrees or credentials in their fields that you can check. See if their names appear in other reliable sources, in bibliographies on your topic, or in reference books in your college's library. Check whether the site's author gives an e-mail address for questions or comments. | **From anonymous authors or authors without identifiable credentials.** Chat rooms, discussion groups, bulletin boards, and similar networks are questionable when they don't give credentials or other qualifying information. |
| **From reliable print sources.** Online versions of the *New York Times, Time* magazine, and other publications that are produced by the publisher are just as reliable as the print versions. | **Secondhand excerpts and quotations.** Materials that appear on a site that is not the official site of the publisher (such as a quotation taken from the *New York Times*) may be edited in a biased or inaccurate manner. Such sources may be incomplete and inaccurate. |
| **Well supported with evidence.** The information is presented in a balanced, unbiased fashion. | **Unsupported or biased.** These sites carry declarations and assertions that have little or no supporting evidence. |
| **Current.** The site's information is regularly updated. | **Outdated.** The site's information hasn't been updated in a year or more. |

# 34

# Using Sources and Avoiding Plagiarism

## 34a  How do I use sources well?

Using sources well means using QUOTATIONS (34h), PARAPHRASES (34i), and SUMMARIES (34j) to create a synthesis of those materials and your own thoughts. It also means documenting your sources and avoiding PLAGIARISM. Generally, you'll begin this process after you've located most of your sources and evaluated them (Chapter 33), written a WORKING BIBLIOGRAPHY (32h), and taken content notes. Of course, during the process of DRAFTING, you might discover the need to do some additional research, and that's fine. Be careful, though, to avoid a trap into which we see some writers fall—endlessly researching to put off the challenging work of drafting.

A crucial part of using sources well is using correct documentation (Chapters 35–36). **Documentation** means making two types of entries in your research paper each time you use a source:

1. Writing a parenthetical citation for each quotation, paraphrase, and summary you take from sources (for examples in MLA STYLE, see 35c; for APA, see 36c).

2. Composing a BIBLIOGRAPHY for the end of your paper. MLA calls this list of sources WORKS CITED, while APA calls it REFERENCES. This list needs to include full bibliographic information on each source from which you have quoted, paraphrased, and summarized in your paper (for examples, see 35d for MLA style and 36f for APA).

Today's bibliographies differ from those of the past. The root word *biblio-* means "book," so traditionally, the bibliographic information referred to a book's title, author, publisher, and place and year of publication. In the age of digital technology, researchers include in their bibliographies not only print sources but also electronic sources.

Documentation is vital for three reasons. It tells readers where to find your sources in case they want to consult those sources in greater depth or verify that you've used them properly. It lends credibility and weight to your writing, strengthening your ethos as someone who has done the careful work needed to develop well-supported papers. It also gives credit to others for their work. A **documentation style** refers to a specific system for providing information on sources used in a research paper. Documentation styles vary among the disciplines. This handbook presents two documentation styles in Chapters 35 and 36.

# 34b  What is plagiarism?

**Plagiarism** is presenting another person's words, ideas, or visual images as if they were your own. Plagiarizing is like stealing: It is a form of academic dishonesty or cheating. Plagiarism is a serious offense that can be grounds for a failing grade or expulsion from a college.

In the workplace, plagiarism can get you fired and hinder your being hired elsewhere. Plagiarism at work also has legal implications; words, ideas, and images, especially those that describe or influence business practices and decisions, are *intellectual property*. Using someone else's intellectual property without permission or credit is a form of theft that may land you in court. Furthermore, plagiarism in any setting—academic, business, or civic—hurts your credibility and reputation. Quick Reference 34.1 lists the major types of plagiarism.

---

## Quick Reference 34.1                                 ■ ■ ■ ■ ■

### Types of plagiarism

You're plagiarizing if you . . .

- Buy a paper from an Internet site, another student or writer, or any other source and pass it off as your own.

- Turn in any paper that someone else has written, whether the person has given it to you, you've downloaded it from the Internet, or you've copied it from any other source.

- Change selected parts of an existing paper and claim the paper as your own.

- Neglect to put quotation marks around words that you quote directly from a source, even if you document the source.

- Copy or paste into your paper any *key terms, phrases, sentences,* or *longer passages* from another source without using documentation to tell precisely where the material came from. This is equally true for both library-based sources and sources you find on the Internet.

- Use *ideas* from another source without correctly citing and documenting that source, even if you put the ideas into your own words.

- Combine ideas from many sources and pass them off as your own without correctly citing and documenting the sources.

- Take language, ideas, or visual images from anyone (colleagues, companies, organizations, and so on) without obtaining permission or crediting them.

⊕ **ESOL Tip:** Perhaps you come from a country or culture that considers it acceptable for students to copy the writing of experts and authorities. Some cultures, in fact, believe that using another's words, even without citing them, is a sign of respect or learning. However, this practice is considered unacceptable in American and most Western settings. It is plagiarism, and you need to avoid it by using the strategies we discuss in this chapter. ●

## 34c   How do I avoid plagiarism?

You can avoid plagiarism two ways. First, be very systematic and careful when you take content notes and when you quote, paraphrase, or summarize materials. Second, become comfortable with the concept of DOCUMENTATION, which you need each time you use a source. Quick Reference 34.2 describes the main strategies you can use to avoid plagiarism.

---

**Quick Reference 34.2**  ■ ■ ■ ■ ■

### Strategies for avoiding plagiarism

- Use DOCUMENTATION to acknowledge your use of the ideas or phrasings of others, taken from the sources you've compiled on your topic.

- Become thoroughly familiar with the documentation style that your instructor tells you to use for your research paper. To work efficiently, make a master list of the information required to document all sources that you quote, paraphrase, or summarize according to your required documentation style.

- Write down absolutely all the documentation facts that you'll need for your paper, keeping careful records as you search for sources. Otherwise, you'll waste much time trying to retrace your steps to get a documentation detail you missed.

- Use a consistent system for taking CONTENT NOTES, making sure to maintain the distinction between your own thinking and the ideas that come directly from a source. Perhaps use different colors of ink or another coding system to keep these three uses of sources separate:

  1. Quotations from a source (documentation required)

  2. Material paraphrased or summarized from a source (documentation required)

  3. Thoughts of your own triggered by what you've read or experienced in life (no documentation required)

- Write clear, perhaps oversized, quotation marks when you're directly quoting a passage. Make them so distinct that you can't miss seeing them later.

- Consult with your instructor if you're unsure about any phase of the documentation process.

---

Another important way to avoid plagiarism is to dive willingly into any interim tasks your instructors build into research assignments. For example, many instructors set interim deadlines such as a date for handing in a WORKING BIBLIOGRAPHY (32h). Further, some instructors want to read and coach you about how to improve one or more of your research paper drafts. In some cases, they might want to look over a research log (32d), content notes, and/or photocopies of your sources.

Never assume that your instructor can't detect plagiarism. Instructors have keen eyes for writing styles that are different from the ones students generally produce and from your own style in particular. They recognize professionally drawn visuals and charts. Instructors can access Web sites that electronically check your submitted work against all material available online. Further, services such as http://www.turnitin.com allow instructors to check your writing against hundreds of thousands of papers for free or for sale on the World Wide Web and the Internet. (Also, that site adds your paper to its huge database of student papers so that no one can plagiarize your work.) Moreover, when instructors receive papers that they suspect contain plagiarized passages, they can check with other professors to see whether a student paper looks familiar.

## 34d How do I work with Internet sources to avoid plagiarism?

Online sources can both greatly help researchers and create new possible problems. Because it's so easy to download source materials, it's potentially easy to misrepresent someone else's work as your own, even if you don't intend to be dishonest.

You might be tempted to download a completed research paper from the Internet. *Don't.* That's intellectual dishonesty, which can get you into real trouble. Or you might be tempted to borrow wording from what you wrongly consider an "obscure" Internet source. *Don't.* Not only is this intellectual dishonesty, but instructors will easily detect it. Quick Reference 34.3 suggests ways to avoid plagiarism when you're working with digital or online sources.

## 34e What don't I have to document?

You don't have to document common knowledge or your own thinking. **Common knowledge** is information that most educated people know, although they may need to remind themselves of certain facts by looking up

## Quick Reference 34.3

■ ■ ■ ■ ■

### Guidelines for avoiding plagiarizing online sources

- Never cut material from an online source and paste it directly in your paper. You can too easily lose track of which language is your own and which comes from a source.

- Keep material that you downloaded or printed from the Internet separate from your own writing, whether you intend to QUOTE, SUMMARIZE, or PARAPHRASE the material. Be careful how you manage copied files. Use another color or a much larger font as a visual reminder that this isn't your work. Just as important, make sure that you type in all of the information you need to identify each source, according to the documentation style you need to use.

- Copy or paste downloaded or printed material into your paper only when you intend to use it as a direct quotation or visual. Immediately place quotation marks around the material, or set off a long passage as a block quotation. Be sure to document the source at the same time as you copy or paste the quotation into your paper. Don't put off documenting the passage until later because you may forget to do it or do it incorrectly.

- Summarize or paraphrase materials *before* you include them in your paper. If you have printed or downloaded Internet sources to separate files, don't copy directly from those files into your paper. Summarize or paraphrase the sources in a different file, and then paste the summaries or paraphrases into your paper. Document the source of each passage at the same time as you insert it in your paper. If you put off this task until later, you may forget to do it or get it wrong.

- Use an Internet service to check a passage you're not sure about. If you're concerned that you may have plagiarized material by mistake, try submitting one or two sentences that concern you to http://www.google.com. To make this work, always place quotation marks around the sentences you want to check when you type them into the search window.

information in a reference book. For example, here are a few facts of common knowledge that you don't need to document.

- Bill Clinton was the US president before George W. Bush.
- Mercury is the planet closest to the sun.
- Normal human body temperature is 98.6 degrees Fahrenheit.
- All the oceans on our planet contain salt water.

A very important component of a research paper that doesn't need documentation is **your own thinking,** which is based on what you've learned as you built on what you already knew about your topic. It consists of your ANALYSIS, SYNTHESIS, and interpretation of new material as you read or observe it. You don't have to document your own thinking. Your own thinking helps you formulate a THESIS STATEMENT and organize your research paper by composing TOPIC SENTENCES that carry along your presentation of information.

# 34f  What must I document?

You must document everything that you learn from a source. This includes ideas as well as specific language. Expressing the ideas of others in your own words doesn't release you from the obligation to tell exactly where you got those ideas—you need to use complete, correct documentation. Here's an example in action.

### SOURCE

Park, Robert L. "Welcome to Planet Earth." *The Best American Science Writing 2001*. Ed. Jesse Cohen. New York: Ecco-Harper, 2001. 302–08. Print. [This source information is arranged in MLA documentation style.]

### ORIGINAL (PARK'S EXACT WORDS)

The widespread belief in alien abductions is just one example of the growing influence of pseudoscience. Two hundred years ago, educated people imagined that the greatest contribution of science would be to free the world from superstition and humbug. It has not happened. (304)

### PLAGIARISM EXAMPLE

Belief in alien kidnappings illustrates the <u>influence of pseudoscience</u>. In the nineteenth century, educated people imagined that science would <u>free the world from superstition</u>, but they were wrong.

Even though the student changed some wording in the example above, the ideas aren't original to her. To avoid plagiarism she's required to document the source. The underlined phrases are especially problematic examples of plagiarism because they're Park's exact wording.

### CORRECT EXAMPLE (USING QUOTATION, PARAPHRASE, AND DOCUMENTATION)

Robert Park calls people's beliefs in alien kidnapping proof of "the growing influence of pseudoscience" (304). Centuries of expectation that science would conquer "superstition and humbug" are still unfulfilled (304). [This citation is arranged in MLA documentation style.]

The writer of the correct example above has used Park's ideas properly through a combination of quotation and paraphrase and documentation. For example, she correctly quotes the phrase "the growing influence of pseudo-science," and she paraphrases the statement "Two hundred years ago, educated people imagined that the greatest contribution of science would be to free the world," rephrasing it as "Centuries of expectation that science would conquer." She also gives the author's name in the sentence and twice includes parenthetical citations, which would lead the reader to find the source on the WORKS CITED page. Sections 34g through 34j explain exactly how to use sources effectively and document correctly.

## 34g How can I effectively integrate sources into my writing?

**Integrating sources** means blending information and ideas from others with your own writing. Before trying to integrate sources into your writing, you need to ANALYZE and SYNTHESIZE your material. Analysis requires you to break ideas down into their component parts so that you can think them through separately. Do this while reading your sources and reviewing your notes. Synthesis requires you to make connections among different ideas, seeking relationships and links that tie them together.

## 34h How can I use quotations effectively?

A **quotation** is the exact words of a source enclosed in quotation marks. Well-chosen quotations can lend a note of authority and enliven a document with someone else's voice. You face conflicting demands when you use quotations in your writing. Although quotations provide support, you can lose coherence in your paper if you use too many of them. If more than a quarter of your paper consists of quotations, you've probably written what some people call a "cut and paste special"—merely stringing together a bunch of someone else's words. Doing so gives your readers—including instructors—the impression that you've not bothered to develop your own thinking and you're letting other people do your talking.

In addition to avoiding too many quotations, you also want to avoid using quotations that are too long. Readers tend to skip over long quotations and lose the drift of the paper. Also, your instructor might assume that you just didn't take the time required to PARAPHRASE or SUMMARIZE the material. Generally, paraphrases and summaries are more effective for reconstructing someone else's argument. If you do need to quote a long passage, make absolutely sure every word in the quotation counts. Edit out irrelevant parts, using ellipsis points to indicate deleted material (29d). Quick Reference 34.4 provides guidelines for using quotations.

---

### Quick Reference 34.4                                    ■ ■ ■ ■ ■

#### Guidelines for using quotations

1. Use quotations from authorities on your subject to support or refute what you write in your paper.

2. Never use a quotation to present your THESIS STATEMENT or a TOPIC SENTENCE.

3. Select quotations that fit your message. Choose a quotation for these reasons:
   - Its language is particularly appropriate or distinctive.
   - Its idea is particularly hard to paraphrase accurately.
   - The source's authority is especially important to support your thesis or main point.
   - The source's words are open to interpretation.

4. Never allow quotations to make up more than a quarter of your paper. Instead, rely on paraphrases (34i) and summaries (34j).

5. Quote accurately. Always check each quotation against the original source—and then recheck it.

6. Integrate quotations smoothly into your writing.

7. Avoid PLAGIARISM (34b–34d).

8. Document quotations carefully.

---

### ■ Making quotations fit smoothly with your sentences

When you use quotations, the greatest risk you take is that you'll end up with incoherent, choppy sentences. You can avoid this problem by making the words you quote fit smoothly with three aspects of your writing: grammar, style, and logic. Here are some examples of sentences that don't mesh well with quotations, followed by revised versions.

**SOURCE**

Goleman, Daniel. *Emotional Intelligence.* New York: Bantam, 1995. 9. Print. [This source information is arranged in MLA documentation style.]

**ORIGINAL (GOLEMAN'S EXACT WORDS)**

These two minds, the emotional and the rational, operate in tight harmony for the most part, intertwining their very different ways of knowing to guide us through the world.

**INCOHERENT GRAMMAR PROBLEM**

Goleman explains how the emotional and rational <u>minds "intertwining</u> their very different ways of knowing to guide us through the world" (9). [Corrected: Goleman explains how emotional and rational minds mix "their very different ways of knowing to guide us through the world" (9).]

**INCOHERENT STYLE PROBLEM**

Goleman explains how the <u>emotional minds based on reason</u> work together by "intertwining their very different ways of knowing to guide us through the world" (9). [Corrected: Goleman explains how the emotional and rational minds work together by "intertwining their very different ways of knowing to guide us through the world" (9).]

**INCOHERENT LOGIC PROBLEM**

Goleman explains how the emotional and rational minds <u>work together</u> by "their very different ways of knowing to guide us through the world" (9). [Corrected: Goleman explains how the emotional and rational minds work together by combining "their very different ways of knowing to guide us through the world" (9).]

**CORRECT USE OF THE QUOTATION**

Goleman explains how the emotional and rational minds work together by "intertwining their very different ways of knowing to guide us through the world" (9). [This citation is arranged in MLA documentation style.]

After writing sentences that contain quotations, read the material aloud and listen to whether the language flows smoothly and gracefully. Perhaps you need to add a word or two placed in brackets (29c) within the quotation so that the wording works grammatically and effortlessly with the rest of your sentence. Of course, make sure your bracketed additions don't distort the meaning of the quotation. For example, the following quotation comes from the same page of the source quoted above. The bracketed material explains what the phrase *these minds* refers to in the original quotation—this helps the reader understand what was clear in the context of the original source but isn't clear when quoted in isolation.

ORIGINAL (GOLEMAN'S EXACT WORDS)

In many or most moments, these minds are exquisitely coordinated; feelings are essential to thought, thought to feeling.

QUOTATION WITH EXPLANATORY BRACKETS

"In many or most moments, these minds [emotional and rational] are exquisitely coordinated; feelings are essential to thought, thought to feeling" (Goleman 9). [This citation is arranged in MLA documentation style.]

Another way to create a smooth integration of a quotation into your sentence is to delete some words, always using an ellipsis where the deletion occurs (29d). You also might delete any part of the quotation that interferes with conciseness and the focus you intend in your sentence. When you use an ellipsis, make sure that the remaining words accurately reflect the source's meaning and that your sentence structure still flows smoothly.

QUOTATION WITH ELLIPSIS

Goleman contends that, generally, "these two minds, the emotional and the rational, operate in tight harmony . . . to guide us through the world" (9). [This citation is arranged in MLA documentation style.]

In the preceding example, the words "for the most part, intertwining their very different ways of knowing" have been deleted from the original material so that the quotation is more concise and focused.

### ◼ Using quotations to enhance meaning

Perhaps the biggest complaint instructors have about student research papers is that sometimes quotations are simply stuck in, for no apparent reason. Whenever you place words between quotation marks, they take on special significance for your message as well as your language. Without context-setting information in the paper, the reader can't know exactly what logic leads the writer to use a particular quotation.

Furthermore, always make sure your readers know who said each group of quoted words. Otherwise, you've used a *disembodied quotation* (some instructors call them "ghost quotations"), which reflects poorly on your writing.

SOURCE

Wright, Karen. "Times of Our Lives." *Scientific American* Sept. 2002: 58-66. Print. [This source information is arranged in MLA documentation style.]

**ORIGINAL (WRIGHT'S EXACT WORDS)**

In human bodies, biological clocks keep track of seconds, minutes, days, months and years. (66)

**INCORRECT (DISEMBODIED QUOTATION)**

The human body has many subconscious processes. People don't have to make their hearts beat or remind themselves to breathe. "In human bodies, biological clocks keep track of seconds, minutes, days, months and years" (Wright 66).

**CORRECT**

The human body has many subconscious processes. People don't have to make their hearts beat or remind themselves to breathe. However, other processes are less obvious and perhaps more surprising. Karen Wright observes, for example, "In human bodies, biological clocks keep track of seconds, minutes, days, months and years" (66).

Rarely can a quotation begin a paragraph effectively. Start your paragraph by relying on your TOPIC SENTENCE, based on your own thinking. Then, you can fit in a relevant quotation somewhere in the paragraph, if it supports or extends what you have said.

Another strategy for working quotations smoothly into your paper is to integrate the name(s) of the author(s), the source title, or other information into your paper. You can prepare your reader for a quotation using one of these methods:

- Mention in your sentence directly before or after the quotation the name(s) of the author(s) you're quoting.

- Mention in your sentence the title of the work you're quoting from.

- Give additional authority to your material. If the author of a source is a noteworthy figure, you gain credibility when you refer to his or her credentials.

- Mention the name(s) of the author(s), with or without the name of the source and any author credentials, along with your personal introductory lead-in to the material.

Here are some examples, using the original source material from Karen Wright on this page, of effective integration of an author's name, source title, and credentials, along with an introductory analysis.

**AUTHOR'S NAME**

**Karen Wright explains that** "in human bodies, biological clocks keep track of seconds, minutes, days, months and years" (66).

### AUTHOR'S NAME AND SOURCE TITLE

**Karen Wright explains in "Times of Our Lives" that** "in human bodies, biological clocks keep track of seconds, minutes, days, months and years" (66).

### AUTHOR'S NAME AND CREDENTIALS

**Karen Wright, an award-winning science journalist, explains that** "in human bodies, biological clocks keep track of seconds, minutes, days, months and years" (66).

### AUTHOR'S NAME WITH STUDENT'S INTRODUCTORY ANALYSIS

**Karen Wright reviews evidence of surprising subconscious natural processes, explaining that** "in human bodies, biological clocks keep track of seconds, minutes, days, months and years" (66).

**Alert:** After using an author's full name in the first reference, you can decide to use only the author's last name in subsequent references. This holds unless another source has that same last name. ●

**EXERCISE 34-1**  Working individually or with a group, read the following original material, from page 60 of "What Makes You Who You Are" by Matt Ridley in *Time* (2 June 2003). Then, read items 1 through 5 and explain why each is an incorrect use of a quotation. Next, revise each numbered sentence so that it correctly uses a quotation. End each quotation with this MLA-style parenthetical reference: (Ridley 60).

#### ORIGINAL (RIDLEY'S EXACT WORDS)

Human beings differ from chimpanzees in having complex, grammatical language. But language does not spring fully formed from the brain; it must be learned from other language-speaking human beings. This capacity to learn is written into the human brain by genes that open and close a critical window during which learning takes place. One of those genes, FoxP2, has recently been discovered on human chromosome 7 by Anthony Monaco and his colleagues at the Wellcome Trust Centre for Human Genetics in Oxford. Just having the FoxP2 gene, though, is not enough. If a child is not exposed to a lot of spoken language during the critical learning period, he or she will always struggle with speech.

#### UNACCEPTABLE USES OF QUOTATIONS

1. Scientists are learning more about how people learn languages. "Human beings differ from chimpanzees in having complex, grammatical language" (Ridley 60).

2. People might assume that individuals can acquire speaking abilities through hard individual work, "but language must be learned from other language-speaking human beings" (Ridley 60).

3. Helping the language learning process "by genes that open and close a critical window during which learning takes place" (Ridley 60).

4. In 2002, one gene important for language development "has recently been discovered on human chromosome 7 by Anthony Monaco and his colleagues" (Ridley 60).

5. Parents should continually read to and speak with young children, because "if children are not exposed to a lot of spoken language during the critical learning period of childhood, they will always struggle with speech" (Ridley 60).

## 34i How can I write good paraphrases?

A **paraphrase** precisely restates in your own words and your own writing style the written or spoken words of someone else. Select for paraphrase only the passages that carry ideas you need to reproduce in detail. Because paraphrasing calls for a very close approximation of a source, avoid trying to paraphrase more than a paragraph or two; for longer passages, use SUMMARY instead. Expect to write a number of drafts of your paraphrases, each time getting closer to effectively rewording and revising the writing style so that you avoid PLAGIARISM. Quick Reference 34.5 provides guidelines for writing paraphrases.

---

**Quick Reference 34.5** ■ ■ ■ ■ ■

### Guidelines for writing paraphrases

1. Decide to paraphrase authorities on your subject to support or counter what you write in your paper.

2. Never use a paraphrase to present your THESIS STATEMENT or a TOPIC SENTENCE.

3. Say what the source says, but no more.

4. Reproduce the source's sequence of ideas and emphases.

5. Use your own words and writing style to restate the material. If some technical words in the original have no or awkward synonyms, you may quote the original's words—but do so very sparingly.

6. Never distort the source's meaning as you reword and change the writing style.

7. Expect your material to be as long as, and often longer than, the original.

8. Integrate your paraphrases smoothly into your writing.

9. Avoid plagiarism (34b–34d).

10. Enter all DOCUMENTATION precisely and carefully.

Here's an example of an unacceptable paraphrase and an acceptable one.

**SOURCE**

Hulburt, Ann. "Post-Teenage Wasteland?" *New York Times Magazine* 9
Oct. 2005: 11-12. Print. [This source information is arranged in MLA
documentation style.]

**ORIGINAL (HULBURT'S EXACT WORDS)**

[T]he available data suggest that the road to maturity hasn't become as
drastically different as people think—or as drawn out, either. It's true that
the median age of marriage rose to 25 for women and almost 27 for men
in 2000, from 20 and 23, respectively, in 1960. Yet those mid-century figures were record lows (earnestly analyzed in their time). Moreover, Americans of all ages have ceased to view starting a family as the major
benchmark of grown-up status. When asked to rank the importance of
traditional milestones in defining the arrival of adulthood, poll respondents place completing school, finding full-time employment, achieving
financial independence and being able to support a family far above actually wedding a spouse or having kids. The new perspective isn't merely an
immature swerve into selfishness; postponing those last two steps is good
for the future of the whole family (11).

**UNACCEPTABLE PARAPHRASE (UNDERLINED WORDS ARE PLAGIARIZED)**

Data suggest that the road to maturity hasn't changed as much as
people think. True, the median age of marriage was 25 for women and 27
for men in 2000, up from 20 and 23 in 1960. Yet those 1960 figures were
record lows. Furthermore, Americans have stopped regarding beginning
a family as the signpost of grown-up status. When they were asked to
rank the importance of traditional benchmarks for deciding the arrival
of adulthood, people rated graduating from school, finding a full-time
job, gaining financial status, and being a breadwinner far above
marrying or having kids. This new belief isn't merely immature
selfishness; delaying those last two steps is good for the future of
the whole family (Hulburt 11).

**ACCEPTABLE PARAPHRASE**

According to Ann Hulburt, statistics show that people are wrong when
they believe our society is delaying maturity. She acknowledges that
between 1960 and 2000, the median age at which women married rose
from 20 to 25 (for men it went from 23 to 27), but points out that the early

figures were extreme lows. Hulburt finds that Americans no longer equate adulthood with starting a family. Polls show that people rank several other "milestones" above marriage and children as signaling adulthood. These include finishing school, securing a full-time job, and earning enough to be independent and to support a family. Hulburt concludes that we should regard postponing marriage and children not as being selfish or immature but as investing in the family's future (11). [This citation is arranged in MLA documentation style.]

The first attempt to paraphrase is not acceptable. The writer simply changed a few words. What remains is plagiarized because the passage keeps most of the original's language, has the same sentence structure as the original, and uses no quotation marks. The documentation is correct, but its accuracy doesn't make up for the unacceptable paraphrasing. The second paraphrase is acceptable. It captures the meaning of the original in the student's own words.

**EXERCISE 34-2** Working individually or with your peer-response group, do the following:

1. For a paper on the place of censorship in the coverage of military conflicts, paraphrase the following paragraph from page 65 of *Regarding the Pain of Others* by Susan Sontag (New York: Farrar, 2003). Start with words mentioning Sontag, and end with this parenthetical reference: (65).

   **ORIGINAL (SONTAG'S EXACT WORDS)**

   There had always been censorship, but for a long time it remained desultory, at the pleasure of generals and heads of state. The first organized ban on press photography at the front came during the First World War; both the German and French high commands allowed only a few selected military photographers near the fighting. (Censorship of the press by the British General Staff was less inflexible.) And it took another fifty years, and the relaxation of censorship with the first televised war coverage, to understand what impact shocking photographs could have on the domestic public. During the Vietnam era, war photography became, normatively, a criticism of war. This was bound to have consequences: Mainstream media are not in the business of making people feel queasy about the struggles for which they are being mobilized, much less of disseminating propaganda against waging war.

2. In one of your sources for a current research assignment, locate a paragraph that is at least 150 words in length and write a paraphrase of it. If you have no such assignment, choose any material suitable for a college-level paper. Your instructor may request that you submit a photocopy of the original material, so make a copy to have on hand.

# 34j   How can I write good summaries?

A **summary** differs from a PARAPHRASE (34i) in one important way: A paraphrase restates the original material completely, but a summary provides only the main point of the original source. A summary is much shorter than a paraphrase. Summarizing is the technique you'll probably use most frequently in writing your research paper, both for taking notes and for integrating what you have learned from sources into your own writing.

As you summarize, you trace a line of thought. This involves deleting less central ideas and sometimes transposing certain points into an order more suited to summary. In summarizing a longer original—say, ten pages or more—you may find it helpful first to divide the original into subsections and summarize each. Then, group your subsection summaries and use them as the basis for further condensing the material into a final summary. You'll probably have to revise a summary more than once. Always make sure that a summary accurately reflects the source and its emphases.

When you're summarizing a source in your CONTENT NOTES, resist the temptation to include your personal interpretation along with something the author says. Similarly, never include in your summary your own judgment about the point made in the source. Your own opinions and ideas, although they have value, don't belong in a summary. Instead, jot them down immediately when they come to mind, but separate them clearly from your summary. Write your notes so that when you go back to them you can be sure to distinguish your opinions or ideas from your summary. On a computer, highlight your personal writing with a screen of yellow or some other color, or use an entirely different font for it. Quick Reference 34.6 provides guidelines for writing good summaries.

---

### Quick Reference 34.6   ▪ ▪ ▪ ▪ ▪

#### Guidelines for writing summaries

1. Use summaries from authorities on your subject to support or refute what you write in your paper.

2. Identify the main points you want to summarize and condense them using your own words without losing the meaning of the original source.

3. Never use a summary to present your THESIS STATEMENT or a TOPIC SENTENCE.

4. Keep your summary short.

5. Integrate your summaries smoothly into your writing.

6. Avoid PLAGIARISM (34b–34d).

7. Enter all DOCUMENTATION precisely and carefully.

Here's an example of an unacceptable summary and an acceptable one.

**SOURCE**

Tanenbaum, Leora. *Catfight: Women and Competition.* New York: Seven Stories, 2002. 117-18. Print. [This source information is arranged in MLA documentation style.]

**ORIGINAL (TANENBAUM'S EXACT WORDS)**

Until recently, most Americans disapproved of cosmetic surgery, but today the stigma is disappearing. Average Americans are lining up for procedures—two-thirds of patients report family incomes of less than $50,000 a year—and many of them return for more. Younger women undergo "maintenance" surgeries in a futile attempt to halt time. The latest fad is Botox, a purified and diluted form of botulinum toxin that is injected between the eyebrows to eliminate frown lines. Although the procedure costs between $300 and $1000 and must be repeated every few months, roughly 850,000 patients have had it performed on them. That number will undoubtedly shoot up now that the FDA has approved Botox for cosmetic use. Even teenagers are making appointments with plastic surgeons. More than 14,000 adolescents had plastic surgery in 1996, and many of them are choosing controversial procedures such as breast implants, liposuction, and tummy tucks, rather than the rhinoplasties of previous generations.

**UNACCEPTABLE SUMMARY (UNDERLINED WORDS ARE PLAGIARIZED)**

Average Americans are lining up for surgical procedures. The latest fad is Botox, a toxin injected to eliminate frown lines. This is an insanely foolish waste of money. Even teenagers are making appointments with plastic surgeons, many of them for controversial procedures such as breast implants, liposuction, and tummy tucks (Tanenbaum 117-18).

**ACCEPTABLE SUMMARY**

Tanenbaum explains that plastic surgery is becoming widely acceptable, even for Americans with modest incomes and for younger women. Most popular is injecting the toxin Botox to smooth wrinkles. She notes that thousands of adolescents are even requesting controversial surgeries (117-18). [This citation is arranged in MLA documentation style.]

The unacceptable summary above has several major problems: It doesn't isolate the main point. It plagiarizes by taking much of its language directly from the source. Examples of plagiarized language include all the underlined phrases.

Finally, the unacceptable summary includes the writer's interpretation ("This is an insanely foolish waste of money") rather than objectively representing the original. The acceptable summary concisely isolates the main point, puts the source into the writer's own words, calls attention to the author by including her name in the summary, and remains objective throughout.

**EXERCISE 34-3**   Working individually or with your peer-response group, do the following:

1. Summarize the following paragraph from pages 29–30 of "Vanishing Before Our Eyes" by Edward O. Wilson in *Time* (24 Apr. 2000). Start your summary with a phrase mentioning the author, and end with this parenthetical reference: (29-30).

   **ORIGINAL (WILSON'S EXACT WORDS)**

   > By repeated sampling, biologists estimate that as few as 10% of the different kinds of insects, nematode worms, and fungi have been discovered. For bacteria and other microorganisms, the number could be well below 1%. Even the largest and most intensively studied organisms are incompletely cataloged. Four species of mammals, for example, have recently been discovered in the remote Annamite Mountains along the Vietnam-Laos border. One of them, the saola or spindlehorn, is a large cowlike animal distinct enough to be classified in a genus of its own. Earth, as far as life is concerned, is still a little-known planet.

2. Write a summary of your paraphrase of the Sontag material in Exercise 34-2. Use the parenthetical reference given there.

3. Write a summary of a passage from a source you're currently using for a paper assigned in one of your courses. If you have no such assignment, choose any material suitable for a college-level research paper. Your instructor might request a photocopy of the material you're summarizing, so make a copy to have on hand.

# 34k   Which verbs can help me weave source material into my sentences?

The verbs listed in Quick Reference 34.7 can help you work quotations, paraphrases, and summaries smoothly into your writing. Some of these verbs imply your position toward the source material (for example, *argue, complain, concede, deny, grant, insist,* and *reveal*). Other verbs imply a more neutral stance (for example, *comment, describe, explain, note, say,* and *write*). For many examples of effective use of such verbs, see the student research papers presented in sections 35e and 36h.

## Quick Reference 34.7

### Verbs useful for integrating quotations, paraphrases, and summaries

| | | |
|---|---|---|
| acknowledges | discusses | organizes |
| agrees | distinguishes | points out |
| analyzes |   between/among | prepares |
| argues | emphasizes | promises |
| asks | endeavors to | proves |
| asserts | establishes | questions |
| balances | estimates | recognizes |
| begins | explains | recommends |
| believes | expresses | refutes |
| claims | finds | rejects |
| comments | focuses on | remarks |
| compares | grants | reports |
| complains | illuminates | reveals |
| concedes | illustrates | says |
| concludes | implies | sees |
| confirms | indicates | shows |
| connects | informs | signals |
| considers | insists | specifies |
| contends | introduces | speculates |
| contradicts | maintains | states |
| contrasts | means | suggests |
| declares | negates | supports |
| demonstrates | notes | supposes |
| denies | notices | thinks |
| describes | observes | wishes |
| develops | offers | writes |

# 35

# MLA Documentation with Case Study

## 35a What is MLA style?

The Modern Language Association (MLA) sponsors the **MLA style**, a documentation system widely used in English and humanities courses that writers follow to tell readers what SOURCES they used in conducting their research and how to find those sources. MLA style requires you to document your sources in two connected, equally important ways.

---

### Important MLA Style Changes

As part of our continuing efforts to ensure that this book provides the most current information on documentation styles, the guidelines and examples in this chapter have been adapted from the Third Edition of *The MLA Style Manual and Guide to Scholarly Publishing* (2008). According to the MLA's Web site, this edition of the *MLA Style Manual* provides documentation style guidelines that will be used in MLA publications beginning in 2009. Thus, the guidelines in the sixth edition of the *MLA Handbook for Writers of Research Papers* should only be followed until the seventh edition is released in spring 2009. If you need more information regarding MLA style updates, check http://www.mla.org.

Although MLA citations should include the minimum amount of information necessary to allow readers to locate the original source, there are several new requirements for entries in Works Cited lists:

- Include the **medium of publication** for each entry, such as "Print" or "Web."
- Include the URL *only* when the reader probably could not locate the source without it.
- Include both an issue and volume number for scholarly journals.
- Use italics for titles instead of underlining for all Works Cited entries.

See Quick Reference 35.1 for more guidance on these requirements.

---

1. Within the text of the paper, use parenthetical documentation, as described in section 35b. Section 35c shows twenty models of in-text parenthetical documentation, each for a different type of source.

2. At the end of the paper, provide a WORKS CITED list of the sources you used in your paper. Title this list "Works Cited." It should include only the sources you've actually used in your research paper, not any you've consulted but haven't used. Section 35d gives instructions for composing a Works Cited list, followed by models, each based on different kinds of sources (book, article, Web site, and so on) that you might use.

For an example of a research paper that uses MLA-style parenthetical documentation and a Works Cited list, see section 35e. As you read the research paper, notice how the two requirements for crediting sources work together so that readers can learn the precise origin of QUOTATIONS, PARAPHRASES, and SUMMARIES.

## 35b What is MLA in-text parenthetical documentation?

MLA-style **parenthetical documentation** places SOURCE information in parentheses within the sentences of your research papers. Also called an *in-text citation*, this information is given each time that you quote, summarize, or paraphrase source materials. It signals materials used from outside sources and enables readers to find the originals.

If you include an author's name (or, if none, a shortened title of the work) in the sentence to introduce the source material, you include in parentheses only the page number where you found the material.

For readability and good writing technique, try to introduce names of authors (or titles of sources) in your own sentences. If you don't include this information in your sentence, you need to insert it before the page number, in parentheses. There is no punctuation between the author's name and the page number.

When possible, position a parenthetical reference at the end of the quote, summary, or paraphrase it refers to—preferably at the end of a sentence, unless that would place it too far from the source's material. When you place the parenthetical reference at the end of a sentence, insert it before the sentence-ending period. If you're citing a quotation enclosed in quotation marks, place the parenthetical information after the closing quotation mark but before sentence-ending punctuation.

The one exception to this rule concerns quotations that you set off in BLOCK STYLE, meaning one inch from the left margin. (MLA style requires that quotations longer than four typed lines be handled this way.) For block quotations, put the parenthetical reference after the period.

## **35c** What are MLA guidelines for parenthetical documentation?

This section shows examples of how to handle parenthetical documentation in the text of your papers. Most of these examples show the author's name or the title included in the parenthetical citation, but remember that it's usually more effective to include that information in your sentences in the paper itself.

### 1. Paraphrased or Summarized Source—MLA

According to Brent Staples, IQ tests give scientists little insight into intelligence (293). [Author name cited in text; page number cited in parentheses.]

In "The IQ Cult," the journalist Brent Staples states that IQ tests give scientists little insight into intelligence (293). [Title of source, author name, and author credentials cited in text; page number cited in parentheses.]

IQ tests give scientists little insight into intelligence (Staples 293). [Author name and page number cited in parentheses.]

### 2. Source of a Short Quotation—MLA

Given that "thoughts, emotions, imagination and predispositions occur concurrently . . . [and] interact with other brain processes" (Caine and Caine 66), it is easy to understand why "whatever [intelligence] might be, paper and pencil tests aren't the tenth of it" (Staples 293).

Coles asks, "What binds together a Mormon banker in Utah with his brother, or other coreligionists in Illinois or Massachusetts?" (2).

### 3. Source of a Long Quotation—MLA

A long quotation in MLA style consists of more than four typed lines. It's set off block style, indented one inch or ten spaces from the left margin. Never put quotation marks around a set-off quotation because the indentation and block style communicate that the material is quoted. At the end of an indented quotation, place the parenthetical reference after the end punctuation mark.

Gray and Viens explain how, by tapping into a student's highly developed spatial-mechanical intelligence, one teacher can bolster a student's poor writing skills:

The teacher asked that during "journal time" Jacob create a tool dictionary to be used as a resource in the mechanical learning center. After several entries in which he drew and described tools and other materials, Jacob confidently moved on to writing about other things of import to him, such as his brothers and a recent birthday party. Rather than shy away from all things linguistic--he previously had refused any task requiring a pencil--Jacob became invested in journal writing. (23-24)

### 4. One Author—MLA

Give an author's name as it appears on the source: for a book, on the title page; for an article, directly below the title or at the end of the article.

One test asks four-year-olds to choose between one marshmallow now or two marshmallows later (Gibbs 60).

Many nonprint sources also name an author; for CDs or DVDs, for example, check the printed sleeve or cover. For an online source, look at the beginning or end of the file for a link to the author, or at the site's home page. (For more information about citing electronic sources, see items 18 through 20.)

### 5. Two or Three Authors—MLA

Give the names in the same order as in the source. Spell out *and*. For three authors, use commas to separate the authors' names.

As children get older, they begin to express several different kinds of intelligence (Todd and Taylor 23).

Another measure of emotional intelligence is the success of inter- and intrapersonal relationships (Voigt, Dees, and Prigoff 14).

### 6. More Than Three Authors—MLA

If your source has more than three authors, you can name them all or use the first author's name only, followed by et al., either in a parenthetical reference or in your sentence. In MLA citations, do not underline or italicize *et al.*

Emotional security varies, depending on the circumstances of the social interaction (Carter et al. 158).

### 7. More Than One Source by an Author—MLA

When you use two or more sources by an author, include the relevant title in each citation. In parenthetical citations, use a shortened version of the title. For example, in a paper using two of Howard Gardner's works, *Frames of Mind: The Theory of Multiple Intelligences* and "Reflections on Multiple

Intelligences: Myths and Messages," use *Frames* and "Reflections." Shorten the titles as much as possible, keeping them unambiguous to readers and starting them with the word by which you alphabetize each work in your Works Cited list. Separate the author's name and the title with a comma, but do not use punctuation between the title and the page number. When you incorporate the title into your own sentences, you can omit a subtitle, but never shorten the main title.

> Although it seems straightforward to think of multiple intelligences as multiple approaches to learning (Gardner, *Frames* 60-61), an intelligence is not a learning style (Gardner, "Reflections" 202-03).

### 8. Two or More Authors with the Same Last Name—MLA

Use each author's first initial and full last name in each parenthetical citation. This is the only instance in MLA style where you use an initial in a parenthetical reference. If both authors have the same first initial, use the full name in all instances.

> According to Anne Cates, psychologists can predict how empathetic an adult will be from his or her behavior at age two (41), but other researchers disagree (T. Cates 171).

### 9. Work with a Group or Corporate Author—MLA

When a corporation or other group is named as the author of a source you want to cite, use the corporate name just as you would an individual's name.

> In a five-year study, the Boston Women's Health Collective reported that these tests are usually unreliable (11).

> A five-year study shows that these tests are usually unreliable (Boston Women's Health Collective 11).

### 10. Work Listed by Title—MLA

If no author is named, use the title in citations. In your own sentences, use the full main title and omit a subtitle, if any. For parenthetical citations, shorten the title as much as possible (making sure that the shortened version refers unambiguously to the correct source), and always make the first word the one by which you alphabetize it. "Are You a Day or Night Person?" is the full title of the article in the following citation.

> The "morning lark" and "night owl" connotations are typically used to categorize the human extremes ("Are You" 11).

## 11. Multivolume Work—MLA

When you cite more than one volume of a multivolume work, include the relevant volume number in each citation. Give the volume number first, followed by a colon and one space, and then the page number(s).

> By 1900, the Amazon forest dwellers had been exposed to these viruses (Rand 3: 202).

> Rand believes that forest dwellers in Borneo escaped illness from retroviruses until the 1960s (4: 518-19).

## 12. Material from a Novel, Play, Poem, or Short Story—MLA

When you cite material from literary works, providing the part, chapter, act, scene, canto, stanza, or line numbers usually helps readers locate what you are referring to more than page numbers alone. Unless your instructor tells you not to, use Arabic numerals for these references, even if the literary work uses Roman numerals. For novels that use them, give part and/or chapter numbers after page numbers. Use a semicolon after the page number but a comma to separate a part from a chapter.

> Flannery O'Connor describes one character in *The Violent Bear It Away* as "divided in two--a violent and a rational self" (139; pt. 2, ch. 6).

For plays that use them, give act, scene, and line numbers. Use periods between these numbers. For short stories, use page numbers.

> Among the most quoted of Shakespeare's lines is Hamlet's soliloquy beginning "To be, or not to be: that is the question" (3.1.56).

> The old man in John Collier's short story "The Chaser" says about his potions, "I don't deal in laxatives and teething mixtures . . ." (79).

For poems and plays that use them, give canto, stanza, and line numbers. Use periods between these numbers.

> In "To Autumn," Keats's most melancholy image occurs in the lines "Then in a wailful choir the small gnats mourn / Among the river swallows" (3.27-28).

## 13. Bible or Sacred Text—MLA

Give the title of the edition you're using, the book (in the case of the Bible), and the chapter and verse. Spell out the names of books in sentences, but use abbreviations in parenthetical references.

> He would certainly benefit from the advice in Ephesians to "get rid of all bitterness, rage, and anger" (*New International Version Bible*, 4.31).

He would certainly benefit from the advice to "get rid of all bitterness, rage, and anger" (*New International Version Bible*, Eph. 4.31).

## 14. Work in an Anthology or Other Collection—MLA

You may want to cite a work you have read in a book that contains many works by various authors and that was compiled or edited by someone other than the person you're citing. Your in-text citation should include the author of the selection you're citing and the page number. For example, suppose you want to cite the poem "Several Things" by Martha Collins, in a literature text edited by Pamela Annas and Robert Rosen. Use Collins's name and the title of her work in the sentence and the line numbers (see item 12) in a parenthetical citation.

In "Several Things," Martha Collins enumerates what could take place in the lines of her poem: "Plums could appear, on a pewter plate / A dead red hare, hung by one foot. / A vase of flowers. Three shallots" (2-4).

## 15. Indirect Source—MLA

When you want to quote words that you found quoted in someone else's work, put the name of the person whose words you're quoting into your own sentence. Give the work where you found the quotation either in your sentence or in a parenthetical citation beginning with *qtd. in.*

Martin Scorsese acknowledges the link between himself and his films: "I realize that all my life, I've been an outsider. I splatter bits of myself all over the screen" (qtd. in Giannetti and Eyman 397).

Giannetti and Eyman quote Martin Scorsese as acknowledging the link between himself and his films: "I realize that all my life, I've been an outsider. I splatter bits of myself all over the screen" (397).

## 16. Two or More Sources in One Reference—MLA

If more than one source has contributed to an idea, opinion, or fact in your paper, cite them all. An efficient way to credit all is to include them in a single parenthetical citation, with a semicolon separating each block of information.

Once researchers agreed that multiple intelligences existed, their next step was to try to measure or define them (West 17; Arturi 477; Gibbs 68).

## 17. Entire Work—MLA

References to an entire work usually fit best into your own sentences.

In *Convergence Culture*, Henry Jenkins explores how new digital media create a culture of active participation rather than of passive reception.

### 18. Electronic Source with Page Numbers—MLA

The principles that govern in-text parenthetical citations of electronic sources are exactly the same as the ones that apply to books, articles, or other sources. When an electronically accessed source identifies its author, use the author's name for parenthetical references. If no author is named, use the title of the source. When an electronic source has page numbers, use them exactly as you would the page numbers of a print source.

> Learning happens best when teachers truly care about their students' complete well-being (Anderson 7).

### 19. Electronic Source with Paragraph Numbers—MLA

When an electronic source has numbered paragraphs (instead of page numbers), use them for parenthetical references, with two differences: (1) Use a comma followed by one space after the name (or title); and (2) use the abbreviation *par.* for a reference to one paragraph or *pars.* for a reference to more than one paragraph, followed by the number(s) of the paragraph(s) you are citing.

> Artists seem to be haunted by the fear that psychoanalysis might destroy creativity while it reconstructs personality (Francis, pars. 22-25).

### 20. Electronic Source Without Page or Paragraph Numbers—MLA

Many online or digital sources don't number pages or paragraphs. Simply refer to those works in their entirety. Here are two examples referring to "What Is Artificial Intelligence?" by John McCarthy; this Web site does not use page numbers or paragraph numbers. Include the name of the author in your sentence; it is also helpful to include the title.

> According to McCarthy, the science of artificial intelligence includes efforts beyond trying to simulate human intelligence.

> In "What Is Artificial Intelligence?" John McCarthy notes that the science of artificial intelligence includes efforts beyond trying to simulate human intelligence.

## 35d  What are MLA guidelines for a Works Cited list?

In MLA-STYLE DOCUMENTATION, the Works Cited list gives complete bibliographic information for each SOURCE used in your paper. Include only the sources from which you quote, paraphrase, or summarize. Never include sources that you consulted but don't refer to in the paper. Quick Reference 35.1 gives general information about the Works Cited list. The rest of this chapter gives models of many specific kinds of Works Cited entries.

| Quick Reference 35.1 | ■ ■ ■ ■ ■ |

## Guidelines for an MLA-style Works Cited list

### TITLE
Use "Works Cited" (without quotation marks) as the title.

### PLACEMENT OF LIST
Start a new page numbered sequentially with the rest of the paper, following the Notes pages, if any.

### CONTENT AND FORMAT
Include all sources quoted from, paraphrased, or summarized in your paper. Start each entry on a new line and at the regular left margin. If the entry uses more than one line, indent the second and all following lines one-half inch (or five spaces) from the left margin. Double-space all lines.

### SPACING AFTER PUNCTUATION
When typewriters were common, it improved readability to leave two spaces after punctuation at the end of a sentence. Computers have made this practice no longer necessary. The *MLA Handbook* uses one space, as does this book. Either style is acceptable. However, you should use two spaces if that's the style your instructor prefers. Always put only one space after a comma or a colon.

### ARRANGEMENT OF ENTRIES
Alphabetize by author's last name. If no author is named, alphabetize by the title's first significant word (ignore *A, An,* or *The*).

### AUTHORS' NAMES
Use first names and middle names or middle initials, if any, as given in the source. Don't reduce to initials any name that is given in full. For one author or the first-named author in multiauthor works, give the last name first. Use the word *and* with two or more authors. List multiple authors in the order given in the source. Use a comma between the first author's last and first names and after each complete author name except the last. After the last author's name, use a period: Fein, Ethel Andrea, Bert Griggs, and Delaware Rogash.

Include *Jr., Sr., II,* or *III* but no other titles and degrees before or after a name. For example, an entry for a work by Edward Meep III, MD, and Sir Richard Bolton would start like this: Meep, Edward, III, and Richard Bolton.

### CAPITALIZATION OF TITLES
Capitalize all major words and the first and last words of all titles and subtitles. Don't capitalize ARTICLES (*a, an, the*), PREPOSITIONS, COORDINATING CONJUNCTIONS (*and, but, for, nor, or, so, yet*), or *to* in INFINITIVES in the middle of a title.

continued >>

## Quick Reference 35.1  (continued)  ■ ■ ■ ■ ■

### SPECIAL TREATMENT OF TITLES

Use quotation marks around titles of shorter works (poems, short stories, essays, articles). Italicize titles of longer works (books, periodicals, plays).

When a book title includes the title of another work that is usually italicized (as with a novel, play, or long poem), the preferred MLA style is not to italicize the incorporated title: *Decoding* Jane Eyre. For an alternative that MLA accepts, see item 20 on page 394.

If the incorporated title is usually enclosed in quotation marks (such as a short story or short poem), keep the quotation marks and italicize the complete title of the book: *Theme and Form in "I Shall Laugh Purely": A Brief Study.*

Drop *A, An,* or *The* as the first word of a periodical title.

### PLACE OF PUBLICATION

If several cities are listed for the place of publication, give only the first. MLA doesn't require US state names no matter how obscure or confusing the city names might be. For an unfamiliar city outside the United States, include an abbreviated name of the country or Canadian province.

### PUBLISHER

Use shortened names as long as they are clear: *Random* for *Random House.* For companies named for more than one person, name only the first: *Prentice* for *Prentice Hall.* For university presses, use the capital letters *U* and *P* (without periods): Oxford UP; U of Chicago P

### PUBLICATION MONTH ABBREVIATIONS

Abbreviate all publication months except *May, June,* and *July.* Use the first three letters followed by a period (*Dec., Feb.*) except for September (*Sept.*).

### PAGE RANGES

Give the page range—the starting page number and the ending page number, connected by a hyphen—of any paginated electronic source and any paginated print source that is part of a longer work (for example, a chapter in a book, an article in a journal). A range indicates that the cited work is on those pages and all pages in between. If that isn't the case, use the style shown next for discontinuous pages. In either case, use numerals only, without the word *page* or *pages* or the abbreviation *p.* or *pp.*

Use the full second number through *99.* Above that, use only the last two digits for the second number unless to do so would be unclear: 113-14 is clear, but 567-602 requires full numbers.

continued >>

## Quick Reference 35.1 (continued) ▪ ▪ ▪ ▪ ▪

### DISCONTINUOUS PAGES
A source has discontinuous pages when the source is interrupted by material that's not part of the source (for example, an article beginning on page 32 but continued on page 54). Use the starting page number followed by a plus sign (+): 32+.

### MEDIUM OF PUBLICATION
Include the MEDIUM OF PUBLICATION for each Works Cited entry. For example, every entry for a print source must include "Print" at the end, followed by a period (if required, certain supplementary bibliographic information like translation information, name of a book series, or the total number of volumes in a set should follow the medium of publication). Every source from the World Wide Web must include "Web" at the end, followed by a period and the date of access. The medium of publication also needs to be included for broadcast sources ("Television", "Radio"), sound recordings ("CD", "LP", "Audiocassette"), as well as films, DVDs, videocassettes, live performances, musical scores and works of visual arts, and so on. (See examples 34–96.)

### ISSUE AND VOLUME NUMBERS FOR SCHOLARLY JOURNALS
Include both an issue and volume number for each Works Cited entry for scholarly journals. This applies both to journals that are continuously paginated and those that are not.

### WORKS CITED INFORMATION REQUIRED FOR ONLINE SOURCES
The following publication information should be listed for all online sources:

1. Name of the author, director, narrator, performer, editor, compiler, or producer of the work. If no author is given, begin the entry with the title of the work.

2. Title of the work. Italicize the title, unless it is part of a larger work. Titles that are part of a larger work should be enclosed in quotation marks.

3. Title of the overall Web site (in italics) if this is distinct from the title of the work.

4. Version or edition of the site.

5. Publisher or sponsor of the site. If this information is not available, use n.p. (for no publisher).

6. Date of publication (day, month, and year, if available). If no date is given, use n.d.

7. Medium of publication. For all online sources, the medium of publication is "Web."

8. Date of access (day, month, and year).

continued >>

**Quick Reference 35.1** (continued) ▪ ▪ ▪ ▪ ▪

**URLs IN ELECTRONIC SOURCES**

Entries for online citations should include the URL only when the reader probably could not locate the source without it.

If the entry requires a URL, enclose it in angle brackets <like this>. Put the URL before the access date and end it with a period. If your computer automatically creates a hyperlink when you type a URL (the text changes color, the URL is underlined, or both) format the URL to look the same as the rest of the entry by changing the font color to black, removing the underline, and making any other changes. In some applications, like Microsoft Word, you can use the command "remove hyperlink," which you can find on the "Insert" menu or by right-clicking on the hyperlink.

If a URL must be divided between two lines, only break the URL after a slash and do not use a hyphen.

## ▪ Following MLA guidelines for specific sources in a Works Cited list

Not every possible documentation model is shown in this chapter. You may find that you have to combine features of models to document a particular source. You'll also find more information in the *MLA Handbook for Writers of Research Papers.* The visual directory on page 390 provides another tool to help you find the Works Cited model you need.

### BOOKS

Citations for books have three main parts: author, title, and publication information (place of publication, publisher, and date of publication).

### 1. Book by One Author—MLA

Bradway, Becky. *Pink Houses and Family Taverns.* Bloomington: Indiana UP, 2002. Print.

### 2. Book by Two or Three Authors—MLA

Edin, Kathryn, and Maria Kefalas. *Promises I Can Keep: Why Poor Women Put Motherhood before Marriage.* Berkeley: U of California P, 2005. Print.

Lynam, John K., Cyrus G. Ndiritu, and Adiel N. Mbabu. *Transformation of Agricultural Research Systems in Africa: Lessons from Andreiya.* East Lansing: Michigan State UP, 2004. Print.

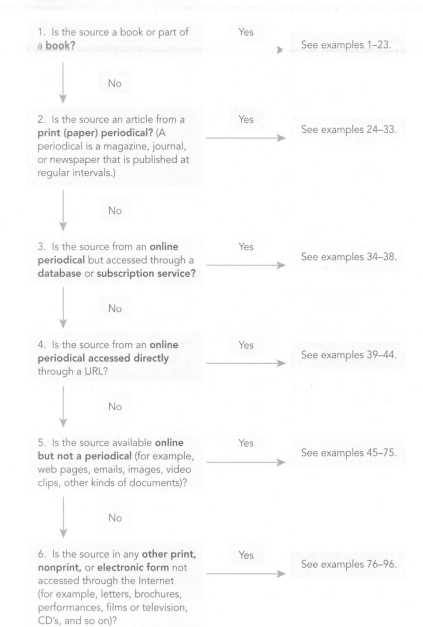

1. Is the source a book or part of a **book?**

Yes → See examples 1–23.

No ↓

2. Is the source an article from a **print (paper) periodical?** (A periodical is a magazine, journal, or newspaper that is published at regular intervals.)

Yes → See examples 24–33.

No ↓

3. Is the source from an **online periodical** but accessed through a **database** or **subscription service?**

Yes → See examples 34–38.

No ↓

4. Is the source from an **online periodical accessed directly** through a URL?

Yes → See examples 39–44.

No ↓

5. Is the source available **online but not a periodical** (for example, web pages, emails, images, video clips, other kinds of documents)?

Yes → See examples 45–75.

No ↓

6. Is the source in any **other print, nonprint,** or **electronic form** not accessed through the Internet (for example, letters, brochures, performances, films or television, CD's, and so on)?

Yes → See examples 76–96.

### 3. Book by More Than Three Authors—MLA

Give only the first author's name, followed by a comma and the phrase *et al.* (abbreviated from the Latin *et alii*, meaning "and others"), or list all names in full and in the order in which they appear on the title page.

Saul, Wendy, et al. *Beyond the Science Fair: Creating a Kids' Inquiry Conference.* Portsmouth: Heinemann, 2005. Print.

### 4. Two or More Works by the Same Author(s)—MLA

Give author name(s) in the first entry only. In the second and subsequent entries, use three hyphens and a period to stand for exactly the same name(s). If the person served as editor or translator, put a comma and the appropriate abbreviation (*ed.* or *trans.*) following the three hyphens. Arrange the works in alphabetical (not chronological) order according to book title, ignoring labels such as *ed.* or *trans.*

Jenkins, Henry. *Convergence Culture: Where Old and New Media Collide.* New York: New York UP, 2006. Print.

---. *Fans, Bloggers, and Gamers: Exploring Participatory Culture.* New York: New York UP, 2006. Print.

### 5. Book by Group or Corporate Author—MLA

Cite the full name of the corporate author first, omitting the first articles *A, An,* or *The.* When a corporate author is also the publisher, use a shortened form of the corporate name in the publication information.

American Psychological Association. *Publication Manual of the American Psychological Association.* 5th ed. Washington: APA, 2001. Print.

Boston Women's Health Collective. *Our Bodies, Ourselves for the New Century.* New York: Simon, 1998. Print.

### 6. Book with No Author Named—MLA

If there is no author's name on the title page, begin the citation with the title. Alphabetize the entry according to the first significant word of the title ignoring *A, An* or *The.*

*The Chicago Manual of Style.* 15th ed. Chicago: U of Chicago P, 2003. Print.

### 7. Book with an Author and an Editor—MLA

If your paper refers to the work of the book's author, put the author's name first; if your paper refers to the work of the editor, put the editor's name first.

Brontë, Emily. *Wuthering Heights.* Ed. Richard J. Dunn. New York: Norton, 2002. Print.

Dunn, Richard J., ed. *Wuthering Heights.* By Emily Brontë. New York: Norton, 2002. Print.

### 8. Translation—MLA

Kundera, Milan. *The Unbearable Lightness of Being.* Trans. Michael Henry Heim. New York: Harper, 1999. Print.

### 9. Work in Several Volumes or Parts—MLA

If you're citing only one volume, put the volume number before the publication information. If you wish, you can give the total number of volumes at the end of the entry. MLA recommends using Arabic numerals, even if the source uses Roman numerals (*Vol. 6* rather than *Vol. VI*).

Chrisley, Ronald, ed. *Artificial Intelligence: Critical Concepts.* Vol. 1. London: Routledge, 2000. Print. 4 vols.

### 10. Anthology or Edited Book—MLA

In the following example, *ed.* stands for "editor," so use *eds.* when more than one editor is named; also see items 9, 11, and 12.

Purdy, John L., and James Ruppert, eds. *Nothing but the Truth: An Anthology of Native American Literature.* Upper Saddle River: Prentice, 2001. Print.

### 11. One Selection from an Anthology or an Edited Book—MLA

Give the author and title of the selection first and then the full title of the anthology. Information about the editor starts with *Ed.* (for "Edited by"), so don't use *Eds.* when there is more than one editor. Give the name(s) of the editor(s) in normal order rather than reversing first and last names. Give the page range at the end.

Trujillo, Laura. "Balancing Act." *Border-Line Personalities: A New Generation of Latinas Dish on Sex, Sass, and Cultural Shifting.* Ed. Robyn Moreno and Michelle Herrera Mulligan. New York: Harper, 2004. 61-72. Print.

### 12. More Than One Selection from the Same Anthology or Edited Book—MLA

If you cite more than one selection from the same anthology, you can list the anthology as a separate entry with all the publication information. Also, list each selection from the anthology by author and title of the selection, but give only the name(s) of the editor(s) of the anthology and the page number(s) for each selection. List selections separately in alphabetical order by author's last name.

Bond, Ruskin. "The Night Train at Deoli." Chaudhuri 415-18.

Chaudhuri, Amit, ed. *The Vintage Book of Modern Indian Literature.* New York: Vintage, 2004. Print.

Vijayan, O.V. "The Rocks." Chaudhuri 291-96.

## 13. Signed Article in a Reference Book—MLA

A "signed article" means that the author of the article is identified. If the articles in the book are alphabetically arranged, you don't need to give volume and page numbers.

Burnbam, John C. "Freud, Sigmund." *The Encyclopedia of Psychiatry, Psychology, and Psychoanalysis.* Ed. Benjamin B. Wolman. New York: Holt, 1996. Print.

## 14. Unsigned Article in a Reference Book—MLA

Begin with the title of the article. If you're citing a widely used reference work, don't give full publication information. Instead, give only the edition and year of publication.

"Ireland." *The New Encyclopaedia Britannica: Macropaedia.* 15th ed. 2002. Print.

## 15. Second or Later Edition—MLA

If a book isn't a first edition, the edition number appears on the title page. Place the abbreviated information (*2nd ed., 3rd ed.,* etc.) between the title and the publication information. Give only the latest copyright date for the edition you're using.

Gibaldi, Joseph. *MLA Handbook for Writers of Research Papers.* 6th ed. New York: MLA, 2003. Print.

## 16. Introduction, Preface, Foreword, or Afterword—MLA

Give first the name of the writer of the part you're citing and then the name of the cited part, capitalized but not underlined or in quotation marks. After the book title, write *By* or *Ed.* and the full name(s) of the book's author(s) or editor(s), if different from the writer of the cited material. If the writer of the cited material is the same as the book author, include only the last name after *By.* Following the publication information, give inclusive page numbers for the cited part, using Roman or Arabic numerals as the source does.

Hesse, Doug. Foreword. *The End of Composition Studies.* By David W. Smit. Carbondale: Southern Illinois UP, 2004. ix–xiii. Print.

When the introduction, preface, foreword, or afterword has a title (as in the next example), include it in the citation before the section name.

Fox-Genovese, Elizabeth. "Mothers and Daughters: The Ties That Bind."
Foreword. *Southern Mothers*. Ed. Nagueyalti Warren and Sally Wolff.
Baton Rouge: Louisiana State UP, 1999. iv-xviii. Print.

### 17. Unpublished Dissertation or Essay—MLA

State the author's name first, then the title in quotation marks (not italicized),
then a descriptive label (such as *Diss.* or *Unpublished essay*), followed by the
degree-granting institution (for dissertations), and, finally, the date. Treat published dissertations as books.

Stuart, Gina Anne. "Exploring the Harry Potter Book Series: A Study of
Adolescent Reading Motivation." Diss. Utah State U, 2006. Print.

### 18. Reprint of an Older Book—MLA

Republishing information can be found on the copyright page. Give the date
of the original version before the publication information for the version you're
citing.

O'Brien, Flann. *At Swim-Two-Birds*. 1939. Normal: Dalkey Archive, 1998. Print.

### 19. Book in a Series—MLA

Goldman, Dorothy J. *Women Writers and World War I*. New York: Macmillan,
1995. Print. Lit. and Soc. Ser.

Mukherjee, Meenakshi. *Jane Austen*. New York: St. Martin's, 1991. Print. Women
Writers Ser.

### 20. Book with a Title Within a Title—MLA

The MLA recognizes two distinct styles for handling normally independent
titles when they appear within an italicized title. (Use whichever style your instructor prefers.) When using the MLA's preferred style, do not italicize the
embedded title or set it within quotation marks.

Lumiansky, Robert M., and Herschel Baker, eds. *Critical Approaches to Six
Major English Works:* Beowulf *Through* Paradise Lost. Philadelphia:
U of Pennsylvania P, 1968. Print.

However, because MLA also accepts a second style for handling such embedded titles, you can set the normally independent titles within quotation marks
and italicize them.

Lumiansky, Robert M., and Herschel Baker, eds. *Critical Approaches to Six
Major English Works: "Beowulf" Through "Paradise Lost."* Philadelphia:
U of Pennsylvania P, 1968. Print.

### 21. Bible or Sacred Text—MLA

*Bhagavad-Gita.* Trans. Juan Mascaro. Rev. ed. New York: Penguin, 2003. Print.

*The Holy Bible: New International Version.* New York: Harper, 1983. Print.

*The Qur'an.* Trans. Abdullah Yusuf Ali. 13th ed. Elmhurst: Tahrike Tarsile
    Qur'an, 1999. Print.

### 22. Government Publication—MLA

For government publications that name no author, start with the name of the
government or government body. Then name the government agency. *GPO* is
a standard abbreviation for *Government Printing Office,* the publisher of most
US government publications.

United States. Cong. House. Committee on Resources. *Coastal Heritage Trail*
    *Route in New Jersey.* 106th Cong., 1st sess. H. Rept. 16. Washington: GPO,
    1999. Print.

---.---. Senate. Select Committee on Intelligence. *Report on the U.S.*
    *Intelligence Community's Prewar Intelligence Assessment of Iraq.*
    108th Cong., 1st sess. Washington: GPO, 2004. Print.

### 23. Published Proceedings of a Conference—MLA

Rocha, Luis Mateus, et al., eds. *Artificial Life X: Proceedings of the Tenth*
    *International Conference on the Simulation and Synthesis of Living*
    *Systems.* Bloomington, IN. 3-7 June 2006. Cambridge: MIT P, 2006.
    Print.

### PERIODICAL PUBLICATIONS—PRINT VERSIONS

Citations for periodical articles contain three major parts: author information,
title information, and publication information.

### 24. Signed Article in a Weekly or Biweekly Periodical—MLA

Brink, Susan. "Eat This Now!" *US News and World Report* 28 Mar. 2005: 56-58.
    Print.

### 25. Signed Article in a Monthly or Bimonthly Periodical—MLA

Fallows, James. "The $1.4 Trillion Question." *The Atlantic* Jan.-Feb. 2008: 36-48.
    Print.

### 26. Unsigned Article in a Weekly or Monthly Periodical—MLA

"The Price Is Wrong." *Economist* 2 Aug. 2003: 58-59. Print.

### 27. Article in a Scholarly Journal

Adler-Kassner, Linda, and Heidi Estrem. "Rethinking Research Writing: Public
    Literacy in the Composition Classroom." *WPA: Writing Program
    Administration* 26.3 (2003): 119-31. Print.

### 28. Article in a Collection of Reprinted Articles—MLA

First include the original publication information, then *Rpt.* and information
about the place the article was republished.

Brumberg, Abraham. "Russia after Perestroika." *New York Review of Books* 27
    June 1991: 53-62. Rpt. in *Russian and Soviet History*. Ed. Alexander Dallin.
    Vol. 14 of *The Gorbachev Era*. New York: Garland, 1992. 300-20. Print.

Textbooks used in college writing courses often collect previously printed
articles.

Rothstein, Richard. "When Mothers on Welfare Go to Work." *New York Times*
    5 June 2002: A20. Rpt. in *Writing Arguments: A Rhetoric with Readings*. Ed.
    John D. Ramage, John C. Bean, and June Johnson. New York: Longman,
    2004. 263. Print.

### 29. Signed Article in a Daily Newspaper—MLA

Omit *A, An,* or *The* as the first word in a newspaper title. Give the day, month,
and year of the issue (and the edition, if applicable). If sections are designated,
give the section letter as well as the page number. If an article runs on noncon-
secutive pages, give the starting page number followed by a plus sign (for example, *23+* for an article that starts on page 23 and continues on a later page).

Green, Penelope. "The Slow Life Picks Up Speed." *New York Times* 31 Jan. 2008,
    natl. ed.: D1+. Print.

### 30. Unsigned Article in a Daily Newspaper—MLA

"Oscars Ready Plans to Deal with Strike." *Denver Post* 31 Jan. 2008: B3. Print.

If the city of publication is not part of the title, put it in square brackets after
the title, not italicized.

"Hackers Hit Northwestern Computer Net." *Pantagraph* [Bloomington] 26 Mar.
    2005: A5. Print.

### 31. Editorial, Letter to the Editor, or Review—MLA

After the author's name or title, provide information about the type of
publication.

"Primary Considerations." Editorial. *Washington Post* 27 Jan. 2008: B6. Print.

Finanger, Emily. Letter. *Outside* Feb. 2008: 14. Print.

Shenk, David. "Toolmaker, Brain Builder." Rev. of *Beyond Big Blue: Building the Computer That Defeated the World Chess Champion,* by Feng-Hsiung Hsu. *American Scholar* 72 (Spring 2003): 150-52. Print.

### 32. Article in a Looseleaf Collection of Reprinted Articles—MLA

Give the citation for the original publication first, followed by the citation for the collection.

Hayden, Thomas. "The Age of Robots." *US News and World Report* 23 Apr. 2001: 44+. Print. *Applied Science* 2002. Ed. Eleanor Goldstein. Boca Raton: SIRS, 2002. Art. 66.

### 33. Abstract in a Collection of Abstracts—MLA

To cite an abstract, first give information for the full work: the author's name, the title of the article, and publication information about the full article. If a reader could not know that the cited material is an abstract, write the word *Abstract,* not italicized, followed by a period. Give publication information about the collection of abstracts. For abstracts identified by item numbers rather than page numbers, use the word *item* before the item number.

Marcus, Hazel R., and Shinobu Kitayamo. "Culture and the Self: Implications for Cognition, Emotion, and Motivation." *Psychological Review* 88 (1991): 224-53. *Psychological Abstracts* 78 (1991): item 23878. Print.

### PERIODICALS—ONLINE VERSIONS FROM SUBSCRIPTION SERVICES

A large (and increasing) number of periodicals are available in digital versions online, as well as in print; some periodicals are available only online. Online periodicals fall into two categories: (1) periodicals you access through a DATABASE or **subscription service** paid for by your library or company, such as EBSCO or FirstSearch, or through an online service to which you personally subscribe (examples 34–38); and (2) periodicals you directly access by entering a specific URL (examples 39–44). Articles you access through a subscription service are the most important for academic research. Of course, many other online sources are not from periodicals; we explain them in examples 45–75.

### 34. Subscription Service: Article with a Print Version—MLA

Jackson, Gabriel. "Multiple Historic Meanings of the Spanish Civil War." *Science and Society* 68.3 (2004): 272-76. *Academic Search Elite.* Web. 7 Mar. 2005.

VandeHei, Jim. "Two Years after White House Exit, Clinton Shaping
Democratic Party." *Washington Post* 21 June 2003, final ed.: A1. *Academic
Universe.* Web. 5 May 2005.

### 35. Subscription Service: Material with No Print Version—MLA

Siemens, Raymond G. "A New Computer-Assisted Literary Criticism?"
*Computers and the Humanities* 36.3 (2002): n. pag. *America Online.* Web.
12 Nov. 2002.

### 36. Subscription Service: Abstract—MLA

The example below is for the same abstract shown in item 33, but here it is accessed from an online database (*PsycINFO*) by means of a library subscription
service. The name of the library shows where the source was accessed, and *10
Apr. 2004* is the date it was accessed.

Marcus, Hazel R., and Shinobu Kitayamo. "Culture and the Self: Implications
for Cognition, Emotion, and Motivation." *Psychological Abstracts* 78 (1991).
*PsycINFO.* Web. 10 Apr. 2004.

### 37. Subscription Service Access with a Keyword: Article in a Periodical with a Print Version—MLA

Electronic versions of sources that also appear in print start with information
about the print version. Here's an entry for a journal article accessed through
a computer service; it also has a print version.

Wynne, Clive D. L. "'Willy' Didn't Yearn to Be Free." Editorial. *New York Times*
27 Dec. 2003: n. pag. *New York Times Online.* America Online. Web.
29 Dec. 2003. Keyword: nytimes.

Information applying to the print version of this article in the *New York Times*
ends with the publication date and information about the online version starts
with the title of the database, *New York Times Online. America Online* is the service through which the database was accessed, and *29 Dec. 2003* is the access
date. The keyword *nytimes* was used to access *New York Times Online.*

### 38. Subscription Service Access Showing a Path—MLA

When you access a source by choosing a series of keywords, menus, or topics,
end the entry with the "path" of words you used. Use semicolons between items
in the path, and put a period at the end.

Futrelle, David. "A Smashing Success." *Money.com* 23 Dec. 1999. America
Online. Web. 26 Dec. 1999. Path: Personal Finance; Business News;
Business Publications; Money.com.

## PERIODICALS—ONLINE VERSIONS ACCESSED DIRECTLY

You can access some online versions of periodicals directly, without going through a paid subscription service. Newspapers and magazines often publish some of their articles from each issue online this way. Often, however, you can't access every single article—or any older articles—without being a subscriber.

### 39. Online Version of a Print Magazine Article—MLA

The example below is for the online version of the same article cited in 25, above. In addition to the print information, include the date you accessed the online version. (If the page numbers from the print version are available, include them, too, after the publication date.)

Fallows, James. "The $1.4 Trillion Question." *The Atlantic.com*. Atlantic
   Monthly Group, Jan.-Feb. 2008. Web. 2 May 2008.

If the article is unsigned, begin with the title.

"Too Smart to Marry." *The Atlantic.com*. Atlantic Monthly Group, 14 Apr. 2005.
   Web. 7 Mar. 2005.

### 40. Online Version of a Print Journal Article—MLA

Hoge, Charles W., et al. "Mild Traumatic Brain Injury in U.S. Soldiers
   Returning from Iraq." *New England Journal of Medicine* 358.5 (2008):
   453-63. Web. 10 Sept. 2008.

### 41. Periodical Article Published Only Online—MLA

Many periodicals are published only online; others have "extra" online content that doesn't appear in print.

Ramirez, Eddy. "Comparing American Students with Those in China and
   India." *U.S. News and World Report*. U.S. News and World Report, 30 Jan.
   2008. Web. 4 Mar. 2008.

Shipka, Jody. "This Was (Not!!) an Easy Assignment." *Computers and
   Composition Online*. Computers and Composition Online, Fall 2007.
   Web. 2 May 2008.

### 42. Online Version of a Print Newspaper Article—MLA

If the article is signed, begin with the author's name, last name first.

Wilson, Janet. "EPA Fights Waste Site near River." *Los Angeles Times*. Los
   Angeles Times, 5 Mar. 2005. Web. 7 Mar. 2005.

If the article is unsigned, begin with the article title.

"Remnant of Revolutionary War Washes Ashore." *CNN.com*. Cable News
    Network, 28 Mar. 2005. Web. 29 Mar. 2005.

### 43. Online Editorial or Letter to the Editor—MLA

"Garbage In, Garbage Out." Editorial. *Los Angeles Times*. Los Angeles Times,
    2 Feb. 2008. Web. 22 Mar. 2008.

Ennis, Heather B. Letter to the Editor. *U.S. News and World Report*. U.S. News
    and World Report, 20 Dec. 2007. Web. 22 Dec. 2007.

### 44. Online Material from a Newspaper or News Site Published Only Online—MLA

Harris, Edward. "Rain Forests Fall at 'Alarming' Rate." *denverpost.com*.
    Denver Post, 3 Feb. 2008. Web. 3 Feb. 2008.

### OTHER INTERNET SOURCES

This section shows models for online sources. For such sources, provide as
much of the following information as you can.

- The author's name, if given.
- In quotation marks, the title of a short work (Web page, brief document,
  essay, article, message, and so on); or italicized, the title of a book.
- Publication information for any print version, if it exists.
- The name of an editor, translator, or compiler, if any, with an abbreviation
  such as *Ed., Trans.,* or *Comp.* before the name.
- The italicized title of the Internet site (scholarly project, database, online
  periodical, professional or personal Web site). If the site has no title, de-
  scribe it: for example, *Home page.*
- The date of electronic publication (including a version number, if any) or
  posting or the most recent update.
- The name of a sponsoring organization, if any.
- The medium of publication.
- The date you accessed the material.
- The URL in angle brackets (< >), only when the reader probably could not
  locate the source without it. If you must break a URL at the end of a line,
  break only after a slash and do not use a hyphen.

### 45. Online Book—MLA

Chopin, Kate. *The Awakening.* 1899. *PBS Electronic Library.* 10 Dec. 1998. PBS.
    Web. 13 Nov. 2008.

### 46. Online Book in a Scholarly Project—MLA

Herodotus. *The History of Herodotus.* Trans. George Rawlinson. 1947. *Internet
    Classics Archive.* Ed. Daniel C. Stevenson. 11 Jan. 1998. MIT. Web. 15 May
    2006.

### 47. Online Government-Published Book—MLA

Start with the name of the government or government body, and then name
the government agency, the title, the work's author (if known), the publication date, the medium of publication, the access date, and the URL, if the
reader needs it.

United States. Cong. Research Service. *Space Stations.* By Marcia S. Smith. 12
    Dec. 1996. Web. 4 Dec. 2007.

MLA also permits an alternative format, with the author's name first, then title,
then government body.

Huff, C. Ronald. *Comparing the Criminal Behavior of Youth Gangs and At-Risk
    Youths.* United States. Dept. of Justice. Natl. Inst. of Justice. Oct. 1998. Web.
    5 Aug. 2008.

### 48. Professional Home Page—MLA

Provide as much of the following information as you can find.

- If available, include the name of the person who created or put up the
  home page. If first and last names are given, reverse the order of the first
  author's name.
- For a professional home page, include the name of the sponsoring organization.
- Include the date you accessed the material.

*Association for the Advancement of Artificial Intelligence.* Web. 17 Mar. 2008.

### 49. Personal Home Page—MLA

Follow guidelines for professional home pages, with the following changes.
Give the name of the person who created the page, last name first. Include the
page's title, if there is one, italicized; if there is no title, add the description
*Home page,* not italicized, followed by a period.

Hesse, Doug. Home page. Web. 1 Nov. 2007. <http://portfolio.du.edu/dhesse>.

## 50. Page from a Web Site—MLA

Provide as much information as you can.

"Protecting Whales from Dangerous Sonar." *National Resources Defense*
    *Council.* NRDC, 9 Nov. 2005. Web. 12 Dec. 2005.

"Abridged History." *Maine Organic Farmers and Gardeners Association.*
    Maine Organic Farmers and Gardeners Assn., 2007. Web. 13 Dec. 2007.

## 51. Entire Internet Site—MLA

*WebdelSol.Com.* Ed. Michael Neff. 2008. Web. 11 Nov. 2008.

## 52. Academic Department Home Page—MLA

Write the name of the academic department, followed by the words *Dept. home
page.* (Do not put any words in quotations or in italics.) Also include the name
of the institution and the date you accessed the page.

Writing. Dept. home page. Grand Valley State U. Web. 26 Feb. 2008.

## 53. Course Home Page—MLA

St. Germain, Sheryl. Myths and Fairytales: From *Inanna* to *Edward*
    *Scissorhands.* Course home page. Summer 2003. Dept. of English,
    Iowa State U. Web. 20 Feb. 2005. <http://www.public.iastate.edu/
    ~sgermain/531.homepage.html>.

## 54. Government or Institutional Web Site—MLA

Home Education and Private Tutoring. Pennsylvania Department of Education,
    2005. Web. 15 Dec. 2005.

## 55. Online Poem—MLA

Browning, Elizabeth Barrett. "Past and Future." *Women's Studies Database*
    *Reading Room.* U of Maryland. Web. 9 June 2003.

## 56. Online Work of Art—MLA

Provide artist, title of work, creation date (optional), the museum or individual who owns it, the place, and the access date.

van Gogh, Vincent. *The Starry Night.* 1889. Museum of Mod. Art, New York.
    Web. 5 Dec. 2003. Keyword: Starry Night.

In this example, the keyword "Starry Night" is what a researcher types into a
search box on the museum's Web site.

## 57. Online Image or Photograph—MLA

As with images from print publications (see item 88), include information about the photographer and title, if known. Otherwise, describe the photograph briefly and give information about the Web site and the access date.

Bourke-White, Margaret. "Fort Peck Dam, Montana." 1936. Gelatin silver print. Metropolitan Museum of Art, New York. Web. 5 Aug. 2008.

## 58. Online Interview—MLA

Pope, Carl. Interview by Amy Standen. *Salon.* Salon Media Group, 29 Apr. 2002. Web. 27 Jan. 2005.

## 59. Online Video or Film Clip—MLA

Reeves, Matt, dir. *Cloverfield.* Trailer. Bad Robot, 2008. Web. 18 Jan. 2008.

## 60. Online Cartoon—MLA

Harris, Sidney. "We have lots of information technology." Cartoon. *New Yorker* 27 May 2002. Web. 9 Feb. 2007.

## 61. Online Television or Radio Program—MLA

Chayes, Sarah. "Concorde." *All Things Considered.* Natl. Public Radio. 26 July 2000. Web. 7 Dec. 2001.

"The Beginning of the End." *Lost.* ABC. 30 Jan. 2008. Web. 1 Feb. 2008.

## 62. Online Discussion Posting—MLA

To cite an online message, give the author's name (if any), the title of the message in quotation marks, and then *Online posting.* Give the date of the posting and the name of the bulletin board, if any. Then give the publication medium, the access date, and, in angle brackets, the URL if needed.

Firrantello, Larry. "Van Gogh on Prozac." Online posting. 23 May 2005. *Salon Table Talk.* Web. 7 June 2005. <http://tabletalk.salon.com/ webx?50@931.xC34anLmwOq.1@.773b2ad1>.

Be cautious about using online postings as sources. Some postings contain cutting-edge information from experts, but some contain trash. Unfortunately, it is nearly impossible to find out whether people online are who they claim to be.

## 63. Real-Time Communication—MLA

Give the name of the speaker or writer, a title for the event (if any), the forum, date, publication medium, access date, and URL if needed.

Berzsenyi, Christyne. Online discussion of "Writing to Meet Your Match: Rhetoric, Perceptions, and Self-Presentation for Four Online Daters." *Computers and Writing Online.* 13 May 2007. AcadlandMoo. Web. 13 May 2007.

### 64. E-Mail Message—MLA

Start with the name of the person who wrote the e-mail message. Give the title or subject line in quotation marks. Then describe the message, including the recipient's name. End with the date of the message and the medium of delivery (*E-mail*).

Pessin, Eliana. "Scottish Writers." Message to Georgia Dobyns. 11 Nov. 2007. Email.

### 65. Part of an Online Book—MLA

Teasdale, Sara. "Driftwood." *Flame and Shadow.* Ed. A. Light. N.p., 1920. *Project Gutenberg.* 1 July 1996. Web. 18 Aug. 2008.

### 66. Online Review—MLA

Travers, Peter. Rev. of *No Country for Old Men,* dir. Joel Coen and Ethan Coen. *RollingStone.* Real Networks, 1 Nov. 2007. Web. 25 Nov. 2007.

### 67. Online Abstract—MLA

Avery, Christopher, et al. "A Revealed Preference Ranking of U.S. Colleges and Universities." NBER Working Paper No. W10803. Oct. 2004. Abstract. Web. 2 Oct. 2008.

### 68. Posting on a Blog—MLA

McLemee, Scott. "To Whom It May Concern." *Quick Study.* 1 Jan. 2008. Web. 14 May 2008.

### 69. Online Sound Recording or Clip—MLA

Komunyakaa, Yusef. "My Father's Love Letters." Poets.org Listening Booth. Academy of American Poets, 5 May 1993. Web. 27 Apr. 2005.

### 70. Online Advertisement—MLA

Samsung. Advertisement. *RollingStone.com.* 8 Nov. 2005. Web.

### 71. Online Manuscript or Working Paper—MLA

deGrandpre, Andrew. "Baseball Destined to Die in Hockey Town." 2002. Unpublished article. Web. 7 Mar. 2005.

## 72. Podcast—MLA

A podcast is an audio recording that is posted online. Include as much of the following information as you can identify: author, title, sponsoring organization or Web site, date posted, and date accessed.

"Business Marketing with Podcast: What Marketing Professionals Should
Know." *Podblaze.com*. The Info Gurus, 13 Oct. 2005. Web. 19 Oct. 2005.

## 73. Online Slide Show—MLA

Erickson, Britta, narr. *Visionaries from the New China*. July 2007. Web. 11 Sept.
2008.

## 74. Online Photo Essay—MLA

Nachtwey, James. "Crime in Middle America." *Time* 2 Dec. 2006. Web. 5 May 2007.

## 75. Online Map, Chart, or Other Graphic—MLA

"Hurricane Rita." Graphic. *New York Times Online*. New York Times. 24 Sept.
2005. Web. 24 Sept. 2005.

### OTHER PRINT, NONPRINT, AND ELECTRONIC SOURCES

## 76. Published or Unpublished Letter—MLA

Begin the entry with the author of the letter. Note the recipient, too.

Irvin, William. Letter to Lesley Osburn. 7 Dec. 2007. Print.

Williams, William Carlos. Letter to his son. 13 Mar. 1935. *Letters of the Century:
America 1900-1999*. Ed. Lisa Grunwald and Stephen J. Adler. New York:
Dial, 1999. 225-26. Print.

## 77. Microfiche Collection of Articles—MLA

A microfiche is a transparent sheet of film (a *fiche*) with microscopic printing that needs to be read through a special magnifier. Each fiche holds several pages, with each page designated by a grid position. A long document may appear on more than one fiche.

Wenzell, Ron. "Businesses Prepare for a More Diverse Work Force." *St. Louis
Post Dispatch* 3 Feb. 1990: 17. Microform. *NewsBank: Employment* 27 (1990):
fiche 2, grid D12.

## 78. Map or Chart—MLA

*Colorado Front Range Mountain Bike Topo Map*. Map. Nederland: Latitude 40,
2001. Print.

## 79. Report or Pamphlet—MLA

Use the format for books, to the extent possible.

National Commission on Writing in America's Schools and Colleges. *The Neglected "R": The Need for a Writing Revolution.* New York: College Board, 2003. Print.

## 80. Legal Source—MLA

Include the name of the case, the number of the case (preceded by *No.*), the name of the court deciding the case, and the date of the decision.

Brown v. Board of Ed. No. 8. Supreme Ct. of the US. 8 Oct. 1952. Print.

## 81. Interview—MLA

Note the type of interview—for example, "Telephone," "Personal" (face-to-face), or "E-mail."

Friedman, Randi. Telephone interview. 30 Aug. 2008.

For a published interview, give the name of the interviewed person first, identify the source as an interview, and then give details as for any published source: title; author, preceded by the word *By;* and publication details.

Winfrey, Oprah. "Ten Questions for Oprah Winfrey." By Richard Zoglin. *Time* 15 Dec. 2003: 8. Print.

## 82. Lecture, Speech, or Address—MLA

Kennedy, John Fitzgerald. Greater Houston Ministerial Assn. Rice Hotel, Houston. 12 Sept. 1960. Address.

## 83. Film, Videotape, or DVD—MLA

Give the title first, and include the director, the distributor, and the year. For older films that were subsequently released on tape or DVD, provide the original release date of the movie *before* the type of medium. For video downloads, include the download date and the source. Other information (writer, producer, major actors) is optional but helpful. Put first names first.

*Shakespeare in Love.* Screenplay by Marc Norman and Tom Stoppard. Dir. John Maddon. Prod. David Parfitt, Donna Gigliotti, Harvey Weinstein, Edward Zwick, and Mark Norman. Perf. Gwyneth Paltrow, Joseph Fiennes, and Judi Dench. Miramax, 1998. Film.

*It Happened One Night.* Screenplay by Robert Riskin. Dir. and Prod. Frank Capra. Perf. Clark Gable and Claudette Colbert. 1934. Sony Pictures, 1999. DVD.

*It Happened One Night.* Screenplay by Robert Riskin. Dir. and Prod. Frank
Capra. Perf. Clark Gable and Claudette Colbert. Columbia 1934. 2007.
4 Mar. 2008. MPEG file.

### 84. Musical Recording—MLA

Put first the name most relevant to what you discuss in your paper (performer,
conductor, the work performed). Include the recording's title, the medium for
any recording other than a CD (*LP, audiocassette*), the name of the issuer
(*Vanguard*), and the year the work was issued.

Smetana, Bedrich. *My Country.* Czech Philharmonic Orch. Cond. Karel Anserl.
LP. Vanguard, 1975. CD.

Springsteen, Bruce. "Lonesome Day." *The Rising.* Sony, 2002. CD.

Radiohead. "Jigsaw Falling into Place." *In Rainbows.* Radiohead, 2007. MP3
file.

### 85. Live Performance (Play, Concert, etc.)—MLA

*All My Sons.* By Arthur Miller. Dir. Calvin McLean. Center for the Performing
Arts, Normal, IL. 27 Sept. 2005. Performance.

### 86. Work of Art, Photograph, or Musical Composition—MLA

Cassatt, Mary. *La Toilette.* 1890. Oil on canvas. Art Institute of Chicago.

Mydans, Carl. *General Douglas MacArthur Landing at Luzon,* 1945. Gelatin
silver print. Soho Triad Fine Art Gallery, New York. 21 Oct.-28 Nov. 1999.

Don't underline or put in quotation marks music identified only by form, number, and key.

Schubert, Franz. Symphony no. 8 in B minor. Print.

Italicize any work that has a title, such as an opera or ballet or a named
symphony.

Schubert, Franz. *Unfinished Symphony.* Print.

To cite a published score, use the following format.

Schubert, Franz. *Symphony in B Minor (Unfinished).* Ed. Martin Cusid. New
York: Norton, 1971. Print.

### 87. Television or Radio Program—MLA

Include at least the title of the program or series (underlined), the network,
the local station and its city, and the date of the broadcast.

*Not for Ourselves Alone: The Story of Elizabeth Cady Stanton and Susan B.*
*Anthony.* Writ. Andrei Burns. Perf. Julie Harris, Ronnie Gilbert, and Sally
Kellerman. Prod. Paul Barnes and Andrei Burns. PBS. WNET, New York.
8 Nov. 1999. Television.

Supply the title of a specific episode (if any) in quotation marks before the title
of the program (italicized) and the title of the series (if any) neither italicized
nor in quotation marks.

"The Middle of Nowhere." *This American Life.* Prod. Ira Glass. Chicago Public
Radio. KCFR-AM, Denver. 7 Dec. 2007. Radio.

Note that many radio programs also exist as podcasts (see item 72).

### 88. Image or Photograph in a Print Publication—MLA

To cite an image or a photograph that appears as part of a print publication (perhaps as an illustration for an article), give the photographer (if known), the
title or caption of the image, and complete publication information, as for an
article. If the image has no title, provide a brief description.

Greene, Herb. "Grace Slick." *Rolling Stone* 30 Sept. 2004: 102. Print.

### 89. Advertisement—MLA

American Airlines. Advertisement. ABC. 24 Aug. 2003. Television.

Canon Digital Cameras. Advertisement. *Time* 2 June 2003: 77. Print.

### 90. Video Game or Software—MLA

*Guitar Hero III: Legends of Rock.* Santa Monica: Activision, 2007.

### 91. Nonperiodical Publications on CD, DVD, or Magnetic Tape—MLA

Citations for publications on DVD, CD-ROM, or other recording formats
follow guidelines for print publications, with two additions: list the publication
medium (for example, *CD*), and give the vendor's name.

Perl, Sondra. *Felt Sense: Guidelines for Composing.* Portsmouth: Boynton,
2004. CD.

### 92. Materials on CD or DVD with a Print Version—MLA

Before the maturity of the Internet, many print materials were previously stored
on CD-ROMs.

"The Price Is Right." *Time* 20 Jan. 1992: 38. *Time Man of the Year.* CD-ROM. New
York: Compact, 1993.

Information for the print version ends with the article's page number, 38. The
title of the CD-ROM is *Time Man of the Year,* its producer is the publisher

Compact, and its copyright year is 1993. Both the title of the print publication and the title of the CD-ROM are italicized.

### 93. Materials on CD or DVD with No Print Version—MLA

"Artificial Intelligence." *Encarta 2003*. Redmond: Microsoft, 2003. CD-ROM.

*Encarta 2003* is a CD-ROM encyclopedia with no print version. "Artificial Intelligence" is the title of an article in *Encarta 2003*.

### 94. Book in Digital Format—MLA

Many books are now available for downloading from the Internet in digital format, to be read on special players.

Gilbert, Elizabeth. *Eat, Pray, Love*. New York: Viking, 2007. Kindle Edition.

### 95. PowerPoint or Similar Presentation—MLA

Delyser, Ariel. "Political Movements in the Philippines." University of Denver.
 7 Apr. 2006. PowerPoint.

### 96. Work in More Than One Publication Medium—MLA

Shannon, Linda, et al., eds. *Coming of Age. The Advanced Writing Curriculum*
 *Coming of Age Course Descriptions*. Portsmouth: Boynton, 2000. CD-ROM,
 print.

This book and CD-ROM come together. Each has its own title, but the publication information—*Portsmouth: Boynton, 2000*—applies to both.

### ■ Using content or bibliographic notes in MLA style

In MLA style, footnotes or endnotes serve two specific purposes: (1) You can use them for content (ideas and information) that does not fit into your paper but is still worth relating; and (2) you can use them for bibliographic information that would intrude if you were to include it in your text. Place a note number at the end of a sentence, if possible. Put it after any punctuation mark except the dash. Do not put any space before a note number, and put one space after it. Raise the note number a little above the line of words, as shown in the following examples.

TEXT OF PAPER

Eudora Welty's literary biography, *One Writer's Beginnings*, shows us how both the inner world of self and the outer world of family and place form a writer's imagination.[1]

**CONTENT NOTE—MLA**

[1]Welty, who valued her privacy, always resisted investigation of her life. However, at the age of seventy-four, she chose to present her own autobiographical reflections in a series of lectures at Harvard University.

**TEXT OF PAPER**

Barbara Randolph believes that enthusiasm is contagious (65).[1] Many psychologists have found that panic, fear, and rage spread more quickly in crowds than positive emotions do, however.

**BIBLIOGRAPHIC NOTE—MLA**

[1]Others who agree with Randolph include Thurman 21, 84, 155; Kelley 421-25; and Brookes 65-76.

# 35e A student's MLA-style research paper

The following is student writer Andrei Gurov's assignment for an MLA-style research paper.

Write an MLA-style research paper on the general subject of "memory." You are required to write 1,800 to 2,000 words, using a variety of sources. Your final paper is due in six weeks. Interim deadlines for parts of the work will be announced. To complete this assignment, you need to engage in three interrelated processes: conducting research, understanding the results of that research, and writing a paper based on the first two processes. Consult the *Simon & Schuster Handbook for Writers,* especially Chapters 33–35 for guidance on how to complete this assignment, and Chapter 36 for guidance on MLA-style parenthetical citations and Works Cited entries. You may also consult the MLA Web site at http://www.mla.org.

**PAGE 1 OF PAPER**

On the first page of your paper, in the upper right corner, type your last name, followed by a space, and then followed by the numeral 1 placed one-half inch below the top edge of the page and one inch in from the right margin. Next, at the left margin, one inch in from the left side, type the four lines with the information shown on the first page of the sample paper. Finally, type your paper's title centered one double space below the last of the four lines that you just finished typing flush left.

Double-space after the title, and start your paper, indenting the first line of the first—and all—paragraphs five character spaces. The indent in Microsoft Word is a hanging indent of 0.50 for "first line."

## OUTLINES

Even though MLA doesn't officially endorse using outlines, some instructors, including Andrei Gurov's, require that students submit formal outlines with their research papers. The traditional formal outline follows long-established conventions for using numbers and letters to show relationships among ideas. A less traditional formal outline includes these elements but also includes the planned content for a research paper's introductory and concluding paragraphs. Both the traditional and the less traditional outlines can be sentence outlines (composed entirely of complete sentences) or topic outlines (composed only of words and phrases). In your outlines, however, never mix the two styles.

This outline is for Andrei Gurov's research paper about déjà vu. To format the outline, he used the less traditional outline, which was what his instructor preferred and asked her class to use. In the name-page number line in the upper right corner of his outline, Andrei typed his last name, left one space, and then typed the lowercase Roman numeral *i* for the page number, the conventional way of indicating any page that comes before the first page of the essay itself. He placed that information one-half inch from the top of the page and made sure it ended one inch in from the right edge of the paper. He then left a half-inch space below the name-number heading and centered the word *Outline*. The thesis statement in the outline matches the last sentence of the first paragraph of his paper.

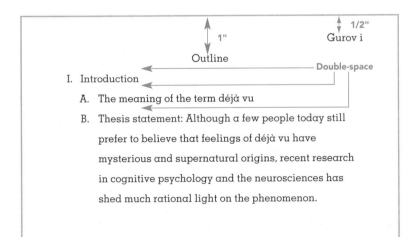

1/2"

Gurov i

1"

Outline

Double-space

I. Introduction

  A.  The meaning of the term déjà vu

  B.  Thesis statement: Although a few people today still prefer to believe that feelings of déjà vu have mysterious and supernatural origins, recent research in cognitive psychology and the neurosciences has shed much rational light on the phenomenon.

II. Percentage of people who report experiencing déjà vu

III. Misunderstandings of the phenomenon of déjà vu

    A. Precognition

    B. False memory

IV. New psychological and medical theories of déjà vu

    A. Human sight's two pathways

    B. Implanted memories

        1. Natural: from old memories long forgotten

        2. Manipulated: from subliminal stimulation

        3. Inattentional blindness

V. Conclusion

    A. Many years of paranormal explanations of déjà vu

    B. Scientific research after 1980

    C. Much promise for further research

## PAGE NUMBERING AFTER THE FIRST PAGE OF THE PAPER

In the upper right corner, type your last name, followed by a space, and then followed by the Arabic numeral of the page in sequence (2, 3, and so on). Place this name-number heading one-half inch below the top edge of the page and one inch in from the right margin. Number the pages consecutively, including the last page of your Works Cited. Many writers use the "header and footer" word-processing function that inserts last names and sequential page numbers, updating automatically. This feature is especially convenient during revision, when your writing causes your pages to fall differently than they originally did.

↕ 1"

Andrei Gurov

**Put identifying information in upper left corner.**

Professor Ryan

English 101, Section A4

12 December 2007

**Use 1/2-inch top margin, 1 inch bottom and side margins; double-space throughout.**

↓ ½"
Gurov 1

Déjà Vu: At Last a Subject for Serious Study

**Center title**

"Brain hiccup" might be another name for *déjà vu*, French
for "already seen." During a moment of déjà vu, a person
relives an event that in reality is happening for the first time.
The hiccup metaphor seems apt because each modern
scientific explanation of the déjà vu phenomenon involves a
doubled event, as this paper will demonstrate. However, such
modern scientific work was long in coming. In his article "The
Déjà Vu Illusion," today's leading researcher in the field, Alan
S. Brown at Southern Methodist University, states that "for over
170 years, this most puzzling of memory illusions has intrigued
scholars" but was hampered when "during the behaviorist
era . . . the plethora of parapsychological and psychodynamic
interpretations" multiplied rapidly (256). Thus, notions of the
supernatural and magic halted the scientific study of déjà vu
for almost two centuries. By the first quarter of the twentieth
century, it began again slowly. Although a few people today
still prefer to believe that feelings of déjà vu have mysterious
or supernatural origins, recent research in cognitive
psychology and the neurosciences has shed much rational
light on the phenomenon.

**Quotation marks around phrases show they appeared separately in the source.**

**The ellipsis indicates words omitted from a quotation.**

continued >>

(Proportions shown in this paper are adjusted to fit space limitations of this book. Follow
actual dimensions discussed in this book and your instructor's directions.)

Some people report never having experienced déjà vu, and the percentages vary for the number of people who report having lived through at least one episode of it. In 2004, Brown reports that of the subjects he has interviewed, an average of 66 percent say that they have had one or more déjà vu experiences during their lives (*Experience* 33). However, in early 2005 in "Strangely Familiar," Uwe Wolfradt reports that "various studies indicate that from 50 to 90 percent of the people [studied] can recall having had at least one such déjà vu incident in their lives."

Perhaps part of the reason for this variation in the range of percentages stems from a general misunderstanding of the phrase *déjà vu,* even by some of the earlier scientific researchers twenty or more years ago. Indeed, in today's society, people throw around the term *déjà vu* without much thought. For example, it is fairly common for someone to see or hear about an event and then say, "Wow. This is déjà vu. I had a dream that this exact same thing happened." However, dreaming about an event ahead of time is a different phenomenon known as *precognition,* which relates to the paranormal experience of extrasensory perception. To date, precognition has never been scientifically demonstrated. As Johnson explains about dreams, however,

> . . . there is usually very little "data," evidence, or documentation to confirm that a Precognition has taken place. If a person learns about some disaster and THEN [author's emphasis] tells people that he/she has foreseen it the day before, that may or may not

**Header has student's last name and page number.**

**World Wide Web source has no page numbers or paragraph numbers.**

**Use block indent of 1 inch (or ten spaces) for a quotation longer than four typed lines.**

continued >>

Gurov 3

be true, because there is usually not corroborative confirmation of what the person claims.

Thus, precognition, a phenomenon talked about frequently but one that has never held up under scientific scrutiny, is definitely not the same as déjà vu.

False memory is another phenomenon mislabeled *déjà vu*. It happens when people are convinced that certain events took place in their lives, even though the events never happened. This occurs when people have strong memories of many unrelated occurrences that suddenly come together into a whole that's very close to the current experience. It seems like a déjà vu experience. This occurs from the "converging elements of many different but related experiences. When this abstract representation, which has emerged strictly from the melding together of strongly associated elements, happens to correspond to the present experience, a déjà vu may be the outcome" (Brown, *Experience* 160). To illustrate lab-induced false memory, Brown in *Experience* cites investigations in which subjects are shown lists of words related to sleep; however, the word *sleep* itself is not on the list. In recalling

the list of words, most subjects insist that the word *sleep* was indeed on the list, which means that the memory of a word that was never there is false memory. This is exactly what happens when well-intentioned eyewitnesses believe they recall certain criminal acts even though, in fact, they never saw or experienced the events at all (159).

In the last twenty years especially, new theories have come to the fore as a result of rigorous work from psychological and medical points of view. In *Experience,* Brown surveys the literature and concludes that this relatively young field of

Introductory phrase smoothly leads into direct quotation.

Put only page number in parentheses when author is named in text.

continued >>

Gurov 4

investigation is dividing itself into four categories: (1) dual processing, (2) memory, (3) neurological, and (4) attentional. This paper briefly discusses the first and second as each relates to the third. Next, I discuss the fourth as it relates to the second.

Brain-based studies of the human sense of sight are one heavily researched theory of déjà vu that has been partially explained in the last two decades. Such studies focus on the dual pathways by which the sight of an event reaches the brain (Glenn; Carey F1). For example, the left hemisphere processes information from the right eye and the right hemisphere processes information from the left eye. The brain is incapable of storing data with respect to time and is only able to "see" events in relation to others. Each eye interprets data separately, at the same precise time. According to research, the human brain can perceive two visual stimuli at one instant as long as they are "seen" less than 25 milliseconds apart. Since the human brain is capable of interpreting both signals within this time, when events are perceived normally, they are seen and recognized by the brain as one single event (Weiten 69, 97-99, 211).

Occasionally, however, the neurological impulses that carry data from each eye to the brain are delayed. As Johnson explains, the person might be fatigued or have had his or her attention seriously distracted (as when crossing the street at a dangerous intersection). As a result, one signal may reach the brain in under 25 milliseconds, while the other signal is slowed and reaches the brain slightly more than 25 milliseconds later. Even a few milliseconds' delay makes the second incoming signal arrive late--and, without fail, the brain interprets the

*Put author and page number in parentheses when author is not named in the sentence.*

*Paragraph summarizes several pages of source material, as parenthetical citation shows.*

continued >>

stimuli as two separate events rather than one event. The person thus has the sensation of having seen the event before because the brain has recognized the milliseconds-later event as a memory.

Implanted memories is another well-researched explanation for the déjà vu phenomenon. Examples of this originate in both the natural and the lab-induced experiences of people. For instance, perhaps a person walks into the kitchen of a new friend for the first time and, although the person has never been there before, the person feels certain that he or she has. With hypnosis and other techniques, researchers could uncover that the cupboards are almost exactly like those that the person had forgotten were in the kitchen of the person's grandparents' house and that the scent of baking apple pie is identical to the smell the person loved when walking into the grandparents' home during holidays (Carey F1).

Thomas McHugh, a researcher at MIT, believes he has even discovered the specific "memory circuit" in the brain that is the source of this kind of déjà vu (Lemonick). This circuit allows people to complete memories with just a single cue. For example, you can remember much about a football game you saw even if someone just mentions the two teams involved. Sometimes, however, the circuit "misfires," and it signals that a new memory is actually part of the pattern of an old one.

Wolfradt describes a lab-induced experiment in which psychologist Larry L. Jacoby in 1989 manipulated a group of subjects so that he could implant a memory that would lead to a déjà vu experience for each of them. He arranged for his subjects to assemble in a room equipped with a screen in front. He flashed on the screen one word so quickly that no one was

continued >>

Gurov 6

consciously aware they had seen the word. Jacoby was certain, however, that the visual centers of the brain of each subject had indeed "seen" the word. Later, when he flashed the word leaving it on the screen long enough for the subjects to consciously see it, everyone indicated they had seen the word somewhere before. All the subjects were firmly convinced that the first time they had seen the word, it absolutely was not on the screen at the front of the room they were in. Some became annoyed at being asked over and over. Since Jacoby's work, lab-induced memory research has become very popular in psychology. In fact, it has been given its own name: *priming*.

Inattention, or what some researchers call "inattentional blindness," is also an extensively researched explanation for the déjà vu experience. Sometimes people can see objects without any impediment right before them but still not process the objects because they're paying attention to something else (Brown, *Experience* 181). The distraction might be daydreaming, a sudden lowering of energy, or simply being drawn to another object in the environment. As David Glenn explains in "The Tease of Memory":

> Imagine that you drive through an unfamiliar town but pay little attention because you're talking on a cellphone [sic]. If you then drive back down the same streets a few moments later, this time focusing on the landscape, you might be prone to experience déjà vu. During your second pass, the visual information is consciously processed in the hippocampus [of the brain] but feels falsely "old" because the images from your earlier drive still linger in your short term memory.

continued >>

Gurov 7

The busy lifestyle today would seem to lead to many distractions of perception and thus to frequent experiences of déjà vu; however, these are no more frequently reported than any other causes reported concerning déjà vu.

One compelling laboratory experiment studying inattention is described by Carey in "Déjà Vu: If It All Seems Familiar, There May Be a Reason." He recounts a test with many college students from Duke University in Durham, North Carolina. The students were asked to look at a group of photographs of the campus of Southern Methodist University in Dallas, Texas, that were flashed before them at a very quick speed. A small black or white cross was superimposed on each photograph, and the students were instructed to find the cross and focus on it (F6). Brown in *Experience* explains that the researchers assumed that the quick speed at which the photographs had been shown would result in no one's having noticed the background scenes. A week's time passed, and the same students were shown the pictures again, this time without the crosses. Almost all insisted that they had been to the college campus shown in the photos, which was physically impossible for that many students since they lived in Durham, North Carolina, and the college in the photographs was in Dallas, Texas (182-83). This means that the scenes in the photographs did indeed register in the visual memories of the students in spite of the quick speed and the distraction of looking only for the crosses.

The worlds of psychology and neurology have learned much since the age of paranormal interpretations of déjà vu experiences, starting around 1935. That is when rational science energetically began its disciplined investigations of

Concluding paragraph summarizes paper.

continued >>

Gurov 8

brain-based origins of the déjà vu phenomenon. Concepts

such as dual processing of sight, implanted memories, and

inattentional blindness, among other theories, have gone far in

opening the door to the possibilities of many more inventive

theories to explain incidents of déjà vu. The leading researcher

in the field today, Alan S. Brown, is among the strongest voices

urging a vast expansion of investigations into this still relatively

unexplored phenomenon. He is optimistic this will happen,

given his whimsical remark to Carlin Flora of *Psychology Today:*

"We are always fascinated when the brain goes haywire."

Gurov 9

Works
Cited
begins
on a
new page.
Double-space
throughout.

List sources in
alphabetical
order.

Divide a URL
only after a
slash.

Works Cited

Brown, Alan S. *The Déjà Vu Experience: Essays in Cognitive
    Psychology.* New York: Psychology, 2004. Print.

---. "The Déjà Vu Illusion." *Current Directions in Psychological
    Science* 13.6 (2004): 256-59. Print.

Carey, Benedict. "Déjà Vu: If It All Seems Familiar, There May
    Be a Reason." *New York Times* 14 Sept. 2004: F1+.
    *LexisNexis.* Web. 11 Nov. 2007.

Flora, Carlin. "Giving Déjà Vu Its Due." *Psychology Today*
    Mar.-Apr. 2005: 27. *Academic Search Premier.* Web.
    7 Nov. 2007.

Glenn, David. "The Tease of Memory." *Chronicle of Higher
    Education* 23 July 2004: A12. Print.

Johnson, C. "A Theory on the Déjà Vu Phenomenon." 8 Dec.
    2001. Web. 20 Nov. 2007. <http://mb-soft.com/public/
    dejavu.html>

continued >>

Gurov 10

Lemonick, Michael D. "Explaining Déjà Vu." *Time* 20 Aug. 2007.

   *Academic Search Premier.* Web. 5 Dec. 2007.

Thompson, Rebecca G., et al. "Persistent Déjà Vu: A Disorder of

   Memory." *International Journal of Geriatric Psychiatry*

   19.9 (2004): 906-07. Print.

Weiten, Wayne. *Psychology: Themes and Variations.* Belmont:

   Wadsworth, 2005. Print.

Wolfradt, Uwe. "Strangely Familiar." *Scientific American Mind*

   16.1 (2005): 32-37. *Academic Search Elite.* Web. 7 Nov. 2007.

**36**

# APA Documentation with Case Study

## 36a   What is APA documentation style?

The American Psychological Association (APA) sponsors a DOCUMENTATION system widely used in the social sciences. APA style involves two equally important features that need to appear in research papers: in-text citations and references.

For an example of a research paper that uses APA-style in-text citations in parentheses and a References list, see section 36h. As you read the paper, notice how the two requirements for crediting sources work together so that readers can learn the precise origin of the material that is quoted, paraphrased, and summarized.

## 36b  What are APA parenthetical in-text citations?

The APA-STYLE DOCUMENTATION guidelines here follow the recommendations of the *Publication Manual of the American Psychological Association,* Fifth Edition (Washington, DC: American Psychological Association, 2001) and *APA Style Guide to Electronic References* (Washington, DC: American Psychological Association, 2007). For possible updates to information, you may wish to check the APA's Web site at http://www.apastyle.org.

APA style requires parenthetical IN-TEXT CITATIONS that identify a SOURCE by the author's name (or a shortened version of the title if there is no author) and the copyright year. For readability and a good writing style, you can often incorporate the name, and sometimes the year, into your sentence. Otherwise, place this information in parentheses, located as close as possible to the material you quote, paraphrase, or summarize. Your goal is to tell readers precisely where they can find the original material.

APA style requires page numbers for DIRECT QUOTATIONS and recommends them for PARAPHRASES and SUMMARIES. Some instructors expect you to give page references for paraphrases and summaries, and others don't; so find out your instructor's preference to avoid any problems in properly crediting your sources.

Put page numbers in parentheses, using the abbreviation *p.* before a single page number and *pp.* when the material you're citing falls on more than one page. For a direct quotation from an electronic source that numbers paragraphs, give the paragraph number (or numbers). Handle paragraph numbers as you do page numbers, but use *para.* or ¶ (the symbol for paragraph) rather than *p.* or *pp.*

The APA *Publication Manual* recommends that if you refer to a work more than once in a paragraph, you give the author's name and the date at the first mention and then give only the name after that. An exception occurs if you're citing two or more works by the same author, or if two or more authors have the same last name. In such cases, each separate citation must include the date to identify which work you're citing.

## 36c  What are APA guidelines for in-text citations?

The following numbered examples show how to cite various kinds of sources in the body of your research paper. Remember, though, that you often can introduce source names, including titles when necessary, and sometimes even years, in your own sentences rather than in the parenthetical IN-TEXT CITATIONS.

## 1. Paraphrased or Summarized Source—APA

People from the Mediterranean prefer an elbow-to-shoulder distance from each other (Morris, 1977). [Author name and date cited in parentheses; note comma.]

Desmond Morris (1977) notes that people from the Mediterranean prefer an elbow-to-shoulder distance from each other. [Author name cited in text; date cited in parentheses.]

## 2. Source of a Short Quotation—APA

A recent report of reductions in SAD-related "depression in 87 percent of patients" (Binkley, 1990, p. 203) reverses the findings of earlier studies. [Author name, date, and page reference in parentheses immediately following the quotation.]

Binkley (1990) reports reductions in SAD-related "depression in 87 percent of patients" (p. 203). [Author name followed by the date in parentheses incorporated into the words introducing the quotation; page number in parentheses immediately following the quotation.]

## 3. Source of a Long Quotation (and Format of Quotation)—APA

Incorporate a direct quotation of fewer than forty words into your own sentence and enclose it in quotation marks. Place the parenthetical in-text citation after the closing quotation mark and, if the quotation falls at the end of the sentence, before the sentence-ending punctuation. When you use a quotation longer than forty words, set it off in block style indented one-half inch or five spaces from the left margin. Never enclose a set-off quotation in quotation marks because the placement in block style carries the message that the material is quoted. Place the parenthetical reference citation one space after the end punctuation of the last sentence.

### DISPLAYED QUOTATION (FORTY OR MORE WORDS)

Jet lag, with its characteristic fatigue and irregular sleep patterns, is a common problem among those who travel great distances by jet airplane to different time zones:

> Jet lag syndrome is the inability of the internal body rhythm to rapidly resynchronize after sudden shifts in the timing. For a variety of reasons, the system attempts to maintain stability and resist temporal change. Consequently, complete adjustment can often be delayed for several days—sometimes for a week—after arrival at one's destination. (Bonner, 1991, p. 72)

### 4. One Author—APA

In a parenthetical reference in APA style, a comma and a space separate a name from a year, and a year from a page reference. (Note: Examples 1 through 3 are also citations of works by one author.)

> One of his questions is "What binds together a Mormon banker in Utah with his brother, or other coreligionists in Illinois or Massachusetts?" (Coles, 1993, p. 2).

### 5. Two Authors—APA

If a work has two authors, give both names in each citation.

> One report describes 2,123 occurrences (Krait & Cooper, 2003).

> The results that Krait and Cooper (2003) report would not support the conclusions Davis and Sherman (1999) draw in their review of the literature.

When you write a parenthetical in-text citation naming two (or more) authors, use an ampersand (&) between the final two names, but write out the word *and* for any reference in your own sentence.

### 6. Three, Four, or Five Authors—APA

For three, four, or five authors, use the last names of all the authors in the first reference. In all subsequent references, use only the first author's last name followed by *et al.* (a Latin term meaning "and others"). Note that *et al.* is followed by a period and is not italicized.

> **FIRST REFERENCE**
> In one study, only 30% of the survey population could name the most commonly spoken languages in five Middle Eastern countries (Ludwig, Rodriquez, Novak, & Ehlers, 2008).

> **SUBSEQUENT REFERENCE**
> Ludwig et al. (2008) found that most Americans could identify the language spoken in Saudi Arabia.

### 7. Six or More Authors—APA

For six or more authors, name the first author followed by *et al.* in all in-text references, including the first.

> These injuries can lead to an inability to perform athletically, in addition to initiating degenerative changes at the joint level (Mandelbaum et al., 2005).

## 8. Author(s) with Two or More Works in the Same Year—APA

If you use more than one source written in the same year by the same author(s), alphabetize the works by their titles for the References list and assign letters in alphabetical order to the years—(2007a), (2007b), (2007c). Use the year-letter combination in parenthetical references. Note that a citation of two or more such works lists the years in alphabetical order.

> Most recently, Torrevillas (2007c) draws new conclusions from the results of eight experiments conducted with experienced readers (Torrevillas, 2007a, 2007b).

## 9. Two or More Authors with the Same Last Name—APA

Include first initials for every in-text citation of authors who share a last name. Use the initials appearing in the References list. (In the second example, a parenthetical citation, the name order is alphabetical, as explained in item 12.)

> R. A. Smith (2008) and C. Smith (1999) both confirm these results.

> These results have been confirmed independently (C. Smith, 1999; R. A. Smith, 2008).

## 10. Work with a Group or Corporate Author—APA

If you use a source in which the "author" is a corporation, agency, or group, an in-text reference gives that name as author. Use the full name in each citation, unless an abbreviated version of the name is likely to be familiar to your audience. In that case, use the full name and give its abbreviation at the first citation; then, use the abbreviation for subsequent citations.

> This exploration will continue into the 21st century (National Aeronautics and Space Administration [NASA], 2004). [In subsequent citations, use the abbreviated form, NASA, alone.]

## 11. Work Listed by Title—APA

If no author is named, use a shortened form of the title for in-text citations. Ignoring *A, An,* or *The,* make the first word the one by which you alphabetize the title in your References. The following example refers to an article fully titled "Are You a Day or Night Person?"

> Scientists group people as "larks" or "owls" on the basis of whether individuals are more efficient in the morning or at night ("Are You," 1989).

### 12. Reference to More Than One Source—APA

If more than one source has contributed to an idea or opinion in your paper, cite the sources alphabetically by author in one set of parentheses; separate each block of information with a semicolon, as in the following example.

> Conceptions of personal space vary among cultures (Morris, 1977; Worchel & Cooper, 1983).

### 13. Personal Communication, Including E-Mail and Other Nonretrievable Sources—APA

Telephone calls, personal letters, interviews, and e-mail messages are "personal communications" that your readers can't access or retrieve. Acknowledge personal communications in parenthetical references, but never include them in your References list at the end of your paper.

> Recalling his first summer at camp, one person said, "The proximity of 12 other kids made me—an only child with older, quiet parents—frantic for eight weeks" (A. Weiss, personal communication, January 12, 2005).

### 14. References to Retrievable Online Sources—APA

When you quote, paraphrase, or summarize an online source that is available to others, cite the author (if any) or title and the date as you would for a print source, and include the work in your References list.

> It's possible that similarity in personality is important in having a happy marriage (Luo & Clonen, 2005, p. 324).

### 15. Reference to an Online Source with No Pages—APA

If an online source doesn't provide page numbers, use the paragraph number, if available, preceded by the abbreviation *para.* It is rare, however, to number paragraphs. If you can't decipher a page or paragraph number, cite a heading if possible.

> (Anderson, 2003, para. 14)

> (Migueis, 2002, Introduction)

### 16. Source Lines for Graphics and Table Data—APA

If you use a graphic from another source or create a table using data from another source, provide a note at the bottom of the table or graphic, crediting the original author and the copyright holder. Here are examples of two source lines—one for a graphic from an article, the other for a graphic from a book.

**GRAPHIC USING DATA FROM AN ARTICLE—APA**

*Note.* The data in columns 1 and 2 are from "Advance Organizers in Advisory Reports: Selective Reading, Recall, and Perception" by L. Lagerwerf et al., 2008, *Written Communication, 25*(1), p. 68. Copyright 2008 by Sage Publications. Adapted with permission of the author.

**GRAPHIC FROM A BOOK—APA**

*Note.* From *The Road to Reality: A Complete Guide to the Laws of the Universe* (p. 270), by R. Penrose, 2005, New York: Alfred Knopf. Copyright 2004 by R. Penrose. Reprinted with permission of the publisher.

# 36d What are APA guidelines for writing an abstract?

As the APA *Publication Manual* explains, "an abstract is a brief, comprehensive summary" (p. 12) of a longer piece of writing. The APA estimates that an abstract should be no longer than about 120 words. Your instructor may require that you include an abstract at the start of a paper; if you're not sure, ask. Make the abstract accurate, objective, and exact. Actually, as you study the social sciences, you may become familiar with effective abstracts because many disciplines have online abstracts of longer sources. See 36g for guidelines on formatting an abstract page. The student paper in 36h has an abstract you can study as an example.

# 36e What are APA guidelines for content notes?

Content notes in APA-style papers add relevant information that can't be worked effectively into a text discussion. Use consecutive Arabic numerals for note numbers, both within your paper and on any separate page following the last text page of your paper. Try to arrange your sentence so that the note number falls at the end. Use a numeral raised slightly above the line of words and immediately after the final punctuation mark. See 36g for instructions on formatting the Footnotes page.

# 36f What are APA guidelines for a References list?

The REFERENCES list at the end of your research paper provides complete bibliographic information for readers who may want to access the sources you draw on for your paper.

Include in a References list all the sources you QUOTE, PARAPHRASE, or SUMMARIZE in your paper so that readers can find the same sources with reasonable effort. Never include in your References list any source that's not generally available to others (see item 13 in 36c). Quick Reference 36.1 presents general format guidelines.

## Quick Reference 36.1 ▪ ▪ ▪ ▪ ▪

### Guidelines for an APA-style References list

**TITLE**

The title is "References" (centered without quotation marks, italics, or underlining).

**PLACEMENT OF LIST**

Start a new page. Number it sequentially with the rest of the paper and place it immediately after the body of the paper.

**CONTENTS AND FORMAT**

Include all quoted, paraphrased, or summarized sources in your paper that are not personal communications, unless your instructor tells you to include all the references you have consulted, not just those you have to credit. Start each entry on a new line, and double-space all lines. APA recommends that student papers follow journal formatting by using a *hanging indent* style: The first line of each entry begins flush left at the margin, and all other lines are indented. The hanging indent makes source names and dates more prominent. Type the first line of each entry full width, and indent subsequent lines one-half inch. The easiest way to do this is using the word processor's ruler bar.

Shuter, R. (1977). A field study of nonverbal communication in Germany, Italy, and the United States. *Communication Monographs, 44,* 298–305.

**SPACING AFTER PUNCTUATION**

APA calls for one space after end-punctuation marks.

**ARRANGEMENT OF ENTRIES**

Alphabetize by the author's last name. If no author is named, alphabetize by the first significant word (ignore *A, An,* or *The*) in the title of the work.

**AUTHORS' NAMES**

Use last names, first initials, and middle initials, if any. Reverse the order for all authors' names, and use an ampersand (&) before the last author's name: Mills, J. F., & Holahan, R. H.

Give names in the order in which they appear on the work (on the title page of a book or under the title of an article or other printed work). Use a comma between each author's last name and first initial and after each complete name except the last. Use a period after the last author's name.

**DATES**

Date information follows the name information and is enclosed in parentheses. Place a period followed by one space after the closing parenthesis.

continued >>

## Quick Reference 36.1   (continued)   ■ ■ ■ ■ ■

For books, articles in journals that have volume numbers, and many other print and nonprint sources, the year of publication or production is the date to use. For articles from most general-circulation magazines and newspapers, use the year followed by a comma and then the exact date that appears on the issue (month and day for daily and weekly publications, month alone for monthly and bimonthly publications, and season for quarterly publications). Capitalize any words and use no abbreviations. Individual entries that follow show how much information to give for various sources.

### CAPITALIZATION OF TITLES
For book, article, and chapter titles, capitalize the first word, the first word after a colon between a title and subtitle, and any proper nouns. For names of journals and proceedings of meetings, capitalize the first word, all nouns, verbs, adverbs, and adjectives, and any other words four or more letters long.

### SPECIAL TREATMENT OF TITLES
Use no special treatment for titles of shorter works (poems, short stories, essays, articles). Italicize titles of longer works (books, names of newspapers or journals). If an italic typeface is unavailable, draw an unbroken line beneath the title *and* beneath the punctuation.

Don't drop any words, such as *A, An,* or *The,* from the titles of periodicals (such as newspapers, magazines, and journals).

### PUBLISHERS
Use a shortened version of the publisher's name except for an association, corporation, or university press. Drop *Co., Inc., Publishers,* and the like, but retain *Books* or *Press.*

### PLACE OF PUBLICATION
For US publishers, give the city and add the state (use the two-letter postal abbreviations listed in most dictionaries) for all US cities except Baltimore, Boston, Chicago, Los Angeles, New York, Philadelphia, and San Francisco. For publishers in other countries, give city and country spelled out; no country name is needed with Amsterdam, Jerusalem, London, Milan, Moscow, Paris, Rome, Stockholm, Tokyo, and Vienna. However, if the state or country is part of the publisher's name, omit it after the name of the city.

### ABBREVIATIONS OF MONTHS
Don't abbreviate the names of months in any context.

continued >>

## Quick Reference 36.1 (continued) ■ ■ ■ ■ ■

### PAGE NUMBERS

Use all digits, omitting none. For references to books or newspapers only, use *p.* and *pp.* before page numbers. List all discontinuous pages, with numbers separated by commas: pp. 32, 44–45, 47–49, 53.

### REFERENCES ENTRIES: BOOKS

Citations for books have four main parts: author, date, title, and publication information (place of publication and publisher). Each part ends with a period.

AUTHOR  DATE        TITLE

Wood, P. (2003). *Diversity: The invention of a concept.*

PUBLICATION INFORMATION

San Francisco: Encounter Books.

### REFERENCES ENTRIES: ARTICLES

Citations for periodical articles contain four major parts: author, date, title of article, and publication information (usually, the periodical title, volume number, and page numbers). Each part ends with a period.

AUTHOR          DATE        ARTICLE TITLE

Wood, W., Witt, M. G., & Tam, L. (2005). Changing circumstances, disrupting

                         VOLUME  PAGE
         PERIODICAL TITLE        NUMBER  RANGE

habits. *Journal of Personality and Social Psychology, 88,* 918–933.

### REFERENCES ENTRIES: ELECTRONIC AND ONLINE SOURCES

Styles for documenting electronic and online sources continue to evolve. The *APA Style Guide to Electronic References* (Washington, D.C.: American Psychological Association, 2007) is available on the APA Web page http://www.apastyle.org/elecref.html and is the best source for current guidelines on these formats. This guide updates the *Publication Guide of the American Psychological Association* (5th ed.).

When citing electronic or online sources, include the name(s) of author(s) the same way as for books and journals. Always include the publication date in parentheses after the author(s) name(s), followed by a period. Titles of books, periodicals, and whole Web sites should be italicized; titles of articles or pages in a Web site should not use italics. Articles retrieved online should always list the volume and issue number; this is a change from previous APA guidelines.

You then include retrieval information for the electronic source. For articles with DOI (Digital Object Identifier) numbers, this is simply the letters "doi" followed by a colon, then the number.

continued >>

## Quick Reference 36.1 (continued) ▪ ▪ ▪ ▪ ▪

For nearly all other references, retrieval information begins with the words "Retrieved from," sometimes followed by the date you actually retrieved it, then the URL and, occasionally, additional information, such as database names.

Here are three examples of electronic source entries. The first is for an article that does not have a DOI number. Because it is for a permanent version of the article, you don't include a date in your "retrieved from" statement.

AUTHOR       DATE                    ARTICLE TITLE

Overbye, D. (2005, June 28). Remembrance of things future: The mystery

                     ONLINE
                 NEWSPAPER TITLE       RETRIEVAL INFORMATION

of time. *The New York Times*. Retrieved from http://www.nytimes.com

Notice that the only punctuation in the URL is part of the address. Don't add a period after a URL.

The second example is for an electronic article that has a DOI number.

                      AUTHOR                    DATE      ARTICLE TITLE

Aglinta, A. K., Tantelff-Dunn, S., & Renk, K. (2007). Interpretation of teasing

                                    PUBLICATION INFORMATION

during early adolescence. *Journal of Clinical Psychology, 63*(1), 23–30,

          DOI

doi: 10.1002/jclp.20302

A third example is for an article from a Web site. Because Web sites may change, the retrieval statement includes the date retrieved as well as the URL. This example has no author.

                  ARTICLE TITLE                      DATE

Think again: Men and women share cognitive skills. (2006).

             PUBLICATION INFORMATION        RETRIEVAL INFORMATION

American Psychological Association. Retrieved January 18, 2006,

                              URL

from http://www.psychologymatters.org/thinkagain.html

The following samples of entries may appear in an APA References list. You can find others in the *Publication Manual of the American Psychological Association* or at http://www.apastyle.org. For quick help deciding which example you should follow, use the following visual directory.

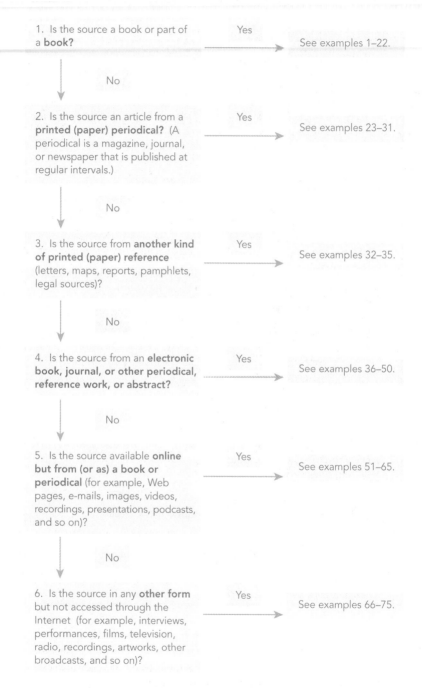

1. Is the source a book or part of a **book?**   Yes → See examples 1–22.

No ↓

2. Is the source an article from a **printed (paper) periodical?** (A periodical is a magazine, journal, or newspaper that is published at regular intervals.)   Yes → See examples 23–31.

No ↓

3. Is the source from **another kind of printed (paper) reference** (letters, maps, reports, pamphlets, legal sources)?   Yes → See examples 32–35.

No ↓

4. Is the source from an **electronic book, journal, or other periodical, reference work, or abstract?**   Yes → See examples 36–50.

No ↓

5. Is the source available **online but from (or as) a book or periodical** (for example, Web pages, e-mails, images, videos, recordings, presentations, podcasts, and so on)?   Yes → See examples 51–65.

No ↓

6. Is the source in any **other form** but not accessed through the Internet (for example, interviews, performances, films, television, radio, recordings, artworks, other broadcasts, and so on)?   Yes → See examples 66–75.

## PRINT REFERENCES—BOOKS

### 1. Book by One Author—APA

Note that all entries use the hanging indent style: The first line of an entry is flush to the left margin, and all other lines in the entry are indented one-half inch.

Bradway, B. (2002). *Pink houses and family taverns.* Bloomington: Indiana
    University Press.

### 2. Book by Two Authors—APA

Edin, K., & Kefalas, M. (2005). *Promises I can keep: Why poor women put
    motherhood before marriage.* Berkeley: University of California Press.

### 3. Book by Three or More Authors—APA

For a book by three to six authors, include all the authors' names. For a book by more than six authors, use only the first six names followed by *et al.*

Lynam, J. K., Ndiritu, C. G., & Mbabu, A. N. (2004). *Transformation of
    agricultural research systems in Africa: Lessons from Kenya.* East
    Lansing: Michigan State University Press.

### 4. Two or More Books by the Same Author(s)—APA

Arrange references by the same author chronologically, with the earlier date of publication listed first.

Jenkins, H. (1992). *Textual poachers: Television fans and participatory culture.*
    New York: Routledge.

Jenkins, H. (2006). *Convergence culture: Where old and new media collide.* New
    York: New York University Press.

### 5. Book by a Group or Corporate Author—APA

Cite the full name of the corporate author first. If the author is also the publisher, use the word *Author* as the name of the publisher.

American Psychological Association. (2001). *Publication manual of the
    American Psychological Association* (5th ed.). Washington, DC: Author.

Boston Women's Health Collective. (1998). *Our bodies, ourselves for the new
    century.* New York: Simon & Schuster.

### 6. Book with No Author Named—APA

*The Chicago manual of style* (15th ed.). (2003). Chicago: University of Chicago
    Press.

### 7. Book with an Author and an Editor—APA

Brontë, E. (2002). *Wuthering heights* (R. J. Dunn, Ed.). New York: Norton.

### 8. Translation—APA

Kundera, M. (1999). *The unbearable lightness of being* (M. H. Heim, Trans.). New York: HarperPerennial. (Original work published 1984)

### 9. Work in Several Volumes or Parts—APA

Chrisley, R. (Ed.). (2000). *Artificial intelligence: Critical concepts* (Vols. 1–4). London: Routledge.

### 10. Anthology or Edited Book—APA

Purdy, J. L., & Ruppert, J. (Eds.). (2001). *Nothing but the truth: An anthology of Native American literature.* Upper Saddle River, NJ: Prentice Hall.

### 11. One Selection from an Anthology or an Edited Book—APA

Give the author of the selection first. The word *In* introduces the larger work from which the selection is taken. Note that names are inverted only in the author position; in all other circumstances, they are written in standard form.

Trujillo, L. (2004). Balancing act. In R. Moreno & M. H. Mulligan (Eds.), *Borderline personalities: A new generation of Latinas dish on sex, sass, and cultural shifting* (pp. 61–72). New York: HarperCollins.

### 12. Selection from a Work Already Listed in References—APA

Provide full information for the already-cited anthology (second example below), along with information about the individual selection. Put entries in alphabetical order.

Bond, R. (2004). "The night train at Deoli." In A. Chaudhuri (Ed.), *The Vintage book of modern Indian literature* (pp. 415–418). New York: Vintage Books.

Chaudhuri, A. (Ed.). (2004). *The Vintage book of modern Indian literature.* New York: Vintage Books.

### 13. Signed Article in a Reference Book—APA

Use *In* to introduce the larger work from which the selection is taken.

Burnbam, J. C. (1996). Freud, Sigmund. In B. B. Wolman (Ed.), *The encyclopedia of psychiatry, psychology, and psychoanalysis* (p. 220). New York: Holt.

## 14. Unsigned Article in a Reference Book—APA

Ireland. (2002). In *The new encyclopaedia Britannica: Macropaedia* (15th ed.,
Vol. 21, pp. 997–1018). Chicago: Encyclopaedia Britannica.

## 15. Second or Subsequent Edition—APA

A book usually doesn't announce that it's a first edition. However, after the first edition, the edition number appears on the title page. In your entry, place the abbreviated information (*2nd ed., 3rd ed.,* and so on) after the title and in parentheses.

Gibaldi, J. (2003). *MLA handbook for writers of research papers* (6th ed.). New
York: Modern Language Association.

## 16. Introduction, Preface, Foreword, or Afterword—APA

If you're citing an introduction, preface, foreword, or afterword, give its author's name first. After the year, give the name of the part cited. If the writer of the material you're citing is not the author of the book, use the word *In* and the author's name before the title of the book.

Hesse, D. (2004). Foreword. In D. Smit, *The end of composition studies*
(pp. ix–xiii). Carbondale: Southern Illinois University Press.

## 17. Unpublished Dissertation or Essay—APA

Stuart, G.A. (2006). *Exploring the Harry Potter book series: A study of adolescent
reading motivation.* Unpublished doctoral dissertation, Utah State
University.

## 18. Reprint of an Older Book—APA

O'Brien, F. (1998). *At Swim-Two-Birds.* Normal, IL: Dalkey Archive Press.
(Original work published 1939)

You can find republishing information on the copyright page.

## 19. Book in a Series—APA

Give the title of the book but not of the whole series.

Goldman, D. J. (1995). *Women writers and World War I.* New York: Macmillan.

## 20. Book with a Title Within a Title—APA

Never italicize a title within a title, even though it would appear in italic typeface if it were by itself.

Lumiansky, R. M., & Baker, H. (Eds.). (1968). *Critical approaches to six major English works:* Beowulf *through* Paradise Lost. Philadelphia: University of Pennsylvania Press.

### 21. Government Publication—APA

Use the complete name of a government agency as author when no specific person is named.

U.S. Congress. House Subcommittee on Health and Environment of the Committee on Commerce. (1999). *The nursing home resident protection amendments of 1999* (99-0266-P). Washington, DC: U.S. Government Printing Office.

U.S. Senate Special Committee on Aging. (1998). *The risk of malnutrition in nursing homes* (98-0150-P). Washington, DC: U.S. Government Printing Office.

### 22. Published Proceedings of a Conference—APA

Rocha, L., Yaeger, L., Bedau, M., Floreano, D., Goldstone, R. & Vespignani, A. (Eds.). (2006, June). *Artificial life X: Proceedings of the tenth international conference on the simulation and synthesis of living systems.* Bloomington, IN. Cambridge: MIT Press.

### PRINT REFERENCES—PERIODICALS
### 23. Article in a Journal with Continuous Pagination—APA

Give the volume number, italicized after the journal title. In the 2001 edition of the APA style manual, only the volume number appears. The new (2007) APA style for electronic references directs writers also to include the issue number in parentheses, immediately after the volume number. We have followed that new practice in the example below.

Tyson, P. (1998). The psychology of women. *Journal of the American Psychoanalytic Association, 46*(3), 361–364.

### 24. Article in a Journal That Pages Each Issue Separately—APA

Give the volume number, italicized with the journal title. Give the issue number in parentheses; don't italicize it and leave no space before it. Note that the new APA practice now uses this style for journals with continuous pagination, too (see item 23).

Adler-Kassner, L., & Estrem, H. (2003). Rethinking research writing: Public literacy in the composition classroom. *WPA: Writing Program Administration, 26*(3), 119–131.

### 25. Signed Article in a Weekly or Biweekly Periodical—APA

Give year, month, and day for a periodical published every week or every two weeks. Don't use the abbreviation *p.* (or *pp.*) for magazines or journals.

Brink, S. (2005, March 28). Eat this now! *U.S. News & World Report,* 56–58.

### 26. Signed Article in a Monthly or Bimonthly Periodical—APA

Give the year and month(s) for a periodical published every month or every other month. Insert the volume number, italicized with the periodical title. Put the issue number in parentheses; don't italicize it, and don't put a space before it.

Fallows, J. (2008, January/February). The $1.4 trillion question. *The Atlantic, 301*(1), 36–48.

### 27. Unsigned Article in a Weekly or Monthly Periodical—APA

The price is wrong. (2003, August 2). *The Economist, 368,* 58–59.

### 28. Signed Article in a Daily Newspaper—APA

Use the abbreviation *p.* (or *pp.* for more than one page) for items from newspapers.

Green, P. (2008, January 31). The slow life picks up speed. *The New York Times,* p. D1.

### 29. Unsigned Article in a Daily Newspaper—APA

Oscars ready plans to deal with strike. (2008, January 31). *The Denver Post,* p. B3.

### 30. Editorial, Letter to the Editor, or Review—APA

Primary considerations. (2008, January 27). [Editorial]. *The Washington Post,* p. B6.

Finanger, E. (2008, February). [Letter to the editor]. *Outside,* 14.

Shenk, D. (2003, Spring). Toolmaker, brain builder. [Review of the book *Beyond Big Blue: Building the computer that defeated the world chess champion*]. *The American Scholar, 72,* 150–152.

### 31. Article in a Looseleaf Collection of Reprinted Articles—APA

Hayden, T. (2002). The age of robots. In E. Goldstein (Ed.), *Applied Science 2002. SIRS 2002,* Article 66. (Reprinted from *U.S. News & World Report,* pp. 44–50, 2001, April 23).

## OTHER PRINT REFERENCES

### 32. Published and Unpublished Letters—APA

In the APA system, unpublished letters are considered personal communication inaccessible to general readers, so they don't appear in the References list. Personal communications are cited only in the body of the paper (see also item 66).

Williams, W. C. (1935). Letter to his son. In L. Grunwald & S. J. Adler (Eds.), *Letters of the century: America 1900–1999* (pp. 225–226). New York: Dial Press.

### 33. Map or Chart—APA

*Colorado Front Range Mountain Bike Topo Map* [Map]. (2001). Nederland, CO: Latitude 40.

### 34. Report or Pamphlet—APA

National Commission on Writing in America's Schools and Colleges. (2003). *The neglected "R": The need for a writing revolution* [Report]. New York: College Board.

Student Environmental Coalition. (2005). *Reduce, reuse, recycle* [Brochure]. Normal, IL: Author.

### 35. Legal Source—APA

Include the name of the case, the citation (usually a volume number, publication title, and page) or a record number, the name of the court deciding the case (if other than the US Supreme Court), and the year of the decision. The following example shows the citation for a published case. See Appendix D of the APA *Publication Manual* for other types of legal citations.

Brown v. Board of Educ., 347 U.S. 483 (1954).

## ELECTRONIC AND ONLINE SOURCES

In general, APA recommends giving the same information, in the same order, as you would for a print source: author name(s), date of publication, title, and publication information (title, volume, issue, pages). Then you add as much retrieval information as others will need to locate the source. This retrieval information may include a DOI number (see example 39) or it may consist of a "Retrieved from" statement along with a URL. In certain cases, you may also need to include the date you retrieved the information.

- DOI (Direct Object Identifier): These numerical codes are sometimes assigned to online journal articles and are typically located on the first page of the online article or included in the database. The DOI for an article will be the same even if the article appears on many different Web sites.

As a result, you don't use a URL or a "retrieved from" statement if a source contains a DOI. Include the number after the publication information. Note: This is a change from earlier APA formats.

- URL: You should include the full URL for most works accessed online, including any articles that don't have a DOI. If the material is only available by search or subscription, include the URL of the home page up to the first slash. If a URL must be divided on two or more lines, only break the address before slashes or punctuation marks (except within "http://"). Don't use a hyphen, underlining, italics, angle brackets, or an end period.

- Databases: A retrieval line is not needed for materials located on widely available databases like library subscription services. If, however, the source is difficult to locate, include the name of the database in the retrieval line.

- Retrieval date: Include the date you retrieved the information only if the item does not have a publication date, is from an online reference book, or is likely to be changed in the future (such as a prepublication version of an article, a Web page, or a Wiki). Note: This is a change from the previous APA style. APA recommends citing the "archival" or permanent version of a source whenever possible. Usually, an archival version is one that either has appeared in print, has a volume and issue number, or has a specific publication date. APA has determined that retrieval dates are unnecessary for archival versions.

Treat information from an online source that your readers can't readily retrieve for themselves—for example, an e-mail message—as a personal communication. Never include it in your References list; instead, cite it in the text with a parenthetical notation saying it's a personal communication. (Also see example 66.) If you have a scholarly reason to cite a message from a newsgroup, forum, or electronic mailing list that is available in an electronic archive, then see example 52 or 53.

### ELECTRONIC BOOKS

### 36. Entire Electronic Book—APA

Provide information about the print version, if available. The retrieval statement gives the specific URL of the work.

Adams, H. (1918). *The education of Henry Adams.* New York: Houghton Mifflin.
　　Retrieved from http://www.columbia.edu/acis/bartleby/159/index/html

### 37. Chapter from Electronic Book—APA

Gembris, H. (2006). The development of musical abilities. In R. Colwell (Ed).
　　*MENC handbook of musical cognition and development.* New York:
　　Oxford University Press (pp.124–164). Retrieved from Ebrary database
　　at http://site.ebrary.com.bianca.penlib.du.edu/

In this example, the name of the database (Ebrary) is given, along with the initial part of the URL where the book was specifically found.

### 38. Thesis or Dissertation—APA

Stuart, G. A. (2006). *Exploring the Harry Potter book series: A study of adolescent reading motivation.* Retrieved from ProQuest Digital Dissertations. (AAT 3246355)

The number in parentheses at the end is the accession number.

### ELECTRONIC JOURNALS
### 39. Article with DOI Assigned—APA

Gurung, R., & Vespia, K. (2007). Looking good, teaching well? Linking liking, looks, and learning. *Teaching of Psychology, 34*(1), 5-10. doi: 10.1207/s15328023top3401_2

### 40. Article with No DOI Assigned—APA

Pollard, R. (2002). Evidence of a reduced home field advantage when a team moves to a new stadium. *Journal of Sports Sciences 20*(12), 969–974. Retrieved from http://0-find.galegroup.com.bianca.penlib.du.edu:80 /itx/start.do?prodId=AONE

No retrieval date is included because the final version of the article is being referenced.

### 41. In-press Article—APA

*In-press* means that an article has been accepted for publication but has not yet been published in its final form. Therefore, there is no publication date, and the retrieved from statement includes a date.

George, S. (In press). How accurately should we estimate the anatomical source of exhaled nitric oxide? *Journal of Applied Physiology.* doi:10.1152/japplphysiol.00111.2008. Retrieved February, 2008 from http://jap.physiology.org/papbyrecent.shtml

### OTHER ELECTRONIC PERIODICALS
### 42. Newspaper Article—APA

Wilson, J. (2005, March 5). EPA fights waste site near river. *Los Angeles Times.* Retrieved from http://www.latimes.com/news/science/environment /la-me-moab05.html

### 43. Online Magazine Content Not Found in Print Version—APA

Shulman, M. (2008, January 23). 12 diseases that altered history. [Online exclusive]. *U.S. News and World Report*. Retrieved January 28, 2007, from http://health.usnews.com/articles/health/2008/01/03/12-diseases-that-altered-history.html

### 44. Web Page or Article on Web Site—APA

Think again: Men and women share cognitive skills. (2006). *American Psychological Association*. Retrieved January 18, 2006, from http://www.psychologymatters.org/thinkagain.html

### ELECTRONIC REFERENCE MATERIALS
### 45. Online Encyclopedia—APA

Turing test. (2008). In *Encyclopædia Britannica*. Retrieved February 9, 2008, from http://www.britannica.com/bps/topic/609757/Turing-test

Because the reference is to a work that may change, a retrieval date is included.

### 46. Online Dictionary—APA

Asparagus. (n.d.). *Merriam-Webster's online dictionary*. Retrieved February 9, 2008, from http://dictionary.reference.com/browse/asparagus

### 47. Online Handbook—APA

Gembris, H. (2006). The development of musical abilities. In R. Colwell (Ed). *MENC handbook of musical cognition and development*. New York: Oxford University Press. 124–164. Retrieved October 8, 2007, from http://0-site.ebrary.com.bianca.penlib.du.edu/lib/udenver/Doc?id=10160594

### 48. Wiki—APA

Machine learning. (n.d.). Retrieved January 5, 2008, from Artificial Intelligence Wiki: http://www.ifi.unizh.ch/ailab/aiwiki/aiw.cgi

Note that (n.d.) means "no date."

### ELECTRONIC ABSTRACTS
### 49. Abstract from Secondary Source—APA

Walther, J.B., Van Der Heide, B., Kim, S., Westerman, D., & Tong, S. (2008). The role of friends' appearance and behavior on evaluations of individuals on Facebook: Are we known by the company we keep? *Human Communication Research 34*(1), 28–49. Abstract retrieved April 20, 2008 from PsycINFO database.

### 50. Abstract Submitted for Meeting or Poster Session—APA

Wang, H. (2007). Dust storms originating in the northern hemisphere of Mars.
AGU 2007 Fall Meeting. Abstract retrieved from http://www.agu.org
/meetings/fm07/?content=program

## OTHER ELECTRONIC REFERENCES

### 51. Personal or Professional Web Site—APA

Hesse, Doug. (2008, November). Home page. Retrieved November 21, 2008, from
http://http://portfolio.du.edu/dhesse

Association for the Advancement of Artificial Intelligence. (2008, March).
Retrieved March 17, 2008, from http://www.aaai.org

Because material on a Web site may change, use a retrieved from date.

### 52. Message on a Newsgroup, Online Forum, or Discussion Group—APA

Boyle, F. (2002, October 11). Psyche: Cemi field theory: The hard problem made
easy [Msg 1]. Message posted to news://sci.psychology.consciousness

### 53. Message on an Electronic Mailing List (Listserv)—APA

Haswell, R. (2005, October 17). A new graphic/text interface. Message posted
to Writing Program Administrators electronic mailing list, archived at
http://lists.asu.edu/archives/wpa-l.html

APA advises using *electronic mailing list,* as Listserv is the name of a specific
software.

### 54. Course Home Page—APA

St. Germain, S. (2003, Summer). Myths and fairytales: From *Inanna* to *Edward
Scissorhands.* Retrieved February 20, 2005, from http://www.public.iastate
.edu/~sgermain/531.homepage.html

### 55. Blog (Web Log) Post—APA

McLemee, S. (2008, January 1). To whom it may concern. Message posted to
http://www.artsjournal.com/quickstudy/

### 56. Video Web Log Post—APA

APA treats every video posted online as a Video Web log, which suggests a regular series of postings. In fact, many videos are not produced in Web log format. Still, we present the APA format. Also see 59, for online television
programs or movies.

Tobias, R. (2008, February 7). *Ranching the new West*. [Video file]. Video posted to http://www.lifeonterra.com/

Wesch, M. (2007, January 31). *Web 2.0 . . . the machine is us/ing us*. [Video file]. Video posted to http://www.youtube.com/watch?v=6gmP4nk0EOE

### 57. Online Digital Recording—APA

Komunyakaa, Y. (2005). My father's love letters. Retrieved March 7, 2005, from the Academy of American Poets Web site: http://www.poets.org /poems/poems.cfm?prmID=2065

### 58. Audio Podcast—APA

Business marketing with podcast: What marketing professionals should know (2005, October 13). *Podblaze*. Podcast retrieved http://business.podblaze.com/

### 59. Online Television Program—APA

If producers or directors can be identified, list them in the author position. Include the episode title, if any, and the title of the series. If it is a one-time program, list only the title.

Bender, J. (Director/Producer). (2008, January 30). The beginning of the end. *Lost*. Video retrieved February 1, 2008, from http://dynamic.abc.go.com /streaming/landing

### 60. Online Advertisement—APA

Samsung. (2005, November). [Advertisement]. Retrieved from http://rollingstone.com

### 61. Computer Software or Video Game—APA

Provide an author name, if available. Standard software (Microsoft Word) and program languages (C++) don't need to be given in the References list.

*Guitar hero III: Legends of rock*. (2007). [Video game]. Santa Monica: Activision.

### 62. Brochure—APA

US Department of Agriculture. (2007). *Organic foods and labels*. [Brochure]. Retrieved December 8, 2008, from http://www.ams.usda.gov/nop /Consumers/brochure.html

### 63. Policy Brief—APA

Haskins, R., Haskins, R., Paxson, C., & Donahue, E. (2006). *Fighting obesity in the public schools*. Retrieved from http://www.brookings.edu/~/media /Files/rc/papers/2006/spring_childrenfamilies_haskins/20060314foc.pdf

### 64. Presentation Slides—APA

Alaska Conservation Solutions. (2006). *Montana Global Warming* [PowerPoint slides]. Retrieved from http://www.alaskaconservationsolutions.com/acs /presentations.html

### 65. Graphs, Maps, Other Images—APA

New York Times Online. (2005, September 24). *Hurricane Rita.* [Interactive map]. Retrieved from http://www.nytimes.com/packages/html/national /20050923_RITA_GRAPHIC/index.html

### OTHER NONPRINT REFERENCES
### 66. Interview—APA

In APA style, a personal interview is considered personal communication and is not included in the References list. Cite the interview in the text with a parenthetical notation saying that it's a personal communication.

Randi Friedman (personal communication, June 30, 2007) endorses this view.

Because a published interview is recoverable by readers, treat it as you would a journal or magazine article, depending on its place of publication.

Zoglin, R. (2003, December 15). Ten questions for Oprah Winfrey. *Time,* 8.

### 67. Lecture, Speech, or Address—APA

Kennedy, J. F. (1960, September 12). Speech to the Greater Houston Ministerial Association, Rice Hotel, Houston, TX.

### 68. Motion Picture—APA

Capra, F. (Director/Producer). (1934). *It happened one night* [Motion picture]. United States: Columbia Pictures.

Capra, F. (Director/Producer). (1999). *It happened one night* [Videocassette]. (Original motion picture released 1934)

Madden, J. (Director), Parfitt, D., Gigliotti, D., Weinstein, H., Zwick, E., & Norman, M. (Producers). (2003). *Shakespeare in love* [DVD]. (Original motion picture released 1998)

### 69. Music Recording—APA

Smetana, B. (1975). *My country* [Recorded by the Czech Philharmonic Orchestra with K. Anserl conducting]. [Record]. London: Vanguard Records. (1975)

Springsteen, B. (2002). Lonesome day. On *The rising* [CD]. New York: Columbia Records.

Radiohead. (2007). Jigsaw falling into place. On *Rainbows* [MP3]. Radiohead.

### 70. Live Performance—APA

Miller, A. (Author), & McLean, C. (Director). (2005, September 27). *All my sons* [Theatrical performance]. Center for the Performing Arts, Normal, IL.

### 71. Work of Art, Photograph, or Musical Composition—APA

Cassatt, M. (1891). *La toilette* [Artwork]. Chicago: Art Institute of Chicago.

Mydans, C. (1999, October 21–November 28). *General Douglas MacArthur landing at Luzon, 1945* [Photograph]. New York: Soho Triad Fine Art Gallery.

Schubert, F. (1822). *Unfinished symphony* [Musical composition].

### 72. Radio or Television Broadcast—APA

Burns, K. (Writer/Producer), & Barnes, P. (Producer). (1999, November 8). *Not for ourselves alone: The story of Elizabeth Cady Stanton and Susan B. Anthony* [Television broadcast]. New York and Washington, DC: Public Broadcasting Service.

If you're citing a television series produced by and seen on only one station, cite its call letters.

### 73. Information Services—APA

Chiang, L. H. (1993). *Beyond the language: Native Americans' nonverbal communication.* (ERIC Document Reproduction Service No. ED368540)

### 74. Advertisement—APA

Swim at home. (2005). [Advertisement]. *The American Scholar 74*(2), 2.

### 75. Images—APA

If you're reproducing an image in your paper, follow the guidelines for graphics in item 16 in 37c. Include the citation in the body of your paper. If you're only referring to an image, cite the photographer or illustrator (if known), the title (or a brief description of the image), and source information.

Arthur Miller in 1961. (2005). [Photograph]. *The American Scholar 74*(2), 123.

## 36g   What are APA format guidelines for research papers?

Ask whether your instructor has instructions for preparing a final draft. If not, you can use the APA guidelines here.

### GENERAL INSTRUCTIONS—APA

Use 8 1/2-by-11-inch white paper. The APA *Publication Manual* recommends double-spacing for a final manuscript of a student research paper. Set at least a one-inch margin on the left (slightly more if you submit your paper in a binder) and leave no less than one inch on the right and at the bottom.

Leave one-half inch from the top edge of the paper to the title-and-page-number line (*header*). Leave another one-half inch (or one inch from the top edge of the paper) before the next line on the page, whether that's a heading (such as "Abstract" or "Notes") or a line of your paper.

**Alert:** Most word-processing programs set the top and bottom margins at one inch as their default. Also, they generally set the "header" function at a default of one-half inch. Therefore, formatting the margins for your paper is probably less troublesome than it might seem. You simply need to check the default settings. ●

Use indents of one-half inch for the first line of all paragraphs, except in an abstract, the first line of which isn't indented. Don't justify the right margin. Indent footnotes one-half inch.

### ORDER OF PARTS—APA

Number all pages consecutively. Use this order for the parts of your paper:

1. Title page
2. Abstract (if required)
3. Body of the paper
4. References
5. Appendixes, if any
6. Footnotes, if any
7. Attachments, if any (questionnaires, data sheets, or other material your instructor asks you to include)

### TITLE-AND-PAGE-NUMBER LINE FOR ALL PAGES—APA

Use a title-and-page-number line on all pages of your paper. Leaving a margin of one-half inch from the top edge of the paper, type the title (use a shortened version if necessary), leave a five-character space, and then type the page number. End the title-and-page-number line one inch from the right edge of the paper. Ask whether your instructor wants you to include your last name in this title-and-page-number line. The "header" feature on a word-processing program will help you create the title-and-page-number line easily.

## TITLE PAGE—APA

Use a separate title page. On it, begin with the title-and-page-number line described above, using the numeral *1* for this first page. Then, center the complete title vertically and horizontally on the page. Use two or more double-spaced lines if the title is long. Don't italicize or underline the title or enclose it in quotation marks. On the next line, center your name, and below that center the course title and section, your professor's name, and the date.

🚫 **Alerts:** (1) Use the following guidelines for capitalizing the title of your own paper and for capitalizing titles you mention in the body of your paper. (For capitalization of titles in the References list, see Quick Reference 36.1.)

(2) Use a capital letter for the first word of your title and for the first word of a subtitle, if any. Start every noun, pronoun, verb, adverb, and adjective with a capital letter. Capitalize each main word in a hyphenated compound word (two or more words used together to express one idea): *Father-in-Law, Self-Consciousness.*

(3) Don't capitalize articles (*a, an, the*) unless one of the other capitalization rules applies. Don't capitalize prepositions and conjunctions unless they are four or more letters long. Don't capitalize the word *to* used in an infinitive. ●

## ABSTRACT—APA

See 36d for advice about what to include in an abstract of your paper. Type the abstract on a separate page, using the numeral *2* in the title-and-page-number line. Center the word *Abstract* one inch from the top of the paper. Don't italicize or underline it or enclose it in quotation marks. Double-space below this title, and then start your abstract, double-spacing it. Don't indent the first line.

## SET-OFF QUOTATIONS—APA

Set off (display in BLOCK-STYLE form) quotations of forty words or more. Double-space to start a new line for the quoted words, indenting each line of the (double-spaced) quotation one-half inch or five spaces from the left margin. Don't enclose the quoted words in quotation marks.

If you're quoting part of a paragraph or one complete paragraph, don't indent the first line more than one-half inch. But if you quote two or more paragraphs, indent the first line of the second and subsequent paragraphs one inch from the text margin.

When the quotation is finished, leave one space after the sentence-ending punctuation, and then give the parenthetical citation. Begin a new line to resume your own words.

REFERENCES LIST—APA

Start a new page for your References list immediately after the end of the body of your paper. Use a title-and-page-number line. Drop down one inch from the top of the paper and center the word *References.* Don't italicize, underline, or put it in quotation marks. Double-space below it. Start the first line of each entry at the left margin, and indent any subsequent lines one-half inch from the left margin. Use this "hanging indent" style unless your instructor prefers a different one. Double-space within each entry and between entries.

NOTES—APA

Whenever you use a content note in your paper (36e), try to arrange your sentence so that the note number falls at the end. The ideal place for a note number is after the sentence-ending punctuation. Use a numeral raised slightly above the line of words and immediately after the final punctuation mark.

Put any notes on a separate page after the last page of your References list. Use a title-and-page-number line. Then, center the word *Footnotes* one inch from the top of the paper. Don't italicize or underline it or put it in quotation marks.

On the next line, indent one-half inch and begin the note. Raise the note number slightly (you can use the superscript feature in your word-processing program), and then start the words of your note leaving no space. If the note is more than one typed line, don't indent any line after the first. Double-space throughout.

# 36h A student's APA-style research paper

Shawn Hickson wrote the following research paper in response to an assignment calling for a research paper about an interesting aspect of contemporary life that psychologists have studied.

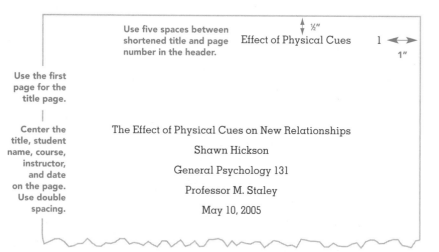

Use five spaces between shortened title and page number in the header.

Effect of Physical Cues    1

½"

1"

Use the first page for the title page.

Center the title, student name, course, instructor, and date on the page. Use double spacing.

The Effect of Physical Cues on New Relationships

Shawn Hickson

General Psychology 131

Professor M. Staley

May 10, 2005

↑ 1" ↕ ½"
Effect of Physical Cues 2 ←→
1"

Abstract

**Place abstract, if required, on the second page.** Communication via the Internet has allowed people to form friendships and relationships in new ways. Research shows that individuals respond to new acquaintances at least partly according to how attractive they perceive the new friends to be. The absence of physical cues in Internet chat rooms or e-mail discussions means that people form impressions that are less affected by superficial factors. As the Internet changes, however, these differences may diminish.

Double-space

←→
1"

---

Effect of Physical Cues 3

The Effect of Physical Cues on New Relationships

Over the past 20 years, the Internet has enabled people to meet others from around the world with a few simple keystrokes. Occasionally, these interactions extend beyond the confines of chat rooms and e-mail discussions, so that individuals arrange to meet in person. Of course, people have learned to be cautious because others online can easily misrepresent themselves and their intentions. Nonetheless, lasting friendships, romances, and even marriages have resulted from first interactions that have happened online. Surprisingly, research shows that compared with people who meet face to face, those who meet on the Internet develop a greater liking for each other (McKenna, Green, & Gleason, 2003). This result is an example of a larger phenomenon: The

APA STYLE: 1-inch margins; double-space throughout

INTRODUCTION

APA-STYLE IN-TEXT CITATION: Doesn't require page numbers for a paraphrase or summary; check whether your instructor prefers that you include them

continued >>

(Proportions shown in this paper are adjusted to fit space limitations of this book. Follow actual dimensions discussed in this book and your instructor's directions.)

THESIS
STATEMENT:
Gives paper's
focus

presence or absence of physical characteristics during first

meetings can influence how people respond to each other.

FIRST
HEADING

Judging People by Appearances

It can be troubling to know that something as shallow as

PARA-
GRAPH 2:
Provides
background
information

someone's physical attractiveness can affect how people treat

that person. However, the truth is that even if people do not

mean to judge others based on their appearance, they tend to

APA-STYLE
INTEGRATED
CITATION:
Author name
cited in text;
date cited in
parentheses

do so. Dion, Berscheid, and Walster (1972) showed research

participants pictures of stereotypically attractive and

unattractive individuals and then asked them to judge the

people in the photographs according to several personality

traits. The researchers found that the more attractive a person

was judged to be, the more desirable traits that person was

judged to have. For example, people might believe that

beautiful women are smarter or that handsome men are more

clever. Several studies found that individuals assume that

attractive people will agree with them more often than those

who are unattractive; they assume that the attractive person

will be more like them (Miyake & Zuckerman, 1993).

PARA-
GRAPH 3:
Provides
further
examples
of thesis

Even when people are young, appearance colors how

others perceive them. Studies of preschoolers show that both

peers and teachers treat children differently on the basis of

their physical appearances. Both expect attractive children to

be more active socially, and teachers believe that attractive

children have more academic potential (Kachel, 1996). Perhaps

more astounding, some controversial research shows that

children's physical appearances may affect how their very own

parents treat them (Bakalar, 2005).

continued >>

Effect of Physical Cues    5

Attractiveness has a different importance for men and women. While both sexes value physical attractiveness in brief relationships, men tend to view it as vital in long-term relationships. In contrast, women tend to regard other qualities more highly, especially financial stability and high social status (Singh, 2004).

PARA-GRAPH 4: Provides information and bridges to next paragraph

However, for men and women alike, physical cues at the first meeting can shape not only impressions but also behaviors. Snyder, Tanke, and Berscheid (1977) showed male participants a picture of either an attractive or an unattractive female and then asked the men to rate her personality traits. Results of this initial rating were very similar with those obtained by Dion et al. (1972). Snyder's group next took the study one step further. Each male participant then had a phone conversation with a female participant who he thought was the female from the picture. In these conversations, men treated their phone partners as if the women possessed the characteristics they believed went along with the photograph. However, the men really knew nothing about the women; they had assigned the women traits simply on the basis of a photograph. Even more interesting, women responded in a manner that was consistent with the images that were being projected onto them. Attractive women who were treated as if they were unattractive actually behaved as if they were, and vice versa. What happened was a clear example of a self-fulfilling prophecy (Snyder et al., 1977). Judgments based on appearance clouded other realities.

PARA-GRAPH 5: Summarizes research findings

Replaces names with et al. because this is second reference to same work with multiple authors

Meeting on the Internet

Meeting people online, especially through e-mail or in a chat room, obviously differs from meeting them face to face

SECOND HEADING

Effect of Physical Cues    6

PARA-
GRAPH 6:
Explains
research
found on the
Internet

because there are no physical cues, only other people's words. Do people meeting in that environment engage one another differently? A study conducted by McKenna et al. (2003) suggests that they do. McKenna and colleagues divided participants into two groups: an experimental group and a control group. All participants had two separate conversations, one in person and the other online. Both conversations took place with the same person. Those in the control group knew this, but those in the experimental group believed they were talking with two different people. Participants in both groups

Creates
clarity by
using
letters in
parentheses
to identify
factors

then rated the quality of the interactions on three factors: (a) the quality of the conversations, (b) the degree to which they felt they had gotten to know the other person, and (c) how well they liked the other person in general. For the control groups, the ratings were similar in all categories, for both in-person and online conversations. However, differences emerged with the participants who thought they had been interacting with two different people, not the same person: They consistently rated the Internet partner higher in all three categories.

PARA-
GRAPH 7:
Interprets
findings
summarized
in previous
paragraph

One probable explanation for this occurrence is that Internet interactions do away with traditional physical judgments. Attractiveness, extreme shyness, speech impediments, and many other superficial factors can hinder people from expressing their true selves and accepting others who are deficient in one area or another (McKenna et al., 2003). Because early judgments determine how two people will interact, a physical meeting makes it harder for some individuals to become comfortable and disclose themselves at the same level as they would in a situation where physical cues don't matter.

continued >>

Effect of Physical Cues    7

By the time people engage in online romantic relationships, according to researcher Malin Sveningsson (2002), they have already established a written relationship based on common interests. They know each other on a basis other than that of physical characteristics. Most people who enter chat rooms do so with the hope of making "contact with people, getting into a rewarding discussion, or just small-talking and having a good time in general" (p. 49). Those who meet on Internet chat sites or electronic mailing lists nearly always come together over a shared interest. A chat room frequenter named Richard explained his reasons for taking part in online conversations: "When you enter a place like that, you just want somebody to talk to . . . so you actively [look] for people who [have] something to say. And all the time you [make] comments just to find someone who [has] something to tell" (p. 50). Women and men are nearly equal in their use of the Internet for purposes of community. The Cyber Dialogue group found that about 27% of women and 31% of men first went to the Internet to "join an online community" and that 85% of women and 82% of men came to believe that "the Internet community is an important part" of their lives (Hawfield & Lyons, 1998). It appears, then, that the primary motivation for both men and women is not physical but rather communicative.

Attractiveness is hardly the only physical quality by which men and women judge others. Broad features of identity such as race, gender, and ethnicity can also trigger uninformed responses. Researcher Lisa Nakamura (2002) found that when a person's race is revealed on the Internet, he or she can be just as subject to prejudicial assumptions as if the

PARA-GRAPH 8: Explains interests of people meeting online

APA-STYLE IN-TEXT CITATION: Requires page number for direct quotation; uses *p.* not *page*

Shawn uses brackets in quotation to show that she (not the speaker) has altered wording to improve clarity

Uses statistics to illustrate example

PARA-GRAPH 9: Gives other factors that influence relationship

continued >>

reality had been revealed face to face. Because of this, some people online deliberately try to mask their race or sex. They want others to judge them by what they say and think rather than by how they look, especially in a first encounter.

PARA-GRAPH 10: Explains how increased use of images and sounds changes nature of online meetings

Whether Internet communication will continue to support first meetings that occur purely in writing is uncertain. With the increased use of digital images and audio, the Internet has begun to provide more and more physical cues. Participants in chat rooms tend to request images earlier as a sign of interest. People can post false photographs or videos, of course, but deception complicates any desired face-to-face meeting later on. Further, the sound of a person's voice shapes others'

APA-STYLE IN-TEXT CITATION: Includes paragraph or screen number for direct quotation from online source without numbered pages

perceptions. When voice communication over the Internet becomes more prevalent, it is likely that our stereotypical notions will return. Dr. Clifford Nass of Stanford University has predicted that when voice becomes a part of online interaction, people will "apply gender stereotypes" (Eisenberg, 2000, para. 6). Nass says that people tend to interpret the female voice as being "less accurate," with deeper male voices projecting authority. Some voices are perceived as more attractive than others, too.

## Conclusions

CONCLU-SIONS: Final segment summarizes main points and looks to the future

Research on Internet relationships suggests that communication without visual cues can increase people's acceptance of one another. In face-to-face meetings, people form impressions based solely on physical appearance, impressions that influence both the way they treat others and the way those people respond. People who are treated well, for example, tend to take on positive characteristics. Because Internet conversations rely more heavily on the quality of

continued >>

Effect of Physical Cues    9

communication than on superficial factors, meeting online
allows people to suspend judgments based on appearance.
This advantage may disappear as images and sounds
increasingly accompany online meetings. Perhaps society
would be healthier if people judged others not by their looks
but by their character as expressed in words and ideas;
however, the current tendency to treat stereotypically
attractive and unattractive people differently shows the
remoteness of that ideal.

Effect of Physical Cues    10

### References

Bakalar, N. (2005, May 3). Ugly children may get parental short
   shrift. *The New York Times,* p. F7.

Dion, K., Berscheid, E., & Walster, E. (1972). What is beautiful is
   good. *Journal of Personality and Social Psychology, 24*(3),
   285–290.

Eisenberg, A. (2000, October 12). Mars and Venus on the Net:
   Gender stereotypes prevail. *New York Times.* Retrieved
   from http://www.nytimes.com/2000/10/12/technology
   /12VOIC.html

Hawfield, K., & Lyons, E. (1998). Conventional wisdom about
   women and Internet use: Refuting traditional
   perceptions. Retrieved March 25, 2005, from
   http://elab.vanderbilt.edu/research/papers/html
   /studentprojects/women/conventional_wisdom.html

Begins
References
on new page

Double-
spaces
throughout

Lists
References in
alphabetical
order by
author

Provides a
source that
appears only
on the Web

continued >>

Kachel, J. (1996, March). Good looks count during childhood.
    *Brown University Child and Adolescent Newsletter, 12*(3).
    Retrieved April 7, 2005, from Academic Search Elite
    database.

McKenna, K. Y., Green, A. S., & Gleason, M. E. (2003).
    Relationship formation on the Internet: What's the big
    attraction? *Journal of Social Issues, 58*(1), 9–31.

Miyake, K., & Zuckerman, M. (1993). Beyond personality
    impressions. *Journal of Personality, 61*(3), 411–436.
    doi: 10.1111/1467-6494.ep9402021314

Nakamura, L. (2002). *Cybertypes: Race, ethnicity, and identity
    on the Internet.* New York: Routledge.

Singh, D. (2004). Mating strategies of young women: Role of
    physical attractiveness. *Journal of Sex Research, 41*(1),
    43–54.

Snyder, M., Tanke, E. D., & Berscheid, E. (1977). Social
    perception and interpersonal behavior: On the self-
    fulfilling nature of social stereotypes. *Journal of
    Personality and Social Psychology, 35,* 656–666.

Sveningsson, M. (2002). Cyberlove: Creating romantic
    relationships on the Net. In J. Fornäs, K. Klein,
    M. Ladendorf, J. Sundén, & M. Sveningsson (Eds.), *Digital
    borderlands: Cultural studies of identity and interactivity
    on the Internet* (pp. 48–78). New York: Lang.

Provides
source
information
for chapter
in a book

# Writing About Literature

## 37a  What is literature?

Literature includes fiction (novels and short stories); drama (plays, scripts, and some films); poetry (poems and lyrics); as well as nonfiction with artistic qualities (memoirs, personal essays, and the like).

Writing about literature generates insights about your reading. It helps you understand other people, ideas, times, and places. It shows you how authors use language to stir the imaginations, emotions, and intellects of their readers. Finally, writing is a way to share your own reading experiences and insights with other readers.

Sometimes instructors ask students to answer questions that deal with material on a literal level, that is, to tell exactly what is said on the page. If a question asks what happens in the plot or what a passage is saying, you need to answer with a SUMMARY or PARAPHRASE of the work. If a question asks about the historical context of a work, or asks for biographical or situational information about the author, you probably need to do some research and then report exactly what you find.

More often, assignments call for making INFERENCES. Making inferences means reading "between the lines" to figure out what is implied but not stated. This reading skill is especially crucial for reading literature because it tends to "show" rather than to "tell." Inferential thinking is necessary when your instructor asks you to discuss why a character does something for which the author provides no explicit reason. It's necessary when your instructor asks you to explain the effect of images in a poem, to discuss how a work implies the author's stance on a social issue, or to analyze how the author depicts the role of women, men, or specific ethnic groups.

Writing effective papers about literature involves more than summarizing the plot. It involves CRITICAL THINKING and SYNTHESIS. In such papers, you state a CLAIM (an observation or a position about the work of literature) and convince your readers that the thesis is reasonable. To be effective, your papers must be thorough and well supported. For support, you make direct references to the work, by SUMMARIZING, PARAPHRASING, and QUOTING specific passages and by explaining precisely *why* and *how* the selected passages support your interpretation.

## 37b How do I write different types of papers about literature?

When you read, look for details or passages that relate to your thesis. Mark up the text as you read by selectively underlining passages or by writing notes, comments, or questions in the margin. Alternatively, take notes separately.

### WRITING A PERSONAL RESPONSE

In a personal response paper, you explain your reaction to a literary work or some aspect of it. You might write about why you did or did not enjoy reading a particular work; discuss whether situations in the work are similar to your personal experiences; explain whether you agree or disagree with the author's point of view and why; or answer a question or explore a problem that the work raised for you.

### WRITING AN INTERPRETATION

An interpretation explains the message or viewpoint that you think the work conveys. Most works of literature are open to more than one interpretation. Your task, then, is not to discover the single right answer. Instead, your task is to determine a possible interpretation and provide an argument that supports it. The questions in Quick Reference 37.1 can help you write an effective interpretation paper.

---

### Quick Reference 37.1 ■ ■ ■ ■ ■

#### Questions for an interpretation paper

1. What is a central theme of the work?
2. How do particular parts of the work relate to the theme?
3. If patterns exist in the work, what might they mean? Patterns include repeated images, situations, words, and so on.
4. What meaning does the author create through the elements listed in Quick Reference 37.2?
5. Why might the work end as it does?

---

### WRITING A FORMAL ANALYSIS

A formal analysis explains how elements of a literary work function to create meaning or effect. Quick Reference 37.2 describes some of the major literary elements that you might expect to use in formal analyses.

To prepare to write a formal analysis, read the work thoroughly, looking for patterns and repetitions. Write notes as you read to help you form insights about these patterns and repetitions.

## Quick Reference 37.2 ▪ ▪ ▪ ▪ ▪

### Major elements of formal analysis in literary works

| | |
|---|---|
| PLOT | Events and their sequence |
| THEME | Central idea or message |
| STRUCTURE | Organization and relationship of parts to each other and to the whole |
| CHARACTERIZATION | Traits, thoughts, and actions of the people in the plot |
| SETTING | Time and place of the action |
| POINT OF VIEW | Perspective or position from which the material is presented—by a narrator, a main character, or another person either in the plot or observing the plot |
| STYLE | How words and sentence structures present the material |
| IMAGERY | Descriptive language that creates mental pictures for the reader |
| TONE | Author's attitude toward the subject of the work—and sometimes toward the reader—expressed through choice of words, imagery, and point of view (Chapter 1) |
| FIGURE OF SPEECH | Unusual use or combination of words, as in metaphor and simile, for enhanced vividness or effect |
| SYMBOLISM | Meaning beneath the surface of the words and images |
| RHYTHM | Beat, meter |
| RHYME | Repetition of similar sounds for their auditory effect |

### WRITING A CULTURAL ANALYSIS

A cultural analysis relates the literary work to broader historical, social, cultural, and political situations. Instructors might ask you to explain how events or prevailing attitudes influence the writing of a work or the way readers understand it.

When you write about literature, certain special elements come into play.

### ■ Using present and past tense correctly

Always use the PRESENT TENSE when you describe or discuss a literary work or any of its elements: *George Henderson* [a character] ***takes*** *control of the action* *and **tells** the other characters when they may speak.* The present tense is also correct for discussing what the author has done in a specific work: *Because Susan Glaspell* [the author] **excludes** *Minnie and John Wright from the stage as speaking characters, she **forces** her audience to learn about them through the words of others.*

Use a PAST-TENSE VERB to discuss historical events or biographical information: *Susan Glaspell **was** a social activist who **was** strongly **influenced** by the chaotic events of the early twentieth century.*

### ■ Using your own ideas and secondary sources

Some assignments call for only your own ideas about the literary work that is the subject of your essay. Other assignments require you additionally to use SECONDARY SOURCES, books and articles in which experts discuss some aspect of the literary text or other material related to your topic.

You might use secondary sources to support your own ideas, perhaps by drawing on the ideas of a scholar who agrees with you or debating the ideas of a scholar who disagrees with you. Or, if you think that you have a new or different interpretation, you might summarize, analyze, or critique what others have written, to provide a framework for your own analysis. You can locate secondary sources by using the process discussed in Chapter 32. A particularly important resource for research about literature is the *MLA International Bibliography,* which is the most comprehensive index to literary scholarship.

As with all source-based writing, you need to DOCUMENT primary sources and secondary sources because you want to ensure that readers never mistake someone else's ideas as yours. Otherwise, you're PLAGIARIZING (see Chapter 34). Most literature instructors require students to use the DOCUMENTATION STYLE of the Modern Language Association (MLA) that we described in Chapter 35. However, check with your instructor.

## 37c Sample student essay

The student essay that follows is a literary analysis of two poems by Claude McKay that draws on SECONDARY SOURCES.

Born in 1889 on the Caribbean island of Jamaica, Claude McKay moved to the United States in 1910 and became a highly respected poet. Paule Cheek, a student in a class devoted to writing about literature, chose to write about Claude McKay's nontraditional use of a very traditional poetic form, the sonnet. A sonnet has fourteen lines in a patterned rhyme and develops one idea. In secondary sources, Cheek found information about McKay's life that she felt gave her further insights into both the structure and the meaning of McKay's sonnets "In Bondage" and "The White City." For your reference, both poems appear on the next page.

## IN BONDAGE

I would be wandering in distant fields
Where man, and bird, and beast, lives leisurely,
And the old earth is kind, and ever yields
Her goodly gifts to all her children free;
Where life is fairer, lighter, less demanding,                    5
And boys and girls have time and space for play
Before they come to years of understanding—
Somewhere I would be singing, far away.
For life is greater than the thousand wars
Men wage for it in their insatiate lust,                          10
And will remain like the eternal stars,
When all that shines to-day is drift and dust.
But I am bound with you in your mean graves,
O black men, simple slaves of ruthless slaves.

## THE WHITE CITY

I will not toy with it nor bend an inch.
Deep in the secret chambers of my heart
I muse my life-long hate, and without flinch
I bear it nobly as I live my part.
My being would be skeleton, a shell,                              5
If this dark Passion that fills my every mood,
And makes my heaven in the white world's hell,
Did not forever feed me vital blood.
I see the mighty city through a mist—
The strident trains that speed the goaded mass,                   10
The poles and spires and towers vapor-kissed,
The fortressed port through which the great ships pass,
The tides, the wharves, the dens I contemplate,
Are sweet like wanton loves because I hate.

Cheek 1

Paule Cheek

Professor Bartlestone

English 112, Section 03

14 March 2008

Words in Bondage: Claude McKay's

Use of the Sonnet Form in Two Poems

The sonnet has remained one of the central poetic forms of the Western tradition for centuries. This fourteen-line form is easy for poets to learn but difficult to master. With its fixed rhyme schemes, number of lines, and meter, the sonnet form forces writers to be doubly creative while working within it. Many poets over the years have modified or varied the sonnet form, playing upon its conventions to keep it vibrant and original. One such writer was Jamaican-born Claude McKay (1889-1948).

The Jamaica of McKay's childhood was very different from turn-of-the-century America. Slavery had ended there in the 1830s, and McKay was able to grow up "in a society whose population was overwhelmingly black and largely free of the overt white oppression which constricted the lives of black Americans in the United States during this same period" (Cooper, *Passion* 5-6). This background could not have prepared McKay for what he encountered when he moved to America in his twenties. Lynchings, still common at that time, were on the rise, and during the Red Scare of 1919 there were dozens of racially motivated riots in major cities throughout

continued >>

(Proportions shown in this paper are adjusted to fit space limitations of this book. Follow actual dimensions given in this book and in your instructor's directions.)

Cheek 2

the country. Thousands of homes were destroyed in these riots,
and several black men were tortured and burned at the stake
(Cooper, *Claude McKay* 97). McKay responded to these
atrocities by raising an outraged cry of protest in his poems.
In two of his sonnets from this period, "The White City" and
"In Bondage," we can see McKay's mastery of the form and his
skillful use of irony in the call for social change.

McKay's choice of the sonnet form as the vehicle for his
protest poetry at first seems strange. Since his message was a
radical one, we might expect that the form of his poetry would
be revolutionary. Instead, McKay gives us sonnets--a poetic
form that dates back to the early sixteenth century and was
originally intended to be used exclusively for love poems. The
critic James R. Giles notes that this choice

> is not really surprising, since McKay's Jamaican
> education and reading had been based firmly
> upon the major British poets. From the point quite
> early in his life when he began to think of himself
> as a poet, his models were such major English
> writers as William Shakespeare, John Milton,
> William Wordsworth. He thus was committed from
> the beginning to the poetry which he had initially
> been taught to admire. (44)

McKay published both "The White City" and "In
Bondage" in 1922, and they are similar in many ways. Like
most sonnets, each has fourteen lines and is in iambic
pentameter. The diction is extremely elevated. For example,
this quatrain from "In Bondage" is almost Elizabethan in its
word choice and order:

continued >>

> For life is greater than the thousand wars
>
> Men wage for it in their insatiate lust,
>
> And will remain like the eternal stars,
>
> When all that shines to-day is drift and dust.
>
> (lines 9-12)

If this level of diction is reminiscent of Shakespeare, it is no accident. Both poems employ the English sonnet rhyme scheme (a b a b c d c d e f e f g g) and division into three quatrains and a closing couplet. McKay introduces a touch of his own, however. Although the English sonnet form calls for the "thematic turn" to fall at the closing couplet, McKay defies convention. He incorporates two turns into each sonnet instead of one. This allows him to use the first "mini-turn" to further develop the initial theme set forth in the first eight lines while dramatically bringing the poem to a conclusion with a forcefully ironic turn in the closing couplet. Specifically, in "The White City," McKay uses the additional turn to interrupt his description of his "Passion" with a vision of "the mighty city through a mist" (9). In "In Bondage," he uses the additional turn to justify his desire to escape the violent existence that society has imposed on his people.

McKay also demonstrates his poetic ability through his choice of words within his customized sonnets. Consider the opening of "In Bondage":

> I would be wandering in distant fields
>
> Where man, and bird, and beast, lives leisurely,
>
> And the old earth is kind, and ever yields
>
> Her goodly gifts to all her children free;
>
> Where life is fairer, lighter, less demanding,

continued >>

> And boys and girls have time and space for play
>
> Before they come to years of understanding--
>
> Somewhere I would be singing, far away. (1-8)

The conditional power of *would* in the first line, coupled
with the alliterative *wandering*, subtly charms us into a
relaxed, almost dreamlike state in which the poet can lead us
gently through the rest of the poem. The commas in the second
line force us to check our progress to a "leisurely" crawl,
mirroring the people and animals that the line describes. By
the time we reach the eighth line, we are probably ready to join
the poet in this land of "somewhere . . . far away."

Then this optimistic bubble is violently burst by the
closing couplet:

> But I am bound with you in your mean graves,
>
> O black men, simple slaves of ruthless slaves.
>
> (13-14)

In "The White City" McKay again surprises us. This time,
he does so by turning the traditional love sonnet upside down;
instead of depicting a life made endurable through an
overpowering love, McKay shows us a life made bearable
through a sustaining hate:

> I will not toy with it nor bend an inch.
>
> Deep in the secret chambers of my heart
>
> I muse my life-long hate, and without flinch
>
> I bear it nobly as I live my part.
>
> My being would be a skeleton, a shell,
>
> If this dark Passion that fills my every mood,
>
> And makes my heaven in the white world's hell,
>
> Did not forever feed me vital blood. (1-8)

continued >>

If it were not for the presence of "life-long hate" in the third line, this opening would easily pass as part of a conventional love sonnet. However, as the critic William Maxwell notes in "On 'The White City'," the first quatrain is "designed to ambush those anticipating another rehearsal of love's powers." The emotion comes from "deep in the secret chambers" of the speaker's heart (2), it allows him to transcend "the white world's hell" (7), and it is a defining "Passion." Once again, however, McKay uses the couplet to defy our expectations by making it plain that he has used the form of the love sonnet only for ironic effect: "The tides, the wharves, the dens I contemplate, / Are sweet like wanton loves because I hate" (13-14).

McKay's impressive poetic ability made him a master of the sonnet form. His language could at times rival even Shakespeare's, and his creativity allowed him to adapt the sonnet to his own ends. His ironic genius is revealed in his use of one of Western society's most elevated poetic forms to critique that same society. He held that critique so strongly that shortly after publishing these poems, McKay spent six months in the Soviet Union, where he met with Communist leaders (Hathaway 282). McKay once described himself as "a man who was bitter because he loved, who was both right and wrong because he hated the things that destroyed love, who tried to give back to others a little of what he had got from them . . ." (qtd. in Barksdale and Kinnamon 491). As these two sonnets show, McKay gave back very much indeed.

continued >>

Cheek 6

Works Cited

Barksdale, Richard, and Kenneth Kinnamon, eds. *Black Writers of America: A Comprehensive Anthology*. New York: Macmillan, 1972. Print.

Cooper, Wayne F. *Claude McKay: Rebel Sojourner in the Harlem Renaissance*. Baton Rouge: Louisiana State UP, 1987. Print.

---, ed. *The Passion of Claude McKay*. New York: Schocken, 1973. Print.

Giles, James R. *Claude McKay*. Boston: Twayne, 1976. Print.

Hathaway, Heather. "Claude McKay." *The Concise Oxford Companion to African American Literature*. Ed. William L. Andrews, Frances Smith Foster, and Trudier Harris. New York: Oxford UP, 2001. 282-83. Print.

Maxwell, William. "On 'The White City.'" *New Negro, Old Left: African American Writing and Communism Between the Wars*. New York: Columbia UP, 1999. *Modern American Poetry*. Web. 5 Mar. 2008 <http://www.english.uiuc.edu/maps/poets/m_r/mckay/whitecity.htm>.

McKay, Claude. "In Bondage." *Literature: An Introduction to Reading and Writing*. 8th ed. Ed. Edgar V. Roberts and Henry E. Jacobs. Englewood Cliffs: Prentice, 2007. 949-50. Print.

---. "The White City." *Literature: An Introduction to Reading and Writing*. 8th ed. Ed. Edgar V. Roberts and Henry E. Jacobs. Englewood Cliffs: Prentice, 2007. 1212. Print.

# 38

# Writing in the Social Sciences

## 38a What are the social sciences?

The social sciences focus on the behavior of people as individuals and in groups. The field includes disciplines such as economics, education, political science, psychology, sociology, and certain courses in geography. At some colleges, history is included in the social sciences; at others, it's part of the humanities.

Some methods used in the social sciences lead to **quantitative research,** which seeks to count things or translate information into numerical data to analyze statistically. Other methods lead to **qualitative research,** which relies on careful descriptions and thorough written interpretations.

In the social sciences, PRIMARY SOURCES include surveys and questionnaires, observations, interviews, and experiments. When writing about information you gather, you analyze and explain what the sources mean or why they're significant.

Surveys and questionnaires systematically gather information from a representative number of individuals. Some writing in the social sciences requires direct observations of people's behaviors. In reporting your observations, tell what tools you used, because they might have influenced what you saw.

You might interview people to gather opinions and impressions. Remember that interviews aren't always reliable because people's memories are imprecise, and their first impulse is to present themselves in the best light. Try to interview as many people as possible so that you can cross-check information. The social sciences sometimes use data from experiments as a source. For example, if you want to learn how people react in a particular situation, you can set up that situation artificially and bring individuals (known as "subjects") into it to observe their behavior.

With all methods of inquiry in the social sciences, you need to be ethical. Professional social scientists must seek explicit written permission from their subjects, and colleges have official panels to review research proposals to make sure the studies are ethical.

The purpose of much writing in the social sciences is explanatory. Writers try to explain both what a behavior is and why it happens. SUMMARY and SYNTHESIS are important fundamental strategies for explanatory writing in the social sciences. INTERPRETATIONS and ANALYSES are common when social scientists write about problems and their solutions.

Social scientists are particularly careful to define their KEY TERMS when they write, especially when they discuss complex social issues. For example, if you're writing a paper on substance abuse in the medical profession, you must first define what you mean by the terms *substance abuse* and *medical profession.* Without defining such terms, you confuse readers or lead them to wrong conclusions.

In college courses in the social sciences, your goal is usually to be a neutral observer, so most of the time you need to use the THIRD PERSON (*he, she, it, one, they*). Using the FIRST PERSON (*I, we, our*) is acceptable only when you write about your own reactions and experiences. Some writing in the social sciences overuses the PASSIVE VOICE (15n and 15o). Style manuals for the social sciences, however, recommend using the ACTIVE VOICE whenever possible.

## 38b What are different types of papers in the social sciences?

A **case study** is an intensive study of one group or individual. If you write a case study, describe situations as a neutral observer. Refrain from interpreting them unless your assignment says that you can add your interpretation to your report. Also, always differentiate between fact and opinion (4d).

Most case studies contain the following components: (1) basic identifying information about the individual or group; (2) a history of the individual or group; (3) observations of the individual's or group's behavior; and (4) conclusions as well as possible recommendations that resulted from the observations.

**Research reports** explain your own original research based on PRIMARY SOURCES. These may result from interviews, questionnaires, observations, or experiments. Research reports in the social sciences often follow a prescribed format: (1) statement of the problem; (2) background, sometimes including a review of the literature; (3) methodology; (4) results; and (5) discussion of findings.

To prepare a **review of literature,** comprehensively gather and analyze the sources that have been published on a specific topic. Sometimes a review of the literature is a part of a longer paper, usually the "background" section of a research report. Other times the entire paper might be an extensive review of the literature.

# 39 .

# Business and Professional Writing

All workplace writing benefits from moving its way through the WRITING PROCESS as it seeks to INFORM or to PERSUADE. Indeed, never before in your writing have the acts of revising, editing, and proofreading carried as much weight as they do in business writing. The slightest error reflects negatively on the writer personally and on the larger world of the company that employs the writer.

E-mail is the primary form of written business communication today. Here are some overriding guidelines for business use.

- Find out whether personal e-mail is tolerated. (You can usually find e-mail policies in an employee manual.) Even if personal e-mail is permitted, realize that monitoring systems in most workplaces can quickly identify such e-mails.

- Ask your supervisor whether there are restrictions regarding the size of attachments that you can send or receive. (Large attachments can overload the computer system at work.) If there are restrictions, alert your recipients about the size of any large attachments before you send them.

- Protect the ID numbers and passwords you're assigned or have created to access your organization's electronic systems. As an employee, you're accountable for all activity conducted on password-protected accounts.

## 39a How do I format and write memos?

**Memos** are usually exchanged internally (within an organization or business). Today e-mail takes the place of most memos, unless the correspondence requires a paper record or signature. The guidelines for writing e-mail also pertain to memos. The appropriate form of communication—paper memos or e-mail—depends on what's customary in your work environment.

The content calls for a beginning, middle, and end, with all parts holding closely to your topic. Don't ramble. If you need more than one or, at most, two pages, change your format into that of a brief report. Here are some guidelines for preparing a memo.

- **Introduction:** Briefly state your purpose for writing and why your memo is worth your readers' attention. Mention whether the recipient needs to take action, making it clear either here or at the conclusion.

- **Body:** Present the essential information on your topic, including facts the recipient needs to know. If you write more than three or four paragraphs, use headings to divide the information into subtopics so that the memo can be scanned quickly.

- **Conclusion:** End with a one- to two-sentence summary, a specific recommendation, or what action is needed and by when. Finish with a "thank you" sentence.

## 39b  How do I write business letters?

Business letters are more formal and official than business e-mails or business memos. Choose to write a business letter, rather than a business e-mail, to add appropriate weight and respect to your message, for ceremonial occasions, and to ensure that your message is placed on the record and thereby becomes part of a "paper trail."

There are some general guidelines for addressing recipients in business letters. Use the full name of your recipient whenever possible. If you can't locate a name, either through a phone call to a central switchboard or on the Internet, use a specific category—for example, "Dear Billing Department." Always use gender-neutral language.

Here are guidelines for the format and content of your business letters.

- **Paper:** Use 8½ × 11-inch paper. The most suitable colors are white, off-white, and light beige. Fold your business letters horizontally into thirds to fit into a standard number 10 business envelope (9½ × 4 inches). Never fold a business letterhead stationery page in half and then into thirds.

- **Letterhead stationery:** Use the official letterhead stationery (name, address, and logo, if any) of the business where you're employed. If no letterhead stationery exists, imitate the format that others have used. If no such tradition exists, center the company's full name, address, and phone number at the top of the page, and use a larger and different font than for the content of your letter.

- **Format:** Without indents, use single spacing within paragraphs and double spacing between paragraphs. All lines start flush left, which means at the left margin. This is called **block style.** An equally acceptable alternative form is called **modified block style** in which the lines for the inside address and the body begin flush left but the heading, closing, and signature begin about halfway across the page.

*ArtsFlamenco*

3B-243 West 21st Street
New York, NY 10011
artsflamenco@msn.com
www.artsflamenco.org

January 11, 2009

Mr. Antonio Alducin
Advisor, Latino Heritage Club
George Washington High School
324 Mapleview Road
Englewood, New Jersey 07631

Dear Mr. Alducin,

We enjoyed speaking with you earlier this week regarding *ArtsFlamenco*'s arts-in-education programs. We can certainly work with you to develop an after-school workshop that ties in elements of Spanish language, culture, music, and dance.

We are enclosing three program plans and their estimated costs. For your further interest, we are also including a DVD showing clips from two of our recent arts-in-education programs. After you have reviewed these materials, please contact us to discuss any questions you might have.

We very much look forward to speaking with you again.

All the best,

*Jorge Navarro*

Jorge Navarro
President and Artistic Director

Encl: 3

*A Section 501(c)(3) New York Not-for-Profit Corporation*

Sample business letter in block style

# 39c   How do I write a resumé?

A **resumé** details your accomplishments and employment history. Its PURPOSE is to help a potential employer (the AUDIENCE) determine whether you'll be a suitable candidate for employment. To make a favorable impression, follow the guidelines for writing a resumé in Quick Reference 39.1; also, examine the sample on page 474.

## Quick Reference 39.1   ■ ■ ■ ■ ■

### Guidelines for writing a resumé

- Place your name, address, e-mail address, and telephone number at the top. If you have a professional Web site or online PORTFOLIO, include the URL.
- Make sure you have a professional e-mail address. No employer will be impressed by beermaster@gmail.com or daddyslittlegirl@hotmail.com.
- Make it easy to read. Label the sections clearly, and target the resumé to the position you want. Help employers see your most significant attributes as quickly and as easily as possible.
- Adjust your resumé to fit your PURPOSE. For example, if you're applying for a job as a computer programmer, you'll want to emphasize different facts than you would if you're applying for a job selling computers in an electronics store.
- Use headings to separate blocks of information. Include the following headings, as appropriate: Position Desired or Career Objective; Education; Experience; Licenses and Certifications; Related Experience; Honors or Awards; Publications or Presentations; Activities and Interests; and Special Abilities, Skills, and Knowledge.
- When you list your work experience, place your most recent job first; when listing education, place your most recent degrees, certificates, or enrollments first.
- Write telegraphically. Start with verb phrases, not with the word *I,* and omit *a, an,* and *the.* For example, write "Created new computer program to organize company's spreadsheets" instead of "*I* created *a* new computer program to organize *the* company's spreadsheets."
- Include only relevant information.
- Tell the truth. Even if you get the job, an employer who discovers you lied will probably fire you.
- Include references, or state that you can provide them on request.
- Fit all of the information on one page. If you need a second page, make sure the most important information is on the first page.
- Use high-quality paper that is white or off-white.
- Proofread carefully; even one spelling error or one formatting error can eliminate you from consideration.

MONICA A. SCHICKEL

1817 Drevin Avenue
Denver, CO 80208
Cell phone: (303) 555-7722
E-mail: mnsschl@wordnet.com
Professional portfolio: www.schickelgraphics.net

OBJECTIVE: Entry level position as a graphic designer or publications assistant

EXPERIENCE

| | |
|---|---|
| 9/08 – present | **Publications Intern** (half-time; paid), *Westword* (Denver, CO) |
| | • Design advertisements |
| | • Prepare photographs for publications |
| | • Lay out the "Tempo" section |
| | • Fact-check, edit, and proofread articles |
| 6/06 - 8/08 | **Customer Service Representative,** Wells Fargo Bank (Aurora CO). |
| | • Sold accounts to customers; made all sales goals |
| | • Created promotional posters |
| 4/03 - 8/05 | Evening Assistant Manager, McDonalds Restaurant (Longmont, CO). |
| | • Supervised 7 cooks and counter workers |
| | • Assured food and service quality |

EDUCATION

| | |
|---|---|
| 8/07 – present | Bachelor of Arts, The University of Denver, expected June 2009 Major: Graphic Arts; Minor: Digital Media Studies |
| 8/05 – 5/07 | AA General Education, Front Range Community College, May 2007 |

SKILLS AND SELECTED EXPERIENCES

- Expert in complete Adobe Creative Suite
- Expert in complete Microsoft Office Suite
- Excellent Spanish language skills
- Illustrator and photographer; have completed several commissions (see portfolio, above)
- Vice President, Student Residence Halls Association
- Cartoonist and Designer, *The DU Clarion* (campus newspaper)
- Excellent customer service skills

REFERENCES: Available on request

Sample resumé

## 39d  How do I write a job application letter?

A **job application letter** (sometimes called a *cover letter*) always needs to accompany your resumé. Avoid repeating what's already on the resumé. Instead, connect the company's expectations to your experience by emphasizing how your background has prepared you for the position. Your job application letter, more than your resumé, reflects your energy and personality. However, there are limits; this is not the place to be too cute or clever.

Each job application letter needs to be tailored to each job. While you can use basic information in multiple letters, one generic letter will not represent you effectively. Among other things, a very general letter tells prospective employers that you didn't care enough to address the specific circumstances of their organizations. Here are guidelines for writing a job application letter; also, examine the sample job application letter on page 476.

- Use one page only.
- Overall, think of your letter as a polite sales pitch about yourself and what benefits you can bring to the company. Don't be shy, but don't exaggerate.
- Use the same name, content, and format guidelines as for a business letter (39b).
- Address the letter to a specific person. If you can't discover a name, use a gender-neutral title such as *Dear Personnel Director*.
- Open your letter by identifying the position for which you're applying.
- Mention your qualifications, and explain how your background will meet the job requirements.
- Make clear that you're familiar with the company or organization; your research will impress the employer.
- End by being specific about what you can do for the company. If the job will be your first, give your key attributes—but make sure they're relevant.
- State when you're available for an interview and how the potential employer can reach you.
- Edit and proofread the letter carefully. If you have to hand-correct even one error, print the letter again.

Monica A. Schickel
1817 Drevin Avenue
Denver, CO 80208

Cell phone: (303) 555-7722
E-mail: mnsschl@wordnet.com
Professional portfolio: www.schickelgraphics.net

May 3, 2009

Jaime Cisneros
Publications Director
R.L. Smith Consulting
2000 Wabash Avenue
Chicago, IL 60601

Dear Mr. Cisneros:

Please consider my application for the graphic designer position currently being advertised on your company's Web site. I believe that my professional experiences, education, and skills prepare me well for this opportunity.

I am currently completing a paid internship at Westword, a weekly features and entertainment magazine in Denver, CO, where I have worked as an effective member of a creative team. My responsibilities have included designing advertisements, laying out sections, and editing photographs. Other related experience includes commissions as an illustrator and photographer. My professional portfolio demonstrates the range and quality of my work. As the enclosed resumé notes, I have additional experience in business environments.

Next month I will earn a BA in graphic design from The University of Denver, where my course of study has included extensive work in graphic design, photography, drawing, and illustration. Simultaneously, I will complete a minor in digital media studies that has included courses in Web design, video editing, and sound editing. I have expertise in all the standard software applications that would be relevant to your position.

I would be pleased to provide further information and to interview at your convenience. The opportunities at R.L. Smith closely match my background and goals, and the prospect of joining your team in Chicago is exciting. I look forward to discussing how I can contribute to your publications department.

Sincerely,

*Monica A. Schickel*
Monica A. Schickel

Sample job application letter

# 40

# Writing for the Public

**Public writing** is intended for people who are reading for reasons other than work, school, or professional obligations. Instead, they read it out of interest or a desire to keep informed. Some public writing is also known as CIVIC WRITING because you're writing to affect knowledge, actions, or beliefs among other citizens in a democratic society.

## 40a How can I understand public writing situations?

Public writing takes a wide range of forms, depending on the situation. The familiar categories of TOPIC, PURPOSE, AUDIENCE, ROLE, and CONTEXT/SPECIAL REQUIREMENTS are especially important for understanding your options and requirements (1b).

Much public writing has the purpose of INFORMING or PERSUADING, and our earlier advice applies. Among other things, this means analyzing your readers and establishing your credibility for them.

"Establishing credibility" means convincing your readers that they need or want to listen to you. Create a strong ETHOS by being accurate and honest and by explaining your connection with the readers. What do you have in common with them?

People also write for the public for the pleasure of expressing themselves. Social networking sites and software like Facebook or MySpace are prime examples of this purpose, as are certain blogs and the online comment sections maintained by many newspapers.

## 40b How do I write for the public?

Reports for the public vary in length, format, and content. An *action brief* from a political organization might consist of a few pages detailing recent developments on an issue of concern, such as a proposed law. Often these are published on Web sites or distributed through e-mail messages.

Write your material in an evenhanded TONE so that your credibility is supported by your fairness. If you want to criticize something, be sure your argument is well reasoned and supported—and that it lacks BIAS or malice toward any person(s) or specific idea(s). This doesn't mean that your writing needs to be limp. Indeed, you can choose writing that's spirited, enthusiastic, and even stirring.

A *policy brief* is a kind of public report in which experts put technical information into a form that nonexperts and decision makers can understand. These days, most of them are published on the Internet. "To brief" someone is to inform them in a concise way. The usual purpose of policy briefs is to persuade people with facts and analysis that support a specific decision. Your readers need to perceive you as objective and careful, basing your position on logic and evidence.

Writers can influence public opinions or actions by decision makers by writing persuasive arguments. Perhaps you want to endorse a new public project or react to a proposal or endorse a law under consideration.

Another type of public writing takes the form of a *letter to the editor* of a publication. When you respond to a previous piece of writing in a publication, always begin by referring precisely to the source, using title, section, and date, if possible.

Many letters to the editor (most often sent as e-mails) propose solutions to a community problem. These letters aim to persuade other readers that a problem exists and that a particular solution isn't only feasible but also the most advantageous of all the possible alternatives. Follow the general guidelines for writing ARGUMENTS (see Chapter 5).

*Editorials* are fairly short arguments that appear in newspapers and magazines. They are also called "commentaries" or "opinion pieces." *Reviews* discuss movies, books, plays, music and so on, explaining and summarizing them for readers and commenting on their quality. All are common forms of public writing.

# Document and Visual Design

## 41a What is visual design?

**Visual design** refers to the appearance of a document (how it looks), as opposed to its content (what it says). Designing documents includes everything from choosing typefaces, heading styles, and colors, to selecting and placing photographs, illustrations, or other graphics.

Chapter 4 explained how to analyze visual images, and the advice there can help you choose images for your own documents. However, visual design involves the relationship between words and images.

Some documents follow formats that are fairly standardized, such as letters, memos, and e-mail messages. Papers you write in academic settings usually follow guidelines established by the Modern Language Association (Chapter 35) or the American Psychological Association (Chapter 36). Other document types—flyers, brochures, annual reports, reports on special projects, programs for concerts or plays, and so on—invite more design creativity and originality.

## 41b What are basic principles of design?

The basic principles of design are unity, variety, balance, and emphasis. Quick Reference 41.1 describes how to check for these principles.

---

**Quick Reference 41.1**     ■ ■ ■ ■ ■

### Checklist for document design

- **Unity:** Do all elements in my document work together visually, such as a consistent font for consistent content? Is there a consistent use of bitmap or vector images?

- **Variety:** Have I introduced elements, where appropriate, that break up monotony, such as headings in a different font from that used in my content? Do these elements add clarity? Do my images add to content?

- **Balance:** Are the elements of my document in proportion to each other, such as equally placed text elements countering or mirroring equally placed images?

- **Emphasis:** Does my document design draw attention to key information, such as framing important text, or placing important elements in the middle or at the top?

---

## 41c How do I design with text?

Text consists of letters and words. To format text, you need to decide which typeface—such as Times or Arial Schoolbook—that you'll use. Also called *fonts,* they come in two major categories. **Serif** fonts have little "feet" or finishing lines at the top and bottom of each letter; **sans serif** (*sans* is a French term meaning *without*) don't. Times New Roman is serif. Arial is sans serif. Highlighting draws attention to key words or elements of a document. You can highlight in various ways, but in all cases, use moderation.

## BOLDFACE, ITALICS, AND UNDERLINING

*Italics* and underlining—they serve the same purpose—have special functions in writing, but they're also useful for emphasis and for headings. **Boldface** is reserved for heavy emphasis.

## BULLETED AND NUMBERED LISTS

You can use bulleted and numbered lists when you discuss a series of items or steps in a complex process, or summarize key points or guidelines. A bulleted list identifies items with small dots, squares, or other shapes and symbols.

## JUSTIFYING

When you make your text lines even in relation to the left or right margin, you're **justifying** them. There are four kinds of justification, or ways to line up text lines on margins: left, right, centered, and full.

Most academic and business documents are left justified, which means that the right ends of the lines are unjustified, or *ragged.* Center, right, and full justification are useful for designing shorter documents (flyers, posters, and so on) because they can attract attention.

## INDENTATION

When you move text toward the right margin, you are **indenting.** Using the ruler line in your word-processing program to control indentations makes it easier to make global changes in your indentation. The top arrow of the bar sets the paragraph indentation, while the bottom arrow sets the indentation for everything else in the paragraph. MLA-style Works Cited pages and APA References pages use *hanging indentations* in which the first line of an entry aligns at the left margin and every following line is indented. Indent bulleted and numbered lists to make them stand out.

## HEADINGS

Headings clarify how you've organized your material and tell your readers what to expect in each section. Longer documents, including handbooks (like ours), reports, brochures, and Web pages, use headings to break content into chunks that are easier to digest and understand. In academic writing, APA style favors headings, whereas MLA tends to discourage them.

## BORDERS

**Borders** are lines used to set apart sections of text. They can take a number of forms, from single lines of varying thickness to patterns. A single rule (a simple straight line, horizontal or vertical) can emphasize breaks between major sections of a long report. Borders around text serve to set off information, as in a table or chart.

## WHITE SPACE

**White space,** the part of your document that has neither text nor visuals, allows readers to read your document more easily and to absorb information in chunks rather than in one big block. White space indicates breaks between ideas and thereby focuses attention on the key features of your document.

Flyers, brochures, posters, reports, Web pages, and similar documents tend to make extensive and varied use of white space because they rely heavily on graphics. Styles change over time, but most current professional designers prefer an uncluttered look with lots of white space.

# 41d How should I incorporate graphics?

Business and scientific reports rely heavily on charts and graphs, as do some research papers. They're compact ways to present large amounts of information. The next three figures illustrate bar graphs, line graphs, and pie charts.

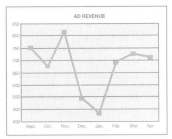

**Bar graphs** compare values, such as the number of different majors at a college, as shown in this graph.

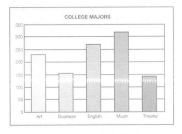

**Line graphs** indicate changes over time. For example, advertising revenue is shown over an eight-month period in this chart.

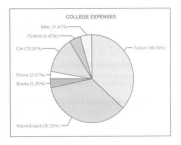

**Pie charts** show the relationship of each part to a whole, such as a typical budget for a college student, as shown in the chart.

**Clip art** refers to pictures, sketches, and other graphics available on some word-processing programs. It can also be downloaded from the Internet, sometimes from free sites, and sometimes for a small fee. Although clip art is rarely, if ever, appropriate in academic writing and business writing, it can add interest to flyers, posters, newsletters, and brochures designed for certain audiences.

In an age of digital cameras, not to mention an age when cell phones have the capacity to take pictures and send them around the world, **photographs** are everywhere. Because you can fairly easily download photographs from a digital camera, you can place them easily into documents. You can also scan photographs from printed photos or from books and articles. The Internet is another source of images; several Web sites (including many at libraries) offer thousands of photographs for free. Most images online, however, are copyrighted, and thus you need to gain permission to use images for any type of publication so you don't plagiarize the material.

# 41e What is page layout?

**Layout** is the arrangement of text, visuals, color, and space on a page. You'll want to arrange these elements so that you follow the basic principles of design (41b) and follow the guidelines in Quick Reference 41.2. Experiment with ideas for

---

### Quick Reference 41.2　　　　　　　■ ■ ■ ■ ■

#### Guidelines for using visuals

- **Design all visuals to be simple and uncluttered.**

- **Use the highest resolution and best images possible.** Small images stretched to fit an area will not look professional and can disrupt a document's design. It's always best to use large pictures and then reduce the size later. Reducing the size of a picture will not harm the resolution, while stretching a picture to make it bigger will.

- **Include a heading or title for each visual.** Doing so helps readers quickly understand what they're seeing.

- **Never use unnecessary visuals.** Make sure all visuals clearly contribute to your PURPOSE. Putting cute clip art on the pages of your writing won't make your reader think your work is well done. However, including a chart that summarizes your findings might.

- **Consider your audience and their sensibilities.** You don't want to offend your readers, nor do you want them to be confused.

- **Credit your source if a visual isn't your own.** Always avoid plagiarism by crediting your source using DOCUMENTATION. If you're using a visual (including a photograph) for a public purpose other than for a class project, you need written permission to use it in your work.

layout by creating a variety of mock-up pages on a computer or by sketching possibilities by hand.

You might also see if any suitable **templates** are available. A template is a professionally designed form that shows you where to place visuals in relation to text; a template has predefined typefaces, heading styles, margins, and so on. Page layout software and most word-processing software have a variety of templates for brochures, flyers, newsletters, and many other types of documents; and several Web sites offer them, too.

## A Message to Multilingual Writers

If you ever worry about your English writing, you have much in common with us and many US college students. Still, we recognize that multilingual writers face special challenges. Depending on how, when, and where you began learning English, you might feel very comfortable with spoken English but not academic, written English. Or you might understand English grammar quite well, but you might struggle with idioms and slang. Multilingual writers' different backgrounds in English will affect the kinds of writing challenges they face.

Most college essays and research papers in the United States are direct in tone and straightforward in structure. Typically, the THESIS STATEMENT (the central message of the piece of writing) is at the end of the first paragraph or, in a longer piece of writing, in the second paragraph. Each paragraph that follows relates in content directly to the essay's thesis statement. Also, each paragraph after the thesis statement needs to begin with a TOPIC SENTENCE that contains the main point of the paragraph, and the rest of the paragraph supports the point made in the topic sentence. The final paragraph brings the content to a logical conclusion that grows out of what has come before.

As you continue writing in English, you might look for interesting ways to blend the traditions and structures of writing in your first language with the conventions of academic writing in the United States. It's important to honor your culture's writing traditions and structures; they reflect the richness of your heritage. At the same time, you can adapt to and practice the writing styles typical in the United States.

Distinctive variations in school writing styles among people of different cultures and language groups have interested researchers for the past thirty years. If you have written academically in languages other than American English, you might notice similarities and differences between the writing you have done in school prior to now and the writing you are asked to do in English. As individuals, we greatly enjoy discovering the rich variations in the writing traditions of our students from many cultures of the world. As American writing teachers, however, our responsibilities call for us to explain what you need to do as writers in the United States. If you were in one of our classes, we would say "Welcome!" and ask you to teach us about writing in your native language. You bring a richness of experience in communicating in more than one language that most US students have never had, and you should be proud of that experience. Using the knowledge of writing in your first language, we could then help you learn how to approach writing effectively in the United States so that you will succeed as a writer and learner in a US college.

Lynn Quitman Troyka
Doug Hesse

# 42

# Singulars and Plurals

## 42a What are count and noncount nouns?

**Count nouns** name items that can be counted: *a radio* or *radios, a street* or *streets, an idea* or *ideas, a fingernail* or *fingernails.* Count nouns can be SINGULAR or PLURAL.

**Noncount nouns** name things that are thought of as a whole and not split into separate, countable parts: *rice, knowledge, traffic.* There are two important rules to remember about noncount nouns: (1) They're never preceded by *a* or *an,* and (2) they are never plural.

Here are several categories of noncount nouns, with examples in each category:

| | |
|---|---|
| GROUPS OF SIMILAR ITEMS | clothing, equipment, furniture, jewelry, junk, luggage, mail, money, stuff, traffic, vocabulary |
| ABSTRACTIONS | advice, equality, fun, health, ignorance, information, knowledge, news, peace, pollution, respect |
| LIQUIDS | blood, coffee, gasoline, water |
| GASES | air, helium, oxygen, smog, smoke, steam |
| MATERIALS | aluminum, cloth, cotton, ice, wood |
| FOOD | beef, bread, butter, macaroni, meat, pork |
| PARTICLES OR GRAINS | dirt, dust, hair, rice, salt, wheat |
| SPORTS, GAMES, ACTIVITIES | chess, homework, housework, reading, sailing, soccer |
| LANGUAGES | Arabic, Chinese, Japanese, Spanish |
| FIELDS OF STUDY | biology, computer science, history, literature, math |
| EVENTS IN NATURE | electricity, heat, humidity, moonlight, rain, snow, sunshine, thunder, weather |

Some nouns can be countable or uncountable, depending on their meaning in a sentence. Most of these nouns name things that can be meant either individually or as "wholes" made up of individual parts.

COUNT      You have **a hair** on your sleeve. [In this sentence, *hair* is meant as an individual, countable item.]

NONCOUNT   Kioko has black **hair.** [In this sentence, all the strands of *hair* are referred to as a whole.]

When you are editing your writing (see Chapter 2), be sure that you have not added a plural *-s* to any noncount nouns, for they are always singular in form.

⬤ **Alert:** Be sure to use a singular verb with any noncount noun that functions as a SUBJECT in a CLAUSE. ●

To check whether a noun is count or noncount, look it up in a dictionary such as the *Dictionary of American English* (Heinle and Heinle).

## 42b How do I use determiners with singular and plural nouns?

**Determiners,** also called *expressions of quantity,* are used to tell how much or how many with reference to NOUNS. Other names for determiners include *limiting adjectives, noun markers,* and ARTICLES. (For information about articles—the words *a, an,* and *the*—see Chapter 43.)

Choosing the right determiner with a noun can depend on whether the noun is NONCOUNT or COUNT (see 42a). For count nouns, you must also decide whether the noun is singular or plural. Quick Reference 42.1 lists many determiners and the kinds of nouns that they can accompany.

⬤ **Alert:** The phrases *a few* and *a little* convey the meaning "some": *I have* **a few** *rare books* means "I have *some* rare books." *They are worth* **a little** *money* means "They are worth *some* money."

Without the word *a,* the words *few* and *little* convey the meaning "almost none": *I have* **few** [or *very few*] *books* means "I have *almost no* books." *They are worth* **little** *money* means "They are worth *almost no* money." ●

## 42c How do I use nouns as adjectives?

### NOUNS USED AS ADJECTIVES

ADJECTIVES in English do not have plural forms. When you use an adjective with a PLURAL NOUN, make the noun plural but not the adjective: *the* **green** [not *greens*] *leaves.* Be especially careful when you use a word as a MODIFIER that can also function as a noun.

The bird's wingspan is ten inches. [*Inches* is functioning as a noun.]

The bird has a ten-inch wingspan. [*Inch* is functioning as a modifier.]

## Quick Reference 42.1

■ ■ ■ ■ ■

### Determiners to use with count and noncount nouns

**GROUP 1: DETERMINERS FOR SINGULAR COUNT NOUNS**

With every **singular count noun,** always use one of the determiners listed in Group 1.

| | | | |
|---|---|---|---|
| *a, an, the* | **a house** | **an egg** | **the car** |
| *one, any, some, every, each, either, neither, another the other* | **any house** | **each egg** | **another car** |
| *my, our, your, his, her, its, their,* nouns with *'s* or *s',* | **your house** | **its egg** | **Connie's car** |
| *this, that* | **this house** | **that egg** | **this car** |
| *one, no, the first the second,* etc. | **one house** | **no egg** | **the fifth car** |

**GROUP 2: DETERMINERS FOR PLURAL COUNT NOUNS**

All the determiners listed in Group 2 can be used with **plural count nouns.** Plural count nouns can also be used without determiners, as discussed in section 42b.

| | | | |
|---|---|---|---|
| *the* | **the bicycles** | **the rooms** | **the idea** |
| *some, any, both, many, more, most, few, fewer, the fewest, a lot of, a number of, other, several, all, all the* | **some bicycles** | **many rooms** | **all ideas** |
| *my, our, your, his, her, its, their,* nouns with *'s* or *s'* | **our bicycles** | **her rooms** | **student's ideas** |
| *these, those* | **these bicycles** | **those rooms** | **these ideas** |
| *no, two, three,* etc.; *the first, the second, the third,* etc. | **no bicycles** | **four rooms** | **the first ideas** |

**GROUP 3: DETERMINERS FOR NONCOUNT NOUNS**

All the determiners listed in Group 3 can be used with **noncount nouns** (always singular). Noncount nouns can also be used without determiners, as discussed in section 42b.

continued >>

### Quick Reference 42.1 (continued)

■ ■ ■ ■ ■

| | | | |
|---|---|---|---|
| *the* | the rice | the rain | the pride |
| *some, any, much, more, most, other, the other, little, less, the least, enough, all, all the, a lot of* | enough rice | a lot of rain | more pride |
| *my, our, your, his, her, its, their,* nouns with *'s* or *s'* | their rice | India's rain | your pride |
| *this, that* | this rice | that rain | this pride |
| *no, the first, the second, the third,* etc. | no rice | the first rain | no pride |

Do not add *-s* (or *-es*) to the adjective even when it is modifying a plural noun or pronoun.

**NO**   Many **Americans** students are basketball fans.

**YES**   Many **American** students are basketball fans.

**EXERCISE 42-1**   Consulting all sections of this chapter, select the correct choice from the words in parentheses and write it in the blank.

EXAMPLE   At the beginning of every school year, all (student, students) <u>students</u> can expect (homework, homeworks) <u>homework</u> that teaches them about the toll-free No Bully hot line.

1. One of the main (reason, reasons) _____ for such a hot line is the change in tempers and violent capacities of (American, Americans) _____ students.

2. Because students are often bullied by a fellow classmate when outside the classroom, it is important that they receive (information, informations) _____ about how to react when confronted by such a threat.

3. Many a child in the (United State, United States) _____ is in danger not only of being teased and taunted by others but also of being the victim of a crime in which (blood, bloods) _____ is spilled, such as from assault or robbery.

4. Because (many, much) _____ classrooms are unsupervised after school, this (time, times) _____ becomes especially dangerous.

5. In a moment of danger, (ignorance, ignorances) _____ can be deadly, so the No Bully hot line was set up to give students (advice, advices) _____ on how to handle bullying and other threatening situations.

# 43

# Articles

## 43a How do I use *a, an,* or *the* with singular count nouns?

The words *a* and *an* are called **indefinite articles.** The word *the* is called the
DEFINITE ARTICLE. Articles are one type of DETERMINER. Articles signal that a
NOUN will follow and that any MODIFIERS between the article and the noun refer
to that noun.

|   |   |
|---|---|
| **a** chair | **the** computer |
| **a** brown chair | **the** teacher's computer |
| **a** cold, metal chair | **the** lightning-fast computer |

Every time you use a singular count noun, a COMMON NOUN that names
one countable item, the noun requires some kind of determiner; see Group 1
in Quick Reference 42.1 (in 42b) for a list. To choose between *a* or *an* and *the,*
you need to determine whether the noun is **specific** or **nonspecific.** A noun
is considered *specific* when anyone who reads your writing can understand exactly and specifically to what item the noun is referring. If the noun refers to
any of a number of identical items, it is *nonspecific.*

For nonspecific singular count nouns, use *a* (or *an*). When the singular
noun is specific, use *the* or some other determiner. Quick Reference 43.1 can
help you decide when a singular count noun is specific and therefore requires
*the.*

⚠ **Alert:** Use *an* before words that begin with a vowel sound. Use *a* before
words that begin with a consonant sound. Go by the sound, not the spelling.
For example, words that begin with *h* or *u* can have either a vowel or a consonant sound. Make the choice based on the sound of the first word after the article, even if that word is not the noun.

|   |   |
|---|---|
| **an i**dea | **a g**ood idea |
| **an u**mbrella | **a u**seless umbrella |
| **an h**onor | **a h**istory book ● |

## Quick Reference 43.1 ■ ■ ■ ■ ■

### When a singular count noun is specific and requires *the*

- **Rule 1: A noun is specific and requires *the* when it names something unique or generally and unambiguously known.**

    **The sun** has risen above **the horizon.** [Because there is only one *sun* and only one *horizon*, these nouns are specific in the context of this sentence.]

- **Rule 2: A noun is specific and requires *the* when it names something used in a representative or abstract sense.**

    Benjamin Franklin favored **the turkey** as **the national bird** of the United States. [Because *turkey* and *national bird* are representative references rather than references to a particular turkey or bird, they are specific nouns in the context of this sentence.]

- **Rule 3: A noun is specific and requires *the* when it names something defined elsewhere in the same sentence or in an earlier sentence.**

    **The ship *Savannah*** was the first steam vessel to cross the Atlantic Ocean. [*Savannah* names a specific ship.]

    **The carpet in my bedroom** is new. [*In my bedroom* defines exactly which carpet is meant, so *carpet* is a specific noun in this context.]

    I have **a computer** in my office. **The computer** is often broken. [*Computer* is not specific in the first sentence, so it uses *a*. In the second sentence, *computer* has been made specific by the first sentence, so it uses *the*.]

- **Rule 4: A noun is specific and requires *the* when it names something that can be inferred from the context.**

    Monday, I had to call **the technician** to fix my computer again. [*A technician* would be any of a number of individuals; *the technician* implies the same person has been called before, and so it is specific in this context.]

One common exception affects Rule 3 in Quick Reference 43.1. A noun may still require *a* (or *an*) after the first use if more information is added between the article and the noun: *I bought **a sweater** today. It was **a** (not *the*) **red sweater.*** (Your audience has been introduced to *a sweater* but not *a red sweater*, so *red sweater* is not yet specific in this context and cannot take *the*.) Other information may make the noun specific so that *the* is correct. For example, *It was **the red sweater that I saw in the store yesterday*** uses *the* because the *that* CLAUSE makes specific which red sweater the writer means.

## **43b** How do I use articles with plural nouns and with noncount nouns?

With plural nouns and NONCOUNT NOUNS, you must decide whether to use *the* or to use no article at all. (For guidelines about using DETERMINERS other than articles with nouns, see Quick Reference 42.1 in 42b.) What you learned in 43a about NONSPECIFIC and SPECIFIC NOUNS can help you choose between using *the* or using no article. Quick Reference 43.1 in 43a explains when a singular count noun's meaning is specific and calls for *the*. Plural nouns and noncount nouns with specific meanings usually use *the* in the same circumstances. However, a plural noun or a noncount noun with a general or nonspecific meaning usually does not use *the*.

> Geraldo grows **flowers** but not **vegetables** in his garden. He is thinking about planting **corn** sometime. [three nonspecific nouns]

### PLURAL NOUNS

A plural noun's meaning may be specific because it is widely known.

> **The oceans** are being damaged by pollution. [Because there is only one possible meaning for *oceans*—the oceans on the earth—it is correct to use *the*. This example is related to Rule 1 in Quick Reference 43.1.]

A plural noun's meaning may also be made specific by a word, PHRASE, or CLAUSE in the same sentence.

> Geraldo sold **the daisies from last year's garden** to the florist. [Because the phrase *from last year's garden* makes *daisies* specific, *the* is correct. This example is related to Rule 3 in Quick Reference 43.1.]

A plural noun's meaning usually becomes specific by its use in an earlier sentence.

> Geraldo planted **tulips** this year. **The tulips** will bloom in April. [*Tulips* is used in a general sense in the first sentence, without *the*. Because the first sentence makes *tulips* specific, *the tulips* is correct in the second sentence. This example is related to Rule 3 in Quick Reference 43.1.]

A plural noun's meaning may be made specific by the context.

> Geraldo fertilized **the bulbs** when he planted them last October. [In the context of the sentences about tulips, *bulbs* is understood as a synonym for *tulips*, which makes it specific and calls for *the*. This example is related to Rule 4 in Quick Reference 43.1.]

## NONCOUNT NOUNS

Noncount nouns are always singular in form (see 42a). Like plural nouns, noncount nouns use either *the* or no article. When a noncount noun's meaning is specific, use *the* before it. If its meaning is general or nonspecific, do not use *the*.

> Kalinda served us **rice.** She flavored **the rice** with curry. [*Rice* is a noncount noun. By the second sentence, *rice* has become specific, so *the* is used. This example is related to Rule 3 in Quick Reference 43.1.]

## GENERALIZATIONS WITH PLURAL OR NONCOUNT NOUNS

Rule 2 in Quick Reference 43.1 tells you to use *the* with singular count nouns that carry general meaning. With GENERALIZATIONS using plural or noncount nouns, omit *the*.

> **NO** The tulips are the flowers that grow from the bulbs.
>
> **YES** Tulips are flowers that grow from bulbs.

## 43c How do I use *the* with proper nouns and with gerunds?

PROPER NOUNS name specific people, places, or things (see 14b). Most proper nouns do not require ARTICLES: *We visited **Lake Mead** with **Asha** and **Larry.*** As shown in Quick Reference 43.2, however, certain types of proper nouns do require *the*.

---

### Quick Reference 43.2  ■ ■ ■ ■ ■

#### Proper nouns that use *the*

- **Nouns with the pattern *the . . . of . . .***
    - **the** United States **of** America
    - **the** Republic **of** Mexico
    - **the** Fourth **of** July
    - **the** University **of** Paris
- **Plural proper nouns**
    - **the** United Arab Emirates
    - **the** Johnsons
    - **the** Rocky Mountains [*but* Mount Fuji]
    - **the** Chicago Bulls
    - **the** Falkland Islands [*but* Long Island]
    - **the** Great Lakes [*but* Lake Superior]

continued >>

| Quick Reference 43.2 | (continued) | ■ ■ ■ ■ ■ |
|---|---|---|

- **Collective proper nouns (nouns that name a group)**
  - **the** Modern Language Association
  - **the** Society of Friends
- **Some (but not all) geographical features**
  - **the** Amazon   **the** Gobi Desert   **the** Indian Ocean
- **Three countries**
  - **the** Congo   **the** Sudan   **the** Netherlands

GERUNDS are PRESENT PARTICIPLES (the *-ing* form of VERBS) used as nouns: ***Skating** is challenging.* Gerunds are usually not preceded by *the*. Use *the* before a gerund when two conditions are met: (1) The gerund is used in a specific sense (see 43a), and (2) the gerund does not have a DIRECT OBJECT.

**EXERCISE 43-1**   Consulting all sections of this chapter, decide which of the words in parentheses is correct and write it in the blank. If no article is needed, leave the blank empty.

EXAMPLE   For (a, an, the) _____ years, people have worked under (a, an, the) the assumption that (a, an, the) the best remedy for (a, an, the) a burn is butter.

1. This kind of treatment seems to be (a, an, the) _____ good idea because butter looks and feels like ointment, but butter doesn't contain (a, an, the) _____ antibacterial property like ointment does.

2. In using butter to treat (a, an, the) _____ burns, you are coating (a, an, the) _____ skin with debris that must be removed later to keep it from interfering with (a, an, the) _____ healing process.

3. In actuality, cold water without ice will not only ease (a, an, the) _____ pain but also prevent scarring and further damage.

4. In fact, (a, an, the) _____ person who keeps the finger submerged for at least several minutes and as long as half an hour will have (a, an, the) _____ least painful or scarred burn, according to doctors.

5. However, if (a, an, the) _____ burn is serious, (a, an, the) _____ first person to be consulted should be a doctor.

# 44

# Word Order

## 44a How do I understand standard and inverted word order in sentences?

In **standard word order,** the most common pattern for DECLARATIVE SEN-TENCES in English, the SUBJECT comes before the VERB.

SUBJECT    VERB

That book    was heavy.

With **inverted word order,** the MAIN VERB or an AUXILIARY VERB comes before the subject. The most common use of inverted word order in English is in forming DIRECT QUESTIONS.

**QUESTIONS THAT CAN BE ANSWERED WITH A YES OR NO**

MAIN VERB    SUBJECT

Was    that book heavy?

AUXILIARY VERB    SUBJECT    MAIN VERB

Have    you    heard the noise?

MODAL AUXILIARY VERB    SUBJECT    MAIN VERB

Can    you    lift the book?

To form a yes-or-no question with a verb other than *be* as the main verb and when there is no auxiliary or modal as part of a VERB PHRASE, use the appropriate form of the auxiliary verb *do.*

AUXILIARY
VERB     SUBJECT     MAIN VERB

Do       you       want me to put the book away?

A question that begins with a question-forming word such as *why, when, where,* or *how* cannot be answered with a yes or no: **Why** *did the book fall?* Some kind of information must be provided to answer such a question; the answer cannot be simply yes or no because the question is not "*Did* the book fall?" Information on *why* it fell is needed: for example, *It was too heavy for me.*

## INFORMATION QUESTIONS: INVERTED ORDER

Most information questions follow the same rules of inverted word order as yes-or-no questions.

QUESTION
WORD     MAIN VERB     SUBJECT

Why       is       that book open?

QUESTION     AUXILIARY
WORD       VERB       SUBJECT     MAIN VERB

What       does       the book     discuss?

QUESTION     MODAL
WORD       AUXILIARY     SUBJECT     MAIN VERB

When       can       I       read the book?

## INFORMATION QUESTIONS: STANDARD ORDER

When *who* or *what* functions as the subject in a question, use standard word order.

QUESTION WORD:
SUBJECT       MAIN VERB

Who       dropped the book?

QUESTION WORD:
SUBJECT       MAIN VERB

What       was the problem?

⚠ **Alert:** When a question has more than one auxiliary verb, put the subject after the first auxiliary verb.

| FIRST AUXILIARY | SUBJECT | SECOND AUXILIARY | MAIN VERB |
|---|---|---|---|
| ⌄ | ⌄ | ⌄ | ⌄ |
| Would | you | have | replaced the book? |

The same rules apply to emphatic exclamations: ***Was*** *that book heavy!* ***Did*** *she enjoy that book!* ●

## NEGATIVES

When you use negatives such as *never, hardly ever, seldom, rarely, not only,* or *nor* to start a CLAUSE, use inverted order. These sentence pairs show the differences, first in standard order and then in inverted order.

**I have never seen** a more exciting movie. [standard order]

**Never have I seen** a more exciting movie. [inverted order]

**She is not only** a talented artist **but also** an excellent musician.

**Not only is she** a talented artist, **but she is also** an excellent musician.

⚠ **Alerts:** (1) With INDIRECT QUESTIONS, use standard word order.

**NO**    She asked **how did I drop** the book.

**YES**    She asked **how I dropped** the book.

(2) Word order deliberately inverted can be effective, when used sparingly, to create emphasis in a sentence that is neither a question nor an exclamation. ●

## 44b How can I understand the placement of adjectives?

ADJECTIVES modify—describe or limit—NOUNS, PRONOUNS, and word groups that function as nouns (see 14e). In English, an adjective comes directly before the noun it describes. However, when more than one adjective describes the same noun, several sequences may be possible. Quick Reference 44.1 shows the most common order for positioning several adjectives.

> ## Quick Reference 44.1 ▪ ▪ ▪ ▪ ▪
>
> ### Word order: cumulative adjectives
>
> 1. **Determiners, if any:** *a, an, the, my, your, this, that, these, those,* and so on
> 2. **Expressions of order, including ordinal numbers, if any:** *first, second, third, next, last, final,* and so on
> 3. **Expressions of quantity, including cardinal (counting) numbers, if any:** *one, two, few, each, every, some,* and so on
> 4. **Adjectives of judgment or opinion, if any:** *pretty, happy, ugly, sad, interesting, boring,* and so on
> 5. **Adjectives of size or shape, if any:** *big, small, short, round, square,* and so on
> 6. **Adjectives of age or condition, if any:** *new, young, broken, dirty, shiny,* and so on
> 7. **Adjectives of color, if any:** *red, green, blue,* and so on
> 8. **Adjectives that can also be used as nouns, if any:** *French, Protestant, metal, cotton,* and so on
> 9. **The noun**
>
> | 1 | 2 | 3 | 4 | 5 | 6 | 7 | 8 | 9 |
> |---|---|---|---|---|---|---|---|---|
> | a | | few | | tiny | | red | | ants |
> | the | last | six | | | | | Thai | carvings |
> | my | | | fine | | old | | oak | table |

# 44c How can I understand the placement of adverbs?

ADVERBS modify—describe or limit—VERBS, ADJECTIVES, other adverbs, or entire sentences (see 14f). Adverbs may be positioned first, in the middle, or last in CLAUSES. Quick Reference 44.2 summarizes adverb types, what they tell about the words they modify, and where each type can be placed.

> ## Quick Reference 44.2 ▪ ▪ ▪ ▪ ▪
>
> ### Word order: positioning adverbs
>
> | **ADVERBS OF MANNER** | • describe *how* something is done <br> • are usually in middle or last position | Nick **carefully** groomed the dog <br> Nick groomed the dog **carefully.** |
> |---|---|---|

continued >>

### Quick Reference 44.2        (continued)        ■ ■ ■ ■ ■

| ADVERBS OF TIME | • describe *when* or *how long* about an event<br>• are usually in first or last position<br>• include *just, still, already,* and similar adverbs, which are usually in middle position | **First,** he shampooed the dog.<br>He shampooed the dog **first.**<br><br>He had **already** brushed the dog's coat. |
|---|---|---|
| ADVERBS OF FREQUENCY | • describe *how often* an event takes place<br>• are usually in middle position<br>• are in first position when they modify an entire sentence (see "Sentence Adverbs" below) | Nick has **never** been bitten by a dog.<br><br>**Occasionally,** he is scratched while shampooing a cat. |
| ADVERBS OF DEGREE OR EMPHASIS | • describe *how much* or *to what extent* about other modifiers<br>• are directly before the word they modify<br>• include *only,* which is easy to misplace (see 21a) | Nick is **extremely** calm around animals.<br>[*Extremely* modifies *calm.*] |
| SENTENCE ADVERBS | • modify the entire sentence rather than just one word or a few words<br>• include transitional words and expressions (see 3g), as well as such expressions as *maybe, probably, possibly, fortunately, unfortunately,* and *incredibly*<br>• are in first position | **Incredibly,** he was once asked to groom a rat. |

🚫 **Alert:** Do not let an adverb separate a verb from its DIRECT OBJECT or INDIRECT OBJECT. ●

**EXERCISE 44-1**   Consulting all sections of this chapter, find and correct any errors in word order.

1. A beautiful few flowers began to bloom in my garden this week.

2. A neighbor asked me, "You did grow all these yourself?"

3. "Yes," I replied, "the roses are my favorite husband's, but the tulips are my favorite."

4. My neighbor, who extremely was impressed with my gardening efforts, decided to grow some flowers of her own.

5. Weeks later, as I strolled by her house, I saw her planting happily seeds from her favorite type of plant—petunias.

# Prepositions

**Prepositions** function with other words in PREPOSITIONAL PHRASES (14m). Prepositional phrases usually indicate *where* (direction or location), *how* (by what means or in what way), or *when* (at what time or how long) about the words they modify

   This chapter can help you with several uses of prepositions, which function in combination with other words in ways that are often idiomatic—that is, peculiar to the language. The meaning of an IDIOM differs from the literal meaning of each individual word. For example, the word *break* usually refers to shattering, but the sentence *Yao-Ming **broke into** a smile* means that a smile appeared on Yao-Ming's face. Knowing which preposition to use in a specific context takes much experience in reading, listening to, and speaking the language. A dictionary like the *Dictionary of American English* (Heinle and Heinle) can be especially helpful when you need to find the correct preposition to use in cases not covered by this chapter.

## 45a How can I recognize prepositions?

Quick Reference 45.1 lists many common prepositions.

## 45b How do I use prepositions with expressions of time and place?

Quick Reference 45.2 shows how to use the prepositions *in, at,* and *on* to deliver some common kinds of information about time and place.

### Quick Reference 45.1

▪ ▪ ▪ ▪ ▪

#### Common prepositions

| | | | | |
|---|---|---|---|---|
| about | below | from | onto | throughout |
| above | beside | in | on top of | till |
| across | between | in front of | opposite | to |
| after | beyond | inside | out | toward |
| against | but | instead of | outside | under |
| along | by | into | over | underneath |
| among | concerning | like | past | unlike |
| around | despite | near | plus | until |
| as | down | next | regarding | up |
| at | during | of | round | with |
| because of | except | off | since | within |
| before | for | on | through | without |
| behind | | | | |

### Quick Reference 45.2

▪ ▪ ▪ ▪ ▪

#### Using *in*, *at*, and *on* to show time and place

**TIME**

- *in* **a year or a month** (*during* is also correct but less common)

    **in** 1995          **in** May

- *in* **a period of time**

    **in** a few months (seconds, days, years)

- *in* **a period of the day**

    **in** the morning (afternoon, evening)

    **in** the daytime (morning, evening) *but* **at** night

- *at* **a specific time or period of time**

    **at** noon          **at** 2:00          **at** dawn          **at** nightfall

    **at** takeoff (the time a plane leaves)

    **at** breakfast (the time a specific meal takes place)

- *on* **a specific day**

    **on** Friday          **on** my birthday

continued >>

**Quick Reference 45.2** (continued) ▪ ▪ ▪ ▪ ▪

PLACE

- *in* **a location surrounded by something else**

  **in** the province of Alberta      **in** the kitchen

  **in** Utah                         **in** the apartment

  **in** downtown Bombay              **in** the bathtub

- *at* **a specific location**

  **at** your house      **at the bank**

  **at** the corner of Third Avenue and Main Street

- *on* **a surface**

  **on** page 20

  **on** the second floor *but* **in** the attic *or* **in** the basement

  **on** Washington Street

  **on** the mezzanine

  **on** the highway

# 45c  How do I use prepositions in phrasal verbs?

**Phrasal verbs,** also called *two-word verbs* and *three-word verbs,* are VERBS that combine with PREPOSITIONS to deliver their meaning. In some phrasal verbs, the verb and the preposition should not be separated by other words: *Look at the moon* [not *Look the moon at*]. In **separable phrasal verbs,** other words in the sentence can separate the verb and the preposition without interfering with meaning: *I threw away my homework* is as correct as *I threw my homework away.*

Here is a list of some common phrasal verbs. The ones that cannot be separated are marked with an asterisk (*).

**SELECTED PHRASAL VERBS**

| | | |
|---|---|---|
| ask out | get along with* | look into |
| break down | get back | look out for* |
| bring about | get off | look over |
| call back | go over* | make up |
| drop off | hand in | run across* |
| figure out | keep up with* | speak to* |
| fill out | leave out | speak with* |
| fill up | look after* | throw away |
| find out | look around | throw out |

Position a PRONOUN OBJECT between the words of a separable phrasal verb: *I threw **it** away.* Also, you can position an object PHRASE of several words between the parts of a separable phrasal verb: *I threw **my research paper** away.* However, when the object is a CLAUSE, do not let it separate the parts of the phrasal verb: *I threw away **all the papers that I wrote last year.***

Many phrasal verbs are informal and are used more in speaking than in writing. For ACADEMIC WRITING, a more formal verb is usually more appropriate than a phrasal verb. In a research paper, for example, *propose* or *suggest* might be a better choice than *come up with*. For academic writing, acceptable phrasal verbs include *believe in, benefit from, concentrate on, consist of, depend on, dream of* (or *dream about*), *insist on, participate in, prepare for,* and *stare at*. None of these phrasal verbs can be separated.

**EXERCISE 45-1** Consulting the preceding sections of this chapter and using the list of phrasal verbs in 45c, write a one- or two-paragraph description of a typical day at work or school in which you use at least five phrasal verbs. After checking a dictionary, revise your writing, substituting for the phrasal verbs any more formal verbs that might be more appropriate for academic writing.

# 45d How do I use prepositions with past participles?

PAST PARTICIPLES are verb forms that function as ADJECTIVES (46f). Past participles end in either *-ed* or *-d*, or in an equivalent irregular form (15d). When past participles follow the LINKING VERB *be*, it is easy to confuse them with PASSIVE verbs (15n), which have the same endings. Passive verbs describe actions. Past participles, because they act as adjectives, modify NOUNS and PRONOUNS and often describe situations and conditions. Passive verbs follow the pattern *be* + past participle + *by: The child **was frightened by** a snake.* An expression containing a past participle, however, can use either *be* or another linking verb, and it can be followed by either *by* or a different preposition.

- The child **seemed frightened by** snakes.
- The child **is frightened of** all snakes.

Here is a list of expressions containing past participles and the prepositions that often follow them. Look in a dictionary for others. (See 46b on using GERUNDS after some of these expressions.)

**SELECTED PAST PARTICIPLE PHRASES + PREPOSITIONS**

| | |
|---|---|
| be accustomed to | be concerned/worried about |
| be acquainted with | be disappointed with (*or* in someone) |
| be composed of | be discriminated against |

| | |
|---|---|
| be divorced from | be made of (*or* from) |
| be excited about | be married to |
| be finished/done with | be pleased/satisfied with |
| be interested in | be prepared for |
| be known for | be tired of (*or* from) |
| be located in | |

## 45e How do I use prepositions in expressions?

In many common expressions, different PREPOSITIONS convey great differences in meaning. For example, four prepositions can be used with the verb *agree* to create five different meanings.

**agree to** means "to give consent": *I cannot **agree to** my buying you a new car.*

**agree about** means "to arrive at a satisfactory understanding": *We certainly **agree about** your needing a car.*

**agree on** means "to concur": *You and the seller must **agree on** a price for the car.*

**agree with** means "to have the same opinion": *I **agree with** you that you need a car.*

**agree with** also means "to be suitable or healthful": *The idea of having such a major expense does not **agree with** me.*

You can find entire books filled with English expressions that include prepositions.

■ ■ ■ ■ **46**

# Gerunds, Infinitives, and Participles

PARTICIPLES are verb forms (see 15b). A verb's *-ing* form is its PRESENT PARTICIPLE. The *-ed* form of a regular verb is its PAST PARTICIPLE; IRREGULAR VERBS form their past participles in various ways (for example, *bend, bent; eat, eaten; think, thought*—for a complete list, see Quick Reference 15.4 in 15d). Participles can function as ADJECTIVES (*a **smiling** face, a **closed** book*).

A verb's *-ing* form can also function as a NOUN (***Sneezing*** *spreads colds*), which is called a GERUND. Another verb form, the INFINITIVE, can also function as a noun. An infinitive is a verb's SIMPLE or base FORM, usually preceded by the word *to* (*We want everyone **to smile***). Verb forms—participles, gerunds, and infinitives—functioning as nouns or MODIFIERS are called VERBALS, as explained in 14d. This chapter can help you make the right choices among verbals.

## **46a**   How can I use gerunds and infinitives as subjects?

Gerunds are used more commonly than infinitives as subjects. Sometimes, however, either is acceptable.

> **Choosing** the right health club is important.

> **To choose** the right health club is important.

🛑 **Alert:**  When a gerund or an infinitive is used alone as a subject, it is SINGULAR and requires a singular verb. When two or more gerunds or infinitives create a COMPOUND SUBJECT, they require a plural verb. ●

## **46b**   When do I use a gerund, not an infinitive, as an object?

Some VERBS must be followed by GERUNDS used as DIRECT OBJECTS. Other verbs must be followed by INFINITIVES. Still other verbs can be followed by either a gerund or an infinitive. Quick Reference 46.1 lists common verbs that must be followed by gerunds, not infinitives.

### Quick Reference 46.1 ■ ■ ■ ■ ■

| Verbs and expressions that must be followed by gerunds | | |
|---|---|---|
| admit | dislike | object to |
| anticipate | enjoy | postpone |
| appreciate | escape | practice |
| avoid | finish | put off |
| consider | give up | quit |
| consist of | imagine | recall |
| contemplate | include | resist |
| delay | mention | risk |
| deny | mind | suggest |
| discuss | miss | tolerate |

Yuri **considered** *calling* [not *to call*] the mayor.

He **was having trouble** *getting* [not *to get*] a work permit.

Yuri's boss **recommended** *taking* [not *to take*] an interpreter to the permit agency.

## GERUND AFTER *GO*

The word *go* is usually followed by an infinitive: *We can **go to see*** [not *go seeing*] *a movie tonight.* Sometimes, however, *go* is followed by a gerund in phrases such as *go swimming, go fishing, go shopping,* and *go driving: I will **go shopping*** [not *go to shop*] *after work.*

## GERUND AFTER *BE* + COMPLEMENT + PREPOSITION

Many common expressions use a form of the verb *be* plus a COMPLEMENT plus a PREPOSITION. In such expressions, use a gerund, not an infinitive, after the preposition. Here is a list of some of the most frequently used expressions in this pattern.

SELECTED EXPRESSIONS USING *BE* + COMPLEMENT + PREPOSITION

| | |
|---|---|
| be (get) accustomed to | be interested in |
| be angry about | be prepared for |
| be bored with | be responsible for |
| be capable of | be tired of |
| be committed to | be (get) used to |
| be excited about | be worried about |

We **are excited about** *voting* [not *to vote*] in the next presidential election.

Who **will be responsible for** *locating* [not *to locate*] our polling place?

🛑 Alert: Always use a gerund, not an infinitive, as the object of a preposition. Be especially careful when the word *to* is functioning as a preposition in a PHRASAL VERB (see 45c): *We are committed **to changing*** [not *to change*] *the rules.* ●

## 46c When do I use an infinitive, not a gerund, as an object?

Quick Reference 46.2 lists selected common verbs and expressions that must be followed by INFINITIVES, not GERUNDS, as OBJECTS.

She **wanted** *to go* [not *wanted going*] to the lecture.

Only three people **decided** *to question* [not *decided questioning*] the speaker.

> ### Quick Reference 46.2 ■ ■ ■ ■ ■
>
> | Verbs and expressions that must be followed by infinitives | | | |
> |---|---|---|---|
> | agree | decline | learn | plan |
> | arrange | demand | like | pretend |
> | ask | deserve | manage | promise |
> | attempt | expect | mean | refuse |
> | beg | hesitate | need | wait |
> | claim | hope | offer | want |
> | decide | | | |

#### INFINITIVE AFTER *BE* + COMPLEMENT

Gerunds are common in constructions that use a form of the verb *be* plus a COMPLEMENT and a PREPOSITION (see 46b). However, use an infinitive, not a gerund, when *be* plus a complement is not followed by a preposition.

> We **are eager *to go*** [not *going*] camping.
>
> I **am ready *to sleep*** [not *sleeping*] in a tent.

#### INFINITIVE TO INDICATE PURPOSE

Use an infinitive in expressions that indicate purpose: *I read a book **to learn** more about Mayan culture.* This sentence means "I read a book for the purpose of learning more about Mayan culture." *To learn* delivers the idea of purpose more concisely (see Chapter 11) than expressions such as *so that I can* or *in order to.*

#### INFINITIVE WITH *THE FIRST, THE LAST, THE ONE*

Use an infinitive after the expressions *the first, the last,* and *the one: Nina is the first **to arrive** [not *arriving*] and the last **to leave** [not *leaving*] every day. She's always the one **to do** the most.*

#### UNMARKED INFINITIVES

Infinitives used without the word *to* are called **unmarked infinitives,** or sometimes *bare infinitives.* An unmarked infinitive may be hard to recognize because it is not preceded by *to.* Some common verbs followed by unmarked infinitives are *feel, have, hear, let, listen to, look at, make* (meaning "compel"), *notice, see,* and *watch.* The verb *help* can be followed by a marked or an unmarked infinitive. Either is correct: *Help me **put** [or **to put**] this box in the car.*

🛇 **Alert:** Be careful to use parallel structure (see Chapter 10) correctly when you use two or more gerunds or infinitives after verbs. If two or more verbal objects follow one verb, put the verbals into the same form.

| NO | We went **sailing** and **to scuba dive.** |
|---|---|
| YES | We went **sailing** and **scuba diving.** |

Conversely, if you are using verbal objects with COMPOUND PREDICATES, be sure to use the kind of verbal that each verb requires.

| NO | We enjoyed **scuba diving** but do not plan **sailing** again. |
|---|---|
| | [*Enjoyed* requires a gerund object, and *plan* requires an infinitive object; see Quick References 46.1 and 46.2 in this chapter.] |
| YES | We enjoyed **scuba diving** but do not plan **to sail** again. ● |

# 46d How does meaning change when certain verbs are followed by a gerund or an infinitive?

**WITH *STOP***

The VERB *stop* followed by a GERUND means "finish, quit." *Stop* followed by an INFINITIVE means "interrupt one activity to begin another."

We **stopped** *eating.* [We finished our meal.]

We **stopped** *to eat.* [We stopped another activity, such as driving, to eat.]

**WITH *REMEMBER* AND *FORGET***

The verb *remember* followed by an infinitive means "not to forget to do something": *I must **remember to talk** with Isa. Remember* followed by a gerund means "recall a memory": *I **remember talking** in my sleep last night.*

The verb *forget* followed by an infinitive means "fail to do something": *If you **forget to put** a stamp on that letter, it will be returned. Forget* followed by a gerund means "do something and not recall it": *I **forget having put** the stamps in the refrigerator.*

**WITH *TRY***

The verb *try* followed by an infinitive means "make an effort": *I **tried to find** your jacket.* Followed by a gerund, *try* means "experiment with": *I **tried jogging** but found it too difficult.*

# 46e Why is the meaning unchanged whether a gerund or an infinitive follows sense verbs?

Sense VERBS include words such as *see, notice, hear, observe, watch, feel, listen to,* and *look at.* The meaning of these verbs is usually not affected by whether a GERUND or an INFINITIVE follows as the OBJECT. *I **saw** the water **rise** and I **saw** the water **rising** both have the same meaning in American English.

**EXERCISE 46-1** Write the correct form of the verbal object (either a gerund or an infinitive) for each verb in parentheses. For help, consult 46b through 46e.

EXAMPLE People like (think) <u>to think</u> that they have a good memory, but everybody shows signs of forgetfulness from time to time.

1. Think about (ride) _____ the railroad to work on a rainy Monday morning.

2. The comfortable reclining seats let passengers (take) _____ a relaxing nap on the way to work.

3. Because of the rain, commuters are forced (bring) _____ an umbrella and a raincoat, along with their usual traveling items.

4. Once they reach their destination, passengers forget that they need their umbrellas and raincoats (walk) _____ the few blocks to work.

5. (Step) _____ out into the rain makes the passengers suddenly realize that they've left their umbrellas and raincoats on the train, which has already left the station.

## 46f How do I choose between *-ing* and *-ed* forms for adjectives?

Deciding whether to use the *-ing* form (PRESENT PARTICIPLE) or the *-ed* form (PAST PARTICIPLE of a regular VERB) as an ADJECTIVE in a specific sentence can be difficult. For example, *I am **amused*** and *I am **amusing*** are both correct in English, but their meanings are very different. To make the right choice, decide whether the modified NOUN or PRONOUN is causing or experiencing what the participle describes.

Use a present participle (*-ing*) to modify a noun or pronoun that is the agent or the cause of the action.

> Micah described your **interesting** plan. [The noun *plan* causes what its modifier describes—interest; so *interesting* is correct.]

> I find your plan **exciting.** [The noun *plan* causes what its modifier describes—excitement; so *exciting* is correct.]

Use a past participle (*-ed* in regular verbs) to modify a noun or pronoun that experiences or receives whatever the modifier describes.

> An **interested** committee wants to hear your plan. [The noun *committee* experiences what its modifier describes—interest; so *interested* is correct.]

**Excited** by your plan, they called a board meeting. [The pronoun *they* experiences what its modifier describes—excitement; so *excited* is correct.]

Here are frequently used participles that convey very different meanings, depending on whether the *-ed* or the *-ing* form is used.

| | |
|---|---|
| amused, amusing | frightened, frightening |
| annoyed, annoying | insulted, insulting |
| appalled, appalling | offended, offending |
| bored, boring | overwhelmed, overwhelming |
| confused, confusing | pleased, pleasing |
| depressed, depressing | reassured, reassuring |
| disgusted, disgusting | satisfied, satisfying |
| fascinated, fascinating | shocked, shocking |

**EXERCISE 46-2**   Choose the correct participle from each pair in parentheses. For help, consult 46f.

EXAMPLE   It can be a (satisfied, satisfying) <u>satisfying</u> experience to learn about the lives of artists.

1. The artist Frida Kahlo led an (interested, interesting) _____ life.

2. When Kahlo was eighteen, (horrified, horrifying) _____ observers saw her (injured, injuring) _____ in a streetcar accident.

3. A (disappointed, disappointing) _____ Kahlo had to abandon her plan to study medicine.

4. Instead, she began to create paintings filled with (disturbed, disturbing) _____ images.

5. Some art critics consider Kahlo's paintings to be (fascinated, fascinating) _____ works of art, though many people find them (overwhelmed, overwhelming) _____.

## 47

# Modal Auxiliary Verbs

AUXILIARY VERBS are known as *helping verbs* because adding an auxiliary verb to a MAIN VERB helps the main verb convey additional information. The most common auxiliary verbs are forms of *be, have,* and *do.* Quick References 15.6 and 15.7 in section 15e list the forms of these three verbs.

MODAL AUXILIARY VERBS are one type of auxiliary verb. They include *can, could, may, might, should, had better, must, will, would,* and others discussed in this chapter. Modals differ from *be, have,* and *do* used as auxiliary verbs in the specific ways discussed in Quick Reference 47.1. This chapter can help you use modals to convey shades of meaning.

---

### Quick Reference 47.1 ▪ ▪ ▪ ▪ ▪

#### Modals versus other auxiliary verbs

- Modals in the present future are always followed by the SIMPLE FORM of a main verb: *I **might go** tomorrow.*

- One-word modals have no *-s* ending in the THIRD-PERSON SINGULAR: *She **could** go with me; he **could** go with me; they **could** go with me.* (The two-word modal *have to* changes form to agree with its subject: *I **have to** leave; she **has to** leave.*) Auxiliary verbs other than modals usually change form for third-person singular: *I **do** want to go; he **does** want to go.*

- Some modals change form in the past. Others (*should, would, must,* which convey probability, and *ought to*) use *have* + a PAST PARTICIPLE. *I **can do** it* becomes *I **could do** it* in PAST-TENSE CLAUSES about ability. *I **could do** it* becomes *I **could have done** it* in clauses about possibility.

- Modals convey meaning about ability, necessity, advisability, possibility, and other conditions: For example, *I **can** go* means "I am able to go." Modals do not describe actual occurrences.

---

## 47a How do I convey ability, necessity, advisability, possibility, and probability with modals?

### CONVEYING ABILITY

The modal *can* conveys ability now (in the present), and *could* conveys ability before (in the past). These words deliver the meaning "able to." For the future, use *will be able to.*

We **can** work late tonight. [*Can* conveys present ability.]

I **could** work late last night, too. [*Could* conveys past ability.]

I **will be able to** work late next Monday. [*Will be able* is the future tense; *will* here is not a modal.]

Adding *not* between a modal and the MAIN VERB makes the CLAUSE negative: *We **cannot** work late tonight; I **could not** work late last night; I **will not be able to** work late next Monday.*

🚫 **Alert:** You will often see negative forms of modals turned into CONTRACTIONS: *can't, couldn't, won't, wouldn't,* and others. Because contractions are considered informal usage by some instructors, avoid them in ACADEMIC WRITING. ●

## CONVEYING NECESSITY

The modals *must* and *have to* convey a need to do something. Both *must* and *have to* are followed by the simple form of the main verb. In the present tense, *have to* changes form to agree with its subject.

You **must** leave before midnight.

She **has to** leave when I leave.

In the past tense, *must* is never used to express necessity. Instead, use *had to.*

PRESENT TENSE  We **must** study today. We **have to** study today.

PAST TENSE  We **had to** [not *must*] take a test yesterday.

The negative forms of *must* and *have to* also have different meanings. *Must not* conveys that something is forbidden; *do not have to* conveys that something is not necessary.

You **must not** sit there. [Sitting there is forbidden.]

You **do not have to** sit there. [Sitting there is not necessary.]

## CONVEYING ADVISABILITY OR THE NOTION OF A GOOD IDEA

The modals *should* and *ought to* express the idea that doing the action of the main verb is advisable or is a good idea.

You **should** go to class tomorrow morning.

In the past tense, *should* and *ought to* convey regret or knowing something through hindsight. They mean that good advice was not taken.

You **should have** gone to class yesterday.

I **ought to have** called my sister yesterday.

The modal *had better* delivers the meaning of good advice or warning or threat. It does not change form for tense.

You **had better** see the doctor before your cough gets worse.

*Need to* is often used to express strong advice, too. Its past-tense form is *needed to.*

You **need to** take better care of yourself. You **needed to** listen.

### CONVEYING POSSIBILITY

The modals *may, might,* and *could* can be used to convey an idea of possibility or likelihood.

We **may** become hungry before long.

We **could** eat lunch at the diner next door.

For the past-tense form, use *may, might,* and *could,* followed by *have* and the past participle of the main verb.

I **could have studied** French in high school, but I studied Spanish instead.

### CONVEYING PROBABILITY

In addition to conveying the idea of necessity, the modal *must* can also convey probability or likelihood. It means that a well-informed guess is being made.

Marisa **must** be a talented actress. She has been chosen to play the lead role in the school play.

When *must* conveys probability, the past tense is *must have* plus the past participle of the main verb.

I did not see Boris at the party; he **must have left** early.

**EXERCISE 47-1**   Fill in each blank with the past-tense modal auxiliary that expresses the meaning given in parentheses. For help, consult 47a.

EXAMPLE   I (advisability) <u>should have</u> gone straight to the doctor the instant I felt a cold coming on.

1. Since I (necessity, no choice) _____ work late this past Monday, I could not get to the doctor's office before it closed.

2. I (advisability) _____ fallen asleep after dinner, but I stayed awake for a while instead.

3. Even after I finally got into bed, I (ability) _____ not relax.

4. I (making a guess) _____ not _____ heard the alarm the next morning, because I overslept nearly two hours.

5. When I finally arrived at work, my boss came into my office and said, "Julie, you (necessity) _____ stayed home and rested if you are sick."

# 47b How do I convey preferences, plans, and past habits with modals?

## CONVEYING PREFERENCES

The modal *would rather* expresses a preference. *Would rather,* the PRESENT TENSE, is used with the SIMPLE FORM of the MAIN VERB, and *would rather have,* the PAST TENSE, is used with the PAST PARTICIPLE of the main verb.

We **would rather see** a comedy than a mystery.

Carlos **would rather have stayed** home last night.

## CONVEYING PLAN OR OBLIGATION

A form of *be* followed by *supposed to* and the simple form of a main verb delivers a meaning of something planned or of an obligation.

I **was supposed to meet** them at the bus stop.

## CONVEYING PAST HABIT

The modals *used to* and *would* express the idea that something happened repeatedly in the past.

I **used to** hate going to the dentist.

I **would** dread every single visit.

**Alert:** Both *used to* and *would* can be used to express repeated actions in the past, but *would* cannot be used for a situation that lasted for a period of time in the past.

    **NO**    I **would** live in Arizona.

    **YES**    I **used to** live in Arizona. ●

# 47c How can I recognize modals in the passive voice?

Modals use the ACTIVE VOICE, as shown in sections 47a and 47b. In the active voice, the subject does the action expressed in the MAIN VERB (see 15n and 15o).

Modals can also use the PASSIVE VOICE. In the passive voice, the doer of the main verb's action is either unexpressed or is expressed as an OBJECT in a PREPOSITIONAL PHRASE starting with the word *by.*

> **PASSIVE** The waterfront **can be seen** from my window.
>
> **ACTIVE** **I can see** the waterfront from my window.
>
> **PASSIVE** The tax form **must be signed** by the person who fills it out.
>
> **ACTIVE** The person who fills out the tax form **must sign** it.

**EXERCISE 47-2** Select the correct choice from the words in parentheses and write it in the blank. For help, consult 47a through 47c.

EXAMPLE   When I was younger, I (would, used to) <u>used to</u> love to go bicycle riding.

1. You (ought to have, ought have) _____ called yesterday as you had promised you would.

2. Judging by the size of the puddles in the street outside, it (must be rained, must have rained) _____ all night long.

3. Ingrid (must not have, might not have been) _____ as early for the interview as she claims she was.

4. After all the studying he did, Pedro (should have, should have been) _____ less frightened by the exam.

5. I have to go home early today, although I really (cannot, should not) _____ leave before the end of the day because of all the work I have to do.

# ■ ■ ■ ■ ■
# Credits

## Text

**Page 4:** From "Trees Are Living Archives" by James S. Trefil, *Smithsonian,* July 1985, pp. 46-54. Copyright © 1985. Reprinted by permission of James S. Trefil. **Page 49:** Reprinted from "Nothing About These Woman Is Real," by Abigail Haworth, *Marie Claire,* July 2005. Copyright © 2005. Reprinted by permission of Abigail Haworth. **Page 50:** Excerpt from "Composers and Patrons in the Classical Era" in *Understanding Music,* 3rd edition, by Jeremy Yudkin. Copyright © 2002. Reprinted by permission of Pearson Education, Upper Saddle River, NJ. **Page 51:** Excerpt from *Three Uses of the Knife: On the Nature and Purpose of Drama* by David Mamet. Copyright © 1998 by Columbia University Press. **Page 56:** Excerpt from "The Study of Humanity" in *Cultural Anthropology,* 1st edition, by Nancy Bonvillain. Copyright © 2006, page 4. Reprinted by permission of Pearson Education, Upper Saddle River, NJ. **Page 58:** Excerpt from page 202 (115 words) from *Hillerman Country* by Tony Hillerman and Barney Hillerman. Reprinted with permission of HarperCollins. **Pages 59-60:** Susan Howard, "Depth of Field," *Newsday,* Jan 1, 1991 Reprinted with permission. **Page 60:** "Making Olive Oil" by Lori de Mori. Copyright © 2004 Weldon Owen Inc., from Williams-Sonoma, *Florence: Authentic Recipes Celebrating the Foods of the World.* Reprinted with permission. **Page 61:** Joshua Foer/National Geographic Image Collection. Reprinted with permission of the National Geographic Society. **Page 62:** Excerpt from *Masterworks: A Musical Discovery,* 1st edition, by D. Kern Holoman. Copyright © 1998. Reprinted by permission of Pearson Education, Upper Saddle River, NJ. **Page 64:** From *The Language of Clothes* by Alison Lurie. Copyright © 1981 by Alison Lurie. Reprinted by permission of Melanie Jackson Agency, Inc. **Page 65:** From *You Just Don't Understand* by Deborah Tannen. Copyright © 1990 by Deborah Tannen. Reprinted by permission of HarperCollins Publishers.

## Art

**Page 16:** Copyright © Google.

# INDEX

Numbers in bold type indicate pages where definitions of key terms can be found.

# NOTES

# NOTES

# NOTES

# NOTES